BRITISH GOVERNMENT

British Government

HIRAM MILLER STOUT

New York · OXFORD UNIVERSITY PRESS · 1953

To my parents

Preface

The literature on the British political system is extensive and includes many excellent works. My purpose in venturing to add to the long shelf of books on this subject has been to provide American readers, principally college and university students, with a description of the present-day structure and practice of British government. While in form and spirit this government is essentially that of the prewar period, the years of conflict and reconstruction have left their marks, and a good many developments of constitutional importance have occurred since 1939. It has seemed, therefore, that a book written in the light of recent developments—postwar elections, the expansion of governmental functions under the welfare state concept, new Commonwealth relations, to mention a few—might fill a need.

The author of a book describing the political system of a country always faces problems of organization. There are usually two or three ways of entering upon the subject and at least as many ways of carrying it forward. The British government presents some special difficulties in this respect. Being the product of a long evolution, it lacks a convenient constitutional birthday from which one can start. Furthermore, its principal governmental institutions do not fall as clearly under either functional or territorial headings as such institutions do in some political systems, for example, the American system with its constitutionally ordained executive, legislative, and judicial organs and its federal, state, and local divisions.

Under the plan I have adopted, the book treats first of the country being studied, its constitution, and the constitutional rights of its citizens. There follows a series of chapters on the structure and functioning of the principal institutions of British government. Succeeding chapters deal with policy and administration in several fields of national importance. The last two chapters discuss the Commonwealth of Nations and the colonial empire.

I am indebted to several persons for valuable suggestions and criticism. Professor William A. Robson of the London School of Economics and Political Science, Professor Charles Aikin of the University of California (Berkeley), Professor R. K. Gooch of the University of Virginia, and Professor William H. Dunham, Jr., of Yale University read the manuscript, and their comments were very helpful. My friends, Dr. H. J. Heneman, Dr. Abbot E. Smith, and Mr. A. J. Rockwell, read parts of the manuscript and gave me useful suggestions. My thanks are due Miss Bernadette Wilson for her assistance in the preparation of the manuscript. I am deeply grateful to my wife for her critical comments on the manuscript and for her encouragement while it was being written. I remain responsible for such errors of fact and interpretation as the book contains.

H. M. S.

Washington, D. C.
November 1952

Contents

BRITISH GOVERNMENT

The Country and Its People

The century between Waterloo and the outbreak of the First World War has often been referred to as the period of the *Pax Britannica*. During that period Great Britain reached a position of pre-eminence among the nations of the world, and its influence was usually decisive in the settlement of major international issues. Britain no longer plays such an important role on the world stage; two vast, continental powers, the United States of America and the Soviet Union, have entered from opposite wings and are taking the leading parts in the dramatic events of the present day. Britain remains, nevertheless, a major world power—important as an industrial nation and as the center of a group of associated states, the British Commonwealth of Nations, and of many dependent territories, the British Empire.

The contributions of the British nation to the modern age are a matter of record. Several countries participated in the expansion of Europe, westward to the Americas, eastward to Asia, and southward to Africa, but none matched Britain in the extent or the permanence of its imperial achievements. British inventors and manufacturers were the first to discover and apply the power resources and machinery which transformed the world's economy. But it is in the fields of law and government that Britain's contributions to modern civilization are the most important and, it is to be hoped, the most enduring. Millions of people around the globe now enjoy the civil liberties embodied in the common law, and they live under democratic political institutions inspired by the British Constitution. The independent judge on the bench of an open court and the speaker in his chair before a free legislature are the monuments of the British nation.

1. *The Geographical Setting*

Because a number of terms are used in referring to Britain, the British Commonwealth, and the British Empire in their various political and geographical aspects, an explanation of nomenclature may be helpful. The 'Commonwealth' consists of a major European power, the United Kingdom of Great Britain and Northern Ireland, and seven independent nations which were formerly colonial dependencies of the United Kingdom and are now referred to as dominions or Commonwealth nations. They are Canada, Australia, New Zealand, South Africa, India, Pakistan, and Ceylon. The 'Empire' embraces the present colonial dependencies of the United Kingdom, such territories as Malta, Nigeria, British Honduras, and the Fiji Islands.

The historical and, in many respects, the political, economic, and cultural center of the Commonwealth and Empire is the United Kingdom. It occupies the island of Great Britain and the northeastern corner of the neighboring island of Ireland. The four principal components of the United Kingdom are England, Scotland, Wales, and Northern Ireland, which, though forming a single state, retain considerable cultural distinctiveness and, except for Wales, some separate political and legal institutions. In the waters surrounding the British Isles are several small islands and island groups attached to the United Kingdom. The Isle of Man, lying in the Irish Sea, has its own governmental organization, and so do the Channel Islands which lie in the English Channel near the French coast. To the west of Scotland are the Hebrides, and to the north the Orkney Islands and the Shetland Islands.

It is the government and political life of the United Kingdom that are the subject matter of this book.* While the official name of the state with which we are concerned is 'The United Kingdom of Great Britain and Northern Ireland,' the terms 'Great Britain' or just 'Britain' are frequently used in referring to it. Sometimes the name 'England' is meant to include the other component parts of the United Kingdom, although never when spoken by Welshmen, Scots, or Ulstermen.

The United Kingdom in its present constitutional form dates from comparatively recent times, but its component parts are ancient nations. England, which passed almost 400 years as a Roman province, fell apart in the early Middle Ages into a number of small kingdoms, but it was permanently reunited about A.D. 900. It brought Wales under its sway in the thirteenth century, and in 1603 England and Scotland were united under a common monarch, King James I of England and James VI of Scotland. A little more than a century later, in 1707, this personal union was replaced by a constitutional one creating the Kingdom of Great Britain. All of Ireland was added by a similar act of union in 1800, after that island had been an English dependency for more than 600 years. The English-Scottish union produced a British amalgam while the Irish union broke down in civil war (1916-21) and Ireland was divided into the autonomous Irish Free State, now the independent state of Ireland or Eire, and Northern Ireland, the latter adhering to the British connection.

Compared with most of the major states of the world, the territory of the United Kingdom is small. It covers 94,300 square miles, an area about the size of Oregon. The island of Great Britain is 750 miles long and is nowhere more than 300 miles in width. The six counties of Northern Ireland are approximately the size of Connecticut.

---

* In this book, 'government' when spelled with a small 'g' refers to the political system or the whole governmental machinery of the state; the spelling with a capital 'G' means the party administration in power.

Except where man's industrial works and his unplanned building have marred the landscape, Britain is an attractive country. Blessed with generous rainfall and the warm currents of the Gulf Stream, it is green the year round. In Wales and Scotland there are mountains, reaching heights of between 3000 and 4000 feet, and the scenic attractions of sparkling streams, quiet lakes, and forests. The Pennines extending from the Scottish border south to the Midlands give northern England some mountainous scenery. In other parts of England ranges of hills vary the topography. The coasts of Britain change from rocky coves and promontories like those of Cornwall and Scotland to the chalk cliffs of Dover and the fens of East Anglia where land and sea intermingle. Along the coast many broad estuaries stretch back into the countryside. Few countries present within so small a territory such a pleasing variety of nature. Poets for centuries have sung the beauties of its hills, lakes, and moors.

Apart from rich agricultural land, Britain's principal natural resources are coal and iron ore. The possession of these, of course, was essential in her growth as a great industrial power. Building stone is extensively quarried, and small amounts of tin have been mined in Cornwall since the days of the Phoenicians. The British Isles have no petroleum, gold, silver, lead, copper, bauxite, or other mineral resources of strategic and commercial importance. Once a land of great forests, the United Kingdom is now an importer of timber and wood products.

Britain's geographical position as an island off the European continent has favored her development. For centuries the English Channel was a sufficient barrier to invasion to give the inhabitants a feeling of security and actually to spare them the devastation suffered time and time again by Continental countries. Secure behind their moat, the English were able to curb royal propensities toward a standing army that might easily have become the weapon of domestic despotism, and they could devote their energies and resources to sea power. They were thus naturally directed toward overseas expansion. The location of Great Britain athwart the trade routes leading to northern Europe has made the country an entrepôt for the rich commerce flowing to and from the countries of this area.

Under modern conditions of war, Britain's island position is much less secure. While the Channel and the sea still impose handicaps to land invasion, they form no barriers to aircraft and long-range missiles. The dependence of the heavily populated British Isles on large imports of food, oil, cotton, timber, and other bulk materials makes the interdiction of sea routes by the airplane and the submarine a serious threat to security.

2. *Population*

The United Kingdom with 50,210,000 people is one of the most densely populated countries of the world. Having a population density of 532 to the square mile it is exceeded only by Belgium and the Netherlands among national states and by Massachusetts and Rhode Island in the United

States. Oregon with approximately the same area has, by contrast, a population density of 16 persons to the square mile.

The population of the United Kingdom is not evenly distributed. England has a population of 41,147,000; Scotland, 5,095,000; Wales and Monmouthshire, 2,596,000; and Northern Ireland, 1,369,000. The density of population in England is 743 per square mile, while in Scotland it is 170. Most of the British people live in cities, and London, Manchester, Glasgow, Liverpool, and Birmingham are the centers of some of the world's largest urban areas.

The growth of population in Great Britain during the past century and a half has been rapid. In 1801, the population was 10,501,000; in 1841, 18,534,000; in 1881, 29,710,000; in 1901, 37,000,000; in 1921, 42,769,-000, and in 1941, 46,605,000.[1] Most of this expansion occurred in the northern and northwestern parts of England where, as Professor Brinton has pointed out, the Industrial Revolution 'effected one of the most rapid and extensive changes in economic geography any country has ever undergone.'[2]

While the population of the United Kingdom has continued to increase in recent decades the rate of growth has slackened as compared with the nineteenth century. In 1944 the British Government, recognizing the importance of population trends for all economic and social planning, appointed a royal commission to examine the subject. The commission, reporting five years later, stated among its conclusions:

> If there is no substantial net migration, the following developments may be confidently predicted, even allowing for a considerable degree of uncertainty about future births:
>
> (i) Total numbers will continue to grow in the near future, perhaps even for another generation. The growth will not be rapid, and the further addition to the population which can be expected is not large.
>
> (ii) The population of working age will remain at about its present size for at least the next thirty years, though it will come to form a somewhat smaller proportion of the total.

---

[1] A decennial census has been taken in the United Kingdom since 1801, except in the year 1941 when the war prevented the usual count. The Registrar-General supervises the taking of the census and issues the subsequent statistical reports.

[2] Crane Brinton, *The United States and Britain* (Cambridge, Mass., 1947), p. 10. 'We in the United States,' he has said, 'often exaggerate the uniqueness of our own economic growth and pioneering. Great Britain in 1770 was not precisely an empty land, but in a century and a half it was to increase its eight million people five and sixfold. The increase was, moreover, geographically uneven. Counties like Dorset or Oxfordshire, for instance, increased very little; Lancashire and Yorkshire grew at an American rate. In 1770 Liverpool was a small town of a few thousands; in a long lifetime thereafter it had become the center of a Merseyside metropolitan area of close to a million. The men who built Liverpool were in some ways as much "pioneers" as the men who built Chicago.'

(iii) The population of young adults (15-39) will show a fall of about 1.4 millions in the next fifteen years.

(iv) The number of old people (over 65) will grow steadily over the next thirty years, the increase amounting to at least 2.3 millions and very probably much more. The proportion of old people to the total will increase considerably.[3]

Noting that the consequences of current population trends may be 'economic, social, psychological, political and strategic,' the commission concluded that the 'industrial progress, the standard of living and the security of the British people, the development and the cohesion of the British Commonwealth, the influence of British ideas, traditions and institutions throughout the world may be affected subtly but powerfully by demographic changes.'[4]

While foreigners recognize certain British types, the people of the British Isles are by no means a pure race. In fact, they are a mixture of several strains, although the Teutonic is the dominant. When the Romans crossed the Channel from Gaul they found the present British Isles inhabited by a Celtic people whom they subdued or drove back into the rough country of Wales and Scotland. Since the Roman colony lasted about 400 years one may suppose that there was considerable intermingling of the indigenous population and the officials, soldiers, traders, and other representatives of the Latin overlord. Meanwhile, a good many of the Celtic people continued to live beyond the sway of the Roman legions.

When the Romans withdrew England was invaded by rough tribesmen from the north German coast—Angles, Saxons, and Jutes. They later had to contest the country with the Danes. Finally, in the memorable year 1066, Duke William of Normandy invaded the island, defeated its Saxon king, Harold, and on Christmas Day was crowned William I, King of England. With William came a large company of noblemen, knights, and retainers, who received the spoils of conquest in the form of feudal estates, princely dignities, and civil and ecclesiastical offices. Two or three hundred years were to pass before Normans and Saxons were welded into a people and the term Englishman could be applied to any inhabitant of the country. England has experienced no large-scale immigration since 1066, although the Scots, the Welsh, and the Irish have continuously made contributions to the racial stock of England. Moreover, a good many French Huguenots were received at the end of the seventeenth century, and after World War II approximately 100,000 Polish soldiers elected to remain in Britain rather than be repatriated.

Students of nationalism recognize that in the creation and continuance of a national group, factors of common language, customs, and traditions are more important than racial origin. On this basis the great majority of

---

[3] Cmd. 7695 (1949), pp. 98-9.
[4] Ibid. p. 100.

the people of the United Kingdom have a sense of British nationality. Within the British nationalism, however, subsidiary national groups have survived. The most numerous are the English, who through long years of contact have imparted a good deal of their approach to political life to the other national groups composing the British state. Writing about the political characteristics of the English, among whom he has lived for many years, the Spanish author-diplomat, Salvador de Madariaga, has said:

> The people of England . . . come to politics with a strong sense of the national scope which politics must have. No doubt, in the heat and passion of political argument they may accuse each other of thinking more of their own class than of the country, but, in comparison with the peoples of other countries, the English are truly patriotic in their political activities, and a national argument is sure to go very deep with them.[5]

Scottish nationalism, always strong in the highlands, expresses itself in the tartan, the kilt, the bagpipe, oatmeal and haggis, and in the observance of distinctive holidays and festivals. Scotland has its own national church, and along the remote lochs and on the islands off the west coast Gaelic is the language of the crofters and fishermen. The Welsh, too, have distinctive customs and traditions. Their Celtic language with its profusion of consonants has never been supplanted among the rural folk. The Scotch-Irish of Ulster form still another subsidiary national group, tenacious of cultural characteristics that link them with Great Britain rather than the rest of Ireland. In their midst is a large minority joined in national spirit and religious faith to the people of Eire.

Scottish and Welsh nationalisms often seek some political expression. Nationalist candidates for Parliament frequently present themselves on platforms calling for greater autonomy for Scotland or Wales, and occasionally one of these candidates arrives at Westminster. There is probably more support in Scotland and Wales for such political devolution than the odd electoral success indicates. The sponsors of the Scottish 'covenant,' calling for a parliament in Edinburgh, claim that more than three-quarters of a million Scots have signed their petitions.[6]

The Scottish and Welsh nationalists complain that the economic development of Scotland and Wales has been neglected and that many young people from their regions must migrate to England in search of opportunity and recognition. If one examines the origins of British men and women prominent in public life it is pretty plain that the Scots have obtained their share of preferment and that the saying, 'All great Englishmen are Scots,' contains a bit of truth. A good many Welshmen have made their mark, too. Of eleven Prime Ministers in the twentieth century, three

---

[5] *Englishmen, Frenchmen, Spaniards* (London, 1928), pp. 156-7.
[6] *The New York Times,* 3 February 1950.

have been Scots and one a Welshman, a high proportion considering the respective populations of the major regions of the United Kingdom.

The United Kingdom, since the establishment of an independent Ireland, has been singularly free of racial groups exercising important influence upon its political life. There has been no Polish vote or Italian vote to which politicians must give attention; there has been no Negro population raising a 'civil rights' problem. Unlike some of the Continental countries, Britain has no ethnic minorities so insistent upon political or cultural autonomy that the very life of the state is at times threatened. In the case of Northern Ireland there is a reverse type of situation, for here the dominant Unionist faction is prepared to use strong measures to maintain the British connection. As indicated, there is considerable Scottish and Welsh national feeling, but neither the voters nor the Parliamentary representatives of Scotland and Wales form racial blocs within the body politic. All British parties have strength in Scotland and Wales, and ethnic issues usually get submerged in larger questions of national policy.

The inhabitants of Britain have always been divided into classes. In Saxon times there existed a social organization of nobility, freemen, villeins, and slaves. With a change of personnel in the nobility and the disappearance of slavery, it continued under the Normans. The rigid feudal structure characteristic of most of Europe passed away early in England. Various social and economic developments brought an end to villenage by the fourteenth century, and the independent, small farmers, the yeomen, became a considerable class of the population. With the growth of towns and cities there developed a thriving middle class, winning rights from Crown and nobility. In England the nobility remained a relatively small group numerically because of the principle that only one person inherited a title and other members of the family were commoners. Thus, the English nobility grew only through new creations by the Crown.

In modern times English society has been stratified into four distinguishable classes. The aristocracy—the hereditary nobility and their connections—still forms a comparatively small group. As a class it has been shorn of most of its political power, but its social standing remains high. Not many titled persons can show family trees deeply rooted in historic soil, for the great majority of peerages date no earlier than the eighteenth century. The more recent creations have brought to the nobility wealth or eminence in science, the arts, or statecraft, which adds to the stature of the class. The sense of *noblesse oblige* has been strong among the British aristocracy and has prevented the development of a socially privileged class divorced from the cultural life of the nation.

At the other end of the scale are the industrial and agricultural workers. The largest class in the nation, they live in the endless rows of unattractive brick houses of Britain's industrial centers or in the usually delightful villages of the rural areas. A literate, hard-working population, they have the dignity of free men. They are a people with a great deal of self-discipline, a willingness to obey constituted authority, and a trust of chosen leaders.

—9

The so-called middle classes consist of two main groups. One group includes several million people engaged in white-collar jobs—clerks, tradesmen, civil servants of the middle and lower grades, and technical workers—and their families. They form 'one of the world's great middle classes.'

Their economic position has been shaken by the inflation consequent upon two wars and by the scarcely corrective deflation of the Great Depression. But they have never suffered as the German middle classes have suffered, and like the rest of the nation they retain a good many of the Victorian ways—more, perhaps, than any other class in Great Britain. They still preach, and what is more, practice, middle-class morality . . . they are, if you like, a type middle class, conservative, unimaginative, hard-working (in spite of their fondness for afternoon tea)—the well-known backbone of the nation.[7]

The other group is referred to by a variety of names—the upper-middle class, the ruling class, the governing class. Several million people fall in this group, and its members comprise the rural gentry and the leaders in the business, professional, and cultural life of the nation. Many of them have attended 'public' schools, and a good proportion have gone to the universities. They have a cultivated manner of speaking, acquired at home and school, which is the most patent characteristic setting them apart from other middle-class folk. Supported by inherited wealth and fairly generous salaries or fees, they have had in the past sufficient affluence to permit them to pursue chosen professions and also to cultivate the arts and sciences. In recent years social and economic changes, particularly high taxation, have dealt severely with the upper-middle class. The jeopardy facing this class is a cause of concern as its members have provided Britain with a large group of independent, liberal-minded leaders who have had a highly developed sense of public duty and the intellectual interest and leisure to participate in and support the country's cultural activities.

Although the groups just discussed are recognizable strata in British society, it must not be assumed that the dividing lines between classes are sharply drawn. The lines are broad, and classes overlap. Moreover, there is a good deal of fluidity in the British social organization. It has always been possible for persons with ambition and enterprise, coupled with ability, to enter a higher social class. Once admitted, they and their families endeavor to make secure their new place by adopting the manners and conventions of the group. Such rigidity as has characterized the British class structure has been weakened considerably since the beginning of this century. Popular education has done much to raise the standards of the laboring classes and to provide them with opportunities for advancement, while other social services have bettered their lot. Excep-

[7] Brinton, op. cit. pp. 81-2.

10–

tionally high inheritance and income taxes have reduced the living standards of the propertied groups. Within two generations England has passed
through a social revolution that has probably produced a greater equality
of income than is to be found in any other large country.

It should be noticed that these social changes are not so much the
result of egalitarian or socialist principles as of the heavy legacies of
two world wars. Even if taxation did not bear with great severity upon
the middle and upper classes their standards of life would be depreciated
by Britain's trading position, which requires constricting the domestic
market in an effort to expand exports and thus earn foreign exchange.

The social changes occurring in Britain have naturally had effects upon
its political life. Until recent years the upper-middle class of British society
formed a real governing class. Its members sat in the House of Commons,
on the judicial bench, and in the council chambers of local government.
They filled the higher places in the Civil Service, they governed the colonial empire, and they represented the United Kingdom in foreign capitals.
The representatives of this class are still prominent in the public life of
the country, but they no longer have the virtual monopoly they had 50
years ago. Members of Parliament and ministers of the Crown with working-class and lower-middle-class backgrounds are not uncommon in present-day Britain. A county or a borough council is usually a pretty faithful
reflection of the social structure of the community. Popular education
and university scholarships have opened doors to the higher ranks of the
Civil Service and to the learned professions, from which come appointments to many public positions. Democracy in modern Britain means
more than a vote for every citizen; it means an opportunity to enter
public life if one has the interest and the ability.

3. Economic Life

Since Napoleon's dismissal of the English as a nation of shopkeepers their
addiction to trade and commerce has been taken for granted. By his day
the English had behind them two or three centuries of growth as a commercial nation. But during that time agriculture was the principal industry of the country and the main vocation of its citizens. It was a diversified
agriculture which provided the Englishman with a fairly broad diet and
good woolen cloth for his back. The story is well known of the series of
inventions and developments that transformed Britain during the century
from 1775 to 1875 from a comparatively small nation of farmers and
traders into the world's greatest industrial and imperial power. The Industrial Revolution did not have sudden adverse effects upon agriculture,
but it embodied political, social, and technological changes which eventually shifted the balance heavily in favor of manufacturing and commerce as the chief occupations of the English people and the principal
cares of their public policies. After the new industrial leaders gained com-
mensurate political power by the Reform Act of 1832 they withdrew
tariff protection from English agriculture with the result that, in the

-11

1870's, when the tramp steamer began to bring the grain from the prairies of the New World to Europe, the agricultural interests were started on a long decline. British prosperity depended upon the relatively cheap imports of food and raw materials and the export of manufactured goods to all parts of the world. With new sources of imports developing—the United States, Canada, Argentina, and Australia—and with a long start as the supplier of the manufactured articles all the world wanted, the terms of trade were greatly in Britain's favor.

The need during World War II to conserve shipping and foreign exchange caused the British government to stimulate domestic agricultural production by every means possible. After the conclusion of hostilities the need was equally great, because high agricultural prices throughout the world made imports costly and kept the terms of trade moving to Britain's disadvantage. By intensive land utilization the British succeeded in raising their domestic agricultural production from approximately one-third to more than one-half of requirements.

The British labor force numbers about 23 million gainfully employed people. By major occupational groups it is distributed as follows:

OCCUPATIONAL DISTRIBUTION [8]

		(In thousands)
Military service		832
Agriculture, forestry, and fishing		1,185
Mining and quarrying		853
Manufacturing industries		8,683
Building and contracting		1,447
Gas, electricity, and water		363
Transport and communication		1,786
Distributive trades		2,650
Professional, financial, and miscellaneous services		3,960
Public administration (national and local)		1,406
Unemployed		201
Males	15,966	
Females	7,400	
Total working population	23,366	23,366

Some eight million of these workers are members of the 730 registered labor unions. Many of these are small, independent unions; however, the great majority of organized workers belong to large unions which in turn are frequently federated with other unions to form industry-wide associations. In 1947, 17 of the 730 registered unions accounted for 67 per cent of the total strength of organized labor.[9] One British union, the Transport and General Workers' Union, is reputed to be the largest labor union in

[8] Adapted from *Ministry of Labour Gazette,* September 1951, p. 359.

[9] 'Trade Unions in Britain,' ID 953, published by British Information Services, December 1949, p. 6.

12–

the democratic world. The great majority of British unions and federations of unions, accounting for about 80 per cent of the organized workers of the nation, are affiliated with the Trades Union Congress. The T.U.C. is directed by a General Council of 25 members, and under a General Secretary it maintains a headquarters organization engaged in administrative, research, and informational activities. The T.U.C. does not control its affiliated members; its policy pronouncements are only advisory. It is, however, a powerful organization, because the strength of its total membership, the standing of its leaders, and the sense of loyalty in the labor movement give the T.U.C. a potency which its constitution belies.

The T.U.C. and its affiliated unions are deeply involved in national politics. They have been closely associated with the Labour Party from the beginning of the party, supplying most of its members and money. In 1948 when the Labour Party had a total membership of 5,422,437, trade-union members numbered 4,751,030. A considerable proportion of the Labour members of Parliament are trade unionists, although the ratio to other occupational groups has been falling since the Party's early days. In the general election of 1918, 49 of 57 successful Labour candidates were trade unionists; in 1945, 119 of 393.[10]

The employers' side of British industry is not so effectively organized for political purposes. There are many trade and business associations, and in the Federation of British Industries they have an influential national organization. The sympathies of most of the members of the individual associations and of the F.B.I. are with the Conservative Party, and a considerable share of the Party's funds are believed to come from these organizations.

Between the wars unemployment was widespread and persistent in Britain. In major industries, mining for example, tens of thousands were out of work for long periods and existed on the 'dole.' Regions such as the Tyneside and South Wales came to be known as depressed areas where the blight of unemployment was chronic. The memory of those days has had a profound effect upon the programs of political parties and the policies of the state. In the programs and policies of both the maintenance of full employment occupies a central place.

Finding work for all has been no problem since the start of World War II. During the war the military forces, munitions plants, agriculture, and the essential services absorbed every available person. Since the close of the conflict, markets at home and abroad and rearmament have kept British industry running at a high rate. Unemployment has been almost nonexistent. Some industries, in fact, have suffered from labor shortages, and the effective deployment of the working force has been a major problem. With the whole population fully employed, there has been little economic pressure on workers to move either geographically or occupationwise.

---

[10] Ibid. p. 6.

4. *Organs of Opinion*

As in every democratic country, the press in Great Britain has an important influence upon the political life of the country. It is the means whereby most of the nation's citizens obtain their news of Parliament, the Cabinet, and the other organs of government. Through it the political leaders of the day carry their views to the country and debate the current issues. Editorials in the press have varying degrees of influence, but there is no doubt about their being read in political circles and helping to shape policies and programs.

The newspapers which are today published in London differ not alone in format but also in character and responsibility. Foremost in almost any category but circulation is *The Times*. Founded in 1785, it has been for more than 150 years a potent influence in British political life. With its classified advertisements on page one and its most important news articles in the middle of the paper, *The Times* has never succumbed to the temptation of becoming a journal popular with the masses. Instead, it is written and edited for the relatively small number of people who have the time and interest to read news and comment on all serious topics of the day. Even under the severe limitations on newsprint that were imposed during World War II and continued for several years thereafter, *The Times* managed to publish a great deal of foreign and domestic news and extensive discussion of leading issues of the day. The time has passed when a leader in 'The Thunderer' could bring down a Government, but *The Times* remains the most influential press organ in the United Kingdom.

Five of London's morning newspapers seek to reach the largest reading public possible. They are *The Daily Express, The Daily Mail, The Daily Herald, The Daily Mirror,* and *The News Chronicle.* Their circulations run from a million and a half to more than four million copies each, and thus they are among the most widely read newspapers in the world. They serve up the news in a sprightly, eye-catching fashion and give considerable space to feature articles, gossip columns, and sports. *The Daily Mail* and *The Daily Express* are Conservative in politics, the latter being a sounding board for the personal and imperialist ideas of its publisher, Lord Beaverbrook. *The Daily Herald* is a supporter of the Labour Party and the *Mirror,* while independent, is anti-Conservative. *The News Chronicle* endeavors to keep alive the political point of view of the Liberals. Except for the *Herald* and the *Mirror,* each of these papers publishes an evening tabloid, under a different name, in which the news is still further condensed and the features of mass appeal given even greater emphasis. The Conservative Party's political views are also expressed in *The Daily Telegraph,* a serious morning newspaper which gives good coverage to foreign and domestic news and publishes thoughtful, responsible editorials. London has its representative of the ubiquitous *Daily Worker,* the organ of the Communist Party. *The Daily Worker* prints news with a communist slant, and in its editorial policy it manages to walk the party line, however many curves or circles it describes. *The Daily Worker* has never been able to establish a reading public comparable to that of any other London newspaper, and it is constantly conducting financial campaigns to keep its presses turning.

Unlike the American press, the Sunday newspapers in Great Britain are mostly independent enterprises not connected with the daily papers. An exception is *The Sunday Express,* which with its circulation of more than three million is an additional platform for Lord Beaverbrook. *The Sunday Times* and *The Observer* are both serious newspapers which devote a considerable amount of space to political news and comments upon the political situation. Several other Sunday newspapers, for example *News of the World, The People,* and *Sunday Pictorial,* are published for the masses and play up stories concerning crime, sports, and the entertainment world.

Because of the short distances involved and the rapid communication facilities available, the London press has been able to serve the whole island of Great Britain. *The Times* appears on the breakfast tables of subscribers throughout the country, and the other London newspapers serve a wide public beyond the limits of the metropolis. This nation-wide circulation has prevented the development in most cities of strong papers dealing with national and foreign affairs and having an editorial policy of influence upon the political life of the country. There are, however, a few important provincial papers which wield considerable influence. One which has an international reputation is *The Manchester Guardian. The Guardian* is an excellently edited newspaper and presents a liberal point of view in its editorial policy. Another strong provincial paper is *The Yorkshire Post,* which adheres to the Conservative Party. Two or three newspapers published in Scotland endeavor to give their readers a coverage of foreign and domestic news, and their editorial opinions are addressed to more than local problems.

In comparing the British press with the American in regard to their respective influences upon political life, one is impressed at once by the point which has just been suggested—namely, the extent to which the London press dominates the scene in Great Britain. Few newspapers in the United States approach the circulation figures of the leading London dailies, and consequently, the American press does not have the possibility of influencing so large a proportion of the country's population. A British politician can pick up on a London newsstand practically all the journalistic comment of the country, and immediately he has the press reaction to current issues and policies.

In spite of its concentration the British press appears to have no greater influence upon political affairs than the more regional American press. This is not surprising when it is recalled that the British press is divided in its political loyalty, with each major party having strong journalistic support. In the number of newspapers, and in the sum of their circulation figures, the Conservatives are ahead, but Labour gets its case to the public through journals partial to its cause and through the fair reporting of the more responsible papers. Circulation figures are not the same as votes cast, as the general elections of 1945 and 1950 affirm. In both elections the Labour Party won Parliamentary majorities in spite of the fact that its principal opposition received greater journalistic backing.

To appraise the influence of the press simply by the outcome of elections would be misleading, however. The newspapers are constantly dealing with current issues and policies—informing and explaining, praising and condemning, noting with satisfaction and viewing with alarm. In these ways they exert a considerable influence. They prompt members of Parliament to ask questions and to initiate debates, and they force political leaders to announce their positions on issues. It seems fair to say that in Britain, as in the United States, the press as a whole plays an indispensable role in the formulation and expression of the public opinion which ultimately controls political parties and Governments but that no section of it can command the voters when they enter the polling booths. On current issues and policy questions the press is one of the powerful influences shaping the attitudes and decisions of politicians.[11]

A summary of the British press and its influence upon political life would be incomplete without mentioning the part played by several weekly journals. The most important of these journals is *The Economist,* renowned throughout the world for the excellence of its comments upon current events as well as its reporting of economic and financial news. Launched more than a century ago, *The Economist* was for a long time an exponent of the Manchester school of political economy. It has moved away from that classic doctrine, but it remains closer to the modern Liberal Party point of view than to that of either the Conservatives or Labourites. Some years ago the ownership of *The Economist* was vested in an independent trust, so its editors are as free from the control of the publisher in their opinions as it is possible to make them. Other journals of opinion which have considerable influence are *The New Statesman and Nation,* usually a supporter of the Labour Party; *The Spectator,* a conservatively inclined journal, and *Time and Tide,* an independent, anti-

---

[11] In Labour Party circles there has been a feeling that the British press has drifted into the hands of a few wealthy individuals who have employed their power in an irresponsible fashion. The Labour Government, acceding in 1946 to such sentiments among its Parliamentary supporters, appointed a royal commission to conduct an inquiry. The Commission heard some 182 witnesses, besides receiving much documentary evidence, on the state of British journalism. Reporting in 1949, it stated: 'There is nothing approaching monopoly in the press as a whole' and that 'between 1921 and 1948 there was a marked tendency away from concentration of ownership in the national press.' The Commission believed, that, except for a few 'quality papers,' the daily press fell short of an ideal standard in reporting the news and that an insufficient variety of intellectual levels was catered to, although an adequate variety of political opinions found voice in the British newspapers. These shortcomings were not attributed to sinister influences but to an attempt to 'give the public what the public will buy.' The Commission saw no solution in state control but on the contrary declared, 'Free enterprise is a requisite of a free press.' It called upon the press to police itself and to seek to improve its own standards of performance. Cmd. 7700 (1949).

socialist organ. *The Tribune,* pungent and disputatious, is the journalistic vehicle of the more leftist members of the Labour Party. None of these journals has a large circulation, but they are widely read in the political and business circles that have the most influence upon public policy.

It is not strictly accurate to include radio in a discussion of organs of opinion in Britain, for broadcasting is a public monopoly and is charged with being objective and nonpartisan. All public radio facilities are owned and operated by the British Broadcasting Corporation, a nonprofit public corporation, controlled by a board of governors appointed by the Government. The news broadcasts of the B.B.C. are an established institution in British life, and they are successful in presenting a fair and balanced account of the events of the day. The B.B.C. allots time to the principal political parties to present their views upon public issues, and it has treated them in a sufficiently equitable manner so that there is no serious dissatisfaction on the grounds of prejudice or censorship.

5. *The Character of British Political Life*

The foregoing pages have described some of the principal characteristics of the environment in which the political institutions of the United Kingdom operate. The form and spirit of a nation's government can only be understood in the context of its geography, the composition of its population, and the economic and cultural activities of its people. The political life of a country is not conducted in a sealed room; it ranges throughout the house and is much affected by activities in other compartments of the total national structure. It would scarcely be argued today, for example, that democratic political institutions could long survive the elimination of a free press, and it is doubtful that an autocratic regime could maintain itself without controlling the organs of public information. The development and the present-day characteristics of British political institutions have been influenced by Britain's insular position, the country's size, the ethnic composition and economic activities of its people, and their social and cultural life.

For several generations British political life has been conducted on a high plane. After the nation recovered from the fears of political and social upheaval engendered by the French Revolution, a reformist movement developed sufficient strength to start attacks on corruption, patronage, and oligarchic privilege. Supported by such diverse influences as the rectitude of the Victorian court, the Nonconformist conscience, and a developing humanitarianism, it raised the tone of British politics. Participation in politics had always been an honorable vocation, one like the Church, the law, or the military service, to which a gentleman could devote his time and talents; and it came more and more to be viewed as an opportunity for service to the common weal.

Until the present century the standards of official life were in the custody of the upper classes whose members occupied the positions from justice of the peace to Cabinet minister. The standards of the former gov-

−17

erning classes have been successfully transmitted to the new groups which the democratization of British institutions has brought into places of power. The new classes in their turn have contributed much in the way of idealism and devotion to the public welfare. British public life remains, therefore, a field of activity in which the standards are high and duty receives more emphasis than personal privilege. There are occasional lapses, to be sure, and in Britain, as elsewhere, officials succumb to temptation and betray their trust. But the corruption and the cynical attitude toward public office which disfigure democratic government in some countries are for the most part absent in the United Kingdom.

Moreover, British political life is conducted, by and large, in good temper. It is vigorous; hard blows are struck and received, and deep bitterness is generated over some issues. Nevertheless, a spirit of tolerance and fairplay is more characteristic of the attitude of political opponents than one of contempt or vindictiveness. The public seems to prefer its politics conducted in this spirit. Sharp practice, however legal, usually brings popular condemnation as unfair and unsportsmanlike.

The tolerance, the willingness to compromise, and the observance of the spirit as well as the letter of the rules which pervade political life in Britain have assisted the nation in surmounting grave problems which would have paralyzed or disrupted less flexible societies. Conditions resulting from the change in Britain's position as a world power and the social revolution which has proceeded in this century might have produced a political intransigence straining constitutional government to the limit. They have not, and this is in large measure due to the traditions and spirit of British political life.

II

The Constitution

The United Kingdom, like every sovereign state, has a constitution. That is, it has a fundamental law, a set of basic political principles which deals in the main with the location and distribution of governmental power, the form and functioning of the organs of government, and the relationship of individuals to the state.

Constitutions of modern democratic states commonly consist of four elements: (a) a written charter or a collection of historic documents, including formal amendments; (b) statutes of constitutional importance; (c) judicial interpretations, and (d) customs and precedents. If the core of the constitution consists of a written document adopted or promulgated at a particular time, the state is said to have a written constitution. If, on the other hand, there is no such single document, the state is considered to possess an unwritten constitution. The importance of such a classification may be easily exaggerated. The 'written' constitutions acquire many unwritten parts, and through the years they become overlaid with legislative amplifications, judicial interpretations, and customary provisions. The 'unwritten' ones usually have important parts committed to paper as charters or broad constitutional statutes. In the course of time the two types come more and more to resemble one another.

The Constitutions of the United States and of Great Britain are spoken of as classic examples of the two types. The core of the American Constitution is the charter drafted at Philadelphia in 1787 and ratified by a sufficient number of states to become operative in 1789. While the document of the Philadelphia Convention remains the starting point for anyone wishing to learn about the Constitution of the United States, in meaning it has developed far beyond the original words. Twenty-two formal amendments have been added, but they represent only a portion of the changes that have been made since 1789. The Congress has enacted many laws that are part of the constitutional fabric—for example, the statutes creating the administrative departments and agencies, the acts determining the succession in the event of the death or removal of both the President and the Vice-President, and the legislation establishing the federal courts system. Furthermore, the Supreme Court in many decisions has amplified and developed the original charter which, being comparatively brief and written for the most part in general terms, has required of the judiciary a weighty duty of interpretation. The fact that a constitution drafted in the stage-coach and sailing vessel era can serve as the nation's fundamental law in the period of airplanes, radio, and atomic power is in large measure because of the constant modernization of the original language by judicial interpretation. Customs have played their part, too. Every day the actions of public officials deepen the grooves of custom so that the machine of state is often guided by them as much as by written rules. The President's Cabinet is an institution organized and continued according to custom, and the role of political parties in the governmental process is largely determined by custom. To understand, therefore, what the Constitution of the United States is at any particular time one must read not only the original document and the amendments thereto but also consult numerous legislative acts and judicial decisions and study the prevailing customs and precedents.

1. *The Elements of the British Constitution*

The 'unwritten' Constitution of Great Britain consists of materials similar to those of the 'written' Constitution of the United States, although the proportions of the ingredients differ. There is no single document comparable to that drafted by the Philadelphia Convention, but there are a number of great historical charters and acts which taken together compose a basic, written law forming part of the Constitution. The most famous, of course, is the Magna Carta of 1215. In this category are the Petition of Right of 1628, the Habeas Corpus Act of 1679, the Bill of Rights of 1689, the Act of Settlement of 1701, the Act of Union with Scotland of 1707, the Great Reform Act of 1832, the Parliament Act of 1911, and the Statute of Westminster of 1931.

Some of these basic documents have more symbolic than intrinsic importance; they have come to represent principles of more general application or of a more liberal character than their authors intended. This is particularly true of the Magna Carta, which through the centuries came to be cited as a guarantee of personal rights and of limitations on royal power more extensive than envisaged by the barons gathered at Runnymede. Such documents are no less important because of this evolution, for it is what succeeding generations believe they represent that makes them vital parts of the Constitution. Some of the historic documents forming part of the Constitution sum up periods of constitutional development or represent the settlement of constitutional struggles. The Bill of Rights of 1689, for example, sets forth in written form the great issues at stake in the constitutional crises of the seventeenth century and was an announcement of the settlement that had been reached. The Statute of Westminster of 1931 summarized, in a sense, several decades of constitutional development in the relations between the United Kingdom and the self-governing dominions.

Legislation forms a large part of the British Constitution. There is scarcely a session of Parliament that does not contribute to the constitu-

laws of constitutional importance enacted by Parliament, judicial interpretations of Parliamentary acts and common-law rights, and the conventions observed by those participating in present-day British political life. All these elements would have to be taken into account should one wish to describe the nature, powers, and functioning of some part of the British political system.

2. *The Amendment of the Constitution*

A constitution must necessarily have some means of amendment. The amending power in Britain is lodged in Parliament, and the British Constitution makes no technical distinction between ordinary legislation and legislation fundamental enough to be considered constitutional. Bills of both kinds go through the same Parliamentary procedure. The British Constitution, therefore, is relatively easy to amend in contrast to the American, which requires action by the Congress and a large proportion of the States.

In actuality, the difference is probably not as great as it seems. It has become generally accepted that Parliament will not pass legislation of a significant constitutional character unless the voters have had an opportunity to express their satisfaction or dissatisfaction with the Government and its legislative majority in a general election. When a Government has a large Parliamentary majority there is naturally a temptation to interpret rather liberally the definition of constitutional issues requiring a new mandate from the voters, and, of course, there is no immediate way of compelling observance of the general rule. At a subsequent general election, however, the voters may show their dislike of constitutional changes considered made without a sufficient mandate by defeating the Government that sponsored them.

It is true, of course, that rarely is a general election merely a referendum on a constitutional matter. Probably the closest to that kind of an election was the one that preceded the passage of the Parliament Act of 1911 when the question of the respective powers of the two legislative houses was the principal issue before the voters. Constitutional and current issues tend to be mixed up in a political campaign, and it would be impossible to say that the results of an election turn solely on one question that is before the electorate. The political opposition, however, can be counted upon to emphasize incidents in which it believes the Government has violated the commonly accepted interpretation of the Constitution, and if it makes a good case for its point of view this fact will undoubtedly influence many voters when they go to the polls.

Some constitutional changes are so generally recognized as necessary that they are not made party issues but are agreed to by both the Government and the Opposition. An example of this type was the Statute of Westminster of 1931 which, in effect, made the British Commonwealth an association of independent states united only in the person of the King. Statutes determining the numerical size of the House of Commons and distributing Parliamentary seats have been dealt with by inter-party agreement.

tional structure statutes that add to or alter the basic la
Examples in this class are statutes establishing governme
and defining their powers, acts determining the qualificatioı
parliamentary and municipal elections, and laws concernin
and powers of local authorities.

The place of judicial decisions in the British Constituti
nificant than it is in the American Constitution. Since Parliaı
legislative supremacy and its enactments are not subject to j
in the American sense, judicial decisions do not bulk so larȝ
pared to the other elements of the Constitution. The British
ever, in interpreting and clarifying the law frequently decl
Constitution is. The civil liberties of British subjects are large
in the common law and thus have been defined and protected ƚ
Freedom of speech, of the press and of assembly, the sanctity
home, and the right of jury trial are common-law rights which
their effective meaning in the long lines of decisions judges
Statutes may redefine or modify the manner of exercising thes₍
such laws are in turn subject to judicial interpretation made
of the many precedents of the past.

One of the most important elements of the British Constitu
of custom and precedent—the conventions of the Constitution
person is well acquainted with a large body of customs and
that govern the form and functioning of British government, hₑ
a faint conception of the nature of the British Constitution. Th
of the monarch in modern Britain is largely determined by custoı
letter of the law has been little changed since the days when the
a working executive and exerted a determining influence upon th
operations of the government. In law, the monarch appoints and
ministers, he has the power to veto legislation, he declares war aı
peace, and he commands the armed forces of the nation. Actuall
know, he either performs these actions only in a nominal sense
them not at all. The transfer of power from the person of the moı
the Crown as an institution and the lapse of royal powers have ı
accomplished by statutes or judicial interpretations but by custo
are equally binding. So strong are the conventional rules of the Conȿ
that it is said that the monarch would assent to a bill abolishing ƚ
position.

The organization and functioning of the Cabinet are largely dete
by custom, for the comparatively recent written law dealing with thi
important institution assumes its existence and place in the constitı
structure and pertains to rather incidental matters, such as the salaı
ministers. Fundamental principles of Cabinet government—the Prime
ister's pre-eminent position, the Cabinet's responsibility to the Hou
Commons, and the collective responsibility of ministers—are establ
by tradition and custom and cannot be cited in the statute books.

In summary, then, the Constitution of the United Kingdom consis
the effective parts of a considerable number of historic charters and stat

—2

In addition to amendment by statutory process, the British Constitution is undergoing constant change through the deepening or abandoning of customs and usages. This is a process which can only be observed at a distance, for naturally a number of incidents are required either to establish a precedent or to indicate that one is no longer valid. As already mentioned, the considerable set of customary rules which establishes the place of the monarch in present-day British government represents amendment by custom and precedent. The requirement that the Prime Minister be a member of the House of Commons represents another change by custom, since it is legally possible for the chief Cabinet minister to be drawn from the House of Lords.

From time to time in Great Britain actions of a Government are denounced in Parliament, in the press, or on the platform as unconstitutional. The critics making such charges mean that the Cabinet is not observing some provision of a well-recognized basic charter or document or has contravened some accepted customary portion of the Constitution. It is not meant, as is frequently the case in the United States, that the highest court of the land has found a legislative act in conflict with a more fundamental written law. In England the remedy open to persons who believe they suffer from unconstitutional actions is the ballot box; no court would entertain a suit challenging as unconstitutional a parliamentary statute or a ministerial action flying in the face of long-established custom. This is not to say that courts will not protect British subjects in the rights they have acquired by statute and long usage, but that these rights may be erased or altered by more recent acts of Parliament. Moreover, a distinction should be drawn between the common-law rights of the subject and customs and precedents affecting the functioning of the governmental organization. The authority of the latter is not to be found in a long line of judicial decisions but in acts of government that have altered and changed the substantive meaning of the law.

The question may be asked: What sanctity does the Constitution have if Parliament may amend it at any time or if an established convention may be broken by politicians temporarily in power? The answer is that the British people treasure their Constitution and are not disposed to see it altered except in ways agreeable to a majority of them. This sentiment is shared by politicians as well as voters. On this matter Professor Ogg said:

> Parliament, after all, is composed of men who, with few exceptions, are respected members of a well-ordered society, endowed with sense, and alive to their responsibility for safeguarding the country's political heritage. They live and work under the restraint of powerful traditions and will no more run riot with the constitution than if it were weighted down with guarantees designed to put it beyond their control. Legally, the constitution is undeniably the most flexible on earth; but actually, it is considerably less fluid than might be inferred from what the writers say. History shows that few systems of government are more grudg-

ingly and conservatively reconstructed by deliberate legislative act. Considered practically, the flexibility of a constitution depends far less upon the procedure of amendment than upon the political temperament of the people.[1]

3. *Phases of Constitutional Development*

In the long period of English history several constitutional phases are discernible. The first phase may be said to have ended with Magna Carta in 1215. It was characterized by the establishment of various primitive institutions of government, the majority of which have survived to this day although their purpose and functions have sometimes changed. The office of the monarch is still an essential part of the government: he is nominally the head of the executive establishment, a participant in the legislative process, and the source of judicial authority. The Great Council survives as Parliament. The successors of the judges sent out on circuit by Henry II to dispense the King's justice continue on these rounds. The Small Council lives on in the modern Ministry and Cabinet and in some of the special courts that grew out of its medieval activities. The sheriffs still represent the Crown in the counties, although their duties are largely ceremonial.

Until 1215 the major constitutional problem was the devising of some means to restrain the tendencies to arbitrary and despotic power on the part of the strong-willed Kings. The medieval nobility, the only class important enough to challenge the royal power, decided to make its rulers subscribe to agreements which set forth the rights of the King's subjects. Hence, they drew up Magna Carta. For a century or more after Magna Carta it was customary for each new King to confirm the obligations set forth in the charter.

Having bound their rulers by agreements, the barons next had the problem of enforcing their observance. Several centuries of constitutional development were required to work out the methods by which the power of the King could be limited and directed in the national interest without employing the sanction of revolution. Parliament slowly developed and gained powers, chiefly that of the purse, that enabled it to restrain the royal authority. It was not until the end of the seventeenth century, however, that the issue of where ultimate power resided was settled and it became clear that Parliament, as the representative of the nation, was the real sovereign. This fundamental constitutional decision was reached after occasional revolts against royal authority, the deposition of several monarchs, the execution of one, and the trial for a decade of a republican form of government.

The date 1689 marks the end of one great constitutional phase and the beginning of another. After 1689 no monarch ever challenged the supremacy of Parliament or considered that he owed his throne to any higher authority than the nation's representatives assembled at Westminster. This is not to say that after 1689 the modern concept of the constitutional mon-

---

[1] Frederic Austin Ogg, *English Government and Politics* (New York, 1936), p. 72.

arch appeared at once. William III, who with his consort Mary succeeded the deposed James II, was a vigorous ruler and a great power in the day-to-day government of the country. But by gradual stages executive power passed into the hands of the King's ministers, and the monarchs ceased to be the active heads of the administrative establishment. The lack of interest in British domestic affairs shown by the first Hanoverian sovereign, George I, and the language barrier between him and his ministers were accidents of history that accelerated the constitutional trend. George III, trying to follow his mother's admonition, 'George, be a king,' endeavored to reassert the exercise of royal authority in the detailed operations of the government, but he never challenged the constitutional principles which underlay the state and the way it functioned. By bribery, by influence, and by the lavish bestowal of favors, George III advanced the royal power at the expense of Parliament, but this was a short interlude which ended when the King's disastrous policies for dealing with the American colonies in revolt failed. From then on, the constitutional development was in the direction of perfecting the means by which a sovereign Parliament could control and direct the executive power of the state.

The device of a cabinet responsible to the legislature was developed to meet the constitutional need. The Cabinet and its functioning grew out of old and established institutions, and indeed today the Cabinet's literal legal position differs little from what it was in the eighteenth century. Precedent upon precedent, however, has changed a collection of individual royal advisers and administrators into a group collectively responsible to one another and to the lower house of Parliament. The King still names the ministers, and theoretically he is free to nominate any person he wishes, but actually he is restricted to the leader of the largest party in the House of Commons as the Prime Minister and the ministerial group proposed by this leader.

While it can be said that there has been no sharp break in constitutional development since 1689, the Great Reform Act of 1832, which broadened the suffrage and made the House of Commons more representative of the nation, marked a turning point of considerable significance. Its meaning was that henceforth the Government must be conducted in accordance with public opinion as expressed in the choice between parties at general elections. Previously a Cabinet enjoying the confidence of the Crown and the House of Lords could usually 'manage' the House of Commons. Ministers through their aristocratic connections and by means of a judicious distribution of patronage could construct a majority which would support them until the Crown transferred its confidence to others or a realignment among the leading politicians occurred. As the size of the electorate increased and as the Parliamentary seats for pocket and rotten boroughs—controlled and unrepresentative electoral districts—disappeared, Cabinets had to look to the more democratic House of Commons for their authority; in order to govern they required a party majority of members representing a body of opinion in the country. The change in the direction of constitutional development wrought by the Act of 1832 was not immediately perceived by the politicians of the time, but within a few years they adjusted themselves to the new order. 'Precedents arising before 1832,' Sir Ivor Jennings has pointed out, 'must be used in rare cases only, for the Reform Act altered the fundamental assumption of the Constitution.' [2]

The process of refinement and adjustment goes on. The modern Constitution is not a static affair. It is constantly growing and changing, and issues within the major framework are always arising. The basic features of the Constitution, however, are firmly set and supported. The overwhelming mass of the people of Britain are content with their constitutional order; they are satisfied that it is well designed to resolve the conflicting interests that modern social life produces. It is flexible enough to adapt itself to new conditions; it is rigid enough to preserve the progress made over many centuries toward those democratic ideals to which the western world still aspires.

4. *Basic Constitutional Principles*

Several basic constitutional principles underlie the modern government of the United Kingdom and condition its functioning. The first: Britain is a constitutional monarchy. The King is, in legal theory, the source of all authority. Members of Parliament are summoned by his proclamation, and this great council of the nation consists of King, Lords, and Commons. Ministers are his servants and together form His Majesty's Government. Judges dispense the King's justice, and military officers command his forces. The monarch is the head of the state churches in England and Scotland. Even the political opponents of the Government are known as His Majesty's opposition. Thus, the authority of the monarchy embraces all elements of power within the nation. The monarch, as we shall see, reigns but does not rule; yet his office unifies and provides a focus of loyalty for all who participate in the governing of Britain.

The adjective 'constitutional' is added to this principle of monarchy to indicate that the King is bound to act according to existing law and custom. He is not free to resume the personal exercise of any royal powers that have lapsed or that may now be employed only upon the advice of his ministers. An attempt by a monarch to do so—to refuse his assent to a Parliamentary bill, to dismiss a personally objectionable minister, to express a personal opinion on a political issue, to grant a peerage not recommended by the Prime Minister—would bring on a constitutional crisis of the first magnitude. The monarch's abdication would be the almost certain outcome of such a crisis.

Next among basic constitutional principles is the concept of Parliamentary supremacy. King, Lords, and Commons in Parliament assembled possess the legal authority to enact laws on any subject. To illustrate by the extreme, Parliament could restrict office-holding to women, suppress all newspapers, and require every citizen to embrace Buddhism. There is no

---

[2] *Cabinet Government,* 2nd ed. (Cambridge, 1951), p. 9.

higher law to which one can appeal against an act of the sovereign Parliament. No judge would declare an act of Parliament null and void. Yet while the legal supremacy of Parliament is incontestable, there are practical limits to its powers. Its acts must have the acceptance of a vast majority of the population else such mighty authority would not be tolerated. Only if Britain were transformed into a police state could sweeping laws repugnant to a majority of its citizens be enforced, regardless of any theory of Parliamentary supremacy. The concentration of legal power in Parliament has the advantages of eliminating many constitutional disputes within the body politic and facilitating the mobilization of the state's authority in times of emergency. It requires, however, a maturity of political action and a sense of responsibility on the part of the governors and the governed. Its abuse would quickly bring the political fabric of the nation down in ruins.

A third basic principle of the Constitution concerns the liberty of the citizen. This liberty is well guaranteed in the United Kingdom. Most democratic states have chosen to list the rights of their citizens in some kind of a constitutional document. The constitutions of the American states of the United States have bills of rights, and the federal Constitution has a similar compilation in the first ten amendments, quickly added in 1791 to remedy what was widely regarded as a defect in the document as originally drafted. The postwar constitutions of Italy, Japan, and the states of Western Germany contain bills of rights, and the constitution of the Fourth French Republic readopted, with some additions, the 'Declaration of the Rights of Man and of the Citizen' of 1789.

The British, too, have a bill of rights enacted by Parliament in 1689 following its adoption by the Convention Parliament the previous year. It does not comprise a complete catalogue of the rights of British citizens, for additional ones depend upon other acts of Parliament and upon the common law as interpreted by the courts. Indeed, the most fundamental of all perhaps, the rule of law, is a common-law principle and appears in no Parliamentary enactment. Wherever found, the rights and liberties of British citizens are as extensive as those of the people of any modern democratic state and are as jealously guarded.

A contradiction may appear to exist between the principles of guaranteed rights and Parliamentary supremacy. If Parliament can amend or repeal any statute, override the decision of any court, and change the common law, what sanctity do personal liberties have? They have only the sanctity of tradition supported by the overwhelming power of public opinion, and this is sufficient. It may be observed, moreover, that in reality it is this sanction that preserves individual liberty in any country. Recent history is strewn with constitutions containing high-flown bills of rights worth no more than the paper on which they were written. Only if Parliament fell into the hands of a group bent on revolution would there be any possibility of the liberty of the citizen being abolished or seriously curtailed.

Although the modern British government does not exemplify the separation of powers which Montesquieu regarded as the great virtue of eighteenth-century English political organization, the judicial branch is nevertheless independent, and this independence is a cardinal principle of the Constitution. In the olden days fearless judges often defied tyrannically minded monarchs, but it was not until the beginning of the eighteenth century that an independent status for the judiciary was officially established. Leaving the appointment of judges with the Crown, the Act of Settlement of 1701 provided for permanent tenure, with removal only upon an address of the houses of Parliament. It also assured the judges fixed salaries. Thus protected, the judiciary has grown in prestige until it is in no danger from any executive or legislative interference.

Finally, the United Kingdom is a unitary state. In contrast to a federal state, it has no territorial subdivisions which have powers placed by a fundamental constitutional agreement beyond the reach of the central government. There are no areas such as the states of the United States, the provinces of Canada, or the states of Australia with powers that are declared in a constitutional act unalterable by the national authority alone. Scotland, it is true, possesses certain separate governmental institutions, and Northern Ireland has its own legislature. The autonomy in these cases, however, rests upon acts of the Parliament at Westminster and could legally, if less certainly as a matter of practical politics, be withdrawn by that body. The principal units of local government, counties and boroughs, are creations, constitutionally, of the national authority, and their boundaries, powers, and governmental organization may be changed by Parliament. In practice, they enjoy considerable autonomy and are not mere administrative subdivisions of the central authority, but this condition is a result of their historical place in the British state and a universal belief in the virtues of local self-government.

5. Recent Constitutional Trends

The history books of the past century reveal that there has been a steady movement toward the democratization of British political institutions. This can be clearly seen in the progressive enlargement of the electorate. Beginning with the Reform Act of 1832 a series of measures has extended the suffrage until today the privilege of voting is enjoyed by almost all adult citizens. The remaining suffrage limitations are few and principally designed to safeguard the privilege itself.

Along with the extension of the suffrage has gone an increase in the power of the elected element in British government. This trend is chiefly to be seen in the declining authority of the House of Lords. By the opening of the twentieth century the House of Lords was definitely the secondary chamber of the Parliament, and its inferior position was confirmed in law by the Parliament Act of 1911. That Act practically removed the power of the peers in financial legislation and limited their power with respect to other kinds of legislation to only one of delay.

When the Labour Government came into office in 1945 there were few political relics of a nondemocratic past which aroused reformers to call for remedial legislation. The Government decided to abolish the 12 university seats in the House of Commons and with them the second vote enjoyed by university graduates, although many critics believed that the democratic principle was doing itself a disservice in this change. The Government also undertook to restrict further the delaying power of the House of Lords. This hereditary chamber continues to exist principally because agreement on the composition and powers of a substitute second chamber has been difficult. Judged by the standards of the proportion of citizens eligible to participate in the basic political process and their opportunities for effective control of the machinery of the state, it may be said that Great Britain is one of the most advanced democracies of the present day.

Among recent constitutional trends, one of great significance is the growing power of the Government, i.e. the Cabinet and Ministry, in the political machinery of the state. This growth in power is largely a result of the increasing complexity and the amount of business of the modern state. A century ago Parliament could debate and decide a considerable number of major questions in each session, and while the Cabinet would be influential in determining the results reached it did not exercise the control over the legislative body that it does today. In the last few decades the volume and complexity of legislation have forced Parliament to rely more and more upon the initiative and guidance of the Government. Practically all legislation today originates in government departments or Cabinet committees and is presented to Parliament for debate and criticism but not for challenges that strike at any of the fundamental features of the legislation. The result is that Parliament is becoming more and more an arena where the Government is criticized and defended. The Government, not Parliament, is the dynamo of the political machine.

This process of aggrandizement on the part of the Government has not gone unchallenged, but it has proved difficult to propose ways and means of restoring legislative initiative and a greater amount of discretion to Parliament. A great deal of modern legislation involves technical matters which can only be drafted by departmental experts, and the member of Parliament, unless he be a specialist in the particular subject involved, is forced to support or oppose as Government and opposition leaders direct. The volume of legislation that Governments wish to enact also contributes to their growing power. They feel compelled to monopolize practically the whole time of Parliament, and the chances of a member squeezing in a non-ministerial bill for Parliamentary consideration are exceedingly slim. Indeed, for several years during and after World War II all time for private members' bills was eliminated, and thus there was destroyed the small opportunity previously existing for non-Governmental legislation.

While the growing power of the Government vis-à-vis Parliament is an important constitutional trend of the present time, it represents in a sense a restoration of a former relationship between the executive and the legislature in the British political system. From the earliest times the initiative and responsibility for political action have been taken by the executive— the King and later the monarch advised by his ministers. As late as the first part of the eighteenth century, Parliament 'was not yet thought of as being in the main a legislative body. Its function was to control the executive, to vote supplies and see that they were prudently spent, to decide the issues of peace and war, and to call ministers to account.' [3] The middle of the nineteenth century when Parliament was more influential in the fashioning of policy was an exceptional period. L. S. Amery has thus explained the Victorian era:

> The mutual interlocking of Government and Parliament had by then been fully achieved. The *laissez-faire* theories of the age in economic matters and the absence of any serious external menace since Trafalgar and Waterloo had reduced the active work, both of administration and legislation, to a minimum. A few broad issues of general policy could be spread over prolonged and eloquent debates. Parliamentary debate as such dominated the attention of the public and created the great Parliamentary figures of that day. In the comparatively evenly balanced and less strictly disciplined Parliament of the time, with both parties and the electorate itself drawn from a limited social stratum, it was not unnatural to conclude that Parliament, which so frequently upset Government, was in fact the body which governed and did so in response to the positive wishes of an actively interested electorate. [4]

Present-day members of Parliament may criticize the Government's actions and policies and these views will be carefully considered by ministers, for it is essential that the Government carry at least its supporters along in a reasonably happy frame of mind. Elections are not won by parties of disgruntled and unenthusiastic candidates. The idea, however, of the Ministry's being a legislative committee operating on a short leash from Parliament is a misreading of the contemporary British Constitution. Circumstances have forced the Government to be the dynamic element in the political structure. The need and wish of the public and its various interest groups for political action, party organization and discipline, the natural desire of private members of Parliament to stand well with prominent ministerial figures who dispense the favors of office, and the politicians' dislike of having expensive election contests forced upon them, all contribute to a strengthening of the Government's position.

Another constitutional trend of recent times is the increased authority of party organizations. This is reflected in the greater amount of discipline exercised by political party leaders and accepted by their Parliamentary supporters. Party leaders have always endeavored to maintain some discipline over their rank-and-file membership in Parliament. They have used persuasion, patronage, and other forms of pressure or inducement to keep their ranks solid. The importance of this kind of organizational work is

---

[3] G. M. Young, in Sir Ernest Barker [ed.], *The Character of England* (Oxford, 1947), p. 93.

[4] *Thoughts on the Constitution* (Oxford, 1947), p. 14.

Adlai E. Stevenson

"The American standard of living is due in no small measure to the imaginative genius of advertising, which not only creates and sharpens demand, but also, by its impact upon the competitive process, stimulates the never ceasing quest of improvement in quality of the product."

Isn't it strange to find people in this country today who criticize advertising and say it should be restricted? Well-meaning people who say that it is unfair competition for a big company to spend more on advertising than a small company.

Ignoring the fact that it is advertising that helps small companies grow big . . . companies like Polaroid, Xerox, Sony and dozens more who have taken on the giants in the marketplace and won their profitable niche.

These people think we should restrict the amount of advertising a company can do—just to be fair.

But, of course, big companies spend more on research and development than little companies, too. And that's even more unfair because it helps develop new products the little companies don't have. So, perhaps, we should also restrict research and development.

It's too bad somebody didn't think of this 40 years ago. Then we'd all still have iceboxes. And you wouldn't have to worry about getting all that frozen food home from the supermarket before it thaws. In your 1967 Model "T."

Magazine Publishers Association
An association of 365 leading U.S. magazines

I start cleaning it. I have brought torn pieces of *Pravda* from the lavatory, and I dunk them in a pan and wipe my floor and "furniture" with fanatical devotion. The problem of cold is more difficult. My prison uniform is simply underwear and dirty dungarees, and canvas boots without laces or socks. The radiator is tepid, and it is November of the coldest winter Europe has known for years. I shiver constantly.

Each day after my one hour of exercise in a small pen on the roof (for this I am allowed an old greatcoat), I go back to my cell. I would like to learn some Russian, but that is not allowed. I have an English pocket dictionary and a pencil, and on the blank page at the end I start a calendar, with crosses to mark the days. Sometimes I have an insane wish to put in several crosses at once as if to make time pass more quickly, but this I resist.

The worst part of loneliness is the beginning. Strange thoughts appear, and my sense of values begins to wobble. I worry about the color of the walls—their grimy Nile green annoys me. After days of work I remove every speck of dirt. My rubbing gives the Nile green a mottled effect, but it is clean, which gives me a sense of victory.

In the impassive Slav faces of my guards I see no hint of human contact, but one day the door opens and a fat girl brings me a cup of tea, and two days later, some extra meat. One of the men catches the idea and he, too, gives me food and cigarettes on the sly. "Not evil but misled." How many times have I heard Penkovsky say that about the Soviet people? It is only the rulers who are evil.

A Visit From Sheila

I AM interrogated every morning and some afternoons. The lieutenant colonel takes over. He drones on for hours about how much he knows of my activities and why I should be sensible and coöperate. I keep repeating that I don't know what it is all about. After a week of this, I am taken to another floor and up to the door of a cell. The lieutenant colonel gives an order, and the guard puts his hand over my mouth and draws back the spy-hole shutter, and the lieutenant colonel says, "Look, Mr. Veen, and tell us if you recognize this man."

I put my eye to the slit and there, sitting on the metal bed, is Penkovsky. No, not Penkovsky, the wreck of Penkovsky. His face is thin and hidden with straggly stubble. He sits motionless with his head down, like a bull after the first wound from the picador has weakened him, when the red strength of his blood is pouring down his shoulders. They have drained Penkovsky of strength by starvation and lack of sleep. I feel sick and wish he would move, but he does not.

I am taken back to the interrogation room, and the lieutenant colonel says through the interpreter, "Well, Mr. Veen, now you have seen the traitor Penkovsky and you

recognized by the presence in Parliament of party officers known as 'whips' whose job it is to keep in touch with all party members, listen to their complaints, mediate on conflicting claims, and, at the right time, produce the votes that are essential to a Government majority or an opposition protest. This kind of activity has gone on for decades.

In former times, however, members of Parliament sometimes rebuffed the whips and voted contrary to the party line. Many such desertions were prompted by conscience, strong feelings that the party position was wrong, or a belief that the best interest of the member's constituency could not be served by party regularity on the issue involved. Sometimes rank-and-file revolts were serious enough to defeat the Government and to enable the opposition to form a Ministry based in part on the rebels' support. Such rejection of the party line has grown more and more infrequent. Party discipline has become stricter and the backbench member more docile.

The change is probably attributable to the inclination of Governments facing rebellion in the party ranks to threaten the members of Parliament with a general election. The dissatisfied member, therefore, is faced with either accepting a policy that he does not like or contributing to the resignation of the Government and his own involvement in a new election. The choice is almost always in favor of subordinating personal preferences or feelings to the party position. The fact that fewer members of Parliament today are individuals of sufficient independent wealth to make the matter of fighting a new election of slight consideration undoubtedly contributes to the current trend toward greater party discipline. A House of Commons composed of persons with independent incomes and established local positions was less amenable to discipline than one constituted of individuals who must weigh most seriously the drain upon their personal means and the threat to their political futures of rebellious conduct. In addition to the cost and inconvenience of contesting a new election, a member out of favor with the party may find the party's support withdrawn from him in his constituency. The party may even nominate and support a new candidate and thus his political situation is rendered exceedingly insecure.

Although the trend toward stricter party discipline has meant that the rank-and-file member of Parliament is a less independent figure, it has contributed to increasing political stability in Britain. Governments are almost never upset on minor issues or through political finagling. A Cabinet backed by a good majority in the House of Commons is certain to stay in power until Parliament runs its natural course or until it encounters some grave issue that brings about a new division in the political opinion of the country. If a Government has only a small majority in the House, it is likely to seek a favorable opportunity for a new appeal to the electorate, for even highly developed party discipline cannot prevent among three or four hundred politicians occasional defections on major issues.

A fourth trend to be noticed concerns the increasing importance in the political system of the Civil Service. The changes and developments that have contributed to the increasing power of the Government have also

−31

enhanced the role of the professional officials, the bureaucrats. The grow-ing volume of legislation and its increasing complexity and technicality have made the politician more and more dependent upon the permanent and professional element in the governmental structure. It has already been mentioned that much of the legislative initiative in British government is taken by the administrative departments. From their experience in the ad-ministration and enforcement of laws, the civil servants draft legislation to extend or to change existing statutes, and these proposals go to Parliament through the political heads of departments, the ministers. Since the bills are Government measures, they rarely are changed in any fundamental aspect, and thus it is the handiwork of the civil servants that is translated into the law of the land.

Not only in the drafting of legislation but also in the formulation of executive policy do the civil servants exercise important power. Ministers at the head of large departments have many involved problems put to them for decision or solution. The information upon which they come to a decision is usually collected and selected by their principal civil servants, and consequently the latter are in a position to guide and suggest the ac-tion of the minister. Weak ministers or ministers more interested in extra-departmental affairs often become little more than the mouthpieces of their permanent officials. The latter from long experience can assemble such strong and convincing arguments in favor of solutions they prefer that only a vigorous personality as the political head of a department can make a real change in policy. Some students of British government feel that the power of the permanent officials is by far the most significant factor in the political system. For example, Ramsay Muir stated some years ago that: 'Bureaucracy has become, during the last century, and especially during the last generation, a far more potent and vital element in our system of gov-ernment than the theories of the textbooks recognize. It has, indeed, be-come the effective and operative part of our system.' [5] Without minimizing the influence of the civil servants or overlooking their power in the case of weak and ineffectual ministers, one may say, however, that a strong Cabinet carrying out a challenging party program can still govern and impose its policies upon the administrative machine.

Another trend of importance, and one giving rise to growing concern, is the increasing use of delegated legislation. This is legislation promul-gated by a Ministry, in the form of orders or regulations, on the authority of a statute passed by Parliament. The necessity of delegated legislation is not in dispute. It is generally recognized that provision must be made for the amplification of statutes to meet varying and special circumstances. 'Much of our social and economic legislation,' L. S. Amery has said, 'covers so vast and detailed a field that no statute, however cumbrous—and many of them are already cumbrous and unintelligible enough—could possibly provide for all contingencies. Some power of ministerial variation

---

[5] *How Britain Is Governed* (New York, 1930), p. 76.

32—

or interpretation is obviously necessary, subject to the attention of Parliament being drawn to what is being done.' [6]

It is this matter of calling the vast amount of delegated legislation to the attention of Parliament that troubles many people concerned about constitutional trends in Britain. The number of orders and regulations issued annually runs into four figures, and Parliament is not organized to review and approve such a volume of subsidiary legislation. A good proportion of these orders and regulations affect the rights and property of private citizens who may have no recourse except to appeal to a minister or an administrative tribunal, either of which is often suspected of bureaucratic bias. There appears to be little possibility of reducing the volume of delegated legislation, but ways to provide safeguards against abuse will be constantly sought during succeeding years by politicians, jurists, and others interested in constitutional problems.

Recent years have seen the increasing use of the public corporation as an administrative instrumentality. The public corporation has been employed to give greater administrative flexibility than can be obtained with the traditional type of department or ministry, to remove some public activities from direct political control, and to establish certain industries formerly in private hands on a reorganized and revitalized basis. The British Broadcasting Corporation, the Transport Commission, the Bank of England, and the National Coal Board are examples of public corporations conducting major activities owned and administered by the state. It will be noted that they nearly all represent new fields of state activity. Additional measures of socialization are likely to produce more public corporations as instrumentalities through which the state exercises ownership and carries out its policies in these particular fields. The rapid growth in the number of agencies of this character has created several problems to which definite solutions have yet to be found. Included in these problems are the matter of the most desirable type of internal organization to be established, the degree of parliamentary supervision over the day-to-day activities of the corporations, and the status of their employees as compared with civil servants and private workers.

Great Britain has always been characterized by vigorous and fairly autonomous local governments. Although, as previously mentioned, the United Kingdom is a unitary state—that is, its local governments are creations of the central government and have no constitutional position that cannot be altered by Parliament—there has existed a strong tradition of local autonomy. Boroughs and counties have had broad powers and a great deal of independence in managing their local affairs. Recent years have seen many inroads into the realm of local government. Some powers and functions have been removed from local control, while most of the rest have been brought under an increasing amount of central supervision. This supervision has been directed toward obtaining a minimum level of

---

[6] Op. cit. p. 50.

service and nation-wide uniformity in various services. The most frequent lever employed by the national government in extending its supervisory power has been the financial grant-in-aid. By offering to pay part of the cost of a local service the national government obtains adherence to certain standard criteria and constant surveillance over the local administration of the activity.

There is considerable feeling in Britain that the removal of functions and the extension of central supervision are sapping the vitality of local political institutions and that initiative is being transferred from the borough or county hall to Whitehall. This belief has some foundation, but centralizing tendencies appear to be inevitable in view of the changes in the social scene that have been taking place. Problems of public health, crime prevention, and transportation do not respect local boundary lines and they can only be dealt with through some centrally directed effort. The British solution has been to change the pattern of local government as little as possible but to introduce uniformity and central control wherever these seem necessary or desirable in the national interest.

As government has affected more intimately the lives of the citizens of Britain, there has been considerable sentiment in favor of some kind of political devolution which would include the establishment of governmental institutions capable of a prompt response to regional needs and problems. This feeling has been stronger in Scotland and Wales than in England, but even to the English it has sometimes seemed that the Parliament at Westminster was too absorbed in foreign and imperial concerns to devote sufficient attention to domestic affairs of regional importance. From time to time suggestions have been advanced that local parliaments on the order of the one seated in Belfast should be established for Scotland, Wales, and two or three large areas in England. To these bodies would be given legislative authority over economic and social matters of principal importance to the inhabitants of the respective regions.

Political devolution of the kind just mentioned has never commended itself to any Government in power at Westminster; no Cabinet has been interested in surrendering authority to any subsidiary parliaments. Moreover, critics have been able to point out that as a practical matter it is extremely difficult to divide authority, federation-wise, in a densely populated and interdependent country like the United Kingdom. While governmental devolution has not traveled far as a question of practical politics, the idea and practice of an increasing amount of administrative devolution have gained considerable support. There has always been some devolution at the administrative level for Scotland and, since 1921, for Northern Ireland. During World War II a regional organization was established for the administration of a number of defense services. When the civil defense organization was established in 1939, Great Britain was divided into twelve regions—ten in England, one in Wales, and one in Scotland. Headed by a regional commissioner reporting to the Ministry of Home Security, each of these areas was designed not only as a unit for the co-ordination of civil defense services but additionally as a region which could function

34–

independently should communications with London be temporarily interrupted. During the course of World War II the regions also became administrative units for services under the Ministries of Supply, Transport, and Food.

Since the war this regional machinery has largely been dismantled. Its place is coming to be taken, however, by the regional administrative services of the nationalized industries and those of several government departments. It is probable that this development will continue and that between the national government and the basic units of local government, the county and the county borough, will appear a layer of regional administrative organizations.

Another constitutional trend of recent years relates to the development of new relations between the United Kingdom and the units of the British Commonwealth and Empire. As the members of the Commonwealth have grown in international importance, their constitutional relationship with Great Britain has changed fairly rapidly. Within the past fifty years Canada, Australia, New Zealand, South Africa, India, Pakistan, and Ceylon have moved from a colonial status, although the first three had already achieved virtually complete self-government in domestic affairs, to the status of independent states legally connected with the United Kingdom only through the tie of a common monarch. Arrival at the independent position known as dominion status had been accomplished by Canada, Australia, New Zealand, and South Africa by the end of World War I, and it was given recognition in constitutional law by the Statute of Westminster of 1931. In 1947 Britain's Indian Empire came to an end, and the two dominions of India and Pakistan replaced it. The next year Ceylon advanced from colonial to dominion status. Also in 1948 two countries left the Commonwealth. Burma, although torn by civil war, decided to seek its destiny outside the Commonwealth group. Ireland's equivocal position within the Commonwealth was ended when the parliament in Dublin repealed the External Relations Act and thus made Ireland entirely independent and disassociated in any legal way with the British Commonwealth.

The desire of India to become a republic but still retain ties with the Commonwealth posed a problem of devising some new formula of association. At a hastily summoned conference of Commonwealth Prime Ministers in April 1949 agreement was reached on a formula by which India recognizes the King as the symbol of Commonwealth unity while adopting a republican constitution. Once again it had been found possible to adapt the constitutional structure of the Commonwealth in such a way that a serious problem was successfully solved without doing great damage to the fundamental nature of this association of states.

III

The British Subject and His Rights

Since in a democracy like Great Britain the citizen plays an essential part in the political process, it is important to indicate who are the citizens of the country, what their constitutional rights are, and how these rights are protected and enforced.

1. *Citizenship*

Citizenship in the United Kingdom is based upon the common-law principle that all persons born within the King's dominions and owing allegiance to him are his subjects. This principle for the acquisition of citizenship is known in legal parlance as the rule of *jus soli*. It is to be contrasted with that known as the *jus sanguinis*. By the latter, parentage determines citizenship, i.e. children of the citizens of a state are themselves citizens regardless of the place of their birth. The rule of *jus sanguinis* is common to most of the Continental states and to other countries where the legal system is derived from Roman law. By statute the United Kingdom extends citizenship to a person born outside His Majesty's dominions whose father was a British subject at the time of the person's birth.[1]

In modern times many countries and territories beyond the British Isles have recognized the King as their sovereign, and therefore the people of these states and territories have been British subjects. Until recently British subjects comprised about a quarter of the world's population. No such union of diverse nationalities and races in a common citizenship had existed since the fall of the Roman Empire. The last few years have seen a considerable dissolution of this world-wide bond of citizenship and its replacement by several individual kinds of citizenship. The present pattern of citizenship within the British Commonwealth of Nations is rather intricate, and only a lawyer skilled in the problem could explain the exact legal status of some nationality groups. Recent developments in, and the general outlines of, the present situation, however, can be indicated.

Canada was the first Commonwealth country to enact legislation that created a separate category of dominion nationals within the generality of British subjects. It did so in 1921 in order that Canadian jurists could be

---

[1] In the event of the annexation of territory, the Crown may extend citizenship by order in council to classes of persons connected with the newly acquired territory.

eligible for election to the Permanent Court of International Justice. The Irish Free State constitution, adopted in 1922, contained a definition of nationality and limited political privileges to citizens thus defined. In 1927 the Parliament of the Union of South Africa passed an act defining Union nationality. These actions were confined to establishing 'mere divisions of British subjects.' [2]

The first real breach in the principle of a Commonwealth-wide citizenship was made by the Free State in 1936 when the parliament of that country declared that the Irish were to be no longer British subjects but only citizens of Ireland. At the same time, the Irish government, by administrative action, provided that British subjects residing in Ireland would not be regarded as aliens but would have substantially the same position as Irish citizens. Outside of Ireland the Irish were regarded as British subjects and treated accordingly.

Canada's enactment in 1946 of a new nationality statute indicated the need of some Commonwealth agreement upon the problems of citizenship. Consequently, a Commonwealth conference of legal authorities was convened in 1947 to consider the matter. The conference agreed that each Commonwealth country should prescribe the conditions governing the admission of persons to its citizenship, that in addition to establishing an individual type of citizenship it should declare all its citizens to be British subjects, and that it should recognize as British subjects the citizens of other Commonwealth members. The special position of Ireland, a good many of whose citizens lived in Commonwealth countries, was to be met by each dominion making an agreement with the Irish government to provide that the Irish should not be considered aliens but should have the same position as British subjects.

Following the conference of experts the Parliament of the United Kingdom passed the British Nationality Act of 1948. This act provided for a citizenship of the United Kingdom and Colonies and declared that the citizens of these areas would be British subjects. All persons who were citizens of other Commonwealth countries would also be recognized as British subjects. In case the term 'British subject' was disliked by any Commonwealth member, the act offered the alternative of 'Commonwealth citizen.' The same year Australia, New Zealand, and Ceylon passed nationality acts based upon the recommendations of the Commonwealth conference. It appeared, therefore, that the pattern of Commonwealth citizenship would develop in such a way that each independent member would establish its own nationality rules and would recognize the citizens of other Commonwealth countries as either British subjects or Commonwealth citizens and accord to them the same general standing within its boundaries as enjoyed by its own citizens.

A break in this pattern occurred, however, when the South African

---

[2] Arthur Berriedale Keith, *Dominion Autonomy in Practice* (London, 1929), p. 58.

—37

Parliament in 1949 passed a nationality act establishing a type of Union citizenship but not declaring its people to be also British subjects or Commonwealth citizens. Then the Indian Constitution of 1950 created a separate citizenship and did not refer to the people of India as possessing a broader Commonwealth status. A further complication was introduced by the repeal of the Irish External Affairs Act, which formally severed whatever tenuous links to the Commonwealth Ireland retained, and by the subsequent Republic of Ireland Act, 1949, passed by the United Kingdom Parliament, which recognized the changed constitutional status of Ireland. The British Government, however, did not follow the logic of declaring Irish citizens to be aliens within the United Kingdom but announced that it would continue to regard them on the same footing as the citizens of other Commonwealth countries. At present the citizenship situation within the Commonwealth stands as follows:

> So far as certain members of the Commonwealth are concerned— for example, the United Kingdom, Canada, Australia, New Zealand and Ceylon—there is a common status of British subject or Commonwealth Citizenship, based upon separate, individual legislation upon an agreed pattern; in regard to certain other members, such as India, there might be not common but similar or even identical status by reciprocity; in regard to others, including South Africa, there might be no such reciprocity; and finally, in regard to countries right outside the Commonwealth, such as Eire, there is the paradox of similarity or identity of status, again by reciprocity.[3]

As with all advanced countries, the United Kingdom provides by law for the naturalization of aliens who desire to become British subjects. There are no racial barriers to the granting of naturalization. An alien who has resided within His Majesty's dominions for five years and within the United Kingdom for one year may apply to the Secretary of State for Home Affairs for a certificate of citizenship. His application must be supported by four sponsors who are British subjects, and he must be of good character and able to speak English. The Home Office investigates the credentials of the applicant, and during the course of the inquiry announces in the personal columns of *The Times* that such an alien is applying for naturalization and invites any information that might prejudice the granting of citizenship. If no unfavorable information is elicited, the Home Office in due course admits the alien to British nationality. An alien so naturalized is entitled to all the rights and privileges of a native-born citizen.[4]

---

[3] K. C. Wheare, 'Is the British Commonwealth Withering Away?' *The American Political Science Review,* September 1950, p. 553.

[4] Under certain circumstances the Home Secretary may revoke the naturalization of an alien. Prior to 1948 he was required to revoke the naturalization certificate of a person convicted of disaffection or disloyalty, but the British Nationality Act of that year made his action discretionary.

2. *Individual Rights*

Possession of civil liberty by the people of free countries is the important thing which separates the democratic world from the lands under dictatorship. Civil liberty is a term employed to sum up a number of basic rights which are so protected and enforced that they cannot be abrogated or invaded except in extraordinary circumstances and then only according to law. There is no official fiat which can override the citizen's rights and subject him to arbitrary or capricious treatment.

England has long been renowned as a country where its citizens enjoy civil liberty. A good part of the present democratic world owes its conceptions of freedom to the liberty developed in England over many centuries. This civil liberty is for the most part embodied in the common law, and wherever the common law has been transplanted it has given the people of that country the inheritance of many struggles against arbitrary power and official usurpation.

The basic liberties which the British subject enjoys are familiar to American citizens whose civil rights flow from the same source. The bills of rights in the state constitutions of the United States and in the federal constitution are, in part, adaptations of famous charters and statutes of English history. Much of the language is identical. Constitution drafters in America were familiar with the Petition of Right, the Bill of Rights, and other documents of English constitutional history, and they had read the works of Locke, Blackstone, Burke, and other illustrious commentaries upon liberty in a free society.

The rights enjoyed by British citizens include freedom of speech, freedom of association, freedom of assembly, freedom from arbitrary arrest and imprisonment, freedom of religion, and freedom of private premises. In addition, and of supreme importance, is the rule of law. It is not defined or stated in any charter or statute but is a pervading principle of the Constitution which is recognized by the Crown, Parliament, and the courts of justice.

Dicey, a distinguished commentator on the Constitution, wrote that the English rule of law had three meanings, which may be summarized: (1) no arbitrary power is recognized in law; (2) 'every man, whatever be his rank or condition, is subject to the ordinary law of the realm and amenable to the jurisdiction of the ordinary tribunals'; and (3) the principles of the Constitution, including individual rights, are to be derived from the decisions of courts in particular cases and not, as in some foreign countries, from statements of general constitutional principles.[5]

A good many constitutional lawyers of the present day regard Dicey's definitions as somewhat obsolete. The rule of law is still an important and vital principle, but it needs restating in the light of present conditions.

---

[5] A. V. Dicey, *Introduction to the Study of the Law of the Constitution,* 9th ed. (London, 1939), p. 183f.

According to a recent statement, the rule of law 'involves the absence of arbitrary power; effective control of and proper publicity for delegated legislation, particularly when it imposes penalties; that when discretionary power is granted the manner in which it is to be exercised should as far as is practicable be defined; that every man should be responsible to the ordinary law whether he be private citizen or public officer; that private rights should be determined by impartial and independent tribunals; and that fundamental private rights are safeguarded by the ordinary law of the land.'[6] Such a statement takes account of developments with respect to administrative law and justice which, as will be discussed later, have important bearings on the rights of citizens.

A full discussion of all the rights of a British subject would require a long and learned treatise. We can take notice, however, of several important rights and indicate their general meaning for present-day British life.

Freedom of speech in Britain permits a person to say or publish anything not banned by law because it is libelous, slanderous, or obscene. Dicey defined the 'right to freedom of discussion' in the following terms: 'Any man may . . . say or write whatever he likes, subject to the risk of, it may be, severe punishment if he publishes any statement (either by word of mouth, in writing, or in print) which he is not legally entitled to make.'[7] In olden times licensing requirements imposed a severe censorship on the press, administered as they were to suppress views disliked by the Crown or powerful ministers. By failing to renew the Licensing Act, Parliament in 1695 established in effect the freedom of the press. The present limitations on speech and press could be extended in such a way as to restrict severely the freedom allowed. For instance, seditious libel, which involves the use of words tending to arouse hatred or contempt for any of the institutions of government, advocating changes in Church or State other than by lawful means, or raising discontent and ill-will among the populace, 'is a very wide offence and could be used to prohibit almost every form of left wing or revolutionary agitation.'[8] In practice, however, the limitations on speech and press are fairly well defined in law and do not operate to impose unjustifiable restrictions.[9] The extent to which the British allow freedom of expression can be seen by any visitor to Hyde Park in London where the soap-box orators hold forth daily on the most controversial questions. Even during wartime there will be speakers denouncing the Government and criticizing its policies in bitter language. The policeman walking

---

[6] E. C. S. Wade and G. Godfrey Phillips, *Constitutional Law,* 4th ed. (London, 1950), p. 58.

[7] Op. cit. p. 240.

[8] E. W. Ridges, *Constitutional Law,* 8th ed. by G. A. Forrest (London, 1950), p. 385.

[9] Under its wartime powers the Government in 1941 suppressed the Communist *Daily Worker* which had been denouncing the conflict with Nazi Germany as an imperialist fraud. Later in the war the ban was lifted. Hitler's attack on the Soviet Union, in the eyes of the *Daily Worker,* had transformed the struggle into democracy's defense against fascism.

by the crowd and hearing himself characterized as an agent of a corrupt and decaying social order will only interfere in case the speaker's language threatens to lead to a breach of the peace.[10]

Freedom of association permits citizens to concert their efforts to obtain objectives on which they are agreed. They may form social clubs; organizations to promote religious, cultural, and business interests; trade unions to strive for improved working conditions; and political parties to seek power within the state. No license or authority from the government is necessary. They can determine their rules of membership and organization, collect money to promote their objectives, own property, and in all lawful ways carry on their activities. The only restriction is that their activities be lawful. Even in this respect a good deal of tolerance is practiced. The Communist Party and various fascist-minded groups, whose ultimate objectives are revolutionary, are permitted to carry on their activities so long as they do not break the peace or interfere with the rights of others.

Freedom of speech and freedom of association would lose much of their significance if there were not also freedom of assembly. This is a basic liberty of British citizens, and they exercise it by meeting in halls and in the open to discuss all kinds of subjects. There is no restriction on freedom of assembly except that persons collecting must conduct themselves peacefully. Trafalgar Square and Hyde Park in London and similar public spaces in other cities are the scenes of demonstrations where speakers harangue the crowds and denounce the governing authorities. Leaders from time to time parade their followers to the Houses of Parliament to present petitions and to lobby with the members in behalf of their causes. In all this the participants, however offensive their views to majority opinion, are within their rights so long as they conduct themselves peacefully.

There is no mark of the totalitarian state that is more repulsive to democratic societies than the practice of arbitrary arrest and imprisonment. In the countries under dictatorship a citizen may be taken from his home by the secret police and committed to prison or forced to spend his days in a camp of slave laborers. Often he will never receive a public trial, and relatives and friends are unable to learn what his fate has been. This sort of despotic practice has been illegal in England for centuries. The common-law courts developed the rule that a person must be charged with a specific crime and must be brought to a public trial within a reasonable time. In the early part of the seventeenth century there was a challenge to this legal principle, and for a time persons were imprisoned without trial, and special courts tried and convicted persons in secret proceedings. The cause of civil liberty won out, however, and freedom from arbitrary arrest and imprisonment was eventually guaranteed in the Habeas Corpus Act passed by Parliament in 1679. Assuming that the principle of the writ of habeas

---

[10] Theaters and moving picture houses are subject to some control through licensing and censorship. Theaters in London, Windsor, and Brighton and new plays are licensed by the Lord Chamberlain. Elsewhere county and borough councils license theaters.

corpus was well established in law, the authors of the Act increased the number of courts that could issue the writ and provided severe penalties for officers holding persons in custody who failed to make a proper and prompt return and for judges who refused to issue the writ when it was applied for.[11] Ten years later the Bill of Rights provided protection against excessive bail being demanded of persons charged with a bailable offense. In Britain no person may be held in prison while the police search for evidence to justify vague suspicions.

During World War II a number of persons, including one member of Parliament, were held in prison without trial under Section 18 B of the Emergency Powers Act. They were persons who before the war had been so active in fascist-type organizations or who had expressed such sympathy for enemy countries that their loyalty was highly suspect. Parliament condoned this invasion of liberty because it had confidence in the ministers who defended the policy as the only practical one in the circumstances. Nevertheless, neither Parliament nor the Government felt happy that resort to such a measure was deemed necessary.[12]

Along with freedom from arbitrary arrest and imprisonment go a number of rights to insure that an accused person receives a fair trial and every opportunity to establish his innocence. The rights concerning criminal trials are substantially the same as those guaranteed in American constitutional law. They include the right to know the charges, the right to have the aid of counsel in presenting a defense, the right to call witnesses and to cross-examine the witnesses of the prosecution, and finally the right to have one's guilt determined by the unanimous vote of a jury of fellow citizens. These rights are deeply embedded in the common law as well as being specified in acts of Parliament, and they are supported by precedents dating back hundreds of years.

Religious liberty has been established in England more recently than some other civil rights, but today it is fully protected. In the sixteenth and seventeenth centuries the concept of tolerating people whose religious faith differed from that of the authorities in power was not understood; religious conformity was considered essential for any well-governed state and hereti-

---

[11] According to Dicey, 'The whole history of the writ of *habeas corpus* illustrates the predominate attention paid under the English constitution to "remedies," that is, to modes of procedure by which to secure respect for a legal right, and by which to turn a merely nominal into an effective or real right.' Op. cit. pp. 220-21.

[12] In a message to the Home Secretary in 1943, Churchill said: 'The power of the Executive to cast a man into prison without formulating any charge known to the law, and particularly to deny him judgment by his peers for an indefinite period, is in the highest degree odious, and is the foundation of all totalitarian governments, whether Nazi or Communist. It is only when extreme danger to the State can be pleaded that this power may be temporarily assumed by the Executive, and even so its working must be interpreted with the utmost vigilance by a Free Parliament. . . Nothing can be more abhorent to democracy than to imprison a person or keep him in prison because he is unpopular. This is really the test of civilization.' Winston S. Churchill, *Closing the Ring* (Boston, 1951), p. 679.

cal beliefs were akin to political treason. In the England of this time there were two principal groups in conflict with the national church—the Catholics and the dissenting sects. Americans will recall that several of the original colonies were founded by representatives of these religious faiths who were prepared to face the perils and rigors of the wilderness rather than conform against their conscience. Toward the end of the seventeenth century, notions of tolerance began to be entertained and gradually the official persecution of nonconforming churches ceased. Nevertheless, it was quite a while before all the disabilities on dissenting Protestants and on Catholics were removed. By the Test and Corporation Acts they were excluded from office-holding and from enjoying some of the other privileges of citizenship, and it was not until 1828 that the repeal of these laws relieved nonconforming Protestants of political disabilities. The next year a Catholic Emancipation Act removed the political restrictions on the members of that faith. Jews were admitted to Parliament in 1858. One of the last restrictions on full religious liberty, the exclusion of nonmembers of the Church of England from the Universities of Oxford and Cambridge, was rescinded in 1871.

We are all familiar with the phrase, 'an Englishman's house is his castle.' It is a succinct way of saying that the citizen's home is a privileged place which may only be entered with his permission or under circumstances defined by law. In Britain, as in the United States, entry into the private home of a citizen by the police authorities requires a warrant issued by a court. This warrant must set forth some legal reason why it is necessary for the police to invade the privacy of the home described. The reason may be to search for a criminal who is suspected of hiding in the premises or to look for contraband articles believed to be within. Whatever the reason it must be sufficiently justifiable to overcome the principle of the inviolability of the citizen's home.

The rights that have been briefly described are not absolute rights. They are qualified when their application in behalf of one person would jeopardize the rights of others and the necessities of organized society. For example, freedom of speech does not entitle one citizen to defame another. The right of assembly ceases when the gathering becomes a riotous mob. The privacy of one's home cannot be used for the conduct of criminal activities. The exceptions, it is important to notice, are defined in law and are not determined arbitrarily by the public authorities. There may be differing interpretations, however, of what the law permits and what the law restricts, and these are cases for the courts to determine. It is frequently necessary for the courts to decide whether certain remarks stated or printed were in fact libelous and how seriously the victims were injured. A court may be required to determine, after hearing many witnesses, whether or not the police were justified in deciding that a crowd of agitators had exceeded the bounds of peaceful assembly. There have been many such cases over the years, so that the precedents are firm guides to what is and what is not conduct permitted by the citizen's basic rights.

−43

3. *The Protection and Enforcement of Rights*

In Britain the citizen's rights are protected and enforced in a number of ways. It is plain that domestic peace and tranquillity are essential if the weak and humble are to be as secure in their rights as the strong and arrogant. The maintenance of a condition of law and order in the United Kingdom is a principal responsibility of one of the chief Cabinet ministers, the Home Secretary. He is charged with keeping the King's peace, which a holder of that office has described as the duty 'to play the honest broker and see that order is preserved at the lowest possible cost in liberty.' [13]

The Home Secretary carries out his duty with respect to personal liberty in several ways. The Metropolitan Police, the force which polices the some eight or nine million people who live in Greater London, are under his jurisdiction, and he must see that they protect and do not invade the rights of the citizen. It is his responsibility to be sure that the police are familiar with the law concerning arrest, public meetings, the sanctity of private homes, and similar matters. The police in other parts of the country do not come directly under the Home Secretary but under the councils of scores of local governments. This distribution of authority is in itself something of a protection to the citizen, since the police with whom he is concerned are responsible not to a distant central government but to one of his own community. The councils of counties and county boroughs have a responsibility similar to the Home Secretary's in insuring that the police forces under their control are guardians of the citizen's rights and not invaders or usurpers of those rights. The British have been very successful in building a police tradition that protects rather than abuses civil liberty. The London Bobbie has a universal reputation as a guardian of the law and a shield of the citizen. Instances of misconduct or invasion of rights by the police are rare in the United Kingdom.

Another duty of the Home Secretary is to receive petitions and memorials for the redress of grievances. As guaranteed in the Bill of Rights, a citizen who considers himself wrongly used may petition the Crown, and his plea will go to the Home Secretary for investigation and remedial action if any seems called for. Furthermore, the Home Office reviews by-laws enacted by local governments for the purpose of seeing whether or not they conflict with the liberty of the subject. A by-law the Home Secretary believes invades an established right may be disallowed by him.

A citizen who feels that his rights have been transgressed has open to him the courts of justice. If he thinks he has been libeled or defamed by the spoken or printed word of someone else he may sue for redress in the proper court. Should he be, in his opinion, unjustly arrested he may seek his release and the punishment of the police officers who invaded his rights. The independence and the high traditions of the judiciary are guarantees

---

[13] J. Chuter Ede, 'Parliament and the Liberty of the Subject,' *Parliamentary Government in Britain* (The Hansard Society, London, 1949), p. 83.

44–

that cases of personal liberty will receive a fair hearing and that the citizen's rights will be scrupulously protected.

Of equal importance with the Home Office, the police, and the courts in protecting personal rights is Parliament. For centuries it has been a forum where grievances could be redressed and where legislation could be enacted to make more secure the rights of the citizen. In its struggle with the Crown to win its own freedom of speech, it was gaining a victory for every citizen of the country. The right of the private member to call attention to cases of official usurpation has meant that there was an assembly in which illegal acts could be brought to the notice of the country. In the modern Parliament the question hour serves as an effective means of protecting civil liberty. At this time the highest authorities of the state can be asked to explain and, if need be, give assurances of remedial action for wrongs affecting the humblest citizen. Many times during a Parliamentary session questions are asked about matters in themselves trivial when compared with the great affairs of state but very real and important for the maintenance of the private citizen's rights. An alert opposition can be counted upon to bring to public notice the infractions of law and the invasions of liberty by public authorities.

None of these institutional guardians of civil liberty would be effective without the support of public opinion. This is basically the force that guarantees the citizen's rights. There is a widespread recognition in Britain that the liberty of one is the liberty of all and that a single instance of injustice weakens the whole fabric of civil rights. Consequently, there has developed a large measure of tolerance and a reluctance to circumscribe the individual, as well as an alertness to official abuse of personal liberty. Public opinion finds its most common expression through the press, and British newspapers are prompt in calling attention to instances where rights appear to have been invaded. They are jealous of their own liberty and are quick to sense what they consider attempts to restrict it. Public opinion also expresses itself at mass meetings, demonstrations in favor of some cause or in protest of some action, and in the speeches of leaders of many public causes. Even in times of greatest emergency the public has insisted upon retaining essential liberties and requiring the authorities to act in conformity with law.

4. Present Dangers to Personal Liberty

During this century there has been some apprehension concerning the maintenance of the traditional personal rights of the citizen. There is no fear of a sudden usurpation by power-hungry ministers or a direct subversion of the Constitution by Parliament or the courts; rather it is a concern about the erosion of the structure of civil liberty by numerous official acts that are individually of slight importance.

It is in the extensive use of delegated legislation and administrative justice that many people in Britain see a threat to personal liberty. Delegated legislation is a term employed to describe the statutory instruments—rules, orders, and regulations—issued by government departments to supplement, amplify, and apply statutes passed by Parliament. Some statutory instruments require confirmation by Parliament before becoming effective; others are operative upon issuance but may be annulled by adverse action of either house taken within a specified time limit. Thirty years ago Professor Laski noted the 'wholesale transference of control from Parliament to the departments,' and observed that 'legislation by reference and by delegation has taken the place of the older method which regulated with a jealous precision each item of official activity.' [14] The trend has continued since that day.

Administrative justice refers to Parliament's practice of conferring judicial powers upon ministers or upon tribunals appointed or controlled by ministers. In connection with the administration of particular statutes, ministers or departmental tribunals are often authorized to hear cases and give decisions affecting the rights and property of private citizens. Administrative justice is practiced extensively under laws pertaining to public health, social insurance, utility regulation, town and country planning, and rent control.

Civil liberty is threatened, according to present-day critics, by the following conditions and practices. Some Parliamentary statutes are drawn in such general terms that the limits of the powers delegated are almost undeterminable. Matters of principle which should be debated and settled in Parliament are left to the discretion of executive and administrative officers. Moreover, the volume and complexity of delegated legislation and the pressure of time render political control through Parliamentary and ministerial scrutiny less effective than it should be. The generality of statutory language often makes it difficult for the courts to apply the *ultra vires* rule, that is, to declare that administrative acts have exceeded the powers granted or the jurisdiction authorized. Furthermore, such generality leads to subdelegation, occasionally three or four removes from the parent statute, which is confusing to the courts and the public. Many enforcement officers possess authority to enter and search private premises without special warrant. Concerning administrative justice, there is lacking in some instances the safeguards that should surround the determination of individual rights. Administrative tribunals are not in all cases as independently constituted as they should be; their methods and procedures do not always conform to the principles of natural justice, and the right of appeal to the ordinary courts on points of law is inadequate. Persons concerned about civil liberty find much to disquiet them in these conditions and practices.

Delegated legislation and administrative justice have not advanced to their present importance without challenge. Almost a quarter of a century ago Lord Hewart, then Lord Chief Justice, published a book, *The New Despotism,* which called attention in vigorous terms to dangers arising from

---

[14] Harold J. Laski, 'The Growth of Administrative Discretion,' *Journal of Public Administration*, April 1923, p. 92.

practices then current. This criticism and others led the Government to appoint a committee to examine and to report on the matter.[15]

Concerning delegated legislation, the Committee on Ministers' Powers concluded in its report that 'whether good or bad the development of the practice is inevitable. It is a natural reflection, in the sphere of constitutional law, of changes in the circumstances of our lives which have resulted from scientific discoveries.' [16] The committee submitted some fifteen recommendations to eliminate abuses and establish safeguards in connection with delegated legislation, including the clear and precise definition of the lawmaking power conferred on ministers, the bestowal in only exceptional circumstances of authority to modify acts of Parliament and to exclude the jurisdiction of the courts, and the adoption of improved procedures for Parliamentary scrutiny of administrative orders. In considering the subject of administrative justice, the committee said that there was 'nothing radically wrong about the existing practice of Parliament in permitting the exercise of judicial and quasi-judicial powers by Ministers and of judicial power by Ministerial Tribunals, but that the practice is capable of abuse, and that dangers are incidental to it if not guarded against, and that certain safeguards are essential if the rule of law and the liberty of the subject are to be maintained.' [17] The safeguards recommended included the maintenance of a distinction between judicial and quasi-judicial functions, the development of a judicial attitude and the employment of judicial-type procedures on the part of ministers and tribunals hearing cases, and the recognition of a broad right of appeal to the ordinary courts of justice.

The committee believed, moreover, that the citizen's opportunities for obtaining redress when injured by the wrongful acts of public officials should be improved. Under the ancient doctrine that the King can do no wrong, it was assumed in law that the Crown, or the State, could not intentionally harm one of its citizens. But a servant of the Crown might act unlawfully and invade the rights of a citizen, and he was personally responsible for his dereliction. The normal remedy for a citizen who believed he had been unjustly injured by an official action was to take proceedings against the public servant. This sometimes was an unsatisfactory method of redress. The official might be unable to pay the damages awarded the private citizen, or it might be manifestly unfair to hold the official responsible for an action performed under general administrative directions. The need for an alternative remedy was recognized in many statutes by allow-

---

[15] Cmd. 4060 (1932), *Report of the Committee on Ministers' Powers.* By its terms of reference the committee was 'to consider the powers exercised by or under the direction of (or by persons or bodies appointed specially by) Ministers of the Crown by way of (a) delegated legislation and (b) judicial or quasi-judicial decision, and to report what safeguards are desirable or necessary to secure the constitutional principles of the sovereignty of Parliament and the supremacy of the Law.'

[16] Ibid. p. 5.

[17] Ibid. p. 115.

ing a citizen to institute proceedings against the Crown, that is, the State itself, by a petition of right. But the granting of such a petition was discretionary, and the citizen had no assurance of being permitted to seek his remedy in this way.

The committee's 'well-balanced paragraphs failed to persuade Parliament to insist upon immediate remedies,' and its recommendations had little influence on subsequent legislation or departmental practice.[18] Before long the requirements of war added greatly to the use of administrative powers; the Government needed broad authority—and much subsidiary law—to deal with the numerous problems involved in a struggle for national survival. After the fighting ended some of the wartime measures were continued in force, and other statutes arising from the Labour Party's program formed the basis for considerable delegated legislation. Consequently, the warning notes have been frequently sounded since 1945. They have been particularly sharp concerning the extension of the Emergency Powers Act, first enacted in 1939, and the passage of a companion measure, the Supplies and Services Act, 1945. Each authorizes the Government to continue or institute by administrative decrees many measures of control and regulation over the economic life of the country.

Although the Conservative Party had been critical of the Emergency Powers Act and the Supplies and Services Act, it found, upon taking office in 1951, that their extension for at least another year was necessary. So much administrative activity, relating particularly to defense and economic affairs, depended upon the authority contained in these statutes that they could not be allowed to lapse before the Government had had an opportunity to examine all existing regulations and to propose to Parliament a new statutory framework to support those regulations still required.

Now no informed person in Great Britain believes that the use of delegated legislation can be denied to Parliament and the Ministry. It is manifestly impossible for the legislature to enact statutes complete in such detail and so anticipatory of all special circumstances that no amplification by the government departments executing them is necessary. When it is public policy, moreover, to plan, manage, and control a good share of the economic and social life of the nation, much administrative action must be performed under the authority of broad statutory powers. Many critics of present practices think, however, that greater circumspection can be introduced into the use of delegated legislation and administrative justice and that additional safeguards in procedures dangerous to individual liberty can be devised.

A few of the restrictions and safeguards proposed in the report of the Committee on Ministers' Powers have been introduced. During the war the Government began the practice of appending explanatory notes to orders and regulations which are involved and technical and the purpose

---

[18] Sir Courtenay Ilbert, *Parliament: Its History, Constitution and Practice,* 3rd ed., rev. by Sir Cecil Carr (London, 1948), p. 74.

48—

of which is not clear unless one is familiar with the matter concerned. The committee's recommendation proposing the creation of a Commons committee to scrutinize delegated legislation laid before the House achieved adoption in 1944 when a select committee was established for this purpose.[19] Out of the work of the select committee grew the Statutory Instruments Act of 1946, which standardized the nomenclature and procedures pertaining to delegated legislation. The term 'statutory instrument' was adopted to cover the subsidiary legislation variously named orders-in-council, orders, warrants, regulations, and rules. The Act fixed at forty days the period during which Parliament may secure by a negative resolution the annulment of a statutory instrument laid before it.

At least in one instance the use of the advisory committee principle as a means of aiding ministers in preparing statutory instruments and in protecting individual rights has been introduced. The National Insurance Act, 1946, requires the minister to submit drafts of regulations he proposes to issue to such a body. The advisory committee reports its views to the minister who must consider them and explain to Parliament if he does not accept them. It is the opinion of a leading authority on administrative law that this type of departmental advisory committee represents 'a new institutional device for scrutinizing regulations which may prove to be of great significance.' It 'may ultimately be found to contain the germs of a solution of the problem of delegated legislation.'[20]

The criticism of the Committee on Ministers' Powers that the private citizen needed a more adequate means of seeking redress when he considered himself injured by public servants has been largely met by the Crown Proceedings Act, 1947. By this statute the Crown accepts a considerable liability for the acts of its servants, and claims against the Crown may be enforced in the courts as of right instead of by permissive proceedings.[21]

While some steps have been taken in recent years to supervise more effectively the lawmaking power of government departments, criticism continues and the problem remains a live one. Some advocates of stricter control of delegated legislation, in the interest of protecting the citizen's rights, desire the abandonment of blanket extensions of such statutes as the Supplies and Services Act; the imposition of time limits on certain types of delegated legislation; and 'a declaration that every official concerned with

---

[19] The House of Lords has had a Special Orders Committee since 1925.

[20] William A. Robson, 'Administrative Law in England, 1919-48,' *British Government since 1918* (London, 1950), p. 122.

[21] Paragraph 1 of the act reads: 'Where any person has a claim against the Crown after the commencement of this Act, and, if this Act had not been passed, the claim might have been enforced, subject to the grant of His Majesty's fiat, by petition of right, or might have been enforced by a proceeding provided by any statutory provision repealed by this Act, then, subject to the provisions of this Act, the claim may be enforced as of right, and without the fiat of His Majesty, by proceedings taken against the Crown for that purpose in accordance with the provisions of this Act.' 10 & 11 Geo. 6, ch. 44.

the enforcement of the law shall be subject to the same rules and customs that govern the activities of the police, from the need to apply to a magistrate for a search warrant to the need to caution a suspect before questioning him.' [22]

The more extensive employment of administrative justice since the examination of the subject by the Committee on Ministers' Powers has emphasized the importance of safeguards to protect individual liberty. About the only noticeable advance in the field of administrative justice is a trend toward 'the adoption of the three-man tribunal as the typical body for dispensing administrative justice.' [23] Judicial powers continue to be conferred on ministers, however, rather than on the more desirable administrative tribunals. Reforms currently advocated include the use of advisory panels to hear the facts in cases coming before ministers, the institution of systematic procedures for appeals, the issuance of reasoned decisions in important administrative cases, and the adoption of personnel methods designed to promote 'a tradition of impartiality among those in the official hierarchy who have to pronounce judgments.' [24]

The British nation faces a serious problem in preserving its traditional personal liberty. The planning and control of a partially socialized economy and the extension of the services of the welfare state, to say nothing of the considerable regimentation necessitated by rearmament programs and by an 'export or die' economy, lead inevitably to many limits being imposed upon the freedom of action of the individual citizen. Government controls, moreover, have a way of advancing into the still unregulated sectors of social and economic life: in order to manage the regulated parts effectively some discipline has to be exerted over the free parts. Totalitarian states have accepted the logic of this situation, and by abolishing personal liberty have left themselves free to plan, order, and control as the higher wisdom of their rulers dictates. In Britain, no major political party nor any responsible politician has considered the totalitarian solution as acceptable. They are presented, consequently, with the problem of finding alternative solutions, of maintaining a highly planned, controlled, and disciplined society while preserving to the individual a great deal of personal freedom. Much can be done by voluntary co-operation. The British people are a law-abiding, socially conscious—some might add long-suffering—nation, although there are signs that the evasion of unpopular measures of rationing and control may be increasing and that the violators do not suffer the censure of their neighbors as once they would have. Voluntary co-operation, however, must be supplemented by controls having legal sanctions, and it is in their administration and enforcement that the pinch with personal liberty is felt.

In preventing the controls from squeezing out the substance of personal

---

[22] *The Economist,* 25 November 1950, p. 866.
[23] William A. Robson, op. cit. p. 127.
[24] *The Economist,* 25 November 1950, p. 867.

liberty, the British have several resources for meeting their problem. As a nation they have a genuine understanding of, and attachment to, the concept of individual freedom. They have the many definitions and ringing declarations of the courts, expounding and defending over the centuries the rights of the subject. They have a Parliament with great traditions of resisting executive usurpation. They have nonofficial institutions and bodies—the press, the universities, the inns of court, the professional societies, the trade unions—which are jealous of their independence and can mobilize powerful forces in the cause of liberty. Even the Civil Service, although frequently accused of preferring administrative convenience to the protection of personal liberty, is not a caste-bound bureaucracy unmindful of individual rights, and it is certainly not engaged in a conspiracy to destroy the private citizen's freedom. With these resources at hand, one may be reasonably optimistic concerning the ability of the British nation to preserve its basic liberties in spite of the heavy pressures placed on the governing mechanism by domestic and international problems.

IV

Crown and Monarchy

Except for the decade of the Puritan Commonwealth, the institution of monarchy has existed in the British Isles since Roman times. It has undergone, however, as fundamental an evolution as any other part of the British polity. Her Majesty Queen Elizabeth II is quite a different kind of monarch from William the Conqueror, Henry VIII, Queen Anne, or George III.

The strictly legal position of the King (or Queen) has changed little in the past few centuries. He heads the executive branch of the government, and he has important legislative and judicial powers. The King appoints and dismisses ministers, he commands the country's armed forces, he declares war and makes peace, he bestows peerages on commoners, and his assent is required to convert into laws the bills passed by Parliament. His Majesty, by all appearances, owns, commands, or disposes of the resources of a mighty empire. The actuality, however, is far removed from the letter of the law. Gradually through the years the personal power and influence of the monarch have been reduced and, whereas once he was the real executive of the state, that place is now occupied by the Crown.

1. *The Crown*

The monarchical office is still referred to as the Crown, but more commonly the term is used in a broader sense. Today the Crown embraces those elements of the British governmental organization wielding executive and administrative power. They include the King, the Cabinet, ministers outside the Cabinet, and the Civil Service. While the Crown's powers are primarily executive and administrative, it also plays an important part in the legislative process and has judicial-type responsibilities as well.

The powers of the Crown are derived from two principal sources, the royal prerogative and statutes enacted by Parliament. The royal prerogative, in the words of Dicey, is 'the residue of discretionary or arbitrary authority which at any time is legally left in the hands of the crown.' [1] In olden days this was a vast amount of power. Monarchs, while in theory never absolute, governed with little restraint beyond their own consciences and the fear of provoking revolution. From time to time, however, limita-

---

[1] A. V. Dicey, *Introduction to the Study of the Law of the Constitution*, 9th ed., p. 424.

tions were applied to the royal power, so that it came to be circumscribed in many particulars by law and custom.

In the medieval period the great landowners, the barons, were sometimes powerful enough to wring agreements from the sovereign, the Magna Carta being the outstanding example. Later, as social and economic life developed in England, other groups and classes accumulated power and influence—the Church, the lawyers, the gentry, and the merchants. So long as the great barons were a potent force with which to be reckoned, these groups often placed their weight on the side of the throne as the guarantor of civil peace and order; but, when royal absolutism threatened, they exerted pressure to restrain monarchical power. In Parliament they had a continuing institution in which they could mobilize their strength and utilize their chief weapon, the granting and withholding of money. The limits of the royal prerogative were a principal issue during the constitutional struggles between King and Parliament in the seventeenth century. James II's insistence upon his dispensing power, the right to ignore or to refuse to enforce acts of Parliament, finally ranged a large part of the country against him and led to his deposition. After 1689 there was no question about the authority of Parliament to limit the royal prerogative.

Following Parliament's success in asserting its mastery, it had less reluctance in conferring additional powers upon the Crown. As ministers assumed more and more of the powers formerly exercised by the monarch personally and as their responsibility to Parliament was gradually established, the legislature was prepared to see the Crown's authority grow. Consequently, during the past two and a half centuries Parliamentary statutes have increasingly added to the powers of the Crown. Today the Crown possesses the prerogative powers that still inhere in the monarch and those powers conferred by Parliamentary legislation, in total a vast reservoir of authority.

A compilation of the powers of the Crown would be an exceedingly lengthy document; it will be sufficient to indicate some of the principal kinds of authority exercised. In the executive field, the Crown appoints ministers, military officers, bishops, civil servants, judges, colonial governors, ambassadors, and other classes of public officials. With a few exceptions, judges for example, these officials serve at the pleasure of the Crown. Within the limits of existing law, the Crown formulates and declares the policy of the British state and issues the proclamations, orders, and directives required for executive and administrative action. The Crown owns and manages a considerable amount of public property. It conducts relations with foreign countries and with the members of the British Commonwealth of Nations, and it administers a vast colonial empire. The postmaster in Glasgow, the clerk in a Manchester labor exchange, the United Kingdom High Commissioner in Canberra, the British consul in San Francisco, and the district officer in Nigeria are all servants of the Crown and are executing its policies and following its administrative instructions.

In the legislative sphere, the Crown prepares bills and pilots them through Parliament. It drafts and issues a large volume of subsidiary legislation in the form of orders-in-council, statutory orders, and regulations. The Crown's judicial powers include the appointment of judges and the members of quasi-judicial tribunals and the right to pardon or reprieve convicted offenders. Furthermore, the highest court of appeal for colonial cases and for cases heard in ecclesiastical courts is an organ of the executive establishment, the Judicial Committee of the Privy Council.

The total of the Crown's political power is symbolized by the person of the monarch, and the forms and procedures of British government are consonant with this notion. The formalities have changed little since the days of Queen Anne. The monarch opens Parliament with an address from the throne which announces a legislative program for the coming session. *Rex* or *Regina* is often the prosecutor of law violators and the party to civil suits involving the state. A crown plus the initials of the reigning monarch form the emblem of public property; one sees them on post-office vans, government buildings, and military stores. Mail is franked with the phrase, 'On Her Majesty's Service.' [2]

The powers of the Crown are wielded by the Government of the day. The ministers composing the Government take the decisions and give the orders that activate the powers of the Crown, and the King acts only on the advice of his ministers. This is the situation in the United Kingdom and, save India, in the other self-governing members of the Commonwealth. In Canada, Australia, New Zealand, South Africa, Pakistan, and Ceylon, other ministers wield the powers of the Crown, all in the name of a common monarch. India, as a republic, recognizes the King as the Head of the Commonwealth and the symbol of its unity.

2. *The Monarchy*

Before discussing the personal position of the sovereign in the modern concept of the Crown it will be well to set down the rules and practices governing the occupancy of and the succession to the throne. The monarchy is regarded as a perpetually occupied office, as the words, 'The King

---

[2] As an example of the ancient forms fitted to a modern situation, the charge of treason, under an act of 1351, against William Joyce, the Lord Haw-Haw of the Nazi radio, is interesting. In part, it read, 'that he, whilst "an open and public war was being prosecuted and carried on by the German realm and its subjects against our lord the King and his subjects, then and on the said several days traitorously contriving and intending to aid and assist the said enemies of our lord the King against our lord the King and his subjects, did traitorously adhere and aid and give comfort to the said enemies . . . by broadcasting to the subjects of our lord the King propaganda on behalf of the said enemies of our lord the King." ' *The Economist,* 8 October 1949, p. 766. The source of the definition of treason in the Constitution of the United States will be recognized from the quotation above. Sect. 3, Art. III begins: 'Treason against the United States, shall consist only in levying war against them, or in adhering to their enemies, giving them aid and comfort.'

is dead; long live the King,' indicate. The death or abdication of one monarch immediately brings his successor to the throne. The succession in the United Kingdom is vested in the House of Windsor, a name adopted during World War I to relieve the House of Hanover of any suggestion of German connections. The Hanoverian line was brought to the throne by the Act of Settlement of 1701 which provided that, should the Princess Anne, accepted as the successor to William and Mary, fail to have direct heirs, the crown should pass to a granddaughter of James I, Sophie, who had married the Elector of Hanover, or to her descendants, provided they were Protestants. Queen Anne, who ascended the throne in 1702, had many children, but none survived her, so upon her death in 1714 Sophie's son, the King of Hanover, became King of Great Britain with the name of George I.

Within the royal family the crown descends by the rule of primogeniture, with a male heir preferred to a female. In the absence of a direct male heir the throne may pass to a daughter or a sister, and certainly the British people, remembering that England was never more peaceful at home and feared abroad than during the long reigns of Elizabeth and Victoria, view with no alarm the ascension of a Queen.

While the wife of a King is known as the Queen, the husband of a Queen in her own right does not become the King. Thus, the wife of King George VI was styled Queen Elizabeth, but when their daughter succeeded to the throne Prince Philip, the Duke of Edinburgh, did not become the King. The Queen's consort may assist his wife in performing some of her official duties, as Prince Albert aided Queen Victoria, but she is the sovereign and must assume the responsibilities of the throne.

Although disputed claims to the throne have arisen several times in English history, there have been no challenges to the rights of the present line for more than two hundred years. James II, expelled in the Glorious Revolution of 1688, maintained an exiled court in France, and his son and grandson each attempted, in 1715 and 1745, to regain the British throne by raising the Scottish clans. In 1745 Bonnie Prince Charlie captured Edinburgh and led his followers as far south as Derby, but there they despaired of the venture and later at the Battle of Culloden, near Inverness, the Stuart hope was forever extinguished.

Some time after a monarch's succession to the throne a coronation ceremony is held in Westminster Abbey, although he has officially reigned from the moment of his predecessor's demise or abdication. In this religious ceremony the highest ecclesiastical dignitary of the kingdom, the Archbishop of Canterbury, anoints and crowns the new sovereign and charges him with the responsibility of performing his duties wisely and faithfully, and the monarch in turn swears to rule according to the laws and customs of the realm. The King sits in a large wooden chair beneath which is the Stone of Scone, carried away from Scotland by Edward I where it had been used for the coronation of Scottish kings and where it was known in legend as the stone upon which Jacob had pillowed his head the night of his heavenly vision.[3]

The royal style and titles conferred upon the monarch at his coronation have undergone several changes in the past century to bring them into conformity with constitutional realities. Queen Victoria was crowned Queen of Great Britain and Ireland, and in 1876 she added the title Empress of India. After the creation of the Irish Free State in 1921 a change in punctuation was required to indicate the separation of Eire from the United Kingdom, and in 1949 further amendment was necessary because of the decision of the Dublin government to sever its formal tie with the British Commonwealth. The title Emperor of India was relinquished in 1947 when that country was divided into the two Dominions of India and Pakistan. Thereafter the style and titles of the monarch began as follows: 'George VI, by the Grace of God, of Great Britain and Northern Ireland and the Dominions beyond the Seas King; Defender of the Faith. . .' [4] This wording remains the legal formula, but changes in the royal titles were foreshadowed in the accession proclamations of Queen Elizabeth II. In London she was proclaimed 'Queen Elizabeth the Second, by the Grace of God Queen of this Realm and of all Her other Realms and Territories, Head of the Commonwealth, Defender of the Faith. . .' Australia and New Zealand also used the revised wording, but in Canada and South Africa the older formula was followed. It is probable that some Commonwealth agreement will be sought which will cause the royal titles to reflect the latest constitutional developments affecting this group of self-governing states. The Statute of Westminster, 1931, recognized the interest of all the dominions in the throne by providing that a change in the sovereign's style and titles requires their consent.

When a monarch is unable to perform his duties because of a brief illness or travel abroad, he appoints Counsellors of State to discharge the sovereign's office or such royal functions as may be specified in letters patent. The Counsellors are usually five senior members of the royal family. Counsellors of State were appointed when King George VI was absent from England for many weeks on trips to Canada and the United States and to South Africa, and again in 1951 when he underwent surgery. The Regency Act, 1937, which authorizes the naming of Counsellors of State, also provides for the appointment of a regent in case the monarch becomes to-

---

[3] Several Scottish nationalists, seeking to call attention to their cause, stole the Stone of Scone from Westminster Abbey at Christmas, 1950. Despite an intensive search by Scotland Yard and the appeals of leading Scots, it was several months before the perpetrators of the theft delivered up the Stone. It was restored to its place beneath the Coronation Chair.

[4] The title Defender of the Faith was conferred on Henry VIII by the Pope, and the Tudor King retained it after his break with the Roman Church. Until 1800, in George III's reign, British monarchs included the title King of France in their official nomenclature, a relic of the days when the Plantagenets fought for land and glory across the Channel.

tally incapacitated. The last regency occurred during the long illness of George III when his son, later George IV, acted for him. In case the succession brings a minor to the throne, a regent serves until the sovereign attains his or her majority.

A constitutional crisis involving the throne arose in 1936 when Edward VIII decided upon a marriage regarded by the Government as unacceptable to opinion in Britain and the Commonwealth. During several weeks of secret parleying both King and Government remained adamant, and the only solution was the abdication of Edward in favor of his eldest brother. With a skillful hand and a minimum strain on the Constitution, Prime Minister Stanley Baldwin arranged the abdication of Edward, a new status as Duke of Windsor for the former King, a suitable financial provision, and the succession of George VI. The correctness with which Baldwin appraised public opinion in this issue may be gauged from the fact that so doughty a champion as Winston Churchill could arouse little sympathy for the King's romantic plight. The majority of the public was satisfied that the new King and his popular Queen fulfilled more adequately the standards of social rectitude expected of the royal family in the present age.

Until the end of the seventeenth century there was no differentiation between the royal finances and the public treasury. Under William III, however, Parliament began providing for the royal family in an appropriation known as the civil list. It was so called because the appropriation to the King included the salaries of the diplomatic, administrative, and judicial officers of the state as well as the sovereign's personal expenses. Today the civil list is a sum fixed from time to time, usually on the monarch's accession, to meet only the expenses of the sovereign and the other members of the royal family. At George VI's accession in 1936 the King was granted £410,000 annually, free of income tax. In 1951 he received what amounted to an increase of £40,000 a year by the Government's transfer of certain charges on the civil list to other appropriations. For example, the King was relieved of paying the salaries of the Yeomen of the Guard, the colorful 'Beefeaters' familiar to all visitors to the Tower of London. Parliament in 1952, upon the recommendation of a select committee, set the civil list for Queen Elizabeth II at £475,000 and granted £40,000 annually to the Duke of Edinburgh. Annuities for most of the other members of the royal family are payable under the Civil List Act, 1937. It is customary for Parliament to increase the allotments to younger members of the royal family as they reach maturity, establish homes of their own, and assume heavier public duties.[5]

---

[5] The hereditary revenues of the Crown, which are surrendered by each sovereign in return for a civil list, bring into the Exchequer considerably more than is granted to the royal family. When there is a Prince of Wales, i.e. the eldest son of the monarch and heir apparent, he receives, except during his minority, the income from the feudal estates of the Duchy of Cornwall.

3. *The Role of the Sovereign*

Let us now consider the personal position of the monarch in the modern concept of the Crown. He has already been described as a symbol of political authority. Does his position have any more meaning than the eagle on the seals and accouterments of government in the United States?

It is fundamentally correct to speak of the monarch as a symbol. He stands for the majesty, the authority, the unity of the British nation, and in each of the units of the Commonwealth and Empire, except India, he represents its statehood. Since the same person is King in all units of the Commonwealth, again excepting India, he is a focus of kinship and loyalty for millions of people living on all continents of the world. As a living symbol he is more interesting than an inanimate one. His picture and that of his family are known to his subjects, notice is taken of his travels and his activities, and his voice, now carried instantaneously to millions, is familiar to their ears. For the people of the United Kingdom and at least those of British descent overseas the King represents all the memories of the past, ties of the present, and hopes of the future that they share.

In addition to being a symbol the King is an influence in the government of Britain. The convention that the monarch acts always on the advice of his ministers is too well established for it to be broken, but he may play a part in shaping that advice. In the frequently quoted words of Bagehot, he has 'the right to be consulted, the right to encourage, the right to warn'; and the author added, 'a king of great sense and sagacity would want no others. He would find that his having no others would enable him to use these with singular effect.' [6] Or, as stated by Winston Churchill, 'Under the British Constitutional system the Sovereign has a right to be made acquainted with everything for which his Ministers are responsible, and has an unlimited right of giving counsel to his Government.' [7] He is well informed on important aspects of public business, and he confers with his ministers frequently.[8] Opportunities naturally arise for a suggestion, a word of caution, or a note of encouragement. Ministers are at liberty to disregard any royal views given to them, but they are not likely to do so without carefully weighing their value. For one thing, the sovereign's counsel is impartial. The King is seeking no party advantage, nor is he concerned with intra-party intrigues. Moreover, the experience of the monarch in public affairs often extends beyond that of his ministers; he can recall

---

[6] Walter Bagehot, *The English Constitution,* World Classics ed. (London, 1928), p. 67.

[7] Winston S. Churchill, *Their Finest Hour* (Boston, 1949), p. 379.

[8] Harry Hopkins wrote after lunching with Their Majesties on 30 January 1941: 'The King discussed the navy and the fleet at some length and showed an intimate knowledge of all the high-ranking officers of the navy, and for that matter, of the army and air force. It was perfectly clear from his remarks that he reads very carefully all the important dispatches and, among other things, was quite familiar with a dispatch which I had sent Sunday night through the Foreign Office.' Robert E. Sherwood, *Roosevelt and Hopkins* (New York, 1948), p. 251.

similar problems in the past and remind his current advisers of decisions made by their predecessors.

Writing on the advantages of the constitutional monarchy, just after the death of King George VI, Clement Attlee said:

> Yet another advantage is that the monarchy, being continuously in touch with public affairs, acquires great experience. A party leader who becomes prime minister has, as a rule, been out of office for some years. He has no doubt kept himself as fully informed as possible and, on coming into office, can avail himself of the experience of the civil service, but this is not the same thing as having access, year after year, to all the secret papers.
>
> King George VI was a very hard worker and read with great care all the state papers that came before him. . . A prime minister discussing affairs of state with him was talking to one who had a wider and more continuous knowledge than anyone else.[9]

Naturally the amount of influence wielded by a monarch depends a great deal upon his or her personality. An able, wise King probably will wield considerable influence, while a less competent sovereign will have a proportionately slighter influence. It is usually impossible to tell until quite a while after a King's death the real weight that he carried in the councils of the nation. His meetings with his ministers are strictly confidential, and he never speaks publicly except in words prepared or authorized by the Government. The King's personal feelings on some issues may be surmised, but the reciprocal loyalty of monarch and ministers makes any attribution of opinion to the sovereign a gross breach of good faith. It is a standing rule of the House of Commons that any question touching on the personal views of the sovereign is out of order. Long after events and individuals have passed from the scene, the biographies of monarchs and the memoirs of their ministers give instances of royal influence upon the policies and actions of cabinets. The voluminous *Letters of Queen Victoria* show her close attention to affairs of state and the vigor of her advice to ministers, many of whom were equally strong personalities. Toward the end of her long reign (1837-1901) ministers were dealing with a personage so deeply enshrined in the hearts of her subjects that to have ignored her views would have been politically dangerous.[10]

---

[9] *Life*, 18 February 1952.

[10] The character of the present-day constitutional monarchy was largely developed during Victoria's reign, and the Prince Consort was a decisive influence in determining the nature of the royal office. In an appreciation, 'Queen Victoria and the Monarchy,' on the occasion of the fiftieth anniversary of her demise, the following was said about her role in public affairs after the Prince Consort's death: 'Through the long years of deep seclusion she maintained an unflagging attention to public affairs, much to the distress of her Ministers who had to journey or send their papers to and fro between London and Osborne and London and Balmoral. This insistence that she should be consulted on even small points of policy proved how well she had learned her duties from the Prince Consort; for he, not wishing to appear to interfere in

In one political situation the monarch still has a positive role to play. That is in the designation of a new Prime Minister. Upon the defeat of a Government in the House of Commons or in a general election, the Prime Minister customarily submits his resignation to the King and advises him to request the leader of the opposition to form a Ministry. The King's choice usually is confined to a member of Parliament who has been the recognized leader of the opposition and head of the 'shadow cabinet,' and this person's accepted position insures his ability to form a Government that will be supported by the House of Commons. Occasionally, however, the party situation may be somewhat confused, and the King will have to exercise a measure of discretion in choosing the political leader he sends for. Such a situation existed when the Conservative Prime Minister, Bonar Law, resigned because of ill health on 20 May 1923. Two Conservative leaders with high claims to the succession, Sir Austen Chamberlain and Lord Curzon, were passed over by King George V because he was informed that neither had the full support of the party rank and file. Curzon's peerage was advanced as a disqualification in his case, although a minister of the time has written that this was more of an excuse than a reason.[11] In the circumstances the King sent for Stanley Baldwin, who was able to form a Government.

The situations in which a monarch will have to exercise some choice in the selection of a Prime Minister are likely to be rare as long as a two-party system is characteristic of British politics. Should a three- or multiple-party system develop, the King's function of choosing a chief minister could take on considerable significance. He would of necessity become involved in the bargaining and maneuvering that accompany the construction of the coalition Governments that the system almost inevitably produces. Between the wars there was a possibility of at least a three-party system becoming established, and the position of the King, while technically that

---

policy, yet anxious to exert the influence of the Crown, had developed, almost perfected, the art of counsel. Every important State paper passed through his hands, drawing from him words of caution or promptings that more might be done: between 1853 and 1857 he filled 50 folio volumes with his comments on the Eastern question alone! This conception of the functions of a constitutional monarch he passed on to the Queen: the monarchy might be unable to initiate policy (Prince Albert was never foolish enough to try to recover abandoned prerogatives) but it could enforce reconsideration of policy, and so, for the rest of the reign, the Queen's life was one of continuous labour. In this way her influence on policy, especially foreign policy, was maintained. She was—and she would not have thought the title unbecoming to a constitutional monarch—the one politician who was always in office, and towards the end of her reign her experience of politics exceeded that of any of her statesmen. Even Dilke, who was no friend of the monarchy, admitted that the Queen's "immense experience" gave her a peculiar, if still limited, right to interfere.' *The Times,* 22 January 1951.

[11] 'The final decision was, to the best of my belief, made mainly on the issue of . . . personal acceptability. . . If a constitutional precedent was created, it was largely as the *ex post facto* cover for a decision taken on other grounds.' L. S. Amery, *Thoughts on the Constitution* (London, 1947), p. 22.

of broker advised by the principals, would almost certainly have grown in importance in so far as the selection of a Prime Minister is concerned. The eclipse of the Liberal Party, however, has reduced the monarch's role to the mechanical one of designating as Prime Minister the leader of the larger of the two principal parties. Only in the event of an issue's splitting party ranks or creating good-sized minor parties could this power of the King take on real significance.

There are two other personal prerogatives, to use the term of Sir Ivor Jennings, which deserve consideration.[12] One is the right of the sovereign to dismiss his ministers, and the other concerns his right to dissolve Parliament —whether he can do so without ministerial advice and whether he may accept or reject such advice. Before 1832 the King's right to exercise these prerogative powers on his own discretion was generally accepted. Since then they have become as inoperative as his right to veto a Parliamentary bill. The reasons which dictate, under the modern Constitution, the removal of these prerogative powers from the sphere of personal discretion are plain. A Cabinet cannot remain in power unless it is supported by the House of Commons; without that support it cannot levy taxes, spend money, or pass legislation. If a monarch, displeased by ministerial policies, dismissed a Ministry supported by the House of Commons, he would have to find other ministers to carry on the administration. Should he succeed, these ministers would immediately have to appeal to the electorate in the hope of obtaining a Parliamentary majority so they could govern. Whether they failed or succeeded, the King would be labeled as a partisan, and what he had done once for an opposition he would be expected to do again. In short, the sovereign's neutral position would be fatally compromised. The same reasoning prevents a sovereign from dissolving Parliament except when advised to do so and requires him to grant a dissolution when the Prime Minister so advises. To dissolve Parliament without ministerial advice would be tantamount to a dismissal of the Ministry, and the King would then become involved in party politics as explained above. If the King refused a dissolution to a Prime Minister, he would be substituting his judgment about the need for and the timing of a general election for that of his chief minister.

While it may be argued that the sovereign still possesses his prerogative rights of dismissal and dissolution, the precedents of the past century indicate that they have lapsed as matters of personal discretion. There are two or three debatable cases concerning the dismissal of Ministries in the early part of the nineteenth century, but the last clear instance was in 1783. No sovereign has refused to accept a Cabinet's advice on dissolution for more than a century, and since 1918 the submission of such advice has been established as a privilege of the Prime Minister alone. In 1924 King George V granted a dissolution of Parliament to Ramsay MacDonald

---

[12] *Cabinet Government,* 2nd ed. (Cambridge, 1951), pp. 368-95.

although he led a minority Government, just deprived of its working majority by the defection of the Liberal Party, and there had been general elections in each of the two preceding years.

4. *The Value of the Monarchy*

The question may be raised of why maintain the monarchy when the King's actual power is so slight and when democratic principles are basic in the political institutions of the country. To many foreigners reared in a republican atmosphere the British monarchy appears at best an expensive bit of antiquarianism. Republican sentiment has appeared in England from time to time, although it has never been strong or influential enough to endanger the continuation of the monarchy. During Queen Victoria's long mourning for the Prince Consort there was some republican feeling expressed, but it dissolved in the great affection she enjoyed in the latter years of her reign.

Undoubtedly a principal reason for the continuance of the monarchical form of government in Britain is the strength of tradition, and Britain is a land where tradition does have strength. As mentioned at the beginning of this chapter, there has always been a King or Queen reigning in the British Isles except for the brief trial of republican institutions during the Commonwealth (1649-60). The institution of monarchy is something with which all Britons have grown up; it is a part of their heritage and their culture. They have shaped it so that it does not interfere with their political or social development, and they see no reason to substitute some other institution which might prove far less satisfactory.

There are reasons other than tradition for retaining the monarchy. One is the practical usefulness of the sovereign as the ceremonial, nonpartisan head of the state. All countries employing the parliamentary type of government have found it necessary to have a head of their state—someone who represents the nation as a unit, in whose name the important acts of state are taken, and who serves as the referee in the party contests for control of the government. Countries without monarchies have usually given the title 'President' to their head of state. Thus, the Presidents of France, Italy, and Ireland occupy positions comparable to that of the King of England in terms of duties and responsibilities.

The British consider their monarch a more satisfactory occupant of a position of this kind than his republican counterparts. For one thing, the presidents are almost invariably veteran politicians who still represent to many of their fellow-countrymen a particular partisan allegiance, although the figures chosen for such posts have usually won respect beyond the limits of their own parties. Moreover, it is sometimes difficult for these presidents to act the role of political neutrality their position requires. Having usually been active in politics all their lives, they are restive when they smell the smoke of political battle. Charges of favoritism arise, and the president may become *persona non grata* to one or more of the parties of the country. Also, it occasionally happens that the president is not

62-

especially impressive as the head of a state; some appear a little ridiculous being king for a term. The hereditary monarch, unless a complete fool, carries with him a good deal of dignity which reflects credit upon the country and its people.

When compared with an office of the American type, the British feel that their monarch has definite advantages in his role of head of state. The two offices are entirely dissimilar, of course, but as a kind of elected monarch in his ceremonial and representational duties, the President of the United States is never able to divest himself of his partisan character. His political opponents can seldom join too wholeheartedly in activities in which the President is participating in his role as head of the nation lest they add to his stature as a party leader and competitor for votes.

The British believe that a modern democratic state has two positions which cannot be satisfactorily combined: one is that of titular, ceremonial head of the state, representing the nation in functions and activities above party divisions; the other is that of political leader—the head of a party espousing controversial policies and programs and the issues of electoral contests. For the first position they consider their hereditary monarch is eminently satisfactory. As the contemporary representative of a dynasty he symbolizes the continuity of national life and the links of the present with the past. He can speak for or appeal to the nation in those causes that have no partisan aspect and in which political opponents can join without sacrificing any competitive advantage.

It is not an easy job. It involves an almost constant round of official and social functions—speaking at dedicatory ceremonies, reviewing troops, receiving distinguished visitors to the country, launching ships, and attending public dinners. During the war years many of the more social activities of the monarch were dispensed with, but the burden of other duties increased considerably. King George VI was unsparing in undertaking any duty in which his presence would contribute to the morale of the public and encourage further patriotic endeavors.

In the discharge of the monarch's duties as head of state he has the assistance of other members of the royal family. They assume a burden of official and social responsibilities almost as great as his. Younger members of the family are gradually trained in the art of being a public figure and start performing their duties at an early age. They sponsor worthy charities, speak at civic celebrations, and visit factories, mines, and shipyards. Commenting on his activities as Prince of Wales, which included several extensive overseas tours, the Duke of Windsor said, 'The number of memorial trees I planted, if they have survived the vicissitudes of climate and the depredations of man, must today constitute a substantial forest. And the number of public buildings and institutions whose cornerstones I laid would comprise, could they be brought together, a sizeable city.' [13]

---

[13] *A King's Story: The Memoirs of the Duke of Windsor* (New York, 1951), p. 212.

In recent years the monarchy has taken on added significance as a bond of unity of the United Kingdom, the autonomous dominions of the Commonwealth, and the colonial empire. As the dominions attained a status of independence, the controlling links running from London to Ottawa, Canberra, Wellington, and Capetown were gradually dropped, and with the passage of the Statute of Westminster each dominion stood forth as a sovereign equal of the mother country. What remained to join them was an acceptance of the crown as a common link. As the symbol of this crown, the King ties together many millions of people living on all continents of the globe.

Each of the dominions, except the Republic of India, has a Governor-General who is the personal representative of the King in that country and his duties are comparable to those of the monarch in the United Kingdom. In the appointment of a Governor-General, the King is advised by his dominion ministers. It was formerly customary to select as Governors-General distinguished figures in the United Kingdom, but in recent years the appointment of native sons to these posts has become common. Australia started the practice and it has been followed by all the dominions except Ceylon. Canada made the change in 1952 when Vincent Massey was recommended as the successor to the retiring Governor-General, Lord Alexander.

The value of the monarch as a link with the colonial empire is probably as important as his functions in connection with the Commonwealth. While some of the colonial dependencies are in a fairly advanced state of governmental and social development, many of them are lands inhabited by primitive peoples whose concepts of political institutions are still in the tribal stage. To them, being joined to a distant country by ties of personal fealty and loyalty to an actual monarch is a conception they can understand and value. It corresponds to their own relationship to native chiefs, and it undoubtedly gives them a greater sense of loyalty to the Empire as a whole.

Recent Kings have considered that one of their responsibilities was to travel to parts of the Commonwealth and Empire and keep alive the links between the mother country and the daughter nations on other continents. Shortly after ascending the throne, King George VI and Queen Elizabeth traveled to Canada and toured all provinces of that dominion. They also took advantage of their presence on this side of the Atlantic to visit the United States. The war interrupted further royal visits, but in 1947 they went to South Africa. Projected visits to Australia and New Zealand had to be abandoned because of the King's illness. Queen Elizabeth II and her consort were en route to these dominions and Ceylon when her father's death recalled her to London to ascend the throne. Tours by other members of the royal family, broadcasts by the monarch to all his subjects, and palace receptions in London for dominion ministers are all means whereby Commonwealth ties are expressed.

Before the First World War, the British monarch played an influential role in the foreign policy of the United Kingdom. While the policy of the

64–

country was definitely determined by the Cabinet, the monarch took a special interest in foreign affairs and probably exerted more influence in this field than in any other. Queen Victoria, it will be remembered, corresponded regularly with her numerous connections in other royal houses and discussed with them affairs of state. Since many of them reigned in countries where the monarch was a determining force in foreign policy, the Queen's views and counsel probably found their way into national policies. The abolition of many of the ruling dynasties after World War I limited the opportunities for royal contacts, and in Britain itself the King became less influential in this field of public policy. The monarchy is still utilized, however, to strengthen foreign attachments and to promote British interests abroad. The Franco-British alliance embodied in the Treaty of Dunkirk (1947) was undoubtedly symbolized more effectively to the French by the nearly contemporaneous visit of Princess Elizabeth and her consort, the Duke of Edinburgh, to Paris than by Ernest Bevin's presence at the signing of the treaty. The close relations existing between Britain and Norway, and to some extent the other Scandinavian countries, have been strengthened by the royal ties uniting the countries.

In addition to foreign policy, the monarchy has been utilized to promote British commercial interests throughout the world. It will be recalled that Edward VIII spent a great deal of his time, while Prince of Wales, in the role of salesman for Britain. Travels to the United States, South America, the Far East, and various European countries were designed to create good will and further the reception of commercial interests in those regions. There is, of course, no way of measuring how successful royal endeavors of this kind are, but it is obvious that they obtain for Britain a tremendous amount of advertising in connection with the opening of trade fairs and commercial exhibits in foreign countries. Many governments follow the practice of promoting national prestige by foreign visits of leading politicians, outstanding military figures, or perhaps a battleship, and the British have a high card to add to their hand when they can include a prince or princess in the entourage.

To sum up, the British have found the institution of monarchy no handicap to the development of a democratic constitution and positively an aid in the operation of that constitution. Without the monarchy, some office to perform the duties now carried on by the King would have to be created and an uncrowned head of state would sacrifice the benefits of prestige and historical continuity. The King serves as a disinterested adviser to successive ministers and his presence is an added guarantee that all national interests will be considered in the formulation of policy. It is doubtful that a more satisfactory bond of Commonwealth membership could be devised than that now existing in the monarchy. The monarchy is not essential to the continuance of the links between Britain and her overseas dependencies, but colonial rule is probably facilitated by the tie of loyalty to the Crown. Finally, the monarchy is useful in strengthening links with foreign countries where royal houses still exist and in advertising British political and commercial prestige in foreign quarters.

To the British, these advantages add up to enough to justify the cost of maintaining the royal establishment. The cost amounts to a little more than one million dollars annually, which works out at about one ten-thousandth of the budget of the British government. From the money provided in the civil list the King maintains considerable establishments at three or four royal residences and does a great deal of official entertaining. Much of this expense would devolve upon the state if there were an elected official performing his duties in place of the hereditary monarch.

Unless there is a revolutionary change in the political and social life of Great Britain, it is a safe prediction that the monarchy is a permanent institution. It has survived the transformation of Britain from a country with an aristocratic government to a democracy with a high degree of socialization, and the monarchy is probably more popular today with the great majority of the citizens than at any time during this period of change.

V

The Cabinet

When the great constitutional struggles of the seventeenth century subsided no doubt was left concerning the supremacy of Parliament over the King. Nevertheless, the King remained a vital part of the machinery of government, and it was necessary that some mechanism be developed whereby Parliamentary supremacy could be made effective. Constitutional struggles of such intensity that the end could only be deposition of the King were not satisfactory as a means of asserting the dominance of Parliament and concurrently conducting the business of the state. The solution of this problem was found in the institution known as the Cabinet. It functions in such a way that Parliament retains ultimate control over the executive but the latter is sufficiently free to govern with vigor and effectiveness.

1. *The Origin of the Cabinet*

The Cabinet of the modern British government has a long genealogy. It goes back to the courts of medieval English kings where there developed an inner circle of the Great Council known as the Curia Regis. This, the Small Council, was a group of officials and aides who were in more or less regular attendance upon the monarch and who performed the day-to-day work necessary to the government of the kingdom. There was not a sharp differentiation in the kinds of business coming before the two councils; both advised the King on policy, sat as a court, and approved royal requests for additional financial aid. Between meetings of the Great Council, the Small Council discharged their common responsibilities.

In the course of time certain specialized functions performed by the Small Council produced new institutional arrangements. Its judicial work led to the establishment of the common-law court of King's Bench and the Chancery for equity cases, and its responsibilities in connection with financial administration, the receipt and auditing of the sheriffs' returns, produced the Exchequer. Its legislative function largely passed to Parliament when in the thirteenth and fourteenth centuries that institution developed out of the Great Council. Meanwhile, the Small Council's advisory and administrative duties continued and indeed became more important as the social and economic life of the country expanded.

By the opening of the Tudor period (1485) the Council, soon to be known as the Privy Council, was a powerful official group composed of the King's chief advisers and ministers and conducting the central administration of the state. Although its responsibilities were principally concerned with executive policy and administration, it still retained—and has to this day—a more general competence which gave the Council judicial and legislative functions as well. Gradually, the Privy Council grew to a size which made it unwieldy as a body for day-to-day administration. During the reign of Charles II the Council sometimes had as many as fifty members. Consequently, it became the practice of kings to consult with an inner group called the Cabinet, so denominated because of its meeting in the monarch's office of that name. The persons forming the Cabinet were usually high officers of state and the members of important administrative committees of the Council.

At the end of the seventeenth and the beginning of the eighteenth centuries a dozen or so ministers composed the Cabinet. They were selected by the monarch without particular regard to common ties or understanding of mutual responsibility. He appointed and dismissed them individually, and they did not feel any sense of collective responsibility for the advice they gave the King or for the conduct of the state's business.[1] The sovereign came to appreciate, however, that matters ran more smoothly and the relations between King and Parliament were more harmonious when his ministers were all drawn from the same Parliamentary faction and were able to command a majority in the Houses of Parliament. William III is credited with having composed the first one-party ministerial group, the Whig 'junto' of 1696, but he did not follow this practice consistently and he did not regard as necessary a constant agreement on policy between his Cabinet and the majority of Parliament.

The reign of Queen Anne (1702-14) was, in a constitutional sense, a continuation of that of William III. Cabinets contained representatives of both parties more often than not, and their members remained personally responsible to the sovereign and not to Parliament. 'The people of Queen Anne's time,' Adams said, 'did not yet see the connection between the three elements of the problem, the parliamentary majority, the cabinet, and the successful carrying out of government policy. The events of her

---

[1] Of the Cabinet of this time, George Burton Adams wrote: 'There was a group of executive and administrative offices of more or less high rank and power whose holders belonged to the privy council, and who sometimes had cohesion enough to stand together against opposition attacks in parliament. But there was no definite notion as yet that these officers formed an organized body within, but distinct from, the council, having as a group a special, or even a semi-official, relation to the formation and direction of policy. A given man was put into office because he was an influential leader in parliament and the nation, and the king asked his advice for the same reason, but he grouped together as he pleased those men whom he wished to consult in a body, leaving out some of the great office-holders and including on occasion some who were not among them.' *Constitutional History of England* (New York, 1921), p. 369.

reign and the experience gained, however, were rapidly making clear both the dependence of cabinet and policy upon parliament and the greater strength and stability of a party ministry over a coalition.'[2]

The advent of the Hanoverian dynasty produced conditions favorable to the further development of the Cabinet. Because leading Tories had conspired to restore a Stuart sovereign, the Whigs had a monopoly of political power and ministries were drawn from their ranks exclusively. George I, who was in his fifties when he succeeded to the English throne, was principally interested in the affairs of the German states, and was content to leave the domestic business of his new kingdom to his ministers. Reduced to conversing in Latin because he knew no English and few of his ministers spoke German, the King left off attending and presiding at Council meetings and thus opened the way for a ministerial chairman, a prime minister. One was soon available in the person of Sir Robert Walpole.

During the rest of the eighteenth century the Cabinet assumed more and more of the characteristics of the modern body of that name, but it was not a plotted, conscious development. The monarch, ministers, and Parliament responded to situations as they occurred, and they gradually developed the mechanism whereby Parliament could exercise effectively the supremacy won in the seventeenth century. So gradual was the evolution of the Cabinet in the constitutional structure and so large a part did custom and convention play in determining its organization and functioning that contemporary observers were hardly aware of the changes taking place. It was not until the early part of the nineteenth century that the true nature of the modern Cabinet was generally understood.

During the time around 1700 when the Cabinet was first emerging as a separate organ of government, it was viewed suspiciously by the houses of Parliament. Paradoxically, in the light of the Cabinet's later place in the Constitution, at that time it appeared to make less secure Parliament's control of the executive. The secrecy surrounding its business and Parliament's inability to identify the author of specific advice to the sovereign caused the politicians outside the Cabinet circle to look askance at its growing importance. Consequently, Parliament in passing the Act of Settlement, 1701, included two provisions designed to improve its means of enforcing executive responsibility. The first required that Privy Council affairs should be transacted in the Council and not in informal Cabinet meetings and that ministers should provide evidence of their responsibility for official acts by appending their signatures. The second provided that officers and pensioners of the Crown should not be eligible to sit in the House of Commons, a measure intended to reduce ministerial power in the House and also to prevent that body from being subverted by bribes in the form of offices and pensions. It is fortunate for the future development of the Cabinet system that neither of these provisions became effec-

---

[2] Ibid. p. 380.

tive, for they would have inhibited greatly its growth. Parliament quickly recognized that both provisions would be more harmful than beneficial and repealed them the next year. It later passed a modified version of the second measure, declaring the holder of any Crown office created after 25 October 1705, and of certain other offices, ineligible to sit in the House of Commons, and depriving a member accepting ministerial office of his seat but permitting him to seek re-election. This statute, until amended by laws passed in 1919 and 1926, required a number of ministers upon appointment to vacate their seats in the House of Commons and submit themselves to new contests at the polls. Since 1926 all ministerial appointments have been exempted from this requirement.

2. *The Privy Council*

All during the time that the Cabinet was taking on its modern form the official position of ministers was that of Privy Councillor. The Cabinet itself had no legal standing, and its collective acts were officially those of the Privy Council. This is substantially the situation today. The Privy Council continues to exist as the official advisory body of the monarch, and when he meets formally with his ministers he is holding a meeting of the Privy Council.

The Council now is a body of about 300 members who never assemble together except on some ceremonial occasion such as the coronation of a king.[3] Appointments to the Council are made by the King upon the advice of the Prime Minister, and they go to ministers, ambassadors, judges, and others prominent in official life. It is necessary for all Cabinet ministers to be Privy Councillors since they must subscribe to the oath required of the Crown's chief advisers. In recent years it has been the custom to admit to the Council all ministers who head departments. For other public figures, membership is usually given in recognition of valuable services to the state and is announced in the Honours List at either New Year's or on the King's Birthday. Once appointed a person remains permanently a member of the Council. Privy Council membership is indicated by the use of 'Right Honourable' before and 'P.C.' after a member's name.

All business of the Council is transacted by ministers who are currently in power, and three of them constitute a quorum. Most of the Council's activity is simply that of giving legal effect to certain decisions reached by the Cabinet. These decisions become legal acts as proclamations or as orders-in-council, literally orders issued by the King after consultation with the Privy Council. The orders are ordinarily executive action authorized by the royal prerogative or by an act of Parliament. Their nearest American counterpart is an executive order of the President.

The procedure of an ordinary Privy Council meeting, as described by a former Lord President, is as follows:

---

[3] About 40 members of the Privy Council are dominion citizens.

When the King holds a Council, those whose presence is required receive a summons in the traditional form, which runs: 'Let the messenger acquaint the Lords and Others of His Majesty's Most Honourable Privy Council that a Council is appointed to be held'—at such and such a place and time. . . What happens at a Council depends on the business to be done, but as a rule the proceedings follow a straight-forward course. First of all, before the Council begins, the Lord President is received in Audience. The other Counsellors then enter and, having bowed and shaken hands with the King, take up their position. They stand in a line, headed by the Lord President, who has a List of Business, as the agenda is called. The items in this are already known to His Majesty, who as they are read out by the Lord President, approves them or gives any other directions that may be needed. When the business is finished, the proceedings become rather less formal. There is some general conversation: then the Counsellors withdraw, leaving as they entered in accordance with their precedence.[4]

Although the business of the Council is today largely formal and its principal administrative responsibilities have been transferred elsewhere, it retains a few duties. They are discharged, for the most part, by permanent or special committees. A number of official committees supervising and allotting money for scientific research report to the Privy Council, and others are concerned with the licensing standards of various professions, such as the medical and architectural. The Judicial Committee, established in 1833, is in effect the highest court of appeal of the British Empire, and it also gives the Crown legal advice on certain questions referred to it.

While the Privy Council continues to be the executive body possessing a legal standing and authority, the actual power resides in the inner group, the Cabinet. The Cabinet usually contains between 15 and 20 members, and they are the leading figures of the party, or coalition of parties, which has a majority in Parliament. As members of Parliament they guide and direct the legislative program in the two houses, and as occupants of the principal executive posts in the governmental organization they control and administer the state's affairs. The size of the Cabinet is not rigidly fixed. The holders of certain offices are invariably members but others may or may not be included. The determination of the exact size of the body is made by the leader of the Cabinet, the officer known as the Prime Minister.

3. The Prime Minister

The development of the office of Prime Minister has paralleled the evolution of the Cabinet itself. Early Cabinets, it will be remembered, were a

---

[4] Herbert Morrison, 'The Privy Council Today,' *Parliamentary Government in Britain* (London, 1949), pp. 62-3.

more or less miscellaneous collection of ministers appointed by the monarch because of their ability, political influence, or personal loyalty to the sovereign. These ministers did not recognize anyone of their number as being pre-eminent, although of course the holders of the most important offices had a certain standing that the others did not enjoy. Gradually, however, the Cabinet came to be organized under a leading figure who was the most influential in determining the composition of the Cabinet and who in turn exacted a loyalty from his colleagues. George I's practice of absenting himself from ministerial councils contributed to the development of the premiership as well as of the Cabinet. 'The result was to transform what had been a mere inner group of royal advisers into a board of government with an independent existence of its own. Having lost its natural president, it was inevitable that it should find one of its own, a "prime minister" in fact, upon whom would fall the task of co-ordinating policy, which before had been the king's.' [5]

Sir Robert Walpole is usually spoken of as the first Prime Minister and, although the office has evolved considerably since his day, there are good reasons to so identify him. When he was appointed to ministerial office in 1721—he had also served from 1714 to 1718—he took the position of First Lord of the Treasury, as his successors have usually done. At the Treasury he had much patronage to dispense, and this was valuable in maintaining Parliamentary support. Walpole did not accept elevation to the peerage as had previously been the practice of nearly all important ministers who were commoners when appointed. He chose to direct and manage Parliament from his seat in the lower house. Furthermore, because most of the ministers were in the Lords, Walpole became the advocate and defender of ministerial policy on all matters, much as a modern premier accepts responsibility for the whole range of governmental affairs. Finally, he set the precedent of resigning when he no longer enjoyed the support of the House of Commons. Defeated twice within a week, early in 1742, Walpole submitted his resignation. A half-hearted attempt was made to impeach him, but Parliament soon realized that its main object—to compel a change in ministerial policy—had been achieved by Walpole's resignation. 'The new method of enforcing ministerial responsibility had been affirmed once and for all. No attempt was ever afterwards made to revive impeachment for this purpose. It had been discovered that the proper way to enforce ministerial responsibility is to compel a minister to resign.' [6]

The scores of Cabinets since Walpole's day have all been headed by a Prime Minister who has been the recognized leader of the group. The leadership, however, is quite different from that of the American President in relation to his Cabinet. The Prime Minister is the principal member of a group of ministers who all serve as advisers of the Crown. His pre-

[5] K. R. Mackenzie, *The English Parliament* (Penguin Books, 1950), p. 81.
[6] Ibid. p. 85.

eminence among his colleagues comes not from any nation-wide election but from his recognized position as head of his party in Parliament and the chief figure in the Cabinet.

Until the present century the office of Prime Minister was unknown to the written law. The person selected by the monarch to form and to head a Cabinet took for himself the position of First Lord of the Treasury, and this gave him a legal authority as a minister of the Crown. The post of First Lord of the Treasury has for long had only nominal departmental duties connected with it, so Prime Ministers have been able to devote their whole attention to the general problems of policy and administration. Prime Ministers may occasionally take the additional responsibility of other ministerial offices. Lord Salisbury and Ramsay MacDonald both served as their own Foreign Secretaries; Churchill occupied the position of Minister of Defence as well as that of First Lord of the Treasury from 1940 to 1945 and again for a period in 1951 and 1952.

The King's designation of a Prime Minister, as has previously been explained, is normally limited to the leader of the political party having a majority in the House of Commons. Only when the leadership of the majority party is for some reason unsettled or when the party situation in the House is confused does the King exercise a real choice, and then he would be guided in the main by the advice of the retiring Prime Minister. Ordinarily the voters know who the Prime Minister would be should the party in power suffer a defeat in a general election. He is the leader of the opposition in the House of Commons and the head of the 'shadow Government.'

The formal qualifications for the position are simple. The Prime Minister must be an adult British subject who either is or who can quickly become a member of one of the houses of Parliament. Also, he either is or must immediately become a Privy Councillor.

The personal qualifications which bring a man to this high position are more difficult to describe. Prime Ministers have varied as much in talent and temperament as Presidents of the United States. Nevertheless, two generalizations may be made. First, Prime Ministers are invariably veteran politicians. One would have to go back to the younger Pitt, who became Prime Minister at the age of 24, to find an exception. In the twentieth century all Prime Ministers, apart from Lord Salisbury (1895-1902), have been long-time members of the House of Commons before appointment— Arthur J. Balfour for 28 years; Henry Campbell-Bannerman, 38 years; Herbert Asquith, 22 years; David Lloyd George, 26 years; Andrew Bonar Law, 23 years; Stanley Baldwin, 15 years; Ramsay MacDonald, 18 years; Neville Chamberlain, 19 years; Winston Churchill, 40 years; and Clement Attlee, 22 years. Moreover, all these men, except MacDonald, had occupied ministerial posts in previous Cabinets. Several had had long periods of high ministerial experience before attaining the premiership. Lloyd George, Chamberlain, and Churchill, for example, had all been Chancellors of the Exchequer—sometimes regarded as the second Cabinet post—in earlier Ministries. Just as the prospects of the brilliant political amateur attaining the Presidency in the United States are not bright, they are even less so in the case of the Prime Minister's office.

Secondly, all modern Prime Ministers have possessed some quality of leadership that has brought them to the top among many aspiring politicians. It has not often been the same kind of leadership. In a Churchill it consists of the type of political genius that makes the person the outstanding national figure of his generation. Lloyd George had many of the same gifts—great vitality, mental brilliance, political acumen, and exceptional oratorical powers. Less striking types of leadership are exhibited in Prime Ministers such as Baldwin, Chamberlain, and Attlee. Baldwin's strength probably lay in his seeming embodiment of national virtues and weaknesses: a kind of John Bull cartoon come to life. Chamberlain won leadership by applying his gifts as an administrator with unswerving persistence and determination. Attlee's mild and unpretentious public nature hides a strong character revealed in private councils. He is skillful in negotiation and has a will capable of acting decisively when necessary. When he took office in 1945 it was frequently said that he was a party compromise between the more vigorous and assertive rivals, Morrison and Bevin; such a view proved to be an underestimation of Attlee's powers of leadership.

Sometimes a Prime Minister's popularity declines while he is in office; his type of leadership becomes outmoded and is found to be unsuitable to changing circumstances. Thus, in 1940, Chamberlain, while exhibiting in war the same dogged and conscientious determination he had shown in pursuing 'peace in our time,' was found to lack the flexibility of mind, the sense of great issues, and the power to inspire which the times called for. Churchill possessed these in a superlative degree, and it would be generally agreed that his leadership was a primary factor in rallying the free world during the darkest days of the war. Many of his countrymen, however, found his qualities as a war leader less appropriate to times of peace, and they could vote against his continuance in office even as the cannonades of victory were booming.

While the country may, in a sense, reject a Prime Minister, he does not necessarily forfeit his party leadership. A party's defeat in a general election is usually regarded as a vote of no confidence in the Government as a team of ministers and not a rebuff to the Prime Minister alone. The former Prime Minister becomes the leader of the opposition and often expects to sit again on the Treasury bench as the head of a Ministry. His position as party leader is reasonably secure until he is ready to relinquish it voluntarily. He usually takes this step when he wishes to retire from the kind of active political life that being Prime Minister or opposition leader imposes upon him. Baldwin, after serving three times as Prime Minister, decided in 1937 to accept a peerage and turn over to Chamberlain the leadership of the Conservative Party and with that the highest ministerial post.

The duties of a Prime Minister are akin to those performed by the chief executive of any major democratic state, although he exercises most of them in close collaboration with his Cabinet colleagues. Unlike the President of the United States, who determines the extent to which he will consult with members of his executive family, the Prime Minister is the leader but not the master of a group, and he is bound to observe the rights of those who jointly share responsibility with him.

In some Cabinets, the Prime Minister stands out more prominently than in others; occasionally the times require a type of personal leadership that would not be acceptable in other periods. Harry Hopkins, reporting to President Roosevelt during a visit to London in 1941, declared that *Churchill* is the government in every sense of the word. . .'[7] A few months later, however, Hopkins was able to observe the difference between the authority of a Prime Minister and a President of the United States. At the Atlantic Conference in August 1941, he saw 'both the President and the Prime Minister in operation away from their home bases. He remarked on the fact that whereas Roosevelt was completely on his own, subject only to the advice of his immediate and self-selected entourage, which advice he could accept or reject, Churchill was constantly reporting to and consulting the War Cabinet in London, addressing his communications to the Lord Privy Seal, who was then Clement Attlee. During three days more than thirty communications passed between the *Prince of Wales* and Whitehall. . .'[8]

As chairman of the Cabinet the Prime Minister participates in the discussions of policy matters coming before that body. His voice is the most influential, but the decisions reached must be ones that commend themselves to the group as a whole. Here strong qualities of leadership are required, for usually several of his colleagues will be powerful political figures and they will represent varying shades of opinion within the party. Advocates of extending the state's social services will contend with believers in financial retrenchment; critics and defenders of issues of foreign policy will have their say; proponents of reform in local government will argue with supporters of the *status quo*. The Prime Minister must guide his colleagues to decisions they can all conscientiously defend and ones that will be supported by the party in and out of Parliament.[9] In addition to the regular Cabinet meetings the Prime Minister attends and participates in some meetings of Cabinet committees. He is the chairman of the Defence Committee and may attend other committee meetings. He also must give occasional attention to ministers outside the Cabinet.

---

[7] Robert E. Sherwood, *Roosevelt and Hopkins* (New York, 1948), p. 243.

[8] Ibid. p. 361. H.M.S. *Prince of Wales* was the battleship on which Churchill traveled to the Newfoundland rendezvous. A few months later it was sunk by Japanese air attack off Malaya.

[9] Viscount Samuel, who has had long experience in high political office, described Ramsay MacDonald as a 'good chairman of the Cabinet, carefully preparing his material beforehand, conciliatory in manner and resourceful. In the conduct of a Cabinet, when a knot or a tangle begins to appear, the important thing is for the Prime Minister not to let it be drawn tight; so long as it is kept loose it may still be unravelled. MacDonald was skilful in such situations. . .' *Memoirs* (London, 1945), pp. 214-15.

The Prime Minister's power of appointment is not as extensive as the American President's, but it is considerable nevertheless. All ministerial positions are within his gift, and they run to 80 or 90. He will either select new occupants or be consulted by the minister principally concerned when there are vacancies in the chief diplomatic, military, judicial, and ecclesiastical offices. Advised by the Permanent Secretary of the Treasury who is the Head of the Civil Service, the Prime Minister appoints the Permanent Secretary or Permanent Under Secretary, the Deputy Secretary or Deputy Under Secretary, and the principal establishments officer in each of the government departments. Finally, there are a good many special appointments in which the Prime Minister is interested—governors-general and United Kingdom high commissioners in the Dominions, British representatives to important international organizations, and board members of nationalized industries. He will certainly be consulted about many of these, and frequently the choice will be his.

The Prime Minister must devote a considerable part of his time and attention to Parliamentary business. He sometimes makes the opening speech in the debate on a principal measure of the Government's legislative program. Occasionally he will give the House of Commons a review of recent developments in major policy fields; Churchill's periodic summaries of campaigns, the relations of Britain and her allies, estimates of conditions in the enemy's camp, and the meetings of the principal wartime leaders will long be remembered for their content and their phrasing. In peacetime when events and opinions can be reported and discussed more openly there is less need for authoritative statements at periodic intervals by the Prime Minister, but occasions arise nevertheless when it is desirable for him to speak for the Government as a whole and bring together the many threads of program and policy. In addition, the Prime Minister is expected to reply to questions in the House of Commons when these pertain to general policy matters. Whether or not he has questions to answer, he is usually present on the Treasury bench at the opening of each day's session, and he remains for the question hour and for any major debate which follows. His Parliamentary duties also require occasional attendance at meetings of the party members when policy issues are to be discussed. Once in a while dissension arises among the backbench members: the privates in the Parliamentary army feel that their officers are not sufficiently solicitous of rank-and-file sentiment. A hearing before the commander-in-chief may be necessary to restore harmony and prevent the spread of disaffection which could be troublesome on crucial votes.

The other powers and duties of the Prime Minister are numerous and varied. He can allocate to ministers subjects and responsibilities not provided by statute, and even where they are allocated by statute he can have them transferred from one department to another by order in council. He has audiences with the King at which Government policy is discussed. There are from time to time Commonwealth and foreign conferences in which he is the leading participant for the United Kingdom. A flying trip to Washington, such as Attlee made in December 1950, may be deemed necessary to discuss Anglo-American views on important issues. He takes part in the affairs of his political party, meeting with committees and addressing the annual conference. He broadcasts over the radio, either in the interest of his party or to inform the country at large about important political developments and policies. He receives deputations of aggrieved trade unionists, housewives, civil servants, or other interest groups that are not satisfied unless their complaint has been heard by the Prime Minister. Finally, there are many public ceremonies and dinners at which the Prime Minister must speak or at least must make an appearance.

The Prime Minister's salary is £10,000 a year. He receives a residence, the famous No. 10 Downing Street, which is both home and office. He also has an office in the Palace of Westminster which he can use while the House of Commons is meeting and where he can confer with members of his own party or the opposition. Since 1917 the Prime Minister has had the use of a country estate, Chequers, for week ends and short holidays. A former Prime Minister, not in receipt of a salary as a minister or as Leader of the Opposition, is entitled to a pension of £2000 a year.

4. *The Cabinet*

'It is a peculiarity of our Constitution,' Sir Ivor Jennings has said, 'that the principles governing the formation and working of the Cabinet and its relations with Parliament can be stated with hardly any reference to the law.' [10] The composition, powers, and functioning of the British Cabinet are governed largely by the unwritten, the conventional part of the Constitution. It was not until 1937, more than 200 years after the Cabinet began to be identified by name, that Parliament took statutory notice of this important institution.[11] Then the chief purpose was to establish some uniformity in the compensation of ministers of various ranks. The Ministers of the Crown Act, 1937, named a number of 'Cabinet rank' ministers as entitled to a salary of £5000 a year, but it did not attempt to specify a fixed size for the Cabinet.[12]

The Labour Cabinet at the beginning of 1951 consisted of 18 members, and the Conservative Cabinet named by Churchill after the general election in October had 16 members. In size these were typical modern Cabinets. Some Cabinets in this century have been as large as 23 members, but it is usually agreed that a group of more than 20 is too unwieldy for effi-

---

[10] *Cabinet Government,* 2nd ed. (Cambridge, 1951), p. 79.

[11] 'The cabinet, the prime minister, and the ministers of the crown have at last been recognized by statute and have been given a status in British constitutional law.' Harlow J. Heneman, 'Ministers of the Crown and the British Constitution,' *The American Political Science Review,* October 1937, p. 929.

[12] Upon taking office in 1951 Churchill announced that: 'During the period of rearmament or for three years, whichever ends first, Ministers who are entitled by statute to a salary of £5000 a year will draw £4000 a year. During the same period the Prime Minister will draw £7000 instead of his statutory salary of £10,000.' *The Times,* 31 October 1951.

cient operation. There has been some feeling that even a Cabinet of between 15 and 20 is too large and that a group of 10 or 12 would be more satisfactory. It is difficult, however, to reduce the Cabinet below 15 without leaving out heads of important departments or sacrificing distinguished figures of the governing party.

During both the First and Second World Wars it was found necessary to create within the Cabinet an inner circle of ministers primarily concerned with the great issues of military strategy and diplomacy which had to be under constant review or which called for rapid decision. In setting up the first so-called War Cabinet, Lloyd George declared that the war could not be fought by a Sanhedrin. Churchill in the Second World War had the same opinion, and he and seven, later six, of his Cabinet colleagues comprised an inner group devoted to the day-to-day conduct of the struggle.[13] The War Cabinet came to an end in May 1945, when the Labour Party withdrew from the wartime coalition in order to contest the general election in July. When the new Prime Minister, Clement Attlee, formed a Cabinet, he reverted to the prewar tradition and included nearly 20 members.

Along with the Prime Minister, there are several other ministers who are invariably members of the Cabinet. One of these is the Chancellor of the Exchequer, the head of the Treasury. As the minister responsible for the fiscal policy of the Government, he is essential to any group of ministers. An equally essential figure is the Secretary of State for Foreign Affairs, who as the name indicates is in charge of the external relations of the United Kingdom.

The office of Secretary of State has been subdivided through the years and today there are eight ministers who are Secretaries of State with various specialties. Besides the Secretary of State for Foreign Affairs, those for Home Affairs, Colonies, and Commonwealth Relations are always members of the Cabinet. In addition, the Secretary of State for Scotland is frequently included. Churchill in 1951 appointed a Secretary of State for Co-ordination of Transport, Fuel, and Power with a seat in the Cabinet. The Secretary of State for War and the Secretary of State for Air were commonly members of prewar Cabinets along with the First Lord of the Admiralty, but with the establishment in 1946 of the office of Minister of

---

[13] In practice several other ministers attended the War Cabinet with fair regularity, because the Prime Minister included them whenever business pertaining to their departments was being considered. Winston S. Churchill, *The Hinge of Fate* (Boston, 1950), p. 88. This expansion also occurred in the case of the Lloyd George War Cabinet. According to Jennings, 'Though the War Cabinet contained only five or six members its sessions tended to resemble public meetings. Departmental ministers and their advisers were summoned to all meetings at which their affairs were under discussion, and as many as thirty-five persons are known to have been present, some sitting on tables and improvised chairs in odd corners. Though the War Cabinet alone was collectively responsible in the widest sense, every minister (and his adviser) wanted to see that his department got fair play, especially with Mr. Lloyd George in the chair.' *Cabinet Government,* 2nd ed. (Cambridge, 1951), pp. 69-70.

Defence the heads of the three service departments were dropped from Cabinet membership.

There are several old positions which have long ceased to have important administrative duties connected with them but which are often included within the Cabinet as a means of adding important party figures who are virtually ministers without portfolio. These are the Lord President of the Council (i.e. the Privy Council), the Lord Privy Seal, the Paymaster-General, and the Chancellor of the Duchy of Lancaster. Another invariable member is the Lord Chancellor, who is the presiding officer of the upper chamber and also the head of the judicial system. Except for the Chancellor of the Duchy of Lancaster, the present Cabinet includes the ministerial positions that have been named as well as the Minister of Labour and National Service, the Minister of Health, the Minister of Housing and Local Government, and the President of the Board of Trade. The holders of the offices in this last group are usually members of the Cabinet, but one or more of them may be displaced by such officers as the Minister of Agriculture and Fisheries, the Minister of Education, the Minister of Supply, or the Minister of Fuel and Power. The inclusion or exclusion of ministers depends to some extent upon the prestige of the persons involved and to some extent upon the importance of a ministry in the policies of the Government as a whole.

Beyond the circle of the Cabinet, there is a group of ministers who occupy important administrative positions but who, either on grounds of party standing or because of the departments they head, do not rate inclusion in the Cabinet. At present there are 22 such ministers. They are the Chancellor of the Duchy of Lancaster, the First Lord of the Admiralty, the Secretary of State for War, the Secretary of State for Air, the Minister of Transport and Civil Aviation, the Minister of Supply, the Minister of Food, the Minister of National Insurance, the Minister of Fuel and Power, the Minister of Education, the Postmaster-General, the Minister of Agriculture and Fisheries, the Minister of Works, the Minister of State for Colonial Affairs (a deputy for the Secretary of State for the Colonies), the Minister of State (a deputy for the Foreign Secretary), the Minister of State for Economic Affairs, the Minister of Pensions, the Attorney-General, the Lord Advocate, the Solicitor-General, the Solicitor-General for Scotland, and the Minister of State for Scotland.

There is still a third group, that of junior ministers. These are members of the majority party in Parliament who serve as assistants to the heads of departments and ministries and who are usually known as Parliamentary Secretaries to these ministries. All these ministers form the Government of the day.

What are the criteria employed by the Prime Minister in choosing his ministerial colleagues? There are several, and they are much like those which guide a President of the United States in selecting his Cabinet. In the first place, there are always a few prominent party leaders who must be included. They usually have been ministers in previous administrations; two or three probably have been contenders for the party leadership and the Prime Minister's office. They have, as a rule, many friends in Parliament and positions of standing within the party. The Prime Minister must invite them to take important portfolios—Lord President of the Council, Chancellor of the Exchequer, Foreign Secretary, or Lord Chancellor. To ignore them or to offer them posts below their rank in party circles would be to risk serious dissension.

Secondly, there are wings or factions of the party to be satisfied. In any two-party system of government, the major parties are always coalitions, in a sense, of factions, groups, and interests. The Prime Minister must attempt to bring the leading representatives of party factions into his official family. Both left-wing and right-wing elements must receive office. A Labour Prime Minister must see that the trade unions and the co-operative movement are sufficiently recognized in ministerial appointments. A Conservative Prime Minister must try to include those who take their inspiration from Herbert Spencer and those who think their party must be progressive or perish. Furthermore, he has agricultural and industrial interests to consider in choosing his ministers.

A proper representation of geographical areas is not as strong a requirement as it is in some countries, but it cannot be ignored by a British Prime Minister. The Secretary of State for Scotland always comes from north of the border, and it is sometimes politically desirable to include other Scots in the ministerial family. The Welsh, too, usually have claims for representation. Rising young leaders must be given an opportunity for ministerial experience, for unless they are included there may be mutterings and revolts among the backbenchers. Finally, places must be found for a few peers. By limiting the number of ministers in certain categories who can sit in the Commons, the Ministers of the Crown Act, 1937, indirectly requires that some peers be given office. A Prime Minister would probably wish in any event to include a few distinguished members of the House of Lords, and in the upper chamber he will need Government spokesmen and pilots of legislative measures.[14]

While the Prime Minister has 80 or 90 ministerial positions at his disposal, the claims always exceed the supply, and he must necessarily disappoint some persons and special groups within his party. Honors and appointments to public office outside the Ministry can sometimes assuage the feelings of the most important or worthy individuals who are excluded.

If a Government is in office for a considerable period of time a Prime Minister usually finds it necessary to reconstruct the Ministry periodically. Illness, retirement, and death create vacancies which must be filled. Ministers may prove to be inept and have to be demoted or removed; junior ministers may show unexpected ability and thus deserve advancement. Occasionally changes are made mandatory by criticism within Parliament or

---

[14] The Conservative Cabinet in 1952 contained 7 peers, an unusually large number. Lord Alexander, Lord Ismay, and Lord Cherwell were not leading party members but owed their selection to association with Churchill before or during World War II.

by the press. The critics will not be appeased until the Prime Minister sacrifices one or two of his colleagues or reconstructs his official family.

Churchill has given us an account of the reconstruction of a Ministry which illustrates the problems faced by a Prime Minister in such an undertaking and the considerable negotiating that is involved.[15] He has written that early in 1942 he 'could feel the tension in political circles growing. There was a demand that the Government should be "strengthened." "New blood," it was said, should be added.'[16] Churchill decided, therefore, to reconstruct the Ministry. A high place had to be found for Sir Stafford Cripps who had returned from the embassy in Moscow and who was the 'most noticeable new blood available.' A Ministry of Production was projected, and the minister-designate, Lord Beaverbrook, had views concerning his new powers that made accommodation with other departments difficult. It was necessary to transfer several ministers to other positions, and a few had to be dropped from office. Informing those to be excluded from the Ministry was an invidious task, as Churchill's account shows. 'It is with very deep regret on every ground, personal and public,' he wrote to Lord Moyne, 'that I find myself compelled to make a change in the Colonial Office. The considerable reconstruction of the Government which events and opinion alike require makes it necessary for me to give Attlee the Dominions Office, which many have pressed should be held by a member of the War Cabinet. That being so, I am anxious that Cranborne should take your place, and I feel sure from all I know of you and from your previous conduct in this war that you will be willing to fall in with my wishes and needs.'[17]

In the reconstruction of the Government Churchill possessed the advantages of his strong position as national leader and the critical nature of the times, which caused politicians to subordinate personal ambition and factious interest. On the other hand, he had the problems of a coalition Ministry in which the cement of party loyalty does not exist and the due claims of all groups must be recognized. After two or three weeks of negotiations the Prime Minister had his reorganized team in place. The War Cabinet was reduced from eight to seven members, with two new faces appearing, and there were eight other changes among ministers of Cabinet rank.

All members of a Ministry receive their offices by nomination of the Prime Minister, and they serve at his pleasure. As a group, they leave office when the Prime Minister submits the Ministry's resignation to the King. The Prime Minister takes this action when his Government no longer has the support of the House of Commons. Nowadays a Ministry's fate is usually determined by a general election. If the election places the ministerial party in a minority in the House, the Prime Minister seldom waits for the new Parliament to meet but resigns at once. He may resign if his

---

[15] *The Hinge of Fate* (Boston, 1950), pp. 74-91.
[16] Ibid. p. 74.
[17] Ibid. p. 80.

Government is defeated in the House of Commons on an important issue; more probably, however, he will advise the King to dissolve Parliament in order to ask the electorate for a Parliamentary majority. Governments do not resign because of defeats in the House of Commons on minor issues or because of adverse votes in the House of Lords unless such rebuffs signify a party split that is beyond healing.

5. *The Duties of a Cabinet Minister*

A Cabinet Minister can be said to have three principal fields of activity. In the first place, he is a member of the Cabinet circle which meets regularly under the chairmanship of the Prime Minister and which considers the principal policy questions before the Government. He is called upon to read memoranda and take his part in the discussion of these issues, and in the end he will have to participate in the decisions which the Cabinet reaches and share responsibility for them. These decisions he is loyally bound to support, both in Parliament and before the public. If he finds that he cannot conscientiously support the decisions reached by the Prime Minister and the rest of his colleagues, his course is to resign from his ministerial position and either become a critic within his own party or join the opposition. Before the Second World War, Anthony Eden as Foreign Secretary found himself less and less in agreement with the ideas of Neville Chamberlain and a majority of the Conservative Cabinet on the policies to be followed concerning the Fascist dictatorships on the Continent, and consequently resigned his office. Eden did not leave the Conservative Party, but he joined Churchill and a number of other non-ministerial members of the party in a faction critical of the Cabinet's foreign policy. In 1951 Aneurin Bevan, Minister of Labour, resigned from the Attlee Cabinet because of disagreements arising out of budgetary policy and Britain's re-armament program. Two other members of the Government, Harold Wilson, President of the Board of Trade, and John Freeman, Parliamentary Secretary of the Ministry of Supply, followed Bevan's example. They remained within the party fold and agreed to vote with the Government on divisions threatening its continuance.[18]

A second function of a Cabinet Minister is to serve as the head of one of the principal government departments. The holders of the three or four sinecure offices do not head major departments but all the other Cabinet members do. As a department head the minister is responsible for the policies pursued by his department and for its administrative efficiency. He must decide policy issues that arise within the department, he must give instructions to his principal subordinates, and he must supervise its activities to such an extent that he knows it is being administered in proper fashion.

---

[18] It is customary for a minister resigning from the Government to make a statement in Parliament explaining his action. On this occasion, if a member of the House of Commons, he takes a traditional 'resignation seat,' the first one below the gangway on the third bench.

From time to time he is called upon to reply to questions in Parliament about the policies of his department and matters of administration that have been criticized. To assist him in his departmental duties he has a junior minister, usually known as a Parliamentary Secretary, and a Permanent Secretary who is the principal civil servant of the department. It is to the latter that the minister looks for the efficient management of departmental business, but it is the minister who must accept the responsibility for all acts of commission or omission.

There is a third field of activity, namely, that of party politics. The minister is usually a leading member of his political party; indeed, it is probably his pre-eminence in party councils that has given him a claim to Cabinet rank. His party duties require attending party conferences where he will advocate and defend policies within his field of departmental interest, speaking at party rallies and in behalf of Parliamentary candidates, and participating in party councils where campaign tactics, policy statements, and similar matters are discussed.

If a Cabinet member effectively discharges the above-mentioned duties he is certain to have a busy day. His duties as a Cabinet minister require a considerable amount of time for the study of papers and for conferences and discussion. The management of a major government department is a big job in itself. Party activity requires conferences with other leaders, the preparation and delivery of speeches, and time spent in travel and meetings. The successful Cabinet minister is the one who can so organize his affairs that each of these fields of activity is properly served and that he stands out as a wise counselor, a competent administrator, and a popular party leader.

As a group, the Cabinet meets usually twice a week at the residence of the Prime Minister, 10 Downing Street. There, around a large table with the Prime Minister as chairman, the members discuss issues and reach decisions. The taking of votes in Cabinet meetings appears to be rare; ministers usually discuss their problems until agreement is found. Concerning Cabinet procedure, Jennings has written:

> The Cabinet itself is a committee, and it comes to its conclusions in much the same way as other committees. That is, it talks around a subject until some compromise suggests itself. Only when there are fundamental divergencies does the majority override the minority. The problem of securing agreement is greater in the Cabinet, partly because of the fundamental importance of its decisions, and partly because . . . it is the duty of the dissenting minority either to resign or to support the decision of the majority. Resignations may entail the breaking up of the Cabinet and, in addition, a party split. Great efforts are therefore made to secure agreement. Compromise is the first and last order of the day.[19]

---

[19] *Cabinet Government,* op. cit. p. 243.

The Cabinet's discussions and decisions are confidential, and no member is at liberty to attribute particular views to any other member.[20] Once a decision has been reached all members are bound to support it by their public statements and by their administrative actions. The rule of Cabinet solidarity was established early in the nineteenth century, and with one exception has been consistently followed. The exception occurred in the case of the coalition Government under Ramsay MacDonald in 1931. This Government included several Liberals who were not prepared to support the protectionist policy favored by the other members of the Ministry. Since these Liberals felt that the country's crisis was sufficiently grave to justify their support of the general program of the Government and since their participation was desired by the other ministers in the interest of national unity, they were allowed to remain through an 'agreement to disagree.' This arrangement did not prove satisfactory for long, and its repetition is unlikely.

6. *The Cabinet Secretariat*

Until the time of the First World War, the Cabinet conducted its meetings without an agenda and with no record of decisions reached. The only person permitted to make notes of the Cabinet's transactions was the Prime Minister, who did so to assist him in preparing a letter to the King. This informality was found unsatisfactory during the First World War. In fact, it had led to a number of ministerial misunderstandings in the years before the war. Lord Hankey, the first Secretary to the Cabinet, has gathered some of these instances, including the following revealed in a note from Lord Hartington's private secretary to Gladstone's private secretary in 1882:

My dear Eddy—

Harcourt and Chamberlain have both been here this morning, and *at* my chief about yesterday's Cabinet proceedings. They cannot agree about what occurred. There must have been some decision, as Bright's resignation shows. My Chief told me to ask you what the devil *was* decided for he be damned if he knows. Will you ask Mr. G. in more conventional and less pungent terms?

Yours ever, ——— [21]

---

[20] The rule of secrecy extends to the proceedings of previous Cabinets, and a former minister who wishes to reveal his attitude on some issue must seek the sovereign's permission and release from his Privy Councillor's oath through the Prime Minister then in office. Defending the rule, in a comment on Aneurin Bevan's revelation of a position he took in the Labour Cabinet of which he was a member in 1951, *The Times* said: 'It is vitally important to the working of the Cabinet system that Ministers should feel free to state their views with not only complete but also enduring privacy. If they had reason for fearing that their attitude on a particular topic would later be revealed publicly, free and frank discussion in Cabinets would become impossible.' 8 August 1952.

[21] Lord Hankey, *Diplomacy by Conference* (New York, 1946), pp. 66-7.

84–

On another occasion, the Duke of Devonshire, when upbraided by Joseph Chamberlain for failing to stand by what the latter believed was a Cabinet agreement, wrote back: 'As you know, I am rather deaf, and I am afraid, sometimes inattentive. I certainly altogether failed to understand that . . . a decision was even provisionally taken of such importance as that to which you refer, and it must have been taken after very little discussion.' [22]

The pressures falling on the Cabinet after the outbreak of war in 1914 soon revealed the inadequacies of its methods of transacting business. Discussions and the taking of decisions were frequently handicapped because Cabinet members were uninformed of some subject to be raised, and often it was essential that decisions reached by the Cabinet be stated with precision and exactitude. Consequently, Lloyd George, when he became Prime Minister in 1916, 'took over for the purposes of the Cabinet, lock, stock, and barrel, the whole of the methods and apparatus of the Committee of Imperial Defence.' [23] The usefulness of the Committee's secretariat was so apparent that it was continued after the war and is now a permanent appendage of the Cabinet. Contributing greatly to the secretariat's successful start and to its development as an indispensable part of the machinery of British government was the ability of the first Secretary to the Cabinet, Sir Maurice (later Lord) Hankey. For more than 20 years he served successive Cabinets in this position, and during most of that period he held the additional posts of Clerk of the Privy Council and Secretary of the Committee of Imperial Defence, as well as serving as secretary of several imperial conferences.

Under the guidance of the Prime Minister, the Cabinet secretariat prepares an agenda of business to come before the body and circulates to Cabinet ministers any memoranda or committee reports that they should see before undertaking to discuss items on the agenda. It keeps minutes of Cabinet meetings and advises members of decisions reached in the meetings. It also serves the Cabinet committees which give a preliminary examination to most of the issues which come before the whole body. It would be virtually impossible today for the Cabinet to conduct its business properly without the services of the secretariat.

During the Second World War the Cabinet Offices were expanded to include besides the Secretariat proper an Economic Section and a Central Statistical Office. The first maintains a constant watch on economic trends and developments as they affect the British situation and advises the Cabinet of their purport. It prepares the annual *Economic Surveys,* which are reports of developments and forecasts of what may be expected over the whole range of domestic and foreign economic affairs. The *Economic Surveys* complement the regular budget statements on the British government's financial condition made by the Chancellor of the Exchequer. The Central Statistical Office was established 'to produce a developing statistical series,

---

[22] Ibid. p. 68.
[23] L. S. Amery, *Thoughts on the Constitution* (London, 1947), p. 79.

general and comprehensive in nature, to be an index to economic and social trends.' [24] As a result of its work, published in the *Monthly Digest of Statistics,* the basic facts and figures about the British economy are well recorded and presented.

7. Cabinet Committees

For many years it has been the practice of the Cabinet to use committees to help it discharge its responsibilities. Some of the Cabinet committees are permanent bodies; others are *ad hoc* groups created to deal with a special problem or a critical situation. The number and the composition of the committees are largely determined by the Prime Minister, and he is guided by his own working methods, the nature of the problems which his Cabinet faces, and the talents and temperaments of his ministerial associates. In order not to derogate from the joint responsibility of the Cabinet, the activities of the committees are not publicized, and even the exact membership is rarely revealed. As an exception, however, the ministers composing the permanent Defence Committee were listed at the time the national defense machinery was reorganized in 1946.

Cabinet committees serve several purposes. They provide a means whereby certain problems and issues can be studied and discussed by the ministers most concerned before they are brought before the whole Cabinet. It obviously assists consideration of a subject in Cabinet meetings if the principal issues involved have been identified and thrashed out by a smaller ministerial group and agreed recommendations submitted. Cabinet committees are also useful to co-ordinate policy and administration. The political, economic, social, and administrative implications of a complex problem can be investigated by the ministers most concerned and ways found to mobilize their efforts and eliminate conflicting or duplicating programs. Furthermore, committees can be employed to keep a critical problem under continuous review. It would be difficult and inefficient for the whole Cabinet to concentrate its attention for any extended period on one aspect of national policy, but a ministerial committee can be charged with such a responsibility. Finally, by including non-Cabinet ministers when appropriate, the committee system can extend the Cabinet's co-ordinating activity to wider areas of governmental affairs.

Committees customarily report to the whole Cabinet. They seek to submit agreed reports and recommendations, but a minister who dissents from the action of a committee to which he belongs may raise the matter in a Cabinet meeting. There, under the chairmanship of the Prime Minister, a resolution of the difficulty will be sought. The views of the committee majority may win the approval of the rest of the Cabinet, and in this case the dissenting minister must accommodate himself to the general verdict or, if he believes this impossible, resign. Before a minister is placed in the

---

[24] Herman Finer, 'The Central Planning System in Britain,' *Public Administration Review,* Autumn 1948, p. 244.

position of either submitting to a policy decision to which he strongly objects or resigning, pains will be taken to work out a solution acceptable to all.

One of the important standing committees is the Legislation Committee, formerly known as the Home Affairs Committee. The functions of the Legislation Committee are to give a policy review to all bills proposed by ministers, make recommendations to the Cabinet on legislative priorities, and to consider the Parliamentary procedure to be followed in obtaining the passage of bills. In 1940 there was established the Lord President's Committee 'with the cardinal purpose of bringing into regular and unifying contact the many departments involved with home and economic problems so that they might unitedly prosecute the main lines of policy required of them by the War Cabinet.' [25] It has remained an important committee to deal with the co-ordination of domestic policy, although the sterling convertibility crisis of 1947 led to the establishment of a Committee on Overseas Economic Policy which took responsibility for certain economic affairs formerly within the jurisdiction of the Lord President's Committee. Other responsibilities for co-ordinating and supervising economic policies and programs, formerly entrusted to a Home Economic Committee under the chairmanship of the Lord President, passed also in 1947 to a new committee under the Minister of Economic Affairs, then Sir Stafford Cripps. These committees were later succeeded by an Economic Committee dealing with both internal and external economic policy.

One of the largest and most important of the standing groups is the Defence Committee. With the Prime Minister as chairman, it includes the Minister of Defence, the Lord President of the Council, the Foreign Secretary, the Chancellor of the Exchequer, the Minister of Labour, the Minister of Supply, the First Lord of the Admiralty, and the Secretaries of State for War, Air, Commonwealth Relations, and Colonies. The Defence Committee concerns itself with the 'organization for national defence in its broader aspect, including both current questions of high policy in the sphere of defence, and also the preparation of plans over the whole field of government activity, both civil and military, for mobilizing the entire resources of the nation in a major war.' [26] It is advised by the Chiefs of Staff Committee consisting of the professional heads of the three military services.

In connection with the Cabinet's committees it should be noted that their membership and responsibilities change in response to the problems facing the Government and to the methods of operation of Prime Ministers. The system remains a flexible one. Nevertheless, the practice of using committees is well established, and every Cabinet will have groups analyzing, recommending, and co-ordinating policy in the major fields of governmental activity.

---

[25] Finer, op. cit. p. 242.
[26] Cmd. 6923 (1946), *Central Organization for Defence.*

The British Cabinet has proved to be a highly successful governmental institution. Over a period of more than 200 years it has been adapted by successive political leaders of the nation to meet the requirements of the time. The constitutional conventions which largely determine the Cabinet's organization and methods of functioning have been firm and rigid enough to maintain it as a responsible agent of a democratic society, yet they have been sufficiently flexible to permit the growth and changes that new conditions and circumstances have called for.

The Prime Minister's office offers scope for high leadership. Occupying it, an incumbent of strong qualities can be a powerful influence in world affairs. The position, however, is so related to the rest of the Cabinet that the Prime Minister must act with the advice and consent of a group of ministers publicly known and responsible to a free Parliament.

Like other parts of the British Constitution, the Cabinet is a changing, evolving institution. During the course of the twentieth century there have been such developments as the establishment of the Cabinet Office administered by a permanent secretary, the creation of several continuing ministerial committees, and the appointment of ministers to co-ordinate the work of two or more departments. Moreover, the problem of directing the national effort during two world wars temporarily caused radical alterations in the Cabinet's structure and operations. We can expect additional innovations as the institution responds to the future requirements of British politics and to the creative ability of future statesmen.

VI

Parliament: The House of Commons

Governmental institutions of great antiquity are comparatively rare in contemporary civilization. Most of them were founded in the modern period of history, and a goodly proportion within this century. Even in ancient countries such as China, India, and Egypt, or Mexico and Peru in the Western Hemisphere, the present-day institutions of government are of comparatively recent origin, and in the oldest of European states there are few executive, legislative, or judicial organs of venerable age. There are traces, of course, of earlier political forms and practices in the modern governments of all states, for revolutions can never clear the ground completely and build anew. But by and large the institutional changes in most countries have been profound and sweeping.

England has never experienced revolutionary changes of such character and permanence that the continuity of her political institutions has been broken. The long history of the monarchy has been mentioned; that of the courts will be noted later. The legislative branch has an unbroken history of almost equal length. Only the Icelandic *Althing* can challenge the claim of the British Parliament to be the world's oldest legislative assembly, and in view of the latter's numerous progeny the title 'Mother of Parliaments' indisputably belongs to it.[1] In this and the two succeeding chapters we shall deal first with the composition, organization, and powers of the House of Commons and the House of Lords and then with Parliament as a functioning institution in the scheme of contemporary British government.

1. *Historical Background*

Historians place the origin of Parliament among the institutional developments of the thirteenth century, although the body which emerged during that period had roots in the Norman and Saxon monarchies. In the thirteenth century the kings called together on various occasions not only the chief magnates of the realm, a traditional practice, but also knights from

---

[1] 'In the past 100 years there have grown from the Mother of Parliaments, at Westminster, not far short of 50 daughter Parliaments within the family circle of the Commonwealth. . . All the Parliaments of the Commonwealth—Federal Parliaments, State Parliaments, Provincial Parliaments, and the Legislatures of Colonies with elected or unofficial majorities—are built without exception upon the model of Westminster.' *The Times,* 2 November 1949.

the shires and burgesses from the towns. The purpose in assembling these enlarged councils was not the consideration and enactment of legislation in the modern sense but the obtaining of consent to new tax levies, since even in the thirteenth century it was a constitutional principle, sometimes honored in the breach, that the King could impose no new burden without the approval of the Great Council. The knights and the burgesses were added to the Council because the economic groups from which they were drawn represented a fertile source of royal taxation, and they could give military, political, and administrative support to the monarchy.

There was little sense of the representative principle at this time, and no one had in mind establishing a national body that reflected the sentiment or opinions of the country as a whole. The idea of representation was implicit, however, in the method by which the enlarged Great Council was constituted. Since it was impractical to summon to a Council meeting all knights and burgesses, the kings in their writs to the county sheriffs instructed that a small number, usually two or four, be selected for the purpose of attending a Great Council.

Two assemblies of the thirteenth century are singled out as 'model' parliaments, precursors of later developments.[2] In 1265 Simon de Montfort, the leader of a baronial revolt, summoned in the king's name a council consisting of the great lay and ecclesiastical magnates and also two knights from each shire, two citizens from each city and two burgesses from each borough. In 1295 Edward I summoned a council which contained all the above-named elements and, in addition, representatives of the lower clergy. It would be a mistake to stress the 'model' character of either of these parliaments, for there were other occasions during this century when knights and burgesses were summoned and the practice of including the lower clergy ceased after 1332. What is significant about several of the late thirteenth-century parliaments is that the Great Council had been enlarged to include representatives of other estates of the realm and that they were summoned by the king 'to discuss together with the magnates the affairs of our kingdom.' Thus, the Great Council became not only a body of important territorial lords performing their tenurial obligation of proffering individual advice to the monarch but a more representative national assembly whose members could consult with one another and assume a corporate existence.

During the following century it became customary to summon the new elements to every Parliament. In the beginning there was no division of Parliament into separate, organized groups; indeed, the knights and burgesses probably stood beyond the outer circles of the Council and their

---

[2] In medieval usage the term parliament meant an assembly to discuss important matters, and it was employed in several countries of western Europe. 'Clearly the essence of parliament is discussion, and when the word is first applied to the great councils of the English Kings it is in order to emphasize their deliberative function.' K. R. Mackenzie, *The English Parliament* (Penguin Books, 1950), p. 12. The name was commonly used in England after the middle of the thirteenth century.

contribution to its deliberations was little more than to signify assent to what the magnates of the realm were willing to concede to the King. It seems likely that parliamentary organization in England proceeded in much the same way as it did on the Continent, with the nobility forming one group, the ecclesiastical prelates another, and the knights and burgesses a third. Gradually, however, the first two groups, whose property interests were much the same, coalesced into one house, and the Commons—that is, the representatives of the commonalty of England, the people of the shires and towns—into a second. By the end of the fourteenth century this process had been completed and the bicameral Parliament was an established institution.

Through the centuries there has been a transfer of power from the Lords to the Commons, from the upper house to the lower. This transfer has gone on despite the fact that for several centuries the great majority of the individuals who were personally powerful and influential in the affairs of the country were members of the House of Lords. The thing which has been crucial in establishing the dominance of the Commons is the financial power which it gained and has held. Early in Parliamentary history the House of Commons won the right to primacy in the consideration of tax levies asked by the King. By the end of the fourteenth century a Parliamentary formula for grants, 'by the Commons with the advice and assent of the Lords,' was in use, and in 1407 Henry IV agreed that such grants, 'should be reported to him only in the manner accustomed, that is to say, by the mouth of the Speaker of the Commons.' [3]

It took several centuries and many bitter quarrels and tests of strength to establish parliamentary, or, in practice, House of Commons, dominance in the financial affairs of the State. Kings from time to time attempted to circumvent the power that control of the purse gave to Parliament, but in the end they were always forced to admit defeat. They revived old levies that had passed from use, they sold titles and monopolistic rights, they exacted forced loans, and they occasionally accepted foreign subsidies, but they were always defeated because their financial resources were inadequate to carry on an expanding and growing governmental organization. After the constitutional trials of strength in the seventeenth century no monarch ever attempted to conduct a government in defiance of Parliament or from financial sources not voted by Parliament.

As control of the purse led to a change of balance within the parliamentary structure, so the growth of the House of Commons in importance led to its attractiveness to men seeking political careers. Throughout the nineteenth century, as the suffrage was extended, the prestige of the House rose, and by the end of the century it was by all odds the more important chamber. This supremacy was given formal recognition in the Parliament Act of 1911, and the House of Commons has guarded its status so jealously that it has been able to discover no satisfactory way of reforming, and thus

---

[3] Ibid. p. 67.

making more representative, the membership of the House of Lords. Indeed, it is likely that some members of the House of Commons would prefer to abolish the second chamber rather than share authority more evenly.

2. *The Composition of the House of Commons*

The House of Commons consists of 625 members who are elected for a term of five years. It usually happens, however, that Parliament is dissolved before the five-year term expires, and members are continuously faced with the possibility of a general election.

The size of the House is determined from time to time in accordance with parliamentary acts for distributing seats to territorial districts known as constituencies. At the beginning of this century it consisted of 707 members, but the abolition of the Irish seats after the creation of the Free State in 1921 reduced the House to 615. In 1945 the size was increased to 640 members in order to give representation to areas that had grown in population since the last distribution of seats. The redistribution scheme in effect at the general election of 1945 was a temporary one, and Parliament in 1948 enacted legislation fixing the size of the House at 625 members and apportioning these seats to redrawn constituencies. Each constituency returns one member to the House of Commons. Until the most recent electoral act, there were 15 double member constituencies, but these have been eliminated.

With the House having a membership of 625, each member represents approximately 80,000 persons. This compares with a figure of about 350,-000 which a member of the lower house of the United States Congress represents. Each British constituency is a compact area bounded by lines that usually have some historical or administrative significance. Districts are known by name rather than number, which is the practice in the United States, and the name is commonly taken from the most important geographical or governmental unit within the constituency. Thus, Clement Attlee represents Walthamstow, West, a district in the East End of London; Winston Churchill sits for Woodford, an area to the northeast of London; Hugh Gaitskell is the M.P. for Leeds, South, and Anthony Eden's constituency is Warwick and Leamington. While all the constituencies have approximately the same population, they naturally vary a great deal in area. Many urban constituencies are small sections of congested cities, while some of the rural constituencies, especially in Scotland, cover vast expanses of sparsely populated territory.

The House of Commons elected in 1945 was the last to include a group of members representing the British universities. This unusual kind of representation was begun in 1604 when James I, on the suggestion of Sir Robert Cecil and Sir Edward Coke, granted parliamentary seats to the Universities of Oxford and Cambridge. For a long time they were the only universities represented. In 1918 the number of university seats was fixed at 15, and they were distributed in the following way: Oxford, 2; Cambridge, 2; the University of London, 1; the Scottish universities, 3; the English provincial universities, 2; the University of Wales, 1; the University of Dublin, 2; the National University of Ireland, 1, and the University of Belfast, 1. The three seats representing Dublin and the National University were eliminated after the establishment of the Irish Free State (1921). The university members were elected by the graduates of the universities, who thus had two votes, one in their residential constituency and another as university alumni. In choosing the university members, the voters used the single transferable vote method.

The Representation of the People Act of 1948 eliminated the university representation and the second vote of the eligible graduates, who numbered 228,769.[4] The Opposition charged the Labour Government with failure to honor the agreement of the Speaker's Conference which had considered the provisions of the bill and had recommended the retention of the university seats. While some of the Conservative criticism can be discounted as normal opposition tactics, there was reason to question the Government's decision to terminate the university representation. The universities almost invariably sent distinguished representatives to the House of Commons, and though in recent years they were usually members of the Conservative Party, they frequently were known for their liberal and public-spirited point of view. On the whole, they were a broadminded group of representatives who contributed to the best traditions of the House.[5] Although the Conservative Party had pledged itself to restore the representation of the universities, the Churchill Government decided, in view of its small majority after the general election of 1951 and the many problems facing Parliament and the ministry, to postpone introducing legislation on this subject and to make such legislation effective upon the next Parliamentary dissolution.

With the abolition of the university constituencies, representation in the House of Commons is based completely upon a single principle for the first time in several hundred years. Each member of Parliament represents a territorial area of approximately a standard number of inhabitants.

What sorts of people sit in the House of Commons? Like most democratic assemblies of the present era, the House is composed of members of varying ages, backgrounds, and occupations. After the general election of 1951, the age distribution of 313 Conservative M.P.'s was as follows: one per cent in the group 21 to 29; 22 per cent, 30 to 39; 37 per cent, 40 to 49; 29 per cent, 50 to 59, and 11 per cent above 60. Their Labour opponents were an older group, the distribution for 274 members being: one

---

[4] H. G. Nicholas, *The British General Election of* 1950 (London, 1951), p. 2.

[5] Among the 12 serving in the 1945 Parliament were Sir John Anderson (now Lord Waverley), who rose in the Civil Service to be Permanent Under Secretary of the Home Office, served as Governor of Bengal, and during the war was successively Lord Privy Seal, Home Secretary, Lord President of the Council, and Chancellor of the Exchequer; Sir Arthur Salter, widely known as a civil servant, League of Nations official, Oxford University professor, and wartime minister, and Sir A. P. Herbert, noted humorist and playwright. These three denominated themselves as independents. By winning a by-election, Salter returned to Parliament in 1951 as a Conservative.

per cent, 21 to 29; 10 per cent, 30 to 39; 31 per cent, 40 to 49; 28 per cent, 50 to 59, and 30 per cent above 60.[6] Among the Conservatives, 59 per cent were university trained, 27 per cent at Oxford and 21 per cent at Cambridge. Thirty-three per cent of the Labourites attended a university, but only 9 per cent and 5 per cent, respectively, were educated at Oxford and Cambridge. Sixty-four per cent of the Conservative M.P.'s received their secondary education at a 'public' school, 24 per cent at Eton, while the percentage for the Parliamentary Labour group was 11. About a quarter, 24 per cent, of the Labour members had had only an elementary school education. In 1936, the formal education of 49 per cent of Labour M.P.'s had been limited to an elementary school, and only 17 per cent were university trained.[7]

The occupations of members of the House constitute a long list. In 1951, there were 65 lawyers on the Conservative side, 58 of them barristers, while 30 lawyers, including 23 barristers, sat on the Labour benches. 'At least 100' Conservative M.P.'s were company directors, and 24 were engaged in banking, brokerage, and insurance. Thirty were farmers. The writing profession, usually journalism, claimed 32 Conservatives and 42 Labourites. Fifty-eight Labour members were trade union officials, a considerable reduction from the proportion during the party's early days. Comparing the House of Commons in the 1950's with the prewar Parliament, *The Economist* concluded that the changes 'are more striking in the Labour than in the Conservative party. The Tories have fewer land owners, merchants and manufacturers, and rather more journalists than they used to have; but otherwise they are much the same. The Parliamentary Labour party is better educated than it was; it is very well versed in local government; it has fewer trade union officials and has acquired a large number of lawyers and journalists.'[8]

3. *The Member and His Constituents*

In 'representing' his constituents the member of Parliament must be active in their behalf. He must see that local views are considered when legislation is being discussed in committee or debated in the House. He must call to the attention of ministers the claims of his area for public works or for special assistance and he must try to prevent developments to which there is local objection.[9] The member receives many personal appeals from con-

---

6 *The Economist,* 26 January 1952, p. 916.

7 Ibid. p. 195.

8 Ibid. p. 196.

9 The M.P. for Newbury, for example, protested the location of a bomber base for the use of the United States Air Force near the town. After being informed by the Secretary of State for Air that the Cabinet ministers concerned had discussed his objection but found no suitable alternative, the member said: 'The Cabinet has made its decision. We lose Greenham and Crookham commons and Newbury has to face the nuisance of a bomber base near the town. But no one in Newbury or the district

94–

stituents who want him to inquire into some matter or prod a government department. Some of these he can dispose of by referring them to the proper departments for action. Others may require a question put to a minister in the House of Commons, or the raising of the subject on the adjournment of the House. Members of Parliament must make frequent visits to their constituencies—some make a practice of going every week end—in order to gather local opinion and to receive requests for assistance of one kind or another. They pay particular heed to the leaders of their constituency party organization and its affiliates, but they are available to all local residents who have a problem to discuss.

While the kind of activity described absorbs a good deal of the time of a member of Parliament, he is less influenced by local interests than a Congressman in Washington. The circumstances of political life and the British tradition tend to make him more national and less parochial in his point of view. To begin with, geographical and sectional interests play a less significant part in British politics than they do in a continental country like the United States. The United Kingdom is a relatively small, homogeneous country where the sense of sharing a common welfare is generally understood. Parliament does not divide into the farm, silver, oil, and other blocs characteristic of the United States Congress, because Britain does not have vast areas in which special economic interests, cutting across party lines, are dominant. There is some disposition for M.P.'s from mining areas, centers of shipbuilding, or farming districts to speak for these sectional interests, and there are, of course, occupational or functional interest groups —trade unionists, brewers, publishers, retired military officers, and others. Also, the Scottish and the Welsh members form groups with a community of interest. None of these sectional interests takes, however, the all-or-nothing stands that sometimes occur in Washington. To do so would bring it into conflict with the Parliamentary parties, and this suggests a second difference between the British and American political situations bearing on this matter.

Party discipline is much stronger at Westminster than on Capitol Hill. An M.P. who took an adamant position on behalf of a local or sectional interest that his party was not supporting would put himself in the bad graces of the party managers and conformity or expulsion might soon be the choice before him. When the continuance of the Ministry in power depends upon mustering safe majorities on every vote, party leaders cannot permit members to indulge themselves in pursuing conflicting local interests. An American legislator may embarrass and frustrate his party leadership and the President, but he only indirectly threatens their continuance in power.

A member of the House of Commons, therefore, is required to support

---

wishes to delay essential defence preparations, and it seems to me that we must now accept with good grace this Cabinet ruling made for strategic reasons.' *The Times*, 11 April 1951.

a national as contrasted with a local or sectional point of view. Such pressure as he desires to exert on behalf of a local interest must ordinarily be done within his party, and by combining with other M.P.'s who have like or similar interests he may influence party policy; his advocacy must stop short, however, of transgressing the party line in Parliament. 'Log-rolling' tactics may be tried, but they are not likely to prove successful. As Jennings has pointed out, 'it always has to be remembered that no proposal passes the House of Commons without the consent of a Government in which the Chancellor of the Exchequer plays a prominent part. No Government omits electoral conditions from its calculations; no Government fails to pay attention to suggestions from the Whips that certain proposals would "do their men good in their constituencies." But one man's meat is another man's poison; or, to be more exact, one man's income is another man's expenditure. What the Government spends through one Department it must collect through the Treasury. The electoral conditions which the Government keeps in mind are those of a very substantial part of the country.' [10]

Finally, the antecedents of Parliament and the Congress continue to have influence upon these bodies and upon popular attitudes toward them. The medieval concept of Parliament as a council of the great and wise assembled to deliberate upon the affairs of the kingdom still prevails to a degree. The House of Lords has always been constituted on the basis of status and rank. Composing the lower house on the basis of geographical representation has been somewhat a matter of convenience, and the notion that its members are delegates for particular local areas has not been stressed. The readiness of voters to accept nonresident candidates indicates that representation of local views is not as important as supporting party principles and general policies of interest to a constituency. The principle underlying the composition of the Congress of the United States was the representation of organized political entities, the states, and that traditional concept still has wide acceptance among members of the national legislature and their constituents. To push this distinction too far would be a mistake; British M.P.'s are not unmindful of local interests, and United States Congressmen often subordinate the special affairs of their states and districts to national considerations.

Probably members of both Parliament and the Congress would agree that Edmund Burke's famous address to his Bristol constituents declared their ideal with respect to the relationship between a representative and the voters. The words of Burke were:

> Certainly, gentlemen, it ought to be the happiness and glory of a representative to live in the strictest union, the closest correspondence, and the most unreserved communication with his constituents. Their wishes ought to have great weight with him; their opinion high respect; their business unremitted attention. It is his duty to sacrifice his repose,

---

[10] *Parliament* (Cambridge, 1948), p. 30.

his pleasures, his satisfactions, to theirs; and above all, ever, and in all cases, to prefer their interest to his own. But, his unbiased opinion, his mature judgment, his enlightened conscience, he ought not to sacrifice to you, to any man, or to any set of men living. These he does not derive from your pleasure; no, nor from the law and the constitution. They are a trust from Providence, for the abuse of which he is deeply answerable. Your representative owes you, not his industry only, but his judgment; and he betrays, instead of serving you, if he sacrifices it to your opinion. . .

Parliament is not a congress of ambassadors from different and hostile interests; which interests each must maintain, as an agent, and advocate, against other agents and advocates; but parliament is a deliberative assembly of one nation, with one interest, that of the whole; where, not local purposes, not local prejudices, ought to guide, but the general good, resulting from the general reason of the whole. You choose a member indeed: but when you have chosen him, he is not a member of Bristol, but he is a member of parliament.

4. *The Qualifications and Privileges of Members*

Almost any British subject, 21 years of age or more, is legally qualified to sit in the House of Commons. Those ineligible include all members of the peerage except the Irish nobility, clergymen of the Churches of England and Scotland and the Roman Catholic Church, persons holding offices of profit under the Crown, and undischarged bankrupts.[11] Ministers of the Crown, it should be added, are exempted by statute from the ban on holders of offices of profit. Since the enfranchisement of women in 1918, they have been eligible to sit in the House, and several score have been elected in the past 30 years. Twenty-one women candidates were successful in the general election of February 1950, and 17 won seats in October 1951.

Members of the House have important privileges. During, and for 40 days before and after, a Parliamentary session they are immune from arrest arising from a civil suit; they cannot be challenged in a court of law for any statements made within the House; they are exempt from jury duty; they receive the expenses of travel between Westminster and their constituencies, and they have a franking privilege. Valuable as these are, they are not as important as they were in the days when Parliament and the Crown were in frequent conflict. Then the Speaker's claim, upon the submission of his election for royal approval, to 'the ancient and undoubted rights and privileges of the Commons' had substantive meaning to nearly every member. Freedom from arrest in a civil action became well established in the Tudor period, but freedom of speech for members of the House of Commons was still a disputed privilege under the Stuarts and was

---

[11] While these categories seem reasonably precise, there is in practice a good deal of confusion about the eligibility of candidates and members. See below, pp. 206-7.

not secure until the enactment of the Bill of Rights in 1689. This statute declared, 'That the freedom of speech, and debates on proceedings in Parliament, ought not to be impeached or questioned in any court or place out of Parliament.' [12]

Besides the privileges due to members as individuals, the House of Commons in its corporate capacity has the right to protect its dignity from the calumnies of a member or a person outside. It may do this by the expulsion of a member or by the punishment of contempt by admonition or imprisonment. The procedure starts with a member offering a motion which calls attention to the alleged contempt, and if the Speaker considers that a *prima facie* case has been presented, the matter is referred to the Committee of Privileges, a group of ten senior members. This committee inquires into the case, and when it reports the House decides whether a breach of privilege has been committed and the action called for. A nonmember, say a newspaper reporter considered guilty of contempt for an article about Parliamentary affairs, may be ordered to appear at the bar of the House to receive an admonition or to be sentenced to imprisonment. The duration of imprisonment is limited to the remaining length of the Parliamentary session.

It is possible that in protecting its privileges the House may come into conflict with the ordinary courts. The courts are prepared to recognize that the House has the right to protect its dignity and orderly procedure by punishment for contempt, but they object to the House's being the judge of its own jurisdiction. Instances of disputed jurisdiction are rare; Parliament usually takes a tolerant view of criticism and does not push its claims beyond reason, and the courts are disposed to accept a Parliamentary action to protect its privileges as justified.[13]

Until this century members of the House of Commons received no com-

---

[12] The Constitution of the United States provides that senators and representatives 'shall in all cases, except treason, felony and breach of the peace, be privileged from arrest during their attendance at the session of their respective Houses, and in going to and returning from the same; and for any speech or debate in either House, they shall not be questioned in any other place.' Art. i, sect. 6.

[13] There appear to be periods when members of Parliament become hypersensitive and discover many alleged breaches of privilege. One such occurred during the second session of the Parliament elected in 1950. It led *The Times* to chide the members of Parliament for their undue sensitivity to criticism and to recall to them a statement of the Committee of Privileges in 1948. 'The Committee is of the opinion that it is not consistent with the dignity of the House that penal proceedings for breach of privilege should be taken in the case of every defamatory statement which, strictly, may constitute a contempt of Parliament. While recognizing that it is the duty of Parliament to intervene in the case of attacks which may tend to undermine public confidence in and support of the institution of Parliament itself, the Committee thinks it important that, on the one hand, the law of Parliamentary privilege should not be administered in a way which would fetter or discourage the expression of opinion or criticism, however prejudiced or exaggerated such opinions or criticisms may be, and that on the other hand, the process of Parliamentary investigation should not be used in a way which would give importance to irresponsible statements.' *The Times,* 1 August 1951.

pensation for their services from the national treasury, but in 1911 Parliament enacted legislation setting £400 as their annual salary.[14] The compensation was increased in 1937 to £600 and in 1946 to £1000. While the present salary is naturally some help to the less affluent members, it still leaves many of them with the necessity of seeking additional employment. The obtaining of suitable employment is frequently a problem because parliamentary duties require a great deal of the time of conscientious members. Some members follow journalistic pursuits, as this is an occupation that permits them to capitalize on their official position and work at the odd times when not attending the House. Many members of the Labour Party retain positions as trade union executives, and M.P.'s with professional training usually carry on their practices while serving in Parliament.

It seems likely that the issue of paying members a sufficient amount to support themselves as full-time legislators will have to be faced before long. The number of people with independent incomes or with established professional practices that permit them to devote a major part of their time to parliamentary pursuits is steadily declining under the weight of heavy taxation. At the same time the expenses of parliamentary membership are rising. A member of the House must devote a great deal of time and correspondence to the affairs of his constituency, and many members spend their small salary on secretarial assistance and other essential office expenses. At present, members have no office space or clerical assistance provided, and they must meet their constituents and conduct their public business in the lobbies, libraries, or dining rooms of the Houses of Parliament.

Some members of Parliament have been reluctant to make membership in the House of Commons a full-time, salaried position for fear that candidates would be attracted principally because of the compensation involved. This might happen in some cases, but the hardship placed on conscientious members and the temptations confronting all of them today appear more serious than the danger of self-seeking candidates. Faced with the necessity of earning a living, some members are tempted to exploit their official position for private gain. This is particularly true of those who supplement their official salary by earnings from journalistic activities. The House was compelled to expel a Labour member in 1947 for

---

[14] Until the seventeenth century it was customary for members of the House of Commons to receive wages from their constituents. 'The last person known to have received wages regularly as a member was Andrew Marvell, the poet. He was member for Hull during the first 18 years of Charles II's reign, having been returned, not by the people of Hull, but by the mayor and aldermen; and he richly earned his wages by sending regularly, almost to the day of his death, letters to his good friend the mayor, conveying information about proceedings in parliament, and about London affairs generally.' Sir Courtenay Ilbert, *Parliament: Its History, Constitution, and Practice,* rev. by Sir Cecil Carr (London, 1950), p. 142.

having revealed confidential information to a newspaper for which he was working.[15]

As just mentioned, the House may expel a member who is considered unqualified to sit there. Curiously, there is no procedure for a member simply to resign from the House. If a member desires to resign, he has himself appointed to an archaic position known as the stewardship of the Chiltern Hundreds. By accepting appointment to this nominal position, the member makes himself ineligible for further service in the House because an old statute automatically disqualifies any member of Parliament who accepts an office of profit under the Crown. Enacted at a time when Parliament was endeavoring to keep members from being subverted by receiving royal favors, the statute still is in force. Parliament makes exceptions, it is important to add, for the large body of its membership holding ministerial office.

5. *The Officers of the House*

The presiding officer of the House is known as the Speaker. He is a member elected by the House and in practice he is chosen by the party in power at the time the office falls vacant. Customarily a Speaker is re-elected until he dies or resigns for age, and he is sometimes returned to new parliaments without opposition.[16] The Speaker's office is one of great honor and dignity, which compensates his constituency for what practically amounts to loss of representation. The earliest Speakers—and the office dates from the fourteenth century—were appointed by the King, and today the Speaker's election is subject to the formality of royal approval.[17] Originally the individual who spoke for the Commons in dealings with the Crown, the Speaker is now the impartial presiding officer of the House, and his external representation of his fellow members is purely formal.

---

[15] Estimating that for the average M.P. the expenses of Parliamentary membership were probably near £400 a year, *The Economist* said: 'It is better that the majority of MPs should have outside work than that we should be governed by professional politicians; but the salary paid should not be such that many MPs are very hard up, or having to work desperately long hours in order to avoid being hard up. It should even be enough to enable a few devoted members—not just the elderly, the single and the unemployable—to give all their time to parliamentary work. No one wants people to put up for election for the sake of the money; it is better that most men should have to make some financial sacrifice by becoming MPs. But the sacrifice should not be such that able people consider it prohibitive. And that is the point which seems to be quickly approaching.' 28 July 1951, p. 197.

[16] The Conservatives opposed the incumbent Speaker, a Liberal, in the general election of 1895, and considered offering a rival candidate to the House when the time came to re-elect the presiding officer. They did not do so, however, and even continued him in office after they formed a Government. The Speaker was also opposed in the elections of 1935, 1945, and 1950. In the last instance the Speaker's opponent was an independent candidate.

[17] The last disapproval occurred in 1679 when Charles II objected to the election of Sir Edward Seymour.

100–

Once elected, the Speaker divests himself of partisanship and becomes an umpire administering without favor the established rules of the House and a guardian of the rights of all its members. He lives in a well-appointed apartment in the Palace of Westminster and receives a salary of £5000 a year. When he quits the office it is customary to grant him a pension and for the Crown to offer him a peerage.

When it becomes necessary to choose a new Speaker, the leaders of the majority party canvass their membership with great care in order to designate the person best qualified to occupy the office. The qualifications are a thorough knowledge of the rules and practices of the House and demonstrated personal traits of tact, patience, and judicial temperament. It is customary for the majority party leaders to consult with the opposition and obtain its approval of the member selected for Speaker. Occasionally the opposition decides to nominate a candidate from its own ranks. In 1951, for example, the Labour Party contested the election of W. S. Morrison, a Conservative, who was chosen by 318 votes to 251. Attlee promptly congratulated the new Speaker and promised him 'the full support of the Opposition in maintaining order and the authority of the Chair.' [18]

The Speaker must have the confidence and respect of all members. Douglas Clifton Brown, the Speaker from 1943 to 1951, made the following comments about his office on the occasion of his re-election in 1945:

> . . . I have to try to see that the machine runs smoothly. The Speaker can help here, in the Chair and behind the Chair. I have to see that Government business, while I am not responsible for it, is not unduly hampered by wilful obstruction. I have to see that minority views have a fair hearing. . . Of course, there will be various shades of opinion on all sides of the House, and all these have to be considered when one is calling speakers. Free speech and fair play for all must be my main study. . . As Speaker, I am not the Government's man, nor the Opposition's man. I am the House of Commons' man, and I believe, above all, the back benchers' man. . . As Speaker, I cherish the dignity of the office very much: I wish to uphold it, and I shall.[19]

The other officers of the House are the Clerk and his two assistants, the Sergeant-at-arms and his deputies, the Chaplain, and the Chairman and Deputy Chairman of Committees. The Clerk and the Sergeant-at-arms, with their assistants, are appointed by the King upon the nomination of the Prime Minister, and their tenure is for life. The Chaplain is appointed by the Speaker. The Chairman and the Deputy Chairman of Committees are elected by the House, which means in effect that they are chosen by the majority party, and they retire upon a change in Government.

---

[18] *The Times,* 1 November 1951.
[19] 413 *H.C. Debates* 5s., cols. 7-8.

In addition to these officers, there are several others whose positions and duties grow out of the party organization of the House. They are important in the direction and control of the chamber's business—the debate and passage of legislation and the criticism and defense of the Government. When one considers that Parliament may enact approximately 75 public bills during a session, and that some of them will be exceedingly complicated measures, it is plain that the time allowed for debate must be closely controlled and rationed. A House of Commons of more than 600 members could spend months discussing such controversial topics as the nationalization of the iron and steel industry or changes in the structure of local government. The House does not get deeply involved because its time and the pace of legislative consideration are managed by the Government.

The individual in charge of planning and arranging the Parliamentary schedule is the Leader of the House of Commons, always a strong figure in the Cabinet and sometimes the Deputy Prime Minister. The Leader of the House must be a good organizer, popular with fellow members, and sensitive to currents of opinion among the backbenchers. He is assisted in his work by the whips.[20] The Government side has a chief whip who holds the position of Parliamentary Secretary of the Treasury, five whips who have official positions and receive salaries as Lords Commissioners of the Treasury, and three assistant whips who are unpaid. Their job is to keep in touch with all party members in the House, mollifying the rebellious and encouraging the faithful. The whips are responsible for guaranteeing the attendance of sufficient members for crucial debates and divisions. They send to party members a weekly program of the business to come before the House, and they indicate the importance of each item by a system of underscoring—one line, fairly important; two lines, highly important; and three lines, most important. No member who desires to retain his standing with the party can ignore a 'three-line whip.' If he absents himself from a sitting after such a summons has gone out, save for a very good reason, he is in effect severing his party connection.

The other side of the House is equally well organized. The chief figure is the Leader of the Opposition. He is the member who would in all probability become Prime Minister upon a change of Government, and he may have held that office in the past. So important is the position of Leader of the Opposition regarded that he is paid an official salary of £2000 a year. He is assisted in his party duties by whips who perform the same functions among the opposition members that the Government whips carry out on their side. The opposition whips are not paid salaries in addition to their ordinary Parliamentary compensation, but they expect to become Treasury officials when their party achieves power.

---

[20] The origin of the term whip is attributed to Edmund Burke who once described the efforts of ministers to assemble their supporters for an important debate by the hunting-field phrase of 'whipping them in.' The 'whipper-in' eventually became abbreviated to whip.

The whips of the two sides of the House arrange much of the business of the chamber. They agree upon the time to be allotted for debate and upon the number of speakers from each side. Some of these agreements, made, as the saying is, 'behind the Speaker's Chair,' or 'through the usual channels,' stage-manage important debates and insure that the leading actors get an opportunity to deliver their pieces.

6. *Committees of the House*

The committee system of the House of Commons is less highly developed than in legislative bodies in the United States. Nevertheless, the House has a number of committees, and their work is important.

It is customary for the House to transact much of its business in the Committee of the Whole House, which is the entire membership of the House sitting under less formal rules of procedure than is the case in a regular session. For example, motions do not need to be seconded, a member may speak more than once, and a motion to put the question can be moved at any time. In Committee of the Whole House, the Speaker leaves his chair and the House is presided over by the Chairman or Deputy Chairman of Committees. In addition to the Speaker leaving the chair, the change in status is also marked by the removal of the mace, the richly ornamented rod, surmounted by a crown, which rests on the table in front of the Speaker whenever the House is in regular session and which is the symbol of his office. The Committee of the Whole House is designated the House in Supply when bills dealing with the appropriation of money are under consideration and the House in Ways and Means when taxation measures are being considered.

Besides the Committee of the Whole House, the House of Commons employs four other types of committees—namely, select committees, sessional committees, standing committees, and committees on private bills. Select committees are named for the purpose of examining a particular subject and reporting to the House, and a score or more may be set up in a parliamentary session. Usually composed of 15 members, they choose their own chairmen and keep records of their proceedings. The membership of a select committee may be designated by the Committee of Selection, or it may be named in the motion proposing the committee's establishment. Sessional committees are select committees that are chosen for the life of a parliamentary session, and there are normally about ten in existence. The Committee of Selection, a body of 11 members chosen at the beginning of a session to make appointments to other committees, is a sessional committee, and others are the Committee on Standing Orders, on Statutory Instruments, and the Committee on Public Accounts.

Standing committees exist to relieve the Committee of the Whole House of some of its legislative burden, and they have no functional specialties determining the bills referred to them. Designated Committees A, B, C, D, and the Scottish Committee, they consist of a group of 20 members chosen by the Committee of Selection, plus from 10 to 30 particularly qualified members added for the consideration of each bill referred to a committee. The standing committees are appointed at the beginning of a new Parliament and continue until that Parliament is dissolved. Committees on private bills consist of four members (except that on unopposed private bills which has five members) who sit in a quasi-judicial capacity to weigh the merits of measures dealing with special interests, for the most part, the powers of local authorities. They, too, are appointed by the Committee of Selection. The party membership on all committees is roughly proportionate to the party standings of the whole House.[21] Apart from those on private bills, Parliamentary committees do not, as a rule, hold the extensive hearings customary with American legislative committees, and they are not generally served by the professional staffs found in Washington and some state capitals.[22]

In recent years as Parliament has found the pressure on its time increasing in severity, there have been numerous proposals to develop a more extensive committee system than now exists. It has been pointed out that much time could be saved and more expert knowledge be brought to bear on certain classes of legislation if the parliamentary membership were broken down into a number of functional committees which would discuss legislation in detail and study amendments and revisions. By the present practice, bills receive committee consideration, but these bodies are large and their work is not specialized. Bills going to the Committee of the Whole House are sometimes allotted relatively brief periods of debate and parts of them may be passed over entirely because parliamentary time limits must be rigidly observed. The House, however, has been reluctant to transfer major responsibility to small committees, preferring to keep the whole House the arena of debate in place of a section of its membership. Cabinets, too, have never looked with much favor on an extension of the committee system. It is easier for ministers to keep pending legislation under control if it is considered in the Committee of the Whole House where they are present and where the Government's forces can be easily mobilized against unwanted amendments and changes.

It seems likely, though, that the committee system will have to be more extensively used if the House of Commons is going to consider with any adequacy the volume of legislation that now comes before it. The increasing technicality of many pieces of legislation also argues for the greater use of committees. Not all members can be well versed on public finance, the social services, national defense, local government, and other major areas of legislation. It is possible, however, for a few members to concentrate in a special field and become sufficiently qualified to guide the deliberations of their fellow-members when their specialty is discussed. This kind

---

[21] The majority party does not choose the chairmen of standing committees; they are drawn from a panel of not less than 10 members nominated by the Speaker.

[22] The Counsel to the Speaker gives the Committee on Statutory Instruments professional advice, and the Comptroller and Auditor-General serves the Committee on Public Accounts.

of specialization occurs to a considerable extent at the present time. Members concentrate on foreign affairs, colonial problems, education, and other subjects and do most of their study and speaking when these matters are before the House. They do not have, however, a formalized system that insures they will be heard and have some influence when appropriate legislation is introduced and debated.

7. *The Time and Place of Meeting*

Parliament assembles annually in early November and continues in session until the late summer of the following year. A long holiday lasting from shortly before Christmas until about the first week of February is customary, and briefer recesses are taken later in the year. Several hundred years ago, the summoning of Parliament was something the kings tried to avoid, and Parliament eventually required its meeting every three years by the Triennial Act of 1694. Almost contemporaneously it made annual Parliaments essential by limiting the life of important laws and appropriations to one year. No such stratagems have been necessary for a long time as the constant meeting of Parliament is essential to the life of the country.

The House of Commons may adjourn by its own action at any time, as may the House of Lords. Adjournments do not affect the status of pending business. Annual sessions are brought to an end by a prorogation of the King, acting, of course, upon the advice of the Prime Minister. When Parliament is prorogued, action on pending business ceases, and a bill that has not passed all the necessary stages in both houses must be introduced again. A dissolution of Parliament occurs when the Prime Minister requests this action of the King, and it at once sets in motion the machinery of a general election. Until 1867 the death of the monarch acted to dissolve Parliament and to require a general election. Nowadays the same Parliament continues. Should the houses be adjourned or prorogued at the time of the sovereign's death, they immediately meet, and the members take a new oath of allegiance.

The House of Commons sits in a newly built chamber that replaced the one destroyed by a German bomb on 10 May 1941. From that date until completion of the new chamber in 1950, the House met in the peers' chamber, although the imminence of air raids drove it to Church House in the precincts of Westminster Abbey on a number of occasions.

The new House is in the traditional British style of a wide center aisle with tiers of benches rising from the floor on each side. Each tier of benches is divided midway by a side aisle termed the gangway. At the entrance to the chamber from the lobby of the Palace of Westminster is a railing known as the bar of the House. It is guarded by the Sergeant-at-arms; no one but a member may pass beyond this point, although occasionally persons are invited to address the House from outside the bar. It will be recalled that Benjamin Franklin once spoke to the House from this point when he was a colonial agent in London. At the opposite end from the bar is the Speaker's chair, a massive wooden chair on a raised platform. In front of the Speaker and between the two front rows of benches is a large table at which the clerk and his assistants sit. The leaders of the Government sit on the front bench, frequently called the Treasury bench, on the Speaker's right hand, while across the big table on the opposite front bench sit the leaders of the opposition. Members who hold ministerial positions, or who have held such positions when their party was in power, occupy seats behind the principal party figures. On the upper benches and below the gangway on either side sit the nonministerial and junior party members. These are the 'backbenchers' who talk and vote but are less influential in parliamentary affairs than their colleagues. Members of minor parties must find seats below the gangway, and they sit on the ministerial or opposition side according to their feelings toward the Government of the day.

When the House was discussing plans for rebuilding the bombed chamber some members argued that its physical size should be enlarged and individual desks and chairs provided. Since the old chamber only supplied seating space for 346 members there was obviously some merit in reconstructing it to allow at least all members to be present at one time. It was finally decided, however, to reproduce the original chamber, although some concessions in the way of improved lighting, heating, and ventilation were agreed to. Winston Churchill, Prime Minister at the time the rebuilding plan was adopted, argued persuasively that the structural form of the House and its intimate atmosphere had great influence upon the conduct of its business. He said in this respect:

> There are two main characteristics of the House of Commons which will command the approval and the support of reflective and experienced Members. They will, I have no doubt, sound odd to foreign ears. The first is that its shape should be oblong and not semi-circular. Here is a very potent factor in our political life. The semi-circular assembly, which appeals to political theorists, enables every individual or every group to move round the centre, adopting various shades of pink according as the weather changes. I am a convinced supporter of the party system in preference to the group system. I have seen many earnest and ardent Parliaments destroyed by the group system. The party system is much favoured by the oblong form of Chamber. It is easy for an individual to move through those insensible gradations from Left to Right, but the act of crossing the Floor is one which requires serious consideration. I am well informed on this matter, for I have accomplished that difficult process, not only once but twice. Logic is a poor guide compared with custom. Logic, which has created in so many countries semi-circular assemblies with buildings that give to every Member, not only a seat to sit in, but often a desk to write at, with a lid to bang, has proved fatal to Parliamentary Government as we know it here in its home and in the land of its birth.

> The second characteristic of a Chamber formed on the lines of the House of Commons is that it should not be big enough to contain all

its Members at once without over-crowding, and that there should be no question of every Member having a separate seat reserved for him. The reason for this has long been a puzzle to uninstructed outsiders, and has frequently excited the curiosity and even the criticism of new Members. Yet it is not so difficult to understand if you look at it from a practical point of view. If the House is big enough to contain all its Members, nine-tenths of its Debates will be conducted in the depressing atmosphere of an almost empty or half-empty Chamber. The essence of good House of Commons speaking is the conversational style, the facility for quick, informal interruptions and interchanges. Harangues from a rostrum would be a bad substitute for the conversational style in which so much of our business is done. But the conversational style requires a fairly small space, and there should be on great occasions a sense of crowd and urgency. There should be a sense of the importance of much that is said, and a sense that great matters are being decided, there and then, by the House.[23]

Compared to most legislative bodies, the House of Commons maintains a high standard in debate and deportment. Perhaps few contemporary members reach the oratorical heights of a Burke or a Fox, but a House accustomed to Churchill's magnificent use of language does not have to make deep apology to past generations. There are numerous first-class speeches delivered in every session, and usually the general level of debate is high. The rules of the House forbid the reading of speeches, although members may speak from notes.

The British sense of propriety and the respect in which the Speaker is held result in the House being a well-behaved assembly. Occasionally the Speaker is forced to reprove a member for the intemperance of his remarks, and once in a great while he finds it necessary to 'name' a member, an action which results in the offending person's immediate expulsion from the sitting. Some years ago an unruly member attempted to run out of the chamber with the mace; such conduct, it scarcely needs to be said, was universally deplored.[24]

It is only in this century that Parliament has undertaken an official publication of its debates. The House of Commons began keeping a journal

---

[23] 393 *H.C. Debates* 5 s., cols. 403-4.

[24] In the spring of 1951 the House passed through an unusually tempestuous period. The Conservative opposition began exploiting the procedural possibilities for the delay and obstruction of business, particularly its right to debate statutory instruments, through 'prayers' or motions for their annulment, at the end of a day's sitting. The object was pretty plainly the harassment—and physical exhaustion—of the Government which, because of its small Parliamentary majority, was compelled to keep its party members present until the early hours of the next morning. Tempers wore thin, and the Speaker had difficulty in maintaining orderly sessions. Opposition tactics, however, began to appear to a good deal of the public as unworthy of the critical period through which the country was passing, and after the Easter recess the campaign was discontinued.

of its proceedings in 1547—the Lords began in 1509—but this became simply a record of official actions. Down until the early years of the nineteenth century there was no regular reporting of speeches. For a long time, in fact, it was against the rules of the House for its clerks to take notes on speeches, although there was a good deal of unauthorized reporting and publication of debates. In 1809 a private publisher, T. C. Hansard, acquired a parliamentary record known as *Debates* which was being produced by William Cobbett as a supplement to his *Weekly Political Register*. For a hundred years 'Hansard' recorded the debates and proceedings of Parliament, although this private publication was subsidized by the state after 1877. In 1909 'Hansard' was replaced by an official publication, *Parliamentary Debates*. The name 'Hansard' continues in popular use when reference is made to the proceedings of Parliament.[25]

Besides *Parliamentary Debates* there are other official publications which are issued to inform the members of Parliament and the public. Such Parliamentary committees as those on estimates and public accounts submit reports which are published. Royal commissions, commissions of inquiry, and various special committees publish their findings and recommendations. These are usually presented to Parliament 'by command of His Majesty,' which means at the instance of a minister. Command papers are numbered serially. The longer of these official documents are bound in blue paper covers and are commonly referred to as 'blue books.' From time to time ministers submit to Parliament compilations of documents, statements of policy, and records of negotiations, and when ordered printed by the House of Commons they are known as 'white papers.' The Foreign Secretary, for example, may submit the record of the negotiations preceding the conclusion of a treaty. All these official papers are published by His Majesty's Stationery Office, a department under the Treasury.

The House of Commons permits the press to report its proceedings and provides a gallery above the Speaker's chair for the use of correspondents. On the whole, Parliamentary activities are extensively publicized by the British press. *The Times* publishes detailed accounts of the proceedings of each House, and other newspapers report them with varying degrees of completeness. The weekly journals regularly report and comment on Parliamentary affairs, and the B.B.C. gives a summary of Parliamentary business. Even *Punch,* Britain's leading magazine of humor, includes a feature 'Impressions of Parliament.' What is said and done in Parliament is readily available for all who are interested.

There is not a free legislative assembly meeting anywhere in the world but that owes a debt to the House of Commons. In the older dominions representatives of their respective populations sit in chambers that are virtual replicas of the original at Westminster, and the functioning of these

---

[25] *Parliamentary Debates* is a record of words spoken in Parliament. There is no comparable practice to that of the U.S. Congress of permitting members to 'extend their remarks' in the *Congressional Record* or to insert material prepared by non-members.

assemblies bears almost as close a resemblance to the parent body. The younger dominions are just establishing their independent institutions, but it is a safe prediction that their national legislatures will use the House of Commons as a model in many particulars. In all democratic countries, whether or not they employ the responsible cabinet type of government, evidence of the organization, procedure, and traditions of the House of Commons is discernible. The House of Commons stands as a great monument to the right and authority of freely elected representatives to assemble together, to speak, and to resolve upon action for the public weal.

VII

The House of Lords

Although a lineal descendant of the Great Council of Norman England, the House of Lords is today the upper house only in a ceremonial and courtesy sense. Effective legislative power has long since passed to the House of Commons, and to it Ministries hold themselves accountable. This disproportion in the power and influence of the two chambers is a reflection of the changes in the social and political life of Britain which have transformed it from a nation ruled by a King and the aristocracy to one governed by broad popular consent. Some written but many unwritten parts of the Constitution have relegated the House of Lords to its present inferior status.

1. *The Membership of the House*

In order to describe the composition of the modern House of Lords, it is necessary to say something about the class of British society known as the nobility. From Saxon days there have been individuals possessing a right to share in the councils of state because of personal status and hereditary position. During the formative years of Parliament the more important barons and clergy received from the King individual writs of summons, and they continued to claim this privilege. If summoned to one Parliament they considered that they were entitled to attend all future Parliaments and that this privilege passed to their heirs. This group of individually summoned magnates became recognized as the hereditary peerage. In the course of time gradations of rank among the greater barons were introduced, and five ranks have now existed for several hundred years. The lowest and most numerous is that of baron, and in ascending order the others are viscount, earl, marquess, and duke. While these ranks have some social and ceremonial significance they are unimportant politically: each peer has one vote in the House of Lords.[1]

---

[1] The title of duke was introduced in England by Edward III, marquess by Richard II, and viscount by Henry VI. The title of earl, equivalent to the continental rank of count, was of Saxon origin, while the title of baron was held by the tenants-in-chief of the Norman kings. The title lord is a generic term applicable to any member of the nobility. Barons are always addressed as lords, but a viscount, earl, marquess, or duke is usually called by his appropriate title. The wives of peers are collectively addressed as ladies, but individually they are usually given their appropriate rank:

The power to grant titles of nobility has always belonged to the royal prerogative, and the granting instrument is a patent which sets forth the rank of the holder and the manner in which the title shall pass to his descendants. The inheritance of a title must conform to the law governing the transmission of landed property, and the nearest male heir is the usual successor. There are a few ancient 'baronies by writ' which descend to heirs general, thus permitting a female to inherit the title.

There are about 850 members of the peerage now entitled to sit in the House of Lords. Most of these are peers of the United Kingdom, although there is a small company of English, Scottish, and Irish peers whose titles date from the time when England, Scotland, and Ireland were independent countries. Creations after 1707, when England and Scotland were united, were in the peerage of Great Britain, and those after 1800 in the peerage of the United Kingdom.

Noblemen with only Scottish or Irish titles do not all sit by right in the House of Lords, but in accordance with the respective acts of union they choose some of their membership to represent them. The 16 representative peers from Scotland are selected by the 40-odd Scottish peers for the duration of a Parliament, while the representative Irish peers are chosen for life. Since the establishment of the Irish Free State in 1921 there have been no elections among the Irish peerage to fill vacancies in the ranks of the 28 representative peers accorded Ireland in the Act of Union, 1800; there are today six having seats in the House of Lords, and as Lord Chancellor Jowitt said while discussing in the House the effects of the Republic of Ireland Act of 1949, 'the Irish representative peers are a gradually dying race.' He added that the remaining ones would continue to be members of the House of Lords. A number of peers of Scottish or Irish origin also possess more recent titles of nobility in either the peerage of Great Britain or that of the United Kingdom and are thus entitled to membership in the House of Lords on this basis.

Occasionally there is a titled member of the House of Commons. Such a member is either an Irish peer not chosen to represent the whole body of the peerage of Ireland or the heir of a peer and using a courtesy title.[2] Scottish peers not elected to the House of Lords are not eligible to sit in the Commons.

---

duchess for the wife of a duke, marchioness for the wife of a marquess, countess for the wife of an earl, viscountess for the wife of a viscount, and lady for the wife of a baron. Two other titled groups, knights and baronets, are not members of the peerage and do not sit in the House of Lords. The title baronet was introduced by James I in 1611, and it is an hereditary honor. The holder of a baronetcy uses the prefix Sir before his Christian name and follows his surname by Bt. or Bart. Knighthoods are not hereditary. Their holders precede their Christian names by Sir, and the wives of knights, as well as those of baronets, use the title lady.

[2] Lord Palmerston in the last century and Earl Winterton, who represented a Sussex constituency from 1901 until 1951, are examples of Irish peers elected to the House of Commons. The heir of a peer of high rank may use one of his father's lesser titles as a courtesy title. Thus, the present Marquess of Salisbury sat in the House of Commons as Viscount Cranborne.

Some titles of nobility may descend through a female heir, and there are today about 20 peeresses in their own right. Despite the strenuous endeavors of some of these ladies to win summonses to the House of Lords, the male peers have not seen fit to admit them. As peeresses in their own right they are ineligible to seek election to the House of Commons. This disability does not extend to the wives of peers; the American-born Lady Astor, for example, long represented Plymouth in the lower chamber.

The nobility in England has always been a comparatively small class. Seven earls and 51 barons were summoned to the Parliament of 1295. Until the Stuart period the number of lay peers in Parliament was usually about 50, although it once fell to 23. Since the seventeenth century peerages have been granted more freely, and most present-day titles are comparatively recent creations. Unlike the Continental nobilities, a title descends to only one individual and all other descendants of the title-holder are commoners.

The selection of new peers is made by the Government of the day, and the names are recommended to the King by the Prime Minister. The grant of new peerages is usually announced in the Honours List published at New Year's and on the King's Birthday. A special occasion such as the coronation of a new monarch may bring forth an honors list.[3]

In olden times Kings conferred peerages on persons who had rendered valuable services to the crown and the state and upon favorites of the court. Eighteenth-century sovereigns were co-operative in helping prime ministers who enjoyed their confidence to 'manage' the House of Commons by the judicious award of honors. This trafficking in honors largely disappeared under the new conditions introduced by the Reform Act of 1832 and the nineteenth century's higher standards of political morality. Toward the end of the century, however, there were rumors that the needs of party leaders for ample campaign funds had given rise to a rather unsavory commerce in connection with the bestowal of peerages. For £50,000 subscribed to a party fund, the gossip ran, one could 'purchase' a barony. The matter was debated in Parliament several times, resolutions were passed, and finally in 1922 the Government appointed a royal commission to investigate and submit recommendations.

The commission uncovered no corruption, but it believed that the procedures followed in the award of honors should be safeguarded against abuse and that an act should 'be passed imposing a penalty on anyone promising to secure, or to endeavor to secure, an honor in respect of any pecuniary payment or other valuable consideration, and on any person

---

[3] A new peer selects his own title. He has considerable latitude, although the names of counties and principal towns are usually associated with earls, marquesses, and dukes. Many new peers use their own surnames, sometimes adding a place name connected with their life or exploits; thus, Air Marshal Tedder became Lord Tedder; Field Marshal Sir Bernard Montgomery, Viscount Montgomery of Alamein; Stanley Baldwin, Earl Baldwin of Bewdley; and Sir William Beveridge, Lord Beveridge.

promising such payment or consideration in order to receive an honor.'[4] The Government accepted the recommendations of the commission, and since that time there has been much less criticism of 'political' honors. Some of these honors are admittedly rewards for faithful service to a party, but today the recipients must be persons of sufficient prominence and reputation to be adjudged eligible on other than narrow, partisan grounds.

Politicians are only one class of persons considered for inclusion in an honors list. It has always been customary to reward distinguished military heroes with titles, and the names of Marlborough, Nelson, Wellington, Haig, and Jellicoe are examples of this practice. Several of the prominent British military figures of World War II had their services rewarded by patents of nobility. These included Field Marshals Sir Alan Brooke, Sir Bernard Montgomery, Sir Archibald Wavell, Sir Harold Alexander, Admiral Sir A. B. Cunningham, and Marshal of the R.A.F. Sir Arthur Tedder. Distinguished diplomats and civil servants are sometimes awarded peerages, and notable figures in the fields of art, literature, and science are occasional recipients. Tennyson, Bryce, Kelvin, Lister, Rutherford, and Keynes are examples.

A person may decline to accept a peerage, although the heir to a title has no choice when it descends to him. As the House of Commons has become the more important of the two chambers, most influential politicians have preferred to continue their careers there and have been unwilling to accept translation to the Lords. Gladstone never accepted a peerage, and Lloyd George took one only a short time before his death; Winston Churchill has preferred to remain a commoner. Sometimes a political figure who is past his prime and who feels unequal to future campaigning lets it be known that he is prepared to accept a peerage, and if he is on good terms with the chief whip of the Government and the Prime Minister he is likely to be so rewarded.

A small number of the male relatives of the reigning sovereign are customarily members of the House of Lords. At present they are the Queen's husband, the Duke of Edinburgh; her two living uncles, the Duke of Windsor and the Duke of Gloucester; and her cousin, the Duke of Kent. The royal dukes only attend the House on ceremonial occasions and never participate in debates or vote.

Besides the members of the lay nobility, the House of Lords also contains a remnant of the clerical estate, the lords spiritual, which was a large element in medieval times. The Archbishops of Canterbury and York, the Bishops of London, Durham, and Winchester, and 21 other bishops of the Church of England are members of the House. The 21 bishops are the most senior, according to appointment, of the 28 occupants of English sees.

In addition, there are nine lords of appeal in ordinary who hold life peerages. The lords of appeal were first introduced into the House in 1876 for

---

4 Cmd. 1789 (1922). See below, pp. 197-8.

the purpose of assisting with the judicial duties that fall to the Lords as the highest court of appeal. They are invariably distinguished lawyers.

Members of the House of Lords possess the same privileges and immunities with respect to freedom of arrest while attending to their parliamentary duties and of liability for what they may say in their chamber as do members of the House of Commons. In olden times they possessed certain other privileges, but these have become inoperative through lack of use or legal change. One of the last, the right of a peer charged with a criminal offense to be tried by his fellow lords, was abolished by statute in 1948. This privilege, it may be said, had not been used very frequently, and the lords did not consider they were losing much of value. Peers came to feel that their chances were usually better before an ordinary jury than before their own House where fellow members were not impressed by titles or ancestral lineage. Although the peers nowadays have no privileges not accorded members of the House of Commons, they suffer what may be considered certain disadvantatges. They are not eligible to vote in parliamentary elections, although they can in local elections, and they receive no remuneration for attendance in Parliament.

2. *The Organization and Procedure of the House*

The chamber of the House of Lords is a richly decorated room to the right of the central lobby in the Palace of Westminster. It is built in the style customary of British parliamentary chambers, that is, with benches rising in several tiers along the sides of the chamber. At the head of the chamber is a dais for the throne of the King or Queen. Below this and between the rows of benches is a large, rather shapeless divan known as the woolsack. It is upon this that the presiding officer of the House, the Lord Chancellor, sits. The benches to his right are occupied by peers who support the current Government, while opposite, on his left, sit the members of the opposition. There are cross benches reserved for the use of the bishops who attend. As in the House of Commons, ministerial members occupy the front bench on the Government side and the leading figures of the opposition take the front bench across the central aisle. After a German bomb destroyed the chamber of the House of Commons in 1941, the Lords moved to another room in the Palace of Westminster in order to permit the Commons with its larger attendance to occupy their chamber. With the completion of the new Commons chamber, the Lords returned to occupy their red benches.

The House of Lords is less highly organized than the House of Commons. Matters of formal organization and procedure are embodied in standing orders which may be amended by the House. The Lord Chancellor as the presiding officer is little more than a moderator, and questions concerning procedure are decided by votes of the House. He has a vote as a peer but no casting vote in case of a tie. Since the atmosphere of the House of Lords is one of dignity and calm, there is little call for a strong presiding officer armed with elaborate rules of procedure. In debate members address themselves to 'My lords' and not to the Lord Chancellor. The House has several clerical and ceremonial officials who are well versed in its procedure and ritual.

When Parliament is called into session by royal proclamation the House of Lords assembles at the same time as the House of Commons, and its sessions are terminated by a prorogation. While Parliament is in session the upper house may meet and adjourn on its own motion. The peers meet daily, usually Monday through Thursday, at two-thirty o'clock when the Lord Chancellor takes his seat on the woolsack, and they ordinarily adjourn two or three hours later. Only three peers are needed for a quorum.

The committee system of the House of Lords is more simple than that of the House of Commons. The Lords conduct some of their business in the committee of the Whole House, which is the membership present operating under less formal rules of procedure than obtain when the House is in regular session and presided over by the Lord Chairman of Committees, a Government supporter. The House has no standing committees except one for textual revision to which bills are referred after passing the Committee of the Whole House. Sessional and select committees are utilized for the consideration of special kinds of legislation or for the gathering of additional information upon pending bills. Sessional committees may consist of all members present during a session or of smaller parts of the House membership. There are a number of select committees on private bills, consisting of five peers, appointed in each session.

The political parties in the House of Lords are organized with leaders and whips. A peer indicates his party allegiance by accepting or rejecting the whip. Party discipline is less strict than in the lower house, because the life of the Ministry does not depend upon the maintenance of a majority and the peers do not have constituents to whom they must justify their Parliamentary actions. Party leaders in the Lords keep in contact with the respective leaders in the Commons in order to plan the legislative program and to concert their Parliamentary tactics.

Besides its legislative work the House of Lords has two judicial functions. One, the trial of impeachments on charges preferred by the House of Commons, is no longer of importance. The last impeachment occurred in 1805, 'and the procedure may now be regarded as obsolete. Impeachment in the seventeenth and early eighteenth centuries was a means for "liquidating" opponents. The ballot boxes are now available for political opponents and the criminal courts for criminals.' [5]

The second judicial function, that of serving as a court of appeal, is of great importance. Subject to certain exceptions, the House of Lords is the final court of appeal for civil and criminal cases tried in the courts of England and Wales, and Northern Ireland, and for civil cases tried in

---

[5] W. Ivor Jennings, *Parliament* (Cambridge, 1948), p. 381.

Scotland. In theory the same body which legislates is the appellate court, and any peer is legally qualified to participate in the judicial activity of the House. The practice, however, is quite different. For more than a century the performance of the judicial function has been confined by custom to the law lords, who are the Lord Chancellor, the nine Lords of Appeal in Ordinary, and those peers who have held high judicial office.

3. *The Parliament Acts of 1911 and 1949*

Until the early years of this century the legislative powers of the House of Lords were nominally the same as those of the House of Commons. In actuality, however, the Lords had ceased to be as influential in law-making and had accepted the role of a secondary chamber. This change in the relative importance of the two houses had proceeded throughout the nineteenth century as successive extensions of the suffrage had made the Commons more and more representative of the total population of Britain and as democratic principles had won greater acceptance. A measure of the change in the relative importance of the two chambers is indicated by the fact that during the nineteenth century it became increasingly inconvenient for the Prime Minister to be a member of the House of Lords. Disraeli as the Earl of Beaconsfield headed his second Government from the House of Lords and Lord Rosebery and Lord Salisbury were Prime Ministers at the turn of the century, but it is significant that twenty years later the noble status of Lord Curzon was regarded as a disqualification for the highest political office and that the King was advised to entrust the Government to a commoner, Stanley Baldwin.

The change in the respective powers of the two Houses of Parliament, which was occurring in practice, was confirmed in law by the Parliament Act of 1911. The enactment of this statute was made necessary by the action of the predominately Conservative House of Lords in rejecting the Finance Bill of 1909 introduced by the Liberal Government of the time. The income and inheritance tax provisions of the bill were designed to fall heavily upon the wealthy elements of the country.

It had been virtually an unwritten provision of the Constitution that the Lords accepted without change the financial legislation passed by the House of Commons, so the action of the upper chamber in 1909 created a constitutional crisis. Asquith, the Prime Minister, advised the King to dissolve Parliament, and a general election was held. The Liberal Ministry was returned with a majority, and the House of Lords bowed to the electoral decision. Nevertheless, the Government decided to eliminate the possibility of such a crisis arising again by setting forth in law what it considered to be the correct constitutional relationship between the two Houses of Parliament. A bitter legislative battle ensued; but after another general election, fought on the issue of the peers versus the people, and the Prime Minister's threat to advise the King to create enough new peers to insure a Government majority in the Lords, the upper house admitted defeat and the Parliament Act was passed.[6]

The Parliament Act declared, first, that any measure passed by the House of Commons and rejected by the House of Lords would become law upon receiving the royal assent, provided it had been passed by two more successive sessions of the Commons within two years. Secondly, the act provided that any money bill, passed by the House of Commons, would become law upon receiving the royal assent after it had been before the House of Lords for 30 days. A money bill was defined to include measures dealing with taxation, appropriations, loans, and audits. The Speaker of the House of Commons was empowered to decide, in case of dispute, whether or not a bill was a money bill. A third provision of the Act reduced the statutory life of a parliament from seven to five years. The practical effect of the Parliament Act, therefore, was to give the House of Lords a delaying power of two years over all legislation except financial bills, and with respect to the latter its delaying power was limited to 30 days.

The Labour Government which came into office in 1945 expected to have difficulty with the overwhelmingly Conservative House of Lords in enacting its program of nationalizing a number of the large industries of Britain. The Lords accepted with only inconsequential amendments the bills to nationalize the Bank of England, the coal industry, the domestic transportation services, the cable and wireless system, and the units of the gas and electric power industries remaining in private or municipal hands. The statutes for these nationalizations were passed by early 1948 and there remained only the iron and steel industry on the Government's original legislative program.

Because of the complexity of the problems which iron and steel nationalization presented and because of the excellent record the industry was establishing in the postwar battle for production, the less doctrinaire socialists in the Government appeared content to digest the rather full meal of nationalization already swallowed and postpone dealing with iron and steel until a later time. This tactic, however, was not acceptable to some of the more radical elements of the Labour Party who pressed for action. Anticipating that the House of Lords might reject a steel nationalization bill and wishing to retain the support of a united party, the Government leaders decided to restrict the Lords' powers further in order to insure the passage of a bill before the life of Parliament expired. Consequently, in late 1947 the Government introduced a bill, which passed the House of Commons, to limit the delaying power of the House of Lords to one year instead of two. Although expecting the Lords to reject such a measure, the Government planned to pass it under the provisions of the

---

[6] The threat to advise the Crown to create enough new peers to obtain a favorable majority had been used in 1832 when the Great Reform Bill was before Parliament. In 1712 Queen Anne created 12 Tory peers in order to overcome the Whig opposition to the Treaty of Utrecht.

Parliament Act of 1911 and still have time to enact steel nationalization over the objections of the upper house before a general election would constitutionally be necessary.

At this point the Conservative opposition in the House of Lords proposed to the Government that instead of proceeding with a bill simply to limit the Lords' powers, the question of the reform of its membership be considered as well. The Government accepted the suggestion and early in 1948 a series of conferences of the leaders of all parties was held, but no agreement was reached. According to the opposition leader in the House of Lords, the Marquess of Salisbury, the talks 'broke down because a fundamental difference arose between the Government and the Conservative Party in respect of the functions which a Second Chamber in this country should perform.'[7] The Government proceeded, therefore, with its bill to limit the delaying power of the Lords to one year. On 9 June 1948, after a postponement of several months, the bill was considered on second reading in the Lords and defeated 177-81. Passed by two subsequent sessions of the House of Commons, it received the royal assent as the Parliament Act, 1949.[8]

4. *Reform of the House of Lords*

The proposal of the Conservative opposition in 1948 for an all-party consideration of a reform of the upper house was by no means a novel idea. For half a century, at least, leading statesmen have been suggesting changes in the composition and powers of the House of Lords, and proposals have been debated in Parliament many times. The Parliament Act of 1911 declared that a reform of the composition of the upper chamber should follow the abridgment of its powers. Nothing was accomplished, however, before the outbreak of the First World War, which postponed the consideration of domestic problems of this kind for several years. In 1918 a Parliamentary commission under the chairmanship of Lord Bryce produced a plan for a reconstituted second chamber. The Bryce Plan proposed to reduce the House to 327 members serving 12-year terms. Eighty-one of these members were to be selected from the hereditary peerage by a standing committee of both houses, and the remaining 246 were to be chosen by 13 district electoral colleges composed of members of Parliament from the respective areas into which the country was to be divided for this pur-

---

[7] *The Times,* 9 June 1948.

[8] The Parliament Act, 1949, was the third bill to be enacted under the provisions of the Parliament Act, 1911. The two others were the Government of Ireland Act, 1914, and the Established Church (Wales) Act, 1914. Neither became effective, however, for the outbreak of war in 1914 caused the Government to introduce a bill suspending them. The first was replaced by the Government of Ireland Act, 1920, and the second by the Welsh Church Act, 1919. The procedure of the Parliament Act, 1911, was also invoked for two additional measures between 1912 and 1914. The first, the Temperance (Scotland) bill, was eventually passed by the House of Lords after a compromise on some of its provisions, and the Plural Voting bill was dropped before enactment because of the war.

pose. This proposal failed to elicit any general support, and with the Conservatives in power most of the time between the wars, no serious attempt was made to deal with the problem. The Labour Party's contribution to the discussion during this time was to advocate the establishment of a unicameral legislature.

In spite of the lack of progress on reconstituting the House of Lords, there is general recognition of the fact that a hereditary legislative chamber is an anachronism in a modern democratic state. When practical measures of reform are considered, however, a dilemma has arisen which has proved insurmountable. That dilemma is this: if the membership is made more representative of the whole nation, particularly by adding elected members, the House of Lords should have, or will claim, important legislative powers, and thus may become a rival to the Commons; on the other hand, unless the House has an important role in the legislative process, it will not attract the kind of membership which a reform of its composition would be designed to accomplish. The party leaders conferring in 1948 made some progress in removing this dilemma by tentatively agreeing that 'The Second Chamber should be complementary to and not a rival to the Lower House, and, with this end in view, the reform of the House of Lords should be based on a modification of its existing constitution as opposed to the establishment of a Second Chamber of a completely new type based on some system of election.' [9] Furthermore, they agreed, in principle, that the reformed House should be composed of appointed 'Lords of Parliament,' life peers drawn from the hereditary nobility and other groups 'on grounds of personal distinction or public service.' The reference of these conclusions concerning the composition of the House to the Parliamentary parties was contingent, however, on the leaders finding some basis of agreement on the powers of a reformed chamber. The search was unsuccessful. Their differences came down to the number of months during which a reformed House could delay the passage of Commons approved bills, and the Conservatives declared that 'On the principle to be applied in deciding what that period should be, there is really a fundamental difference between the Government and the Opposition.' [10]

The reforming plans that have been advanced are usually based on the idea of reducing the hereditary element in the Lords and at the same time leavening the resulting group by life peers or long-time members selected for their professional or vocational qualifications. There are already precedents for such changes in the composition of the House. The Irish and Scottish peers do not all sit as of right in the House but elect individuals from their membership to represent them. Not all bishops of the Church of England are members of the House, only the 24 senior bishops, and they hold what are in effect life peerages. Also, the nine lords of appeal in ordinary are a professional element holding life peerages. Thus, it is

[9] Cmd. 7380 (1948). *Parliament Bill*, 1947, p. 3.
[10] Ibid. p. 5.

frequently proposed that the present hereditary peers of Great Britain and the United Kingdom could choose a representative group which would be supplemented by long-term or life members representing the professions, industry, and labor.

Other proposals combine a reform of the House of Lords with the establishment of some kind of a 'social' or 'economic' chamber. Such a body would be composed of the representatives of various interest groups—farmers, businessmen, professional people, trade unionists, consumers. It might have an advisory role with respect to the work of the 'political' legislature, or it might share power in some fashion. These proposals have never attracted much support, and the practical difficulties of devising a workable and acceptable scheme, if the chamber has any important powers or influential position, are great. As Professor Barker has said, the 'essence of the State, and equally of the divisions of the State, is a common territorial citizenship, which unites the residents in a common area for the common handling of the common questions that concern them all in their common capacity as neighbors.' [11]

The representation of social or functional groups at the top of the governing structure would tend to atomize the national society, and their chamber would be an arena of conflicting special interests where differences rather than similarities would be at a premium. Furthermore, the attempt to separate the powers of government into political, social, and economic spheres would lead to serious complications. Foreign affairs, presumably, are primarily a political matter, but where does one place authority with respect to tariffs, trade agreements, and monetary policy? In the domestic field, the maintenance of law and order would probably be classed as political. Can it be divorced, however, from social policy concerned with education, slum clearance, juvenile delinquency, and kindred welfare subjects?

This brief discussion can merely suggest some of the difficulties involved in schemes to change radically the basis of representation for a legislative chamber. The British are prone to move cautiously when remodeling their governmental institutions, and they probably will do so in the case of the House of Lords. They realize that it is a part of their Constitution that needs to be brought into closer consonance with the political and social life of modern Britain. Until there is fairly general agreement, however, that they can dispense with a second chamber altogether or replace the House of Lords with a more useful body, they are apt to confine their reforming efforts to tinkering with the existing structure.

5. *The Case for and Against the House*

An objective evaluation of the House of Lords as a political institution requires a standard against which it can be measured. We have no universal standard, for constitution-makers in devising the second chambers of na-

---

[11] Ernest Barker, 'British Ideas of a Social Parliament,' *The American Political Science Review,* March 1950, p. 21.

tional legislatures have sought varying ends and given these bodies the functions they believed appropriate to the ends. In some cases they have sought to create a chamber of a more conservative temper and less subject to popular pressures than the lower house, and they have endowed it with powers of delay and revision. In other instances they have desired to provide for the special representation of the major subdivisions of the country, and they have given the second chamber sufficient authority to compel a consideration of the interests concerned. Other constitution-drafters have sought to establish checks on the exercise of executive power and have so armed the second chamber.

Since the modern British Parliament is the product of a long evolution, the purposes to be served by the House of Lords and its powers in the governmental system have undergone a great deal of change. From a place where the landed aristocracy exerted its due strength it has become a chamber where wealth and position, derived now from many sources, have a voice but not much power. This transformation has proceeded gradually as the social environment in which the political system operates has changed.

The conference of which Lord Bryce was chairman agreed on four functions that a second chamber of the British Parliament should perform. They were:

1. The examination and revision of bills brought from the House of Commons, a function which has become more needed since, on many occasions, during the last thirty years, the House of Commons has been obliged to act under special rules limiting debate.

2. The initiation of bills dealing with subjects of a practically non-controversial character which may have an easier passage through the House of Commons if they have been fully discussed and put into a well-considered shape before being submitted to it.

3. The interposition of so much delay (and no more) in the passing of a bill into law as may be needed to enable the opinion of the nation to be adequately expressed upon it. This would be specially needed as regards bills which affect the fundamentals of the Constitution or introduce new principles of legislation; or which raise issues whereon the opinion of the country may appear to be almost equally divided.

4. Full and free discussions of large and important questions, such as those of foreign policy, at moments when the House of Commons may happen to be so much occupied that it cannot find sufficient time for them. Such discussions may be all the more useful if conducted in an assembly whose debates and divisions do not involve the fate of the executive Government.[12]

Before World War II Jennings wrote about the conclusions of the Bryce commission, 'It is by no means certain that if an equally representative Conference had been held twenty years later these propositions would have

---

[12] Cmd. 9038 (1918), p. 4.

secured the same unanimity.' [13] This observation is probably more true today. The Conservative Party would settle for a second chamber endowed with such powers, but the Labour Party would consider them unacceptable. Labour would undoubtedly wish to restrict the first proposition to technical and drafting amendments and to exclude major matters of substance as falling within the competence of the upper house. Concerning the third point, it would challenge the right of the House of Lords to determine the need for and the length of delay 'to enable the opinion of the nation to be adequately expressed.' This was the problem which brought the conference of party leaders to naught in 1948. The Labour members believed that the procedures of the Parliament Act of 1911 permitted 'a House of Lords hostile to the Government of the day to render the legislative programme of the Government ineffective in the fourth and fifth sessions of a quinquennial Parliament.' [14] Hence reducing the period of possible delay was necessary. To the Conservatives, it was important to maintain a delaying power sufficient to force a Government, three or four years after attaining office, to forego highly controversial legislation or to seek a new mandate from the electorate.

Lacking any universal standard by which to evaluate the House of Lords and any agreement among the political parties on the proper composition and powers of a second chamber, we can only record some of the principal deficiencies and merits of the present House as they appear to British and foreign observers.

Its defects, if described without qualification, are serious ones. The anomaly of having a legislative chamber constituted in these democratic days on the hereditary principle has been mentioned. There is no reason to suppose, of course, that the eldest son of a politically gifted peer will inherit his father's qualifications in that regard. Perhaps environmental factors will give a son certain interests that he would not otherwise possess, but there is little assurance that this will be true. If he does have an interest in politics, he may find his inheritance a handicap, since the more active life of a member of the House of Commons usually attracts the young man with a flair for politics and he stands the chance of being translated to the upper chamber at a time when he is in line for political advancement in the Commons. [15] The chief ministerial posts are today usually awarded to members of the House of Commons because it is important that most of the leading ministers be present in the lower chamber to sup-

---

[13] Op. cit. p. 425.

[14] Cmd. 7380 (1948). *Parliament Bill, 1947*, p. 4.

[15] A case in point was that of Lord Hailsham, who at the time of his succession was Quintin Hogg, M.P., and a leading member of the Conservative opposition in the House of Commons. Hogg, regretting the necessity of quitting the House of Commons, wrote to the Prime Minister requesting legislation to make translation to the House of Lords dependent on a summons from that body. Attlee replied, 'I fully understand your feelings and I must say that I have much sympathy with you,' but he refused to promise to introduce any bill as suggested by Hogg. *The New York Times*, 10 September 1950.

122–

port the Government's legislative measures and to reply to opposition criticism.[16]

The small attendance characteristic of the present House of Lords is also cited against the body. The attendance customarily runs from 50 to 100. Occasionally, when some important debate is scheduled, the attendance will rise to 200 or 300 peers, but hundreds of the eligible members never appear on the floor of the House. On the second submission in 1948 of the important Parliament Bill, the vote in the Lords rejecting the measure was 218 to 36.

A further criticism of the present House is based on the fact that the Conservative Party has by far the largest number of adherents. In the nineteenth century, the Conservatives and Liberals were about equally represented, but as political issues were drawn more sharply on economic and social lines, the hereditary peerage inclined increasingly toward the Conservative side. A large number of Liberal peers left the party over the Irish Home Rule issue in 1886, and the Liberal Party remained weak in the House of Lords thereafter. With the decline of the Liberal Party and the rise of Labour, the disproportionate balance in the upper chamber became more marked. A small company of Liberal peers remained true to their party and some joined the Labour Party, but the majority of them found their way into the Conservative fold.

During its periods in office, the Labour Party has redressed the balance slightly by awarding peerages to party members or to outstanding nonparty individuals with Labourite sympathies. Labour has found it difficult, however, to build up a large and loyal following in the House of Lords. Its leaders usually prefer to continue in the more active political life of the Commons, and some who are prepared to retire to a less demanding career are opposed in principle to joining the peerage. Some, too, consider that a title involves a more expensive style of living than they can afford, and there are others who do not care to commit their descendants to membership in a hereditary nobility. The Labour Party has usually had to select elderly and heirless politicians and trade union leaders or go to the professions where party ties are not so pronounced.

While the case against the House of Lords based on composition, on the slight interest shown by the majority of its members, and on its one party dominance is abstractly overwhelming, there are points in its favor which to a considerable extent right the balance. In the first place, the peers who regularly attend the sessions of the House are, on the whole, an able group of political figures. The territorial nobility has exhibited little interest in Parliamentary life so that the majority of the peers who frequent the House of Lords are men who have been in active politics or some form of public service, or who are distinguished representatives of

---

[16] Churchill said that he considered Sir Philip Cunliffe-Lister, later Lord Swinton, 'made the serious mistake of quitting the House of Commons for the House of Lords in November, 1935, thus stultifying one of the arguments for his transfer to the Secretaryship of State for Air.' *The Gathering Storm*, p. 128.

some aspect of national life. Thus, in practice, the work of the House is conducted by a much more representative body than the formal composition of the House would indicate.

The standard of discussion and debating is probably the highest of any legislative chamber in the world. Its membership includes individuals who are recognized authorities upon almost every subject that comes before Parliament.[17] A debate on foreign affairs will include speakers who have held important diplomatic posts, former viceroys and governors-general, and others who have had broad experience in conducting the external relations of the United Kingdom. Speaking from experience and conviction and having no constituents or special interests to represent, they can take a national viewpoint as no other responsible group can. Consequently, the House of Lords has considerable value as a forum for the consideration of great public issues. While it is divided politically and in an unbalanced fashion, the upper house is rarely sharply or bitterly partisan. Its members are not looking forward to a general election with the same concern as are members of the House of Commons and they do not see in their political opponents individuals whom they will soon meet in a contest for votes.[18]

The value of the House of Lords as a chamber to amend and revise bills coming from the Commons is debatable, but on the whole its activity is generally beneficial. A good deal of its work is for the purpose of correcting technical defects appearing in bills during or after their passage through the lower house. Ministers and their departmental advisers frequently utilize consideration in the House of Lords in order to tidy up a measure that has been subject to numerous amendments while passing through the Commons and to repair previously unnoticed defects of drafting. Consideration by the peers also offers an opportunity for the Government to introduce any of those changes it is prepared to accept after promising in the House of Commons to take amendments under advisement.

---

[17] The high standard of debate on public issues ied Lord Cecil to defend the present composition of the House for this purpose. He wrote during the 1948 controversy: 'As far as discussion is concerned, its performances have been generally approved. They have been marked by expert knowledge, clothed in clear and sometimes eloquent language. That is because its membership includes experts on every topic of public interest, who are compelled to express themselves in a way that ordinary educated individuals—normal citizens—will be able to understand. It is this combination of experts with non-experts that makes the Lords' debates so valuable, and it would be a pity to destroy it. I suggest, therefore, that for purposes of discussion no important change should be made in the composition of the House. True, it involves the use of the hereditary principle in order to obtain the non-expert element. But for that purpose the principle works well and does no harm.' *The Spectator,* 13 February 1948.

[18] Reviewing the record of the Parliament elected in 1945, *The Economist* said: 'On the whole, defence, colonial policy, Commonwealth affairs and general economic policy have been discussed on a much more informed and authoritative plane in the upper than in the lower house. Lord Keynes on the American loan, the India debate, the debates on the Parliament Bill, on Marshall Aid, and on devaluation far outstripped in brilliance and insight their counterparts in the lower house.' 14 January 1950.

There is little question about the value of the kinds of work just mentioned. More controversial is the adoption of non-ministerial amendments that affect the substance of a bill. As Jennings has said, 'What one side regards as common-sense the other considers to be blatant politics in the worse sense.' [19] In general, the peers only amend or revise bills in major particulars when they believe public opinion supports them or will rally to their side. Their defense of this practice is weakened by the fact that they are more apt to insist upon amendments when a Labour Government is in office than when there is a Conservative one. Nevertheless, it is apparent that on occasion the peers have correctly gauged opinion and amended bills in a way that improved them. In 1948, for example, the peers rejected a provision in the Criminal Justice Bill which would have abolished the death penalty in murder cases for an experimental period of five years. Public opinion appeared to support the peers' amendment, and the Government dropped the controversial clause when the bill was again considered in the House of Commons.

One useful activity of the House of Lords is to consider private bills and provisional order confirmation bills. The latter are bills giving approval to departmental orders laid before the House. The work of private bill committees takes much time, and it brings no political renown to those who sit on them. Much of this labor is assumed by peers since about half the private bills introduced at each Parliamentary session first go to the House of Lords. Without this service, members of the House of Commons would be much more severely burdened than they are. Provisional order confirmation bills are also divided about equally between the houses, and in this respect the peers relieve the members of the lower chamber of a good deal of tedious but important work.

The House of Lords may well undergo some reform before many years have passed. Almost all British political institutions have been changed when their salient characteristics have lost touch with the current life of the country. It will be a test of statesmanship to devise a reform of the House of Lords that eliminates its anachronistic features, while at the same time preserving its useful qualities: the intelligent discussion of public issues and the insertion of the amount of delay in lawmaking that insures against the worst mistakes.

---

[19] Op. cit. p. 427.

VIII

Parliament: A Functioning Institution

In its formative period Parliament had no initiative in legislation. It was convened by the King to hear what additional revenue he required and what changes in the law he and his justices proposed to make, and the function of the members was to give their assent to these propositions. Gradually, however, Parliament began to petition for the redress of grievances and for changes in the law of the land, and it was made plain on numerous occasions that parliamentary consent to royal proposals was contingent upon the King's action in meeting these requests. Sometimes the resulting legislation differed considerably from what the petitions contained, for the medieval kings considered themselves qualified to legislate and had no hesitancy in making changes in the parliamentary drafts. Nevertheless, in time Parliament gained the right of initiative in lawmaking, until finally it was the King who assented rather than proposed.

1. *Parliamentary Procedure*

While Parliament was gaining and consolidating its power, the two Houses were also developing rituals and rules to govern and guide their internal business. Their rituals pertain to such matters as the opening and closing of sessions of Parliament, the start of a day's sitting in each House, the conduct of relations between the two houses, and modes of address employed by members to one another.

The opening of a new Parliament is one of the most colorful of the ceremonies at Westminster. With each House assembled in its own chamber, the ceremony begins when an official known as the Gentleman Usher of the Black Rod knocks on the door of the Commons chamber and, upon being admitted, asks the members to attend the Lord Chancellor in the peers' chamber. There, after hearing the royal summons read, the members of the Commons are invited by the Lord Chancellor, speaking for the Lords Commissioners, to return to their chamber and choose a Speaker. The election of the Speaker proceeds by a bit of pantomime which ends when the person chosen, making a show of reluctance and unworthiness, is escorted to his chair by two members. The next day the Speaker, wearing a bob wig and accompanied by many members of the House, announces his election at the bar of the Lords' chamber. The Lord Chancellor signifies the royal approval of the choice. Then the Speaker demands recog-

126–

nition of 'the ancient and undoubted rights and privileges of the Commons,' an assurance which the Lord Chancellor gives. After leading the members of the Commons who have attended him back to their chamber, the Speaker retires to don a full bottomed wig and his robes of office. He then reports to the House that his election has received royal approval and that he has laid claim to the rights and privileges of the Commons.

The Speaker's election completed, the members of the Commons take an oath of allegiance and sign the roll.[1] The following day Black Rod commands the members of the Commons—or the few who can find a place to stand—to return to the upper house to hear the King's speech. The monarch usually opens Parliament in person, riding from Buckingham Palace in a state coach and attended by members of the royal family, palace officials, and an escort of the Household Cavalry. From the throne the King reads a brief message which comments on the general state of the country and indicates the principal legislative measures which will be introduced by his ministers. After hearing the King's speech the members of the Commons return to their chamber where, with the Speaker in the chair, they give a first reading to a 'Bill for the Better Suppressing of Clandestine Outlawries,' a stage property which is used every year in this ceremony to demonstrate that the House of Commons has the right to consider legislation before receiving the King's recommendations.[2] That out of the way, the House is ready to debate and adopt a reply of thanks to the Gracious Speech of His Majesty.

The ceremonies just sketched form part of a considerable body of Parliament ritual which leaves its impress upon the participants and is felt by the members of the public who may read descriptions in the newspapers or hear them over the radio. Some ceremonials symbolize constitutional victories won by Parliament in past centuries, and in days when totalitarian regimes exist not far from London it is well to have reminders that democratic liberties were usually dearly bought. Other ceremonies establish links between the present generation of royalty, ministers, lords, and commoners, and their many predecessors; the current re-enactment takes its place as only another scene in the long pageant of British history. Perhaps the curious inversion of meaning in many of these ceremonies makes them all the more significant. For example, everyone knows that when at the opening of Parliament the King, resplendent in robes of state or in military uniform, reads his speech before the peers, who have gathered clothed in their ermine-decorated robes, he is reading a statement of policy written by some of the comparatively colorless group of commoners who have been able to crowd into the Lords' chamber on this occasion. Their power and authority are underscored by the apparently minor role they play in the spectacle.

---

[1] The oath runs: 'I, John Doe, swear by Almighty God that I will be faithful and bear true allegiance to Her Majesty Queen Elizabeth II, her heirs and successors, according to law. So help me, God.'

[2] This practice was started in 1743. What measures were then proposed remain a mystery, because the contents of a bill are only revealed on its second reading.

Ceremonial and precedent govern a good deal of the procedure of Parliament and influence the spirit of its activities.[3] Even more controlling are the rules of the two houses. Each house is empowered to adopt, amend, repeal, and enforce its rules, and each has a considerable body of standing orders which determine the procedure for different kinds of bills, the allocation of time for private members' business, the appointment of committees, the adjournment of sittings, and similar matters. There are in addition sessional orders and resolutions which are readopted at the beginning of each Parliamentary session. In the House of Commons the rules are declared, interpreted, and enforced by the Speaker. In his interpretation he has the help of the Clerk and the Clerk-Assistant of the House of Commons, who are invariably skilled parliamentarians, and of Counsel to the Speaker. One holder of the office of Clerk-Assistant, Sir Thomas Erskine May, prepared an authoritative collection of the rules and customs of the House which is constantly quoted on disputed points of order.[4] Proposals for changes in the rules go to the sessional Committee on Standing Orders for consideration. In the upper chamber the Lord Chancellor applies the rules to the business before the House, but he does not have the final authority of the Speaker and his rulings may be changed by votes of the House. The Lord Chancellor in his capacity as a presiding officer is assisted by the Clerk of the Parliaments who is always an authority on rules and procedure.

2. *Parliamentary Legislation: Public Bills*

Parliament devotes a great part of its time to the debate and passage of legislation. While its authority in this respect is well established, it is important to note that in modern times the initiative in proposing legislation has largely passed from the hands of the non-ministerial members of Parliament into the hands of the Government. Consequently, the measures that Parliament debates and passes are, with few exceptions, those introduced by ministers and sponsored by the Government of the day. Although this dominance of the Government tends to depreciate the legislative work

---

[3] Changes in social manners and habits sometimes make it difficult to maintain old Parliamentary customs. For example, in 1951 a member of the House of Commons questioned the practice, dating from the eighteenth century, which requires the member who desires to raise a point of order with the Chair during a division to remain 'seated and covered.' He pointed out that the days when all members wore top hats were gone, and that in a hunt for a hat of some kind 'the chase is often undignified and even unseemly.' He was supported by a woman member who said that some representatives of her sex 'often came into the House with headgear which was not noticeable.' The suggestion was made that the Serjeant at Arms keep a 'Parliamentary hat' for the use of members wishing to raise a point of order. The Speaker said he wanted to consult all sections of the House before changing 'so old a practice.'

[4] The 15th edition of *Sir T. Erskine May's Treatise on Privileges, Proceedings and Usage of Parliament,* edited by Lord Campion, a former Clerk of the House of Commons, was published in 1950.

of Parliament to a less important place than it occupied in the nineteenth century, it restores, in a sense, the relationship which formerly existed between the executive and the legislature. The old formula that laws are enacted by the King-in-Parliament has been given its former meaning, with Crown now substituted for the King.

In describing the legislative work of Parliament, it is useful to distinguish immediately between two kinds of bills that are considered and enacted. These are public bills and private bills, and there is a separate procedure for each. Public bills are legislative measures which have a general application, i.e. they relate to the country as a whole and affect all persons or interests coming under their provisions.[5] Private bills have only a limited territorial application and relate to some special interest. Many private bills deal with the rights and powers of local authorities and have no effect beyond the municipality named in the bill.

There is a sub-category of public bills known as private members' bills. These are bills of general application introduced by a private member, i.e. a non-ministerial member of Parliament. They represent the last vestige of Parliament as a legislative body where any member may introduce a proposal and seek the support of a majority to get it enacted into law. The procedure for bills of this kind will be described later, and it will then be seen that the opportunities for legislation by private members are not numerous.

Before describing the Parliamentary procedure for public bills, we should consider the sources of proposals which are to be translated into law. In a technical sense, the principal source is the Government. All public bills are introduced on its behalf with the exception of the relatively few private members' bills. The Government is prompted to introduce bills for a variety of reasons. It must introduce and pass a number of annual measures in order to keep the machinery of the state running. These include the Finance Bill, the Appropriation Bill, the Consolidated Fund Bills, the Expiring Laws Continuance Bill, and the Army and Air Force Bills. Then there are usually a few policies or administrative activities dependent on legislation of definite duration which must be extended or amended by new statutes.

With a good share of Parliamentary time absorbed by these obligatory measures, the Government has the problem of allotting the balance in the most satisfactory way. It must introduce several bills to fulfill its election promises and to satisfy major interests supporting the party. Furthermore, nearly every government department has one or more bills, arising from its administrative experience, which it is trying to get enacted. A number of these will get introduced during a Parliamentary session, and the choice will depend upon how important they appear to the Cabinet, how con-

---

[5] Financial measures fall in the class of public bills. The Parliamentary procedure with respect to financial bills has been largely omitted from this chapter in order to discuss in Chapter IX the whole subject of central government finance.

troversial they are, how much time is available, and how influential different ministers are. Frequently these bills will have been discussed with, and perhaps initiated by, departmental advisory committees, groups of governmental and private specialists appointed on either a continuing or *ad hoc* basis by ministers.[6] In addition, unforeseen events and emergencies necessitate the introduction of a few bills in every Parliamentary session. Bills may originate, moreover, with pressure groups, either existing organizations or ones formed to sponsor a particular measure. By arousing enough interest both within Parliament and outside, they persuade the Government to prepare and introduce the bills they are advocating.

Some proposals for legislation are made by royal commissions. These are committees established by the Government to investigate and to report upon subjects of public interest. Usually the subjects are ones which require the collection and weighing of considerable evidence, activities which the regular committees of Parliament do not have time to undertake. Royal commissions are customarily composed of members of Parliament and private citizens, and an attempt is made to give representation to all interested groups and shades of opinion. A well-known public figure is usually named as chairman, and a civil servant from an interested department serves as secretary. A commission will hear witnesses, sometimes scores of them, and receive written statements from many individuals and organized groups. It finally prepares a report with recommendations of the executive or legislative action it deems desirable. Dissenting members often submit one or more minority reports. Occasionally a royal commission prepares a draft bill.

While Governments are sometimes accused of appointing royal commissions to avoid the necessity of taking unpalatable policy decisions, the practice on the whole is a highly commendable one. Performing the kind of work that is frequently done by legislative committees in the United States, they are rarely charged with political bias and their methods of gathering information are always above reproach. The effort to compose a commission of all shades of opinion sometimes results in a set of straddling conclusions, but even when this happens the collected evidence and the discussion of the problem have value. Ministers, of course, are under no obligation to accept the recommendations of a royal commission, but the political opposition and outside interest groups usually see to it that some action results. In practice, royal commissions are the source of a substantial amount of parliamentary legislation.

---

[6] Concerning the use of advisory committees, an American scholar has said: 'While the departmental or interdepartmental advisory committee is not the most significant agency affecting policy formation, its real importance has seldom been properly stressed. Much more attention has been given to the royal commissions and parliamentary committees that work in public. . . The evidence indicates that these advisory agencies have exerted considerable influence, although its exact extent is difficult to appraise.' Charles Aikin, 'The British Bureaucracy and the Origins of Parliamentary Policy, II,' *The American Political Science Review,* April 1939, pp. 225-6.

Whether a bill arises out of the election commitments of the dominant party, the administrative activities of a department, or the recommendations of a royal commission, it will receive Cabinet consideration before being introduced in Parliament. Cabinet consideration will first be given, in most cases, by one of the Cabinet committees. For example, a bill to introduce conscription for the armed forces would probably be first considered, as a matter of policy, in the Defence Committee of the Cabinet. Here the major issues of policy involved would be discussed and decided upon. A proposal of this importance would certainly go before the entire Cabinet and changes in some of its major features might result from this consideration. Meanwhile, it is likely that the most interested minister would be holding consultations with outside groups or bodies which could be expected to have strong views upon such a subject. A Labour Government would undoubtedly want to sound out the trade unions and receive their opinions before proceeding with the bill in Parliament. Once Cabinet approval has been given, the minister who will introduce and sponsor the bill in Parliament will have the measure drawn up in its proper form. This will be done by Parliamentary Counsel of the Treasury, the authority on form and language for public bills. Finally, the Legislation Committee of the Cabinet must give its approval to this draft bill.

These preliminary steps completed, a minister will introduce the bill in the House of Commons and ask for the reading of the measure.[7] Introduction consists of having the title of the bill printed on the order paper for the day and handing a copy, or a dummy supplied by the Public Bill Office of the House, to the Clerk at the table. The Clerk reads the title of the bill, and this constitutes its first reading. The bill is immediately printed and circulated to the members of the House. On rare occasions the Government reverts to a procedure which was once universal, namely, requesting leave to introduce a bill. The purpose of this action would be to enable a minister to make a statement concerning the reasons for introducing the bill and to permit the opposition an opportunity to speak against it at this stage. After the Government and the opposition have made their statements, the House would vote to allow the introduction of the bill, a formality which the Government's majority would guarantee.

Nonfinancial bills may be introduced in the House of Lords as well as in the House of Commons, and any peer may present a bill without giving notice. Except for private bills, not many measures are introduced in the upper house, however. Occasionally a bill that raises no political issues of importance will be introduced in the Lords where its provisions are apt to receive more consideration than time will permit in the lower house. For example, in 1949 the Government introduced in the Lords a Patents

---

[7] In form a bill consists of a long title setting forth the purposes for which legislation is desired; a short title; the clauses giving the main provisions of the bill, and the schedules, containing details of the measure and lists of bodies and statutes affected. Occasionally a bill contains a preamble which sets forth assertions about the necessity of the proposed legislation.

and Designs Bill, the subject matter of which was technically important but not politically divisive.

At the first reading in the Commons a date is set for the second reading. This is theoretically the next Monday, but in practice it is a time selected by the leaders managing the Government's legislative program. The second reading is the occasion for a debate upon the general principle involved in the measure. The minister most concerned with the bill usually starts the debate, moving 'that the bill be now read a second time.' In the example of a bill on military conscription, the Minister of Defence would probably introduce the debate, and he would explain the background of the measure, why the Government wishes it passed, and develop the principal policy issues involved. Some leading member of the opposition would follow, probably a former minister who has some competence in the subject matter of the bill. He might move to amend the minister's motion by striking out 'now' and adding 'on this day six months,' or some time beyond the expected end of the session. Alternatively, he might propose a substantive amendment to the policy embodied in the bill. Then would ensue a general debate in which many members on both sides of the House would participate, and it would end with a minister winding up for the Government. Backbench members who wish to speak on the bill must take their chances of 'catching the Speaker's eye,' and an individual M.P. may spend many hours in 'bumping,' that is, rising for recognition and then resuming his seat when passed over, before being called to deliver his views.

Upon the conclusion of the debate, there would be a division, a vote on the measure. An adverse vote would mean, of course, that the Government would have to resign or seek from the King a dissolution of the House of Commons. A favorable vote would mean that the bill goes to a committee for further consideration. A measure of special importance and any financial bill would go to the Committee of the Whole House, while other bills would be referred to one of the standing committees of the House. A bill dealing only with Scotland would automatically go to the standing committee known as the Scottish Committee, and for such bills even the second reading is a formality.[8]

In committee, the bill would be taken up and debated clause by clause, and it might suffer changes and amendments at this stage. These changes and amendments would have to be agreed to by the Government, for it could always insist upon its original version and among its own supporters make the matter one of confidence in the Ministry. Upon the completion of its deliberations, the committee reports to the full House. If no amendments have been made in committee the bill is ordered read a third time; if amended, it enters the report stage. Further amendments may be proposed at this stage.

The next step is for the bill to receive a third reading, which is little

---

[8] Cmd. 7308 (1948).

132–

more than an opportunity for both sides to state their positions again. No substantive amendments are in order. Rejection on third reading is unlikely since the crucial vote has been taken at the second reading.

The bill now goes to the House of Lords for its consideration, and much the same procedure is followed there. If the House of Lords amends the bill in any particular, it must be returned to the House of Commons for consideration of these changes. Often they are accepted by the Commons; if they are not, the dissenting House sends to the Lords a statement of its disagreement. In case the House of Lords will not retreat from its position, the bill must fail, but since the peers rarely insist upon changes that are objected to by a majority of the House of Commons, the views of the latter are almost certain to prevail. For many centuries there was a procedure whereby, in cases of disagreement, the two houses would appoint 'managers' who would attempt to reconcile the differences, a method similar to that practiced by the Congress of the United States when the Senate and the House of Representatives appoint conference committees. Parliament has not used this procedure for almost a hundred years. It will be recalled that under the provisions of the Parliament Act of 1911 the power of the House of Lords to delay a money bill is limited to one month, so unless the Lords propose an amendment of obvious validity their action on such a bill will have no effect upon the lower house.

After differences between the two houses have been resolved, the bill is ready for the royal assent. Although this is a matter of form today—the royal veto has not been employed since 1707 when Queen Anne refused her assent to a bill—the royal assent is a recognition of the legal situation that legislation is a function of the King-in-Parliament. It is given by three commissioners appointed by the Lord Chancellor for this purpose, and the ceremony used is one that has come down from medieval England. After a clerk of the House of Lords reads the commission authorizing the assent —usually a number of bills receive the assent in one ceremony—the Clerk of the Crown reads the title of each bill, and the Clerk of the Parliaments gives the approval in the appropriate Norman-French phrase. For the ordinary public bill he says, *Le Roy le veult*. For a supply bill, one appropriating money to the Crown, he declares, *Le Roy remercie ses bon sujets, accepte leur benevolence et ainsi le veult*. In olden times the monarch's disapproval of a bill presented for his assent was expressed in the words, *Le Roy s'avisera*. With the royal assent the bill has become a law, and two copies, printed on special vellum, are deposited respectively in the Rolls of Parliament and in the Public Record Office.[9]

It will be noted that the principal opportunities for debate occur on the second reading of a bill and in the committee stage. Debate on these occasions might stretch out interminably but for parliamentary rules known

---

[9] A Statute Law Committee has been engaged in recent years in preparing a new edition of *Revised Statutes*. In 1948 Parliament passed a bill prepared by the Committee to eliminate obsolete and superseded laws enacted between 1235 and 1800. A second bill will cover the period 1800 to 1948. *The Times,* 15 December 1949.

as closure. The simplest form of closure is a motion that the question be put to a vote by the Speaker or, in committee, by the chairman. He will not entertain such a motion, however, until he is satisfied that an adequate discussion has taken place and that the opposition has had an opportunity to state its case. When a complicated bill is before the House of Commons, it is customary for the Government to work out a timetable to control the progress of the measure. It sometimes resorts to closure by compartments or a 'guillotine' motion. Under this procedure debate is permitted for a limited time and then the question is put. Opposition agreement to legislative timetables is occasionally obtained through 'the usual channels,' that is, the party whips.

Debate may be further restricted by the Speaker's authority under the standing orders of the House to select, at the report stage, proposed amendments for discussion. This form of limitation of debate, called 'the kangaroo' because it jumps over some amendments, is also exercised by the chairmen of committees. The Speaker or chairman does not give the reasons for his choice but simply announces the amendments he has selected for debate. This power is vested in the presiding officer in order to insure that the most important amendments and those raising issues not previously debated are reached. Closure is frequently criticized for the rather ruthless way it limits debate and prevents many members from presenting their views, but it is difficult to see how a Government could place a legislative program on the statute books without resort to procedural control of this kind. 'The closure, the kangaroo, and the guillotine,' Sir Ivor Jennings has said, 'are the instruments for driving legislation through at a reasonable pace.' [10]

It may be noticed that parliamentary closure rules obviate filibustering, at least in the manner occasionally practiced in the United States Senate. From time to time, nevertheless, members attempt to obstruct the business of the House. They may offer dilatory motions asking for the adjournment of the House or of a committee, call the Speaker's attention to the absence of a quorum, which is 40 members, or attempt to 'talk out' an objectionable bill. These measures, however, are of little avail when the Government majority desires that the business before the House progress. Also, irrelevant speech-making is soon halted by Mr. Speaker. He is obliged to give opposition members a fair chance to state their case, but he is the guardian of the majority's rights as well.

Let us turn now to the procedure for private members' bills, which were mentioned earlier. Any member of the House of Commons may introduce a bill, either by giving notice of the title of the bill or by a motion made at the beginning of public business on Tuesdays and Wednesdays for leave to bring in a bill. The latter method is known as the ten minutes rule from the fact that the speeches for and against the motion are limited to that length of time. Not many members take advantage of their right to intro-

---

[10] *Parliament*, op. cit. p. 237.

duce bills, because their efforts are largely futile, apart perhaps from some publicity, unless assured time for a second reading. The standing orders allot a number of Fridays throughout a session for private members' business when bills can receive second readings, although Governments are rather prone to invade this time when their own schedule is pressed. At any rate, the normal time available will suffice for the consideration of about 20 private members' bills. For the opportunity of a second reading the members of the House draw lots. When one of the fortunate members has no bill which he wishes to sponsor, he may agree to introduce the bill of a member less lucky in the ballot.

After introduction the bill follows the usual procedure for a public bill. If opposed by the Government, the bill probably dies an early death, for it is not likely to survive the second reading. If the Government has no objection to the bill, it may win sufficient support throughout the House to surmount all the hurdles of procedure and receive the royal assent. During the bill's passage through Parliament its sponsor must be alert lest some procedural fault terminate his ambition to be the author of a statute. Sir A. P. Herbert, independent member for Oxford University from 1935 to 1950, has related some of the problems facing the M.P. who is endeavoring to pilot a private member's bill to a safe haven. The private member, he has written, 'begins to think better of Whips and others in authority.'

> For he has to do himself so many bits of drill which he has always seen done by the Whips before—and they seemed so easy then. If he wants to prevent his Bill being 'talked out' he must butt in at the right moment and move 'that the Question be now put.' If there is a division, he can no longer stroll into the Lobby indicated by the Whips, chatting airily with a friend. He is in charge now: he must organize and lead. He must arrange for one of his supporters to be the other 'Teller' (two 'Tellers,' one for each side, stand outside each Lobby, and one counts the Members as they come out); he must decide which of them will take the 'Aye' Lobby and which the 'No,' and make sure that the other fellow knows where to go (which, in the excitement, may be very necessary). Then he must remember to give the names of his 'Tellers' to the Speaker, which is easily forgotten, and, if forgotten, ruins all. Even now he dares not scurry off to his 'Telling' post at the Lobby door. He must wait in the Chamber and make sure that a few Members shout 'Aye!' (or 'No!') when the Speaker puts the question for the last time two minutes later. If this is not done the division is 'off'—and the Member is an ass. Then, breathless and excited, he must press through the crowd of Members surging into the Chamber to vote, and take his place for the counting. Then, when the figures have been handed to the Clerk at the Table here is the ritual announcement. The four Tellers line up, bow, and advance one pace. The senior Teller on the winning side announces the figures. The

Speaker repeats them, and the Tellers bow again, if possible together. It all sounds simple, and looks simple, when the Whips do it; but, after much experience, one can still make mistakes, and I confess that I have rarely done the bowing to my satisfaction.

If he gets a majority for his Second Reading, the unofficial Member has a long steeplechase before him—Committee upstairs—the Report Stage—Third Reading. His Whips, of course, if he is a party man, are still his guides, philosophers, and friends, and will advise him in the background, but many things he can only do for himself.

He is now a Minister in miniature, and must use the same arts— know when to accept an amendment and when to stick his toes in, how to keep his friends eager and his enemies calm. Many a Minister, I dare say, has been glad of this training.[11]

During the last war, the Government decided that it must monopolize the entire legislative time of the House of Commons, and consequently it abolished the periods for considering private members' bills. This privilege has since been restored, but the time allotted for the consideration of these bills is so limited that very few ever get to the point of receiving the royal assent.[12]

3. *Parliamentary Legislation: Private Bills*

The second principal class of parliamentary bills, private bills, must go through the major stages of other legislation, but the procedure differs considerably from that pertaining to public bills. As mentioned previously, private bills deal with a special situation or a limited locality, and the great majority concern the rights and powers of local authorities. Since such rights and powers cannot in some instances be abridged or modified except by parliamentary action, it is necessary to introduce a bill for this purpose.

Before a private bill can be considered by Parliament, a petition setting forth the purpose of the proposed legislation and the estimate of any costs involved must be submitted to the Examiner of Petitions for Private Bills of either the House of Commons or the House of Lords. The sponsor of the legislation must also notify the government department most concerned

---

[11] A. P. Herbert, *Independent Member* (New York, 1951), pp. 65-6.

[12] Of 23 private members' bills given a first reading on 28 January 1949, 5 eventually were enacted into law. Various fates attended the 18 which perished between introduction and the royal assent. Only 11 survived the second reading stage. The Government's disapproval and the lack of Parliamentary time disposed of several. The promise on the part of the Government to meet the purposes of the bill by administrative action caused two to be dropped. The House of Commons defeated two by free votes on second reading. Several of the private members' bills introduced were concerned with the protection of animals. They included bills to abolish fox hunting, to limit the time worked by pit ponies, to license pet shops, to prevent cock fighting, and to regulate the docking and nicking of horses.

with the project and all affected interests. If one of the Examiners of Private Bills certifies that these requirements have been complied with, the petition with the bill attached may be introduced in Parliament. Of the private bills presented at a parliamentary session approximately half are introduced in each House. Should no opposition develop to a private bill, it proceeds through the various legislative stages without attracting any particular attention. At the committee stage, it goes to a committee on unopposed bills which gives it perfunctory consideration. Should the bill be opposed, it is referred to one of a number of private bill committees which are appointed in each House at the beginning of a parliamentary session. Private bill committees in the House of Commons are composed of four members and in the House of Lords of five members. Members of Parliament do not, as a rule, care for service on these committees, since they take much time and bring little public recognition. All non-ministerial members of the two Houses are eligible to serve on these committees unless they have interests or constituents who would be affected by bills under consideration.

The procedure in private bill committees is quasi-judicial. The sponsor and opponents of a bill, e.g. a municipal government and the private corporations or private individuals affected, employ legal counsel to present their arguments, and expert witnesses frequently testify to the merits or defects of a proposed bill. Sometimes the hearings are quite involved and protracted. In the end the committee decides whether the purpose of the bill as declared in its preamble is or is not desirable; if a favorable decision is reached, the committee considers the detailed provisions of the bill. A bill favorably considered by a committee is then reported to the House with or without amendments. A favorably reported bill almost invariably has a smooth passage from then on. It may possibly be opposed during its passage through the second House, but such opposition is not common.

The procedure for private bills relieves Parliament of a great deal of legislative work which is of interest to only a limited number of people. Except for the members serving on private bill committees, no other members of Parliament are required to participate beyond procedural formalities. A second merit of the procedure lies in the provision for a quasi-judicial hearing which brings out the advantages and disadvantages of the proposal without the bill becoming a political issue in the usual sense.

The need for private bill legislation has been reduced somewhat by the increasing use of provisional orders and statutory schemes. The first are orders issued by a government department upon the request of a local authority; when approved by Parliament they have statutory effect. Each year these orders are compiled into a number of provisional orders confirmation bills, which are passed by Parliament. In most instances, they go through without objection, but should any exception be taken to a provisional order, it would become invalid and the party sponsoring it would then have to proceed through a private bill. Statutory schemes are plans or programs for the development of a municipal service which are submitted by a local authority to a minister, who after consideration may either approve, reject, or amend the scheme. If approved, it is usually then laid before Parliament and becomes legally binding. The method of statutory schemes is extensively used in connection with such municipal functions as education, town and country planning, and public health.

In a consideration of Parliament's legislative function, mention should be made of lobbying, i.e. the efforts of persons or organizations to influence the legislature in behalf of their special interests. This kind of activity is not as prevalent at Westminster as it is in some capitals. There appear to be two reasons for the relative absence of lobbying activities. One, and the more important, is the strict control the Cabinet maintains over legislative measures; the cultivation of a member by a lobbyist would be largely in vain however sympathetically he reacted. The second reason is that many of the interests concerned with influencing Parliament are well represented by spokesmen there. Several dozen salaried officials of trade unions sit on the Labour side of the House of Commons, and on the benches opposite are company directors and members connected with various business interests. Other M.P.'s take a special interest in such matters as agriculture, shipbuilding, local government affairs, veterans' welfare, and housing. These members exert their influence in party councils, but party discipline prevents them carrying their advocacy beyond the point which the leadership is prepared to accept.

Although lobbying activities are a relatively minor problem at Westminster, and Parliament has never considered registration or other control measures necessary, there are many societies and organizations presenting their causes and programs to the members of Parliament. Some of them have draft bills ready for any sympathetic M.P. who happens to win an opportunity to sponsor a private member's bill. By and large, however, their principal targets must be the Government or the big movements behind its party organization—say, the T.U.C. in the case of Labour—and not individual members of Parliament.[13]

4. *The Critical Function of Parliament*

It has been estimated that, apart from financial business, about two-fifths of Parliament's time is devoted to the consideration of bills.[14] The balance

---

[13] A few years ago there was some concern about the activities of 'contact men,' individuals who claimed to be able to procure permits, licenses, and exemptions more expeditiously than ordinary applicants could. When appointing a committee to inquire into their activities, the Prime Minister said, 'There is also a type of contact man who appears to make an improper use of the facilities of the House,' and he announced that the Speaker had consented to review 'the existing rules as to the admission of strangers to the precincts of the House.' *The Times,* 4 February 1949.

[14] Jennings, op. cit. p. 5.

of its time is given to other activities which are as necessary as legislation in the functioning of democratic government. One of these is the statement and debate of major policy issues. It is important in the conduct of democratic government that there be frequent occasions when the authorities in power state their purposes and objectives and when their opponents have an opportunity to challenge these and to point out what they consider to be errors and deficiencies of policy. In Great Britain, Parliament serves as the principal stage for this kind of policy review.

There are several stated occasions when the general policy of a Government is declared and debated, and during the course of a Parliamentary session other opportunities arise for debates on important aspects of public policy. The King's speech at the opening of Parliament, prepared by his ministers, serves as a general declaration of the aims and intentions of the Government, and in the ensuing debate on the speech there is an opportunity for ministers to explain their policies more fully and for their opponents to criticize. The budget speech of the Chancellor of the Exchequer is another occasion when the general lines of Government policy are exposed and when the opposition can turn its heaviest guns upon the ministerial position. It is customary to have two or three full-dress debates on foreign policy during a parliamentary session.

The 26 Parliamentary days allotted to supply—the estimates of expenditure for the next financial year—provide opportunities for policy debates. By custom the topics for most of these debates are selected by the opposition; such matters as munitions production, colonial development, assistance to agriculture, and the public housing program may be taken up in connection with the pertinent estimates submitted by the Government. The debates are not concerned with detailed financial proposals but focus on a series of policies and programs reflected in the estimates. Furthermore, debates on the second reading of important pieces of legislation—for example, changes in the powers of the House of Lords or bills to nationalize important industries—may become general critiques of Government policy, even though the issue itself is not so broad. For the Government, all these occasions are opportunities to inform the rank-and-file party members in Parliament of its aims, but more importantly they serve to enlighten and persuade the public. For the opposition, these debates are useful to stimulate party members and to win converts among the voters.

Parliament considers that it has a right to hear from ministers the first statement of any significant governmental policy. Unlike the custom in the United States, British ministers rarely hold press conferences or give interviews; they consider that the place for them to make statements of policy or voice opinions is in the parliamentary chamber of which they are a member. The opposition in Parliament would object strenuously to a curtailment of its privilege of challenging ministers in face-to-face debate on policy questions. Of course, ministers as well as other members of Parliament make frequent public speeches, both to their constituents and to

−139

other audiences, and such addresses may contain announcements and explanations of important policy matters. When they do, the policies discussed will undoubtedly be raised soon in one House or the other and defended or criticized there.[15]

In summary, then, Parliament serves today as a forum in which the Government, at periodic intervals, declares the aims of its policies and the opposition exposes ministerial deficiencies and proposes alternative solutions. The public is regularly being informed of what the Government is trying to do, and voters are able to judge the merits of the arguments put forward by ministers and their opponents.

Usually parliamentary procedure requires that a vote—a division—follow a major debate on policy issues. If the debate follows the King's speech from the throne, the vote is on the Government's request to make a reply of thanks to His Majesty. This the opposition will endeavor to amend. On other occasions the debate may be on the second reading of a bill or on a motion of censure introduced by the opposition. In Committee of Supply the opposition will move to reduce the estimate under consideration for a department or a service by a nominal amount, say £100.

Whatever the parliamentary procedure that occasions the vote, the size of the Government's majority is usually indicative of the success attained by the respective sides in the preceding debate. Almost invariably party discipline is sufficiently strong to win a majority for the Government, and the most the opposition can hope for is to reduce the Government's vote from its normal strength. A small majority on a critical vote shows that the Government made a poor case for its policy and that it has lost the confidence, at least temporarily, of some of its own party members. In describing a debate in the House of Commons at the time of the invasion of Norway in 1940, Churchill has pointed out that the Chamberlain Ministry, although winning a majority, failed to convince the House of the correctness of its policy. 'The Government had a majority of eighty-one, but over fifty Conservatives voted with the Labour and Liberal oppositions, and there was no doubt that in effect, though not in form, both the debate and the division were a violent manifestation of want of confidence in Mr. Chamberlain and his Administration.' [16] Chamberlain quickly recognized this loss of confidence, and a few days later Churchill became Prime Minister in his stead.

A word should be said about voting in Parliament. The initiative in forcing a vote, or division, is usually taken by the opposition. The oppo-

---

[15] Sir Stafford Cripps, former Chancellor of the Exchequer, was subject to some criticism for announcing the devaluation of the pound sterling on 18 September 1949, in a radio broadcast. Although Parliament was not sitting, the Government quickly consented to an opposition demand that it be recalled for a debate on devaluation and its consequences.

[16] *The Gathering Storm*, p. 660.

sition under the direction of its leader challenges the Government by contesting the passage of a bill or resolution, by seeking to amend Government measures, or by moving a formal motion of censure. Occasionally the Government forces a division by a motion of confidence if it feels that its own supporters are getting a little out of hand. When the Speaker, or the Chairman of Committees if the House is in Committee of the Whole House, puts the question, he calls for the ayes and nays and announces what seems to be the result. If objection is raised, he calls for the House to divide. Bells ring in all the public rooms of the Parliament building to call the members to the chamber. Members have two minutes to reach the chamber before the doors are closed. The Speaker or Chairman again puts the question. The members then march into one of two lobbies adjoining the chamber, one for those supporting the Government and one for those opposing it. Two whips from each side act as tellers. In case of a tie, the Speaker or Chairman of Committees has a casting vote, and he uses it to keep alive the issue under consideration.

When the Government has only a small majority in the Commons, a division can be a dramatic occasion. The whips of each side get out every member who is physically able to attend, and sometimes they rouse an ailing member from his bed of pain. In the Parliament elected in 1950 the Government won a number of divisions by majorities of from one to fifteen votes. Pairing is practiced, i.e. a member desiring to be absent at the time of an important vote agrees with an opposition member, through the whips, that neither will appear for the division. Occasionally the Government 'takes off the whips' and permits a free vote. This may be done when the issue is one about which the party has no policy position. Questions of public morality which cut across party lines are sometimes settled, at least so far as Parliament can settle them, by free votes.

5. *The Question Hour*

The Government is not only challenged and required to defend itself in formal debates throughout a Parliamentary session but it is regularly subjected to the questions of private members. In the House of Commons the first 45 minutes after the opening formalities of four daily sessions a week are set aside for questions directed at ministerial members. The procedure of the House provides that any non-ministerial member may submit through the Clerk at the table a maximum of three questions to be answered by the Government. Two days' notice must be given. Printed on the order paper for the day, questions may deal with matters of high policy or with relatively insignificant incidents of bureaucratic arrogance or inefficiency. No question, however, may accuse a minister of bad faith or impugn his motives.

A minister may refuse to answer a question if he believes the public interest would not be served by a discussion of the subject matter at that time. Occasionally, ministers do state that they are not in a position to

–141

answer a question.[17] It is sometimes deemed undesirable to discuss matters being negotiated with other countries, and the Foreign Secretary will say that he is not in a position at this time to give the information requested. Ministers, as a rule, do not care to avail themselves of the privilege of refusal for the inference can rarely be avoided that the Government has something to conceal or is embarrassed by the question. A refusal to answer is almost certain to lead to questions in the future, so it is usually deemed preferable to meet the issue when first raised.

Questions are directed to the minister responsible for the policy or activity inquired about. Thus, a question about the size of the military forces would be directed to the Minister of Defence and answered by him. A question about the socialized medical service would be directed to the Minister of Health who would give the reply. A question about a broad policy matter would probably be answered by the Prime Minister or perhaps the minister responsible for leading the Government majority in the House. In case a minister to whom a question is directed cannot be present in the House, the answer will be given by the parliamentary secretary of the department. The parliamentary secretary will also answer questions if the minister is sitting in the House of Lords. The answers to questions which cannot be reached because of time limitations are printed in the Parliamentary proceedings of the day.

The Government sometimes uses the Question Hour to squelch a rumor or to correct a piece of false information. A co-operative member will ask a question which a minister will answer in a forthright fashion.

If a questioner is dissatisfied with the answer he receives, he may follow up his inquiry with supplementary questions. Other members may join him in putting supplementary questions. These must definitely be related to the original question and not raise new issues. The Speaker of the House enforces this rule very strictly. Occasionally he is forced to reprove a member for attempting to make a statement in place of asking a supplementary question. Some members acquire considerable skill in the phrasing of both original and supplementary questions, and through the choice of words and phrases their queries carry overtones that do not escape the House or the public.

The replies of a minister to a series of questions in the House of Commons suggest an omniscience that is, of course, beyond the ability of any minister. A Foreign Secretary on the same day may answer questions concerning Great Britain's relations with France, the Government's policy as declared in some organ of the United Nations, and the activities of an obscure consul in South America. He is able to give answers to such diversified questions because the necessary inquiries have been made and the

---

[17] On 12 December 1949, a Labour M.P. asked the Minister of Supply 'whether this country was now able to manufacture the atomic bomb.' The Minister replied, 'It would not be in the public interest for me to answer this question.' 470 *H.C. Debates* 5s., col. 2337.

replies prepared by civil servants of the Foreign Office. They write out the answers and the minister reads them in the House. When supplementary questions arise the minister is on his own, and sometimes the difference between a successful and an unsuccessful minister depends upon the skill with which he deals with questions in the House. The clumsy handling of questions by a minister will almost certainly cause the opposition to press the attack more vigorously, and a poor performance repeated on several occasions can damage the prestige of a Government. Quick thinking, caution, and a proper amount of frankness are requisites during the time a minister is on his feet in the question hour.

As a device for holding a Government to account for its policies and administrative activities the question period is highly successful. During a parliamentary session a Government will have to answer several hundred questions posed by sharp and eager critics. Granted that many questions are frivolous and some insignificant when placed along side the great issues of the day, it is nevertheless true that much important information is elicited and many bureaucratic blunders exposed. The Question Hour is a way of keeping government from becoming indifferent to the impact of administration upon the private citizen and his interest. The highest minister of state can be called upon to explain an incident of bureaucratic callousness affecting some plain citizen in a remote part of the country. In these days when the public is increasingly dependent upon the services of the state and the life of the private citizen is more and more ordered by laws and regulations, it is of value to have a procedure whereby the frictions in the administrative machine are quickly called to the attention of the most responsible officials of the nation. The few hours of parliamentary time devoted to this purpose each week are well spent in keeping government responsive to the problems and desires of ordinary citizens.

Should the minister's replies to the original question and then the supplementary questions still leave the interrogating member dissatisfied, he may give notice that he intends to raise the matter upon adjournment. Then at the end of the day's session, when the motion to adjourn is open to debate, the questioner may pursue his subject in direct form. The minister, of course, has an opportunity to reply. While many of these adjournment debates deal with matters of limited interest, they sometimes are concerned with an important policy question, and an alert opposition can give the Government some uncomfortable moments. The right of members to raise matters upon adjournment is another means of holding the Ministry accountable and of enabling Parliament to exercise its critical responsibility.[18]

The House of Lords also has time set aside for directing questions to ministers and for their replies. Moreover, it is possible to institute a debate

---

[18] After the question period at the opening of a daily session a member may move to adjourn to consider 'a definite matter of urgent public importance.' If the Speaker is satisfied that the member's topic can be included under this definition and 40 M.P.'s support the motion, the usual order of business is suspended.

in the House of Lords on almost any public issue. The procedure is for a member of the House to ask for a discussion and to 'move for papers.' This requires the ministerial members of the House to agree to a time for the discussion of the issue and to prepare all relevant material that may be needed in the debate. Under the liberal rules of the House, such debates range widely and insure that the question gets a thorough airing. The standard of discussion is high, and anyone troubling to read the speeches that are made will probably have a better understanding of the question than he could obtain in almost any other way. Such debates are not pressed to a vote, and it is customary for the one who raised the issue to ask at the end of the debate for leave to withdraw his motion. His purpose has been served by getting the matter discussed and by leaving to public opinion the decision whether or not the Government made an adequate defense of its policy. Since many of the debates in the House of Lords are conducted by recognized authorities upon the questions at issue, the Government cannot be insensitive to the impressions created about the correctness or effectiveness of its policies.

The importance of Parliament as a forum for the discussion and debate of public issues and the criticism of ministerial action has taken on increasing significance at the same time that its legislative responsibility has declined. It has been pointed out that the initiative in legislation has been taken by the Cabinet and the administrative departments which ministers head. The opportunity for a private member of Parliament to sponsor legislation is very restricted, and the chances of such legislation being enacted are small. The private member's function today, therefore, is to contribute to the discussion of proposals placed before Parliament and to maintain a vigilant eye upon the stewardship of the Government. He cannot sponsor important legislation, but he can see to it that such legislation as is passed represents the best thought of Parliament and that it is administered as efficiently and as fairly as possible.

IX

National Finance

For many decades now the amount of money collected from the people of Britain in the form of taxes and the sums spent by their government departments have steadily increased. Today it is estimated that about 40 per cent of the total of all incomes in the United Kingdom passes through the Treasury. The use for public purposes of such a large proportion of the current wealth of the country cannot fail to have its effect upon the whole national life. In a sense, therefore, when Parliament and the Cabinet are considering the collection of revenue and the appropriation of funds they are dealing with the entire national budget, for the disposition of what is left in private hands will be greatly affected by public policy.

Parliament gained its position of supremacy by obtaining control over the nation's purse. It early acquired the power to determine the amount of revenue to be collected and the kinds of levies to be imposed to produce this revenue. It extended its control, too, over the purposes for which public money was spent. In modern times the financial power of Parliament has been complete: every tax, duty, or impost paid by the citizen must have been voted by Parliament and every shilling spent by a government department must have been appropriated by the legislature.

1. *The Formulation of Financial Policy*

Parliament concerns itself with the following aspects of public finance—the raising of revenue, the appropriation of the money collected, the issue of money to the spending authorities, and the auditing of the government's financial transactions. In determining the amount of money to be raised, the ways in which this is to be done, and the purposes for which the revenue is to be spent, Parliament is guided by the Cabinet. The Cabinet formulates financial policy, submits to Parliament proposals for raising revenue and for spending it, and steers measures through the legislature until they are enacted into law. The initiative in financial matters, as in other policy areas, is taken by the Ministry; Parliament's function is to debate, criticize, and finally approve what the Cabinet recommends.

The minister responsible for financial policy is the Chancellor of the Exchequer. He naturally occupies one of the most important positions in the Government, and he has considerable scope for formulating and pursuing policies reflecting his views and convictions on public finance.

However, he must convince the Prime Minister and the rest of the Cabinet of the correctness of the policies he wishes to follow, and there must be a general co-ordination of financial policy and policies in the fields of trade, social services, national defense, and, in fact, all major areas of governmental activity. A desire by the Minister of Housing and Local Government to embark upon a large-scale program of public housing requires co-ordination from the start with the Chancellor's financial policies, or a decision by the Minister of Defence that the Royal Air Force should be re-equipped with new planes cannot be taken until the financial aspects are examined and approved. Thus it comes about that the Chancellor of the Exchequer is a potent influence in every field of public activity. Major questions of financial policy will come before the Cabinet as a whole; less important issues will be discussed and decided by the Chancellor and the minister or ministers concerned.

In reaching decisions on financial policy the Chancellor of the Exchequer and the Cabinet must bear in mind Parliamentary sentiment. If their majority in the House of Commons is economy-minded, they must seek to hold down government expenditure and taxation, and perhaps find some way of reducing the more unpopular taxes. Proposals for increasing expenditure in particular kinds of activity must be considered in relation to party policy and Parliamentary opinion. Outside organizations have views to be considered, too. Many business groups—bankers, manufacturers, exporters, shipowners, and merchants, to mention some of the principal ones—are deeply interested in general financial policy and in detailed aspects affecting their activities. For example, the method of assessing motor license fees in accordance with nominal horsepower determined for many years engineering design in the British automotive industry. The trade unions can be counted on to have strong opinions about the ways of raising revenue and the purposes for which it is expended. The development of financial policy, therefore, requires considerable balancing of forces within the Government, within Parliament, and among the general public.

2. *The Financial Departments*

The Chancellor of the Exchequer discharges his responsibilities as minister of finance through several departments of the British government. The most important from a policy standpoint is the Treasury. It is nominally headed by a board, but the Chancellor of the Exchequer is the minister in effective charge. He is regularly assisted by a junior minister, the Financial Secretary of the Treasury, and during some periods there has been a Minister for Economic Affairs. The director of the Treasury's staff and the chief advisor to the Chancellor is the Permanent Secretary, who holds the most important post within the Civil Service. The Treasury is a comparatively small department, having about 1500 employees. More than 200 of these are in the highest class of the Civil Service, the Administrative

Class.[1] A postwar addition to the Treasury is the Central Economic Planning Staff. Under a Chief Planning Officer, this Staff concerns itself with the formulation of basic economic policies and with the co-ordination of economic programs throughout the government.

The other departments over which the Chancellor of the Exchequer exercises general supervision are the tax collecting and the disbursing departments. Taxes are collected by the Inland Revenue Department and the Customs and Excise Department, and money is disbursed by the Paymaster-General and the Exchequer.[2] These agencies do not have policy-making functions, so their management is largely in the hands of permanent civil servants. The Customs and Excise Department and the Inland Revenue Department are headed by boards; the Paymaster-General's Office by a minister, the Paymaster-General, and the Exchequer and Audit Department by the Comptroller and Auditor-General. The Post Office, although headed by its own minister, the Postmaster-General, is controlled by the Treasury in matters of finance. The Post Office is the collecting agent for some taxes, and its postal, telephone, and telegraph services produce revenue going into the government's general account.

3. *The Authorizing of Expenditure and Revenue*

The procedures through which an annual financial program for the British government is developed and given statutory effect are rather involved, and the discussion here will omit some technicalities and concentrate on the main steps. Some of the present practice is the product of past constitutional relationships between the executive and the legislature. The requirement, for example, that the House of Commons first consider financial business in a Committee of the Whole House harks back to the days when the King occasionally sent for the journal of the House to learn the views of its members and when the Speaker was regarded as more of a royal than a Parliamentary servant. Other procedures date from specific reforms introduced over more than a century. Parliamentary 'common law,' or traditions and usages long observed, has also contributed.

The British government's fiscal year extends from 1 April to 31 March. It is inaugurated by one of the highlights of every Parliamentary session, namely, the budget speech of the Chancellor of the Exchequer. This speech, given soon after 1 April, contains a general review of the government's financial condition, a statement of the tax program for the coming

---

[1] Before the First World War the Treasury carried on its activities with about 140 employees. The increase in 40 years to 1500 is a measure of both the expansion of governmental activity in Britain and the enlarged role of the Treasury in financial and general economic affairs.

[2] In 1949 the Board of Inland Revenue observed the centenary of its founding. During 100 years its total collections rose from £33 million annually to £2 billion. Its original staff, obtained by combining 3 boards (Stamps, Taxes, and Excise) charged with tax collection, numbered about 5000; today it employs 53,000.

year, and an outline of proposed expenditures.[3] A considerable amount of drama is associated with the speech because the Chancellor never reveals prior to this address the changes in taxes which he proposes to make. Financial circles have always eagerly awaited the Chancellor's revelations, but today the ordinary citizen is almost equally interested to know whether purchase taxes will be increased or decreased or how much of a levy is going to be added to the prices of cigarettes and beer. All new taxes and increased rates of existing taxes announced by the Chancellor in his speech become effective immediately, although many months may elapse before Parliamentary sanction has been obtained.

Naturally a great deal of preparatory work has gone on before the beginning of the fiscal year. On the side of governmental expenditure, the Treasury sends a circular to all government departments in October requesting their estimates for the coming fiscal year. These are supposed to be ready by 15 January. In the preparation of these estimates considerable consultation goes on between the Treasury and each of the departments. Treasury officials have the task of keeping the requests of the departments within the framework of the Government's financial policies. They know, therefore, the kinds of additional expenditure that can be authorized and the areas in which cuts will have to be imposed. This consultation proceeds between the permanent officials of the Treasury and of the various departments, and ministers will ordinarily be concerned only when important issues arise. The departments frequently feel that the Treasury is very parsimonious and takes a narrow view on many questions. The Treasury for its part considers that there is often a lack of understanding of the general financial problems of the government and a failure to appreciate that every minister's request for additional funds cannot be allowed. In the end, a Treasury decision is controlling unless overruled by the Cabinet.

In February the estimates are submitted to the House of Commons in large printed volumes. Those for the civil services and revenue departments, grouped into classes, are submitted by the Financial Secretary of the Treasury and those for the military services by the Minister of Defence. The estimates appear as a list of about 150 sets of figures known as 'votes.' Although several votes may pertain to the same department, each deals with a fairly distinct service or governmental activity. There is a standard form in which the votes are presented. First a statement of the total sum of the vote is given, then follows a list of the subheads under which the vote will be accounted for, and finally detailed figures in explanation of the amount requested are set forth.

No estimate or request for expenditure can be considered by Parliament unless it is submitted by the Ministry. This rule of considering no measures to spend money unless they are proposed by the Crown was first adopted

---

[3] In 1952, because of a serious financial situation and the need to institute remedial measures as soon as possible, the Government advanced the budget speech to 11 March.

148–

in 1706, and it has the effect of giving the Government control over all expenditure.

The House of Commons considers the estimates in a Committee of the Whole House known as the Committee of Supply or the House in Supply. This committee, established at the opening of a Parliamentary session in response to the demand in the King's speech for a grant of supply, is presided over by the Chairman of Committees or his deputy. The House also appoints a select committee which examines a few of the estimates, taking different departments in turn so that all the estimates in the course of time get a more thorough screening than is possible from the Committee of Supply. By a standing order of the House, 26 days of Parliamentary time are allotted for considering the estimates. They are usually the first order of business on successive Thursdays between February or March and August. At the end of the discussion on a vote, the Committee adopts or rejects the vote and then reports to the House.

When the votes are considered in committee a member of the House may move a reduction in the amount proposed by the Government, but he cannot move an increase. To do the latter would be to violate the rule that no expenditure can be considered unless submitted by the Crown. It is possible, however, for a member to suggest that a larger sum be substituted and the whole committee may induce the Government to submit a revised estimate. By and large, though, the estimates pass through the committee virtually as submitted by the Government. Discussions in the Committee of Supply do not ordinarily arouse much interest. The consideration of a few votes may bring out a large attendance, but usually the House is sparsely populated during the sittings of the committee. Since the figures are rarely subject to change, the debates resolve themselves into criticisms and defenses of policies and activities of the offices whose expenditures are under consideration. The topics of these debates are chosen, according to a practice of long standing, by the opposition party. The votes for the Ministry of Food may well bring out criticisms of the Ministry's bulk purchasing practices or of meat negotiations with Argentina. The debate on the army votes may center on recruiting practices or on the utilization of conscripted soldiers.

There is not time to consider all the votes in the Committee of Supply, and a large proportion of them are accepted without any debate. On the last two allotted days the chair is authorized to put the questions to dispose of all the remaining votes in committee and on report in the House. All that remains is for the members to register their approval or disapproval on each class of the estimates.

Governmental activities must be carried on and money spent before Parliament has finished considering the estimates for the fiscal year. This situation leads the House of Commons, in March, to authorize the Government to spend from each vote a limited amount. In general, the Government gets provisional authority to pay salaries and spend money for other purposes until about the first of August when the Parliamentary session will be coming to an end. Concurrently with this authority to spend under each vote, the House, acting in Committee of Ways and Means, passes resolutions authorizing the Government to draw money from the Consolidated Fund.[4] For several months after the opening of the fiscal year, therefore, the Government is operating on provisional authorizations both to spend and to draw revenue for these expenditures.

After the Committee of Supply has concluded its consideration of the estimates and reported to the House, the Committee of Ways and Means resolves to grant out of the Consolidated Fund money to make good the supply granted to the Crown. When this formal action is reported, the House orders the Appropriation Bill brought in. The Appropriation Bill authorizes the issue of sufficient money from the Consolidated Fund to meet the estimated expenditure, and it appropriates all money granted by Parliament since the Appropriation Act of the previous year. In appropriating money the bill repeats the order of the estimates. As a consequence, departments must keep their expenditures within the limits of the pertinent votes and they are not free, except as authorized by the Treasury or Parliament, to transfer sums from one vote to another.

At the same time that the House of Commons is considering the estimates it is also reviewing the Government's proposals for raising revenue. The Government's intentions in this regard are announced, as previously mentioned, in the budget speech of the Chancellor of the Exchequer. He discloses in this address the proposed rates of taxation and the amounts which he estimates the various sources of revenue will produce. His proposals are embodied in some 15 or 20 resolutions, and all but the last are moved and passed the night of the budget speech. The last forms the basis of discussion of fiscal policy in the Committee of Ways and Means until the Finance Bill is brought in. This measure embodies all the tax resolutions of the year and is the authority under which the revenue departments collect the money to support the government and its activities.

Thus, several months after the beginning of a fiscal year the House of Commons is prepared to authorize in the Appropriation Bill the expenditure of money and in the Finance Bill the raising of revenue. These two bills go through the usual stages of public bills and are then sent to the House of Lords. Action in the House of Lords is purely perfunctory. Since the enactment of the Parliament Act of 1911 the Lords have only 30 days in which to consider financial bills and, in practice, they take little notice of them. The House of Lords has conceded to the lower chamber supremacy in financial matters and limits its interest to other aspects of public policy.

---

[4] The authority to draw money from the Consolidated Fund to make good the supply voted on account is formally given in the Consolidated Fund (No. 2) Bill. The second and third readings of the bill are occasions for the debate of any general administrative questions. The Consolidated Fund (No. 1) Bill, passed earlier, authorizes the issue of money to cover supplementary estimates for the financial year just ending. Both bills may empower the Treasury to borrow money.

It sometimes happens that events arise to upset the financial planning of the Chancellor of the Exchequer. A war may start, and it may be necessary to increase sharply the expenditures of several ministries and to levy additional taxes. To meet such a situation the Chancellor presents a revised budget to the House of Commons. Should a department and the Treasury considerably miscalculate the likely expenditure required by a new service or an administrative activity, a supplementary estimate will be submitted to the House of Commons. For example, when the National Health Service was inaugurated there were few guideposts to its probable cost. The original estimates proved inadequate, and supplementary ones had to be submitted.

Not all expenditures must be appropriated annually. Some are permanent charges on the Consolidated Fund. These include interest on the public debt, the salaries of judges, and the civil list, i.e. the income of the monarch and other members of the royal family. Similarly, most taxes are not reconsidered annually but stand at fixed rates. Any of these items, however, are subject to change if the Government so recommends and Parliament approves.

4. Current Expenditure and Taxation

The budget of the United Kingdom for the financial year 1952-3 was balanced at £4,661,375,000. This represents a marked increase over prewar budgets and, of course, the figure is astronomical in relation to nineteenth-century finance. With revenue estimated at the figure given and expenditure at £4,230,562,000, the Chancellor of the Exchequer predicted a surplus of £430,813,000. The total expenditure was divided roughly as follows: £2180 million for the civil departments, £48 million for the Post Office and the revenue-collecting departments, £1377 million for the military services, and £625 million for service of the national debt and miscellaneous items. Apart from the military services and interest on the national debt, the social services constitute the biggest items of expenditure, amounting to £1471 million. The principal ones and their estimated cost in the financial year 1952-3 were: the National Health Service, £393 million; the Ministry of National Insurance, £219 million; the National Assistance Board, £97 million; the Ministry of Pensions, £84 million; the Ministry of Education, £259 million; the Ministry of Labour, £20 million; the Ministry of Food, £250 million; and the Ministry of Housing and Local Government for public housing, £60 million.

The money expended is raised principally by taxation. During times of national emergency, war periods for example, the government borrows heavily, but ordinarily its policy is to balance its current expenditures by income from various kinds of taxes and payments for services.[5] The prin-

---

[5] The Treasury balances its books on an annual basis, and any appropriations not spent by 31 March lapse. 'An Act of 1875 requires the Treasury to prepare within fifteen days after the expiration of every financial year an account of the

cipal kinds of levies are income and surtaxes, estate or inheritance taxes, excises, sales or purchase taxes, customs duties, and licenses.[6] The necessities of British financial policy in recent years have made the rates of most of these taxes and duties exceedingly high by any standard of comparison. The basic rate of the tax on personal incomes has risen from the few pennies of a century ago to nine shillings sixpence in the pound, or 47.5 per cent of a person's income. People of modest means receive various exemptions which lower this rate, but by American standards the British income tax falls with considerable severity upon the working-class population. It also rises steeply, and for the largest annual incomes the rate is 19 shillings sixpence in the pound, or 97.5 per cent.[7] Nearly all articles sold at retail, except those necessary for a fairly minimum standard of living, bear a purchase tax which rises to 100 per cent on goods classed as luxuries. The smoker contributes heavily to the public treasury with the result that 20 cigarettes cost approximately 60 cents in American money. About the only customary source of revenue which the British Treasury foregoes is an annual property tax on land and its improvements. This field of taxation has been left to the local governments which are partly supported by property taxes.

The money collected by the revenue agencies is deposited to the Treasury's account in the Bank of England. In Scotland, six private banking establishments, used annually in turn, serve as government depositories. With only a few exceptions the money goes into an account known as the Consolidated Fund. It is upon this fund that the Exchequer draws when

---

public income and expenditure of the United Kingdom, showing the surplus of income or excess of expenditure during the year. If there be a deficit, it must be met in the following year by virtue of the Finance Act of 1930. If there be a surplus of income, the surplus must be paid to the National Debt Commissioners, and applied by them towards purchasing, redeeming or paying off the national debt.' Sir Courtenay Ilbert, *Parliament: Its History, Constitution, and Practice,* rev. by Sir Cecil Carr (London, 1950), p. 81.

[6] For the financial year 1952-3 the Chancellor of the Exchequer estimated that the various revenue sources would produce the following amounts:

Inland Revenue	
Income tax	£1,804,225,000
Surtax	123,000,000
Inheritance taxes (death duties)	175,000,000
Profits and excess profits taxes	457,000,000
Stamp duties and miscellaneous	59,500,000
Customs and Excise	
Customs	1,043,500,000
Excise	772,000,000
Other Revenues	
Motor vehicle duties	64,150,000
Miscellaneous other receipts	163,000,000
Total Revenue	£4,661,375,000

[7] In the fiscal year 1948-9, there were 86 persons in the United Kingdom who were left with an annual income exceeding £6000 ($16,800) after payment of taxes. In 1938-9 there were 6560.

152–

it makes payments authorized by the Appropriation Act of Parliament.

The agent of the British government in most of its financial operations is the Bank of England. Founded in 1694, it was until 1946 a privately owned and managed institution, although its relation with the Treasury had for a long time been close. Indeed, for decades before the Bank's nationalization it had operated virtually as an adjunct of the Treasury. No great change took place, therefore, when the state bought the interest of the Bank's shareholders and the governors became appointees of the Crown. The Bank of England serves as the custodian of public funds and as the Treasury's agent in borrowing money and operating the controls on foreign-exchange transactions.

5. *The Comptroller and Auditor-General*

The final stages of the financial process are the control of the issue of public money and the auditing of the government's accounts. These are primarily the responsibility of an officer known as the Comptroller and Auditor-General. His office dates from 1866 when the Exchequer and Audit Departments Act of that year combined what had formerly been two separate departments. Appointed by the Crown, the Comptroller and Auditor-General has a status comparable to that of a judge. His salary is not appropriated annually but is a permanent charge on the Consolidated Fund, and he can only be removed from office by an address of the two Houses of Parliament. He is responsible for seeing that no money is expended except as authorized by the annual Appropriation Act and that no illegalities occur in the collection, custody, or expenditure of public funds. 'He might not be unfittingly described,' Jennings has said, 'as the grand protector of red tape.'

> He insists that due formality be observed in everything; not because red tape is attractive in itself, but because it is merely a term of abuse for proper control. Parliament by legislation, the House of Commons by resolution, the Public Accounts Committee by its reports, and the Treasury by minutes, has laid down a long series of complicated rules whose purpose is to secure responsibility to Parliament and freedom from corruption, waste and inefficiency.[8]

The Comptroller and Auditor-General reports to the Public Accounts Committee of the House of Commons. This body, whose first appointment was moved by Gladstone in 1861, is a select committee of 15 members named at the beginning of each annual session of Parliament. According to custom, a senior member of the opposition party is the chairman. Working from reports submitted by the Comptroller and Auditor-General, the committee in a series of meetings examines Treasury officials and the accounting officers of other departments. It then issues one or more reports noting unsatisfactory financial practices and making recommenda-

---

[8] *Parliament* (Cambridge, 1948), p. 320.

tions for changes. For example, in 1949 the committee called attention to the growing practice of Parliament granting considerable sums each year to independent or semi-independent bodies, such as the Medical Research Council and the University Grants Committee, whose accounts are not subject to the strict auditing of the regular government departments. The Public Accounts Committee of the 1951-2 session recommended more urgent efforts to reduce tax evasion. The Treasury comments on the reports and indicates the measures it has taken to meet the committee's criticisms.

With a record of almost a century behind it, the Public Accounts Committee has established a good reputation as a guardian of probity and regularity in financial matters. 'Though it receives little attention from the Commons and from the press, the procedure it has evolved and the authority its views carry ensure publicity and action in the places that most matter.' [9]

6. *The Role of the Treasury*

Two features of British government finance are deserving of comment. One concerns the role of the Treasury. This department has long occupied the central position with respect to public finance. During the nineteenth century the Treasury regarded itself as the champion of economy and efficiency in public administration, and it guarded the national purse from the spending proclivity of the other departments of government. According to the standards of Gladstone and his contemporaries, a Chancellor of the Exchequer measured his success by the amounts of money he left with the taxpayers, who were considered better judges of how their incomes should be spent or invested than the financiers and economists of the government.

The principle of Treasury control became firmly implanted at this time. This principle is difficult to define precisely, but it means in general that the Treasury must be consulted and its approval obtained by all other ministries for any policy or administrative action having financial implications. Since a large percentage of policies and administrative actions have financial implications, the Treasury's views must be sought on numerous and frequent occasions. Many instances arise during the preparation of the estimates for submission to Parliament when Treasury guidance must be requested and followed. Its views must be considered by departments planning new programs, because the need for increased staff, purchases of supplies and materials, and other administrative expenses will almost certainly arise. Treasury control is the dominant influence in personnel administration; the numbers of civil servants, their pay, and most of the conditions of their service are determined mainly by the Treasury.

The Treasury exerts constant pressure for economical administration, although some believe it to be less firm nowadays than it was half a cen-

---

[9] Basil Chubb, *The Control of Public Expenditure* (Oxford, 1952), p. 193.

tury ago. Two World Wars have had their influence. Normal standards of economical administration cannot be maintained when the nation is fighting for survival. The British Treasury is not extravagant even in war-time, but obviously many items of expenditure and departmental methods must be quickly approved that would normally be subjected to consider-able scrutiny. Furthermore, a change in administrative practice, introduced after 1920, appears to have weakened Treasury control somewhat. Prior to that date each department had an accounting officer who had supreme authority, subject only to the minister, for all financial matters. He was the Treasury's man in each department and was looked to for the enforcement of economy as well as financial regularity. Beginning about 1920 the post of accounting officer was joined with that of permanent secretary, the purpose of the change being to make a minister's chief advisor on policy matters also the official responsible for the financial effects of policy. There is considerable feeling today that permanent secretaries do not assume their second role, that of the stern accounting officer, with sufficient fre-quency and that, moreover, the Treasury is not viewed with the terror familiar to an older generation of civil servants.[10]

Treasury control may not be the awesome thing it was 50 years ago, but it is still a force to be reckoned with in British financial administration. In the preparation of budget estimates and in subsequent administrative actions pressure for economy is exerted. In addition, the Treasury en-deavors to promote economical administration by positive approaches as well as the more negative ones of reducing estimates and disallowing pro-posed expenditure. Its Organization and Methods Division seeks to elimi-nate waste and inefficiency by advising the departments concerning better forms of administrative organization and improved ways of transacting business.

What has been said above about Treasury control refers to its respon-sibility to promote administrative efficiency and economy, that is, the per-formance of public business with a minimum of waste. There is another aspect of Treasury control, which is its attitude toward major policies in-volving increased expenditure. The Treasury is generally critical, or at least other departments think so, of proposals that call for greater outlays of money. To some extent the Treasury can resist such proposals, but the

---

[10] 'The admirable intention of this combination of roles was to ensure that there would be no divorce between responsibility for policy and for the financial con-sequences of that policy. The object, as stated by Sir Warren Fisher, the Permanent Secretary to the Treasury at that time, was that "all Heads of Departments should work together as a team in the pursuit of economy in every branch and every detail of the public service."

'This departure was altogether unexceptionable so long as heads of departments could be counted upon as allies of economy and believers in prudent housekeeping. But that basic assumption, which appears so axiomatic in the twenties, ceased to be wholly valid; and the delegation of Treasury control must be regarded in retrospect as the main reason why it ceased to be valid.' The Economist, 2 December 1950, p. 958.

final decision involves more than the views of the financial department and depends upon the interplay of political forces. The Chancellor of the Exchequer is a member of the Cabinet, which is based upon a party majority in Parliament, and he may find it necessary and desirable to approve the larger estimates the Government as a whole considers good policy.

In this century the demands for increased expenditure have usually overcome the Treasury's braking influence. Since at least 1906, when the Liberals came to power, the trend has been toward the expansion of the state's services, and many governmental functions have been added as well as older ones expanded. The Welfare State is by its nature expensive. Treasury control as applied to policy operates today, therefore, in a context considerably different from that of the nineteenth century.

If the Treasury's traditional authority over expenditure arising from policy considerations has been somewhat shorn, its responsibility has expanded greatly in another direction, namely, economic planning. The Treasury entered this field in a large way during the Second World War when the assets and the productive resources of the nation had to be fully mobilized and when the civilian economy had to be rigorously controlled. After 1945 the economic problems facing the country were almost as great as those of the war years. The export trade had to be rapidly restored in order that Britain could pay for the imports needed to sustain its people and its industries. It was necessary to limit these imports to essential raw materials and manufactured products. A large and carefully planned investment program had to be launched to repair the ravages of war and to insure an expanding output by British industries. Agreements for the orderly reduction of the claims of Britain's creditors, the holders of sterling balances, had to be negotiated. While all these things were being done the domestic economy had to be carefully managed to maintain an acceptable standard of living and to prevent inflation from robbing British industry of its power to compete in world markets.

The responsibility for economic planning to deal with these large and interrelated problems fell largely on the Treasury. The Chancellor of the Exchequer became the director of the nation's economy, and he was charged with the co-ordination of the activities of several departments that had parts to play in carrying out the Government's program. He has the assistance of a Chief Planning Officer, the head of the Central Economic Planning Staff which was joined to the Treasury in 1947. For the information and data required in drafting plans and programs the Central Economic Planning Staff can call upon the Economic Section of the Cabinet Office and the Central Statistical Office, two wartime agencies which have been continued. Probably the economic life of no nation has been as fully recorded and documented as that of the United Kingdom in the past ten years. Co-ordination between government and industry is sought through the Economic Planning Board. Under the chairmanship of the Chief Planning Officer, the Board is composed of the permanent secretaries of the Board of Trade and the Ministries of Labour, Materials, and Supply; representatives of the Treasury and the Economic Section of the Cabinet Office; and six nonofficial members, three trade union and three management representatives.

The Treasury today, therefore, is not only the department supervising the financial affairs of the British government, but it is also the controller of a tightly managed national economy. It could probably relax some of its controls in a world generally at peace and trading with relative freedom. Even in such favorable circumstances, considerable economic planning will continue, and the Treasury's responsibility will remain heavy.

7. The Role of Parliament

The second feature of British government finance to be specially considered is the part played by Parliament. Parliament possesses the ultimate authority in financial affairs, and its failure to act—to provide for revenue and to vote appropriations—would soon bring the machinery of state to a grinding stop. Nevertheless, in practice the control of Parliament is more formal than real. There are several reasons for this condition.

In the first place, the initiative in financial matters, as in other fields of policy, is taken by the Cabinet, and Parliament may only criticize and attempt to alter what is proposed by the Government. The ministerial majority in the House of Commons can be counted upon to sustain the Cabinet's financial program and to vote down any major threats coming from the opposition. The Cabinet, and particularly the Chancellor of the Exchequer, have taken into account the views of their party in the formulation of their policies, so they do not have to expect serious trouble with their own supporters as the financial measures are debated. Few members of the majority party are disposed to join the opposition over a financial issue; to do so would threaten the life of the Ministry and probably precipitate a general election.

In the second place, Parliament has little time in which to delve deeply into the Government's financial proposals. The 26 days of debate allotted to the estimates allow only a superficial examination of most of them. Timetables must be rigidly observed or the House of Commons would not complete its review and pass the necessary legislation. The result is that debate is centered on policy issues reflected in the estimates of a number of the departments, but any detailed consideration of their financial affairs is impossible.

Parliament, moreover, is inadequately organized to deal with financial measures any more effectively than it does. The estimates and the resolutions on revenue proposals are considered in Committees of the Whole House where detailed examination is impractical. There are no small committees on appropriations and taxation engaged in a constant consideration of the purposes for which money is to be spent, the manner in which the administrative departments are carrying out their financial responsibilities, and the ways in which the funds needed by the government are to be raised. In this particular, the contrast with the United States Congress is quite marked. The House of Commons is served by no appropriations or finance committee which, with the aid of a supporting staff and after hearing administrative officials and private interest groups, can bring in bills to its house that have been largely drafted by the committee. Congressional control of finance is real, as any administrative official who has had to defend his agency's budget estimates before an appropriations committee can testify.

Since the early years of this century, when budgets began to increase appreciably, Parliament has sought some means of exerting closer control over public expenditure. Members were satisfied that the Comptroller and Auditor-General and the Public Accounts Committee were guarantors of honesty and conformity to law and rule in the handling of public monies, but they believed some additional machinery could be devised to eliminate waste and promote administrative efficiency. Consequently, in 1912 a select committee was established to examine the estimates submitted to the House of Commons. The outbreak of war in 1914 ended the life of the Estimates Committee, but the huge outlays required for military purposes and rumors of wasteful expenditure led to a demand for more rigorous Parliamentary control. In 1917, as a result, the Government agreed to the appointment of a National Expenditure Committee to examine current expenditure and to recommend economies consistent with policy. It prepared a number of reports on the efficiency of departments and services, and it investigated cases of alleged waste and poor administration. The National Expenditure Committee was abolished in 1920, but the following year strong sentiment in the House of Commons induced the Government to agree to re-establish the Select Committee on Estimates. This committee existed until 1939, when war again ended the publication of detailed estimates. While it produced some useful reports, the committee, for various reasons, never stood high in Parliamentary or ministerial esteem.

At the start of World War II the Government acceded to Parliamentary desire for the creation of another National Expenditure Committee. It was an influential body of 32 members who performed much of their work through subcommittees. Inquiries were undertaken and reports made on major administrative problems, such as war contracts and the civil defense organization, as well as on cases of waste and inefficiency. Matters for investigation were proposed by committee members, other M.P.'s, and by private citizens. Although some of the committee's activities were controversial and ministers occasionally felt that it was intruding upon the sphere of their responsibility, it performed, in general, a useful service. The committee partly took the place of a Parliamentary opposition during a period when the demands of national unity and coalition Government quieted some of the usual forms of criticism.

With the cessation of hostilities, the National Expenditure Committee was disbanded, and the House of Commons re-established the Estimates Committee, which has remained a part of Parliament's machinery of financial control. By its terms of reference, the Estimates Committee was directed 'to examine such of the Estimates . . . as may seem fit to the Committee . . . to suggest the form in which the Estimates shall be presented . . . and to report what, if any, economies consistent with the policy implied in those Estimates may be effected therein.' The committee, a body of 36 members, has built its working methods on those developed by the National Expenditure Committee. Although the estimates submitted to the House of Commons are the take-off point for the committee's work, it chooses only a few matters for investigation during each Parliamentary session. 'It does not try to do the Treasury's job all over again. While it is interested in the money figures which represent the cost of action, it goes straight to the questions of organization and methods which lie behind the figures. It is more interested in the department's memoranda and explanations of organization, work, and results than in the money figures into which they can be translated.' [11]

In the Public Accounts Committee and the Estimates Committee, the House of Commons has developed two bodies which aid it in discharging its financial responsibilities. Parliament lacks, however, a method of reviewing the whole range of annual expenditure. The Public Accounts Committee insures that the money granted by Parliament has been spent on the objects intended and in the ways prescribed. The Estimates Committee maintains a campaign against inefficient administrative organization and methods. The remaining gap, which some members of Parliament believe exists, is between the work of these committees and the policy debates which occur when the House is in Supply.

While the search for some means of making Parliamentary consideration of the problems of public finance more meaningful has continued for at least half a century, successive ministries have been generally unreceptive to proposed reforms. Chancellors of the Exchequer wish their carefully prepared programs to receive Parliamentary approval with no substantial changes. Supported by the Government's majority in the House of Commons, they prefer consideration of the estimates and revenue measures in committees of the Whole House where important issues can be made matters of confidence. Smaller committees would probably be more difficult to manage, and their members might acquire an authority which ministers would find difficulty in resisting. Cabinets, on the whole, have been opponents of changes in Parliamentary organization and procedure which tend to weaken their control over the business they have mapped out for enactment, and they are especially sensitive about relaxing authority over financial measures.

While the centralization of financial responsibility in the executive may be criticized for relegating Parliament to too perfunctory a role, it has the virtue—and it is an important one—of providing the nation with a coherent, integrated plan covering its revenue and its expenditure. After policy has been determined by the Treasury, and on major issues by the

---

[11] Basil Chubb, op. cit. p. 166.

Cabinet, there is a settled program for the coming fiscal year. It will not be twisted out of shape by log-rolling in the legislature or by failure to levy the taxes deemed necessary. When a Chancellor of the Exchequer opens his budget and predicts that at the end of the next fiscal year there will be a surplus or a deficit of a certain amount, that figure is very likely to be realized. Unexpected occurrences may intervene to falsify his prediction: business conditions may change markedly and reduce tax receipts, or a war may start and necessitate greatly increased expenditure. Barring such major eventualities, which would require a revision of the budget during the year, there is a strong presumption that his expectations will prove accurate. At least it is known that no important alterations will be made by Parliament. There is no uncertainty about what the administrative departments will have to spend or concerning the taxes to fall on the citizen.

The British system of public finance does not eliminate popular control as much as the appearances suggest, despite the rather nominal role of Parliament. The Chancellor of the Exchequer, in preparing his program, is influenced by party policy and the views of his ministerial colleagues, who are politicians sensitive to public opinion. Moreover, he must prepare a program acceptable to the Government's majority in the House of Commons. That majority is usually large enough so that he is not beholden to every bloc and faction, but nevertheless he cannot flaunt the views of influential sections of the Parliamentary party. If sentiment within the party is strongly in favor of a considerable increase in expenditure on national defense, a Chancellor of the Exchequer who ignored this opinion would soon find himself in a difficult situation. The Prime Minister would undoubtedly see that this intra-party difference was resolved before the budget was presented to Parliament. While the opposition's views on financial questions do not weigh heavily in the Chancellor's calculations, he will take care that he gives it no issues about which its members can make political capital. The financial program laid before Parliament, therefore, is one that has been prepared with political realities very much in mind. The procedures under which the annual budget is drafted and those governing the translation of the estimates and revenue measures into law emphasize legislative self-restraint and executive initiative and responsibility, but they are no less democratic because of these features.

In another respect the British system is commendable. That is the way it focuses Parliamentary debate and criticism on policy questions. Adequate controls have been developed to insure that estimates of expenditure will be pruned for waste and 'padding,' that administrative inefficiency will be reduced to the extent possible in such a large organization, and that dishonesty will be detected. Parliament can rely on the Treasury, the Comptroller and Auditor-General, and the Committees on Estimates and Public Accounts to maintain a constant watch on the departments. What the House of Commons does is to bring into the arena of public discussion the policies reflected by the figures of national finance. When the estimates are before the Committee of Supply the opposition selects a number of votes which provide springboards for attacks on ministerial policies and programs. Its calls for economy are not generally directed at departmental waste or inefficiency but at the nature and scope of Government policy. This, it is suggested, is meaningful criticism, for in the modern state substantial economies can only be obtained by the curtailment of services and the reduction of programs. It must not be assumed that opposition criticism is always pointedly directed or that it selects the most important targets; members of Parliament often fritter away time on the trivial and unimportant. The point is that there is much to be said for a national legislature, in discharging its responsibilities with respect to finance, centering its attention on the policy issues represented by the numerical symbols, and leaving to better equipped instruments the search for administrative economy.

X

Political Parties

While most of the institutions of British government can be traced in origin to the medieval period of history, one which is modern is the political party. It is no less important for its comparatively recent development. The British political system, as it has functioned for about two centuries and a half, can only be understood with reference to political parties. Political parties formulate principles and define issues, nominate and elect candidates to the House of Commons, organize voters for campaigns and the casting of ballots on polling day, and divide Parliament into a group conducting the King's Government and an opposition group prepared to assume power if the Ministry should fall.

1. *Historical Background of the Party System*

Before 1700 there was always factionalism in English political life. Monarchs were supported in their policies by royal servants and courtiers who could usually assemble many adherents. An opposition would develop from time to time, grouping itself around some powerful magnate who was out of royal favor or some combination of noblemen who sought to seize power for themselves. Such factional struggles were represented when a baronial party forced King John to subscribe to Magna Carta at Runnymede, when Yorkists and Lancastrians fought the Wars of the Roses with the throne as the prize, and when the youthful Lady Jane Grey died in the Tower— a pawn in the struggle between rival Tudor factions. This kind of factionalism bears only superficial resemblance to the modern system of political parties. The groups involved rarely held together for any length of time, their ties were usually personal, and their methods of persuasion were the sword, the dagger, or the headman's ax.

Modern political parties began to develop in England in the seventeenth century when the concept became accepted that men could differ over important political issues without being disloyal to the basic principles of the Constitution. This tolerance of opposing political views was essential before parties could emerge from the realm of temporary factionalism or conspiracy. The end of the seventeenth century was a favorable period for the notion of political tolerance to take root. Englishmen had spent twenty years in the middle of the century fighting each other, violently arguing constitutional ideas, and trying a radically different form of polity. By

1660 the majority of them were ready to desist and to try to live with most of their fellow citizens on a basis of accommodation. After they had rid themselves of a king, James II, whose policies threatened to divide them into irreconcilable factions again, they were prepared to sheathe their swords and keep their rivalries within bounds. The political leaders of the country had, in Parliament, an institution where they could debate and contest with one another for the right to control the policies of the state. They all stood to gain more from bloodless warfare than from contests in which the stakes were supreme power or complete destruction. Consequently, in this atmosphere of toleration, men began to group themselves according to certain political principles, often basic and strongly held but not revolutionary in character.

The first division turned primarily on the issue of royal power, and in many ways was a continuation of the civil war differences between Cavaliers and Roundheads. The Cavalier point of view was generally that royal power, although it must be limited, should not be resisted. The Cavaliers believed strongly in the maintenance of the royal prerogative and the established church. Their opponents, while not anti-monarchical, thought that illegal power should be resisted and that toleration of non-subversive religious sects should be permitted. The abuse of the royal prerogative by James II alarmed so many of the royalist party that they were prepared to join their opponents, the Whigs, in the Glorious Revolution of 1688. Through the change of sovereigns the Whigs were able to establish the kind of monarchy they conceived to be proper. Old party differences reappeared, and the royalists, now known as Tories, were always under some suspicion while the succession issue was important. It was not until the middle of the eighteenth century, long after the Hanoverian dynasty was firmly established on the throne, that they recovered and were strong enough to battle the Whig oligarchs for place and power within the constitutional framework of a limited monarchy. This they proceeded to do throughout the late eighteenth and early nineteenth centuries.

Although the Whigs and Tories were modern political parties in comparison to the factional groupings of former centuries, they were nevertheless very different from twentieth-century parties. In the first place, they were in no sense mass organizations spread through every borough and county. The suffrage, it will be remembered, was still very restricted, and the great body of the people did not participate in the political process. In the second place, few fundamental political, economic, or social principles divided the parties. The leaders of both came from the aristocratic governing classes and accepted all the tenets of these classes. By and large, political division occurred in terms of traditional and personal loyalties, and the spoils of office were the principal prizes in the contest. The strength of the Tories lay in the country squires and among the rural clergy of the Established Church, who were socially connected with the landed gentry. The Whigs represented an alliance between some of the powerful noblemen of the kingdom and the rich business interests centered in London and the few other considerable cities of the time.

While this circumscribed rivalry between Whigs and Tories was being carried on in the late eighteenth and early nineteenth centuries, the economic and social changes introduced by the industrial revolution were transforming Britain in a way that was bound to be reflected in the political affairs of the country. New classes of the population were gaining wealth and economic power. Population movements were draining villages all over England and creating crowded industrial centers. Manchester, Sheffield, and Birmingham, which had been sprawling villages, were becoming large towns. Rapidly mounting industrial production and commercial ties with all corners of the globe were changing the ways in which a large proportion of the British people gained their livelihood.

These developments were reflected in the party situation during the first half of the nineteenth century. Against the strenuous opposition of the Tories, the Whigs in 1832 achieved an enlargement of the electorate which admitted some of the new business and commercial classes to the suffrage. They naturally considered the Whig Party to be the political vehicle best suited to advancing and protecting their interests. The Tory squirearchy became even more loyal to its political allegiance as it saw threats to the landed interest in the rapid rise of the manufacturing and commercial classes.

For two or three decades after 1832 the parties went through a period of realignment and consolidation from which emerged two strong groups calling themselves Liberals and Conservatives respectively. These parties divided the vast majority of the British electorate almost equally until the time of the First World War.

During the latter half of the nineteenth century the political rivalry was dramatized by the two great party leaders of the time, Gladstone and Disraeli. With each succeeding enlargement of the electorate and through the natural increase in the population of Britain, the Conservative and Liberal ranks swelled until each became a mass party, counting its supporters in the millions.

Generally speaking, the Conservatives tended to be strongest in the rural areas where the social system connected with the landed estate and the parish church continued to exist. The party, however, enlisted in its ranks many of the middle classes who pursued professions or business occupations in the cities. The Liberals continued to include a good deal of the old Whig aristocracy, but increasingly the party was based upon the manufacturing and commercial interests and the wage earners in mine and factory. It was also strong among religious nonconformists, particularly in Northern England, Wales, and in parts of Scotland. Toward the end of the nineteenth century the issue of home rule for Ireland drove a deep cleavage into the ranks of the Liberal Party, and many of its upper-class elements joined with the Conservatives to form a combination known as the Unionist Party. The Liberals recovered from this schism, however, and in 1906 won the largest Parliamentary majority ever enjoyed by a party up to that time. Under the leadership of Campbell-Bannerman, and then Asquith after 1908, the Liberal Ministry carried through Parliament the

164–

most far-reaching legislative program that Britain had seen for decades. Obstructed by a Conservative majority in the House of Lords, the Liberals faced the issue of Parliamentary reform, and after two general elections succeeded in enacting the Parliament Bill of 1911. They were in power when the war began in 1914, and for a year a Liberal Ministry remained solely in charge. The intensity and the probable duration of the struggle caused the parties, however, to form a coalition Government in 1915 under Asquith as Prime Minister. Dissatisfaction with his leadership resulted in a reorganization of the coalition the next year, and David Lloyd George became the Prime Minister. Toward the close of the war, divided counsels appeared within the Liberal Party concerning the advisability of continuing the coalition when the conflict should end, and in 1918 the party split into two groups under the leaders Lloyd George and Asquith.

In the meantime a development was occurring which was to work a radical transformation in the political party situation. This development was, of course, the growth of the Labour Party to the position of a separate national party. The Labour Party traces its origin to several late nineteenth-century movements interested in political action to advance socialist ideas or working-class representation in Parliament. In 1900 four of them, the Independent Labour Party, the Social Democratic Federation, the Fabian Society, and the Trades Union Congress, held a meeting in London to concert their plans. They established the Labour Representation Committee, of which Ramsay MacDonald became the secretary, and they hoped to elect a group of M.P.'s who would speak especially for the wage-earning classes of the population. It is worth noticing that the great majority of the early leaders of the Labour Party took their inspiration not from Marx and Engels but rather from William Morris, Robert Owen, the Christian Socialists, the Fabians, and other British reformers. Thus, the Labour Party has never had the Marxist cast of some of the Continental socialist movements.

Only two of the Committee's 13 candidates were elected in 1900, but, in 1906, 27 were successful. In Parliament they co-operated with the Liberal Party, and this alliance continued until the close of the First World War. In 1918, however, a Labour Party was formally organized under a constitution which brought together in a federation the trade union, the socialist, and the co-operative movements. By and large, the trade unions supplied the votes and the money for the new party while the socialist movement, strong in certain intellectual circles, furnished doctrine and leadership.

2. *Party Politics between the Wars*

When Parliament was dissolved after the armistice of 11 November 1918 and the first general election since 1910 was held, the party situation took the following form. The Conservatives and a part of the Liberal Party put forward candidates on a coalition basis and announced their intention to continue the wartime co-operation with Lloyd George as Prime Minister.

The faction of the Liberal Party under Asquith ran candidates as the bona-fide representatives of the party. The new Labour Party came forward with its own slate of candidates and contested the election independently. The result was an overwhelming victory for the coalition; it won 478 seats in a total of 707. The great majority of these 478 seats were held by Conservatives; in fact, they had a majority over all other parties combined. The independent Liberals—the Asquith group—won only 28 seats, while the Labour Party obtained 63.

In 1922 the coalition, which had lasted longer than almost anyone had expected, broke apart, and for the succeeding general election the Conservatives decided to resume their independent position. They had opposed to them the two factions of the Liberal Party and the new Labour Party. Efforts had been made to heal the breach in the Liberal Party, but many differences separated the two factions, not the least being the rivalry of the leaders, Lloyd George and Asquith. In the general election of 1922 the Conservatives won a majority over all the opposing parties, and Bonar Law, who had formed a Government upon the resignation of the Coalition Cabinet, remained the Prime Minister. He was succeeded the next year by Stanley Baldwin, who decided to dissolve Parliament and seek a mandate for the introduction of tariff protection. This was an issue upon which all Liberals, with their long tradition of loyalty to free trade principles, could unite, and the two wings of the party were brought together to fight the general election of 1923 in unison. The Labour Party, which had seen its popular vote rise from the 2,224,945 of 1918 to 4,236,733 in 1922, was naturally determined to contest the election as an independent party and to seek for itself a Parliamentary majority. It did not achieve that goal, although it increased its Parliamentary representation from 142 to 191. The Conservatives gained slightly in popular votes but lost 86 seats in the House of Commons. The reunited Liberal Party polled a vote in excess of that achieved by the two wings the year before and gained 45 additional seats. After this election the Conservatives remained the largest party in the House of Commons, but the result clearly showed a repudiation on the part of the electorate of the policy upon which the Conservatives had gone to the country. The King, therefore, asked the leader of the Labour Party, the second in Parliamentary strength, to form a ministry. It was the first time this party had held the seals of office. Tacitly supported by the Liberals and pursuing a noncontroversial program, the Labour Government with Ramsay MacDonald as Prime Minister remained in office for almost a year.

Although two general elections had been held within a short period of time, it was recognized on all sides that the Parliamentary situation was definitely unsatisfactory and that another general election would be necessary before a stable Government could be established. This general election was precipitated when the Liberals withdrew their support from the Government on an issue of curbing communist activities in Britain. In the general election of 1924 the Labour Party polled 5,487,620 votes, almost a million above its 1923 poll, but its representation in the House of Commons was cut from 191 to 151. The Liberals were again a poor third in the race. With a large Parliamentary majority, the Conservatives formed a Government and Stanley Baldwin became Prime Minister again.

Baldwin's Conservative Government lasted almost the constitutional limit of a Parliament. As the time approached when a general election would have to be held, the three parties began announcing their programs and establishing positions for the coming contest. The Conservatives pointed to their record of the past five years and appealed to the electorate for another majority to continue a strong and stable government. The Labour Party, although it would have to overcome a large Conservative majority in the House of Commons, also appealed for a victory which would enable it to carry out a clear-cut program. This program was framed in reasonably moderate terms. It contained little that was revolutionary, and the party advocated in general the extension of domestic policies which had been in existence for 20 years. The Liberals attempted to re-establish themselves as a major party. They conducted a vigorous campaign, utilizing the considerable war chest which Lloyd George had collected and which he controlled.

The general election of 1929 resulted in a sharp rebuff to the Conservatives. They polled almost a million more votes than in 1924, but their parliamentary strength dropped from 400 seats to 260. Labour's popular vote soared to a figure almost equal to that of the Conservatives and won 288 seats for the party. The Liberals almost doubled their popular vote, but they had slight success in winning seats. They had 46 at the time of the dissolution, and they gained 13 by the election to give them a total of 59. Eight seats were won by Independents or representatives of minor parties.

Baldwin resigned the premiership, and the King invited MacDonald to head a Government again. He formed a Ministry from among the more moderate elements of the Labour Party and undertook to govern without a formal understanding with the Liberals who held the balance of power in the House of Commons. The Government attempted no radical domestic legislation so it was able to count on Liberal support. It pursued a vigorous foreign policy, and in this field it enjoyed considerable Parliamentary and popular support. During its two years in office, however, the economic storm which followed the stock market crash of 1929 began to gather, and the Labour Government was faced with the necessity of taking measures to enable Britain to survive the coming troubles. MacDonald's Cabinet was divided on the nature of the proper measures to be pursued. In general, the issue was whether more or less orthodox fiscal policies should be followed or whether the Government should assume financial risks and push boldly ahead. If the former course were chosen, severe reductions in government expenditure were necessary, and these would fall heavily on the social services. If the second course were adopted, the threats to the stability of the pound and Britain's position in international trade were likely to be serious and national bankruptcy might be the final result.

Unable to get agreement within the Cabinet on the course to follow, MacDonald resigned as Prime Minister, but he was immediately requested by the King to form a coalition Government to include the Conservative and Liberal parties. This action of the Prime Minister and party leader created a crisis in the Labour ranks. Several of MacDonald's Cabinet colleagues followed him into the new Government, but other prominent members of the party and almost all the Labour M.P.'s opposed his action. MacDonald, Snowden, Thomas, and the others who supported the coalition were expelled from the Labour Party, and Arthur Henderson was chosen as the new leader. Parliament was soon dissolved, and a general election ensued. The coalition, calling itself the National Government, appealed to the electorate for a general mandate to take those measures which seemed required to protect Britain from the economic depression settling over the world and to fortify her financial position. The Labour Party, criticizing the emergency measures which had been taken by the National Government, offered a program more radical and socialist in character than any which had been presented up to this time. The Liberals, who had all supported the formation of the coalition and the emergency acts which it had taken, broke into three factions when the election was called. One group, terming themselves National Liberals and led by Sir John Simon, fully supported the new Government, including its intended policy of tariff protection. A second group, with Sir Herbert Samuel as leader, supported the National Government on all issues except the introduction of higher tariffs. Lloyd George led still a third faction, which criticized the holding of the general election and took up a position in opposition.

The results of the 1931 election were an overwhelming victory for the National Government. It won 556 of a total of 615 seats and thus had the largest Parliamentary majority a Government ever enjoyed in the House of Commons. Of the 556 Nationalists, 470 were Conservatives, 35 were National Liberals, 33 were Liberals, 13 were National Labourites, and 5 were Independent members. Labour's representation in Parliament was decimated. The party won only 52 seats, although its popular vote of 6,649,630 was only about 1,750,000 below the poll of 1929. In addition to the 52 Labour members, the Parliamentary opposition consisted of the Lloyd George family—the former Prime Minister, his daughter, his son, and his son's brother-in-law—and three Independent members. The Parliamentary situation was actually so lopsided as to be a source of embarrassment to the Government.

In the Government formed after the general election of 1931 Ramsay MacDonald remained as Prime Minister. But with the Conservatives supplying the overwhelming voting strength of the Government, it was bound to be dominated by the policies of that party. The Conservative leader, Stanley Baldwin, became increasingly Prime Minister in fact, although not in name. For almost four years this anomalous situation continued while the Prime Ministership fell to the lowest level known in a hundred years. Finally in 1935, MacDonald, abused as a renegade by his former Labour

168–

associates and contemptuously tolerated by the majority of Conservative politicians, resigned from office and was succeeded by Baldwin.

Although the five-year life of Parliament did not expire until 1936, the new Prime Minister decided to call a general election in the autumn of 1935. At the time of the dissolution the Government had 505 supporters in the House of Commons of whom 451 were Conservatives. The opposition had grown to 94, chiefly through the decision of the Samuelite Liberals to cross the House in 1933. The campaign was not an exciting one, and issues of foreign policy held first place in party manifestoes and in campaign speaking. The Nationalist candidates supported the policy of League of Nations sanctions to halt the Italian war against Ethiopia, and this was a position that the Labour Party could not oppose. It was forced to criticize the Government for its dilatoriness in advocating international sanctions and for its lack of vigor in foreign affairs. Labour urged the reduction of armaments at a time when the Fascist menace on the Continent was causing grave concern to a few far-seeing politicians. The opposition Liberals took a position not much different from that of the Labour Party, although they continued to advocate their traditional policy of free trade.

The general election of 1935 was a clear victory for the Nationalist coalition. It won 431 seats out of a total of 615. In this majority the Conservatives had 387, the National Liberals 33, National Labour 8, and there were 3 Independents. The opposition was composed of 154 Labour members, 17 Liberals, 4 Independent Liberals, and 9 other members, including one Communist. Although the title of National Government was retained, the Ministry was almost wholly Conservative and the party situation took on a more normal complexion. There were no differences of principle between the Conservatives and their minor allies, the National Liberals and the National Labourites. On the opposition side of the House, the Samuelite and Lloyd George Liberals continued to maintain positions independent of Labour and each other.

In 1937 Stanley Baldwin ended his long leadership of the Conservative Party, accepted a peerage, and entered the House of Lords. Baldwin passed on to Neville Chamberlain, his successor as party leader and Prime Minister, the large Conservative majority won in 1935. It was a strong and united party, although Winston Churchill and the few who supported him formed a group becoming increasingly critical of the Government's foreign policy and its tardy steps toward British rearmament. These critics were reinforced in 1938 by Anthony Eden's resignation as Foreign Secretary. They represented no serious threat to the Chamberlain Government, but they did provide a rallying point for those who saw danger in the trend of events in Europe.

3. Recent Party History

From the summer of 1938 British politics were dominated by the tense diplomatic atmosphere created by the threats of Hitler and Mussolini. Upon the outbreak of war in 1939, the Government received almost unanimous support for its decision to appease no more, and Parliament readily enacted the war measures asked by the Ministry. During the period of the 'phony' war in the winter of 1939 and 1940 considerable dissatisfaction developed over the slow tempo of mobilization. Chamberlain, handicapped by his diplomatic miscalculations prior to the beginning of hostilities, appeared inadequate to give the kind of leadership which victory would require. This dissatisfaction quickly came to a head when the Germans seized Denmark and Norway and the allied counter-measures proved to be feeble and ineffective. The reconstitution of the Government to provide inspiring and aggressive leadership was an obvious need. Negotiations were opened with the opposition political leaders, and it soon became apparent that Winston Churchill was the only one who could head a Government acceptable to all parties. Consequently, Chamberlain resigned and Churchill accepted the King's commission to form a coalition to carry on the war. He selected the leader of the opposition, Clement Attlee, as Deputy Prime Minister and formed a new ministry of Conservatives, Liberals, and Labourites. Besides himself and Attlee, he picked three others to compose a war cabinet to manage the day-to-day direction of the struggle. This Government lasted until victory was achieved in Europe in May 1945. During that time the parties followed an electoral truce, not contesting Parliamentary seats which fell vacant because of death or resignation. The strengths of the parties in Parliament thus remained constant throughout the war.

As success for the allied cause became certain, the Labour Party grew restive and eager to resume its freedom of action. Churchill proposed that the coalition continue in order to achieve victory over Japan and to deal with immediate postwar problems, but the leaders of the Labour Party decided to withdraw and obtain their independence. There was agreement that a general election should be held inasmuch as ten years had elapsed since the electorate had had an opportunity to go to the polls. Upon the withdrawal of the Labour ministers from the Government, Churchill formed a 'caretaker' ministry and announced a general election for 5 July 1945.

The Labour Party campaigned for a mandate which would authorize it to make some significant changes in Britain's economic and social life. It proposed the introduction of a planned economy to insure each citizen an increasing measure of social well-being. A number of the basic industries and services of the British state were to be transferred from private to public ownership and management. The Conservatives had a much less formal program than their Labour opponents, and they based a great deal of their campaign upon the importance of continuing Churchill as Prime Minister until the war in the Far East should be concluded and until the basic issues of peace should be decided.

The results of the election were surprising to the people of Britain and to the world at large. The Labour Party won a large Parliamentary majority, 393 of the 640 seats in the House of Commons. The Conservative opposition numbered only 189. The Liberal Party was reduced to 12 seats, its smallest representation in history. Two Communists were elected to the House. From the debacle of 1931, when the divided and demoralized Labour Party had been reduced to 54 seats, it had come back within 14 years to the position of winning a strong Parliamentary majority and forming a Government independent of any outside support. The country had given Labour the mandate for which it had asked.

As the time drew near when the life of the Parliament elected in 1945 would come to an end, much speculation arose concerning the date of a general election. After four years in power the Labour Party had carried through a monumental legislative program and had redeemed all the pledges given in the campaign of 1945. It had encountered strong opposition to a bill adding the iron and steel industry to the nationalization list, and the Government had started a measure to reduce the delaying power of the House of Lords to one year in order to complete action on the iron and steel bill before the expiration of the life of Parliament. Some Labourites were eager that there be no dissolution before this legislative action was complete. Others whose enthusiasm for the nationalization program had begun to wane and who feared future economic difficulties gave their counsel for an early election. These conflicting views within the party became pronounced at the time of the devaluation crisis in September 1949. The advocates of an early election believed that the party should go to the country before rising prices and discontent among the laboring classes, which were expected to follow devaluation by a few months, became serious issues. They were prepared to sacrifice iron and steel nationalization at this time in the hope that Labour would win a new mandate and could then reintroduce the bill to transfer the industry to public hands. Others in the party advised postponing an election until the country had recovered from the shock of devaluation and until the expected beneficial effects in terms of increased exports and rising gold and dollar reserves would restore the voters' confidence in Labour's management of the British economy. The Prime Minister, who had the final word on the timing of the general election, kept his own counsel. Nevertheless, an electioneering atmosphere developed throughout the country, since all politicians realized that a decision would have to be made soon and the battle joined. Attlee finally announced that the Parliament in recess over the Christmas holidays would not meet again and that a general election would be held on 23 February 1950.

A record number of candidates filed nomination papers for the general election of February 1950. The Labour and Conservative parties contested virtually every seat in the House of Commons. The Liberal Party, making a valiant bid for a comeback, nominated 475 candidates. Even the Communists, whose electoral activities no one took seriously, entered 100 candidates in the race. No important issue developed during the campaign. The Labour Party pointed to its record during the past five years and contrasted the full employment of the postwar period with the depressed conditions under Conservative Governments prior to 1939. The Conservatives challenged few of the economic and social objectives of the Labour program but contended that the Government had been wasteful and inefficient in its management of British affairs. The forecasts about the outcome predicted a close race, but how very close was surprising to all. Labour won 13,266,592 popular votes; the Conservatives, 12,502,567, and the Liberals, 2,621,548. Representation in the House of Commons was Labour 315, Conservatives 298, and Liberals 9. When all the counting was finished Labour had a majority of six over all other parties. Never before had the balance in the House of Commons been so close.

For about a year and a half the Labour Government carried on with its small Parliamentary majority. Although continuous and vigorous Conservative opposition placed the Labour members under considerable strain, they maintained their ranks and repelled all major challenges. The near deadlock in Parliament, however, was unsatisfactory to the parties and fed agitation in the constituencies for a general election to clarify the situation. Finally, Prime Minister Attlee announced in a broadcast: 'I consider that the time has now come to ask the electors for a renewal of confidence in the Government and to give it adequate Parliamentary support in order to deal with the important issues with which the country is faced at home and abroad.' [1] Parliament was dissolved on 5 October 1951, and the general election set for 25 October.

The party machines were ready for battle. Altogether 1376 candidates were nominated. The Labour and Conservative Parties, with their allies, contested nearly every seat in the House of Commons. The Liberals decided to concentrate their efforts and nominated only 100 candidates. The campaign proved to be largely a continuation of the one in 1950. About the only new issue was a Conservative charge that Labour bungling had led to the loss of Britain's oil properties in Iran and to trouble with Egypt over British bases in the Suez Canal zone. The Labourites replied by characterizing their Tory opponents as out-of-date imperialists who would embroil the country in costly local wars; some accused Churchill of being a 'war-monger.'

In the general election of 1951 the pendulum swung the other way, but not very far. The Conservatives and their allies captured 321 seats, while Labour won 295. Six seats were won by Liberals and three by independent candidates. Thus, the Conservatives had a majority of 17 over all other parties. In popular votes, Labour had a very slight margin. The party polled 13,949,105 votes, or 48.7 per cent of the total; the Conservatives, 13,730,642, or 48 per cent; the Liberals, 730,552, or 2.5 per cent. The Communist Party, which contested ten seats, received only 21,640 votes, and all its candidates had to forfeit their election deposits.

When the result of the election was clear, Attlee immediately resigned, and the King invited Churchill to form a Government. The new Prime Minister invited the small Liberal group to ally itself with the majority

---

[1] *The Times,* 20 September 1951.

172–

party, but the offer was refused. The Parliamentary Labour Party re-elected Attlee as its leader, and he thus became the official Leader of the Opposition.

4. *The Composition and Distribution of Parties*

The adult population of the United Kingdom, viewed from the standpoint of its political allegiance, appears to be about equally divided into Labourites and Conservatives. Each party can count on a base strength of approximately ten million voters. While these voters are not found in sharply defined packages, there are, nevertheless, geographical areas and social groups in which each is strong.

The Labour Party, as we would expect, is dominant in the major industrial areas of Great Britain. In a wide belt stretching diagonally across the island from South Wales to the Tyneside there are constituencies which regularly return Labour members to Parliament. There are, in addition, mining and manufacturing districts in Scotland and in other parts of England where the Labour Party has great strength. In London, the working-class districts north, east, and south of the old City are strongholds of the party. In social distribution, Labour can count on a high proportion of all trade unionists voting for it and a great many of the unorganized workers. It also attracts some middle-class support in the large centers of population.

The Conservative Party is strongest in the counties of southern and central England which are primarily agricultural areas. It is also strong in those parts of northern England and Scotland which are not highly industrialized. The party counts enough loyal voters to win it seats in a good many of the big metropolitan areas, especially in the constituencies of a suburban nature. By social groups, it unites the business and farming elements of the population and a high proportion of the professional classes. The Conservatives have also enjoyed the support of a large percentage of the farm laborers and the village population throughout the country. Even in a number of industrial and mining areas there are considerable groups of Conservative voters. In Northern Ireland it has a traditional dominance in all classes except the nationalists who consider that their first loyalty is to the republic to the south.

While a map of the United Kingdom by counties or constituencies shows a high concentration of Labour or Conservative strength in particular areas of the country, it would be misleading to conclude that the other party is hopelessly weak in these areas. In fact, party strength is fairly well distributed, and the so-called 'solid' Labour or Conservative territories are often closely divided. According to an analysis made after the 1950 election, 'In Durham and Tees-side, which sent back a solid block of Labour members, the Labour poll was only sixty percent of the total; in the Yorkshire woollen district it was only the merest fraction over half; in the Black Country it was less than fifty-four percent; even in the industrial areas of

−173

South Wales it was less than two-thirds of the whole.'[2] In the areas which regularly return Conservatives, the Labour strength usually rises to 40 or 45 per cent of the voting population. Neither the Conservative nor the Labour Party considers its cause so hopeless in any constituency of Great Britain that it offers no candidate in a general election. There is no 'solid South' in the United Kingdom where one party has overwhelming strength. Even in Northern Ireland the Unionist (Conservative) vote in 1950 was only 62.7 per cent of the total.

The Liberal Party, which polled more than two and a half million votes in 1950, is widely distributed geographically. In that election, 'English counties and boroughs accounted for over a million each, 2,104,871 in all, distributed over 369 constituencies of every kind. The typical Liberal vote was a figure of five or six thousand, not varying greatly in borough or county, North or South.'[3] About the only concentration of Liberal strength occurs in Wales, where formerly the party was dominant. Labour, however, has won away most of the miners in the south and the Liberals are able to return only four or five M.P.'s. There is a good deal of Liberal strength in Scotland, but it was not sufficiently concentrated in 1950 to carry more than two constituencies against the Labourites and Conservatives. The present-day Liberal Party brings together people belonging to all classes of British society. The party has always had a good following among noncomformist religious groups.[4]

As a result of the 1951 general election the future of liberalism as an organized political force is uncertain. The party's popular vote fell to 730,552, and only six of its candidates were successful. Approximately three-fourths of the voters supporting the Liberal Party in 1950 cast their ballots for the candidates of other parties in the next general election, and the Conservatives were apparently the chief beneficiaries. It is problematical how many of these voters would return to their previous allegiance if they had Liberal candidates to support. Moreover, a party without prospects of forming a Government finds it difficult to attract new adherents and to maintain an organization in competition with the major party machines.

The Communist Party has never been large in Britain, and it shows no signs of growing, despite the considerable agitation in which it indulges. Its membership is supposed to be about 40,000, and it collected 91,684 votes in the 1950 election. With ten candidates entered in the general election of 1951, the Communist Party received only 21,640 votes. Geographically, its strength is in the poorer industrial areas of London, the

---

[2] *The Economist,* 11 March 1950.

[3] H. G. Nicholas, *The British General Election of* 1950 (London, 1951), p. 300.

[4] Nicholas describes the Liberal voters of 1950 as constituting 'a remarkably diversified minority.' He states: 'Analyses of the composition of Liberal voters, as revealed in B.I.P.O. [British Institute of Public Opinion] polls, show that to a greater degree than any other party the Liberal Party seems to have drawn its support evenly from both sexes, all ages, all classes and all occupations.' Ibid. p. 300.

Clydeside, and South Wales. It also enjoys some support in the mining areas of Durham and Scotland. Outside of the working classes it has a sprinkling of members who are in professional activities.

5. *Party Principles and Policies*

Labour presents itself as the party of democratic socialism. The socialist objectives of the party embrace the public ownership of the basic industries of the state and those economic enterprises that are natural monopolies. These include the power resources of the country, coal and electricity, the iron and steel industry, the major services of transportation and communications, and the natural monopolies of gas and water supply. In all, the Labour Party considers that roughly 20 per cent of the economic life of the country should be publicly owned and managed. For the remaining 80 per cent the Labour Party is prepared to continue private ownership but only under a considerable degree of governmental regulation which requires it to conform to the economic planning of the state. Thus, private business is subject to controls on investment, on the location of industry, and on the allocation of its output between the domestic and export markets. Through financial and trade controls a Labour Government would plan the economic life of the nation and bring thousands and thousands of individual business enterprises into conformity with its general program.

According to Labour Party policy, economic planning and control should be directed by a democratically chosen government. The party believes that through persuasion a majority of the population can be won to the Labour program and that a regular accounting, in the form of the traditional electoral system, should be given to the voters of the country. The regulation and control which a socialist economy requires should not, in the view of this party, impinge upon any of the basic civil liberties of the citizen. Freedom of discussion and the right of criticism are to be safeguarded, and the socialist way must win its victory in free competition with other programs. The Labour Party, therefore, considers itself directly opposed to communist philosophy, however much their economic and social objectives may be alike. There is no place in the philosophy of the Labour Party for control by a dictatorial group or for the repressive measures of the police state. Moreover, the democratic socialist, declares one of the leading journals supporting the Labour Party, 'does not accept the Communist view that the State should plan in detail all production and distribution. It is not our aim either to compel everyone to do the work we think he is best suited to, or to provide people with goods according to our definition of their needs. That is slavery. Under proper safeguards, most people prefer to sell their labour and to buy their goods in a free market. What the democratic Socialist is determined to achieve is that the freedom of the market is a genuine freedom, and this demands interference with the price system at many points.' [5]

---

[5] *The New Statesman and Nation,* 6 November 1948, p. 391.

Of equal importance with its economic objectives are the social welfare goals advocated by the Labour Party. It believes that the state has a responsibility to insure a constantly improving standard of living for all citizens of the country. Since the wage-earning classes have the lowest standard, measures must be taken to give them an increased share of the national product. Complete equality of income is not an aim of the party, but it desires to narrow the gap between the highest and the lowest levels of personal income. 'The method adopted to achieve greater equality has been twofold,' one of Labour's leading publicists has said. 'On the one hand there has been a substantial increase in the wages of the lower paid workers secured partly by trade union action and partly by direct Government intervention and arbitration in the case of unorganized workers. On the other, taxation has been used as an instrument to bring about a substantial redistribution of the national income.' [6]

All classes of the population, but particularly the wage-earning classes, must be protected, the party believes, from the various menaces which are prevalent in a modern industrial society. These include the threat of unemployment, dependency in old age, accidental injury while working, inadequate income for family life, and the inability to obtain proper medical attention. Against all these social ills, it is Labour Party policy to devise and extend remedial measures. This program is the content of the welfare state. In popular language it is designed to safeguard the individual citizen from the cradle to the grave. Furthermore, Labour theory goes beyond guarantees of minimum protection and endorses more positive objectives. The latter include greater educational opportunities for all classes of the population and increased cultural and recreational facilities.

Labour Party theorists have given much attention to foreign policy. Historically, the party has been a critic of nationalism and imperialism, holding that these forces lead to wars in which the common people suffer and the big capitalists profit. There have always been strong pacifist elements in the party who believe in the virtues of peace for its own sake and in the ideals of world co-operation. Before World War II Labour gave strong support to the League of Nations, worked for the reduction of armaments, and sought to foster the pacific settlement of international disputes. It believed that as the laboring classes won greater political power throughout the world the prospects for peace and good relations would be enhanced.

The nature of the international scene since 1945 has forced the party to change some of its policies if not its objectives in foreign affairs. It has discovered that working-class populations under communist dominance, while they might protest loudly their belief in peace and good relations, pursue policies which violate many of the sacred precepts of British Labour philosophy. Consequently, the Labour Party, although still regarding the maintenance of peace, the pacific settlement of international disputes, and

---

[6] Francis Williams, 'The Program of the British Labour Party; an Historical Survey,' *The Journal of Politics,* May 1950, p. 192.

the reduction of armaments as prime objectives, sees that these goals can best be obtained through the traditional methods of alliances with like-minded powers, patient diplomacy, and strong national defenses. The acceptance of these policies in foreign affairs has caused considerable soul-searching in the party, and it is with a good deal of reluctance that Labour conferences have endorsed the use of force to maintain British interests overseas, the continuance of conscription at home, and the support of a defense establishment that is a heavy burden upon the British economy.

In keeping with its international aims, the Labour Party has always maintained connections with socialist parties in other countries. Following World War II and Labour's sweeping victory in the general election of 1945, the party stood forth as the strongest and most mature social democratic movement in Europe. It endeavored to give advice and encouragement to the socialist parties in the Continental countries and to keep them from being submerged by the aggressive communist forces on the left and from conservative groups on the right.[7] An international branch in the party headquarters maintained close liaison with the socialist parties of Italy, France, and the Scandinavian countries. In Germany, the Social Democrats were encouraged to rebuild German political life and to espouse causes similar to the policies of Labour in Great Britain. Contact with socialist groups on the Continent was also promoted through the Trades Union Congress which endeavored to aid the socialist labor movements in becoming rallying centers of working-class interests.

On the whole, the Labour Party has been only moderately successful in its efforts to assume the leadership of European socialism. The weakness and divisive tendencies of most of the socialist parties on the Continent have not given British Labour much of a force to build upon, and the necessities of foreign policy have frequently caused Labour Governments of the United Kingdom to be more concerned about political stability than about socialist progress. The temperamental and psychological differences which always affect Anglo-Continental relations appear in the case of British Labour's contacts with socialists across the Channel. Indeed, British trade unionists often seem to be more nationalistic in their attitudes and feelings and more distrustful of foreigners than the Conservatives. Only with the trade unionists and the social democrats of Scandinavia do the British Labourites have sufficient temperamental affinity to work together easily. British Labour, therefore, despite its strong position at home after 1945, has not supplied the leadership of a European socialist movement that many expected it would. If Britain's economic condition had been stronger following the war, the Labour Party might have had a more effec-

---

[7] An example of the Labour Party's support of Continental socialists was its grant in 1948 of £1000 to the party organ of French socialism, *Le Populaire. The Times,* 19 May 1949. In 1951 the National Executive Committee of the Labour Party endorsed the establishment of a fund by the Socialist International to promote the development of social democratic parties in Asia, and it offered an initial contribution of £1000. *The Times,* 26 July 1951.

tive influence in strengthening and encouraging European socialist parties. As it was, the exigencies of the British situation sometimes forced the Labour Government to follow policies that many in the Continental nations regarded as hesitant and cautious if not unco-operative and selfish.

The Conservative Party represents itself as the party of capitalism and free enterprise. It contrasts the socialist principles of its Labour opponents with its own belief in the private ownership of property and the usefulness of the profit motive in Britain's economic life. 'A true property-owning democracy,' the party's 1950 election manifesto asserted, 'must be based upon the wide distribution of private property, not upon its absorption in the State machine.' [8]

The party is opposed in principle to the ideas of shaping the British economy by planning and of using extensive controls to direct the efforts of the nation's productive forces. While Conservative thought is thus opposed to planning and the use of controls, Conservative policy is by no means so positive on these matters. For one thing, the realities of Britain's position as a manufacturing and trading nation have forced the Conservatives to accept a great deal of governmental planning and direction. The freedom possible when Britain was a more wealthy power and had an enormous cushion of overseas investments is simply not feasible today. Secondly, the Conservatives have in the past accepted a good deal of unofficial planning and control through cartels and trade associations. Their belief in the virtues of competition and free enterprise has never been carried to the point of condemning all control and direction of the economy. What they do oppose is the policy of state capitalism pursued by their major opponents. They think that socialist planning is a highly inexact science, that it produces an unwieldy bureaucracy, and that it is more apt to stultify the creative and productive forces of the nation than release them.

The Conservative position on the issues that grow out of the concept of the welfare state is equivocal. The Conservatives by no means oppose the intervention of the state to obtain and guarantee a more abundant life for all citizens of the country. Indeed, Conservatives on the platform frequently claim credit for either proposing or instituting many of the social welfare measures now in operation. The Conservatives profess a belief in a policy of full employment, social insurance to protect individuals and families against the vicissitudes of modern life, greater educational opportunities, and a rising standard of living for all classes of the population. For example, their general election manifesto in 1950 contained such ringing declarations as, 'We regard the maintenance of full employment the first aim of a Conservative Government'; 'We are determined to give a solid base of social security below which none shall fall and above which each must be encouraged to rise to the utmost limit of his ability'; and 'We

---

[8] *The Times,* 25 January 1950.

178–

pledge ourselves to maintain and improve the Health Service.' [9] They differ from their Labour opponents on the means and the rate by which many of these goals are to be obtained, but they do not condemn them as being false objectives.

In the field of foreign affairs, the Conservative Party has always presented itself in unblushing fashion as the party of a vigorous nationalism. It makes no apology for the British Empire, and declares that the future of the United Kingdom depends upon the development of the colonies under British leadership and the continuation of Commonwealth ties. It has never had pacifist tendencies nor has a sentimental internationalism pervaded its councils. It has stood for the assertion of British interests overseas and the maintenance of British prestige in international affairs. The Conservative Party has endorsed British participation in international organizations, such as the League of Nations and the United Nations, but it has never regarded such collective security arrangements as substitutes for a militarily strong Britain, alliances with like-minded powers, and close Commonwealth and imperial links.

Conservative policy statements place heavy emphasis upon the United Kingdom's relations with the dominions and with the dependent empire. In the early part of this century many Conservatives cherished the hope that the British Empire could be developed on some kind of a federal basis which would enable it to speak with one voice to the world. Some of them envisaged a global British federation as an enormous protected trading area. The federation idea had no great appeal to the dominions, which wished to establish themselves as independent states in world affairs, and to the United Kingdom it had impractical features because of essential trade relations with non-empire countries. It lives on in the pronouncements of Lord Beaverbrook, but he has little influence in determining orthodox Conservative policy. Nevertheless, the Conservative Party regards itself as a special guardian of imperial interests and desires to foster the remaining ties among the Commonwealth nations and the links between the United Kingdom and the colonies.

The Liberals have endeavored to find a general policy position between those of the Labour and Conservative parties. They have preserved as much of the inherited radical tradition as possible, championing the freedom of international trade, progressive social advances at home, protection of civil liberties, and enlightened colonial policies. The Liberals draw a line between themselves and the Labourites on the issue of socialism. The party professes to believe in the private ownership of property and the private management of British industry. It accepts a large measure of state intervention in the economic sphere, but this is to stop short of public ownership and management. On the other side, the Liberals separate themselves

---

[9] *The Times,* 25 January 1950. Before the 1951 general election, Winston Churchill declared, 'We Conservatives take our stand on basic minimum standards below which nobody should be allowed to fall, but above which everybody should have the fullest opportunity to rise.' *The Sunday Times,* 21 October 1951.

−179

from the Conservatives on the issue of freedom for business interests to organize to control production, fix prices, and allocate markets. The Liberals think that both the Labour and Conservative parties believe in a closely controlled economic order and that they differ only over whether trade unionists and bureaucrats on the one hand, or bankers and industrialists, on the other, shall hold the reins of power. As a substitute for either of these economic regimes the Liberal Party proposes a kind of partnership of management and labor in industrial affairs. Private ownership and management would remain, but through representative councils and profit-sharing schemes the workers would achieve a stake in the businesses in which they are employed. The Liberals advocate strictly drawn legislation against business monopolies and restrictive trade practices.

Traditionally less interested than the Conservatives in foreign policy and imperial affairs, the modern Liberal Party has developed no novel policies in these fields. The party stands for co-operation with all friendly powers and supports participation in international organizations to promote peace, freer economic relations, and rising living standards. It maintains slight contacts with Continental parties which share its general point of view, but they are all so weak in their respective countries that such liaison arouses little enthusiasm among the participants nor does it attract much notice in other circles. Some of the party's leaders have strongly advocated closer relations among the states of Western Europe, and the party endorsed the establishment of the Council of Europe.

The Liberal Party favors more constitutional reforms than either of the major political parties. Because the single-member constituency system of voting works to the disadvantage of third parties, the Liberals are ardent proponents of a change to some kind of proportional representation. They believe, with probably considerable justification, that the adoption of the alternative vote or proportional representation employing multiple-member constituencies would lead to a large increase in their Parliamentary representation and give them a balancing role in the House of Commons. Thus, the party forming a Government would have either to offer a coalition to the Liberals or hold office at their sufferance. Other constitutional changes which are proposed in Liberal policy statements include a reform of the House of Lords, a reorganization of the Cabinet and the administrative departments, and a devolution of authority from Westminster to Scotland and Wales.

Another third party, the Co-operative Party, is closely associated with Labour, and their aims and objectives overlap in most fields of public policy. It does, however, present a national program of its own, and it sponsors some Parliamentary candidates. The Co-operative Party, like the Labour Party, believes in the nationalization of all natural monopolies, such as the railways and the gas and electricity services. It also favors the nationalization of some of the heavy industries, including iron and steel, shipbuilding, and chemicals. It opposes nationalization of those industries and trades where it believes consumer control, through co-operative principles,

180—

is practicable. So far it has been able to accept all the nationalization measures of Labour Governments, but the two parties might part company on future nationalization proposals. In 1950 the objections of the Co-operative Party caused the Labour Party to revise a proposal for the nationalization of insurance to a plan of 'mutualization.' In other fields of domestic policy and on foreign policy the Co-operative Party is a staunch ally of Labour.

A schismatic socialist group, the Independent Labour Party, has maintained a separate existence although its Parliamentary representation in the House elected in 1945 merged with the Labour Party after the death of its leader, James Maxton. At its annual conference in 1950 the I.L.P. decided to continue its electoral activity, declaring that the Labour Party was disposed to carry out 'Tory policy.' According to the I.L.P., 'the Labour Party performs a vital, militant role when in Parliamentary opposition, but concerns itself only with attempting to run capitalism at home and maintain the Empire abroad while holding office.' The I.L.P., consequently, believed, after failing to elect any candidates in 1950, that it 'should remain an independent political organization, fighting elections wherever possible and thus providing a real Socialist alternative to the electorate.' [10] It nominated four candidates in the general election of 1951, but none was elected.

As befits a party which has no prospect of being saddled with the responsibility for what it advocates, the Communist Party proclaims the most radical set of policies to be placed before British voters. It does not advocate the immediate establishment of a communist state on the model of Soviet Russia, although that is undoubtedly its ultimate goal, but it declares for the most extreme version of the principles and policies proposed by other parties. Thus, in its election manifesto in 1950, the Communist Party advocated general wage increases, the taxing of profits until 'the rich really squeal,' price cuts, the abolition of sales taxes on all commodities except luxuries, increases in family allowances and all pensions, and the nationalization of land and many additional industries. In the field of foreign affairs it repeats verbatim the propaganda line of Moscow. During the general election campaign of 1950 the party's general secretary declared that the Communists 'would repudiate the North Atlantic Treaty, outlaw the atomic bomb and begin negotiations for world peace.' [11] The constitutional changes the Communists propose include the establishment of Scottish and Welsh parliaments, a reduction of the voting age to 18, and abolition of the House of Lords.

From reading the party manifestoes and hearing the leaders of British political parties, one might conclude that real differences of opinion separate the major British parties, and this would be a correct conclusion. Nevertheless, it would be an incomplete conclusion should one overlook

---

[10] *The Times,* 10 April 1950.
[11] *The New York Times,* 17 February 1950.

the substantial measure of agreement that exists and the beliefs that they share. Leaving aside the desire of the Liberals for proportional representation, there are no major constitutional issues which divide the parties. All are satisfied with the role of the monarchy in modern British life, all believe in Parliamentary supremacy and in the present methods of Cabinet government, all insist upon the independence of the judiciary, all support the neutrality of the Civil Service, and all recognize the need for some reform of local government. The only important constitutional issue on which they find agreement difficult is the reform of the House of Lords, and in this matter both the Conservatives and the Labourites wish to make changes in the composition and the powers of the second chamber.

Although the division between the major parties is most sharp on domestic issues, particularly those concerning the nationalization of industry and the degree to which the state shall plan and control the economic life of the country, there are not irreconcilable differences between the parties. The Conservatives are prepared to accept most of the nationalization steps which Labour has taken; they have only committed themselves to restore the iron and steel industry and the road haulage service to private ownership. In the field of the social services, there is little disagreement in principle although there is much disputing about costs and priorities. Foreign affairs do not raise deeply contentious issues; indeed, there tends to be more criticism of foreign policy within the ranks of each party than there is between the leadership of the two. Both parties believe in fostering Commonwealth relations and in developing the colonial empire. Differences arise in regard to the speed at which constitutional changes should be introduced in the colonies, but the necessity for political advances is not seriously questioned.

It is this large measure of agreement which gives British political life a high degree of stability and which enables power to be transferred from one party to the other without shocks to the fabric of the state. A change of the party in power is more likely to involve a change of rate in the pursuit of various common goals and objectives than a radical change of policy. A party coming into office accepts in general what its predecessor has done; it proceeds to build from that point in accordance with its principles and policies.

182–

XI

Party Organization and Finances

The organization of British political parties has two aspects—namely, the organization of voters throughout the country and the organization of party members in Parliament. The two are intimately related: voters are organized to elect candidates to the House of Commons, and a Parliamentary party must keep in close touch with the national party organization if its strength is to be maintained. The two party organizations, the national and the Parliamentary, are interlocked by a number of common officers, by the contacts of the central offices with party leaders in Parliament, and by the annual conferences in which representatives of both participate.

1. *National Party Organizations*

The country-wide organization of political parties was stimulated by the enlargements of the electorate in the nineteenth century. Before that time there was little need for party organization outside Parliament because the number of voters was small and many members of the House of Commons came from rotten or pocket boroughs which were controlled by patrons or small cliques of local notables. Moreover, in the county constituencies the voters were scattered, and the maintenance of continuing organizations would have been impeded by the poor communications of that period. The abolition of the rotten and pocket boroughs and the addition of hundreds of thousands, and later millions, of voters to the electoral rolls changed the situation and produced conditions inviting the formation of nation-wide party organizations.

The first organizations to appear were registration societies. Their mission was to get the names of all eligible voters on the registration lists since the Reform Act of 1832 made such enrollment a prerequisite to voting. The registration societies canvassed the electorate, reminding the forgetful and stimulating the apathetic among the voting population. They did not concern themselves with nominating candidates or conducting campaigns.

The Liberal Party advanced beyond the stage of registration societies when it started organizing urban voters for the purposes of selecting candidates and planning campaign strategy. The basic unit of organization was the ward caucus, embracing all the Liberal voters living in a ward. The caucus selected a ward committee which in turn was represented in a city-wide convention. Introduced in Birmingham by Joseph Chamberlain, the

Liberal scheme of organization quickly proved its worth and was soon imitated throughout the country. The Conservatives saw the need of a more effective organization than that provided by the registration societies, and they hastened to bring their supporters together into local groups. While the organizing movement developed more rapidly in the large cities, it spread before long into the rural areas.

The next step was to join the hundreds of local party associations into national organizations. The Conservatives were first to do this, establishing in 1867 the National Union of Conservative and Constitutional Associations. The National Liberal Federation was founded ten years later.

The national organization of the Conservative Party continues to be based upon local associations. There is one in each Parliamentary constituency, and it is composed of all persons who contribute to the local party fund. The members of an association are organized by branches or polling districts. Each Conservative association is an autonomous unit, making and amending its rules, choosing its officers, 'adopting,' that is selecting, its Parliamentary candidate, and picking its candidates for local government elections. All members are eligible to attend an annual meeting at which officers are chosen and reports read. The major work of an association, however, is conducted by an executive council and a smaller finance and general purposes committee.

The constituency associations are linked together in the National Union of Conservative and Unionist Associations. They are represented in one of the National Union's 12 area councils, its central council, and at its annual conference. The purposes of the National Union are primarily to promote and rally the Conservative interest throughout the country; its duties with respect to the constituency associations are advisory and not controlling. However, its Standing Advisory Committee on Parliamentary Candidates has the power to withhold the Conservative label from unapproved prospective candidates.

At the pinnacle of the national organization is the leader of the party, who is the Prime Minister if the Conservatives are in power or the Leader of the Opposition if they are not. He is elected, when the position falls vacant, by the Conservative members of both houses of Parliament, prospective Parliamentary candidates, and the executive committee of the National Union of Conservative and Unionist Associations. His position is one of great power and influence within the party. The party leader determines Conservative policy on the important issues of the day. In doing so he has the benefit of advice from Parliamentary colleagues and party committees, but he alone pronounces the authoritative views of the Conservative Party. No one else can commit the party in policy matters. Moreover, he selects the chairman of the party, who is the head of the Central Office and responsible for maintaining an efficient and financially well-supported organization.

The Central Office is a permanent headquarters which keeps in touch with the constituency associations and endeavors to make all the general preparations and provide the resources required for waging a successful

184–

election campaign. It advises local groups on organizational problems and party tactics.[1] It undertakes the study of public issues and publishes the reports in pamphlets and booklets. The Central Office arranges speaking engagements and in other ways helps local associations to promote the party cause. It interviews persons desiring to stand for Parliament and maintains a roster of names from which recommendations can be made when a constituency association lacks a suitable local candidate. Because parties always need money to carry on their activities, the Central Office is constantly soliciting likely contributors. As the time of a general election approaches, and particularly during the official campaign period, the activities of the Central Office are greatly accelerated. It uses all the arts of publicity to put the Conservative case to the voters and to arouse enthusiasm among party workers.

The Central Office is connected with the constituencies through the system of election agents, who form a corps of professional political workers. Ideally the Central Office would like to have a full-time agent in each constituency. For the 1950 general election the Conservatives came close to this goal, having full-time party officials in 527 of the 542 constituencies in England and Wales and in most of the Scottish constituencies.[2] The party's agents, who are organized in the National Society of Conservative and Unionist Agents, are employed by individual constituency associations, but they are subject to considerable supervision by the Central Office. The Central Office conducts a training program for agents and gives examinations for certificates of proficiency. The profession has three levels—the organizer, the certificated organizer, and the certificated agent. The party has adopted salary scales for election agents, ranging from £400 to £800 a year, and they are covered by a pension scheme to which an agent and his constituency association contribute on an equal basis.

In the constituency the agent is in charge of all the party's political activity. He manages the local party headquarters, directs the work of paid canvassers and subscription collectors, arranges speaking engagements and other appearances for the candidate, contracts for printing and advertising, and accounts for the money collected and spent in an election. In discharging his responsibilities, he must act with skill and tact in order to elicit as much volunteer support as possible and to avoid any political mistake that would harm the prospects of his party's candidate. Between the constituency agent and the Central Office there is a regional headquarters in the charge of a Central Office agent. The latter has a staff of specialists who are available to help in local situations, and who are concerned with

---

[1] For example, in 1950 the Conservative Central Office advised the Montgomeryshire Conservative Association, according to its chairman, not to oppose the constituency's M.P., Clement Davies, leader of the Liberal Party in the House of Commons. *The Times,* 19 December 1950. This advice was probably given in conformity with a strategical plan to incorporate as much of the Liberal strength as possible into the Conservative camp.

[2] H. G. Nicholas, *The British General Election of* 1950 (London, 1951), p. 24.

women's activities, youth organizations, labor groups, party publicity in the area, and similar matters. In cities containing several constituencies there is usually a chief agent to co-ordinate and to supplement the work of the individual agents. In all, the Conservatives have a quite complete organization extending from several hundred election agents to the general director or national agent in the party's Central Office.

Once a year the Conservative Party convenes a conference attended by the national officers and several thousand delegates from local associations. They meet for several days to hear speeches by the party leaders and by representatives of various groups and classes of voters—farmers, students, housewives, businessmen, and anti-socialist trade unionists. The conference debates resolutions on national issues proposed by delegates, but those adopted have no binding force. They do not become a party platform to which the leader and his Parliamentary colleagues are committed. Nevertheless, the debates and the resolutions indicate party sentiment and influence future policy pronouncements by the leadership. Since the annual conference has no national candidates to nominate, it lacks some of the drama and tension of an American party convention. It succeeds, however, in stimulating hundreds of rank-and-file delegates to work more ardently for victory in the next election. A description of a recent annual conference as 'a rally rather than a conference, the signal for a demonstration of enthusiasm rather than a serious discussion of the aims and content of Conservative policy' fits the typical national meeting of Tory politicians.[3]

The Conservative Party has devoted a good deal of attention to organizational matters in the last few years, and there appears to be general agreement that considerable success has rewarded its effort. Some Labour Party politicians were disposed to attribute their loss of Parliamentary seats in the general election of 1950 to an improved organization and direction of the Conservative machine. The Conservatives, for their part, have been stimulated by the challenge of the effective organization with which they compete.

The history of the organization of the Labour Party—as distinguished from the political trends and movements which produced it—begins with the establishment of the Labour Representation Committee in 1900. In February of that year delegates from the Trades Union Congress and three socialist groups met and formed the Committee in order to 'devise ways and means for securing an increased number of Labour members in the next Parliament.' The three socialist groups were the Social Democratic Federation, the Independent Labour Party, and the Fabian Society. The first was a rather ineffectual organization started in 1881 to propagate the doctrines of Karl Marx. 'By 1900,' according to an historian of the period, 'it was already a spent force with no future ahead of it.'[4] The Independent

[3] *The Economist,* 21 October 1950, p. 617.
[4] D. C. Somervell, *British Politics since* 1900 (New York, 1950), p. 23.

186–

Labour Party was founded in 1893 by James Keir Hardie, a Scottish miner who had been elected to Parliament the previous year. Along with two other M.P.'s elected in 1892, Keir Hardie held himself aloof in the Commons from the few so-called 'Lib-Labs,' who were Liberal Party members of working-class background. The I.L.P. members failed to secure re-election in 1895, but they had established an organization which continued.

The Fabian Society sprang from different roots than the other two socialist groups and was destined to play a more influential part in the development of the Labour Party. Started in 1884 by some members of the London intelligentsia, it was soon propagating socialist ideas with much energy and literary skill. In its early days, the activities of the Fabian Society brought together such persons as George Bernard Shaw, H. G. Wells, Graham Wallas, and Sidney and Beatrice Webb. The Webbs had a wide acquaintance in political and literary circles and for several decades exerted through their personal contacts, public services, and writings a great influence upon their times. The Fabians were originally not much interested in a socialist or working-class party; they believed that because of social and economic developments the trend toward collectivism was irresistible and that what was required was some intellectual group to supply politicians with the practical measures to meet the desires and needs of the masses. The socialist state, in their view, would not be created by revolution but by the progressive adoption of collectivist programs—'the inevitability of gradualness,' to use the frequently quoted words of Sidney Webb.

The trade unions represented at the meeting in 1900 were by no means committed to socialism. Their interest was to increase working-class representation at Westminster with a view to obtaining practical benefits for wage-earners. For this purpose they were prepared to co-operate with the socialist groups and to provide most of the money needed by the Labour Representation Committee.

The Labour Party started, therefore, as a kind of holding company for trade union and socialist organizations. A person did not join the party directly but supported it by virtue of his membership in an affiliated organization. In 1918 a Labour Party Conference adopted a new constitution which announced a more general objective than the election of labor representatives to Parliament and which required appropriate organizational changes. Its new program was 'to secure for the producers by hand or by brain the full fruits of their industry and the most equitable distribution thereof that may be possible, upon a basis of common ownership of the means of production and the best obtainable system of popular administration and control of each industry and service.' To provide a method of membership for producers 'by brain' and those 'by hand' who did not belong to trade unions the conference authorized the formation of local Labour associations of individual members. Several hundred of these associations have been formed. In nearly every Parliamentary constituency nowadays the local Labour Party is a federation of the constituency association, the branches of trade unions, and other affiliated groups.[5] All these organizations are represented on a general committee, which elects the officers and the executive committee of the local Labour Party.

Headship of the national Labour Party is not vested in a leader but in the National Executive Committee, a body consisting of 25 members and a treasurer elected at the annual conference. Twelve members of the committee represent the affiliated trade unions, one represents socialist, co-operative, and professional organizations, seven represent constituency Labour parties, and five women represent their sex in the Labour movement. The committee has a chairman who serves for a year. The leader of the Parliamentary Labour Party is an *ex-officio* member of the National Executive.

The Labour Party holds an annual conference to which come delegates from all affiliated organizations. The annual conference receives reports from its officers, elects the members of the National Executive Committee, hears addresses by the party leaders, and debates resolutions. The debating and voting on resolutions are somewhat more significant activities than they are at a Conservative Party conference, for the Labour conference, in principle, lays down policy to be followed by the Parliamentary party. When the party is in opposition in the House of Commons, the Parliamentary leaders are usually disposed to follow the views of the conference, but a Labour Cabinet finds that the responsibilities of office are not so easily reconciled with policy-making by convention techniques. In practice, therefore, Cabinet ministers and the National Executive co-operate to manage the annual conference and to insure the adoption of resolutions which are generally agreeable to the Government. This frequently calls for a considerable exercise of the arts of practical politics. Many resolutions come from the more radical elements of the party, the constituency associations being particularly productive of resolutions demanding 'more socialism,' 'the elimination of all profits,' or 'an end to the cold war with Russia.' Usually the party chieftains can control the debate and, working through trade union leaders, obtain the passage of acceptable resolutions. Since the number of votes cast by delegates to Labour conferences is equal to the dues-paying membership of their organizations—card voting it is called—the attitude of the big trade unions is frequently decisive. In recent years the card vote of the six largest unions accounted for more than half the votes cast at Labour Party conferences, and the total trade union vote amounted to about 80 per cent of the total. Generally speaking, the unions' delegates are loyal to their political leaders, and a ministerial plea seldom goes unheeded.

---

[5] At the end of 1948 the membership of the Labour Party stood at 5,422,437. Eighty affiliated trade unions contributed 4,751,030 members. There were 629,025 individual members. *The Times,* 19 May 1949.

188–

The Labour Party maintains a central office under the administrative supervision of the party's general secretary. He is selected by the National Executive Committee and approved by the annual conference. The central office, often referred to as Transport House from its location in a London office building of that name, has sections dealing with finance, research, international affairs, and other party interests. It promotes the organization of local Labour parties, carries on membership campaigns, provides speakers for party meetings, issues books, pamphlets, and reports, and in other ways serves as the national headquarters of party activity. Liaison with the party leaders in Parliament, especially the whips, is naturally close.

Like the Conservatives, the Labour Party relies heavily upon a system of election agents to build its strength in the constituencies and to manage the campaigns of its candidates. It has not had as many full-time paid agents as the rival party, but it has been increasing the number of election officials of this kind. For the general election of 1950 the party had 279 full-time agents at work, and they were located, for the most part, in constituencies where the need was the greatest. For example, 101 of the 115 constituencies the central office regarded as marginal had full-time Labour agents.[6]

The national headquarters conducts a training course for persons desiring to become agents. Those passing the course successfully receive Grade A certificates as Labour election agents and are eligible for membership in the National Union of Labour Organisers and Election Agents. A minimum salary of £400 a year has been set. Labour election agents, like Parliamentary candidates, must be approved by the party's National Executive Committee. All agents come under the tactical direction of the National Agent in the central headquarters. Between him and the constituency officials are district organizers who supervise party activity in an area of the country.

Besides their regular organizations British political parties maintain or endorse auxiliary groups formed to enlist particular classes of the voting public or to promote interests compatible with general party policy. An active Conservative organization is the Primrose League, named for Disraeli's favorite flower. Another with a less romantic title is the Ratepayers Association. Youth is catered to in the Young Conservatives movement. The Labour League of Youth is an organization with almost 600 branches throughout the country. There are party clubs at all the universities, and the Labour Party has joined its student clubs into the National Association of Labour Student Organizations. These auxiliary organizations hold rallies, arrange speaking engagements, raise money, and by other means promote the party cause.

Some of the West End clubs of London have a political flavor. The membership of the Carlton Club includes many leading Conservatives within and without Parliament, particularly those who manage the Cen-

---

[6] H. G. Nicholas, op. cit. p. 29.

tral Office. There is also a Conservative Club, and the Reform Club has for many years been a place where Liberal politicians forgather.

All in all, the United Kingdom is highly organized from the standpoint of party politics. Each major party provides local associations which the voter can join and offers him a choice of other political organizations through which he can make his influence felt. The farmer, the housewife, the businessman, the trade unionist, the student, all are encouraged to be active in party affairs.

For some years past there has been a trend in British politics toward the strengthening of party machines, that is, the professional elements in the party organizations have been becoming more important while the voluntary and auxiliary groups have been drawn more closely to the central machinery. The salaried staffs of the national headquarters have grown, they perform more services for local associations and branches, and they supervise more closely all forms of party activity. Efforts have been made to increase the number of election agents and to train them in their work. Elections are contests between highly organized and efficient party machines.

2. *The Parliamentary Parties*

Within Parliament each party is formally organized, holds meetings, chooses officers, and establishes committees. By means of its organizational machinery, the Parliamentary party arrives at policy positions, agrees on Parliamentary tactics, and maintains a cohesive, disciplined group.

The organization of a Parliamentary party differs somewhat according to whether the party is in power or in opposition. In power, a party's principal leaders are ministers, officers of the Crown, and policy-making is largely concentrated in the Cabinet. A major opposition party, however, often admits to the discussion of policy and Parliamentary tactics its private members.

The Parliamentary Conservative Party includes all Conservative members in the two houses of Parliament. A member technically joins by accepting the party leadership, and his connection may cease when he rejects the whip or when as a disciplinary measure it is withdrawn.

The Parliamentary party's head is the party leader, chosen, as previously mentioned, by the party members in Parliament, prospective Conservative candidates, and the executive committee of the National Union of Conservative and Unionist Associations. Once elected, he remains leader until his resignation or retirement from politics. His influence with respect to party policy and Parliamentary tactics is as great at Westminster as it is concerning the program of the national Conservative organization. He must, nevertheless, work in collaboration with the principal members of the party and keep in mind the opinions and sentiments of the backbenchers. When the Conservatives are in office the Prime Minister is the party leader; indeed, he has usually been designated as leader of the party before he undertakes to form a Ministry.[7] Then his chief counsellors on party matters in Parliament are ministerial colleagues and the whips. When the Conservatives are in opposition, the leader is advised by his 'shadow cabinet,' or the consultative committee, which he appoints.

During the period of Churchill's service as opposition leader there was some Conservative criticism to the effect that his attention to the position was neither as continuous nor as detailed as the Parliamentary situation required. There were complaints that the 'shadow cabinet' decided on Parliamentary moves only to have the leader intervene on a different tact and confuse his supporters. Whatever the merits of this criticism, it has to be recognized that no opposition leader can give complete satisfaction to a large body of politicians of varying opinions and temperaments. When a Parliamentary issue arises they react in different ways. Some favor forthright opposition, some prefer harassing the Government by utilizing all the Parliamentary maneuvers permissible, while others argue for a compromise position. The leader must consider these views and then decide the course to be followed. In Churchill the Conservatives had an opposition leader whose eminent reputation and long political career made him less dependent upon the advice of fellow members than the usual party leader.

The party whips play an important part in the Parliamentary organization of the Conservatives, as they do in other parties too. They are the regular link between the leadership and the rank and file. They receive the requests and the complaints of the members, and they seek to satisfy them in so far as that is possible. The whips have the responsibility of mobilizing the party strength in order to execute the Parliamentary moves on which the leadership has decided. When the party is in power they bring promising backbench material to the attention of the ministers, and they are influential in determining appointments and in making recommendations for honors. In office or out, the whips maintain close connections

---

[7] In 1940 Churchill was asked by the King to form a Government while Chamberlain, the retiring Prime Minister, was still leader of the Conservative Party. Churchill's account of the situation and of his reason for succeeding Chamberlain in the leadership is as follows: 'Mr. Chamberlain also thought it right to resign the leadership of the Conservative Party, and I was invited to take his place. I had to ask myself the question—about which there may still be various opinions—whether the leadership of one great party was compatible with the position I held from King and Parliament as Prime Minister of an Administration composed of and officially supported by all parties. I had no doubt about the answer. The Conservative Party possessed a very large majority in the House of Commons over all other parties combined. Owing to the war conditions no election appeal to the nation was available in case of disagreement or deadlock. I should have found it impossible to conduct the war if I had had to procure the agreement in the compulsive days of crisis and during long years of adverse and baffling struggle, not only of the leaders of the two minority parties, but of the leader of the Conservative majority. Whoever had been chosen and whatever his self-denying virtues, he would have had the real political power. For me there would have been only the executive responsibility.' *Their Finest Hour*, p. 496.

with the party's central office so that the tactics of the Parliamentary and the national parties will be co-ordinated.

While in opposition from 1945 to 1951, the Parliamentary Conservative Party had 16 committees concerned with various fields of public business, such as economic policy, national defense, foreign affairs, and colonial policy. These committees made studies of pending legislation and policy questions, and their conclusions had weight in determining the party's position on current issues. The work of the committees provided material for the use of Conservative members in Parliamentary debates. After taking office in 1951, the Parliamentary Conservative Party continued to have about a dozen committees of backbenchers who studied policy issues and who placed their views before the party's leaders.

In or out of power, there are other groups which unite like-minded members and which have varying degrees of influence in formulating Conservative policy. One is the 1922 Committee, which takes its name from the date when the Lloyd George coalition Government was broken up by the Conservatives' resuming their independence. It is a group of backbench members who express to the leadership the views of a large proportion of the rank and file. In the 1940's the Tory Reform Committee united a number of members who desired the party to champion programs which they believed would appeal to liberal and independent voters.

For several reasons arising out of the history and nature of the Labour movement in Britain, the Parliamentary Labour Party is more highly organized than its Conservative rival. Labour, being a federative movement, has had the problem of providing proper representation for various interest groups, and the organizational structure of the P.L.P. has been a partial answer to this need. Moreover, the Labour Party, both within and without Parliament, has not been prepared to vest as much authority in a leader as have the Conservatives. Close organizational ties between the leadership and the rank and file have always been viewed as important, and this attitude became a conviction after the MacDonald episode in 1931 when, to the dismay of many backbench members, the Labour Prime Minister and several of his ministerial colleagues resigned office and immediately entered a coalition Government. There has been a desire, in addition, to keep the Parliamentary party a democratic group in which minority opinions may be aired and the voice of the backbench member heard in party councils. A rather complex organizational structure has resulted from the efforts to satisfy these needs and desires.

The P.L.P., consisting of the Labour members of both houses, elects a party leader at the beginning of each Parliament. Re-election is customary as long as the leader is able and willing to serve.[8] He is the Prime Minister if the party is in power, the Leader of the Opposition if it is not. His posi-

---

[8] A spirited contest occurred in 1922 when Ramsay MacDonald defeated J. H. Clynes 61 votes to 56. By this victory MacDonald, who had begun his political career as the secretary of the Labour Representation Committee in 1900, was placed in a position to become the first Labour Prime Minister in 1923.

tion is not as authoritative as that of the Conservative leader, but it is one of great power and influence nevertheless.

When the party is in power, the P.L.P. also selects a chairman and a vice-chairman for a liaison committee, which additionally includes the Leader of the House of Commons, the chief whip, a representative of the Labour peers, and the secretary of the Parliamentary party, who is not an M.P. The committee, which meets at least once a week, is designed to serve as a connecting link between the Ministry and the backbench members of the party. 'The Committee has several functions: it keeps the Government in touch with Party feeling, tries to head off revolts by mediating between leaders and rank-and-file, arranges for meetings of the P.L.P. and for smaller conferences of Ministers and interested Backbenchers, and generally seeks to soothe ruffled feelings in Party and Government.' [9] The chairman of the liaison committee presides at meetings of the P.L.P. On such occasions party policy may be discussed or ministers questioned about the affairs of their departments. A meeting of the party membership is frequently required when a highly controversial issue is before Parliament and the Labour ministers feel it necessary to have their position fully understood and supported. Votes in a general meeting of the P.L.P. are rare. If the leadership senses a strong current of dissatisfaction with ministerial policy as expounded before the party meeting, it usually shifts its position until a large measure of agreement is obtained.

In 1945 the P.L.P. created some 20 groups of members, presided over by backbenchers, to study and debate policy questions. Each group was concerned, in a general way, with a major field of public policy—foreign affairs, agriculture, public finance, social insurance, health, and similar subjects. Labour members could join the group or groups in which they were interested. Besides the functional groups of the P.L.P., the membership was also divided into area groups. These consisted of Labour members from London, Scotland, Wales, Yorkshire, and other areas of the United Kingdom. They met to consider policy and administrative matters affecting their regions, and they brought the local aspects of current national problems to the notice of the party leadership.

While the functional groups of the P.L.P. were of some service in giving the backbencher a more effective role in Parliament and of keeping the ministry in touch with party sentiment, they were only moderately successful in meeting the problem facing any party in office, that of providing a means whereby the private member can participate in policy formulation without encroaching upon the necessary authority of the Cabinet. In appraising the group system, a student of the P.L.P. has written as follows:

> Those Members of Parliament who expected that the Groups would give them a chance to take part actively in policy-making have had their hopes rudely dashed. From the start the Ministers made it clear

[9] James MacGregor Burns, 'The Parliamentary Labor Party in Great Britain,' *The American Political Science Review,* December 1950, p. 858.

that they did not look on the Groups in this light. The Ministers' reasons for taking this position were twofold: They felt that constitutionally they could not reveal proposed legislation to a few Members before presenting it to the whole House; and they believed that as a practical matter it would be risky to discuss legislative proposals with Backbenchers because the latter might speak for only a narrow minority of the Party, or they might 'leak' to the press, or they might try to obstruct or alter Cabinet proposals. Some Backbenchers have come to feel that the group meetings are a waste of time, or, even worse, that they are a means of keeping the rank-and-file occupied with trivial tasks so that their influence would be minimized.[10]

There are informal or unofficial groups within the P.L.P. as there are in the Parliamentary Conservative Party. Some of these exist in every Parliament, while others are impermanent and disappear with the passing of the issues which prompted their creation. The trade union group, which unites all M.P.'s officially endorsed and financially supported by trade unions, is a permanent Parliamentary group. An influential body within the P.L.P., its members are naturally concerned with policy and legislation which affects the interests of organized labor. Another permanent group is that of the M.P.'s from mining constituencies. In the Parliament elected in 1945, about 15 backbenchers, led by R. H. S. Crossman, formed a 'Keep Left' group. Dissatisfied with the Government's foreign policy and the effects of military expenditure and conscription upon Labour's domestic program, the 'Keep Left' group criticized the Government in party meetings and in the House of Commons, with Foreign Secretary Bevin as their special target. They did not carry their opposition to the point of an open break with the party leadership, and much of their argument was in time deflated by continued Soviet intransigence.

Although the unofficial groups occasionally produce serious divisions within the Parliamentary party and may embarrass a Government at a critical time, they can also serve to strengthen the hand of the leadership. By organizing a body of opinion within the party they indicate to the leaders the strength and importance of dissatisfaction. If a group is revealed to be expressing the views of a good many members, the leadership can consider what compromises it can offer; if, on the other hand, the dissentients are unimportant, the party chieftains can devise ways of outmaneuvering or even destroying them politically. When their party is in power, dissident groups, as a rule, have no desire to bring down the Ministry, so their opposition must stop short of the point where they threaten the Government's majority in the House of Commons. Not all unofficial groups, moreover, are adverse critics of ministerial policy; some of them give strong support to the party leadership. For example, Labour's trade union group, while it is vigilant in looking after its special interests, is a loyal bloc within the

---

[10] Ibid. pp. 859-60.

party and can be counted upon to mobilize its members behind the official leadership.

After the electoral triumph of 1945 the P.L.P. voted to suspend the rather strict standing orders which bound its members. These orders had authorized the P.L.P. to expel a member 'on account of things said or done' in the House of Commons, and they had provided that, 'outside activities, whether in writing or speech, which are contrary to the discipline or constitution of the Party shall be dealt with by the National Executive Committee.' Furthermore, in case of 'persistent refusal to observe the decisions of the Parliamentary Party,' the P.L.P. was to report the erring member to the National Executive Committee, which would consider 'the matter in its constituency and other aspects.' In other words, a rebellious member faced not only expulsion by the P.L.P. but also loss of endorsement as a Labour candidate. The suspension of the standing orders was continued for a few months after the general election of 1951, but embarrassing dissensions among Labour M.P.'s forced their reimposition. The P.L.P. voted unanimously to require each member to support in debate and divisions the position decided by a party majority unless he was prevented by reasons of conscience from doing so.

While the suspension of these standing orders permitted Labour M.P.'s more freedom in Parliamentary debate and action, it did not prevent the leadership from meting out discipline whenever it felt that a member had transgressed beyond the bounds of reason. Action was usually taken first by the National Executive Committee and followed, in Parliament, by the withdrawal of the Labour whip. Several cases of rebellious conduct arose during the period from 1945 to 1950, and in each the party leadership acted decisively. One M.P., John Platts-Mills, was expelled for being the ringleader of a group of 37 Labourites who sent a telegram of good wishes to a fellow-traveling socialist, Nenni, just before the critical election in Italy in 1948. The sympathies of the British Labour Party were with the orthodox and anti-communist wing of the Italian Socialist Party. When taken to task by the party, all the erring members except Platts-Mills pleaded a misunderstanding of the message, recanted, or gave assurances of future good conduct. Platts-Mills was dropped by his constituency party, and he was defeated by the Labour candidate when he fought the general election of 1950 as an independent. Another member, Konni Zilliacus, was expelled in 1949 for advocating views corresponding too closely to those of international communism. In the case of Zilliacus, his constituency party still wished to retain him as its candidate after his expulsion by the National Executive Committee. The issue was carried to the annual conference where the action of the committee was sustained overwhelmingly. He contested his seat as an independent candidate but was defeated by the regular Labour candidate. In May 1949 a considerable number of Labour M.P.'s, including five Parliamentary Private Secretaries, who are members appointed to assist individual ministers in the House, voted against the Government on the Republic of Ireland Bill. Their offense was deemed serious because a three-line whip had gone out. All were warned that they would be reported to the National Executive Committee if they transgressed again, and the Prime Minister ordered the dismissal from office of the five Parliamentary Private Secretaries.

No serious disciplinary cases arose in the Parliament elected in 1950. The small majority possessed by the Government undoubtedly gave the Labour members a heightened sense of responsibility, and they probably noted the lack of success of those expelled from the party who tried to return as independents.[11] It would be incorrect to conclude, however, that the cohesion of the P.L.P. depends upon the fear of disciplinary action. The great majority of the Labour members regularly support the leadership because of loyalty to the party and its program. They trust and respect their leaders; they have a deep and abiding attachment to the 'Cause.' They have little sympathy, unless a matter of conscience is involved, for the rebel who carries his case to the point of dividing the party and aiding the opposition. When the leaders wield their disciplinary powers against such a rebel, the majority of the rank and file consider the action well deserved.

3. *Party Finance*

Political parties require a good deal of money to carry on their activities. In the central offices, there are the continuing expenses of rent, salaries, postage, supplies, and similar items. Printing bills for pamphlets and more extensive party publications add up to considerable amounts. As a general election approaches expenses increase, and during the official campaign they mount rapidly. At such times the parties deluge the country with tracts and proclaim the virtues of their principles and candidates from numerous billboards and hoardings. One expense British political parties are spared is the purchase of radio and television time. The publicly owned B.B.C. makes available broadcasting facilities without charge, and each party is allotted time roughly proportionate to its Parliamentary strength.[12]

The regulation of political party finances has been limited in Britain to the expenditures of individual candidates. By law each candidate for a seat in the House of Commons may expend, from the start of the campaign, a sum of £450, plus 2d. per voter in predominately rural constituencies and 1½d. per voter in urban constituencies. These provisions permit, in practice, expenditures ranging from about £700 to £1000 by each can-

---

[11] The Parliamentary Labour Party in 1950 censured one M.P., Tom Driberg, 'for gross neglect of his Parliamentary duties.' Mr. Driberg spent several months in Korea as a war correspondent during the period when a number of close divisions occurred in the House of Commons. *The Times,* 16 November 1950.

[12] For the 1950 general election campaign the parties agreed to confine themselves to 14 broadcasts—5 for Labour, 5 for the Conservatives, 3 for the Liberals, and 1 for the Communists. The Labour and Conservative Parties had 120 minutes each at their disposal, the Liberal Party had 40 minutes, and the Communist Party 10 minutes. Each party was free to select its speakers for the time allotted.

didate. In the general election of 1950 the total expenditure of candidates amounted to £1,170,114. This sum was expended for the following purposes: agents' fees, 7.7 per cent; clerical assistance, 5.6 per cent; printing, stationery, advertising and postage, 61.1 per cent; committee rooms, 4.6 per cent; personal expenses, 5.5 per cent; and miscellaneous matters, 9.7 per cent.[13]

In the past a good many Conservative candidates were expected to provide most of their campaign expenses from their own pockets. Believing that this practice limited the number of able candidates available, the party conference has established the rule that no candidate, upon adoption, may contribute more than £25 to his constituency association. Conservative members of Parliament are restricted to an annual contribution of £50 to their local associations. The Labour Party has regulated the contributions of trade unions to constituency parties and to candidates' election expenses. Trade unions are authorized to contribute £250 annually to local party organizations in borough constituencies and £300 in county constituencies, and they may pay up to 80 per cent of a candidate's lawful election expenses. The purpose of the restrictions on direct trade union expenditure is to prevent the unions 'from swamping the initiative and independence of the divisional labour parties.'[14]

Between elections local party associations raise money by solicitation and by arranging bazaars, teas, dances, and other social events. This money is employed to maintain the local organization. Continuing party activity is important, since there is no fixed date for elections and the local organizations may have to prepare for a campaign on short notice.

No attempt is made to regulate the receipts and the expenditures of the national party organizations, and they are not required to publish financial statements.[15] The Labour Party voluntarily issues such a statement, but the other parties have not seen fit to emulate its practice.

Concerning the magnitude of the Conservative Party's expenditures and the sources of its income one can only speculate. The party appears to possess ample financial resources, although to those on the inside the coffers may seem far from full. The Conservatives have always relied on individual gifts to support the activities of the party, and it is generally supposed that some wealthy persons contribute fairly substantial amounts. Many of these gifts from businessmen and other persons of large affairs are offered because of party loyalty or in the belief that Conservative Governments will be generally favorable to their interest. Others are subscribed,

---

[13] H. G. Nicholas, op. cit. p. 16.

[14] Ibid. p. 37.

[15] It is occasionally proposed that political parties be required to publish financial statements. For instance, a Labour member moved in the House of Commons on 15 December 1949, 'That, in the opinion of this House, political parties, and all other organizations having political action as one of their aims, should publish annually full and adequate statements of their accounts.' After a caustic debate, in which Conservative and Labour members exchanged accusations about slush funds and trade union subsidies, the motion was carried 213-104. The Times, 16 December 1949.

it is occasionally rumored, in the expectation of some kind of social preferment—a knighthood, a baronetcy, or perhaps a peerage.

Filling the party treasury by what amounts to the sale of honors is not
practiced as fulsomely as it was a generation ago. The generous bestowal
of honors and titles by the coalition Government of Lloyd George and the
concomitant growth of a political fund produced a public scandal which is
remembered by party financiers.[16] They are not apt today to connect too
closely the Honours List and the receipts side of the party ledger. Nevertheless, generous contributors to the Conservative Party can expect to be
considered when the list of persons to be honored 'for political and public
services' is drawn up, and the recipients of honors and titles are obvious
prospects for the Central Office to approach concerning the state of its
treasury.

A considerable amount of the money collected by the Conservative
Central Office is used to subsidize local associations that find it difficult
to meet the expenses of a vigorous campaign. All constituency associations
are obligated to contribute to the funds of the Central Office on an ability
to pay basis. Those having no ability get financial help from the more
affluent associations by the subsidies of the national headquarters. It has
been estimated that, at a minimum, 'two fifths of the associations are
assisted financially by Central Office.' [17]

Not having any considerable wealthy clientele on which to rely, the
Labour Party has had to raise its money in other ways. It has been supported for the most part by affiliation fees. These are paid, on an annual
sixpence per capita basis, by trade unions, co-operative societies, socialist
groups, and other organizations affiliated with the party. The trade unions
supply by far the largest amount.

In the early days of the Labour movement many of the trade unions
used part of the regular dues collected from their members for political
purposes, aiding the Labour Representation Committee and sometimes
supporting members of Parliament. In 1909, however, a court decision,
the Osborne Judgment, declared that money collected for ordinary trade
union purposes could not be spent on political objectives. This decision
threatened to curtail seriously the political activities of the unions and in-

---

[16] Ramsay Muir's account of the origin of this fund was as follows: 'In those years
huge fortunes were being very easily made. Their makers, avid of distinction, were
ready to spend freely what they had easily won. Many of them, also, were inspired
by a genuine enthusiasm for the Coalition Prime Minister, Mr. Lloyd George, who
was at the height of his fame and had become a national idol as the organizer of victory. It seemed natural that, at the end of a colossal struggle, titles and distinctions
should be widely distributed. The Whips (Liberal and Conservative) used their opportunities; and an immense political fund was created. When the Coalition broke
up, in 1922, this fund was divided between the Conservatives (who had supported
the Coalition as a united party) and the Coalition Liberals.' *How Britain Is Governed* (New York, 1930), p. 135.

[17] Allen M. Potter, 'British Party Organization, 1950,' *Political Science Quarterly*,
March 1951, p. 70.

directly to thwart the growth of the Labour movement. Relief came four years later when Parliament authorized the trade unions to establish political funds and to collect assessments from all their members who did not 'contract out' of payment. The Trade Disputes Act, 1927, following the general strike of 1926, amended the law concerning political contributions by limiting the assessment to those trade union members who affirmatively approved, that is, who 'contracted in.' A repeal of the Trade Disputes Act was one of the first things done by the Labour Government when it came into office in 1945, and thus the situation with respect to the political funds of the trade unions was restored to its pre-1927 status.

Besides their assistance to the party by means of affiliation fees and donations, a number of trade unions assume the financial responsibility of Labour candidates, paying a part of their campaign expenses and supplementing their Parliamentary salaries. In the general election of 1950, 140 Labour candidates were sponsored by trade unions. The National Union of Mineworkers paid the expenses of 37 candidates, the Transport and General Workers Union of 19, the National Union of Railwaymen of 13, the Amalgamated Engineering Union of 11, the General and Municipal Workers of 10, and the Union of Shop, Distributive and Allied Workers of 10.[18] In the 1951 general election, 138 Labour candidates were sponsored and financially supported by trade unions. Furthermore, the larger unions usually contribute generously to the general election fund of the Labour Party.

Besides its monetary receipts, the Labour Party receives a great deal of volunteer assistance from the trade unions and other affiliated organizations. This probably goes a considerable way in making up the difference between the allegedly greater financial resources of the Conservative Party and its Labour rival.

Money does not appear to be a determining factor in present-day British politics. The lack of financial support probably handicaps some independent and minor party candidates, but the two major parties are able to get their appeals before the voters in adequate fashion. The Conservatives no doubt are in a position to spend more on election agents and on some forms of nation-wide publicity. To counter this advantage the Labour Party has the assured income of its affiliated organizations, particularly the trade unions, and the unpaid help of their headquarters and local staffs.

---

[18] *The Times,* 8 February 1950.

XII

Parliamentary Elections

One of the most dramatic of all occurrences in the democratic world is a British general election. For about three weeks candidates declaim and exhort from innumerable platforms, and finally some 28 million people go to the polls to select the 625 members of the next House of Commons. In spite of the skill of polltakers and other prophets, the result is never certain. A general election can always produce the startling kind of upset that occurred in 1945 when the party of the victorious war leader, Winston Churchill, was rejected in favor of the Labour opposition.

1. *The Timing of a General Election*

Constitutionally, the maximum life of a House of Commons is five years. It had been set at three years by the Triennial Act of 1694, extended to seven years by the Septennial Act of 1716, and fixed at the present limit by the Parliament Act of 1911. In periods of peace a general election almost always occurs before the five-year period has expired. The two world wars caused Parliament to extend its own life in order to avoid the disruption and political uncertainty of a general election while the military struggle was in progress. The Parliament chosen in 1910 was not dissolved until the end of 1918, and there was no general election in Britain between 1935 and 1945.

In the normal course the choice of a time for a general election is in the hands of the Prime Minister. He has the constitutional authority to advise the King at any time to dissolve Parliament, and this act of dissolution sets in motion the electoral machinery which brings a new Parliament to Westminster. In fixing a date the Prime Minister is naturally guided by his reading of the political situation. As long as he heads a reasonably harmonious ministry supported by a good and loyal majority in the House of Commons he will certainly put off the date of election until close to the five-year limit. If the position of his Ministry is a precarious one, supported only by a narrow majority in the House of Commons, he will probably be disposed to seek an early opportunity for a dissolution and an appeal to the electorate.

In either case, the Prime Minister will attempt to select a date most favorable to his party. Some popular development in the conduct of foreign affairs or a period of domestic prosperity may cause him to feel that the star of his party is in the ascendant and that a general election will return it to power. No party wishes to go to the country when it is under more than the usual partisan criticism of its management of the nation's affairs. Besides the general state of the political situation there are other practical considerations which a Prime Minister must take into account. These include the efficiency of the organization within his party, the size of the campaign treasury, the effect of weather conditions upon voting, and the state of public business in Parliament. In reaching his decision about a general election the Prime Minister has the benefit of advice from leading members of his Cabinet and from important party officials. They, too, are reading the signs of the times and attempting to judge the best date for an appeal to the electorate. While these views will have great weight with the Prime Minister, the choice is essentially his, and no one is authorized to speak for him in this matter.

Almost from the moment a new Parliament assembles party managers and the press begin to speculate about the possibility of a 'snap' election. By this they mean an unexpected dissolution of Parliament and the holding of a general election with a view to catching the opposition off balance and getting a larger Government majority in the House of Commons. While this speculation is a common feature of British politics, there is rarely such a thing as a snap election. The opposition is competent to assay the political situation and can usually predict when a general election is imminent. It knows that a Prime Minister with a good working majority is unlikely to risk a general election in the off chance of making that support overwhelming, and it is aware that a weakly supported Ministry will probably seize the first opportunity for an appeal to the country; consequently, both the party in power and the opposition make their election plans accordingly. Neither one wishes to bring its organization and the enthusiasm of its party workers to a high pitch until just before an election.

It has been mentioned that a dissolution of Parliament starts the machinery for the selection of a new Parliament. This process is initiated by a royal proclamation expressing a desire 'to meet our people and have their advice in Parliament' and calling for the issuance of writs by the Lord Chancellor and the Governor of Northern Ireland summoning members of the House of Lords and the House of Commons. Members of the House of Lords, except the representative peers of Scotland, receive individual writs requesting their presence in a new Parliament. For the House of Commons writs go to the returning officer in each constituency, usually a sheriff, a mayor, or the chairman of an urban district council. By these writs the returning officers are instructed to hold an election to choose a member for a new Parliament.

2. *The Electorate*

Before taking up the procedure for nominating candidates, their campaigns, and the polling, it will be well at this point to consider the electorate which will choose the members of the House of Commons. Although

-201

this electorate today includes virtually every adult citizen of the United Kingdom, this condition of affairs has only recently been true. Until 1928 a quite considerable part of the British public was excluded from the Parliamentary franchise. The expansion of the electorate has taken place as the result of a series of Parliamentary acts which successively have conferred the vote upon large classes of the population.

The first of these acts was the Great Reform Act of 1832, called 'great' not so much because of the additional number of voters added to the electorate but because it marked the end of the aristocracy's monopoly of British political life and started a movement which within a century made the United Kingdom one of the advanced democracies of the world. Prior to 1832 there were two general kinds of Parliamentary franchise. There were county voters who were entitled to elect the two members coming from each shire of the kingdom, except in Wales where each county returned only one member. The county suffrage was limited by an ancient statute of 1430 to 40-shilling freeholders; that is, male citizens who owned property of a rental value of at least 40 shillings a year. In the fifteenth century such an amount was a respectable sum and insured that only substantial citizens of the county would participate in the choice of members of Parliament. While changes in the value of money might have been expected to increase the county franchise, the decline in the number of individuals holding property by freehold, because of the growth of vast landed estates, tended to keep the rural electorate comparatively small. It is estimated that at the time of the passage of the Reform Act of 1832 the county franchise was enjoyed by about a quarter of a million people.

The other class of voters, those having the borough franchise, enjoyed their right as a result of an almost infinite variety of laws and customs which had grown up over a period of several hundred years. There was no universal standard as in the case of the county suffrage, and indeed the qualifications were different in almost every town. What had started out as being a privilege enjoyed by all freemen of a borough had in most cases degenerated into the right of a small clique to choose the two members for the House of Commons. In a few places, Bristol and Westminster notably, the electorate was reasonably large, but these were exceptional communities. In other towns, the franchise was limited to the members of certain trade guilds or to the possessors of certain property rights. A few boroughs had what was called a 'pot-walloper' franchise which conferred the vote upon those male citizens who possessed a domicile where a meal could be cooked. Other places maintained similarly archaic or irrelevant qualifications for voting.

Not only was the suffrage hopelessly out of date and irrational but the method of apportionment of members in the House of Commons was equally in need of reform. Cornwall, for example, had a population in 1831 of about 300,000 and returned 42 county and borough members to the Commons; Lancashire with a population of 1,300,000, returned but

202–

14. Each county, except those in Wales, returned two members irrespective of the population of the county. As long as Britain was predominately rural there was no great injustice in such an apportionment, but by the early part of the nineteenth century there were mining and other industrial areas which caused a considerable concentration of population in a few of the counties.

In addition, numerous towns had come into existence or villages had grown into populous cities, and they had no representation at all except through the county members. Other towns which in past centuries had been flourishing places had lost much of their population and in a few instances had disappeared entirely. Two classic examples, Old Sarum in Wiltshire and Dunwich in Essex, no longer existed; the first was deserted, and the second had slid into the sea. These so-called rotten or pocket boroughs still returned two members each to the House of Commons. The choice was made by someone who owned the land where the borough once stood, and he in effect appointed two people to Parliament. These patrons, as they were known, were not above selling a membership in 'the best club in London.' So brazen was this traffic in the eighteenth century that patrons frequently advertised the Parliamentary seats in their gift and sold them to the highest bidders. More commonly, however, patrons bestowed their seats upon sons, other relatives, or friends and thus had a small block of votes which they could control in the House. Some of the best known members of eighteenth-century parliaments were beneficiaries of the patronage system, among them being the younger Pitt, Charles James Fox, and Edmund Burke. Indeed, there was some disposition to defend the patronage system on the ground that it provided a means whereby worthy young men could get a start in political life. Its abuses, however, were so patent that it could not survive the agitation which led to the Act of 1832.

The changes made in 1832 in the suffrage and in Parliamentary representation probably would have come a few decades earlier had not the French Revolution and the succeeding Napoleonic wars produced a climate in England hostile to any revision of the political system. Before these events there had been considerable agitation for reform and a number of political leaders had advocated changes. After Waterloo came several years of reactionary Tory rule which regarded any mild reform as an invitation to revolution. Social and economic changes were going on, however, which finally necessitated complementary revisions in the political system. A Whig Ministry which came to power under Earl Grey in 1830 was prepared to attack the problem, and two years later it was successful in enacting the Great Reform Bill.

The Act of 1832 based the suffrage in both county and borough constituencies upon the ownership or occupancy of property. In the counties the franchise was extended, in general, to leaseholders and copyholders of land which had a rental value of as much as £10 a year and to tenants-at-will who occupied land of a rental value of £50 a year. In the boroughs

−203

all the archaic suffrage privileges were abolished and the franchise bestowed on all rate-paying occupants of property worth £10 rental a year. The problem of representation was attacked by eliminating members for the 56 boroughs where the population was less than 2000 inhabitants, reducing the representation from two members to one for 30 boroughs having between two and four thousand people, and depriving the City of London of two of its four members. The seats thus made available were apportioned to 42 boroughs which had not previously been represented, and 65 seats were given to the more populous counties. Additional representation was also given to Scotland and Ireland. In effect, the Act of 1832 enfranchised practically all men of means in both the country and the cities; it also reapportioned representation in the House of Commons so that all parts of the nation were represented with some fair degree of equity. The electorate was increased by about half a million voters.

The Act of 1832 was not long on the statute books before agitation began to enlarge the electorate and to make other changes in the voting system. During the 1840's this agitation was carried on by an organization known as the Chartists, so called because the reforms they advocated were embodied in a charter which they urged Parliament to pass into law. The six points of their charter were: universal manhood suffrage, equal electoral districts, the secret ballot, annual parliamentary elections, abolition of property qualifications for the members of the House of Commons, and the payment of salaries to members of the House. The vigor with which the Chartists pressed their program gave the public authorities some concern, but Chartism never took on the character of a revolutionary movement. The Chartists always sought by constitutional means to bring about the reforms in which they were interested, and consequently the barricades never rose in the streets of London as they did with some frequency across the Channel. While the Chartist movement expired without seeing any of its six points adopted, they were all, save one, eventually accepted by Parliament. The exception is that of annual Parliamentary elections, which even the most radical democrats would scarcely think necessary or practical today.

Following the enfranchisement of the middle classes by the Act of 1832, a large proportion of the urban workers were added to the electorate in 1867. This was done by lowering the property qualification for voting in borough constituencies. The act also adjusted representation more equitably by depriving some small boroughs of seats and giving them to more populous towns. In 1884 another extension of the electorate was made by changing the property qualifications for county voters, and as a result the franchise was given to a large number of agricultural workers and miners. The next year there was a further redistribution of seats in the House of Commons. The Act of 1867 had added almost a million voters to the electorate, and the Act of 1884 brought in almost double that number. By these two acts the electorate was increased to about four million voters.

No further change in the franchise or in parliamentary representation was made until 1918. The Asquith Government introduced a bill in 1912 to enlarge the electorate, to abolish plural voting, and to simplify the registration system, but it ran into procedural difficulties and was dropped. Another bill was rejected by the Lords and was eventually shelved because of the outbreak of war in 1914. Many people recognized during the First World War that several million citizens still excluded from the franchise should be given voting rights, and consequently in 1916 a Parliamentary committee, known as the Speaker's Conference since it was presided over by the Speaker of the House of Commons, studied the suffrage situation and made recommendations which were embodied in the Representation of the People Act of 1918.

By this measure all male citizens, 21 years of age and over, were enfranchised. The only exceptions, as popularly stated, were peers, criminals, and lunatics. A vigorous women's suffrage movement which had begun before the war achieved partial success in the Act of 1918. Unwilling to enfranchise all women at once, partly because of the greater number of that sex in the total population, Parliament granted the suffrage to women over 30 years of age if they or their husbands were qualified to vote in local government elections. The changes in the franchise through this Act increased the British electorate from 8,350,000 to 21,300,000. The Act also provided for a general redistribution of seats. It abolished the old distinction between county and borough suffrage and allotted seats to geographical districts—constituencies—on the basis of one member for every 70,000 people in Great Britain and one for every 43,000 in Ireland. The size of the House of Commons rose to 707 members, but with the establishment of the Irish Free State (1921) it was reduced to 615.

The restrictions upon the suffrage of women contained in the Act of 1918 were universally regarded as only temporary. They lasted ten years, and in 1928 the Conservative Government then in power enfranchised all women on the same basis as men by a measure popularly known as the 'Flapper Bill.' Thus, four years short of a century from the date of the Great Reform Act the electorate had been enlarged to a point where all adults, save those in prisons or mental institutions, or eligible to sit in the House of Lords, were entitled to vote.

3. *Parliamentary Representation Today*

During World War II it was accepted that a general election would have to be held as soon as the course of the conflict permitted. In preparation for such an election, Parliament in 1944 increased the number of seats in the House of Commons to 640 to provide additional representation for those areas which had grown in population in the preceding years. This was understood to be a temporary measure until the matter of Parliamentary representation could be restudied after the war. A restudy was undertaken in 1946 by a House of Commons committee under the chairmanship of the Speaker, and it resulted in the Representation of the People Act, 1948.[1]

The Act of 1948 reduced the House of Commons to 625 members to be elected, without exception, from single member constituencies. It re-adjusted the boundaries of a considerable number of constituencies and provided for four permanent boundary commissions to advise changes as population shifts indicated the necessity. Furthermore, the act elimi-nated two long-standing features of the British electoral system, univer-sity representation and plural voting. The 12 seats in the House of Com-mons occupied by members selected by the graduates of British universities were abolished and with them the second vote which these graduates en-joyed. Also eliminated was the second vote possessed by individuals who owned or occupied property in a constituency other than their residential one. Prior to 1918 a voter was entitled to cast a ballot in as many con-stituencies as he had property therein, and since balloting was spread over a week or two it was possible for some individuals to vote in several con-stituencies. In 1918 plural voting had been limited to two ballots per voter; the second ballot was abolished by the Act of 1948. The latest elec-toral law also made identical the requirements for voting in national and local elections. Previously, the local suffrage had been based upon the pay-ment of rates, local taxes, and since in England these are levied upon occupiers of property, not just owners, the suffrage was a broad one. The Act of 1948 placed the local suffrage on a universal citizenship basis, making it the same as the national.

The general election of 1950 saw a House of Commons elected by all the adult citizens of the United Kingdom, with each person who went to the polls casting one vote. In order to cast this vote the citizen had to comply with only one requirement, namely, to have his name on the voting register of his constituency. The registration of voters was introduced by the Act of 1832, and it has remained a permanent feature of the British electoral system. Once a year a list of voters is compiled in each con-stituency by the registration officer, who is either the town clerk of a borough or the clerk of a county council.[2] After the lists are compiled they are posted on the bulletin boards of town halls, churches, and other public buildings, and any voter who finds that his name has been omitted has an opportunity to call it to the attention of the registration officer. He may also protest the inclusion of the name of an unqualified person.

4. The Nomination of Candidates

We shall now return to a consideration of the organization and conduct of a general election. The first thing to be noted is the process of nominat-ing candidates. Regarding the legal qualifications of candidates, we may

---

[1] The Representation of the People Act, 1949, consolidated much of the law re-lating to Parliamentary elections.

[2] The total number of registered voters in the United Kingdom as announced in December 1949 was 34,410,306. *The Times,* 10 December 1949.

state as a general rule that anyone qualified to be a voter may stand for the House of Commons except clergymen of the Churches of England and Scotland and of the Roman Catholic Church, undischarged bankrupts, and persons 'holding an office of profit under the Crown'—except, of course, ministers and the Leader of the Opposition. While this statement is broadly accurate, the law on the subject of the qualifications of candidates and members of the House is, in fact, highly complicated and frequently obscure. It is said that since 1693 there have been enacted 145 statutes pertaining to members' qualifications which are still in force.[3] Not many of these enactments have much relevance to present-day conditions, nor do they operate to disqualify any considerable number of persons. They sometimes lead, however, to embarrassing situations in which an M.P. discovers that because of an archaic statute he is ineligible to hold his seat; after the 1945 general election it was necessary for Parliament to pass acts validating the elections of five members who by a law of 1707 were disqualified from being candidates.

The personal qualifications are similar to those that obtain in any democratic state. It is usually necessary that a candidate have some speaking ability and a manner that attracts rather than repels voters. In former times a candidate had to be prepared to bear a good share of his campaign expenses, either from his own resources or from those of his family and friends, and many candidates in the past have been selected principally because of their ability to finance a political battle. While a candidate with financial means is usually still welcome today, this requirement is not nearly so important. Candidates of the Labour Party have never been expected to finance themselves, and in an effort to present their parties as

---

[3] Geoffrey Bing, 'Candidates and Members,' *The Times,* 13 December 1949. Mr. Bing cites some of the most unreasonable of the existing disqualifications. For example, in 1746, 'as an aftermath of the Jacobite revolt of the previous year, Parliament passed an Act which disqualified, both as an elector and as a Parliamentary candidate, any person in Scotland who had been present twice in the same year at Divine Service in any Episcopal church "whereof the pastor or minister thereof shall not pray in express words for his Majesty by name, and for his Majesty's heirs or successors, and for all the Royal Family." ' This particular disability on voters was removed by the Representation of the People Act, 1948, but its application to Parliamentary candidates was not eliminated. There are a good many anomalies in the laws about clergymen, bankrupts, judges and civil servants. Likewise, the disqualification of government contractors, originally aimed at members of Parliament seeking to make profits out of the American Revolutionary War, leads to occasional complications today. There have been many definitions of 'offices of profit under the Crown,' and Mr. Bing concludes, 'No one can say with certainty which offices disqualify and which do not.'

In 1939 Parliament passed an act permitting persons in the armed forces to stand for the House of Commons and to remain on full pay until nomination day. If elected they could either be released for Parliamentary service or continue on active duty while holding a seat in the House. The Minister of Defence announced in December 1949 that after the next general election the prewar practice would be re-established and that military personnel would have to leave the service before announcing their candidacy. *The Times,* 8 December 1949.

mass rather than class movements, the Conservatives and Liberals have in recent years restricted their candidates' contributions to party funds and proclaimed that ability and probity were the only requirements for standing under their banners. In days past the scion of some noble or aristocratic family was usually regarded as a good candidate. The sons of peers and members of prominent county families had something of a start in election campaigns through the prestige of their names and their connections. In some constituencies a Parliamentary seat might be held by a well-known local family through several generations. As the influence of the governing classes has declined so has the advantage of candidates from this social stratum. It is still of benefit to bear a well-known name, but today it requires more than this to win an election.

The formal requirements in the nomination of candidates are simple. Eight days after the writs of election have been issued, nominations of candidates are made by filing with the returning officer of each constituency papers giving the name, address, and occupation of the candidate and bearing the signatures of two local voters who propose and second a candidate and eight additional voters who 'assent.' There are no party conventions, caucuses, or primaries involved in the nominating process. Each candidate must post £150 which is returned to him if he polls as much as one-eighth of the total vote on election day. The purpose in requiring a deposit is to eliminate freak candidatures. Some Labour candidates have found the requirement of the deposit something of a risk, and for the election of 1945 the party is said to have established an anti-deposit-losing insurance fund to which each candidate contributed £10. The requirement was not changed in the electoral act of 1948, however.[4]

Although the formal nominating process is simple, a good deal of work precedes it. Usually some time before an election each party organization in a constituency has 'adopted' a candidate. The candidate adopted may be a local political figure who has been active in the party's service, or he may be someone from another part of the country who is desirous of entering Parliament. Since there is no residential qualification and by and large voters are not prejudiced against the 'outsider' as a candidate, a considerable number of aspirants who are adopted are not local people.[5] In case no local candidate is available or no well-known person from the outside offers himself, the party organization of the constituency may appeal

---

[4] In the general election of 1950, 319 out of 475 Liberal candidates lost their deposits, 97 out of 100 Communists, and 5 out of 620 Conservatives. No Labour candidate lost his deposit.

[5] Veteran members of the House of Commons frequently have sat for a number of constituencies. Thus, Winston Churchill has successively represented Oldham, Northwest Manchester, Dundee, and the Epping Division of Essex, now Woodford. Gladstone during his long career represented in turn Newark, Oxford University, South Lancashire, Greenwich, and Midlothian. In the general election of 1950, 118 Labor, 139 Conservative, and 148 Liberal candidates were neither residents of the constituency in which they were running nor of adjacent constituencies. H. G. Nicholas, *The British General Election of 1950* (London, 1951), p. 58.

to the national party headquarters to suggest a name. The central head-quarters of all parties keep lists of available candidates, in general young men and women who wish to break into national politics and who are considered promising by the national officers. An individual so proposed negotiates with the local constituency organization, and if the liking is mutual the person is adopted as the candidate. In a good many cases when the central office is called upon to propose a young candidate to a local constituency organization the seat is considered a 'safe' one for the opposition. The candidate will not be discredited if he fails to win; indeed, victory would probably surprise his friends as well as his political foes. He does have an opportunity, however, to show his political qualifications and to run a good race against what will probably be older and more experienced candidates. A strong showing may well lead to his adoption in a more promising constituency at a later date.

However selected, a candidate once adopted begins to promote his prospects among the local voters, a process known as 'nursing' a constituency. This consists of speaking on as many occasions as possible; attending civic celebrations, fairs, and bazaars; making donations to local charities; and in other ways placing himself before the voters in as favorable a light as he can. Thus, come election time, the candidates are usually quite well known to the voters of a constituency. A sitting member, of course, has had numerous opportunities to call his qualifications to the attention of the constituency, but the candidates of other parties have probably been active too, and enter the official campaign under no great disadvantage.

5. *Election Campaigns*

The campaign itself is brief by American standards. It officially begins with the dissolution of Parliament and ends with the election 17 days later, Sundays and holidays excluded. It is conducted through all the means that are available to politicians in democratic countries.

As soon as the Prime Minister announces a dissolution the national and local party organizations leap into action. At the local level each candidate's campaign is usually managed by an agent, a paid official who directs the local party headquarters and who has previously been laying the groundwork for what is hoped will be a successful contest. The agent is truly a professional politician. He studies the electorate, deploys the party workers, watches the strategy of the opposition, and advises the candidate on campaign tactics. A good agent is almost as important as a good candidate in winning an election. Successful agents sometimes are promoted to better paying constituencies or given positions in the central party headquarters.

During the approximately three weeks of the campaign a candidate will speak dozens of times throughout the constituency. His agent will previously have tried to rent suitable halls and to make dates before groups of voters. The speeches of candidates naturally uphold the principles and policies of their respective parties and denounce those of their opponents.

Contrary to the practice in the United States, the audience at British political rallies takes almost as active a part as does the speaker on the platform. It is customary to ask questions of the candidate and for opponents to heckle him. Sometimes a candidate's success in a meeting depends more upon his ability to give a quick answer or to turn the tables on a heckler than it does upon his ability to expound forcibly and cogently his position on great public issues.

In addition to speaking, a candidate endeavors to canvass as many voters as he can. He is assisted in this by workers from his headquarters who proceed from door to door urging voters to go to the polls on election day and to support their candidate. Voters in Britain expect this kind of personal solicitation, and no candidate can afford to neglect it. Campaign advertising includes posters, banners, and sound trucks which proclaim the sterling qualities of a party and its national and local candidates. In addition, each candidate is allowed to send post free one communication to each registered voter of his constituency. This 'election address' is usually a small brochure which gives biographical information about the candidate and explains his views on issues and policies.

The national campaign is directed by the central party headquarters which operates in the manner of a military general staff fighting a great battle. Speakers are directed to strategic areas, and the party's forces are deployed in what is considered to be the most effective manner. The press takes an active part in the campaign, and those newspapers having political leanings support their respective parties by reporting meetings and speeches and by commenting editorially upon the party programs. During the past two decades the radio has played an important part in election campaigns. It is not possible for the parties to 'buy time' for their speakers or to get political advertisements put on the air, since broadcasting is a publicly owned monopoly; they each receive, instead, several opportunities to address the nation through the facilities of the British Broadcasting Corporation. The B.B.C. allots equitable amounts of time which each party may use in the way its central headquarters considers most effective. The campaign is usually opened by broadcasts given by the leaders of the Labour, Conservative, and Liberal parties, and at its close they return to send forth an appeal for victory. In between, other party figures will take to the air and seek to persuade all those who have not made up their minds before polling day. Television was used for the first time in the general election of 1951. Lord Samuel, a senior Liberal statesman, had the distinction of being the first British politician to present a campaign appeal through this medium, and he was followed by Labour and Conservative speakers.

The national headquarters of the major parties are on the alert during the campaign for some startling disclosure or some unexpected tactic which could be turned to profit or, if employed by the opposition, could be damaging. In the election campaign of 1924 the Conservatives made a great deal of the alleged Zinoviev letter which called upon British Communists to subvert the military forces in preparation for revolution. In the 1945 campaign Churchill attempted to picture Professor Harold J. Laski, then

210–

chairman of the Labour Party Executive Committee, as a sinister influence behind the party's Parliamentary leaders and to suggest that a British Gestapo might emerge from a Labour victory. This campaign tactic probably lost more votes than it gained. Few British voters could visualize Professor Laski or Mr. Attlee standing in the shoes of the unlamented Herr Himmler.

6. *The Balloting*

One day, approximately three weeks after a dissolution, the entire electorate of Britain goes to the polls. Each voter has previously received a polling card bearing his polling number and giving the location of his voting place. Formerly these cards were distributed by the candidates, but this work is now the responsibility of the registration officer in each constituency. On arriving at a polling station, which is normally open from 7 A.M. to 9 P.M., a voter presents his card, and it is checked against the register of voters. If his name appears on the register he is given a blank ballot, which is a small slip of paper bearing the name and occupation of each candidate but no party affiliation. The voter's polling number being noted on the ballot, he takes the paper to a screened booth and marks with a cross the candidate of his choice. He then folds the ballot and drops it in a ballot box which is in the custody of the presiding officer of the polling station. This kind of secret ballot was introduced in England by statute in 1872. Formerly voters had assembled at a polling station and voting had been by a show of hands.

The Representation of the People Act of 1918 and a supplementary statute in 1920 made provision for absentee voting, and the Act of 1948 extended the categories of persons eligible to vote in this manner. In general, the statutes make absentee voting available to persons, otherwise eligible, who will be away from their constituencies on polling day because of public service of some kind or for occupational reasons, those who have recently moved to another area, or those who are physically incapacitated. The voting may be performed either through a ballot mailed to a returning officer or by a previously designated proxy. If a voter chooses to vote by proxy he must designate his proxy in advance. The proxy must be a relative or a registered voter of the absent individual's constituency, and no proxy, except in the case of a relative, may cast more than two absentee ballots. Provision for absentee voting has considerable importance for the citizens of Great Britain, since customarily many thousands of them are abroad in military service, in colonial administration, and in business activities. Many additional thousands, such as fishermen and commercial travelers, would find it inconvenient to be at home on polling day.[6]

---

[6] In the general election of 1950, 471,088 absentee ballots were cast, representing 1.6 per cent of all valid votes. While all the parties recognized the importance of encouraging absentee voting by persons eligible to ballot in this way, 'it was the Con-

At the hour set, all polling stations in a constituency are closed, the ballot boxes sealed and sent to the town hall or some other central place where the returning officer of the constituency opens them and mixes the ballots from all polling stations. The ballots are then counted and the result announced. Each candidate is permitted to have one or two watchers during the count of the ballots, but the returning officer and his assistants are the only other persons allowed to be present. Should the balloting result in a tie a recount is made, and if a tie still exists the two candidates involved decide the issue by lot. Before the Representation of the People Act, 1948, the returning officer had a casting vote in case of a tie.

Victory in an election goes to the candidate receiving the largest number of votes, whether or not this is a majority of all votes cast. Since in many constituencies there are three and occasionally four or five candidates, it frequently happens that the victor wins only a plurality of the total vote.

After ascertaining the victorious candidate, the returning officer endorses the election writ and sends it and the ballot papers to the Lord Chancellor's office. The Clerk of the Crown in Chancery prepares a list of the elected members which is transmitted to the Clerk of the House of Commons to form the roll for the next session.

In addition to the limitations upon candidates' expenditures there are a number of other legal provisions designed to insure the fairness of the campaigning, the balloting, and the counting of the votes. In this connection, a distinction is made in Britain between corrupt and illegal electoral practices. Corrupt practices are those involving moral turpitude, such as falsification of the register, theft of ballots, or deliberate miscounting of the votes. Illegal practices are those prohibited by law but not dishonest in themselves, e.g. excessive expenditure by an agent in behalf of his party's candidate.

Should a defeated candidate or one of his supporters believe that the person declared elected is ineligible to sit in Parliament or that some illegality occurred during the campaign, the voting, or the counting of the ballots, he may petition to have the election invalidated. If the challenge is to the legal eligibility of the winning candidate, the House of Commons decides the matter. If, on the other hand, the petitioner charges a corrupt or illegal electoral practice, the accusation is investigated by two judges of the King's Bench Division of the High Court of Justice. Their report to the House of Commons determines the outcome. A serious breach of the electoral laws can result in the forfeiture of the victory as well as a prosecution. Challenges of election results are not common in Britain. For one thing, the candidates' agents are well schooled in the laws governing elections and keep a careful watch on the conduct of their party workers. In

---

servatives who in the vast majority of constituencies made the most of the opportunities so afforded,' H. G. Nicholas stated. He concluded, 'It is very hard not to believe that the Conservatives owe at least 10 seats to the introduction of the postal vote.' Op. cit. pp. 6-9.

the second place, the balloting is fairly simple. There are no 'long ballots' so prevalent in the United States, which with their dozens of names often lead to confusion in marking and counting. Since counting is on a constituency basis, the figures do not run into the hundreds of thousands and even millions as in many American elections. In the British system there is less likelihood of mistakes and errors which could be the basis of a challenge to the result.

7. By-Elections

Between general elections there may be held a large number of elections in individual constituencies. These by-elections occur whenever a seat in the House of Commons is vacated by death, 'resignation' through a member applying for the Chiltern Hundreds, or the elevation of the sitting member to the House of Lords. The procedure followed is identical to that of a general election. A writ of election is issued to the returning officer of the constituency, the candidates are nominated, and the balloting proceeds on the appointed day. Candidates defeated in the previous general election may enter if they are still the adopted choices of their parties, or constituency associations may select new candidates. By-elections are sometimes used to secure the return to the House of Commons of a prominent party leader defeated in a general election. Occasionally a backbench member holding a safe seat will co-operate with the party leadership by vacating his place to provide an opportunity for a former minister to re-enter the House.

By-elections frequently attract considerable attention. If the constituency is one in which the parties are fairly evenly matched, each side will make a great effort to win the vacant seat. Should the Government continue to hold a seat contested in a by-election this result is interpreted as indicating that the Ministry still enjoys the confidence of the country. On the other hand, should the opposition win a seat formerly held by a Government supporter, this may be taken to mean that the Ministry is losing strength. During the life of the Parliament elected in 1945 the Labour Party established the unprecedented record of retaining in by-elections 35 seats which had been won in the general election. Many of these were safe seats, and the Conservative opposition's chances were admittedly slight. Others, however, were hotly contested and the issue in doubt until the ballots were counted. Labour extended its record in the 16 by-elections occurring between the general elections of 1950 and 1951; the party retained the eight seats it had previously held.

In addition to the outcome of by-elections, the increase or decrease of the winning candidate's majority as compared to the previous election is closely watched. If a winning candidate just squeezes through when his predecessor had won the seat by an impressive majority, this result is taken as indicating a change in party fortunes. While political forecasters and the press make a great deal of by-elections, it is clear that the results are affected by much more than the gain or loss in the Government's popularity. The personalities of the candidates influence the voting and many other local factors may enter the situation. A by-election is never a micro-cosm of a future general election.[7]

During both world wars, after coalition Governments had been formed, the major parties agreed upon an electoral truce. By this truce a seat which fell vacant was considered to be the property of the party which had held it, and in the resulting by-election the other party would not present a candidate. During the last war the electoral truce was faithfully observed by both the Conservative and Labour parties, but independent candidates were not restrained from entering a contest when they felt that there was some prospect of success. Once in a while these independent candidates ran as not very effectively disguised representatives of one of the two major parties. Had victory in Europe not permitted the holding of a general election in July 1945 it is probable that the strain on the electoral truce would have been severe and that there would have been occasional violations by local Conservative and Labour organizations even though the national leaders stayed aloof.

8. *Electoral Reform*

Almost 200 years ago Blackstone concluded that the system whereby the people of Britain were represented in Parliament was one of the perfections of the British Constitution. There were dissenters to this view even in his day and, as we have noticed, they grew more numerous and vocal after the fears inspired by the French revolution began to wane. Electoral reformers achieved their first great success with the Act of 1832, and since then they have been a permanent pressure group within British political life. They have advanced under many banners and have shifted their efforts from one target to another—extension of the franchise, fair distribution of Parliamentary seats, protection of the electoral process from influence and corruption, woman suffrage, payment of members, plural voting. What battles still remain to be won?

Many would say that the electoral reform movement has accomplished its mission and that since the passage of the Representation of the People Act of 1948 there is no need for further change. The franchise is broad and democratic, representation is equitably distributed, and the purity of elections is unsurpassed anywhere in the world. A dissatisfied element remains, however, and its grievances are based upon the manner in which the single-member constituency principle often operates to elect 'minority' candidates and upon the way small changes in the popular vote of parties produce exaggerated results in terms of Parliamentary representation.

---

[7] By and large, the total vote of a constituency in a by-election is usually smaller than in a general election. As a general election approaches, however, the proportion of voters going to the polls is likely to rise, particularly in sharply disputed districts. In the last by-election (South Bradford) before the general election of 1950, 87.3 per cent of the registered voters cast ballots.

Some rather horrendous figures can be quoted to state a case against the existing electoral system.

The first problem comes about because there are a good many three- and four-cornered contests in a general election. The seat goes to the candidate polling the most votes; often this is only a plurality and not a majority of all ballots cast. Critics point out that in the constituencies where the victor receives only a plurality, a majority of the voters are being represented by an M.P. whom they voted against. Thus, if Candidate A receives 20,000 votes; Candidate B, 15,000, and Candidate C, 10,000, A will represent a constituency where 5000 more ballots were cast against him than for him. Of 607 contested seats in the general election of 1929 there were three or more candidates for 470 seats, and in 288 of these elections the victor received less than a majority over all rivals. In the general election of 1950, with the Liberals entering 475 candidates, the Communists 100, and with 56 independent and minor party candidates, there were three-cornered contests in most constituencies and four-way fights in a good many. The Conservatives won five seats with between 45 and 50 per cent of the total vote, 13 seats with between 40 and 45 per cent, and 14 seats with between 35 and 40 per cent. The Labour record was about the same. The Liberals captured only two of their nine seats by absolute majorities. Thus, there were approximately 75 seats won by 'minority' candidates in 1950.

The second problem which disturbs contemporary electoral reformers is the way 'the system distorts the national verdict given in a general election, produces the most extravagantly unjust results, turns every election into a gamble, and by doing so exercises an unhealthy influence, almost despite themselves, upon the policy of party leaders.'[8] In the general election of 1922 the Conservatives polled 38 per cent of the votes cast and won 347 seats in the House of Commons; in 1923, they again polled 38 per cent but lost 90 seats; in 1924, they won 47 per cent of the popular vote and the large total of 415 seats, while the Labour and Liberal opposition parties, with 53 per cent of the vote, got 200 seats. In 1929 the Conservatives slumped to 38 per cent of the total ballots and won 253 seats; Labour with only 36 per cent of the popular vote captured 288 seats. The Liberals with 23 per cent of the popular vote won 58 seats. The results of the general elections of 1931, 1935, and 1945 were equally distorted in terms of Parliamentary representation. In 1945 Labour polled 11,900,000 popular votes and won 393 seats; the Conservative Party 8,900,000 and 189 seats, and the Liberals 2,200,000 and 12 seats.

In 1950, however, this distortion of the popular vote did not occur, at least for the two major parties, and Parliamentary seats 'were divided between the parties in exactly the same ratio as their votes.'[9] Labour received 46.1 per cent of the popular vote, the Conservatives 43.4 per cent, the

---

[8] Ramsay Muir, *How Britain Is Governed* (New York, 1930), pp. 168-9.
[9] Nicholas, op. cit., appendix by D. E. Butler, p. 328.

Liberals 9.2 per cent, and other candidates 1.3 per cent. The seats won were: Labour, 315; Conservatives, 298; Liberals, 9; others, 3. This result was at variance with the conclusions of statistical analyses of British election figures which have indicated that with two parties in the race, 'the ratio of seats won by the parties might be expected to be at least the cube of the ratio between the votes cast for them; in other words, if the ratio between the votes was A:B, the ratio between seats would be at least $A^3:B^3$.'[10] The election of 1950 failed to conform to the formula, it is held, because of a slight 'bias' in the electoral system which favored the Conservative Party. The 'bias' is caused by the fact that Labour 'squanders many more votes in piling up huge majorities in absolutely safe seats than the Conservatives whose strength happens to be more effectively spread.'[11] This particular 'bias' did not operate in previous elections for the reason that it was offset by another 'bias,' the slight overrepresentation of normal Labour areas and the underrepresentation of Conservative areas. In 1945, when the average Labour constituency contained 51,000 voters and the average Conservative one 57,000, it took more Conservative votes to win a seat than Labour votes. The redistribution of seats by the Act of 1948 removed this 'bias' of the electoral system. The remaining 'bias' due to Labour's big majorities in a number of safe constituencies continues to exist, and in the general election of 1951 it gave the party a slightly larger popular vote than the winning Conservatives. Labour won 48.7 per cent of the total popular vote and 295 seats in the House of Commons; the Conservative Party received 48 per cent and captured 321 seats. The Liberals, with 2.5 per cent of all ballots cast, won six seats.

The two most favored changes to cure the alleged defects of the present electoral system are the alternative vote and proportional representation. The alternative vote could operate without abandoning the single-member constituency principle. According to this proposal, each voter would indicate, when more than two candidates were seeking election, his preferences—one, two, three. In case no candidate received a clear majority, the second preferences, and if necessary the third preferences, would be counted until one candidate had accumulated an effective majority and thus become the victor.

A scheme of proportional representation would necessitate the creation of multi-member constituencies, usually four-, five-, or six-member areas. Parties could nominate candidates for all seats or any lesser number. A voter would indicate his preferences up to the total number of seats to be filled. In the counting, a quota number—i.e. the votes necessary to elect one member—would be arrived at, and any candidates having this number would be declared elected. Their 'surplus' votes, and the votes of candidates hopelessly outclassed, would be distributed according to the prefer-

---

[10] Ibid. p. 328.
[11] Ibid. p. 331.

ences expressed. This distribution process would continue until all seats were filled.

No reader will be surprised to learn that interest in changing the electoral system is strongest among members of the Liberal Party. Since 1922 the Liberals have consistently failed to achieve a Parliamentary strength proportionate to their popular following. In three-cornered contests the Liberal candidate usually runs second or third, and thus while the party piles up impressive national totals it wins few seats in the House of Commons. Even in 1951 when the party's popular vote fell to 2.5 per cent of the national total, its proportionate share would have amounted to 15 seats. The two largest parties currently have no interest in either the alternative vote or proportional representation. In its younger days the Labour Party endorsed proportional representation, but since it has grown to be one of the two major contenders in the political battle its views have changed. The Conservatives as a party have never favored a change in the electoral system, although proportional representation has been advocated by some elements within the party. Nowadays both Labour and Tory politicians prefer to take their chances on shifting enough popular votes—and only small percentages are necessary—to produce a good working majority in the House of Commons.

When the inequities and distortions of the British electoral system are exposed the case for proportional representation appears strong. Further examination suggests, however, that its adoption would do much more than relate Parliamentary representation accurately to popular voting. It would probably work a fundamental change in the functioning of British government. As it presently operates, the British system is predicated upon the existence of two strong parties, each of which is prepared to form a Ministry on a day's notice. Proportional representation might well result in there rarely being a party with a Parliamentary majority, and under such conditions either coalition or minority Government would be the rule. Coalitions formed to meet some supreme national emergency have functioned well, but their success has not been marked during normal times. Minority Governments depending upon the voting support of a third party have seldom had long or useful lives. Britain probably would pay a big price in political stability for a more accurate representation of the electorate—strong Governments might be rare.

An additional cause of instability might well come from proportional representation. It is almost certain that its adoption would lead to a number of minor parties, groups without broad national programs but devoted to special causes—pacifism, Scottish nationalism, Beaverbrook imperialism, Mosely fascism, and so forth. By concentrating their ballots under proportional representation, minority movements can secure the election of a few members here and there. Possessing no general mandate and subject to no major party discipline these splinter groups would contribute little to effective government or opposition. If numerous and extreme enough they could menace orderly administration.

The British political system as now conducted encourages diverse political interests to seek common ground. Its forces are centripetal. There can be no doubt that as a result some worthy causes are neglected and some courageous spirits are suppressed, but, by the same token, the system prevents many extremists from gaining bargaining positions and requires the great majority of its politicians to represent a broadly conceived national interest.

XIII

The Administration of Justice

In Britain the administration of justice has a long and honorable history, and the judicial system represents one of the most successful endeavors of the English nation. Courts have been sitting in England for centuries, and while they have not always administered a kind of justice that would satisfy modern standards, they have attempted, by and large, to give every man his due and to hold public authorities to previously established rules of conduct. There have been lapses from high standards, and despotically minded kings have abused the judicial system, but still progress has been steady. The supremacy of the law has always won out in the end.

1. *The Law of the Land*

Before undertaking a description of the machinery of justice and the way it functions, it will be well to consider briefly the law that it administers.[1] In general, English courts deal with three kinds of law, namely, the common law, equity, and statute law. The distinctions between these types of law are best indicated by describing their historical origins.

The common law originally evolved from the customary rules and practices of the Germanic tribes that settled in England 1500 years ago. When disputes arose the parties appealed to the customs of their locality, and the tribal elders pronounced the correct interpretation of the local customs. Some Anglo-Saxon law was reduced to written form in the dooms and decrees sanctioned by the king and his council, the witan, but much had to be sought in the decisions of courts, which endeavored to declare what was the custom 'from time when the memory of man runneth not to the contrary.'

But for one development of the Norman period, it is possible that England might have had several systems of common law, each dominant in a particular locality. The development which insured a national common law was the confirmation and extension under Henry II of the practice of sending royal judges to hold court throughout the land. For many decades these judges traveling on circuit had to compete with local courts under the

---

[1] The discussion in this chapter relates mainly to England and Wales. Scotland, as will be mentioned later, has its own jurisprudence and system of courts. In Northern Ireland, judicial organization differs somewhat from the English pattern.

control of feudal magnates who had a vested right to dispense justice. The royal judges finally won out in this contest because of the superior quality of justice they dispensed, and gradually the kings gathered into their hands a monopoly in the judicial field. The royal judges traveling regularly from the King's household tended to bring a uniformity into the rules of the common law. By moving from county to county and then, at the seat of the royal government, having an opportunity to discuss with fellow judges their judicial experience, they built up a body of rules common to Kent as well as Yorkshire.

In the course of centuries the remedies which were available to private litigants in civil suits came to be expressed in a number of forms of legal action. A person who considered himself wronged had to fit his case into one of these forms of action. If he proved the injury to the satisfaction of the court he was awarded money damages as provided by the rules of common law. However, the remedy available at common law sometimes appeared to do less than justice to the injured party. Occasionally the award of money damages was in no way adequate to reimburse the injured party for his loss. For example, if a person had agreed to sell a valuable object and then refused to honor the contract, the would-be purchaser would have a common-law action for damages because of the breach of contract. He would not, however, have the object which he prized and wished to purchase. He could only obtain substantial justice through some action which compelled the defaulter to carry out his bargain. Or, to take another situation, a person might have reason to fear some injury. He could await its occurrence and then sue for damages. The injury, however, might be irreparable, and hence he would desire 'preventive' justice. In medieval times cases of this nature were often carried directly to the king who, as the fountain of justice, could render a decision deemed equitable to both parties. The business of dispensing the King's justice in such cases fell to an official of the court known as the chancellor because he was usually a cleric and thus more learned than the other royal advisers and administrators.

Through these petitions to the monarch and the decisions of the chancellors there grew up a secondary body of law known as equity or chancery justice. In the course of time it came to be formalized into a number of forms of action which were designed to give remedies not available at common law. Since the legal learning of the chancellors was largely in canon law, which in turn was based on Roman law, equity jurisprudence came to have a strong flavor of Roman law. During the later Middle Ages a serious competition developed between the courts administering the two kinds of law, and it looked as though equity might, in civil cases, displace the common law entirely. The common-law lawyers and judges, however, were stubborn in resisting encroachments upon their province, and eventually jurisdictional lines were marked out which left to both systems of law particular kinds of jurisdiction. A litigant in a civil cause had the choice of pursuing his case at common law or at equity, and his decision was based on the nature of the injury suffered and the kind of remedy he

220–

sought. Besides providing remedies unknown to the common law, equity jurisprudence also took jurisdiction over new legal subjects, of which trusts are a good example.

The relation of statute law to the common law and to equity should now be noticed. Common law and equity both developed through judges declaring what was the customary practice of the community as expressed in the decisions of courts. They were, as it is frequently said, judge-made law. Well-established rules came into existence because of the judicial practice of following earlier decisions upon the same subject. A judge did not endeavor to render abstract justice; he declared the rights of the parties in accordance with what his judicial predecessors had determined those rights to be from as far back as the records went. Since cases were rarely identical in all particulars, the judges would use the general rule and then distinguish the case before them to the extent necessary to render justice to the parties. This process of distinguishing from general rules led to the creation of secondary rules until the whole complex field of human relationships was covered by rule after rule.

Sometimes, however, it appeared desirable to announce a new rule of conduct or to make a definite change in the rights and obligations of parties in certain situations. When social and economic developments occurred more rapidly than the judicial practice of building precedent by precedent could keep pace with, the law had to be brought up to date. Thus came about the need for statute law. Medieval kings, acting upon the advice of leading nobles gathered in a Great Council, would on occasion proclaim some new rule. It would supersede the relevant common law and be interpreted and enforced by the courts. After Parliament became an established institution, the members of that body frequently petitioned the king for redress of grievances and for the proclamation of new corrective statutes. Gradually this legislative activity grew until a principal function of Parliament was the consideration of either legislative proposals of the sovereign or measures initiated by members of Parliament. It must not be supposed, however, that the legislative activity of early Parliaments was very considerable; it was not until social life developed to something like its modern complexity that the number of laws enacted rose to substantial proportions.

The statutes that were enacted assumed the existence of the common law and of equity. They were built upon the base of existing jurisprudence. Frequently they changed an established rule of the common law or brought together several lines of judicial interpretation into a new standard rule, but in interpreting the statutes the judges continued to use their common-law precepts. This is the practice of courts today although, of course, the volume of statutory law has been growing very markedly in recent decades. The pace of modern life requires that positive law assume a greater place among the rules governing relationships between citizens.

To sum up, all rights and duties of British citizens in personal relationships that have a public incidence, all property and business relationships, and all relationships between them and persons in positions of authority are determined by the laws of the land. The basic law, both civil and criminal, is to be discovered in the vast body of the common law. A limited number of legal situations are covered by the rules of equity or chancery law. Both the common law and equity are being altered and advanced constantly by statute law. The latter as the most recent declaration of sovereign power always has precedence, but where the statutes are silent the courts fall back on the underlying common law.

The universal application of law, a fundamental principle of the British Constitution, is usually referred to as the rule of law. The rule of law, in this sense, means that the rights and obligations of citizens are always to be determined in open court according to fixed and established rules rather than the caprice or fiat of any authority.

2. *Administrative Law and Justice*

A feature of continental jurisprudence is the existence and use of a body of law known as administrative law. This kind of law regulates the conduct of official business and pertains to the relations of private citizens and their governmental authorities. In Continental countries, and in other nations which have modeled their legal systems upon those of continental Europe, administrative law is dispensed in a separate system of courts. Thus, a French citizen who is involved in a dispute with the taxing authorities will have his case heard and adjudged in an administrative rather than an ordinary court. Should he have the misfortune to be injured by a state-owned vehicle, say a post-office truck, his claim for damages would come before an administrative court and, if successful, he would collect from the government.

Anglo-Saxon jurisprudence has never favored the establishment of a separate body of law or a separate series of courts for the administration of this kind of justice. Following the lead of Dicey, English lawyers long regarded the French *droit administratif* as conferring a privileged status on officials and as affording less protection to the private citizen's rights. They preferred to keep officials, in both their private and public capacities, answerable to the same law as are private citizens, and to maintain the ordinary courts as the usual places for hearing and deciding cases arising out of the performance of administrative functions. In recent years, however, English lawyers have viewed the Continental practice more tolerantly and have been prepared to admit that Britain has, in fact, a large and growing body of administrative law. Its sources, as Professor Robson has written, 'include not only the law controlling public administration (i.e. Statutes, common law and equity), but also the law emanating from the executive organs in the exercise of their duly authorized powers. Thus, statutory instruments, administrative orders and the determinations of administrative tribunals can be as authentic sources of administrative law as legislation and decisions of the Courts. Moreover, just as the usages and conventions of the Constitution form an important part of constitutional law, so the usages and conventions of the Executive form an essential part of administrative law.' [2]

Moreover, there are many administrative 'courts' functioning in England. They have developed on an *ad hoc* basis and form no system comparable to those across the Channel. While cases involving administrative law are often heard in the ordinary courts, a great many of them come, in the first instance, to ministers or to special departmental tribunals. These executive agencies have been designated by statute to hear cases involving particular fields of administrative activity—for example, town planning, rent control, social insurance, and public housing—because it is believed that the efficiency of government and the protection of the citizen's rights can best be served through a special procedure for dealing with disputed questions which arise. Instead of loading the ordinary courts with a great mass of small cases about pension rights or the rental charges of landlords, these matters are heard by administrative officials or tribunals and decisions given. A dissatisfied party may have an appeal to the ordinary courts, at least to the extent of claiming that the original administrative action of which he complains was *ultra vires,* that is, it was not authorized by the statute under which the official or officials acted; he may have an appeal to a higher administrative tribunal; or sometimes there is no right of appeal at all. In hearing and deciding cases administrative officers and administrative tribunals are required to follow a judicial-like procedure, although it is not as formal as the procedural rules of the regular courts. England has, therefore, a large body of administrative law and many administrative 'courts'—ministers, other administrative officials, and special tribunals hearing and deciding cases.

Many persons have been disturbed and alarmed by the growth of administrative law and the jurisdiction conferred upon the bureaucratic machine in place of the ordinary courts of justice. We have already taken note of the fear that basic liberties are being undermined by having personal and property rights determined, to all intents and purposes, by officers of the executive rather than the judicial branch of the government. These officers, it is charged, frequently fall below acceptable standards when acting in a judicial capacity. If not too zealous in promoting departmental policy or partial to the official point of view, their lack of judicial training and the absence of the traditions surrounding the regular courts cause them to impair rights and deliver inequitable decisions. It would be misleading, however, to leave the impression that a great deal of injustice occurs when ministers or other officials hear and determine cases arising in connection with their administrative activities. Ministers and civil servants, by and large, are fair-minded and desire to be just to all parties. The risk comes about in devolving a judicial function upon officers who are

---

[2] William A. Robson, 'Administrative Law in England, 1919-1948,' *British Government since* 1918 (London, 1950), p. 89.

primarily concerned with administrative duties and whose training and competence lie in other lines.

There appears to be no solution to this admittedly serious problem except to improve the quality of administrative justice. The sphere of public administration is constantly expanding, and many of the issues arising between officials and private citizens will continue to be heard and decided by administrative authorities. If throughout the executive establishment there can be developed procedures for hearing cases that are fair and that accord the citizen his elementary rights, and if judicial-mindedness can be instilled into officials exercising judicial duties, then the dangers in the present situation will be removed to a large extent. There are reasonably good prospects of such changes occurring. Awareness of the problem has come in the past two or three decades, and from that should flow remedial action. The institution of a comprehensive system of administrative courts is unlikely, for the British are more apt to proceed in piecemeal fashion.

3. *The Courts of Justice*

Justice is administered in Britain in two principal hierarchies of courts, one for civil cases and one for criminal cases. The lowest civil courts are known as county courts, and there are some 450 of these in England and Wales. They are arranged in circuits and are presided over by a body of 62 county court judges. A county court judge is appointed by the Crown and must be a barrister of at least seven years' experience. The jurisdiction of these courts is limited by the amount of damages which may be claimed and by the value of the property in dispute. A county court may entertain a suit where the amount claimed is less than £200 or where, in equity cases, the value of the property in dispute is not more than £500.

The procedure in the county court is comparatively simple. The parties may employ lawyers, but often they conduct their cases themselves. County court procedure provides for an eight-man jury when the amount in dispute exceeds £5 and one of the parties requests it, but it is unusual for a jury to be employed. The records of each of the county courts are kept by an official known as the registrar. He often succeeds in bringing parties to settle their cases out of court, so the number of county court trials is considerably less than the number of disputes settled there.

Above the county courts is the Supreme Court of Judicature, which is divided into the High Court of Justice and the Court of Appeal. The High Court of Justice has original jurisdiction over civil suits involving claims of any amount and of any kind. Because of the availability of the county courts for minor cases, it is unusual for a party to seek a decision in the High Court of Justice for any but a serious suit. The High Court is organized in three divisions. The Queen's Bench Division is a common-law court which is a direct descendant of the medieval courts established to dispense royal justice. The Chancery Division, as the name suggests, deals with suits involving chancery or equity law. It, too, is a descendant of courts established centuries ago to administer the justice dispensed by the chancellors in the monarch's name. The third division, the Probate, Divorce, and Admiralty Division, deals with cases involving these three subjects which have little in common but the fact that the law is specialized and cannot be conveniently administered by the other two divisions. This division is a consolidation of a number of courts which formerly exercised jurisdiction in these fields.

Each of the divisions of the High Court of Justice has a bench of judges who sit singly or in groups of three, depending upon the procedure of the court. The Queen's Bench Division is headed by the Lord Chief Justice of England and has twenty other judges. The Chancery Division is nominally presided over by the Lord High Chancellor, and there are five other judges. The head of the Probate, Divorce, and Admiralty Division has the title of President, and seven additional judges share the work of this division. By the Judicature Act, 1873, which established the Supreme Court of Judicature, a High Court judge is eligible to sit in any division. Moreover, any division may give, as suitable, remedies based on common law or equity, although in practice the divisions deal with their legal specialties.

From the county courts and from the High Court of Justice appeals may be taken on points of law but not usually of fact to the Court of Appeal. The Court of Appeal consists of the Master of the Rolls and eight other judges. Three judges customarily sit together to hear an appealed case.

The final stage in the civil hierarchy is the House of Lords. Upon application, the House of Lords may grant leave to appeal on a legal point but not on a question of fact. While theoretically the appeal is to the whole House of Peers, actually the legal business is transacted by the Lord Chancellor and the other Law Lords. The hearing of a case is recorded in the ordinary legislative journal of the House, but the procedure is judicial and conforms to that of a supreme court of appeal. Needless to say, the amount involved must be very substantial, or the principle one of great moment, before litigants are disposed to carry cases as high as the House of Lords.

The hierarchy of criminal courts starts with one of the most interesting institutions of English jurisprudence, the justice of the peace. For centuries the Crown has appointed in each county substantial members of the community to the commission to maintain the King's peace. These justices are responsible for trying minor offenses and for examining the charges against alleged criminals to see whether or not there is a sufficient case to hold them for trial by higher courts. Until fairly recent years, the justices of the peace were usually country gentlemen who were important local figures and who were regarded as responsible for the maintenance of order in their communities. Untrained in the law, they dispensed a simple justice in cases involving petty thievery, minor assaults, and violations of local by-laws and ordinances. In this century, the body of justices has been expanded by including men and women from many walks of life, and the social distinction of being a 'J.P.' has been somewhat reduced. It is still, however, a considerable local honor and most justices take their duties seriously.[3]

The jurisdiction of a justice of the peace sitting alone is restricted to cases in which the fine does not exceed £5 or the jail sentence 14 days. Two or more justices may sit as a court known as petty sessions and impose slightly higher fines and sentences. In large cities the system of unpaid and untrained justices has been supplanted by a permanent and paid group of magistrates who would correspond roughly with the police-court judges of many American municipalities. Known in London as metropolitan magistrates and in 16 provincial cities as stipendary magistrates, these judicial officers are barristers appointed by the Home Secretary.

The next stage above the justice of the peace court is a court known as quarter sessions. It is so named because it is convened four times a year. A court of quarter sessions consists of all, or a major proportion of, the justices of the peace in a principal area of local government—an administrative county, a county borough, or certain non-county boroughs. Some boroughs employ a barrister part-time to preside over their court of quarter sessions. Known as a recorder, he is appointed by the Home Secretary. By the Justices of the Peace Act, 1949, a considerable number of non-county boroughs lost their separate commissions of the peace and became petty sessional divisions of the counties in which they are situated. A court of quarter sessions hears cases that are similar in character to those tried summarily in petty sessions but which are of a more serious nature and which will be followed by heavier fines or sentences if the parties accused are found guilty. The court has a right to hear appeals from fines or sentences imposed by single justices.

The most important criminal court of original jurisdiction is the assize court. This court, held periodically in each county town, is a direct descendant of the courts established by the Norman monarchs in their plan to bring the King's justice to the entire realm. The court is presided over by a judge coming from the Queen's Bench Division of the High Court of Justice in London, and his visit to a county town is marked by considerable ceremony. As the representative of the sovereign, the fountain of justice, the assize judge takes precedence over all local officials. His journey from his living quarters to the court is announced by heralds, and the procession is attended by the local dignitaries in their robes and insignia of office.

The jurisdiction of the assize court extends to all serious crimes—such as armed robbery, arson, embezzlement, kidnapping, and murder. Charges against alleged criminals used to be brought to the notice of the assize court by a grand jury which examined the evidence and found it either sufficient for holding the person for trial or not weighty enough to justify a trial. The grand jury is no longer employed in Great Britain, and the

---

[3] There are approximately 19,000 justices of the peace. About 13,100 men and 3700 women are on the active list, including such ex-officio justices as the mayors of boroughs and the chairmen of county and district councils.

indicting process is performed by the justices of the peace who have made a preliminary examination or by the Public Prosecutor, an official of the Crown who endeavors to secure the conviction of alleged criminals. The assize court uses a trial jury of 12 persons in its procedure, and it is the responsibility of the jury to pass judgment upon the guilt or innocence of the person charged as revealed by the evidence presented in court. Questions of law which arise in the course of a trial are decided by the judge.

An appeal from a conviction in an assize court may be taken to the Court of Criminal Appeal. The Court of Criminal Appeal consists of at least three judges drawn from the Queen's Bench Division of the High Court of Justice. Appeals may be taken on any question of law and on a question of fact provided the trial judge or the Court of Criminal Appeal itself agrees. The Court of Criminal Appeal may sustain the lower court, or it may modify the sentence, or if it considers that there has been a miscarriage of justice, quash the verdict entirely. Occasionally, an appeal may be carried from this court to the House of Lords, but only if the Attorney General certifies that some important legal point is involved in the case.

A convicted criminal having exhausted the appellate procedure open to him has only the pardoning power of the Crown as a last resort. This royal prerogative is exercised upon the advice of the Home Secretary. He may reprieve a condemned criminal, he may reduce a sentence, or he may pardon the convicted person.

One special court deserves some mention in connection with the British judicial system. This is the Judicial Committee of the Privy Council. Strictly speaking, the Judicial Committee is not a court at all but an administrative body which advises the Crown on the exercise of the royal prerogative with respect to appeals from colonial and Commonwealth courts. It also advises upon appeals coming from the highest ecclesiastical court of the Church of England, the Court of Arches.

The jurisdiction of the Privy Council grew up in past centuries through the common-law right of subjects living overseas to appeal to the King in Council for the disallowance of judgments by the highest judicial authorities of their colony. In 1833 the hearing of these appeals and the submission of advice to the Crown were lodged in a Privy Council committee. At present the Judicial Committee consists of the Lord Chancellor, the Law Lords of the House of Lords, and distinguished dominion and colonial judges who are privy councillors. It does not have a fixed membership, but usually cases are heard by the same group of jurists who exercise the judicial functions of the House of Lords.

Probably no court in the world hears such a variety of cases and applies so many kinds of law. In a single term it may hear cases from some of the older dominions where the law is substantially like that of Great Britain, from the newer dominion of Ceylon and territories where indigenous systems of law are involved, and from colonies where primitive native law is predominant. Thus, the Judicial Committee will perhaps consider in turn cases from Australia, Nigeria, Ceylon, and Trinidad.[4] The decision by the Judicial Committee is not a court judgment but, in accordance with its constitutional nature, a statement of advice to the Crown either to sustain the dominion or colonial court or to return the case for a new hearing in accordance with the opinion of the Judicial Committee.[5]

Some of the cases coming before the Judicial Committee involve important questions of constitutional law in the dominions. For example, in 1949 the Judicial Committee heard an appeal from the High Court of Australia concerning the power of the Commonwealth Government to nationalize the banking system of the country. Federal legislation on nationalization was challenged by the private banks and three of the states of the dominion as being in conflict with a provision of the Commonwealth constitution. To argue its case the Government of Australia sent the Commonwealth Attorney-General, and the parties in opposition employed a strong company of leading barristers. The decision rendered in this case, controlling on the High Court of Australia, was against the constitutionality of the nationalization statute.

As the dominions have come to the position of full stature in international affairs they have been disposed to limit or abolish the right of appeal to the Judicial Committee of the Privy Council. South Africa, Canada, Pakistan, and India have barred appeals, as did Ireland while it remained a member of the British Commonwealth. Their determination to eliminate the right of appeal to the Privy Council stems mainly from a belief that the procedure is incompatible with the present independent status of the dominions but also in part from objections to the expense imposed upon litigants. The costs in counsel fees, travel to London, and expenses incidental to the hearing are naturally high and can only be undertaken by wealthy litigants. There has been practically no feeling that the Judicial Committee of the Privy Council is affected by any but the highest judicial standards in its hearing and deciding of cases brought before it. At the time the Judicial Committee heard its last appeal from India, the Indian High Commissioner in London said that through two centuries of association 'nothing has impressed the people of India more than the high sense of detachment, independence, and impartiality which have invariably governed the deliberations of the Privy Council.' [6]

---

[4] The Judicial Committee began the Trinity term sittings in 1949 with 45 appeals to be heard. Their origins were as follows: India and Pakistan, 31; Canada, 5; Ceylon, 1; West Africa, 3; Fiji, 2; East Africa, 1; Singapore, 1; and one prize appeal. *The Times*, 14 June 1949.

[5] An American author, writing of the many dissents by justices of the Supreme Court of the United States, has said: 'In Great Britain, the Judicial Committee of the Privy Council always announces its decisions in a single opinion, for the decisions are in the form of advice to the Crown, and it is said that the Crown would be confused by conflicting advice. We attribute more hardihood to our bar, fortunately, than the British to their Crown.' Paul A. Freund, *On Understanding the Supreme Court* (Boston, 1950), p. 8. Yet dissenting opinions are not infrequently given by British judges in the ordinary courts.

[6] *The Times*, 8 February 1950.

228–

4. *The Legal Profession*

Something should be said now about the legal and judicial profession which gives life to the institutions that have been described. The law has always been a highly honored profession in England and its practitioners have played leading parts in the development of British government. Lawyers as a professional group are probably not as prominent in the legislative and executive branches of British government as they are in the United States, but they still are an extremely influential group.

The legal profession in England is divided into two bodies. One group is that of solicitors. These lawyers deal directly with clients, and they may be engaged in a general practice or they may be specialists in particular aspects of the law. They draw legal instruments such as contracts and wills, they advise clients on their legal rights and obligations, and they prepare cases for argument in court. Appearance in the higher courts is restricted to the second legal class, the barristers. The barristers are a much smaller group—some 2000—and are considered, professionally and socially, a somewhat more select body of lawyers. Every barrister belongs to one of the four Inns of Court—Lincoln's Inn, Inner Temple, Middle Temple, and Gray's Inn. These Inns of Court prescribe the legal training which is necessary for admission to the bar, offer instruction to law students, and provide a professional club where members meet and where many have their chambers in the college-like surroundings of the Inn. The origins of the Inns of Court are lost in history, but it seems probable that they started as lawyers' guilds for the purpose of training new members of the profession. The records of Lincoln's Inn go back to 1422, when all the present Inns had been in existence for a century or more.

When a solicitor advises his client to take a case to court or when the client has no option, the solicitor obtains a barrister to make the presentation. This practice is known as briefing, and the brief handed to the barrister will bring a fee varying with the difficulty of the case and the prominence of the barrister. Successful barristers are briefed time and again for important cases, and the sum of their annual fees will amount to very high figures. It is said that Sir Stafford Cripps before he left the active practice of law for a political career was earning approximately £25,000 annually in the courts.

Most of the practice of the barristers takes place in a large collection of castellated buildings on the Strand known as the Law Courts. Here sit the divisions of the High Court of Justice, the Court of Appeal, and the Court of Criminal Appeal. Not far away in the City is the Central Criminal Court, known popularly as 'Old Bailey,' which is the assize court for London. About a mile from the Law Courts in the other direction are the Houses of Parliament where sit the House of Lords and the Judicial Committee of the Privy Council. Barristers accompany the High Court judges when they travel from county to county holding the assizes. There are sev-

—229

eral of these circuits, and barristers specializing in criminal law regularly belong to one of them.

The Crown makes appointments to judicial positions from the ranks of the barristers. The choice in the case of the higher appointments is made by the Prime Minister, who usually consults the Lord Chancellor. The latter selects the puisne judges of the High Court and the county court judges, and as a barrister he has a good acquaintance throughout the profession. In the selection of the more important judges he will probably consult the Prime Minister and perhaps other Cabinet colleagues. Judicial appointments are not, however, regarded as political plums to be awarded to party stalwarts. The most important criteria are a lawyer's standing in his profession and his record as a practicing barrister. The Prime Minister and the Lord Chancellor will undoubtedly give some weight to the political and social views of persons being considered for judicial appointment, and neither Labour nor Conservative ministers are likely to recommend the selection of someone decidedly hostile in political philosophy.

Judges are appointed without term, and this practice of serving during good behavior dates back to the Act of Settlement of 1701. One of the practices which the Stuart Kings indulged in was the removal of unsympathetic judges; consequently, the independence of the judiciary suffered considerably during their reigns. Since the beginning of the eighteenth century there has been no question of the inviolability of the judicial office, and nowadays the removal of a judge for political reasons is unthinkable. The power to remove remains vested in the Crown but may only be exercised upon an address by both Houses of Parliament.[7]

5. An Appraisal of the Judicial System

The quality of a judicial system depends upon the degree to which it is able to maintain a balance between the rights of the individual and the rights of the community. A judicial system must guarantee that parties in civil suits have every reasonable opportunity to advance their claims or protect themselves from unjustified demands. In criminal cases it must assure that an accused person shall not be convicted unless the weight of the evidence points to his guilt beyond any reasonable doubt. The alleged criminal must be afforded sufficient aid and opportunities for defense so that he can match the obviously superior power and resources of law enforcement agencies. On the other hand, there are community rights to be guarded, too. The judicial system must operate so that the public interest is protected through the exercise of necessary restraints and compulsions upon individual citizens and their private corporations. Malefactors must be brought to justice and the public protected from their depredations.

It is a difficult matter to keep the scales of justice reasonably even. Because of the important interests involved, there are always pressures to

---

[7] The last removal of a judge from office occurred in England more than 100 years ago.

change the rules in favor either of stronger private rights or stronger community rights. The twentieth century has seen in several countries the ascendancy of political philosophies which subordinate the rights of the individual to what is represented as the higher social good. The Fascists in Italy and the Nazis in Germany changed the law and reorganized the judicial system in such ways that the community, represented by their political and military authorities, had exceptionally broad and sweeping powers. The same situation exists in Soviet Russia, and a characteristic feature of Communist rule in all the states where that party has seized power has been the establishment of a so-called People's Court to administer a decidedly partial justice.

It is generally conceded by all whose appraisal is based on democratic standards that the British have been unusually successful in maintaining a judicial system which holds a fair balance between private rights and the social interest. The system has its deficiencies, but they soon come to public attention and steps are instituted toward corrective action. Such corrective action sometimes seems unnecessarily delayed, but in dealing with a matter as fundamental as the administration of justice it is undesirable to move precipitantly or in an experimental fashion. Important rights are involved and each change must be carefully studied in advance. In considering judicial reform, the certainty of the law and the stability of its administration are frequently as important as the securing of abstract justice.

Several characteristics of the British judicial system give clues to the reasons for its comparatively high quality. One contributing factor is found in the strong traditions of the legal profession. Lawyers and judges are a professional group with high standards which they jealously maintain. The Inns of Court for the barristers and the Law Society for solicitors are professional associations of high requirements and uncompromising principles. They are quick to debar any member whose methods of practicing reflect discredit on the profession. The judges of British courts, who are selected from among the barristers, are imbued with the standards of professional conduct set forth by these societies. In addition, they have the traditions of the courts to uphold. Behind them are hundreds of years of judicial history during which the judges have usually been courageous in maintaining that all the King's subjects of high and low degree are bound by the law.

Probably the dignity and decorum of British courts contribute to the maintenance of high judicial standards. It is not only a matter of the formality which wigs and robes give to the judge and the barristers arguing before him, but also the solemn and serious manner in which trials proceed. Judges will not permit trials to be converted into theatrical performances, and there is no bullying of witnesses or attempts to get an emotional verdict from a jury. This is not to say that barristers do not make earnest and forceful pleas for their clients, but the proceedings are almost always dignified and consonant with the seriousness of the judicial process. The high standard of courtroom conduct is not confined only to the courts in the capital. The assize courts bring to every county two or three times a year one of the principal judges of the kingdom, and he conducts his court in the provinces in the same spirit as in London. Thus, the standards of the highest courts are transmitted to the provinces.

A third characteristic of the British judicial system which contributes to its high quality is its divorce from active politics. Many British lawyers maintain an interest in political life and participate therein as members of Parliament or of local councils, but usually a lawyer devotes his talents primarily to politics or to the legal profession. A leading barrister can rarely spare much time from his profession for active political life, and an important politician seldom attempts to carry on at the bar. The judges are completely divorced from active politics.[8] Appointed for life terms, they have no interest in keeping active in a party organization or in considering what their fortune will be at the next election. It is contrary to the traditions of the bench for them to indicate publicly any partiality for a political party or for a Government which may be in power. There is thus absent from the British scene the type of judge who is primarily a political leader and who views his judicial career as either an interlude from executive or legislative service or as a stepping stone to higher political office. A result of this tradition is the removal from the minds of judges of those considerations of ambition and political indebtedness which might handicap them in the proper performance of their judicial duties. In addition to security of tenure, the judges receive high salaries which on the whole make them immune to tempting business offers or to any compromise with their duty.[9] All in all, the high prestige which comes from a severely restricted profession, security of tenure, and generous compensation combine to make the judge as free as possible to exercise his calling in the most responsible manner.

Another contributing factor is the comparatively speedy procedure with which trials are conducted in England. This dispatch is largely a result of the rules which govern the conduct of trials, the management of the courtroom procedure by the judge, and the provision for the prompt hearing of appeals. The contrast with American courts with respect to the dispatch

---

[8] The Lord Chancellor is, of course, an exception. As a member of the Cabinet, the presiding officer in the House of Lords, and as the highest judicial authority of the state, he is engaged in executive, legislative, and judicial activities. Since Prime Ministers select leading barristers for this position, professional standards are a sufficient guide to a Lord Chancellor in separating his judicial conduct from his other official duties. Moreover, as a peer he does not face the problem of re-election to Parliament, and he can be less politically minded than most of his ministerial colleagues.

[9] The Lord Chancellor receives £10,000 a year; the Lord Chief Justice, £8000; the Master of the Rolls and the Lords of Appeal in Ordinary, £6000, and the judges of the High Court of Justice, £5000. While salaries of these amounts compare favorably with other official remuneration in England, the difference between the incomes of the judge and the successful barrister has widened appreciably. Judicial salaries were set by the Judicature Act of 1873, and rising prices and taxation have reduced the real income of the judiciary.

of business is marked. Although in the federal system many improvements have resulted from the work of the Judicial Council and the Administrative Office of the United States Courts, as well as from the codes of procedure prepared under the supervision of the Supreme Court, the majority of the state judicial systems are characterized by laborious procedures which put a premium on legal technicalities that delay final decision.

Unlike the situation in the United States, where the rules of procedure are usually determined by legislative bodies in which trial lawyers have a considerable influence, the rules in British courts are made by a committee of judges and barristers known as the Rules Committee. This committee has existed since 1873 and has been successful in maintaining a body of rules which are at once adequate to protect the parties having cases in the courts and to move such cases along with reasonable dispatch. British courts do not get delayed by wrangles of opposing lawyers over such matters as the choosing of a jury, and their decisions are not open to challenge on technical grounds as often happens in the United States. While the judge is, in a sense, an umpire in the proceedings before him, he nevertheless keeps control of the procedure. He is quick to end what are merely dilatory tactics, and he will not allow minor procedural problems to defeat the ends of justice.[10] An appeal taken from a court of original jurisdiction is promptly heard, and it is rarely possible to keep the case alive beyond this appeal. This speedy procedure is particularly true of criminal trials and undoubtedly contributes to the comparatively small amount of major crime in Great Britain. The spectacle of a convicted criminal carrying his case from one court to another over a period of months and sometimes years is unknown in Britain, where even the most serious criminal trials consume only a few days and appeals are disposed of a short time after the original verdict.

No human institution ever achieves perfection, and it is natural that there are features of the British system of administering justice that deserve and receive criticism. Some students of judicial administration believe that the continued use of the justice of the peace as the lowest judicial officer in the criminal hierarchy requires a change. They point out that while the justice of the peace was a satisfactory judicial officer in the days when England was primarily a rural and decentralized country, under present social conditions the office is an anachronism. Appointed by the Lord Chancellor upon the advice of the Lord Lieutenants of the counties, who in turn accept recommendations from advisory committees, the justices of the peace are individuals with some local standing but not necessarily with any particular aptitude for judicial work. A moderate amount of political influence seems to bear upon the original appointment of justices.

---

[10] Governor Thomas E. Dewey, after a visit to the Law Courts in London in 1949, was quoted as follows: 'Your legal procedure is, of course, superb. There are four judges in London doing the same work that we have thirty for in New York. . . Your judges have a great deal more power than ours, and your barristers are especially trained for the particular job they are going to do.' The Times, 19 May 1949.

The justice of the peace was the subject of an investigation by a royal commission which reported in 1948 and which recommended only a few minor changes in the present situation.[11] Some of these were embodied in a bill enacted as the Justices of the Peace Act, 1949. It imposed a retirement limit of 75 years of age on justices, regrouped some of the areas covered by various commissions of the peace, established more precise rules concerning the appointment and conditions of service of magistrates' clerks and stipendiary magistrates, and authorized traveling expenses for 'J.P.'s' when their duties necessitated travel. It is probable that the practice of substituting paid magistrates for justices in the urban areas will continue, and perhaps at some future time a professional corps of judges will replace the present 'J.P.'s' entirely. Defenders of the present system make the point that the justice of the peace court brings the administration of justice for a large number of petty matters into close contact with local conditions. The 'J.P.' through his familiarity with the community is quite capable of rendering substantial justice without professional training in the intricacies of the law. What he needs to know of a technical nature he can learn from his clerk, who not only keeps records but has some professional competence. The system may break down when England ceases to have a semi-retired class of local notables who have sufficient interest and financial means to devote themselves to this kind of work. Then the paid magistracy will have to be extended to all areas of the country.

Another line of criticism is directed toward the expense of judicial proceedings. While the courts are open to all, and there are no political or social restrictions upon using them, there are economic barriers which operate. To carry a case beyond the lowest civil and criminal courts is an expensive enterprise. Counsel fees must be paid and the expense of traveling to London and living there during the proceedings is incurred. Wealthy litigants will not be deterred by such considerations, but parties with modest financial means are often prevented from carrying their cases to the highest courts. This problem has been met to some extent by the provision of legal assistance for parties with only meager financial resources. The Labour Government in 1948 provided by statute for additional assistance to these litigants. This assistance is a help to the least wealthy in the community, but it leaves a considerable number of people with modest financial means handicapped in the use of the courts. Proposals are occasionally advanced for a further decentralization of the judicial system, in order that the higher courts would be more easily accessible to parties outside of London. However, the traditions and practices which for centuries have centered on the location of the highest courts in the capital argue against such a move.

What has been said about the legal and judicial systems applies to all parts of the United Kingdom except Scotland. Scottish law and the system of courts differed from those in England prior to the Act of Union of

---

[11] Cmd. 7463 (1948).

1707, and they were not disturbed by the merger of political sovereignty. The Parliament at Westminster legislates for Scotland but, when necessary, it adapts statutes to the law and the courts of that country. Because of the closer political relations which Scotland maintained with the Continent for several centuries prior to the Act of Union, Scottish law was more affected by Roman law than was the common law of England. There is today no substantial difference in the quality of justice administered in England and in Scotland, but there is a different nomenclature in the court system and the judicial procedure varies to some extent. The Scottish judicial system provides for a hierarchy of civil and criminal courts. From the highest civil court, the Court of Session, there is a right of appeal to the House of Lords. No appeal lies, however, from the highest criminal court, the High Court of Justiciary.

XIV

The National Administration

In the part of London known as Westminster, one of the principal streets is Whitehall, a broad thoroughfare faced with a number of stone buildings which house departments and ministries of the British government. Until fairly recent years practically all the administrative departments could find a place along Whitehall or near by; consequently, the name is often used to suggest the whole bureaucratic apparatus of the British state.

The growth of government during the past few decades has made it necessary to locate the headquarters of a number of administrative services beyond the Whitehall neighborhood, and some of these or important branches of departments have even been placed in the provinces.[1] Along Whitehall or immediately adjacent are still to be found, however, the Treasury, the Foreign Office, the Home Office, the War Office, the Admiralty, and several other of the more important ministries of the state. Downing Street is a short cul-de-sac off Whitehall, and No. 10 and No. 11 are conveniently near the Treasury and the Foreign Office.

There are about 30 departments under responsible ministers through which the British government carries on its principal activities.[2] Some of these are small departments with specialized and limited functions. The majority, however, are large administrative establishments employing from several hundred to many thousands of civil servants and industrial workers. The largest in point of numbers is the Post Office, which employs about 250,000 people or nearly one-third of the ordinary civil servants of the

---

[1] A considerable decentralization occurred during the last war for security reasons and to make room for expanding British and allied military services. Some of the relocated offices did not return to London. Currently, additional decentralization is being undertaken. About 1800 employees of the Foreign Office are scheduled to move to Cheltenham between 1952 and 1955. *The Times,* 21 September 1949.

[2] Omitted are the public corporations which manage nationalized industries or services. They are financially autonomous, and the power of a minister with respect to a corporation is usually limited to the issuance of general directions. There are a score or more of departments, offices, boards, and commissions which are not represented in Parliament by ministers but whose estimates are presented to Parliament. They are thus subject to Treasury control. Their functions, by and large, are specialized and do not involve problems of national policy. Lists of British administrative agencies, classified by the degree of their responsibility to Parliament, are given in W. Ivor Jennings, *Cabinet Government,* 2nd ed. (Cambridge, 1951), Appendix III, pp. 509-30.

national government. The employees of the Post Office are naturally distributed in all parts of the United Kingdom, and comparatively few of them are located in London. On the other hand, a department like the Treasury has nearly its entire staff in Whitehall.

1. *The Origins of the Government Departments*

The evolutionary growth of the British political organization is indicated in no better way than in the histories of the government departments. The development of much of the apparatus of the state from the household offices of the medieval kings is plainly shown in some of the old departments and ministries. For example, the Lord Chancellor, who was originally a chief clerk or scribe for the monarch, gradually became the principal law officer of the Crown, and today he has important duties with respect to the supervision of the judicial system and the appointment of judges. In another case, the administrator of the sovereign's holdings as Duke of Lancaster—possessions added to the Crown in the fourteenth century—became a minister with the title Chancellor of the Duchy of Lancaster.

The expansion of the functions of the state can be traced in the founding and development of the administrative departments. The oldest ones, as we would expect, are concerned with the basic activities of government. They deal with the defense of the kingdom against foreign enemies, the conduct of diplomatic relations, the collection, custody, and disbursing of the public revenue, and the maintenance of domestic peace and order. The newer departments are mainly concerned with the social and economic problems that have confronted the modern state during the past century. They are the problems of supervising and directing the economic activity by which a highly industrialized country sustains its life, regulating its transportation and communication services at home and abroad, and of endeavoring to protect its citizens from the social perils of the modern age.

Pre-eminent among the old departments of state is the Treasury, which existed even before the medieval office of the Exchequer—so-called because of the use of a checkered board on which tax receipts, brought in twice a year by the sheriffs, were counted before a Court. Down until Stuart times the Treasury was in charge of the Lord High Treasurer, but James I decided that this powerful official should share his responsibilities with several other ministers. Consequently, in 1612 he placed the office of Lord High Treasurer in commission, that is, he named a board to supervise the financial department of the state. The last Lord High Treasurer was appointed in Queen Anne's reign; since then the office has always been in commission. The First Lord of the Treasury continued to be the principal minister of the Crown, and his influence and authority grew to encompass the entire ministerial circle. Gradually the management and direction of the Treasury fell primarily upon the Chancellor of the Exchequer, whose office traces back to the twelfth century and his title to the thirteenth. The responsibility at the Treasury of the Junior Lords disappeared in the course

-237

of time and their relations to it became nominal. Thus today the Treasury is headed by the Treasury Board, but the officer who takes most of the actions of the Board is the Chancellor of the Exchequer. The position of First Lord of the Treasury is important to the Prime Minister, for it enables him to control the Civil Service, including appointments to the top places in all government departments. The Junior Lords are whips of the majority party in the House of Commons.

Another ancient office is that of Secretary of State, dating back to the reign of Henry III. Originally a clerical official in the palace establishment, the Secretary became in the course of time one of the more important of the royal ministers. Through him the kings conducted most of their relations with foreign countries, and he came to have a number of responsibilities connected with overseas and domestic affairs. These duties eventually became too heavy for one individual, so the office was divided; from Tudor times to the close of the eighteenth century there were usually two Secretaries of State. Today there are actually eight, each of whom heads a major ministerial department.

The Secretary of State for Foreign Affairs is in charge of the external relations of the United Kingdom. The principal domestic concerns of the office, in so far as they pertain to England and Wales, are in the hands of the Secretary of State for Home Affairs. The division of responsibility between a Foreign Office and a Home Office was made in 1782. In 1794 the military responsibilities of the Secretary of State were transferred to another official, the Secretary of State for War. Since at that time the acquisition or loss of colonies was the usual result of wars with England's Continental rivals, it was logical that the Secretary of State for War should administer the colonial possessions of the nation, a responsibility previously borne by the Home Secretary. Later, as many of the colonies grew to be more than citadels of military power or pawns in the peace conferences after European wars, there was need for an office in London which concerned itself with the political and economic development of the overseas possessions and the relations between them and the mother country. Hence, in 1854, the office of the Secretary of State for the Colonies was established. Following the Indian mutiny and the abolition of the political powers of the East India Company, a new office under a Secretary of State was established to supervise the administration of the populous subcontinent of India. The India Office and the Secretaryship of State ceased to exist when India and Pakistan became independent dominions in 1947. The colonies peopled largely by European races gradually developed into self-governing nations, and this change was recognized in Whitehall by transferring their relations with the United Kingdom to a Secretary of State for Dominion Affairs (1925). The final step in the evolution of a part of the colonial empire into an association of independent states is indicated by the change of the name of the Dominions Office to that of the Commonwealth Relations Office under a Secretary of State for Commonwealth Relations. Out of the office of the Secretary of State for War has come another depart-

238–

ment: in 1917 the importance of the airplane as a military instrument was recognized by the creation of an Air Ministry headed by a Secretary of State for Air. Another branch of the office of Secretary of State is the Scottish Office, established in 1926 when the post of Secretary for Scotland, created in 1885, was raised to the rank of a principal Secretary of State. The Secretary of State for Scotland represents in the British ministry those administrative departments which handle purely Scottish affairs. In 1951, Churchill appointed a Secretary of State for the Co-ordination of Transport, Fuel, and Power. While today each of the Secretaries of State is responsible for a major department of government they are all regarded as occupants of the same office. Statutory powers are conferred upon a Secretary of State, and in theory any one of them is qualified to discharge the functions of the other. In practice, the responsibilities of each are sufficiently extensive to keep him busy without encroaching upon the spheres of his fellow Secretaries of State, and by constitutional convention no one of them would attempt to exercise powers beyond his own department.

The occupant of another old office in the British government is the First Lord of Admiralty. As in the case of the Lord High Treasurer, there was once a Lord High Admiral. His duties were conferred upon a board of commissioners in the reign of Henry VIII. For a period of about 200 years the office of Lord High Admiral was in and out of commission, but since the early eighteenth century the duties have remained vested in a board. The Board of Admiralty of today consists of 11 members who collectively have the responsibility for the administration of the Royal Navy. The First Lord of the Admiralty is in effect the minister of the Navy, although all official transactions are those of the Board and the other members of the Board have departmental responsibilities. The Parliamentary and Financial Secretary of the Admiralty and the Civil Lord are politicians and rank as junior ministers. Five Sea Lords plus two other high-ranking naval officers comprise the professional element on the Board.

The most important royal servant in the medieval monarchy was the Lord Chancellor. He was a chaplain and a secretary of the sovereign, and the keeper of the royal seal. He attended Parliament and became the speaker or presiding officer of the House of Lords, although he was not always a peer. As 'keeper of the King's conscience,' the Lord Chancellor had referred to him the petitions for the exercise of the royal grace and favor, and out of this responsibility arose the chancery courts and the body of law known as equity. Through the centuries he has remained an important official, and in modern times the Lord Chancellor has been the head of the judicial system, the presiding officer of the House of Lords, and a Cabinet minister.

The Curia Regis of the medieval kings developed into a body known as the King's Council and later into the Privy Council, which in Tudor times was a functioning group of royal advisers. The Privy Council had an official known as the Lord President, and this office continues to this day and is occupied by a leading minister of the Crown. Since nowadays the functions of the Privy Council are primarily formal ones, the administrative duties of the Lord President are not heavy. Consequently, the Prime Minister usually bestows the office upon one of his principal lieutenants whom he wishes to keep reasonably free of departmental duties.

Two old offices which are sinecures in modern ministries are those of the Lord Privy Seal and the Chancellor of the Duchy of Lancaster. Their occupants are almost wholly free of administrative duties and are, in effect, ministers without portfolio.

Several Privy Council committees developed into governmental departments with important administrative responsibilities. Students of American history will remember the important role of the Privy Council Committee on Trade and Plantations during the colonial era. This committee eventually became, through several intermediate stages, the Board of Trade under a President who is today the responsible minister of that department. Another Privy Council committee developed into the Board of Education, and from 1899 until 1944 the President of the Board was the minister of education for England and Wales. In the latter year the Board was transformed into the newly organized Ministry of Education. The Ministry of Agriculture and Fisheries, established in 1919, stems from a board of that name and an earlier 'veterinary department' under the Privy Council.

The Board of Trade has been the parent of several present-day departments. In 1917 its responsibilities with respect to labor matters were transferred by statute to a Ministry of Labour. The name of the latter department was changed in 1939 to the Ministry of Labour and National Service when it was given charge of administering the system of military conscription and of other kinds of compulsory service. The Ministry of Transport was created in 1919 to assume the functions of the Board of Trade relating to the regulation of internal transportation and electric power, and in 1939 it took over the Board's responsibilities with respect to shipping. The Ministry's functions have been modified by the nationalization of the domestic transportation services. Before 1939 a department of the Board of Trade had developed plans for the supply and distribution of food during the course of a war. This department was made the Ministry of Food in that year. The Mines Department of the Board of Trade became the Ministry of Fuel and Power in 1942. The new Ministry was given additional responsibilities relating to petroleum, gas, and electric power. Its functions have been considerably modified by the nationalization of the coal mines and the gas and electric industries. Despite the shedding of important responsibilities, the Board of Trade retains a considerable range of functions relating to manufacturing, domestic and foreign trade, patents, and bankruptcy.

Central supervision of local government responsibilities relating to poor relief, sanitation, and health led to the establishment, merger, or abolition of a number of administrative bodies. An independent Poor Law Commission, established with the enactment of the new Poor Law of 1834, gave way to a Poor Law Board under a responsible minister, and the Board in turn was superseded by the Local Government Board (1871).

The latter Board, which had a President as the responsible minister, absorbed several functions with respect to public health exercised by a Privy Council office and by the Home Office. In 1919 the Local Government Board became the Ministry of Health, and in 1951 the Ministry's functions outside the fields of public health and sanitation were transferred to the Ministry of Town and Country Planning, first renamed the Ministry of Local Government and Planning and then the Ministry of Housing and Local Government. The central administration of poor relief passed eventually to the National Assistance Board, an independent commission created in 1948.

The introduction and expansion of various schemes of social insurance finally led to the establishment of the Ministry of National Insurance in 1944. It assumed the functions relating to health insurance performed by the Ministry of Health and those relating to unemployment insurance performed by the Ministry of Labour.

The Law Officers' Department is under the Attorney-General, who has the assistance of the Solicitor-General. They represent the Crown and the government departments before the courts and give legal advice to the Government. Similar functions for Scotland are performed by the Lord Advocate's Department.

With one exception, the remaining major administrative departments of the British government have all been established by statute. The exception is the Post Office which traces its origin to the old prerogative office of the Postmaster-General. The Ministry of Pensions was created in 1916 to administer the pensions system for war veterans. The Ministry of Supply was created in 1939 as a procurement agency for both the civilian and military departments. It has a wide range of functions, including the management of the royal ordnance factories and Britain's atomic energy program. The Ministry of Works, which constructs and maintains public buildings and cares for royal parks and ancient monuments, succeeded in 1942 to the duties of a board, the Commissioners of Works, dating from 1851. In 1945 the Ministry of Civil Aviation was set up as a regulatory agency for domestic flying and as a supervisor of the public corporations engaged in the business of overseas aerial transport. It also constructs and maintains civil airports and provides ancillary services. In 1951 it was merged with the Ministry of Transport. The Ministry of Defence was created in 1946 to co-ordinate military policy and administration. A world-wide scramble for raw materials led in 1951 to the establishment of a Ministry of Raw Materials. Set up to insure an adequate flow of basic products to British industry, it took over functions formerly performed by the Ministry of Supply and the Board of Trade.

2. Departmental Organization

Regardless of historical origin or present nomenclature the internal organization of a British government department is fairly uniform. At the top of its pyramidal structure is the minister. A member of Parliament, he belongs to the party or the coalition of parties having a majority in the House of Commons, and he is regarded as a political figure. Occasionally some person who has not been active in politics is appointed to ministerial office, but then he becomes immediately a member of the ministerial team. He is bound by the conventions which control the operations of the Ministry and its relations to Parliament. If he is a member of the Cabinet he sits in that body under the chairmanship of the Prime Minister, and he is required to support fully and faithfully the decisions and policy pronouncements of the group. A minister who does not belong to the Cabinet circle is nevertheless committed to the Government's program and policy. He serves at the pleasure of the Prime Minister; he leaves office when the Prime Minister decides the Government should resign.

Within the department the minister is responsible for all activities of the organization. Any failures of administration are chargeable to him; by the same token, he is entitled to the plaudits for successful work done by the department. Naturally, a minister cannot personally know about all the activities and operations of a large government department; he must rely upon subordinates in whom he has confidence. A successful minister is one who can develop a competent team of principal assistants and who can so infuse the entire departmental staff with his personality that the organization functions in a creditable manner. Harold Nicolson has written, 'A minister of strong personality immediately alters the whole atmosphere of his department; and in the shaping of events, atmosphere is a far more important element than the written word.' [3]

Below the minister in a typical department are one or two junior ministers, junior in responsibility as well as frequently in age and political experience. They are designated as Parliamentary Under Secretary, Parliamentary Secretary, or Financial Secretary. Like their chief they are members of the controlling party in the House of Commons and sit either in that House or in the House of Lords. The function of the junior ministers is to take charge of some aspects of departmental business and thus relieve their chief of a share of his burden. A Parliamentary secretary may supervise several branches of the internal administration of a department, or he may handle most of the Parliamentary liaison work of the ministry. The latter activity is essential if the minister is a peer and therefore not available to answer questions or speak in debates in the House of Commons. 'The duties of an under secretary,' Winston Churchill wrote, 'are often changed, but his responsibilities are always limited. He has to serve his chief in carrying out the policy settled in the Cabinet, of which he is not a member and to which he has no access.' [4] Writing on this occasion about Anthony Eden's dissatisfaction, while a Parliamentary under secretary at the Foreign Office, with the Government's policy during the 1930's,

---

[3] *The Spectator,* 11 February 1949, p. 181.
[4] *The Gathering Storm* (Boston, 1948), p. 132.

Churchill added that, 'only in an extreme case where conscience and honour are involved is he justified in carrying any differences about foreign policy to the point of public controversy or recognition.' [5]

The nature of a Parliamentary secretary's relationship to his minister came into prominence during the investigations of the Lynskey Tribunal in 1949. The tribunal brought out that one Parliamentary secretary had on occasion overruled the advice of the permanent officials in his department without consulting the minister. When this was revealed the Prime Minister, Clement Attlee, laid down the definite ruling that a junior minister should not override the advice of the permanent officials in his department without reference to his ministerial chief, who alone is responsible to Parliament. Commenting upon this affair and fully endorsing the Prime Minister's statement, Mr. Nicolson wrote as follows upon the proper relations between a minister and his Parliamentary secretary or under secretary:

> The Minister, and the Minister alone, is justified in overriding the opinion of the permanent civil servant. Even in matters specifically allocated to him by the Minister, the Parliamentary Secretary, if he is a prudent man, would not act against the advice of the civil servants without referring the issue to his chief for final decision. The Parliamentary Under Secretary as an institution (and it is an excellent institution) exists for two purposes. On the one hand he is there to relieve the Minister of the less important items of his House of Commons and departmental tasks. On the other hand he is there to learn the business of Government Departments and thereby to qualify himself for more responsible office. Quite certainly he is not there to dictate or determine policy; that is the function of the Minister alone.[6]

Directly below the minister in the departmental chain of command (the Parliamentary secretaries may be regarded as occupying positions of a staff nature) is the permanent secretary or permanent under secretary, the chief civil servant of the department. His position has two aspects. In the first place, he functions as a general manager in charge of the administrative work of the department. The permanent secretary is the head of the entire administrative hierarchy, and he is responsible to the minister for the proper functioning of the organization. The other aspect of his position is that of serving as the chief advisor to the minister on all matters of departmental policy and administration. It is improper for any other departmental official, save the Parliamentary secretaries, to proffer advice to the minister except through the permanent secretary. This pre-eminence in the departmental organization has been objected to by some groups of civil servants, particularly those in the scientific field, who consider that they should have direct access to the minister. They argue that the permanent

---

[5] Ibid. p. 132.
[6] Op. cit. 11 February 1949.

secretary, while admittedly competent in general administration, is not technically qualified to evaluate advice coming up from specialized branches of the department. While this point of view has been expounded, it is not apparent that it has effected any appreciable change in the operations of British government departments. The position of specialist officers has been improved by the introduction of a government-wide scientific service, but the controversy between the generalist, represented by the Administrative Class officers of the Civil Service, and the specialists has not been resolved.

Between the minister and the permanent secretary there must exist mutual trust and confidence. The minister must feel that his policies are being fairly explained to the department and executed in a loyal and wholehearted spirit. He must be confident that he is receiving the most sound and competent advice of which the staff is capable. The responsibility for the establishment of a satisfactory relationship between minister and permanent secretary falls largely on the latter. The permanent secretary must be sufficiently adaptable so that he can work successfully with ministers of varying temperaments and of different political views. Permanent secretaries can do a good deal in subtle ways to train inexperienced or erratic ministers, but if a definite clash of personalities arises or a serious difference over policy mars their relationship it is usually necessary to remove the civil servant.[7] Such instances are not common, for a civil servant rarely reaches the position of permanent secretary without exhibiting the flexibility of mind and temperament necessary to work effectively with ministers of different political attitudes and personal habits. The higher civil servants, Mr. Nicolson has remarked, 'are of sufficient intelligence not to submit to their Minister proposals which they know in advance he would be unable, either from personal or political reasons, to accept. None

---

[7] Winston Churchill records an instance of this kind in the Foreign Office. 'Up to this time and during many anxious years Sir Robert Vansittart had been the official head of the Foreign Office. His fortuitous connection with the Hoare-Laval Pact had affected his position both with the new Foreign Secretary, Mr. Eden, and in wide political circles. The Prime Minister, who leaned more and more upon his chief industrial adviser, Sir Horace Wilson, and consulted him a great deal on matters entirely outside his province or compass, regarded Vansittart as hostile to Germany. This was indeed true, for no one more clearly realized or foresaw the growth of the German danger or was more ready to subordinate other considerations to meeting it. The Foreign Secretary felt he could work more easily with Sir Alexander Cadogan, a Foreign Office official also of the highest character and ability. Therefore, at the end of 1937, Vansittart was apprised of his impending dismissal, and on January 1, 1938, was appointed to the special post of "Chief Diplomatic Adviser to His Majesty's Government." This was represented to the public as promotion, and might well indeed appear to be so. In fact, however, the whole responsibility for managing the Foreign Office passed out of his hands. He kept his old traditional room, but he saw the Foreign Office telegrams only after they had reached the Foreign Secretary with the minutes of the department upon them. Vansittart, who refused the Embassy in Paris, continued in this detached position for some time.' Op. cit. pp. 241-2.

but a moron among civil servants would write the same minute for Lord Margesson as he would write for Mr. Shinwell.'[8]

Below the permanent secretary the departmental organization fans out. Usually the permanent secretary is served by one or two deputy secretaries who supervise various branches of the ministry. They in turn have under them one or more assistant secretaries, and below the assistant secretaries come the principals and assistant principals. All lines of responsibility within the department converge inward and upward to the permanent secretary and through him to the minister.

3. Departmental Reorganization

The departmental organization of the British government, in terms of the number of ministries and their responsibilities, has grown without much plan or direction. As the activities of the state have expanded, the administration of new services has been given to some existing ministry or another one has been established. The result after several centuries of growth, and particularly since the rapid expansion of the sphere of the state in the past few decades, could be nothing less than a total structure lacking both symmetry and efficiency of line. This condition has not gone unnoticed, and from time to time there have been proposals for a reorganization of the departmental structure. Usually these reorganizations have been designed, first, to reduce the number of separate departments and agencies of the national government, and second, to effect a grouping of ministries concerned with associated services or administrative tasks.

One of the most thorough studies of this subject was carried out near the end of the First World War and appeared as the report of the Machinery of Government Committee of the Ministry of Reconstruction.[9] The Haldane Report, as it was called from the name of the committee chairman, proposed that the administrative side of the British government be organized in ten principal divisions—finance, national defense, foreign affairs, research and information, production, employment, supplies, education, health, and justice. The report did not suggest limiting the number of departments to ten, for it was realized that the administrative activities falling under some of these major divisions were so extensive that a single department would be a cumbersome and unwieldy organization. It did intend, however, that there should be a grouping within these fields and that the associated ministries should have their work closely co-ordinated.

While the report of the Machinery of Government Committee was widely endorsed it led to little official action. The departmental organization of the British government between the wars continued to be characterized by its pre-1914 lines of development. Proposals were advanced for the crea-

---

[8] Op. cit. 11 February 1949, p. 181. Lord Margesson and Mr. Shinwell both held the post of Secretary of State for War, the former a Conservative and the latter a Labourite.

[9] Cmd. 9230 (1918).

tion of a number of super-ministries similar to the recommendations of the Haldane Committee, or alternatively there were schemes for the grouping of departments under a non-departmental super-ministry.

The departments concerned with the military services were nearly always selected for one of these two treatments. Concerning military and defense organization, Ramsay Muir wrote between the wars, 'This work is divided between three independent and often mutually jealous departments, the Admiralty, the War Office, and the Air Office.' He pointed out that a measure of co-ordination was provided by the Committee of Imperial Defence but that its usefulness was limited because it was only an advisory body. The result was, according to Muir, 'that in the Cabinet itself, apart from the Prime Minister, there is no one whose business it is to speak for a single defense policy; but there are three members who commonly make it their business to stand up for the claims of their own departments. . .'[10] In the late 1930's, as the necessity for rearming against a patently aggressive Germany became obvious, the importance of co-ordinating the service departments could not be overlooked. The device chosen was the appointment of a co-ordinating minister, the three departments being left with their existing powers and direct representation in the Cabinet. This arrangement soon proved to be far from satisfactory, for the co-ordinating minister was expected to accomplish tasks for which he had insufficient authority. Consequently, when Churchill became Prime Minister in 1940 he created for himself the position of Minister of Defence and in effect became the 'super' minister over the three service departments. This solution was formalized after the war by the establishment of the Ministry of Defence. The Minister of Defence sits in the Cabinet from which the First Lord of the Admiralty, the Secretary of State for War, and the Secretary of State for Air are excluded. Except for controlling such common interests as combined operations, the Joint Intelligence Bureau, and the Imperial Defence College, the Ministry has no operating responsibilities and endeavors to co-ordinate the military establishment and to allocate resources through a number of joint secretariats and joint committees.

During World War II, governmental experience and the need to plan for the future led to a number of official inquiries and reports pertaining to public administration, but they did not prompt the creation of another Haldane Committee to consider the general design of departmental organization. The British government has not been subjected to the kind of examination and analysis carried out in the United States by the Commission on the Organization of the Executive Branch of the Government under the chairmanship of Herbert Hoover. Problems of organization and administrative methods have not been ignored, however.

With the encouragement of the Select Committee on Estimates of the House of Commons, there has been established a Government Organization Committee composed of permanent heads of departments with the

---

[10] *How Britain Is Governed* (New York, 1930), pp. 97-8.

Permanent Secretary of the Treasury as chairman. The committee is not 'attempting a review of the government machine in one huge investigation. The program is to take individual governmental activities which concern a number of departments and to examine them in turn and to correct any faults or misallocation of functions which the examination reveals. It is expected that this task will take some years to complete.' [11]

The 'task force' used by the committee in making its inquiries is the Treasury's Organization and Methods Division. Originally a unit to promote the introduction of modern office machines in the administrative departments, the O and M Division has developed into an important staff agency to study administrative problems and to recommend solutions. Its functions are in many ways similar to those performed by the Administrative Management Division of the Bureau of the Budget in Washington. The Treasury O and M Division works through departmental establishment and organization officers whose staffs are usually divided into branches dealing respectively with personnel management and organization and methods problems. Besides its work for the Government Organization Committee, the O and M Division endeavors to support and stimulate O and M activities throughout the whole governmental machine. Departmental O and M units are not only engaged in lending assistance to operating officials on their day-to-day problems but they undertake systematic reviews of the total structure, functions, and procedures of their ministries. The Treasury aids this work by supplying special staff, compiling and sharing administrative experience, and conducting research into matters of common concern. Altogether a good deal of activity along the lines of repairing and remodeling the administrative machine has been going on during the postwar years.

Other developments have proceeded which may have considerable significance for the departmental organization of British government. One is the practice introduced by Prime Minister Attlee of giving a few of his principal colleagues a co-ordinating responsibility over broad fields of public policy. Thus, the Labour Secretary of State for Foreign Affairs not only headed the Foreign Office but also supervised policy matters with respect to Commonwealth and imperial concerns. The Chancellor of the Exchequer came to have a similar responsibility for economic affairs, and Sir Stafford Cripps, when he held the office, was in journalistic language frequently referred to as Britain's 'economic czar.' The Lord President of the Council took general charge of domestic problems of a noneconomic nature. Each of these ministers performed a co-ordinating role with respect to the policies and programs of several departments.

Churchill continued the practice of designating co-ordinating ministers when he returned to office in 1951. He appointed a Secretary of State for Co-ordination of Transport, Fuel, and Power whose supervision included

---

[11] J. R. Simpson, 'Improving Public Management,' *Public Administration Review.* Spring 1949, p. 106.

the Ministry of Transport and Civil Aviation and the Ministry of Fuel and Power. The Lord President of the Council had a similar responsibility with respect to the Ministry of Agriculture and Fisheries, and the Ministry of Food. The Paymaster-General was given a supervisory role concerning scientific research, particularly atomic research.

Churchill's use of co-ordinating ministers, 'overlords' as the Opposition dubbed them, was challenged as impairing the responsibility of departmental ministers to Parliament. He denied any intention to weaken this 'fundamental principle in our system of Parliamentary democracy,' and said that his only innovation in the practice of designating co-ordinating ministers was to announce publicly 'the specific area of co-ordination assigned to each of them.' [12] Attlee and other critics stated that it was the public designation of the functions of these members of the Government that caused the difficulty of knowing where the responsibility of a co-ordinating minister ended and that of a departmental minister began. While the co-ordinating activities of senior ministers were 'kept within the Government's circle' and covered by the rules of Cabinet secrecy, neither Parliament nor the public was confused about who was responsible for the policy and administration of departments. There was one minister directly responsible and the whole Government was collectively responsible. However, a publicly appointed co-ordinating minister appeared to introduce a new element and to blur the areas of responsibility.

A second development which affects the departmental organization of the government is the establishment of a number of standing committees of the Cabinet to deal with policy matters in particular areas. The Prime Minister and his leading colleagues preside over most of these committees, which thus receive direction from the highest authority. It has been suggested that if the practice of dividing the Cabinet into several permanent committees is found successful there may be a case for increasing the number of departments rather than trying to amalgamate some of them. The Board of Trade, it has been said, would gain in efficiency if it were divided into departments dealing with foreign trade and with domestic industry. The Ministry of Health was in effect divided in 1951 when its principal responsibilities for housing and local government were transferred to the Ministry of Town and Country Planning, now the Ministry of Housing and Local Government. The desirability of subdividing some other departments may become more obvious as the nature of supervision over the nationalized industries becomes clearer.[13]

---

[12] *The Times*, 7 May 1952.

[13] The editors of *The Economist* regard the development of a system of Cabinet committees as sufficiently significant to say that the 'problem that was first authoritatively propounded by the famous Haldane Committee of 1917 appears to be on the way to solution. . . It [the solution] differs from the truer Haldane proposal in that there are no super-Departments; each Department remains equal in the eyes of Parliament. And it differs from the crypto-Haldane proposal in that no Minister is

It seems probable that for some time in the future a considerable amount of experimentation will proceed in Britain in the field of departmental organization. The interlocking character of so many of the government services and activities makes a continuance of separate departments, when co-ordinated only at the Cabinet level, unsatisfactory for efficient administration. At the same time, considerable hesitancy is shown for the establishment of a few super-departments which would be exceedingly difficult for a single minister to manage. It seems likely that the solution will be sought, in part, along the lines marked out by the postwar Labour Government. This would mean a continuance and a development of the Cabinet committee system and the designation of a few of the leading members of the Government as responsible for the co-ordination of policy within a number of broad fields.

In connection with departmental reorganization, it may be noted that the British Cabinet has considerable authority with respect to the management of the administrative machine, including the allocation and transfer of functions. By the Ministers of the Crown (Transfer of Functions) Act, 1946, it is empowered to shift important duties, and the staffs to perform them, from one department to another. The functions of the Ministry of Health concerning public housing and local government supervision were transferred by order-in-council, as previously mentioned, to the renamed Ministry of Local Government and Planning, now the Ministry of Housing and Local Government. Parliament is by no means uninterested in administrative organization and efficiency; the Committees on Estimates and Public Accounts of the House of Commons are constantly inquiring into and reporting on these matters. But by and large Parliament leaves the Government considerable latitude in the organization and management of the administrative establishment. Statutes establishing departments are brief and do not attempt to prescribe organizational forms and procedures. As an example, the Ministry of Defence Act, 1946, consists of six short sections occupying a couple of pages in the statute books. Administrative instruments of various kinds have created and determined the functioning of the internal machinery of the ministry. By contrast, the National Security Act, passed by the United States Congress in 1947 to accomplish much the same purpose, the unification of the military departments, covers 17 pages of text and is much more detailed with respect to powers, duties, and organization.

4. *Administrative Co-ordination*

The British government, like every other large governmental organization, is continuously faced with the problem of co-ordinating its administrative services. With a score or more of large departments, each administering

subordinate to any other (except to the Prime Minister); each remains fully responsible to Parliament for the conduct of his Department and equally entitled to a voice in reaching decisions that concern it.' *The Economist*, 2 October 1948, p. 527.

many programs established by national policy, the problem is huge in its dimensions, and it contains many sub-problems. These include the identification and elimination of competing and nonessential programs, the efficient allocation of manpower and materials, the sharing of facilities where feasible, and the avoidance of undue burdens on the public for information and for compliance with complex administrative procedures. For example, a public housing program, besides raising issues of major policy which will be determined by the Cabinet and Parliament, presents problems of administrative co-ordination. Competing with housing are other important programs, say military rearmament and industrial construction, requiring manpower, materials, and public services, and all could be crippled without careful allocations and priorities. Then there are several departments administering policies which impinge. The Ministry of Labour, for instance, will be interested in the effects of the housing program on the distribution of workers of various categories, the Ministry of Agriculture in the provision of cottages for agricultural workers, and the Board of Trade, the Ministry of Supply, and the Treasury in the purchase of timber and other materials in foreign markets. Since the war, the problems of co-ordination have been especially serious because resources have been so severely strained. It has been necessary to husband foreign exchange and to prevent the dissipation of the country's earnings on programs and activities of secondary importance. With few extra resources in the national cupboard, the dangers of miscalculation and loose control in withdrawing them have been great.

When we come to examine the machinery for the co-ordination of a complicated program we find that it operates at several levels of the administrative organization. Some co-ordination will take place at the ministerial level through the Cabinet, one of its standing committees, or an *ad hoc* committee. These ministerial groups will have the benefit of the advice and study of the Government's Chief Planning Officer and the Economic Section of the Cabinet Offices as well as departmental planning units. They will also be served by the Cabinet Secretariat whose officials know the departments to be consulted and those to be informed of decisions reached. Ministers will be called upon to determine major allocations of resources and to give directions which subordinate official levels can execute.

At the ministerial and lower official levels a principal agency of administrative co-ordination is the Treasury. Through its control over the estimates of expenditure of the various government departments, the Treasury is equipped with authority to eliminate duplication and overlapping of administrative services and to promote efficiency and economy. The annual submission of estimates gives the Treasury an opportunity to examine from a central position the work of all departments and to propose co-ordination where it is lacking. Its Organization and Methods Division can survey administrative trouble spots and suggest changes conducing to greater efficiency. Moreover, the Permanent Secretary of the Treasury as Head of the

Civil Service can obtain the co-operation of the other permanent heads of departments and through them influence all levels of officialdom.

A great many interdepartmental committees represent a further means of administrative co-ordination. They are composed of official members from interested government departments, who discuss administrative problems, propose remedies, and take decisions within their terms of reference. Departments such as the Treasury, the Ministry of Defence, and the Privy Council Office, which are not large operating departments themselves, are the centers of much interdepartmental committee work.

During the war much of the co-ordination of supplies of manpower and materials required by industry was performed by the Ministry of Production. The need during the postwar years for an agency to carry out a co-ordinating function similar to that performed by the Ministry of Production became apparent as shortages remained critical and breakdowns of production threatened. The answer was the appointment in 1947 of a Minister for Economic Affairs to whose office was attached the Chief Planning Officer and his staff. When a few months later the Minister for Economic Affairs, Sir Stafford Cripps, became Chancellor of the Exchequer, the Central Economic Planning Staff moved into the Treasury. 'The central staff,' it has been explained, 'is an addition to, rather than a replacement for, the series of standing ministerial and interdepartmental official committees that had become a standard pattern of war administration.' [14]

Many departments of the British government must carry their organization beyond the headquarters in Whitehall. They require regional, subregional, and, in some cases, local offices for the performance of their functions. Prior to World War II there was no uniform pattern of regional organization, each department creating whatever territorial units appeared best suited to its needs.[15]

In 1939 a civil defense organization was established on a regional basis. Each of the 12 regions into which Great Britain was divided—ten in England, one in Wales, and one in Scotland—had a headquarters which was almost a miniature Whitchall. Under a regional commissioner and his deputy, there were representatives of the principal national departments, and in an emergency cutting communication with London they were prepared to function independently. The commissioner, who reported to the Home Secretary as Minister of Home Security, had direct supervision over the civil defense services, and he acted in an advisory capacity with respect to the regional offices of such ministries as Supply, Food, and Transport. The lines of communication between the regions and London were never

[14] Martha M. Black, 'Aspects of National Economic Planning under the Labour Government,' *The Journal of Politics,* May 1950, pp. 269-70.

[15] For example, the Ministry of Health had 19 districts for the auditing of local government accounts, the Home Office 10 regions for factory inspection, the Ministry of Labour 12 regions, and the Ministry of Transport 6 divisional areas. John A. Fairlie, 'Administrative Regions in Great Britain,' *The American Political Science Review,* October 1937, pp. 938-41.

severed during the war, and no region was required to operate independently.

Although much of the wartime regional organization was dismantled, there has developed since 1945 a counterpart which undoubtedly will remain a permanent feature of the British administrative system. This plan was designed by an interdepartmental committee established by the Treasury in 1946, and it provides for 11 standard regions. Each ministry maintaining a regional organization is required to conform to the standard pattern unless it can demonstrate that its services would be better administered through an individual territorial arrangement. A large measure of conformity has been obtained, and the regional headquarters of almost all ministries are located in the same cities. The present regions have no official comparable to the wartime commissioner to co-ordinate their work. The representatives of the various ministries, however, are in close touch and work together on matters that require their joint action. Since they usually are at the assistant secretary grade of the departmental hierarchy, they have a good deal of responsibility devolved upon them. Disagreements among them have to be referred to London for decision. It appears that much of the interdepartmental co-ordinating machinery of Whitehall is being reproduced in the provinces, although the experimental period is by no means finished.[16]

The British government is by no means a perfectly attuned administrative mechanism. It suffers, as do all large-scale organizations, from failures of co-ordination. It possesses, however, in the Cabinet structure and in the interdepartmental committees on lower official levels satisfactory machinery for achieving co-ordination. When failures occur they are more attributable to conflicts of Governmental policy, sometimes not immediately soluble because of the political interests involved, and to human incapacities than to a lack of co-ordinating machinery.

5. Some Characteristics of British Public Administration

Large-scale public administration in advanced societies exhibits more similarities than differences, and the 'shop talk' of important executive officials from Washington, London, Paris, and probably even Moscow, should they get together, would be about many of the same problems—departmental organization, recruitment and management of personnel, financial controls, and interdepartmental co-ordination. In all likelihood they would discover, after they got each other's terminology straightened out, that their solutions to these problems had a good deal in common. Nevertheless, the administrative services of different countries have national features formed by their historical background and by the political and social environment in

---

[16] Concerning the co-ordinating machinery at the regional level, S. E. Finer has written: 'The arrangements are in fact masterpieces of improvisation. They show what the Civil Service can do, unnoticed, if put to it.' *A Primer of Public Administration* (London, 1950), pp. 81-2.

which they operate. Let us consider several which seem to characterize British public administration.

Almost 50 years ago, A. Lawrence Lowell pointed out a characteristic of British administration, that, 'Of all the existing political traditions in England, the least known to the public, and yet one of those most deserving attention, is that which governs the relation between the expert and the layman.' [17] The tradition is that political power and responsibility shall be vested in the nonexpert layman but that he shall be supported and guided by the expert. The principle of a team of this kind, 'the titular holders of a public post, enjoying the honours, and assuming the responsibility, of office, and a subordinate, who, without attracting attention, supplies the technical knowledge and largely directs the conduct of his chief, extends throughout the English government from the Treasury Bench to the borough council.' [18] The tradition is equally valid today. The ministerial head of a government department is seldom a specialist in the work of the department. Lawyers are appointed as Lord Chancellor and Attorney-General, but it is pure circumstance if the Chancellor of the Exchequer is a financier, the Minister of Health a doctor, or the Minister of Education a teacher. The minister has associated with him the specialists, the permanent secretary of the department, and the other chief permanent officials. Together they administer the department and its services. The combination of the layman and the expert is characteristic of public administration in many democratic states. Cabinet officers in the United States rarely lay claim to special competence in the substantive work of their departments, and they are supported by experts who supply relevant information and who recommend policy and action. Two things, however, are distinctive about British administration in this respect. One is the level to which the expert or specialist group rises. It fills all positions except the two or three ministerial posts in a department, and the minister has a closely organized hierarchy of permanent officials, culminating in the permanent secretary, through which he receives his information and advice. The other is the almost complete responsibility, publicly recognized and accepted, of the political head of a department for the policies and actions of his administrative subordinates. They cannot be questioned by Parliament or its committees about the views they hold or the advice they render to the minister.[19] If Parliament is dissatisfied with the administration of a department or objects to policies being pursued its remedy is to criticize the minister and to try to compel his resignation.

---

[17] *The Government of England,* rev. ed. (New York, 1914), vol. I, p. 173.

[18] Ibid. p. 176.

[19] The authority of the House of Commons Select Committee on Statutory Instruments to require departments to submit memoranda or send officials to explain rules or orders being considered is exceptional. The committee's power of inquiry, however, does not 'include access to the official files or disclosure of the advice given by civil servants to their political chief.' William A. Robson, 'Administrative Law in England, 1919-1948,' *British Government since* 1918 (London, 1950), p. 120.

Both the amateur and the expert elements are essential to successful public administration in a democratic society. The permanent civil servants in Great Britain could administer their departments without ministerial chiefs, and do it quite competently for a time, but before long they would miss the guidance of the politician sensitive to trends of public opinion as expressed in Parliament and the constituencies. Sir William Harcourt once said that a government of civil servants would be very able and efficient but that they would all be hanged from the lamp posts before the end of six months.

In connection with the professional staff in British public administration, there is a further characteristic to be noted. This is the important place which the administrative 'generalist' occupies. The chief permanent officials in a ministry are frequently no more expert in the department's substantive work than is the minister; their forte is general management. 'My own conception of the permanent head of a large Government department,' Sir Warren Fisher, a former Permanent Secretary of the Treasury, once explained, 'is that he is not (except by accident) a specialist in anything, but rather the general adviser of the Minister, the general manager and controller under the Minister, with ultimate responsibility to the Minister for all activities of the department.' [20] The training and experience of Administrative Class officers are designed to fit them for this role. Entering the Civil Service after the liberal education of the university, they are immediately associated with the top hierarchy of the Service, and they move about with considerable frequency from department to department. By the time an officer reaches the rank of permanent secretary he has probably had experience in half a dozen departments, some as different in substantive functions as the War Office and the Board of Trade.[21] We have already mentioned the exception which some of the subject-matter specialists, particularly the scientists in the Civil Service, take to the preferred position that the 'generalist' administrator occupies in the departmental organization. The present tradition, however, is strongly established.

Another characteristic of British administration is the extensive use of committees to direct and co-ordinate administrative activities. At the top of the administrative hierarchy is the Cabinet, a committee of the chief ministers. While it is principally a policy body, the Cabinet is also concerned with administrative matters, directing the execution of programs, allocating responsibilities, and reviewing performance. Some of its committees are likewise charged with not only the co-ordination of policy but also the general oversight of its administration. Below the Cabinet level, the committee method is extensively practiced. It has been mentioned that

---

[20] *Royal Commission on the Civil Service*, 1929-1931, *Minutes of Evidence*, Q. 18960.

[21] This sort of universal competence is exemplified in the career of a prominent civil servant like Sir Arthur Street, who died in 1951. He served in turn as Permanent Secretary of the Ministry of Agriculture, the Air Ministry, and the British Control Commission in Germany, and as Deputy Chairman of the National Coal Board.

some departments, for example the Lord President's Office and the Ministry of Defence, carry on a large share of their work through interdepartmental committees, which set policy within the limits of legislation and Cabinet decisions, allocate funds, and supervise the results achieved. While the committee method has its advantages in terms of the co-ordination of programs being carried on by several departments or agencies, the settlement of jurisdictional problems, and the pooling of administrative experience, it can be used to postpone action and to blur executive responsibility. Churchill complained of the 'boggling, hesitation, changes of policy, arguments between good and worthy people unending' that occurred in the Cabinet and the Military Co-ordination Committee during the winter of the 'phony war.' He declared that 'one could hardly find a more perfect example of the impotence and fatuity of waging war by committee or rather by groups of committees.' [22] Churchill also inveighed against the disposition of ministers and officials to create committees. In a memorandum to the Secretary of State for the Colonies he said on one occasion, 'I should deprecate setting up a special committee. We are overrun by them, like the Australians were by the rabbits.' [23] At another time he asked the head of the Cabinet Secretariat, Sir Edward Bridges, to give him a 'list of all committees of a Ministerial character forming part of the Central government, with any offshoots there may be.' Additionally, he wanted 'all the committees of a departmental nature,' and the information, Churchill said, 'is the prelude to a New Year's effort to cut down the number of such committees.' [24] He probably achieved some reduction, but he was opposing a strong tendency in British administrative practice. Like the old saying that when two or three Englishmen get together they form a club, it can be added that when two or three British officials meet they establish a committee.[25]

To conclude, the people of Britain are served, despite some shortcomings,

---

[22] *The Gathering Storm* (Boston, 1948), p. 580.

[23] *Their Finest Hour* (Boston, 1949), p. 682.

[24] *The Grand Alliance* (Boston, 1950), p. 721.

[25] Writing about the British defense organization, an American, Major General C. F. Robinson, commented on 'the wide use of the committee device in British governmental activities, including military,' and made the following observations:

'The division of activities between the various committees is often hazy, and undoubtedly there is considerable overlapping. The fact that there is no clear-cut hierarchy in their organization, with committees often reporting several ways, is also confusing.

'There can be no logical objection to the committee device, if it is necessary to secure information and advice in several independently organized fields of activity before a proper decision can be reached, provided that there is a chairman with power to make decisions and take action. There is little question that the British system of defense organization secures a higher degree of coordination than that developed in the United States system to date. On the other hand, there is a question whether better organization would not eliminate the necessity for so many committees in the British system and secure quicker and more positive results.' 'British Organization for Defense,' *Public Administration Review,* Summer 1948, pp. 183-4.

by one of the world's best administrative organizations. It is an effective mechanism for carrying out national policy. Lines of authority are generally clear and direct. The civil service is obedient, competent, and honest. Once policy is declared its implementation is rarely vitiated by administrative confusion or official sabotage. In peace and war, the national administration has demonstrated its ability to discharge heavy responsibilities and to maintain a high standard of efficiency.

XV

The Civil Service

Without any doubt much of the success of parliamentary democracy as practiced in Great Britain results from the efficient Civil Service which staffs the departments and ministries. Britain has developed a permanent Civil Service of great professional and technical competence while at the same time managing to avoid most of the evils frequently characteristic of a permanent bureaucracy. The British civil servant is an ordinary member of the community, respected for his position but not regarded with either awe or disdain.

1. *Historical Development*

This satisfactory state of affairs has not always existed in England. Until about a century ago, the patronage system flourished as luxuriously in Whitehall as it did in the Washington of 'King Andrew.' Official positions were filled through political and personal influence, and professional qualifications were often given little consideration. The leading political figures of the time did not hesitate to appoint to government offices their dependent relatives, personal friends, and partisan supporters. This practice was so common that the civil service of the eighteenth and early nineteenth centuries was once described as the outdoor relief system of the aristocracy.

While patronage was the rule in appointments, the corollary doctrine of rotation in office never prevailed. Once appointed, a clerk or an official was practically assured of a position until his death or until he chose to retire. This attitude toward public office stemmed in part from a general recognition of vested rights and also in part from the necessity of continuity in a political system which did not elect administrations at periodic times but was subject to occasional sudden changes of Ministry.

During the early years of the nineteenth century many sharp criticisms and satires were directed toward the evils of the patronage system. For example, several essays from the caustic pen of Thomas Carlyle were devoted to the subject. The first step in reform, however, did not begin with the Home Civil Service but with the appointment of officials to be sent as administrators to India. Parliament required the East India Company to introduce a limited form of open competition in choosing candidates for Haileybury, the training school for officers in the Company's service. This

−257

reform did not last long, but in 1853, when the Company's charter was again before Parliament for renewal, a thorough-going system of competitive selection was provided for the Indian service. Lord Macaulay was the principal sponsor of this change and the architect of the plan of open competition. Meanwhile, a movement to make some changes in the Home Civil Service gathered sufficient strength to cause the Government of the day to institute an inquiry into the methods of appointment. The resulting Trevelyan-Northcote Report, issued in 1853 and submitted to Parliament the next year, recommended the introduction of open competition among recruits for administrative and clerical positions. This proposal was strongly attacked, some critics saying that the principle of open competition and examinations was utopian or that it would fasten a Chinese practice on the British government. Others simply feared the effects of the loss of patronage on their political fortunes. Queen Victoria had misgivings and insisted that care must be taken to prevent open competition from permitting the appointment of socially unsuitable persons in the public service.

Gladstone, who had sponsored the Trevelyan-Northcote inquiry, strongly favored the reform, and there was sufficient support for a change to lead the Government in 1855 to establish a Civil Service Commission of three members. The function of the Commissioners was to examine for junior positions such candidates as the departments might care to nominate and to issue certificates to those deemed qualified. A further step of importance was taken in 1859 when Parliament limited the benefits of a retirement act to officials and clerks appointed after certification by the Civil Service Commissioners. Criticism continued but the reform had been well enough received so that in 1870 the Government could issue an order-in-council making open competition the method of recruitment to virtually all administrative and clerical positions in the Civil Service. From that date there has been no deviation from the general principle that government offices and departments should be staffed by permanent civil servants selected in open competitive examinations.

The development of the Civil Service since 1870 has been largely guided by the recommendations of a number of Royal Commissions which have inquired into the problems of the Service and proposed remedial action. The most recent of these Royal Commissions, under the chairmanship of Lord Tomlin, was appointed in 1929 and issued its report in 1931.[1] It took account of the conditions affecting the Civil Service during World War I and the postwar period. On the whole, it found that the Service was developing along the proper lines. The Commission approved of the reorganization, introduced in 1920, which had substituted a number of all-service—'Treasury'—classes for the former First Division and Second Division clerks and the numerous special classes which had been created in

---

[1] Cmd. 3909 (1931), *Report of the Royal Commission on the Civil Service, 1929-31.*

previous decades. It made recommendations of a minor character on recruitment, remuneration, promotion, retirement, and other Service problems, but no sweeping changes were proposed. The Civil Service at the beginning of World War II was, therefore, essentially the administrative organization developed in the latter half of the nineteenth century and modified slightly at the end of the previous war.

While the Civil Service itself was little changed, the political and social environment in which it operated had changed a great deal. The state was assuming new functions, particularly in the economic and social welfare fields, so that in the decade before 1939 the nonindustrial employees rose 111,000 to a total force of 422,000.[2] The expanded educational opportunities of the previous few decades were opening the upper ranks of the Civil Service to social classes that had not been able to qualify before. The majority of competitors for the highest classes of the Service still came from Oxford and Cambridge, but many of the graduates of these universities who sought entrance to the Civil Service were scholarship students from the less noted secondary schools. Finally, on two occasions between the wars the upper ranks of the Civil Service had been called upon to work under Labour ministries composed of a good many people of social backgrounds that differed from that of the traditional Administrative Class officer. No serious problems resulted, despite the forebodings of some ardent Labourites and ultra-conservatives. A change had occurred, however, for no longer were both ministers and the chief civil servants commonly members of the same social stratum, meeting at school reunions and in Pall Mall clubs.

World War II naturally produced a considerable expansion in the administrative services of the British government. Old departments expanded and several new ministries were established—Food, Supply, Aircraft Production, Home Security, Economic Warfare, and Information—and the number of nonindustrial civil servants rose to more than 700,000. The permanent civil servants were subject, like all other inhabitants of the United Kingdom, to the manpower controls of the Ministry of Labour and National Service, and many who desired to join the military forces were required to remain as civilian administrators. To replace those who were released and to supply thousands of new positions, the departments recruited widely from the business world, the professions and the universities. Most of these wartime civil servants left after the close of hostilities, although to prevent a sudden depletion of administrative staffs the Government required, until 1947, the written approval of a department for any high-ranking official's resignation.

While the conflict was in progress attention was given to the measures which would be required, when victory should be won, to place the Civil Service on a peacetime footing. A number of committees studied various

---

[2] E. N. Gladden, 'The British Civil Service in Transition,' *The American Political Science Review,* April 1949, pp. 335-6.

features of the Civil Service, and their reports began to appear as early as 1943. Many of these proposals have affected the organization and character of the postwar Civil Service.

2. *The Present-Day Civil Service*

The British Civil Service today numbers approximately 700,000.[3] This is an increase of about 250,000 over the Service in 1939. Some 250,000 of these public employees work for the Post Office, which operates the telephone and telegraph services in the United Kingdom as well as the postal service. The balance is distributed among more than 50 departments, offices and ministries which vary in size from the 53,000 employed by the Board of Inland Revenue to the few score who staff the Cabinet Secretariat. By another classification, about 40 per cent are stationed in London and the remainder scattered throughout the country. A plan is in process for moving approximately 50,000 civil servants away from London to the provinces.[4]

Wherever employed, these civil servants belong in general to one of a series of classes arranged hierarchically according to the responsibility of the work performed. There are at present five general or Treasury classes into which the Civil Service is divided. These represent a refinement, introduced in 1920, of a division which had existed since 1870 between administrative officials performing the more responsible kinds of work and clerks carrying out routine duties.

The highest class of the Service, the Administrative Class, is a relatively small group of about 4000 officials who occupy the most important positions in the various government departments. The duties of this class 'are those concerned with the formation of policy, with the co-ordination and improvement of government machinery, and with the general administration and control of the Departments of the Public Service.' [5] The members of the Administrative Class are recruited between the ages of 20½ and 24 by a severe competitive examination, and normally about 100 are appointed to the Service each year. New recruits serve a two-year probationary period and then, if considered satisfactory, advance as rapidly as their industry and talents justify. The Administrative Class is subdivided into the grades of assistant principal, principal, assistant secretary, under secretary, deputy secretary, and permanent secretary. The permanent secretary grade is the highest open to a civil servant, and the holders of these appointments are the general managers of the government departments. Each is responsible to his political chief, a minister, for the efficient operation of the administrative staff on all levels below.

---

[3] On 1 January 1950 the total number of civil servants was 687,350. Cmd. 7887 (1950).

[4] *The Economist,* 26 October 1948, p. 621.

[5] *Report of the Joint Committee on the Organization, etc., of the Civil Service* (1920).

The Executive Class is the next below the peak of the administrative pyramid, and it consists of about 60,000 officials. Executive Class officers occupy positions of considerable responsibility, principally in departments conducting large-scale administrative services for which policy is well established; e.g. departments dealing with the collection, disbursement, and accounting of government funds. The members of the Class were formerly recruited by an open competitive examination given for candidates completing their secondary education. The age limits were 18 to 19. Since the war, military conscription and the larger number of secondary school graduates proceeding to university study have caused the Civil Service Commission to widen the area of recruitment. Competitions are now held for young persons between 17½ and 18½, for those completing their two years of military service, for university graduates, and for former regular service men and women below the age of 45.

Below the Executive Class is the large and important Clerical Class, divided into two principal grades which are designated clerical officer and higher clerical officer. Civil servants of this class perform the great volume of government work involved in receiving and answering correspondence, reviewing and checking forms, maintaining departmental records, and the numerous other types of clerical duties common to public offices. The Clerical Class is recruited from candidates taking an open competitive examination given annually in about 65 centers throughout the United Kingdom, and the age limits are 16½ to 17½. It is thus designed to appeal to boys and girls who have had at least four years of secondary education. There is also a competition for ex-service personnel below the age of 50.

The more routine office work is performed by a class reserved to women and known as Clerical Assistants. They are recruited between the ages of 15 and 16, and candidates must have completed their elementary education. Actually many have gone beyond this educational level.

The fifth class is called the Typist Class. It also is reserved to women, and the entrance ages are from 18 to 33. Proficiency in various stenographic skills is a requisite for this class. It has some seven grades ranging from typist to controller.

The five Treasury classes of the Civil Service perform the administrative and clerical work characteristic of most government offices. In addition, there are a number of departmental and professional classes which are peculiar to one department or to a distinct type of work. Departmental classes exist for the special mechanical and manipulative skills necessary in the Post Office, for much of the work of the Ministry of Labour, and for inspectorships of various kinds. These civil servants are recruited by open competition. The professional classes include officials belonging to a recognized profession, e.g. doctors, lawyers, and engineers, and they are usually selected through competitive interviews. Before the last war the professional and technical staffs were organized on a departmental basis, and they felt that, in comparison with the administrative and clerical classes, they did not receive their just deserts in terms of pay and promotional opportunities. Their complaints were largely met in 1945 by the introduction of all-Service classes for scientists, statisticians, actuaries, accountants, architects, engineers, lawyers, medical officers, and similar professional groups.[6]

Until fairly recent times the British Civil Service had relatively little government-wide integration. Recruitment was administered centrally by the Civil Service Commissioners but all subsequent aspects of personnel administration were handled departmentally. Since about the time of World War I, however, there has been a gradual integration of the entire Service with a vesting of increasing control in the Treasury. The Treasury has obtained this primacy in personnel matters because of its financial responsibility and the direct bearing of size of staff, salaries and wages, pensions, and other aspects of personnel administration upon governmental economy. The reality of Treasury control over the Civil Service was recognized in 1920 when the Permanent Secretary of the Treasury had the additional title 'Head of the Civil Service' conferred upon him. The Permanent Secretary at the time and until 1939, Sir Warren Fisher, was extremely interested in furthering the concept of a government service as opposed to a collection of departmental services united only through centrally controlled recruiting practices and a few common principles. Fisher during his some 20 years in the Treasury broke down many departmental barriers and infused a generation of civil servants with a loyalty to the Service as a whole and only secondarily to their department or ministry. He believed in the fairly frequent transfer of the higher ranking civil servants from one department to another, and in this way he not only combatted departmental autonomy but he opened up broader career opportunities in the Administrative Class of the Service. Fisher was assisted by a provision of an order-in-council of 1920 which made the Permanent Secretary of the Treasury the official to advise the Prime Minister on the appointment of the permanent secretaries of other departments. He was thus in a strategic position to promote an increasing amount of service integration.

The Treasury contains an Establishments Department which is concerned with the management of the Civil Service. This Treasury unit deals with an establishment and organization officer in each government department. He occupies a high place in the official hierarchy of a department, being one of the four civil servants in each administrative agency whose appointment must be approved by the Prime Minister. The functions of his office relate to the placement of new recruits, training, promotion, the recruitment of temporary employees, welfare services, administrative organization and methods, and office accommodation and equipment. It will be noted that both personnel administration and administra-

---

[6] Cmd. 6679 (1945), *The Scientific Civil Service*. The scientific service is divided into three classes: Scientific Officer, Experimental Officer, and Assistant (Scientific). The method of recruitment for the upper grades is normally by a review of candidates' records and interviews.

tive management are the responsibility of one officer. As explained by a Director of the Treasury's Organization and Methods Division, 'Organization and methods and personnel cannot be treated as separate independent elements in management; good personnel management and sound organization and methods must develop side by side.' [7]

The Treasury exercises its control through a review of budget estimates; through Treasury orders, minutes, and circulars dealing with personnel matters; through its supervision of the work of the Civil Service Commissioners; and through the day-to-day advice it gives to departmental establishment officers on cases and problems before them. It also provides the official representation on the National Whitley Council, a body which considers personnel problems affecting the employees of more than one department, and it presents the governmental case on wage and salary claims before the Arbitration Tribunal. A serious difference between a department and the Treasury on a personnel issue can be carried to the ministerial level, but it is the Treasury's point of view, by and large, that is controlling in the management of the Civil Service.

The development of Treasury control over the Civil Service as a whole has not been accepted without challenge. Students of public administration have questioned the advisability of vesting such authority in a department whose primary concern is financial policy and governmental economy. Some of them argue that personnel questions should be considered from a broader point of view and that too often any change or innovation is studied by the Treasury primarily in the light of its cost. Some of the associations of civil servants have been particularly critical of Treasury control. They would prefer to see a more autonomous Civil Service Commission created, with functions embracing the entire field of personnel administration. The suggestion has been made, too, that 'a more logical and possibly less objectionable arrangement might be for the Headship of the Civil Service to be centered on the Secretary to the Cabinet, and primacy to be focused upon the Cabinet Office' since it is 'perhaps more appropriate that the Civil Service should be centered on the office closest to the Prime Minister rather than on that of the Chancellor of the Exchequer.' [8]

It appears doubtful, however, that the position the Treasury has attained concerning the Civil Service will be much altered. The authority of the Chancellor of the Exchequer over the proposed expenditures of government departments is a solidly based fact of the British political system, and the salaries and wages of the hundreds of thousands of government employees are so significant in the computation of public finances that it is difficult to expect controlling authority to be lodged elsewhere. While there is some justification, no doubt, for the criticism that the Treasury gives undue weight to financial considerations in considering personnel matters,

---

[7] J. R. Simpson, 'Improving Public Management,' *Public Administration Review,* Spring 1949, p. 100.

[8] S. B. Chrimes, *English Constitutional History* (London, 1947), pp. 40-41.

it bears at present an onus that would fall, in all likelihood, upon any other office or department having such responsibility. In the course of time a reconstituted Civil Service Commission would probably be regarded as obstructionist by individuals and groups who were unable to convince it of the justice or the practicality of their claims.

3. *Recruitment in the Civil Service*

It will be well to follow this general description of the British Civil Service with an examination of some of its characteristic features. As has been mentioned, recruitment is the responsibility of the Civil Service Commissioners, although they are subject to the general supervision of the Treasury. They announce the examinations, administer them, grade the results, and establish lists from which departments and offices make appointments to vacancies. In the past few years the Commission has been strengthened by the appointment of three additional commissioners. The commissioners, it may be mentioned, are senior civil servants and are not political appointees. The Commission has a staff of about 750.

Two or three general features of the recruiting system are worth noting. In the first place, it is closely integrated with the educational system of the country. Examinations are timed and the age limits for candidates are fixed so graduates of various stages in the educational system are naturally attracted to, and prepared for, Civil Service employment. Thus, recruitment for the Administrative Class is designed to secure graduates of the universities, the Executive Class attracts young men and women who have completed their secondary education, and the Clerical Class is open to those who have finished four years of secondary education. Restrictive age limits mean that young persons considering a Civil Service career have ordinarily about two or three opportunities, at annual intervals, to decide to compete in an examination and seek appointment. The recruitment system therefore tends to make government service an attractive occupational field to young men and women leaving schools and universities.

A second feature of the recruiting system is the reliance on academic types of examinations. Except for certain specialized classes for which particular qualifications are required, the Civil Service tests its applicants by examinations of the kind they have been accustomed to in schools and universities. No special effort is made to relate the examinations to the work of government departments or to particular types of jobs. The examinations are designed to test the knowledge, the mental capacity, the reasoning power, the alertness, and the personal qualities of the candidates. It is believed that this can best be done by examinations covering subject matter with which they are acquainted and in the form which is familiar to them. Another feature of the recruiting system is the considerable use which is made of outside examiners. The Civil Service Commissioners invite established members of the academic profession to assist in the preparation of examinations and in their grading. They also bring in

264–

private citizens to sit on boards giving oral tests or interviewing candidates when a written examination is not considered suitable. The use of members of the academic profession in preparing and grading examinations is another means whereby the Civil Service system is kept closely associated with the educational institutions of the country.

A description of the recruiting process for members of the Administrative Class will illustrate the principles of recruitment in the British system and also show the selection methods for this important group of public officials. The Civil Service Commissioners hold examinations for this Class in the summer of each year. They are open to men and women between the ages of 20½ and 24 who are British subjects.[9]

The Administrative Class examination is given in two ways. By Method I any man or woman who meets the age and citizenship requirements may compete. The examination consists of three principal parts. The first is a written test covering subjects of which any intelligent young man or woman is supposed to have some knowledge. It consists of writing an essay on one of a number of suggested subjects; a language section 'to test the understanding and use of English'; and a Present Day section which includes questions 'on matters of general interest and importance at the present day, cultural, social, economic, political, and scientific.' The purpose of this part is to weed out candidates who are so highly specialized or so indifferent to the world in which they live that they lack means of self-expression or know little of current affairs.

The second part of the examination offers a broad range of academic subjects—77—from which the candidates may choose to answer questions in two or three fields in which they consider themselves to be most competent. The subjects range all the way from Arabic to zoölogy. This part of the examination is designed to test a person's knowledge, comprehension, and reasoning power within fields which he regards as his own specialty. The questions are usually of the essay type and thus, in addition, test a candidate's ability to organize his knowledge, write cogently and persuasively, and show his sense of proportion in dealing with a large subject. This second part of the examination carries the most weight.

The third part consists of two interviews, the first being one in which the candidate appears before a single interviewer for the purpose of eliciting information useful in the second, which is a 45- to 60-minute appearance before a board selected by the Civil Service Commissioners. A final selection board is composed as follows:

It is a large Board, consisting usually of eight or nine members under the chairmanship of the First Commissioner. Three or four retired senior civil servants and one woman member sit regularly, so

---

[9] In addition to the Administrative Class of the Home Civil Service, the Civil Service Commission recruits by the same examination for Branch A of the Foreign Service, Clerkships in the House of Commons, the Statistician Class, and Cadetships in the Government Communications Headquarters.

as to provide continuity as well as experience of the needs of the Service; the current user interest is represented also by the presence of one or other of the serving Establishment Officers, who take it in turn to sit on the Board at our invitation. When candidates for the Foreign Service are being interviewed, the current user interest is represented by one or more serving officers from the Personnel Department of the Foreign Service; and the retired senior officials are ex-Foreign Servants.

The remaining members are chosen so as to represent the interest which the Universities and the general public have in these appointments. There are three panels consisting respectively of University representatives, representatives of business and industry, and representatives of Trades Unions; and the Commissioners try to arrange that one representative of each panel shall always be present, on a rota system. Every Vice-Chancellor and every Head of a College is invited to nominate a representative to sit on the University panel, so that over a series of competitions every University and every College can acquire direct experience of the way in which the Final Selection Board is conducted and the type of candidate for which the Services are looking.[10]

The interview part of the examination is designed to bring out the interests, tastes, and poise of the candidates, and to test 'the candidate's fitness for appointment, as he reveals himself from the standpoint of experienced members of the Service and representatives of the general public, as well as that of critical University tutors.' [11] It is considered to afford some insurance that candidates with high mental capacities but poor personalities will not find their way into the Service. Such an examination is open, of course, to all the objections that are made about interviews and oral tests. In prewar England there was some feeling that this part of the examination gave an undue advantage to candidates who had had greater social privileges than others, and that the examining boards were too much impressed by nice manners. The Civil Service Commissioners have met these criticisms in large part by improving the administration of oral interviews and by broadening the representation on selection boards.

The standing of candidates depends upon the sum of the marks they receive on the three parts of the examination. There is no definite passing grade, and the competitors are allotted to the available vacancies in the order of their examination marks.

Method II of the Administrative Class competition represents an innovation in British Civil Service examinations. It is an adaptation to civilian recruitment of a procedure developed by the War Office for the selection

---

[10] *Report of His Majesty's Civil Service Commissioners for the Period 1st January, 1941 to 31st March, 1949*, p. 33.

[11] Ibid. p. 34.

of army officers. During World War II the War Office put its officer candidates through a series of tests, under the direction of psychological specialists, which were designed to bring out personality traits not adequately revealed in paper examinations or brief interviews. The War Office Selection Board subjected candidates, identified to the examiners only by numbers, to carefully planned situations which were supposed to disclose qualities of leadership, ingenuity, resolution, and emotional stability. On the recommendation of the National Whitley Council's Committee on Post-War Recruitment, the Civil Service is offering Method II as an alternative entry to the Administrative Class for an experimental period of ten years.

Method II requires as a prerequisite 'a full course of study for an honors degree at a recognized University,' and the candidate must have obtained at least second-class honors. So qualified, he is given a written examination embracing a paper on English; General Paper 1, on 'matters of general interest and importance at the present day'; General Paper 2, consisting 'of questions devised to test reasoning power, capacity to perceive implications, and ability to distinguish between the important and the less important'; and a general intelligence test. Candidates qualifying on the written examination proceed to the Civil Service Selection Board for a testing of their personal qualities. For a few years the Civil Service Selection Board assembled the candidates at a country estate, Stoke-d'Abernon, for a two- or three-day period of testing; it now administers its tests in London. The last step in Method II is the appearance of a candidate before the Final Selection Board. The Selection Board, aided by reports on the candidate's success in the two previous steps of the examination, conducts interviews similar to those given in the final stage of Method I, and determines the ranking of the competitors.

Seventy-five per cent of the Administrative Class vacancies to be filled by open competition are allotted to the candidates examined by Method I, and 25 per cent to those examined by Method II. The Civil Service Commissioners hope, 'by the use of a carefully designed system of follow-up reports on the performance in the Service of the successful candidates,' to obtain during the ten-year experimental period enough data 'to compare the selective value of the two methods and to conclude which yields the better results.' Presently they report, 'It is too early yet for us to hazard a guess in which direction the evidence points.' [12]

Candidates selected by each method are listed in the order of their scores and are available for appointment from the top of the list. With the passing of the abnormal period of the postwar years, it is expected that the Administrative Class will have an average of about 100 vacancies annually, so the number who can expect appointment will not be large. The dozen or so candidates at the top of the list can ordinarily select the de-

---

[12] *Report of His Majesty's Civil Service Commissioners for the Period 1st January, 1941 to 31st March, 1949*, p. 12.

partments they would like to enter, but the persons farther down must take such vacancies as are open.

The examination procedure for other classes of the Service is similar to that described above, although it is not so comprehensive and usually omits the oral interview except in the case of specialized kinds of work. The Clerical Class examination, for example, is a written test covering subjects that boys and girls have studied in elementary and secondary schools. It is designed to test their knowledge of English, arithmetic, history, everyday science, and other general subjects. It is sufficiently difficult so that only good students have much chance of making a grade high enough to assure appointment. For some scientific and technical positions, the procedure of the 'unassembled' examination is used, i.e. candidates submit statements of their qualifications which are then examined and rated by the Civil Service Commissioners. Departments are authorized to appoint locally a number of classes of industrial employees. There are regulations by which such employees can be nominated by their departments for establishment, i.e. permanent tenure and pensions. The Civil Service Commission must be satisfied in regard to the employees' ability for the work, nationality, character, and health.

4. *Compensation and Other Personnel Policies and Practices*

After appointment civil servants are compensated according to scales of pay established by the Treasury. Unlike the practice in the United States where the Congress determines civil service pay rates by law, the British Parliament leaves the establishment of the scales of remuneration to executive action. It is customary for each class of the Service to have a broad range of salaries which is broken down into scales for each grade of the class. Thus, the lowest grade of the Administrative Class has a starting salary of £400 a year and rises to £750. The Assistant Secretary grade ranges from £1320 to £1700. Civil servants proceed up each grade scale by annual increments until they reach the top. Usually about midpoint on the scale there is a break known as the 'efficiency bar,' and only civil servants with the better performance ratings, as measured by service records, go beyond this point.

In setting Civil Service salaries and wages, the Treasury endeavors to pay what it considers are approximately the standards of private business. It undoubtedly takes into account some of the features of Civil Service employment which are not characteristic of private employment. Thus, the Treasury considers permanent tenure, reasonably generous provisions for leave, and noncontributory pensions as benefits which the civil servant has above most employees in private industry. In the higher ranks of the Service no effort is made to relate salaries to outside positions of comparable responsibility. The salaries paid to officials of the Administrative Class are fairly high in comparison with other classes of the Service, but they are considerably below what successful professional and business executives would receive.[13] In examining the compensation of civil servants the Royal Commission in 1931 stated that 'the present general standard of remuneration is reasonable in the light of the wage levels now prevailing.' With the rise in prices which occurred during and after the war, the Civil Service level of remuneration had to be raised. A similar situation occurred during World War I and it was met by giving civil servants a bonus determined by the cost-of-living index of the Ministry of Labour. This system of basic pay plus bonus was continued until 1934 when all salaries and wages were consolidated into single rates. During World War II a bonus plan was introduced, and in 1945 all civil servants paid less than £1500 annually were receiving £60 additional. At the beginning of 1952 a substantial increase to compensate for the rise in the cost of living was announced by the Treasury. All civil servants receiving less than £1500 a year benefited, being given a 10 per cent increase on the first £500 of salary, 5 per cent on the next £500, and 2½ per cent on any remuneration above £1000. The annual cost to the Exchequer was estimated at £30 million.

While the Treasury has the authority to fix Civil Service remuneration, differences arising between it and employee associations may be taken to the Arbitration Tribunal, an administrative body which hears and determines wage and salary claims. The case for an increase is presented by an employee association—individual claims are not considered—and the Treasury states the official position. The Government is committed to give effect to all awards made by the Tribunal. As the result of the consideration of many claims, the Tribunal has established several principles governing its awards; for example, a pay increase given one grade usually entitles the supervisory grade above to an increase in order to maintain the pay differential. Although the Tribunal is not required to follow Government policy in making its awards, it is disposed to do so in practice. For example, after the Chancellor of the Exchequer called for restraint in raising personal incomes following the devaluation of the pound sterling in 1949, the Arbitration Tribunal found an excuse to postpone a decision on the claim of the Administrative Class principals and assistant principals to higher salaries.[14]

In 1952 when the Treasury announced a general pay increase for the Civil Service, the official side of the National Whitley Council agreed to a staff side proposal that future claims based on general economic conditions should be negotiated centrally and not with individual unions. It rejected, however, a proposal that pay increases should be granted automatically whenever an index of wage rates rises a certain number of points. The

---

[13] The Government announced in 1949 its intention to raise the salary of the Permanent Secretary of the Treasury to £5000 a year and the salaries of other permanent secretaries from £3500 to £4500. Before the new compensation became effective, however, an anti-inflation policy of holding all salaries and wages to pre-devaluation levels was urged by the Government, and the Civil Service was forced to become a national example.

[14] *The Economist,* 18 March 1950, p. 582.

agreement on central negotiations should reduce the number of claims by employee unions and associations coming before the Arbitration Tribunal.

The advancement of civil servants to higher ranking positions in the Service has always been possible, but until recent years few promotions were made beyond the class to which an official was appointed. While a Clerical Class officer could look forward to reaching the higher grades of his class, his prospects of promotion to the Executive Class were slight. Similarly, an Executive Class officer rarely received promotion to the Administrative Class. Officers in the service could attempt the open competition for the next higher class, but, as the Civil Service Commission has said, the examinations were 'academically exacting, and the candidate entering from the Service was handicapped by lack of time for preparation.' [15] In brief, the barriers between the classes were high and seldom surmounted. Today, because of changes in personnel policy since World War II, the promotional prospects of civil servants are considerably enhanced. The Civil Service Commission regularly holds competitions limited to persons in the service for advancement to the next higher class and a proportion of vacancies in each class is reserved for the successful candidates. For example, Executive Class officers between the ages of 21 and 30 may enter a limited competition for promotion to the Administrative Class, and 20 per cent of the vacancies in the latter class are reserved for the successful competitors. The examination is similar to Method II of the normal open competition for the Administrative Class.

Following his original appointment or promotion to a higher class a civil servant enters upon a two-year probationary period. Treasury regulations provide that no appointment is final until the head of a department is satisfied that an employee has demonstrated his fitness while on probation. For entrants to the Administrative Class there is a further stipulation that the Civil Service Commissioners must have approved final appointment. In exercising their duty in this respect, the Commissioners are guided by the Central Probation Board, which was established in 1946. The Board consists of the First Civil Service Commissioner and three heads of departments. It is empowered to confirm an appointment, recommend a longer trial period in the same or another department, or recommend dismissal.

While the probationary period has always been regarded as a time for the instruction of new employees, a great deal more attention has been paid in recent years to the post-entry training of civil servants. During the war the Select Committee on National Expenditure of the House of Commons called attention to what it regarded as the neglect of this aspect of personnel administration.[16] In 1944 an official report on training made

[15] *Report of His Majesty's Civil Service Commissioners for the Period 1st January, 1941 to 31st March, 1949*, p. 30.

[16] *Organization and Control of the Civil Service*, 16th report, Select Committee on National Expenditure, Session 1941-2.

270–

recommendations which added a further stimulus.[17] As a result, training programs for all classes of employees have been introduced or expanded. They are conducted in the various departments and centrally by the Treasury, depending upon the types of civil servants to be trained and the nature of the courses. A few civil servants are sent to the Administrative Staff College, a private institution established in 1946 for the advanced training of promising young officers from government, business, and the trade unions. Others receive sabbatical leaves for study and observation in industrial establishments or in foreign countries. The Treasury's Director of Training and Education is in charge of overall Civil Service training, and in each department there is a training officer who organizes and supervises particular departmental programs.

Wars create serious problems for governmental services. They disrupt normal recruitment, they introduce many temporary employees to staff expanding offices, and they create large numbers of military veterans with claims for consideration in future employment policies. After World War I the British Civil Service absorbed a great many ex-service men. Some of them satisfied the standards for permanent civil servants, but thousands of others could not qualify and were employed for years on a temporary basis. Principally because of efforts to give employment to as many veterans as possible, the resumption of normal recruitment was postponed for most classes until late in the 1920's. The Government in power during World War II hoped to avoid a similar long period of unsettlement after the close of hostilities and still do justice to the young men and women whose careers had been interrupted by the conflict. Accordingly, the Chancellor of the Exchequer announced early in 1944 that the problems connected with postwar recruitment had been referred to the National Whitley Council for study and recommendation. The report of the Council formed the basis of policy for special recruitment and the treatment of ex-service men and women in the years immediately after the close of hostilities.[18] Instead of giving persons who had served in the military forces a preference in the normal Civil Service competitions, the Civil Service Commission conducted a series of reconstruction examinations. For these the normal age limits were extended to allow for war service, and the Commission devised tests of a less academic character than the usual kind. Moreover, three-fourths of the vacancies in the Administrative Class, two-thirds of those in the Executive Class, and a half of those in the Clerical Class were reserved for the successful competitors in the reconstruction competitions. In the fiscal year 1945-6, 958 persons were recruited through these competitions; in 1946-7, 9760; in 1947-8, 22,276, and in 1948-9, 9278.[19] Meanwhile, recruitment by the normal procedures was resumed, and ex-service men and women were eligible to compete in these competi-

---

[17] Cmd. 6525 (1944).

[18] Cmd. 6567 (1944).

[19] *Report of His Majesty's Civil Service Commissioners for the Period 1st January, 1941 to 31st March, 1949,* pp. 56-7.

tions provided they could meet the age and educational requirements. The British Civil Service, it appears, has dealt justly with the men and women entitled to special consideration because of their war service without appreciably lowering its standards, blocking the recruitment of young people completing their education, or creating a continuing problem of 'temporary' employees.

As previously indicated, the British civil servant has certain prerogatives and privileges which add to the attractiveness of his employment. Once appointed, he is secure in his position unless he proves to be exceptionally inefficient or commits some serious misdemeanor. This security of tenure has no statutory basis and legally the situation remains that all civil servants are employed at the pleasure of the Crown. The principle of security of tenure is firmly established, however, and removals never occur for political or personal reasons. A civil servant can look forward to retiring on a pension which is granted by the Crown.[20] As in the case of tenure, the civil servant has no legal right to a pension, but the assurance of payment is established beyond challenge. Some Civil Service organizations would prefer a pension system to which employees make contributions, since they believe that the present plan really forces them to contribute through lower scales of salaries and wages.

Along with certain privileges, civil servants also have obligations which they must observe. One of the most important concerns political activity. Until recently it has been the rule that all civil servants, except industrial workers in such establishments as the royal arsenals, could vote but could not participate actively in politics. It was not permissible to run for office, speak in behalf of candidates, canvass for votes, contribute to campaign funds, or in other ways engage in partisan political affairs. Many civil servants, particularly those in positions far removed from policy-making, considered these restrictions too severe. In 1949 a committee, appointed by the Government and headed by Sir C. H. Masterman to inquire into this matter, recommended that all the industrial and nonclerical employees of the state be permitted almost complete freedom with respect to political activity, provided it did not interfere with their duties, but that the policy-making, professional, and clerical classes of the Civil Service be limited as in the past.[21] The Government's announcement that it accepted the report as a reasonable guide brought protests from some civil servants' associations whose members were left under the ban. The Government postponed a final decision on the report by stating that the matter was before the National Whitley Council. Later it announced that the restrictions upon political activity would be lifted immediately for the classes

---

[20] The normal retiring age for civil servants was 60 until 1951 when the Treasury proposed to the National Whitley Council that this age be treated as the minimum rather than the normal. This proposal was 'in execution of the Government policy, announced by the Chancellor of the Exchequer in his Budget speech, to encourage older workers to remain in employment.' *The Times,* 13 April 1951.

[21] Cmd. 7718 (1949).

272–

named to benefit in the Masterman Report but that they would remain in effect temporarily for all other civil servants.[22] Participation by civil servants in local government affairs has always been countenanced, at least as long as it did not interfere with the officials' regular duties. For some time departments have been authorized to grant a maximum of 12 days' paid leave to employees desiring to engage in municipal political activity.

A civil servant is required to conduct himself in such a manner that he bring no reproach upon the Service. The use of his position or information gained through his work for personal profit would bring disciplinary action and, if the offense were serious enough, dismissal from the Service. These obligations are well understood by civil servants and there are extraordinarily few breaches committed. The Service is jealous of its reputation, and a civil servant offending the traditions of the Service would find little sympathy among his colleagues.

The British government has never been faced with widespread disaffection among its employees or troubled by many cases of disloyalty. Like all democratic governments following World War II, it has had to consider that the ideological struggle going on in the world might touch its administrative service and that the communist movement might find some recruits in government offices and departments. The revelations of the Royal Commission in Canada investigating subversive activity and the involvement of one British scientist in the Canadian case showed the insidious and dangerous nature of communist infiltration. Conscious of the problem, the Government in March 1948 began a quiet investigation of loyalty in the various ministries and departments and announced that civil servants regarded as untrustworthy would, if employed in positions with access to confidential information, be transferred to less sensitive posts and might be dismissed when reasonable grounds for believing them disloyal were found. Three advisers—two senior civil servants and a former Labour member of Parliament active in public employee affairs—were appointed to assist ministers in reaching decisions in loyalty cases. After the investigation had been under way for several months, the Government revealed that no civil servant had been dismissed on account of communist or fascist connections.[23] Later the Prime Minister stated that '50 persons have received notice that they are thought to come within the scope of the Government's policy in regard to the employment of Communists and Fascists in certain parts of the Civil Service. Of these none have been dismissed, three have resigned and ten have been transferred. Of the rest sixteen have been reinstated, twelve are awaiting transfer, while nine have not yet replied.' [24] In conducting its purge, the Government allowed a hearing to sus-

---

22 *The Times*, 2 November 1949.

23 *The Times*, 8 December 1948.

24 465 *H.C. Debates* 5s., col. 1259. As of 15 March 1950, 48 civil servants had been transferred to other employment, 47 because of membership in or association with the Communist Party and one because of membership in a fascist group. *The Times*, 15 March 1950.

pected officials, but it made no provision for appeal to the courts.[25]

Although women have been employed extensively in the Civil Service for 50 years or more, they have always suffered a certain amount of discrimination. Until fairly recent years there were important areas of the Civil Service which were not open to them. Some progress toward equal opportunity was made as a result of the Sex Disqualification (Removal) Act of 1919 and subsequent resolutions in the House of Commons. By 1940 women were eligible for all ordinary positions in the Service, although the Foreign Service still excluded them. This citadel of conservatism has since been reduced, and in the postwar examinations women have been competing with men. The postwar period has also seen the abolition of the marriage bar, a requirement that women employed in government service resign upon marriage.

Women civil servants continue to suffer discrimination with respect to their compensation since their salaries and wages are approximately 75 to 80 per cent of those paid male officers of the same grade and class. Considerable efforts have been made to achieve equal pay. Many representations on this point were made to the Tomlin Commission, but in reporting in 1931 it confessed, 'we are divided almost equally.' In 1936 the Labour opposition introduced in the House of Commons a motion in favor of equal pay which was only beaten by the Government, upon reconsideration, 149 to 134. The economic and social consequences of introducing equal pay in both the public service and private employment were studied by a royal commission appointed in 1944.[26]

Despite the strong efforts of women's groups and the sympathetic support they have received in Parliament, the Treasury has remained adamant. In view of the party's previous position on this issue, the postwar Labour Government might have been expected to grant equal pay, but it maintained the discrimination on the ground that inflationary measures must be avoided.[27] In 1951 the staff side of the National Whitley Council restated its demand for equal pay to the Conservative Government, proposing a gradual introduction of the change. The Chancellor of the Exchequer took the position that the 'whole question depended on how soon improvements could be achieved in the country's finances.' [28]

Approximately four-fifths of the nonindustrial civil servants belong to Civil Service unions or associations. The first Civil Service unions appeared in the Post Office in the latter part of the nineteenth century, and since then several hundred have been organized covering officials and employees

---

[25] Dr. Klaus Fuchs, a scientist employed in one of the government's atomic energy establishments, confessed in 1950 to violations of the Official Secrets Act and was sentenced to 14 years' imprisonment.

[26] Cmd. 6937 (1946). *Report of the Royal Commission on Equal Pay*, 1944-46.

[27] It is estimated that the cost of introducing equal pay for the approximately 250,000 women civil servants would amount to £10,000,000 annually. *The Economist*, 15 April 1950, p. 820.

[28] *The Times*, 14 December 1951.

in all grades and classes. Some of them, such as the Civil Service Clerical Association, are service-wide, while others are small organizations representing a group or class of specialized employees. Unionism in the Civil Service was considerably encouraged in 1919 when the Whitley Council system was extended to the public service, for it is based upon the principle of bargaining between an employer and organized groups of employees.

Many of the Civil Service associations which were organized in the early part of the twentieth century were affiliated with trade unions in private industry. This relationship imposed a serious strain upon the Civil Service during the general strike of 1926. The Government was determined to break the resort to direct action involved in the strike and, of course, required the support of all government departments to keep essential services operating. None of the Civil Service unions joined forces with the strikers, but some of them refused to volunteer for extra work or to assist the Government in any way beyond the normal duties of their members. The next year Parliament, in enacting the Trade Disputes Act, required all Civil Service associations to dissolve their affiliation with outside trade unionism. This provision of the law was disliked by many of the Civil Service unions and the groups in private industry with which they had been affiliated, and one of the first acts of the Labour Government taking office in 1945 was to repeal the restriction.[29]

The Whitley Council system is a plan for the discussion of employee problems, working conditions, and grievances in councils organized within departments and also on a service-wide basis. In private industry the Whitley councils are composed of representatives of the employer and representatives of the organized employees. In the Civil Service, the employer's place is taken by the chief officials in a department and by representatives of the Treasury in the all-service or National Whitley Council. Some of the departmental councils have been valuable in the discussion and settlement of issues brought before them, and the National Council has some creditable achievements in its record. The plan for the reorganization of the general classes of the Service in 1920 and the policies on recruitment after World War II resulted from discussion and agreement in the National Council. By and large, though, the issues which have come before the National Council and its action upon them have not fulfilled the expectations which were entertained that 'Whitleyism' in the Civil Service might be a vehicle for the improvement of methods and practices in public administration. 'Whitleyism, after its first five years,' in Professor Laski's opinion, 'became little more than a machine for dealing with wage, and similar, claims, and for safeguarding, as far as possible, the rights of seniority in the processes of promotion; it realised little of the hopes it has

---

[29] The Civil Service Clerical Association, which has more than 150,000 members and which until 1927 was affiliated with the T.U.C., chose not to renew its affiliation.

aroused about post-entry training, the search for new talent in the lower grades, or the effort to encourage the lower officials in the hierarchy to contribute their ideas to the common pool of administrative effort.' [30]

5. *The Importance and the Quality of the Service*

While the principle that ministers take personal responsibility for all actions of their departments and the traditional anonymity of civil servants tend to obscure the importance of the Civil Service in the conduct of the British government, no informed citizen is unaware of the vital role it performs. Indeed, in some quarters, there is an inclination to overestimate its power within the political structure. The opinion is occasionally advanced that the civil servants are really the controlling influence in the modern British government and that no body of harassed ministers can establish effective supervision over the professional staff. For example, a generation ago the Webbs were writing: 'The Government of Great Britain is in fact carried on, not by the Cabinet, nor even by the individual ministers, but by the Civil Service.' [31] This view is an exaggeration, but it contains an element of truth with respect to those departments which are not headed by strong and vigorous ministers, and about offices whose ministers are not able to devote sufficient time to departmental duties.

Any body of professional officials possessing the high quality and experience of the British Civil Service would be bound to exert a great deal of influence upon governmental affairs. This influence is no doubt increasing as the problems of government become more complex and their technical aspects more difficult for the layman to master. A Foreign Secretary confronted daily with the involved problems arising in the many organs of the United Nations, in the administration of occupied areas, in trouble spots like the Middle East and Southeast Asia, and in delicate relations with great and small powers must necessarily rely heavily upon the permanent officials of the Foreign Office. What he can do, of course, is to infuse the Foreign Office with a sense of his views and opinions, as formulated and influenced by other members of the Cabinet, so that all decisions and actions of the department are in reasonable accord.

Given the important place which the Civil Service occupies in the British political system, it is worth asking whether its high quality is being maintained and whether in the future the professional element in administration will measure up to the magnitude of the tasks it must shoulder. Will it continue to attract to its ranks a considerable share of the best talent of every generation, and will its members display the same devotion to duty and the willingness to render impartial, anonymous service to successive ministries that their predecessors have? These questions are pertinent, for one reason, because the standards of the Civil Service were set and its

---

[30] Harold J. Laski, *Reflections on the Constitution* (New York, 1951), p. 165.
[31] Sidney and Beatrice Webb, *Constitution for a Socialist Commonwealth of Great Britain* (London, 1920), p. 67.

reputation won in an era when the higher civil servants formed a division of the governing classes that pretty well dominated British political life. This monopoly, of course never complete, has disappeared. The governing classes no longer consist of the aristocracy, the landed gentry and their representatives in Parliament, the Church, the armed forces, and the Civil Service. Nowadays they consist as much or more of trade unionists, professional men, and captains of business, many of whom have risen from humble backgrounds.

Before World War II there was considerable apprehension in the ranks of the Labour Party about the ability of the Civil Service to serve loyally a strong Labour Government, despite the satisfactory relations of ministers and civil servants during the two minority ministries headed by Ramsay MacDonald. Professor Laski wrote in 1938, for example, 'The neutrality of the civil service has not yet been tested by the need to support a policy which, like that of a socialist party, might well challenge the traditional ideas for which it has stood.' [32] He added, 'I do not for a moment suggest that the civil service would not meet such a test with adequacy; I note only that, so far, the need to meet it has not arisen.'

Whether or not the Civil Service of a generation ago would have met the challenge can never be answered decisively, for along with the governing classes the Civil Service has been changing, too.

The Administrative Class is still dominated by graduates of Oxford and Cambridge, but this does not mean that all the new recruits to this Class are necessarily from the social groups which once sent their sons into the Civil Service. The increased educational opportunities of the past few decades are permitting many talented young men and women from the lower social classes to attend the ancient seats of learning and to compete for entrance to the Civil Service. Graduates of the University of London and the provincial universities are winning appointment, too, and they frequently represent social classes formerly excluded from the public service. Promotion from the lower ranks of the Civil Service is still not common, but it is occurring more often than a generation ago and in this way new elements are being introduced into the upper hierarchy.[33]

---

[32] Harold J. Laski, *Parliamentary Government in England* (New York, 1938), p. 261.

[33] The shift in the sources of recruitment is to be seen in data compiled by the Civil Service Commission on the Administrative Class competitions of 1939 and 1948. In 1939 there were 67 successful candidates, and their universities were: Oxford, 31; Cambridge, 30; London, 3; Edinburgh, 2; St. Andrews, 1. In 1948 there were 41 successful candidates by Method I and 10 by Method II. The universities of the 51 were: Oxford, 16; Cambridge, 18; London, 9; Sheffield, 1; Edinburgh, 5; St. Andrews, 1; nonuniversity, 1. More light on social changes affecting Civil Service recruitment is thrown by figures on the pre-university schools attended by the successful competitors in 1939 and 1948. In 1939, for example, 43 had attended a public school (in the British usage) and 24 other types of schools. In 1948, of the 51 successful competitors 22 had attended public schools and 29 other types of schools. Thus, the percentage of public school candidates had fallen from 64 per cent to 43 per cent. The Civil

It is to be expected that some people in Britain view this change with considerable misgiving. They feel that the 'new' people in the upper ranks will not be as well qualified and as jealous of the Service's reputation for integrity and disinterested public service as the more traditional recruits. There appears to be no reason for this apprehension. The entrance qualifications are still high and not greatly changed from those which formerly produced a Civil Service of superior intellectual capacity and great administrative ability. Moreover, the chances of improving the intellectual quality of the Service are probably enhanced by broadening the field of selection. On the score of integrity, no major scandal has touched the Civil Service in recent years. The Lynskey Tribunal, which investigated allegations of influence-peddling and whose revelations forced one minister to resign from Parliament, found no evidence of corruption among the civil servants of the departments involved.[34] It is a remarkable tribute to the integrity of the Civil Service that in the postwar period of austerity and rationing, when the temptations must have been numerous to favor friends in allocating materials, to overlook evasions of foreign exchange regulations, and to show favoritism in other ways, no serious scandals have been disclosed. Few other countries can point to such a record. To those who fear for the future standards of probity in the Civil Service it is worth recalling that the traditions of the Service undoubtedly have great influence upon all who are appointed and that what has been firmly established will not lightly be injured.

A more serious cause for concern about the future quality of the Service lies in the attraction of other careers for promising university graduates. At least a generation ago the opinion was fairly widespread that the Administrative Class was not drawing as many first-rate university graduates as formerly. Sir Warren Fisher expressed his concern on this matter to the Tomlin Commission, and A. D. Lindsay, then Master of Balliol College, Oxford, testified that, 'judging on the impression I get, year in and year out, of the most able young men, and what they go after,' he did not believe the successful candidates measured up to the pre-1914 standard.[35] Whether or not there has been an improvement over the interwar period is a difficult matter to judge. One is inclined to doubt it in view of the

---

Service Commissioners utter a caution against basing 'conclusions too firmly on figures for a single postwar year, and that one which was in many respects abnormal.' They plan to make future analyses of Civil Service recruitment which will determine whether or not the pattern of 1948 is the 'normal' for the postwar period. In this connection it may be noted that in recent years the Civil Service Commission is giving much more attention to personnel research than it had ever done before. Since 1945 it has had a research unit to undertake the preparation of new tests, to follow-up on the performance of successful candidates, and to engage in job analysis. *Report of His Majesty's Civil Service Commissioners for the Period 1st January, 1941 to 31st March, 1949*, pp. 36, 42-3, 73-95.

[34] Cmd. 7616 (1949).

[35] Royal Commission on the Civil Service, 1929-31, *Minutes of Evidence*, Q. 11, 109.

greater opportunities for financial rewards in business and the professions and the increased dependence of the upper and middle classes on earned income as contrasted with inherited wealth. The higher ranking civil servants have suffered a severe loss of real income through the rise in prices since 1939, and while the older officers can rarely leave to seek compensation comparable to their ability, younger men are deterred from entering the Service or prompted to resign for more lucrative employment. It is doubtful, therefore, whether the Government was well advised in postponing salary increases promised in 1949 to the higher ranks of the Civil Service in order to make them an example in its anti-inflation campaign after the devaluation of the pound.[36] The prestige of the Service exerts a strong attractive force, but it will be unable to offset indefinitely great disparity between the rewards of public service and of private business, the bar, and other occupations open to enterprising and talented young men.

The Civil Service Commission is concerned over the ability of the postwar Service to attract candidates of high quality. It has reported that for the Administrative Class competition in 1948 'there were not enough candidates of the right quality to fill the vacancies,' and it has expressed the hope, in the case of the Foreign Service, 'that the fact that in 1948 only a fifth of the vacancies could be filled is only a passing phenomenon.' [37] Declaring that it 'must not hesitate to go into the market and compete with rival employers,' the Commission has endeavored, by lectures and descriptive brochures, to call to the attention of university authorities and students the career opportunities in the Civil Service.[38]

Evaluating the British Civil Service on the basis of its accomplishments during the past decade or so, one would conclude almost certainly that it is still a highly efficient administrative organization. During the war years it performed most competently under the trying conditions of bombing, blackouts, dispersed offices, and shortages of supplies. Many of its senior officers formed the nuclei of new ministries required for war purposes; others, reinforced by temporary appointments, devised and managed elaborate systems of rationing, bulk purchasing, materials allocation, manpower control, censorship, and civil defense. Some even found time for planning postwar measures of reconstruction and development.

Since 1945 the burden on the Civil Service has been almost as heavy as during the war period. Many wartime controls have had to be main-

---

[36] The effect of this action on the morale of the higher ranking civil servants was exposed in an exchange of letters between the Association of First Division Civil Servants (Administrative Class officers) and the Chorley Co-ordinating Committee of Civil Service Unions, and the Prime Minister. *The Times* was led to comment: 'The terms of the letters are such as have never before, perhaps, been used by the higher Civil servants to the head of the Government. That from the First Division Association refers to "the deep sense of injustice that is now felt throughout the ranks of the higher Civil service. . ."' *The Times,* 12 January 1950.

[37] *Report of His Majesty's Civil Service Commissioners for the Period 1st January, 1941 to 31st March, 1949,* p. 43.

[38] Ibid. p. 37.

tained. In addition, the Labour Government's nationalization of industry program and its schemes of social betterment drew heavily upon the resources of the Civil Service in terms of personnel for planning and the establishment and staffing of new administrative organizations. The Civil Service has also been required to devote much of its energy and skill to international affairs. The postwar proliferation of international agencies has not only been an extra responsibility for the Foreign Office but has involved other ministries. The Treasury, the Board of Trade, the Colonial Office, the Ministry of Supply, the Ministry of Defence, the Ministry of Food, and occasionally other departments have been concerned in the political and economic problems arising out of Britain's international position. A conference with American officials over some aspect of the 'dollar gap' may well involve civil servants of the Foreign Office, the Treasury, the Board of Trade, and the Ministry of Fuel and Power. The negotiating and reporting required by such an international body as the Organization of European Economic Cooperation and the many committees of the North Atlantic Treaty powers place heavy tasks on the civil servants of such a central member as the United Kingdom. So far as one can judge, they are discharging them with their traditional skill.

XVI

Local Government

The United Kingdom being a unitary state, there have been no formal constitutional barriers to the national government's exercise of those powers usually considered as local or municipal. Policy and administration with respect to police and fire protection, education, street construction and maintenance, public housing, and similar functions could be transferred completely to Westminster. That they have not been is owing in part to the impracticality of the extreme centralization which would result, but the more important reasons are the long tradition of local self-government and the belief in its importance in a democratic society. For centuries local affairs have been handled locally, and the British people have desired to maintain a distinction between governmental functions primarily national in character and those primarily of local importance.

In the nineteenth century the oligarchic character of local government was considerably modified, and the governing authorities came to be elected by, and responsible to, the majority of citizens in each unit. Meantime, a trend toward the centralization of policy-making and administration developed, and it has continued to the present day. It has occurred not so much as a result of conscious design but as a reaction to the changing environment in which government operates. The great increase in population, the speed of intercommunication, the advances in science and technology, and the ensuing revolution in the concept of the role of government in social and economic affairs, have led to strong centralizing tendencies in the United Kingdom. The autonomy of local governments has accordingly suffered, but they have by no means been reduced to the status of administrative areas or deprived of all initiative.

1. Historical Background

At least three of the present-day units of British local government have roots far back in the past. The county is descended from the Norman unit of that name which was substituted for the Saxon shire. The borough goes back to the middle ages when towns that became commercially prosperous or important for other reasons won royal charters giving them special powers and privileges. The parish was originally an ecclesiastical unit which often followed the boundaries of a Saxon township and which came

–281

to have civil functions because of its convenient size and because most community affairs centered around the activity of the church.

A map of England and Wales at the beginning of the nineteenth century would have shown the country divided into 50-odd counties, in each of which would have been one or more boroughs enjoying certain special powers and rights. Both counties and boroughs were subdivided into many parishes. County affairs were administered by the justices of peace. Appointed by the Crown, these justices were substantial citizens originally selected to maintain the King's peace, but through the centuries they had a number of administrative duties devolved upon them. The boroughs were governed by their 'corporations,' which were almost invariably controlled by small groups of local citizens who chose the mayor, aldermen, and councillors. The parish was administered by a vestry which consisted either of all rate-paying inhabitants or a small body they elected.

The reforming spirit of the 1830's produced the Municipal Corporations Act of 1835 which eliminated a good deal of obsolete legislation pertaining to the boroughs and gave them a standard form of governmental organization. It also democratized the governments of the boroughs, abolishing the oligarchic cliques which had ruled most of them and conferring the franchise on all local taxpayers. As the century progressed the assumption by government of various new activities led to the establishment of special units of local government. Usually the county was considered too large to be a satisfactory area for the administration of these new activities and the parish was often too small. Consequently, nineteenth-century England became overlaid by one after another of road districts, poor law unions, sanitary districts, drainage districts, and various other specialized units of local government. The result of this development was the existence toward the end of the century of a hodgepodge of areas and authorities whose boundaries rarely coincided but whose powers increasingly impinged upon one another.

The demand upon Parliament to take action to rationalize this confusion in the field of local government grew during the latter decades of the nineteenth century and resulted in 1888 in the passage of the Local Government Act. This act established administrative counties as the basic units of local government and conferred important powers upon them. The counties created followed in general the boundaries of the then existing counties, although for administrative convenience the lines did not entirely coincide. Thus, from 1888 there have existed two types of counties—the historical and the administrative. The slightly more numerous administrative counties—there are 59 historical counties and 62 administrative counties in England and Wales—are the important units for governmental purposes. The Act of 1888 exempted the most populous of the boroughs from the jurisdiction of the counties in which they were located and, calling them county boroughs, conferred upon them the powers of an administrative county as well as of a borough. For example, Manchester located in Lancashire is a county borough possessing substantially greater powers of local government than the county.

While the Act of 1888 did a great deal to modernize government and administration at the local level, it did not eliminate all the numerous units and bodies that had grown up for special purposes during the preceding decades. In 1894 a Parliamentary statute achieved considerable reform in this respect. This act provided for the division of the administrative county into rural and urban districts, the former being areas where the population was relatively sparse and the latter areas which were more thickly settled. The governments of the rural and urban districts absorbed practically all powers which did not belong to the counties or boroughs as the result of the Act of 1888, although the parishes were continued with a few minor powers. In 1899 a host of minor authorities within the County of London, with miscellaneous powers and duties, were amalgamated into 28 metropolitan boroughs, plus the old City of London. By the end of the nineteenth century, therefore, the elaborate patchwork quilt of local units had been simplified to the following major pieces: the administrative county, the county borough, the borough, the rural or urban district, and the parish.

2. The Institutions of Local Government

Before passing to a description of the organization of the principal units of local government, it will be desirable to say something about the historical county. As mentioned before, it was continued in existence by the Local Government Act of 1888, although most of its powers were transferred to the administrative county. The historical county remained a unit for two purposes—parliamentary elections and the administration of justice.

The historical county has a number of officers, all of whom are appointed by the Crown. The principal one is the Lord Lieutenant. He is a prominent local person, frequently a peer, who represents the county on public occasions and, in general, performs such ceremonial duties as arise. During World War II the lord lieutenants took an active part in various voluntary movements and sponsored or participated in many local ceremonies connected with the war effort. The official responsibilities of the lord lieutenants are limited to recommending to the Lord Chancellor the names of persons suitable for appointment as justices of the peace and to serving as the chairmen of the local commissions of the peace. Formerly they commanded the local militia, but with the establishment of the Territorial Army this duty has disappeared.

Another official of the historical county is the sheriff. In olden times he occupied an important office, being a principal representative of the royal government in the county. Most of his functions have been transferred to other officials or bodies so that today the office is considerably less significant. The sheriff may serve as the returning officer for parliamentary elections, he summons juries, he attends the justice holding an assize court in the county, and he carries out judgments awarded by the courts. The historical county also has a clerk of the peace who is appointed by the court of quarter sessions. It is customary to appoint as clerk of the peace the same individual who is clerk of the council of the administrative county. Thus, the administrative and judicial records of the county are in the charge of the same official. The last official of the historical county to be noted is the coroner. He investigates cases of unnatural death and presents his findings to a coroner's jury, which in turn reports to the proper judicial authorities. He is appointed by the county council and must be a barrister, solicitor, or physician. Large counties have more than one coroner; there are about 350 such officials in England and Wales.

Turning now to the administrative county, we find a form of government which is the prototype for nearly all units of British local government. The central organ of the county is a popularly elected council, the size of which varies with the population of the county. Some of them are as small as 50 members, while the London County Council has 150 members and the Lancashire County Council 137. The council consists of ordinary councillors elected for three-year terms and aldermen who are chosen by the councillors for six-year terms. The number of aldermen is usually equal to one-third the number of councillors. Aldermen may be chosen from outside the council or from the body of councillors, in the latter case by-elections being necessary to fill the resulting vacancies. The council is presided over by a chairman who may or may not be a member of the council at the time of his election. He has no powers other than those of a presiding officer, although he undertakes such ceremonial duties as fall to the first member of the county council. The council is required to meet at least four times a year; it may meet more often, but frequent meetings of the entire membership are not customary.

A great deal of the work of the council is conducted by committees into which it is broken. Some of these committees are required by Parliamentary statutes, e.g. an education committee, while others are established by the council on its own initiative. Committee members are chosen in a manner similar to Parliamentary practice, that is, slates are prepared by a selection committee and approved by the council as a whole. As it works out, the committees have a considerable amount of control over their own membership. Members of long standing suggest the names of other councillors for vacancies which develop. Important committees may establish subcommittees to deal with portions of their general responsibility. They may also co-opt persons who are not members of the council in order to obtain special experience or wider community representation.

The administrative county requires a considerable body of officials and employees to carry out its activities. The principal officers of the county government include the clerk, the chief constable, the surveyor, the finance officer, the education officer, and the health officer. Each heads a department of county government with supervision over clerks, inspectors, policemen, teachers, engineers, chemists, mechanics, and laborers. The county clerk, while not in authority over the entire administrative organization, serves as a sort of co-ordinating officer. The principal county officers, however, tend to look to the appropriate council committees for guidance and support. Thus, the education officer, while responsible to the council as a whole, deals on a day-to-day basis with the education committee, and his administration of the school system is under regular review by the committee.

As mentioned above, each administrative county is subdivided into urban and rural districts. There are 572 urban districts and 475 rural districts in England and Wales. The governmental institutions in these districts are similar to those of the counties. Each district has a popularly elected council consisting of an appropriate number of councillors. The council elects a chairman who presides over its deliberations. The council is divided into committees which maintain supervision over various district activities. Each district government has a staff of officials and employees who carry out the functions of the unit. Some of the urban districts are quite considerable municipal areas, and they have fairly large administrative services.

Below the rural and urban districts are the smallest units of local government, the parishes, to the number of about 14,000. The parish has a council if its population is of sufficient size to justify it. Otherwise its affairs are transacted in a parish meeting open to all voters of the area. The parish has a clerk who performs such administrative functions as may be required.

The principal units of city government in England and Wales are the county boroughs and the boroughs. Most of these cities trace their histories back hundreds of years, and they are proud of the part they have played in various episodes of British history. Canterbury was an ancient town when Chaucer's pilgrims were journeying to its shrines. Almost 1000 years separate Lady Godiva's famous ride through the streets of Coventry and the attempt of the German Luftwaffe to erase the city from the map. The chronicles of Southampton tell of Henry V assembling his knights and yeomen to invade France as well as of General Eisenhower's armada sailing for the Normandy beaches. A borough is established by royal charter, but its constitution and powers are regulated by the Local Government Act, 1933.

When county government was reorganized in 1888 some 60 boroughs were considered large and important enough to be exempted from the jurisdiction of the counties in which they were located and to be established as county boroughs. Their number is now 83. The governments of county boroughs have a wider range of powers than an administrative county. Other boroughs do not differ a great deal from urban districts except that their charters may contain certain powers and privileges not usually accorded an urban district. For purposes of modern government, these distinctions are usually unimportant.

Borough government follows the usual pattern of English local government. There is a council elected by the voters of the borough, and the council increases its number by the selection of aldermen. The borough council, like the county council, operates chiefly through committees which maintain a constant surveillance over the principal municipal activities. The council elects a presiding officer either from its membership or from the outside, and he bears the title of mayor. The charters of some boroughs give the mayor the additional dignity of being known as lord mayor. As in the case of the chairman of a county council, the mayor's functions, other than those he has as a councillor, are chiefly ceremonial. In boroughs with a long history, the mayor's position is one of considerable dignity and local social importance. He is elected for one year but may be re-elected any number of times. The position frequently is a fairly expensive one for the holder as he is expected to discharge his ceremonial and representational duties on a scale in keeping with the traditions of the city.

The administrative work of the borough is carried on by a body of municipal officials and their subordinate staffs. The principal of these officials is the town clerk, an ancient and honorable office in English communities. Besides keeping the records of the council and of the borough generally, the town clerk, who is usually a solicitor, serves as the coordinating officer for the municipal administration. 'His department,' S. E. Finer has written, 'is a focal point for all co-ordination: and this for two reasons. By controlling and keeping minutes the Clerk alone is in a position to know what all committees are up to, at all times. Secondly, what local authorities may or may not do is so hedged in by law, that a wise council will hardly move a step without consulting their Clerk. An efficient Clerk's department will play in the local councils, the same co-ordinative role, the role of a "collective memory" that the Secretariat does to the Cabinet.' [1] The other officials are practically the same as those found in the government of an administrative county. There is a surveyor, a treasurer, an education officer, a health officer, an engineer, and a chief of police. Each heads an administrative department and supervises a staff of subordinate officials and employees.

3. The Functions of Local Government

Local governments in Britain perform the functions conferred on them by Parliamentary statutes. There is a great volume of legislation conferring powers and prescribing the manner in which they are to be exercised. Besides the statutes bestowing functions upon all local governments or certain classes of them, some local authorities have special powers derived from private acts which they have promoted. Some Parliamentary statutes are specific and impose powers and duties that leave no room for discretion by governments. Others establish minimum standards and allow local authorities possessing greater resources or more initiative to expand their services beyond the required level.

A county borough is described as an all-purpose local authority because it is competent to exercise the many powers conferred by general Parliamentary statutes upon all local governments. The administrative county is

---

[1] A Primer of Public Administration (London, 1950), p. 89.

likewise an all-purpose authority, but it is either required or may exercise the option of delegating some functions to district authorities. It is sometimes referred to, therefore, as a two-tier authority in contrast to the one-tier county borough. While in recent years the district authorities have been receiving some powers by delegation from the county, most of their powers are derived directly from Parliamentary statutes.

Within the limits of Parliamentary legislation the council of a county borough or an administrative county may enact by-laws setting local policy. Such by-laws must have the approval of an appropriate Whitehall department—for example, the Home Office for by-laws dealing with policing and public order or the Ministry of Housing and Local Government for those pertaining to housing. The councils of urban and rural districts and boroughs may pass by-laws, too, but approval by the councils of their administrative counties is necessary. The councils of local governments, however, are not primarily policy-making bodies. Their duties are chiefly of an administrative nature. They discuss, supervise, and review the execution of policy which has been largely determined at Westminster. It is for this reason that the work of council committees is important. In general, there is a committee for each of the major activities of the local government, and it keeps a close surveillance over the administrative work being performed.

Local authorities are empowered to raise money to support their activities by levying taxes known as rates. These are taxes on real property and they are levied on the basis of assessed valuations.[2] The rates fall on the occupants of property whether or not they are the owners. County boroughs, boroughs, and rural and urban districts are called rating authorities, levying taxes for their own expenses and also for other local governments within their rating areas. A county council does not levy rates directly but issues 'precepts' to the rating authorities within its jurisdiction which in turn must add the amounts of these precepts to their own municipal outlays.

The local governments in Britain spend approximately £700 million annually. A little less than half this amount comes from local sources; the balance is provided by the national government in the form of various grants. Some grants are for specific activities, but the bulk of the money is in the form of a grant for general municipal purposes. By the Local Government Act of 1948, local governments share an annual sum, amounting to about £170 million, on the basis of the degree to which each falls below or exceeds a national average of financial capacity. A borough where rateable values are low but the demand for municipal services is high receives more than a borough having larger taxable resources. Some local governments above the national average receive no equalization grants from the Exchequer. Local governments may borrow money but

---

[2] By the Local Government Act, 1948, valuation for rating purposes was transferred from the local authorities to the Board of Inland Revenue.

only for purposes authorized by Parliamentary statutes, and the consent of an appropriate ministry is required.

The accounts of all local governments, except county boroughs and boroughs outside London, are audited by district auditors, who are national civil servants appointed by the Minister of Housing and Local Government. Many county boroughs and boroughs have voluntarily adopted the district audit system, and all of them are required to use it to account for certain Exchequer grants. If a district auditor discovers an illegal expenditure he may levy a surcharge on the account in question, and this surcharge must be repaid by the officials who sanctioned payment. A surcharge may fall on council members who approved an illegal expenditure, as well as on an administrative officer. Local officials may appeal to the Minister of Housing and Local Government or to the High Court of Justice for relief from a surcharge.

A county borough exercises a considerable range of municipal activities. First, it is responsible for the personal protection of its inhabitants and maintains police and fire services for this purpose. During World War II the fire departments of all local governments were placed under the Minister of Home Security in order that they could be used more effectively in controlling air raid damage, but in 1947 the county and county borough authorities were given control of the fire services. Secondly, a county borough is responsible for public health and sanitation. Its duties in this sphere have been limited by the National Health Service, although it has received back some functions, for example, the maintenance of health centers and clinics, as delegations from the national service. The local functions now are principally those of environmental health services, that is, the assuring of clean and sanitary conditions for community life. This involves inspection and the enforcement of regulations relating to sanitation in public places, the collection and disposal of refuse, the maintenance of a sewage system, and the abatement of pollution. Next, a county borough is the local education authority. It maintains primary and secondary schools and often special institutes and training facilities. In addition the county borough has functions dealing with planning and public works. It plans the physical development of the municipality, designating areas for residential and industrial development, locating schools and other public structures, and providing for parks and recreational facilities. The local government constructs and maintains streets, bridges, and the buildings required for its own operations.

Many boroughs in the past have owned and operated public utilities which provided electricity, gas, water, and transportation services. In 1945 a third of the gas production of the country was in municipal hands and two-thirds of the electricity production.[3] The central government's nationalization schemes have absorbed a good many of these municipal enter-

---

[3] J. H. Warren, 'Local Government,' *British Government since* 1918 (London, 1950), p. 201.

288—

prises. The gas and electric power industries have been taken over by public corporations and the local governments paid the balance of outstanding indebtedness on the plants they owned. A number of municipally operated airports have been acquired by the Ministry of Transport and Civil Aviation. However, one activity in this class, public housing, has been expanding, and today nearly all local governments own and manage housing developments of considerable magnitude.

The local government functions that have been summarized in terms of the one-tier county borough belong as well to the two-tier administrative county and its districts, the borough, the urban district, or the rural district. Some functions are administered directly by the county government while others are performed by the districts. The latter are usually responsible for the construction and maintenance of streets and roads, except trunk roads, for street lighting, refuse collection and disposal, for the provision of libraries, parks, bathhouses, and other public facilities, and for the operation of some municipal utilities. The functions of the parish, it may be added, are limited to the maintenance of such local facilities as footpaths, village greens, and parish halls.[4]

4. *Local Government Service*

The local governments of Great Britain employ approximately 1,300,000 persons to perform their various functions. About a million of these employees are laborers and manual workers, not a surprising proportion if it is recalled that much municipal activity falls in the public works field. The remainder includes such categories as teachers, policemen, firemen, clerks, and typists, and the relatively small professional and executive groups.

Until recent years there was considerable diversity in the personnel standards and practices of British local governments. Within certain limits, which will be noted, each county, borough, or district council was free to devise its own employment policies. Some of the larger units had well-developed personnel programs, while in others the employment practices were far below the standards of the national Civil Service. The small staffs of many minor governmental units did not lend themselves to such practices as recruitment through competitive examinations, training programs, and classification and pay schedules. Furthermore, patronage and nepotism were present here and there.

Through the years some uniformity in personnel matters had been imposed on the local governments by national legislation and administrative action. National standards with regard to the qualifications and pay of teachers, policemen, and firemen restricted the autonomy of the local authorities, and the appointment of various professional officers was sub-

---

[4] Under the National Parks and Access to the Countryside Act, 1949, parish councils were directed to survey all public footpaths and bridleways within their boundaries in order that the county authorities could record them on official maps.

ject to the approval of a ministry. These national requirements were enforceable through the inspecting authority of the Whitehall departments and through the financial control inherent in grants from the Exchequer. Professional associations and trade unions also exerted pressure toward standardization in personnel matters. The associations were interested in such officials as engineers, doctors, accountants, and architects. The unions dealt with the local authorities on the conditions of employment for laborers and manual workers. Thus, local councils were circumscribed to a considerable extent in determining personnel policy by official controls administered by the national ministries and by the nonofficial practices of professional groups and trade unions. Their freedom was the greatest with respect to the general administrative and clerical classes.

Municipal employees have pressed for greater uniformity in their conditions of service in the interest both of higher remuneration and of better career prospects. After World War I they obtained the creation of nine regional Joint Councils through which employee associations could meet with the representatives of local councils and negotiate agreements on personnel matters. Only three of these functioned before 1939, but during World War II the others were activated and in 1945 a National Joint Council for the Administrative, Professional, and Technical Staffs of Local Authorities was established. The National Council has produced a general personnel program, the 'Scheme of Service,' for adoption by local governments. The great majority of municipal authorities have accepted the Scheme of Service and their personnel policies and practices are governed by its provisions. In all these efforts to promote the cause of municipal employees the lead has been taken by the National Association of Local Government Officers (NALGO).

The Scheme of Service, which applies to employees receiving less than £700 a year, is not as detailed and precise as the body of orders and regulations governing the national Civil Service. The local governments vary too much in size and resources to be covered by a complete code, and some flexibility must be allowed for special conditions. Moreover, administration by hundreds of separate local authorities would naturally produce some difference. The purpose of the Scheme, therefore, is to introduce as much uniformity as the nature of local government allows and to raise the general standard of personnel administration.

By the Scheme five major classes of local government employees are recognized—the General, the Clerical, the Higher Clerical, the Miscellaneous, and the Administrative, Professional, and Technical. The classification of the service of each local unit on this basis is left with individual municipal governments. The Scheme establishes salary scales for each class of employees, and it sets forth principles and policies pertaining to tenure, training, promotions, political activity, and other personnel matters. Standards of recruitment are prescribed for 16-year-old and 18-year-old candidates who have completed their schooling, but individual local authorities determine and administer their own examinations. Provision has been made for promotional examinations for clerical and administrative officers.

290–

They are administered by the Local Government Examinations Board, an appendage of the National Joint Council, and in their degree of difficulty they represent a considerable advance in the requirements for the higher administrative and executive posts.

The principal executive and professional officers of a local government are appointed by the council upon the recommendation of its committees. Vacancies are frequently advertised and candidates with the requisite qualifications are invited to apply. After an appropriate committee reviews the applications submitted and interviews the most promising candidates, a recommendation is submitted to the council. Whitehall approval is necessary for several positions at the department head level—for example, the Home Office for a chief of police and the Ministry of Health for a health officer.

Local government officers do not have the permanent tenure vouchsafed to civil servants of the national government, but dismissals for personal or political reasons are rare. By national legislation, all local authorities are required to maintain pension plans, which are financed by municipal and employee contributions. Among the higher officers, transfer from one local authority to another is fairly common. By such transfers officers advance to larger units of government that pay higher salaries and offer greater scope for their ability and experience. Pension rights are transferable.

Since the war the local government service, like the Civil Service and other salaried groups, has been adversely affected by rising living costs. In 1951 NALGO submitted a claim to the National Joint Council for a twenty per cent increase in the salaries of its 150,000 members, declaring that the more able officers were resigning to enter private business and that the supply of candidates of good quality was declining.[5] Claims of this kind can be taken to the Industrial Court if no satisfactory agreement is reached in joint negotiations. Higher remuneration will probably be necessary to maintain the quality and efficiency of the local government service. Although career prospects have been improved by the Scheme of Service, the benefits in this respect will not offset comparatively low salaries during a period of rising living costs and full employment.

5. *Local Politics*

The elected officials of English local government are the county, borough, and district councillors, and they occupy part-time, unpaid positions. Local government elections, at least for the county and larger borough councils, are contested on party lines, and party divisions carry over into the organization of the councils. This is rather a new development in British politics, for until fairly recent times party lines were not sharply drawn in local elections. Many candidates ran as independents, the issues were primarily local, and the councils did not divide into permanent governing and opposition elements.

---

[5] *The Times,* 18 January 1951.

The Labour Party has been chiefly responsible for increasing the degree of political organization and activity at the local levels of government and for introducing there national issues.[6] Some of the party's early leaders saw in local politics an opportunity to promote their programs of social welfare and public ownership. They were concerned about ameliorating the conditions of the poor, extending the social services, and expanding governmental activities generally. It was possible, they believed, to utilize the powers of county and borough councils to achieve some of these objectives. Moreover, the councils were good training grounds for Labour politicians. Party members, therefore, were encouraged to participate in local government affairs and to promote welfare programs and what was termed 'gas and water socialism,' i.e. the public ownership of local utilities. The careers of a number of the contemporary national leaders of the party reflect this interest in local politics. Clement Attlee was mayor of Stepney, a London metropolitan borough, and wrote a Fabian Society pamphlet on local government; Herbert Morrison, the author of *How London Is Governed,* was leader of the London County Council for a time, and J. Chuter Ede was for many years a member of the Surrey County Council. Aneurin Bevan, Edith Summerskill, George Isaacs, George Tomlinson, and Hector McNeil are other former Labour ministers who have been active in local government affairs.

The Conservatives reacted slowly to the Labour challenge. Not struggling to establish themselves as a national party, they did not feel impelled to build a base in local government and to bring into close association the political organizations at both levels of government. The Conservative cause was considered adequately represented by the numerous party members and independents who, carrying the credentials of local position and civic interest, offered themselves for election to the councils. Conservative politicians did not regard local elections as the occasion to debate foreign policy, protective tariffs, or the major social and economic problems confronting Parliament. Recent years have seen a considerable change in this Conservative attitude toward local government. More attention must be paid, the party has decided, to local politics. Some Tory leaders believed that Labour's sweeping victory in the general election of 1945 could be explained, in large part, by the work of the well-managed local organizations serving the party and that the Conservatives needed to imitate their opponents' methods.

Another factor inducing a changed attitude was the closer relations of the central and local governments. As the local governments increasingly became agents for the administration of national programs, the distinction between national and local politics was blurred. Policies and programs pertaining to the social services, public assistance, and the nationalization of

---

[6] In London, however, the Conservatives, becoming alarmed at what they considered the radical tendencies of the new London County Council, promoted party alignment along national lines.

industry affected the local governments, and rationing and controls touched every citizen. In consequence, these national issues were carried over into local politics; an election for councillors was an opportunity for the voter to express himself in a way to get the attention of ministers and backbench M.P.'s.

Postwar local government elections, therefore, have been waged on national party lines and national issues have played almost as large a part in them as municipal problems. Writing of the county council elections in 1949, the editors of *The Economist* said: 'These local elections were fought on national issues, by the deliberate choice of the two parties. It was well understood by the party organizers that it was the Labour Government's national record since 1945 which was under judgment and local parties were urged to run their contests as the first of the General Election battles.' [7]

In view of the trend toward linking national and local politics, the predictive value of the council elections is of interest. That they show general tendencies among voters few would dispute. Serious losses by the party in power at Westminster usually presage trouble at the next general election, and by the same token widespread success indicates continued confidence in the Government.

There are definite limits, however, to what can be deduced from the results. In the first place, fewer voters go to the polls in local elections than in Parliamentary elections. Usually about a quarter of the eligible electorate votes. In 1949, as a result of the efforts of the parties to arouse interest and to create something of a general election atmosphere, about 40 per cent of the electorate cast ballots. The percentage of voters going to the polls in a general election is at least 70, and in 1950 it was 84. While local elections are a good sample of the electorate's views, one cannot be sure that the ballots of the nonvoters would fall in the same proportions as those of the voters. Secondly, it is pretty certain that the reaction of voters to a local election is different from that to a general election. They are not voting for or against the continuance of a Ministry in power. A person who will use his local ballot as a kind of protest against the Government might well vote the opposite way when faced with the choice in a general election. Moreover, local issues and personalities affect council elections, and these contests cannot be converted into national referenda however energetically the party machines may try. It should be noted, finally, that the results of local elections, tabulated nation-wise, are seldom clear-cut. The national party headquarters produce figures on seats won and lost, but there is usually a considerable discrepancy between the Labour and Conservative reports. A good deal of this comes about because the affiliation of many candidates is doubtful. Both Labourites and Conservatives claim that some independents and minor party members are really to be counted on their side.

---

[7] 16 April 1949, p. 698.

The geographical distribution of party strengths at the local level of government follows the general lines found in national politics. Labour is strong in the industrial cities and towns, in some of the urban districts with large working class populations, and in many of London's boroughs and satellite communities. The mining districts are strongly Labour, too. The agricultural areas are usually Conservative, and so are most of the towns and urban districts where large scale industry is not predominant. While many borough and county borough councils have Labour majorities, the Conservatives control all but a small number of the administrative counties. After the local government elections in 1949 there were Labour majorities in only seven county councils: London, Durham, Derby, Nottingham, Monmonthshire, Glamorgan, and Carmarthen. In 1952 a sharp swing to the left gave Labour control of five additional counties: Essex, Northumberland, Stafford, West Riding, and Lancashire. The Liberals retained one county, Flint.

6. The Reform of Local Government

Nearly everyone in Britain agrees that some reform of local government is overdue. In structure and functions the present system of local government is not realistically adjusted to the political and social situation. Local government reform, however, happens to be one of the subjects which, like the weather, everyone talks about but nobody does anything about. There has been a good deal of tinkering on the part of Parliament, but no major reorganization has occurred since the acts of 1888 and 1894. In view of the Labour Party's long interest in local government affairs and the experience of several of its leaders in local politics, it is strange that no comprehensive reform measures found a place in the Government's legislative program after 1945. Admittedly the supply of important bills exceeded the limits of Parliamentary time and a comprehensive local government measure would have consumed many days of a session. Nevertheless, the need for reform has been great and the Labour Government's diffidence toward the subject is difficult to explain.

In connection with reform, the first problem encountered is the disparity in size among the units of local government. Apart from London, the largest administrative county is Middlesex with a population of 2,270,000, while the smallest is Rutland with 18,000. County boroughs range from Birmingham's 1,085,000 inhabitants to Canterbury's 25,000. The populations of Middlesex and Birmingham are approximately equal to the aggregate population of the 50 smallest counties and county boroughs. Urban districts range in population from 700 to 200,000 inhabitants. Such disparities make legislation applying to classes of local government quite inappropriate. What is desirable for a great metropolis is probably wholly unsuited to a town of 50,000 inhabitants. The latter has neither the financial resources nor the administrative establishment to accept the responsibilities of a large city.

294–

It is clear that what is required is some equalizing of local government areas. Parliament recognized this need in 1945 and established a Local Government Boundary Commission with the responsibility of creating 'effective and convenient units of local government administration.' Previously all changes in local government boundaries had to be promoted by means of private bills in Parliament, a long and expensive process. Many such bills were introduced, chiefly by county boroughs seeking to extend their boundaries, but they frequently led to bitter and prolonged contests. Administrative counties were reluctant to lose territory and taxable property to the spreading cities, and small boroughs and urban districts disliked losing these assets, and sometimes their identity as well. With the establishment of the Local Government Boundary Commission these requests for changes went to the Commission. After two years of existence it reported:

> Since the establishment of this Commission in 1945 we have received applications for the creation and extension of county boroughs which would have removed substantial areas and resources from counties and involved the disappearance of 66 non-county boroughs, 130 urban districts and 11 rural districts, as well as the absorption of parts of 174 other county districts. The attitude of county councils to these demands is normally one of unqualified resistance, and has culminated in counter-claims for the removal of county borough status from most of the existing county boroughs.[8]

Faced with such a flood of applications, the Commission made a few provisional changes and then stated that it was unrealistic to consider boundary revision apart from the functions of local government units. The Commission came to the conclusion that three principal types of local authority were required. First, there would be counties, which would in general follow present county boundaries except that combinations and divisions of existing units would produce areas having between 200,000 and 1,000,000 inhabitants. Included within this group would be cities having populations between 200,000 and 500,000. Next, there would be a class of 'new' county boroughs, cities with populations between 60,000 and 200,000. Finally, a class of county districts which would include all present noncounty boroughs, urban districts and rural districts, their boundaries adjusted to produce more uniform areas. The Commission proposed a reallocation of functions that would make some counties—the big cities—one-tier authorities, and the rest two-tier. The latter counties would divide their functions with either the 'new' county boroughs or the county districts. The 'new' county boroughs, described by the Commission as 'most-purpose' authorities, would be an intermediate class depend-

---

[8] *Report of the Local Government Boundary Commission for the Year* 1947 (H.M.S.O., London, 1948), p. 7.

ing upon the counties for certain services but still possessing important autonomous functions. For example, the police and fire services would be county functions, but education and many health services would be allocated to the 'new' county boroughs. These proposals did not commend themselves to the Government, and it eventually introduced a bill to abolish the Commission.

The problems of area and functions are closely linked to a third, the optimum amount of centralization to be sought. The centralizing process has advanced rapidly in recent years. Much of it has been a response to changing social conditions. For example, the motor car has transformed living habits and created a need for public services and regulations that did not formerly exist. New views concerning the proper role of the state in economic and social affairs have also conduced to greater centralization.

Whatever the cause, the fact remains that the local governments of Britain have been losing powers and functions to the national government. Some activities have been totally transferred from local to central authority. The Trunk Roads Acts of 1936 and 1946 established a national highway network under the control of the Ministry of Transport, although the counties remain the Ministry's agents for maintenance work. The Electricity Act of 1946 and the Gas Act of 1948 expropriated the municipally owned electricity and gas services and added them to the properties of public corporations, the British Electricity Authority and the Area Gas Boards. The National Health Service Act, 1946, transferred the public hospitals maintained by local governments to new regional authorities. The functions remaining to local authorities for providing poor relief were removed by the National Assistance Act, 1948, and bestowed on the National Assistance Board. In addition to these transfers of function, there has been an increasing amount of Whitehall control imposed on the remaining activities of local government. This control is exercised through the auditing of accounts for services partly financed by Exchequer grants, by the inspection of the performance of these services, by the requirement of obtaining a ministry's endorsement for appointments to key positions in local administration, and by the need to submit development plans for ministerial approval. Such important local services as police, fire protection, education, housing, planning, and public health are all subject to a considerable amount of central control.

Furthermore, within the structure of local government itself the trend has been to move functions from the district and borough level to the county level. Thus, the Education Act of 1944 made the county council the education authority for the whole county; the Police Act, 1946, converted the borough forces into county police forces; the Town and Country Planning Act, 1947, placed the planning function with the county council; and the Fire Services Act, 1947, while dissolving the National Fire Service organized during the war, devolved the service to counties and county boroughs and not to the boroughs and districts which had formerly maintained their own fire departments.

296–

Now many good reasons support the trend toward centralization. The social changes which have made Great Britain a more interdependent community have been mentioned. Administrative efficiency has dictated some transfers from local to central hands. In addition there have been political pressures for more ample and uniform services which could only be supplied by national intervention, involving the complete assumption of a function or its supervision by the central government. Whatever the reason or combination of reasons, the trend raises a serious problem: how to maintain vigorous and flourishing local governments when their powers and functions are constantly being reduced. The British people have always regarded a local government system, endowed with a large measure of autonomy, as one of the cornerstones of their democracy. Its transformation into a field organization of the Whitehall bureaucracy would never consciously be tolerated. Yet this result is possible if the trends of the past few years continue.

These trends are probably having an unsatisfactory effect upon both the political and administrative elements in local government. Membership on county and borough councils holds out less challenge if policy decisions are made in a London department and ministerial approval is required for anything deviating from the national norm. Likewise, ambitious administrative officials may come to feel that the Civil Service or the nationalized industries offer more scope and responsibility than local government service.

In 1949 the Government appointed a committee, composed of officials of ministries having important functions concerning local government and of representatives of associations of local authorities, to examine central-local relations for the purpose of discovering ways of economizing in the use of administrative manpower and of delegating more responsibility to local governments. Adopting 'as a guiding principle that local authorities are responsible bodies competent to discharge their own functions and that they exercise their responsibilities in their own rights,' the committee recommended a number of administrative and statutory changes which would produce 'considerable simplification and loosening of departmental control.' [9] The committee's study and recommendations dealt with central-local relations in such functional fields as education, housing, public health, and civil defense.

Without doubt, periodic surveys by official representatives are a fruitful method of reordering central-local relations, revealing points of friction, and marking for the discard various pieces of bureaucratic apparatus or administrative procedures that no longer serve necessary purposes. A good deal of reform can be accomplished by administrative action, and the Whitehall departments can advance further the cause of a sound municipal structure by proposing amendments to unduly restrictive or out-of-date

---

[9] Cmd. 8421 (1951). *Second Report of the Local Government Manpower Committee.*

-297

statutes when they have the opportunity. There are limits, however, to the results which can be attained by the method of the official survey.

The best answer to the problem of preserving local government as a vital part of the political system lies in an early and comprehensive reform by Parliament. Something along the lines of the Boundary Commission's proposals is indicated. This would include a redrawing of boundaries to create areas satisfying the needs of administration and public interest and control, and a reallocation of functions to give each level of local government some appropriate and important responsibilities. Parliament's task in this respect would not be easy. The vested interests are strong, the various local government associations hold divergent views, and the problems are inherently complicated. But reform is urgent, as a leading newspaper has said, 'to arrest and reverse the decline in this most precious of our political institutions towards mere survival as a picturesque anachronism.' [10]

It will perhaps have been noticed that the reform of local government has been discussed in terms of structure, functions, and inter-governmental relations. The other aspect of reform, honest administration, has not been a serious problem in Britain for many decades. Before the First World War, A. Lawrence Lowell remarked that 'The English towns have, as a rule, been singularly free from corruption.' [11] This statement remains generally true today. Instances of corruption occur, but scandals of the kind which are exposed in American municipalities with unfortunate frequency are rare in Great Britain.

No single reason can be given for the relative lack of corruption in British local government. The reforming spirit of the mid-nineteenth century which led to higher standards in national administration had its influence in the local areas, and the progress of that period has been maintained. Municipal governments have elicited a great deal of unpaid service from their citizens; duty rather than reward has been a characteristic attitude toward membership on a council and work on its committees. The supervision and the auditing controls exercised by the incorruptible civil servants of Whitehall departments have played a part, too. Equally incorruptible has been the judiciary; officers betraying their trust have had to expect prompt and severe punishment. Finally, the permanent officials serving local authorities take pride in their ethical as well as their professional standards. Of them Lowell wrote, 'Their professional character insures efficiency, their effacement shields them from any temptation to achieve a cheap notoriety, and their permanence relieves them from the need of doing personal favours to retain their posts.' [12] As a result of all these influences and factors the standards of official honesty and integrity are high. Local government in Britain shows that favoritism, graft, and jobbery are not irremedial characteristics of municipal affairs.

---

[10] *The Manchester Guardian Weekly,* 8 February 1951.
[11] *The Government of England,* rev. ed. (New York, 1914), vol. II, p. 197.
[12] Ibid. vol. II, p. 201.

7. Local Government in Scotland

Scottish local government was considerably reorganized by the Local Government (Scotland) Act of 1929. This measure made the councils of the 31 administrative counties into which the country is divided the principal authorities for local government purposes. Their functions include the provision of police services for rural areas and small towns, the construction and maintenance of roads, the provision and management of schools, and the administration of various public health and sanitary services. Districts, burghs, and parishes comprise the subdivisions of counties.

Since the act of 1929 there have existed three classes of towns. The four largest cities of the country—Edinburgh, Glasgow, Aberdeen, and Dundee—comprise a group comparable to the county boroughs of England. They exercise the powers of an administrative county. Towns of a class known as large burghs, all with populations above 20,000, have somewhat fewer powers than an administrative county. The county council, for example, is the education authority for a large burgh. The small burghs, those below 20,000 in population, have still more restricted powers.

The popularly elected councils of Scottish local government transact much of their business through committees dealing with various municipal functions. In the towns the ceremonial head of the council is the provost—lord provost in the larger places. He and the bailies, who are also members of the council, serve as magistrates and have some administrative duties. Local government councils have numerous dealings with the Education, Agriculture, and Home Departments of the Scottish Office. These departments exercise their powers of guidance, supervision, and control, under acts of Parliament, in much the same fashion as the corresponding ministries for England and Wales.

XVII

The Government of London

The great metropolitan area known as London contains almost a fifth of the population of the United Kingdom, is the seat of its government and national administration, and is also the commercial and cultural capital of the nation. It is, moreover, the largest and most famous city of the Commonwealth and Empire—the hub around which the affairs of several hundred million people throughout the world revolve.

For many centuries London has occupied a predominant place in the life of Britain. Long before it spread out to its present gargantuan size, London was important enough to tip the balance in civil wars, determine the fate of royal dynasties, and shape national policy at critical times. The old City's influence upon the course of English history has been described in the following way by Professor Trevelyan:

> Such a city, containing more than a tenth of the population of England and a good half of its trained thinking power, placed beside the seat of government at Westminster in juxtaposition so close as to form a single metropolis, could not fail to exercise a decisive influence on the course of English history in the days when the difficulties of travel still isolated Court and Parliament from the other towns and shires of the land. At no time, indeed, did London seek to govern England as Rome had governed Italy or as Athens sought to govern Greece. She accepted the government of England by the Monarchy or by Parliament, so long as the rulers of the land remained at Westminster outside her gates, leaving her ancient municipal liberties undisturbed, and so long as they conducted the religious and foreign affairs of the country in the main in accordance with principles that were popular in London. The Kings and Queens whom she favoured—Henry VIII, Elizabeth, William III and Anne—left behind them political structures that survived. Those who quarrelled with her built for the day— Mary Tudor, the two Charleses and Jameses, and the Protector— though Oliver and the second Charles each owed his rise to power largely to her support.[1]

---

[1] G. M. Trevelyan, *English Social History* (London, 1942), pp. 332-3.

1. *The Many Londons*

A foreigner might suppose that a city of such proportions and influence upon the affairs of a great nation would be organized for governmental and administrative purposes in a model fashion. This supposition would seem the more probable in view of the fact that the metropolis is the capital of a people who have shown great genius as lawgivers and administrators. In truth, however, the British have not, at least in modern times, succeeded in making the government and administration of metropolitan London a conspicuous success, and it remains a place where reforming actions usually trail well behind the needs which give rise to them. Professor Robson, an authority on public administration, has written: 'London is indubitably the largest and most important capital in the world. She is equally clearly one of the worst planned, or rather most unplanned of cities; and her local government administration is unsatisfactory as regards its organization and basic principles.' [2]

The reasons for this state of affairs with respect to political organization and administrative efficiency arise from several sources. For one thing, London's very size creates tremendous problems in municipal organization and administration. The concentration of several million people in a relatively small area and the provision of all the services which an interdependent modern community of this size requires are conditions to be found in few other places in the world. Secondly, the metropolis has always been outgrowing its organizational structure. From medieval times many people whose work and interests centered in the metropolis have spilled over into the surrounding areas and have not been embraced within the boundaries of the municipal organization. London has always had suburbs to complicate its problems. A third cause is found in the multiplicity and strength of vested interests which over the centuries have made change a matter of struggle and compromise. The center has been reluctant to share its authority with growing satellite communities, and the latter have developed in parent counties which have been jealous of the encroachments of the metropolis. Finally, responsibility for action to remedy some of the pressing needs of the metropolis has rested in a central government usually so absorbed in national and imperial concerns that it can seldom be brought to consider the affairs of London.

It happens, therefore, that the London metropolitan area in the middle of the twentieth century is not organized as one municipal government but is a complex with many seats of authority. First of all, there is the ancient City of London, an area of about one square mile on the north bank of the Thames. It is the original London, founded in pre-Roman times and boasting a history of more than 2000 years. Once a place of residence as well as the center of commerce and finance, it is now almost solely the

---

[2] W. A. Robson, *The Government and Misgovernment of London,* 2nd ed. (London, 1948), p. 162.

home of banks, shipping and insurance companies, large business firms, and the commercial services which supplement these undertakings. In the past two centuries its resident population has declined from around 200,000 to about 5000. During the week its streets are thronged with office workers, but at night and on week ends they are almost as deserted as the lanes of a country village.

Surrounding the City on all sides and embracing an area of 117 square miles is the County of London. The county has a population of about 3,500,000. The several other millions of people who live in the metropolis and who consider themselves Londoners are residents of adjoining counties and of municipal units within these counties. The principal administrative unit which embraces most of them is the Metropolitan Police District, covering an area of 692 square miles. The Metropolitan Police District is the London which is counted for census purposes, and it has a population of 8,405,000. There are still other administrative areas which cover much of the metropolis. The region served by the Metropolitan Water Board is somewhat larger than the Police District and so, too, is that of the London Transport Executive. The London Traffic Area, a district subject to traffic regulations prescribed by the London and Home Counties Traffic Advisory Committee and the Minister of Transport, covers 1820 square miles, while the Metropolitan Traffic Area, a district for the licensing of public service vehicles, embraces 2415 square miles. The Port of London Authority administers various important functions connected with the river Thames, and its jurisdiction extends from Teddington eastward to the sea.

2. *The City Corporation*

The City of London, as has been stated, covers a minute area of the metropolis and houses a tiny resident population. Its size and population, however, are in no sense indicative of its importance as a governmental unit. With its ancient history, its great wealth, and the importance in the business world of its constituents, the City still plays a significant role in the political life of the metropolitan area. Its form of government has come down little changed from the Middle Ages, although the services it administers are those of a modern municipality.

The City is governed by three councils known as the Court of Common Hall, the Court of Common Council, and the Court of Aldermen. The Court of Common Hall—the Lord Mayor, aldermen, and liverymen of the several companies of the City of London, in Common Hall assembled—is a sort of town meeting. To be a liveryman a person must belong to one of the City companies, and by such membership one becomes a 'freeman' of the City. These 70 or so City companies—the Goldsmiths, the Fishmongers, the Mercers, the Vintners—were originally trade guilds including within their membership the persons engaged in these businesses or occupations in London. They still are nominally trade guilds, but now the members are for the most part important business figures of the City. Each

302–

City company is organized under a master, wardens, and other officials. The companies have handsome halls within the City where their affairs are conducted, including banquets and other social occasions to which invitations are eagerly sought. Some of the halls were destroyed during the bombing of London in the last war, but these are being restored in their customary magnificence. The City companies administer treasuries running to very large sums, much of the money being devoted to educational activities and other philanthropies with which individual companies have long been associated. The Court of Common Hall brings together the liverymen of the companies only twice a year; the first occasion is for the purpose of electing the sheriffs, the treasurer, the bridgemaster, and the City auditors, and the second of nominating a new Lord Mayor. Concerning the latter duty, their choice is limited to proposing two aldermen who have served as sheriff, and in practice they nominate the two senior aldermen.

The body with the real governing authority in the City is the Court of Common Council, which has 206 members elected from wards into which the City is divided. The electors, who consist of the residents of the City and all persons occupying business premises of more than nominal value, assemble once a year in wardmotes to choose councilmen. The Common Council meets regularly, has committees which deal with different aspects of municipal administration, and votes the annual budget of the City government. It also elects several administrative and ceremonial officials, including the town clerk, the comptroller and City solicitor, the remembrancer, the sword bearer, and the judicial officers of the Mayor's and the City of London Court.

The Court of Aldermen comprises a group of 25 members who are elected for life by the wards and who sit with the Common Council in its deliberations. The aldermen choose a number of City officials, including the clerk to the Lord Mayor, the recorder, the clerk to the Guildhall magistrates, the surveyors, and the steward of Southwark. To qualify for election as a councilman or alderman a person must be a freeman of the City, and in practice he must belong to one or more of the City companies. Elections of councilmen or aldermen are rarely contested.

The Court of Aldermen chooses each year a Lord Mayor, one of the two candidates proposed by the Court of Common Hall. From long before the time when Dick Whittington, as we are told in the nursery rhyme, was thrice Lord Mayor of London, the position has been one of great honor and prestige. Although the Lord Mayor presides at council meetings and takes an active part in municipal affairs, he is not a chief executive, and many of his duties are of a ceremonial kind. He is given an official residence, the Mansion House, where he entertains distinguished visitors to the nation's capital and where many activities connected with the charitable and philanthropic interests of the City are conducted. The Lord Mayor's office is a position which can only be occupied by a person of wealth, for the entertainment obligations far exceed the expenses of £12,500 which are given him. At the time of his induction the City provides a traditional parade, the Lord Mayor's Show, which is one of the attractions enjoyed by the people of the whole metropolis. Riding in a great state coach and wearing his robes and insignia of office, the Lord Mayor goes from the Law Courts, where his choice has been given royal approval, on a circuit of the City. He is accompanied by the other officers of the Corporation and followed by floats and displays which are usually designed to represent some aspect of the City's business interests.

While the medieval pageantry, the numerous ceremonial occasions, and the banqueting are the most obvious features of the municipal life of the City, there is a modern governmental organization which functions behind the showy façade. The City government has a number of municipal functions to perform, and it has a permanent staff of officials and employees to carry them out. It is responsible for the construction and maintenance of most of the streets of the City, and it provides for their lighting and cleaning. The City Corporation controls four bridges over the Thames— the Tower, London, Southwark, and Blackfriars Bridges. It builds and maintains libraries, bathhouses, and a few other public services, and it has its own police force. The corporation has a monopoly of managing public markets within a radius of seven miles from the City. These functions represent a reduction from times past when the City was responsible for navigation on the river and the management of the port and had other powers in places beyond the City boundaries. Its lost functions have passed to the County of London or to special authorities which have been established to administer them.

3. *The County of London*

Three or four hundred years ago the City of London began to break out of its enclosing walls, and the surrounding countryside became the residential area of a growing population. There had been a royal seat at Westminster from Saxon times, and during the centuries a good many people came to live near the palace and the great abbey founded by Edward the Confessor. Gradually, the area between the City and Westminster filled in, and the south bank of the river also became a closely populated district. From the eighteenth century onward the spread of London was constant and rapid. The City boundaries, however, were not extended, and the local government of the area beyond the City was in the hands of a multiplicity of holders whose jurisdiction in most cases was exceedingly small. By the middle of the nineteenth century there were literally hundreds of officials, councils, commissions, and special authorities attempting to govern or administer services in this sprawling metropolitan area. There were justices of the peace of Middlesex who exercised authority in the area; vestrymen of scores of parishes; commissioners of paving, sewers, and lighting who had responsibility for short stretches of public highway and limited local services; poor law guardians; and numerous other authorities. The metropolitan area was a veritable jungle of conflicting and overlapping jurisdictions.

304–

There was scarcely a session of Parliament which did not see the introduction of one or more bills designed to bring some order and efficiency
out of this chaotic situation. Reform, however, was difficult to achieve.
The City Corporation, which had been exempted from the Municipal Corporations Act of 1835, used its considerable political influence to block
any changes which it believed would derogate from its superior position
or would infringe upon any of its rights and prerogatives, and it was unwilling to see the City become the core of a much expanded and more
representative municipal government. The increasing pollution of the
Thames, which made sittings of Parliament and the courts uncomfortable
because of noxious odors, to say nothing of contributing to several serious
outbreaks of cholera, led Parliament in 1855 to create a Metropolitan
Board of Works to have jurisdiction over the sewers, highways, and other
physical aspects of the metropolis. The Metropolitan Board of Works
proved to be an unwieldy and frequently corrupt municipal agency, but it
did succeed in constructing a sewerage system which reduced the pollution of the Thames, in embanking parts of the river, and in laying out some
major thoroughfares. Other municipal activities, however, continued to be
neglected or handled inefficiently by the hosts of parish vestrymen and special commissioners whose unreformed existence went on.

A step forward was finally achieved in 1888 when a County of London
was created by the Parliamentary act establishing the system of administrative counties for the entire country. The County of London extended
over an area of 117 square miles and embraced a population of over three
million. Excluded from its jurisdiction for some functions was the old City,
and beyond its boundaries in nearly all directions there were many thickly
populated areas belonging to adjoining counties. Nevertheless, it covered
a compact urban area, and it inherited the functions of the abolished Metropolitan Board of Works, the justices of the peace, and a number of special authorities. Within its boundaries there still remained numerous parishes whose vestrymen had minor responsibilities within their tiny districts.

The governing body set up by the Act of 1888 consists of a county
council of 150 members, 129 of whom are elected every three years from
43 triple-member districts into which the area is divided. These councillors
add to their number by election 21 aldermen whose terms of office are six
years.[3] The Council thus composed chooses by annual election a Chairman
who in a sense is the mayor of most of London, a Vice-Chairman, and a

---

[3] The aldermen chosen are frequently Council candidates defeated for election or
re-election. It is the usual practice for the political parties to divide the aldermanic
seats in such a way that party strengths, as represented by the popularly elected councillors, are maintained. Concerning their qualifications Herbert Morrison has said:
'My own view is that Aldermen should be regarded as a means of strengthening the
Council, particularly on subjects where the Council as a whole or the party making
the nomination might otherwise be weak. Aldermen should add to the quality and
capacity of the Council and have adequate time for the responsibilities involved.
Looked at from this angle, it is a matter of indifference whether or not they are defeated candidates.' How London Is Governed (London, 1949), p. 62.

Deputy-Chairman. The Chairman and the Vice-Chairman are nominated by the majority party in the Council, while the Deputy-Chairman is proposed by the opposition. The Chairman divests himself of party connections and acts as an impartial presiding officer, much after the manner of the Speaker of the House of Commons. He applies and interprets, with the aid of the Clerk of the Council, the rather elaborate body of standing orders which govern the Council's procedure. The Council operates, like other municipal governments in Britain, through committees which are responsible for various functional activities and which supervise the administrative services of the county.

The Council is divided politically and has a Leader and a Leader of the Opposition. The Leader of the Council serves as the organizing and co-ordinating head of the majority party and as its tactician on policy and procedure. It is the business of the opposition leader to weld his party into a competent body of critics and to take the decisions and make the agreements required by the machinery of the Council. Each council committee has a chairman and a vice-chairman appointed by the majority party. The chairman presides at committee meetings, speaks for the committee in the council, and keeps in touch with the administrative officials concerned with the committee's functional responsibilities. The chairmen of the council's committees, the whips of the majority party, and a group of opposition members, proportionate to their party's number in the council, compose a general purposes committee. It is a kind of steering committee and decides disputes between other committees.

> As a piece of democratic machinery, the London County Council is an outstanding success which compares favourably with any other local authority in the world. Its administration in most fields—there are two or three exceptions—is highly efficient, and its integrity and competence in financial matters unrivalled. Its standing orders are excellent; it devotes a minimum of time and money to ceremony; and in general its proceedings are dignified, orderly and businesslike. The amount of unpaid public service which it evokes from its members is astonishing. The institution of the Leader of the Council and the Leader of the Opposition is a unique and valuable device among local authorities in Great Britain.
>
> The London County Council is probably by far the best organised local authority in England from the point of view of concentration of power, consistency, responsibility and leadership.[4]

The County Council has the responsibility for a considerable number of important municipal functions. It builds and maintains the principal streets and thoroughfares of the county. Sewers and drainage fall within its province. The L.C.C. is the educational authority of the county, constructing and managing primary, secondary, and a number of technical

---

[4] W. A. Robson, op. cit. p. 346.

schools. It is an authority for public housing, and the Council has constructed numerous large-scale housing projects within its own area and also beyond its boundaries on land it has acquired. The L.C.C. has a number of functions relating to public health and sanitation, and it maintains the fire protection service for the county area.

For the financial year 1952-53, the estimated expenditure of the L.C.C. was £67,149,000. Education claimed by far the largest amount, £25,128,285. Other large items of expenditure were: L.C.C. offices (general administrative services), £6 million; Housing, £9.6 million; Health services, £4.3 million; Children's services, £2 million; Fire brigade, £1.6 million; Parks, £1.4 million; Rivers and drainage, £1.5 million; Welfare, £2.3 million; Interest on debt, £5.7 million; Redemption of debt, £2.8 million.[5] The income to cover the County's expenditure came from local property taxes (rates), licenses and fees, payments for municipal services, and Exchequer grants. Percentage-wise the rates were expected to yield 45.5 per cent; Exchequer grants, 29 per cent; housing rents, 11.5 per cent, and miscellaneous sources, 14 per cent.

The County of London has an administrative service of approximately 66,000 officers and employees whose salaries and wages for the financial year 1952-53 were estimated at £29,868,465.[6] Teachers, numbering 18,108, comprised the largest category. The officers and employees of the County are organized in a number of departments, such as finance, health, parks, and education.[7] Each administrative department is headed by one of the 15 permanent, non-political chief officers of the Council. These officers include the Clerk of the Council, the Comptroller of the Council (chief financial officer), the Chief Engineer and County Surveyor, and the Chief Officer of the Parks Department. Besides managing their departments the chief officers are advisors of the Council and its committees. They attend committee meetings, submit reports and recommendations, and answer questions on departmental administration. The chief officers, according to Herbert Morrison, 'carry considerable influence with committees of the Council in the realm where officers should carry influence, namely, that of fact, soundness of administration, and the best method of putting into practice the policy of the Council.'[8] They are appointed by the Council upon the recommendation of an appropriate committee. Their salaries range from £2000 to £3750 a year.

The conditions of service of employees are determined by the L.C.C. except for classes, teachers for example, whose employment is subject to

---

[5] London County Council, *Annual Estimates* 1952-1953, pp. 10-15.

[6] Ibid. pp. 168-9.

[7] The offices of the L.C.C. are located in an imposing stone building on the Thames at the opposite end of Westminster Bridge from the Houses of Parliament.

[8] Op. cit. p. 60. Morrison exonerates the chief officers from any charge of attempting to 'run' the L.C.C. From his experience with administrative officials, in local government and as a minister of Crown, he states that 'as a whole, the officers of the London County Council are the least domineering of them all.'

national legislation or ministerial regulations. The L.C.C. recruits by competitive examinations, and on the whole its personnel policies and practices compare favorably with those of the national Civil Service. Its administrative services have established, in general, a good record for competence and efficiency.

4. *The Metropolitan Boroughs*

From the time the County of London was established it was obvious that some reform in the number and responsibilities of the parish authorities within its boundaries could not long be postponed. More than ten years were to elapse, however, before Parliament and the various interests concerned could agree upon a reform measure. Finally, in 1899 an act was passed which divided the County of London into 28 metropolitan boroughs which absorbed all the parish authorities and many other local bodies within their boundaries and which were given various municipal functions to perform. During the few years of its life, before the passage of the London Government Act, 1899, the London County Council had exhibited a considerable amount of progressive spirit that the more conservative interests in Parliament and in the municipal life of the community felt should be curbed. Consequently, the metropolitan boroughs were established with more power and with more ceremonial trappings than municipal reformers thought necessary. A desire to create counterweights to the County Council figured about as much in their constitution as the demands of effective government.

The metropolitan boroughs vary considerably in size and population. The area of Holborn is 406 acres while that of Woolwich is 8282 acres and that of Wandsworth 9107 acres. Holborn has about 40,000 inhabitants, Wandsworth almost ten times that many. Each metropolitan borough has an elected council with a chairman termed the mayor. The councillors enlarge their numbers by the election of aldermen. The councils have committees to consider and to supervise the administration of the activities for which the metropolitan boroughs are responsible. These activities include the construction and maintenance of streets and sidewalks, street lighting and cleaning, the provision of libraries, bathhouses and other public facilities, the construction and management of public housing properties, and the upkeep of parks, squares, and open spaces. The boroughs are the authorities for a number of inspection and regulatory services in connection with public health and sanitation. Each has an administrative service with a town clerk as the principal officer and with an engineer or surveyor, treasurer, and other necessary officials.

The metropolitan boroughs have a major part to play in the financial administration of the London area. They are the units which levy and collect the local taxes, known as the rates. The London County Council, which spends more than all the boroughs added together, issues demands, known as precepts, on the borough councils to meet its financial needs. These precepts are added to the expenses of the borough governments. In each borough the rates are levied on the occupiers of property according to its assessed or rateable value. Both rateable values and rates vary considerably from borough to borough. In some of the poorer, working-class districts the rateable values are relatively low and the rates high, while the reverse is the case in the wealthier boroughs. In order to reduce the differences in the burden of the rates, an equalizing scheme has been developed whereby the metropolitan boroughs in which the rateable value per head of population exceeds the national average of all local governments, contribute to the borough expenses of the boroughs below the average. The range between the highest and lowest rate levels has thus been considerably reduced, and the burden in relatively wealthy Westminster or St. Marylebone is much nearer to that of Stepney or Bethnal Green. In 1946-7, the City Corporation and the metropolitan boroughs raised £33,234,000 from rates.

Besides local taxation the metropolitan boroughs and the L.C.C. have income from services they provide and from national grants. All the grants are tied to particular municipal activities, such as education, children's services, fire protection, and housing, and are known as *ad hoc* grants. The metropolitan boroughs and the county formerly shared in the distribution of a 'block grant,' which could be used for any municipal function, but the Local Government Act of 1948 established a new method of giving 'untied' financial assistance to local authorities. By the act 'equalization grants' are given on the basis of need to local authorities where the rateable value per head of population is below the national average. The national government becomes, in effect, a rate-payer to the extent necessary to bring a particular local authority up to the national average. Since the metropolitan boroughs and the County of London exceed the national average they receive no equalization grants. The loss to the L.C.C. of income from the former block grants was more than offset by the national government's assumption of financial responsibility for hospital services, under the National Health Service Act, 1946, and for poor relief, under the National Assistance Act, 1948.[9]

All the local authorities are empowered to borrow money for various purposes. The metropolitan borough councils must obtain the approval of the L.C.C. or a national ministry depending upon the purpose of the loan. The L.C.C. must seek Parliamentary sanction.

5. *The Metropolitan Police District*

The County of London, the metropolitan boroughs, and the City constitute the chief municipal units for the metropolitan area. Several important municipal services, however, are administered by separate authorities

---

[9] The Exchequer grants in the L.C.C. budget for 1952-53 were: Education, £12,023,000; Health services, £2,096,070; Housing, £1,942,880; Children's services, £1,077,000; and Fire brigade, £719,320. London County Council, *Annual Estimates 1952-1953*, pp. 10-15.

whose jurisdiction does not coincide with the county and which bear no responsibility to either the L.C.C. or the borough councils. The oldest is the Metropolitan Police District.

Until the establishment of the Metropolitan Police in 1829, the policing of London had been a responsibility of the City corporation and of the numerous parishes and commissions of the peace beyond the City boundaries. It was not a responsibility which they discharged with any marked success. Crimes of various kinds were common, and in times of civil disturbance the only reliable measure was to call out the troops to restore order. In 1829 Sir Robert Peel decided that this unsatisfactory condition of affairs called for a remedy, and he established a police force for a district embracing the entire metropolitan area. The Metropolitan Police District, as fixed later in 1839, was an area with a radius of 15 miles from Charing Cross. The force was made responsible to the Home Secretary of the national government. Sir Robert's fame as a police reformer is immortalized in the name 'Bobbie' by which the London policeman is universally known.

Today the Metropolitan Police District covers an area of almost 700 square miles, thus extending far beyond the administrative County of London. The only separate police force within this district is that maintained by the City, which is organized under a commissioner responsible to the corporation. The City of London force consists of about 1000 officers and constables.

The Metropolitan Police are directed by a Chief Commissioner who is sometimes a retired military officer of high rank and distinction. Before the war, for example, Lord Trenchard, a retired Marshal of the Royal Air Force, was the Chief Commissioner from 1931 to 1935. Below the Chief Commissioner in the headquarters at Scotland Yard is a hierarchy of officers who command and direct the force and its various activities of crime detection and prevention.[10] The force numbers more than 15,000 policemen. The expenditure of the Metropolitan Police District is about £14 million annually, half being paid by the central government and half by the local councils of the District. The force is recruited by competitive examination, and its members have permanent tenure subject, of course, to standards of efficiency and conduct.

In 1933 Lord Trenchard established a training school at Hendon with the object of preparing the most promising young policemen for promotion to the higher ranks of the force. He also introduced a plan of training uni-

---

[10] Neither the Home Secretary nor Scotland Yard has direct control over the provincial police forces, of which there are 130 in England and Wales and 45 in Scotland. Each is organized under its own chief of police and is responsible to its own police authority—the council in county boroughs and a joint committee of councillors and magistrates in counties. Uniformity in pay scales and certain other conditions of service is required as a condition of receiving the 50 per cent grant made by the central government toward the cost of local police forces. As every reader of detective fiction knows, the local police frequently call upon Scotland Yard when they believe their own investigative resources are inadequate to solve a case.

versity graduates for direct appointment as police inspectors, from which rank they would be available for rapid promotion to the higher positions within the service. The Hendon College scheme was abandoned in 1939, partly because the bulk of the force objected to 'direct entry' for persons who had had no experience as a policeman on the beat. A successor school at Ryton in Warwickshire gives training to members of the Metropolitan police and also men from the provincial forces, but a student is required to have had five years' service as a constable and two years as a sergeant before entry. The new college is regarded as a satisfactory institution for the training of policemen to occupy middle-grade positions, but it does not take the place of the former training at Hendon in preparing officers for rapid promotion to controlling positions.[11] Promotions to the grade of inspector in the Metropolitan Police are made by competitive examination.

6. *Other Special Authorities*

One of the most important administrative agencies in the metropolitan region is the Port of London Authority. For many centuries the management of the London docks and the supervision of the river traffic on the Thames were vested in the City corporation. As London grew and the dock area came to extend for many miles below the City, the inadequacy of the Corporation as the controlling authority became recognized. Some agency was needed to undertake the maintenance of existing docks and to plan for the expansion of the port, which handled more water-borne traffic than any other in the world. Finally, in 1908 Parliament created a public corporation known as the Port of London Authority to have the responsibility of constructing all works in connection with the port, maintaining existing facilities, and performing the dredging necessary to keep the Thames navigable.

The Authority has a governing board of 28 members who represent the various interests concerned with the port. These include the City Corporation, the L.C.C., ship owners, merchants, the Ministry of Transport, and the Admiralty. The establishment of the Port of London Authority reduced the jurisdiction of the Thames Conservancy, first constituted in 1857. The Conservancy once had powers over navigation and docking facilities, but now its jurisdiction is limited to the nontidal stretches of the Thames and the river's tributaries. The Conservancy's board consists of 34 members appointed for three-year terms by government departments, the Port of London Authority, the Metropolitan Water Board, and various interested local governments.

Another special authority is the Metropolitan Water Board. From the time that London began to grow beyond the confines of its medieval walls the provision of water has presented a serious problem. Beginning in the eighteenth century there were incorporated a number of private companies supplying water to different parts of the metropolitan region. Their service

---

[11] *The Economist,* 19 February 1949, p. 319.

was never adequate, the metropolis from time to time experienced water famines, and there was always considerable doubt concerning the purity of the supply. The obvious remedy was a single authority empowered to undertake the necessary engineering works to give the metropolitan area an adequate and safe supply of water. Parliament finally recognized this need, after many official inquiries and reports, and in 1903 established the Metropolitan Water Board. It had authority to buy out the private companies then supplying water to parts of the area and to undertake the construction required to supply the metropolis with this essential service. The Board is composed of representatives from the local governments most interested in the service, including the City Corporation, the London County Council, and the councils of the metropolitan boroughs. The Board brings water from considerable distances beyond the limits of the metropolitan area and maintains reservoirs, pumping stations and mains for supplying some eight million people with water service.

One service of great importance in a metropolitan area such as London is that of transportation. Hundreds of thousands of people enter and leave the old City each business day, and for almost two centuries the tendency has been for Londoners to seek residential accommodation farther and farther from the center of the metropolitan area. In modern times transportation services have been provided by the railways, by horse-drawn and then motor bus services, by tramways, and by subways. Each of these modes of transportation was developed by a number of private companies, and there was little planning or co-ordination in their growth or service. The County Council in the early days of its existence expected to be made the transport authority for the area, but Parliament was never prepared to confer the necessary power upon the L.C.C. Consequently, the various services in the hands of private companies continued to exist, although the County Council did take over the operation of some tramway companies.

After several investigations and some ineffective steps toward improving the traffic situation of the metropolitan area, Parliament in 1933 passed the London Passenger Transport Act. This act established a board to take over and operate all the privately owned transportation facilities within a large area, nearly 2000 square miles, centering on the capital. The capital value of the equipment thus acquired amounted to more than £100 million. The act gave the new authority a monopoly of public transportation, except by main line railways and taxicabs, within its area.

The London Passenger Transport Board was composed of a chairman and six other members who were appointed by a body of trustees representing the London County Council and various business and professional associations. Under the direction of the Board, the transportation system of the huge metropolitan area was developed into a highly efficient service. Much new construction was undertaken and equipment was constantly improved. With the nationalization of all internal transportation services by the Transport Act of 1947, the London Passenger Transport Board came under the authority of the Transport Commission and it is now a unit in this vast nationalized undertaking.

312–

7. *Party Politics in London*

Because of the lack of any municipal authority which embraces the entire metropolitan region, the political life of London can only be discussed in terms of its component parts. The most vigorous municipal institution is the London County Council. When it was established in 1888 it attracted much interest from citizens who had been active in municipal reform and in the civic affairs of the area. Election contests in its early history were not directly related to national politics, and it seemed as though parties and issues of a local character might develop. This trend, however, was a brief one. Conservative leaders in national politics became alarmed at what they regarded as the radical tendencies displayed by the London County Council, and they called upon municipal voters to show their allegiance to Conservative policies by choosing party candidates for the L.C.C. Thus, the division in national politics between a Conservative element and a Liberal element was carried over into the municipal field. As at Westminster, the Labour Party in the course of time replaced the Liberals as one of the main contenders for power. A Liberal-Labour group was in control of the Council until 1907 when the Conservatives, under the name of the Municipal Reform Party, won a majority. They controlled the Council until 1934, and since that time Labour has had a majority. The division was very close after the election in 1949, but in 1952 Labour won 92 of the 129 seats. In 1949, the Conservatives received 51 per cent of the popular vote; Labour, 47 per cent; the Liberals, Communists, and others, 2 per cent. In 1952, the respective percentages were 44, 55, and 1.

Municipal elections are now fought by party organizations which are closely allied with their corresponding national parties. This is also true of elections for metropolitan borough councils.

Municipal politics in the London area does not excite the interest that national politics does. In the election of April 1949 for the London County Council slightly more than 40 per cent of the electorate voted in contrast to the 84 per cent casting ballots in the general election of February 1950. The L.C.C. election of 1949, however, brought out the second highest proportion of voters in 40 years. This relatively high percentage reflects in part the interest stimulated by the national political organizations and their desire to make a showing which would encourage their supporters throughout the country. The L.C.C. election, resulting as mentioned in an almost even division between the Conservative and Labour councillors, proved to be an accurate forecast of the national sentiment registered some ten months later.[12]

Beyond the boundaries of the London County Council, elections are fought for the great number of seats on borough, urban district and county

---

[12] In the May 1949 metropolitan borough council elections, 38.2 per cent of the eligible voters cast ballots. By boroughs the percentage voting ranged from 50.2 per cent in Fulham to 25.3 per cent in Shoreditch.

councils which lie, in whole or in part, within the metropolitan area on the same lines as other municipal contests in England. The division is usually between Conservatives and Labourites, although there is a high proportion of independent candidates seeking election.

8. *The Problem of London's Government*

Enough has been said about the government of the metropolitan area to indicate that it is the despair of the municipal reformer. In spite of numerous attempts for more than a century to obtain satisfactory municipal institutions for this region, metropolitan London remains broken into a conglomeration of authorities whose jurisdiction and powers are generally inadequate to their immense responsibilities.

During the war it was obvious that far-reaching plans would be necessary to reconstruct London and to provide the services which its tremendous population required. The damage resulting from bombing and the general dislocations occasioned by the war gave special emphasis to physical planning. The Minister of Town and Country Planning asked both the L.C.C. and the City corporation to prepare planning schemes for postwar reconstruction and development. When produced, neither was regarded as adequate. The plan offered by the City was considered as particularly unsatisfactory, and the Minister, in rejecting it, proposed that another attempt be made. This was subsequently done. Besides requesting plans for the County and the City, the Minister of Town and Country Planning also commissioned Sir Patrick Abercrombie, who had collaborated on the County of London plan, to prepare a scheme for the future development of the London region, an area having a radius of 30 miles from Charing Cross.

The Abercrombie Plan was a comprehensive scheme for the reconstruction and development of the area beyond the County boundaries. It envisaged the movement of about a million inhabitants from inner to outer London and the control of industrial location to prevent future excessive concentrations of population. The plan also dealt with the provision of parks and open spaces and transportation services for the enlarged area.

One of the outstanding features of the Abercrombie Plan was the proposal that several new towns be created, enough to house about 400,000 inhabitants. The development of these satellite communities received Parliamentary endorsement in the New Towns Act of 1946 which authorized the Minister of Town and Country Planning to create public corporations to proceed with their construction. Under the authority of the act, eight corporations were established to develop self-contained towns at distances of 30 to 40 miles from the center of London. The work has proceeded slowly, however, and in 1950 *The Economist* was led to remark, 'At this rate of building the new towns will provide no solution either to the problem of overcrowding or to that of strategic dispersal.' [13]

---

[13] 17 August 1950, p. 305

In 1951 the L.C.C. approved for submission to the Minister of Housing and Local Government a 20-year development plan for the administrative county. Using the earlier county plan and the Abercrombie regional plan as foundations, the new scheme dealt in detail with the county's physical development during the next five years and outlined more generally a program for the 20-year period. The cost of the council's proposals for street and highway construction, schools, parks, slum clearance, and other improvements, was estimated at £27 million annually or a total of £540 million. In approving the plan, members of the L.C.C. noted that its successful realization would depend upon the co-operation of the national government and neighboring authorities, particularly in regard to the housing of several hundred thousand people who cannot be adequately accommodated within the county's boundaries.[14]

The principal difficulty with respect to the satisfactory planning and development of London lies where it has existed for centuries; namely, the lack of a municipal authority with sufficient jurisdiction and power to carry out comprehensive schemes of municipal improvement and to administer the required municipal services. The London County Council has jurisdiction only over the inner circle of the metropolitan area, and its authority is shared with the City Corporation and the councils of the metropolitan boroughs. Beyond its boundaries are scores of separate authorities with diverse and often conflicting interests. Within the Metropolitan Police District, outside of the County of London, are three county boroughs, 35 boroughs, 30 urban districts, four rural districts, and six parishes with councils, besides the County of Middlesex and parts of four other counties. The tendency in recent years to increase the powers of the county councils and county boroughs has aggravated London's problems, for the counties which are partly in the metropolitan area are now responsible for more activities and services than formerly and are more jealous of their powers. Their main concerns are with those areas beyond the metropolitan district, and they do not wish planning for London to encroach upon their own local schemes. Moreover, such regional development as has occurred has produced increased disintegration within London. The regions established by the nationalized industries for their administrative purposes create new one-purpose authorities and the boundaries marked out conform to no existing lines. The hospitals of Greater London, under the National Health Service, are administered by four regional boards. So the cutting up of the London area continues.

What is plainly required is the establishment of a regional authority for Greater London. One such scheme was proposed by Professor Robson before the last war.[15] It envisaged a popularly elected Greater London Council having jurisdiction over an area of about 2400 square miles. The metropolitan boroughs, by this plan, would be consolidated into 10 or 12

---

[14] *The Times,* 14 and 19 December 1951.
[15] Op. cit. pp. 327-402.

units and the boroughs and districts outside the present County of London into about 17 units, all with elected councils. The new regional government would absorb the present county and special authorities. There would be an appropriate division of functions between the regional council and the new district councils.

Some such plan appears to be the solution to the existing jumble of authorities. It would create governmental units adequate with respect to jurisdiction and functions to meet the requirements of metropolitan life. Furthermore, it would preserve local self-government which is suffering erosion as municipal powers are transferred to appointed bodies and to public corporations. The opportunity still exists to transform London, like nineteenth-century Italy, into something more than a geographical expression.

XVIII

Policy and Administration: National Security

One of the primary functions of any government is to provide for the country's national security. So important is this responsibility usually regarded that it has first call upon the human and material resources of the state.

1. *The Security Responsibilities of the United Kingdom*

The British government faces serious problems in endeavoring to assure the national security. Being a densely populated country occupying one island and part of a second, the United Kingdom is particularly vulnerable to being starved out. Consequently, the security of the United Kingdom is not solely a matter of defense against direct attack, but it also means insuring the continuous arrival of supplies to maintain national life. Until the twentieth century Britain's island position was extremely advantageous from the security point of view; since 1066 no foreign invader had successfully obtained a lodgment on its shores, although Napoleon gave the English some anxious times until Nelson won the battle of Trafalgar. The revolution in warfare produced by the airplane, however, has considerably reduced Britain's physical security. During World War II, British cities were heavily bombed, and in any future conflict the certainty of attack by air would have to be accepted.

In addition to the defense of the British Isles and the sea approaches, the United Kingdom has other security commitments of a serious nature. As the leading colonial power in the world it has many overseas possessions for whose security it is primarily responsible. Some of these colonial territories are neither threatened by their neighbors nor by other imperialist powers, and their defense is no great burden upon the United Kingdom. Included within this category are the British colonies in the West Indies, most of the African possessions, and the small islands in the Pacific. A number of others, however, are by no means so secure. Some of them, such as Gibraltar, Malta, and Singapore, are located in areas of high strategic importance, and their military value for defensive or offensive operations is a first consideration in policy with regard to them. Other colonial dependencies occasionally face threats to their internal security which must be met by Great Britain. The postwar situation in Malaya is a case in point.

−317

The United Kingdom's primacy in the British Commonwealth of Nations also imposes security obligations. With the independence of the dominions there is no constitutional responsibility upon the United Kingdom to guarantee the security of these countries, but there is a strong moral obligation and a stronger requirement of self-interest. They have rallied to Britain's side in two world wars, and no British Government could consider being less loyal in a crisis. Together these Commonwealth countries become a formidable military power; separately only the United Kingdom has a large military potential, and that is greatly enhanced by the contributions of the dominions. The United Kingdom, therefore, freely accepts a responsibility in regard to the security of each of the dominions.

A scarcely lighter responsibility is accepted for the security of several independent states whose geographical position is of vital importance to basic British interests. Some of these obligations are embodied in defensive treaties with foreign states; others are assumed through the close interest which Britain takes in their affairs. By the Brussels Treaty of Western Union the United Kingdom is bound in a close military alliance with France, Belgium, the Netherlands, and Luxemburg. This agreement takes its place as one of the basic stones in the security edifice known as the North Atlantic Treaty. Through the latter treaty Britain is militarily committed to the United States, Canada, Norway, Denmark, Italy, and Portugal as well as to its Western Union allies.

In the Middle East, Egypt occupies a special place in British security considerations. As the site of the Suez Canal and the land bridge between Asia and Africa, Egypt must, in British thinking, be a friendly, independent power, and any threat to the security of the Nile Kingdom calls forth a strong British reaction. Hardly less important in British strategic considerations are the independence and friendly attitude of Greece, Turkey, the Arab states, and Iran.

As a permanent member of the Security Council of the United Nations, Great Britain has obligations under the Charter to share in keeping the peace and in guaranteeing the territorial integrity of other members. While the universal security promises of the United Nations have been seriously jeopardized by the unco-operative policies of Soviet Russia and its communist satellites, the British still regard the world organization as an important stabilizing influence and one to which they are committed to give their support.

In summary, the government of the United Kingdom always faces security problems of extreme gravity and complexity. It naturally puts the defense of the British Isles as a first charge upon its resources, but more than any other country it must consider the security of distant colonial dependencies, neighboring states, and strategically placed countries in the Near and Middle East as only slightly less important than its own territory. Britain's security is tremendously enhanced by the close identity of British and American interests in world affairs. The nature of world politics is such that the strategic areas which the British regard as of great importance to their security are in general those of significance to Washington. Without such a community of interest it can hardly be doubted that the security responsibilities of the United Kingdom would be beyond its present resources and capabilities.

2. *Diplomacy*

The government of the United Kingdom undertakes to guarantee the security of Britain and its far-flung interests through diplomacy and through the maintenance of sizable military forces. The diplomatic powers of the British government are derived in general from the royal prerogative. The Crown possesses the power to conduct relations with foreign states, to send and to receive diplomatic representatives, to negotiate treaties, and to declare war and make peace. While these powers may be exercised without reference to Parliament, it is politically necessary that the general conduct of foreign relations and the most important diplomatic actions of the British Government have the approval of a Parliamentary majority.

The control of Parliament over foreign affairs is less restrictive than it is in the case of domestic policies. The relative freedom which the Government has in conducting foreign relations results from the tradition that the Crown should not be closely supervised in this complicated and frequently delicate field of policy. Parliamentary interest in foreign affairs has increased, however, since the First World War, and the Government nowadays feels it necessary and usually desires to keep the Houses of Parliament well informed on foreign relations and to have strong Parliamentary support behind British policies. Moreover, in these times foreign and domestic affairs touch at so many points that no Government can separate them into compartments and assume widely different attitudes with respect to Parliamentary control. A Cabinet today, it is believed correct to say, could not withhold from Parliament a knowledge of commitments of the kind that developed out of the British military conversations with France and Belgium prior to World War I.[1]

On several occasions during a Parliamentary session the two Houses of Parliament stage debates on foreign policy. Some of these occur as the result of ordinary Parliamentary business; other debates are requested by the opposition, following probably an important development in interna-

---

[1] In this case not only was Parliament uninformed but some members of the Cabinet were ignorant, at least until 1912, of how far Britain was obligated. 'The Government's right hand in domestic affairs,' Professor Smellie wrote, 'did not know what its left was doing in foreign affairs. All the things that mattered were conveyed in private and confidential letters from our diplomatic representatives abroad to the Foreign Secretary personally, in his private and unpublished replies and in the interviews which he held with the ambassadors at the Foreign Office in Downing Street.' K. B. Smellie, *A Hundred Years of English Government* (New York, 1937), p. 237.

tional affairs. At such times the Secretary of State for Foreign Affairs, supported by ministerial colleagues, expounds and defends the current policies of the Government, and opposition leaders criticize what they consider to be the mistakes and failures in this field. From such debates the Government senses the extent to which its policies have support throughout Parliament. Debates of this kind in the House of Commons are not followed by divisions unless a resolution or a motion of censure is before the House, but when such is the case the size of the Government's majority is frequently indicative of the popularity of the current foreign policy. In the House of Lords foreign policy debates rarely come to a vote, but they usually evoke able speeches from a number of peers with extensive experience in diplomatic affairs. In the Commons the question hour offers another opportunity for Parliamentary intervention in the field of foreign affairs. Opposition members of the House of Commons frequently ask questions on matters pertaining to foreign relations, and these are answered by the Foreign Secretary or one of his ministerial assistants. If the Foreign Secretary deems it undesirable to answer a question he so states, and the House is usually tolerant of this reticence when it recognizes that delicate negotiations are in progress which might be jeopardized by premature disclosures.

Although the treaty-making power is in no sense shared with Parliament and no legislative ratification is required to make a treaty valid, it is customary for important agreements with foreign nations to be laid before Parliament for debate and approval. After the First World War the Labour Party advocated the debate and approval of all important treaties before their conclusion by the Government, but this practice has not been established and Labour Governments in office have followed much the same policy as other Governments. When the North Atlantic Treaty was being negotiated the Government refused to accept a Labour member's suggestion that the pact be debated in Parliament before signature. The Lord President of the Council, Herbert Morrison, stated: 'We shall follow the customary British Parliamentary practice. The provisional signature of the document is the responsibility of the Government. As I have said before, there follows, however, the responsibility of the House of Commons to ratify or not to ratify, and that will give an appropriate opportunity for Debate.' [2] Parliamentary ratification may be taken as assured, of course, for disapproval of a treaty signed by the Crown would be tantamount to overthrowing the Government. Less important treaties are negotiated and signed by the Crown and are not referred to Parliament for approval or ratification. The Government assumes that the general confidence in which it is held by the House of Commons extends to the negotiation and signature of such agreements.

The minister responsible for the conduct of foreign relations is the Sec-

---

[2] 462 *H.C. Debates* 5s., col. 1400.

320–

retary of State for Foreign Affairs. This office is naturally one of the most important Cabinet positions and its occupant is always a leading member of the Government. In this century the position has been held by such outstanding figures as Sir Edward Grey (afterwards Earl Grey of Fallodon), Lord Curzon, Sir Austen Chamberlain, Anthony Eden, and Ernest Bevin. While the Foreign Secretary has considerable freedom in the formulation of policy and the conduct of relations with other countries, he is nevertheless a member of the ministerial group and takes no important step without the approval of his Cabinet colleagues. It is necessary for him to work in a relationship of mutual trust and confidence with the Prime Minister who bears responsibility for the Government's total policy. If a Prime Minister and his Foreign Secretary find that their views on foreign policy diverge, the latter has no course but to resign. A situation of this kind occurred just before World War II when Prime Minister Chamberlain's inclination toward appeasement was unacceptable to Anthony Eden, the Foreign Secretary. Eden was succeeded by Lord Halifax, but Chamberlain took over much of the direction of foreign affairs and his ill-fated journeys to negotiate a settlement with Hitler are well remembered.

Since the First World War the burden of work falling upon a Foreign Secretary has been so heavy that it has been necessary for him to have the assistance of one or two other ministers. Between the wars one minister usually relieved the Foreign Secretary of much of the business connected with the League of Nations. With the establishment of the United Nations this practice has continued, and a Minister of State usually heads the British delegation to the General Assembly and conducts other important United Nations business. Besides the Minister of State, the Foreign Secretary is assisted by two junior ministers, Parliamentary Under Secretaries of State for Foreign Affairs. They relieve the Foreign Secretary of some of his departmental responsibilities and substitute for their chief in Parliamentary debates and during the question hour.

The Foreign Office is the department headed by the Secretary of State for Foreign Affairs, and it is organized in much the same way as other ministries, although the proportion of senior and policy-making officials is higher than in the typical administrative agency. Except for the Secretary of State, the Minister of State, and the two Parliamentary Under Secretaries of State, all other officials are permanent officers. The highest ranking is the Permanent Under Secretary of State for Foreign Affairs. Like his counterparts in other ministries, he is responsible for the efficient management of the Foreign Office, and he is the Secretary's principal advisor on policy matters. Currently, the Foreign Office has an additional Permanent Under Secretary who is in charge of the German Section.

Reporting to the regular Permanent Under Secretary of State are the Deputy Under Secretary of State (Political), who has charge of United Nations matters, and the Deputy Under Secretary of State (Economic), who supervises four departments dealing with foreign economic relations.

There are nine Assistant Under Secretaries of State who report directly to the Permanent Under Secretary or through a Deputy Under Secretary. The Assistant Under Secretaries supervise a group of departments, the departments being the basic units of Foreign Office organization. Nine of the departments are concerned with political matters in different areas of the world, e.g. the American Department, the African Department, and the Far East Department. Other departments handle such matters as passports, Foreign Office personnel, cultural relations, consular activities, and communications.

The Foreign Office is represented overseas by members of the Foreign Service. The functions of the Foreign Service, in the words of an examination announcement of the Civil Service Commission, are 'to represent His Majesty's Government in foreign countries and to be their channel of communication with foreign governments; to promote good relations with foreign countries; to protect British interests and to foster British trade.' The announcement adds for the enlightenment of candidates for the Foreign Service, 'The art of diplomacy consists of making the policy of one government understood and, if possible, accepted by other governments.'

Britain formerly had a diplomatic service which was a separate corps of officials, but in 1921 it was amalgamated with the personnel of the Foreign Office to form a unified service. A further reform was accomplished at the close of World War II. This was based on recommendations contained in a white paper which said that new conditions in international affairs required changes in Britain's representation in foreign countries. 'Economics and finance have become inextricably interwoven with politics; an understanding of social problems and labour movements is indispensable in forming a properly balanced judgment of world events. The modern diplomat should have a more intimate understanding of these special problems, and greater opportunities to study them than he usually possessed in the past. His training and experience must be wider.' [3] Besides broadening the service to include officers concerned with economic problems, cultural affairs, and informational activities, the latest reforms amalgamated the diplomatic, commercial, and consular branches.

The Foreign Service consists of four branches. All members of the Service are recruited by competitive examinations administered by the Civil Service Commission, and they occupy permanent, pensionable positions. Members are liable for service at home or abroad.

Branch A or the political branch has a strength of about 750 officers. They staff the political departments of the Foreign Office and fill the principal diplomatic positions abroad—the posts of ambassador, minister, counsellor, secretary, consul-general, and consul. The grades, salaries, and titles of Branch A are given below:

---

[3] Cmd. 6420 (1943).

322–

Grade	Pay Scales	Title
9	£ 400-£ 560	Third and Second Secretary, Vice
8	£ 615-£ 750	Consul
7	£ 950-£1250	First Secretary, Consul
6	£1320-£1700	
5	£1700	Posts ranging from Counsellor and
4	£2000	Consul-General to Minister, Am-
3	£2250	bassador, Under Secretary of
2	£2500	State
1	£3500	

(Members of the Service stationed abroad receive living allowances which vary with their posts and responsibilities. Women officers' salaries are slightly lower for each grade of the Service.)

Admission to Branch A of the Foreign Service is open to any British subject between the ages of 20½ and 24 who can meet the examination requirements. The competitions for entry are administered by the Civil Service Commission, and the testing procedures are similar to those used for the Administrative Class of the Home Civil Service, with Method II being employed for candidates who have at least a second-class honors degree from an approved university. Successful candidates are sent abroad at public expense to study and gain fluency in European languages. They are examined again upon their return, and those passing are appointed to the Foreign Service in a probational status. Besides their language study, young officers receive instruction in the work of diplomacy, the organization of the Foreign Office and diplomatic missions, and in the relations of the Foreign Office to other government departments. Later stages of their training may include refresher courses in the Foreign Office, instruction in oriental languages, attachments to the Office of Commonwealth Relations or some other ministry, and attendance at the Imperial Defence College.

Branch B of the Foreign Service comprises the officers who perform the administrative work connected with the Foreign Office and the missions abroad. Its personnel is comparable to the Foreign Service Staff officers of the American Foreign Service. Branch B consists of approximately 1500 employees classified in six grades ranging from Clerical Officer to Deputy Accountant General. About half serve in London and half abroad. Admission to Branch B is through competitive examinations given to young men and women between the ages of 16 and 18½. Transfer from Branch B to Branch A is possible.

Branch C consists of about 500 stenographic and typist positions. Transfer to Branch B is open to its members. Branch D comprises about 85 men who are resident messengers and custodial employees in overseas missions. Courier service between London and British embassies and legations is performed by the Corps of Queen's Messengers. The corps numbers about 50, many being retired military officers.

Like other diplomatic services, the British Foreign Service has been subjected to considerable criticism on the grounds that most of its members come from the upper classes of society and that they are not sufficiently attuned to social developments at home. The Labour Party was for long critical of British representation abroad, and many Labourites advocated a thorough overhauling of the Foreign Service when their party came into power. However, the reforms mentioned above have met many of their criticisms, and the leaders of the postwar Labour Government were generally satisfied with the service. A few noncareer ambassadors were appointed, but in general the Labour Government did not disturb the regular advancement of career officers.[4]

Although not strictly a part of the regular diplomatic organization of the British government, the Commonwealth Relations Office and the United Kingdom high commissioners in dominion capitals constitute a subsidiary foreign relations service. There is a fairly regular rotation of officers between London and Ottawa, Wellington, New Delhi, and the other capitals. The Commonwealth Relations Office undertakes to keep the dominions informed of trends in the formulation of British foreign policy and through it consultation is conducted on all issues of Commonwealth interest. This consultation may take place in London where all the dominions are represented by high commissioners, or it may take the form of British high commissioners in dominion capitals consulting with the various dominion governments. Foreign policy frequently is an important item on the agenda of Commonwealth conferences. Moreover, some important questions in the field of foreign affairs occasionally form the subject matter of a conference of Commonwealth foreign ministers. One such was held at Colombo, Ceylon, in January 1950 to consider Far Eastern problems. While the practice of consultation with the dominions sometimes delays the formulation of foreign policy by the United Kingdom and also may involve the adoption of a compromise point of view, the British regard the extra strength coming from an agreed Commonwealth position as usually justifying the cost. It is not always possible, however, for complete agreement to be achieved through the process of consultation, and the United Kingdom and various dominions sometimes take opposing positions in the United Nations and in other international organizations. Such differences seldom occur on issues of the highest importance.

3. *Military Forces*

In addition to diplomacy, the United Kingdom undertakes to guarantee its security through the maintenance of sizable military forces. British

---

[4] It was occasionally suggested that the trade union background of Foreign Secretary Bevin and many of his Labour colleagues accounted for this recognition of the vested rights of a career organization. It is more probable that the Labour Government discovered in the Foreign Service a specially able and loyal group of officials and believed that British interests might well be injured by the use of professionally untrained and untried diplomatic representatives.

political leaders subscribe to the belief that diplomacy unsupported by military power can never be effective in assuring the security of a country like the United Kingdom. While never justifying the characterization of a militaristic power, Britain in modern times has always been prepared to use force if diplomatic means fail to accomplish the ends of national policy.

The powers of the British government in the raising and maintenance of military forces are completely adequate. The Crown has inherited from the royal prerogative the power to declare war and to command and direct the military forces of the nation, and Parliament regularly bestows the additional authority required to maintain the Army, Navy, and Air Force. Because the cost of supporting military forces and fighting wars was one of the chief financial burdens to be borne by the country, Parliament early took an interest in this matter and today supervises the general direction of military policy and considers the financial obligations involved. The size of the military forces, their pay, the cost of their equipment, and the broad outlines of military organization are determined by the appropriations of Parliament. It would be possible for a Government to pursue briefly military policies that were contrary to the wishes of Parliament, but it would soon need to seek financial support from the legislature. Moreover, the Army Act, which is essential to the legal conduct of the Army and the discipline of the forces, is a statute which must be renewed annually by Parliament. Hence, general military policy is subject to the same parliamentary control and scrutiny as other Government policy; this is to say, the Cabinet must conduct military policy in such a way that it has the continuous confidence of the House of Commons.

In time of war Parliament bestows additional powers upon the Government. During World War I this was done principally by the Defence of the Realm Act, and in 1939 Parliament passed the Emergency Powers Act. These statutes were designed to enable the Government to mobilize the full resources of the United Kingdom in the prosecution of the war, and they authorized the taking of many actions by administrative order which in peacetime would have required acts of Parliament. Thus, in World War II the British Government was authorized to introduce and administer by order such matters as food rationing, the allocation of raw materials and supplies to industry, civil defense regulations, the requisitioning of private property for military purposes, the incarceration without trial of potentially dangerous persons, the censorship of postal and telegraph communications, the requirement of civilian identity cards, and the control of travel to and from the United Kingdom. A totalitarian dictatorship could scarcely have wished for more sweeping powers than those possessed by the Government of the United Kingdom during World War II. They were freely given, and, in general, never abused. Parliament remained to keep watch on their exercise, and the courts were always available to see that administrative action was within the law. The ability of members of Parliament to ask questions and to criticize meant that abuses of power through misdirected zeal or malevolence were brought to light,

—325

and the judiciary required military and civilian authorities to exercise their powers in accordance with the principles of British justice.

In time of peace, general military policy is formulated and decided upon by the Cabinet, subject of course to existing legislation. One of the most important Cabinet committees is that on defense. It is presided over by the Prime Minister and includes the Minister of Defence, the Lord President of the Council, the Chancellor of the Exchequer, the Foreign Secretary, the First Lord of the Admiralty, the Secretary of State for War, the Secretary of State for Air, the Minister of Labour, and the Minister of Supply. All important policy questions—for example, the size of the military forces, the continuance or abolition of conscription, the general disposition of the forces throughout the world—come before this committee for discussion and decision. Issues of great import will also come before the full Cabinet, but because of the high rank of the ministers sitting in the Defence Committee it is not likely that the Cabinet will have different views from this group.

Military policies requiring Parliamentary approval are presented to the legislature, like other policy proposals, by a responsible minister who explains and defends the Government's position. Thus, the financial cost of the military services is included in the estimates submitted by the Minister of Defence and are considered by Parliament until they eventually find a place in the Appropriation Act. Nonfinancial defense policy matters probably will be presented to Parliament and defended there by this Minister. If new or amending legislation is involved, the Government introduces a bill which goes through the usual procedure for public bills.

Parliament takes considerable interest in military policy, and the debates in both houses are usually informing reviews of the Government's stewardship. The opposition is ordinarily interested to see that the country is getting its money's worth from the large sums appropriated for the military services, and it directs its criticism to all aspects of the subject. While the Government is normally prepared to reveal almost all information concerning the military establishment, there are naturally some subjects which must be concealed for security reasons and cannot be safely made the subject of partisan debate. Even in such cases, the Government frequently recognizes that the opposition has a right to know the general situation with respect to the country's defenses. The Prime Minister takes the occasion, therefore, to convey to the Leader of the Opposition and probably a few of the latter's closest colleagues information which cannot be disclosed in public. The Prime Minister is under no constitutional obligation to take the Leader of the Opposition into his confidence, nor is the Leader of the Opposition obliged to accept information in this way if he feels that he would limit his future usefulness as a critic of the Government; but the practice is followed from time to time in order that debates on military policy may center on real issues and not concern themselves with points that could readily be answered but for security restrictions.

326–

4. *The Development of the Defense Organization*

The British have given a good deal of attention to the problems involved in creating the proper organization, both in periods of peace and of war, to consider military policy and to provide for its implementation. Their efforts, some of them experimental, are worth describing in some detail. The year 1904 may be taken as a starting point, for then the inadequacies of British governmental machinery for planning, directing, and supporting extensive military operations, revealed in the Crimean War and later in the Boer War, finally brought about some remedial measures. The principal change at this time was the establishment of the Committee of Imperial Defence. It was organized as an advisory and consultative Cabinet committee under the presiding authority of the Prime Minister and with a permanent secretariat.

For several years prior to the outbreak of war in 1914 the Committee concerned itself with reviewing British strategic plans and with formulating the policies that should become operative shortly before and after engaging Britain's principal potential enemy, the German Empire. Aspects of the total problem—the defense of India, defense against invasion, naval strategy—were undertaken by subcommittees and integrated by a co-ordinating committee. The finished plans were 'incorporated in a document known as the War Book, in which the responsibility of every Government Department under every heading of war emergency action was laid down both for a Precautionary Stage and a War Stage. It was designed to show every Department, not only what it had to do itself, but what other Departments were doing in the matter. Every piece of legislation; every set of instructions; every order, letter, cable, telegram, including those to fleets, military stations, the Dominions, India and the Colonies (some taking the form of dormant instructions in their possession) was drafted and kept ready for issue.' [5] The co-ordination of the plans of the United Kingdom and the dominion and Indian governments was achieved through the exchange of staff officers, ministerial visits—including attendance at meetings of the Committee of Imperial Defence—and discussions at the Imperial Conferences of 1907, 1909, and 1911.

For the first few months of the 1914-18 conflict the day-to-day management of the British war effort was carried on by the full Cabinet of 21 members, but experience soon proved that no body so large and composed of members with so many diverse departmental preoccupations could give the continuous direction to strategic operations and plans that was required. The Prime Minister established, therefore, a War Council of eight members, which was practically the Committee of Imperial Defence but included a leading member of the Conservative opposition, Balfour, and the chiefs of staff of the army and navy. The War Council adopted the practice of the Committee of Imperial Defence of working from an agenda, which the Cabinet had never done, and it utilized the services of the Com-

---

[5] Lord Hankey, *Government Control in War* (Cambridge, 1945), p. 27.

mittee's secretary. A political crisis resulting in the formation of a coalition Government also led to the scrapping of the War Council in favor of a Cabinet committee, called the Dardanelles Committee. Although created to consider the critical matters involved in the Dardanelles campaign, the committee began perforce to deal with the many interrelated phases of the war. It consisted of 12 ministerial members and the two chiefs of staff. The secretary and his assistants of the former War Council continued to serve the new committee.

The Dardanelles Committee gave way, late in 1915, to a new Cabinet committee intended to supervise the total war effort. The War Committee, as it was known, grew from six to 13 members. It was served by the same secretariat as its predecessors.

Dissatisfaction within the Cabinet, Parliament, and the country led in December 1916 to a reorganization of the Government with Lloyd George succeeding Asquith as Prime Minister. Lloyd George immediately reshaped the top machinery for directing the nation's war efforts. Abolishing the War Committee, he created a War Cabinet of himself and four other members—Bonar Law, Chancellor of the Exchequer; Lord Curzon, Lord President of the Council; and Lord Milner and Arthur Henderson, Ministers without Portfolio. The War Committee's secretariat became the secretariat of the Cabinet, preparing an agenda for meetings, keeping minutes, and distributing Cabinet reports and papers to the appropriate ministries.

The War Cabinet had several advantages over its predecessor bodies as an effective instrument for directing the war. Being the Cabinet, it did not have to refer important decisions to a larger group as had the previous committees. It was small enough to meet daily, and its members, with the exception of the Chancellor of the Exchequer, were free of heavy departmental responsibilities. Moreover, they could individually seek to resolve thorny interdepartmental problems and head *ad hoc* committees without involving the whole Cabinet. Ministers outside the War Cabinet were called in whenever a subject concerning their responsibilities was on the agenda.

> The War Cabinet therefore became in effect the Supreme Control in commission with the Prime Minister as the dominating and directing force, but it was supplemented by this system of delegation, which provided a safeguard against congestion of business.[6]

With a reversion after victory to the prewar Cabinet system the Committee of Imperial Defence was re-established, in late 1919, and again began the study of military and strategic problems and the formulation of policy proposals. As before, various questions were remitted to subcommittees, and the co-ordinating committee integrated and consolidated their work for presentation to the Cabinet. One important organizational development occurred in 1923. That was the creation of a Chiefs of Staff Committee composed of the three service heads of the armed forces and

---

[6] Lord Hankey, op. cit. p. 41.

presided over by the Prime Minister or a deputy. Supplemented later by a Joint Planning Committee and a Joint Intelligence Committee, the Chiefs of Staff Committee prepared the plans to give effect to the policy decisions recommended by the Committee of Imperial Defence and approved by the Cabinet. The co-ordination of the work of the Committee of Imperial Defence and the Chiefs of Staff Committee was insured by the use of a common secretariat.

By 1935 the British defense organization represented a highly satisfactory mechanism for the study and determination of broad policy issues and their elaboration into military plans for the armed services. Much of the planning remained in a paper stage, for the emphasis of successive Governments during the interwar years was more on disarmament and military economy than on preparing for a future major conflict; but nevertheless the consideration and planning of defense matters went forward. A war book along the lines of that developed before 1914 was kept up to date. The book 'was an administrative document listing the hundreds of telegrams and messages, which were drafted in advance, which had to be sent all over the world, giving orders about mobilization, censorship, blockades, control of aliens and other matters when war became imminent.'[7]

Where the organization exhibited a weakness was in the 'absence from the machinery of the Committee of Imperial Defence of a guiding hand to formulate a unified defence policy for the three Services.'[8] The Admiralty, the War Office, and the Air Ministry were each represented in the Cabinet, and their respective ministers prosecuted departmental claims at the highest political level. Although agreement was achieved on most major policy questions through the medium of the Committee of Imperial Defence, and on the implementing plans through the Chiefs of Staff Committee, there remained an area where co-ordination was rare and confusion common. To fill this need there was appointed in 1936 a Minister for Co-ordination of Defence. The position was not endowed with sufficient powers to achieve a great deal, and the first occupant, Sir Thomas Inskip, was described by Churchill as 'an able lawyer, who had the advantages of being little known himself and knowing nothing about military subjects.'[9]

When war came in 1939 the British governmental system adapted itself much more quickly to its new burdens than had been the case in 1914. In accordance with earlier planning, the Committee of Imperial Defence was

---

[7] *The Times,* 4 December 1951. Just before the outbreak of the Second World War, the Government was reluctant to translate the war book into action for fear of heightening international tensions, Lord Ismay revealed during a debate on a new Home Guard Bill. 'We did not pay dearly for that lack of timely preparation,' he said, 'because in the first six months of the war it was "a phoney war" and the war book . . . served its purpose admirably when the signal came.'

[8] Cmd. 6923 (1946).

[9] Winston S. Churchill, *The Gathering Storm* (Boston, 1948), p. 200. Churchill was considered for the position, but the Conservative party leaders were not then ready to receive him back in the fold.

dissolved and a War Cabinet established. The Chamberlain War Cabinet differed, however, from that created by Lloyd George in the later years of World War I. It consisted of ten or eleven members, including the Minister for the Co-ordination of Defence and the three service ministers; only two members did not head important government departments, and there were no representatives of the Parliamentary opposition. The Chiefs of Staff attended Cabinet meetings as professional advisors, and the secretariat which had served the Cabinet and the Committee of Imperial Defence undertook this role for the War Cabinet.

The catastrophic military events of the spring of 1940 resulted in major changes in the British organization for directing the war effort. The Minister for the Co-ordination of Defence, finding his position superfluous, had resigned just before the German descent upon Norway, and the Prime Minister placed Churchill, as the senior service minister, in the chair of the Military Co-ordination Committee, which was composed of the political heads of the Admiralty, the War Office, and the Air Ministry. Churchill quickly decided, however, that only a person with the Prime Minister's prestige could satisfactorily preside over this committee at a time of fast-moving and fateful operations. To this Chamberlain agreed. Churchill, moreover, was desirous of bringing the Chiefs of Staff Committee directly under the supervision of the Prime Minister or his deputy, for he considered that the committee's position 'as a separate and largely independent body' was a 'fatal weakness of our system of conducting war at this time.' [10]

Plans for reorganizing the War Cabinet were suddenly submerged by a political crisis which brought about the resignation of Chamberlain and the naming of Churchill as head of a Government supported by the Conservative, Labour, and Liberal parties. Churchill now had an opportunity to create his own organization for the management and direction of the war. He elected to head a small War Cabinet of five members, only one of whom, Lord Halifax, the Foreign Secretary, was in charge of a major department of government. Assuming the additional position of Minister of Defence, Churchill presided over a Defence Committee consisting of several ministers concerned with military affairs and munitions production and including the Chiefs of Staff and the Chief of Combined Operations. He also superintended the work of the Chiefs of Staff Committee, although he did not often preside over its meetings. The War Cabinet, the Defence Committee, and the Chiefs of Staff Committee were all served by a common secretariat.

A few features of the British organization for the control and direction of the nation's military effort during World War II should be noted. In the first place, Churchill believed, as did Lloyd George before him, that supreme political authority should be vested in a small War Cabinet of strong ministers capable of sharing the responsibility for major policy de-

---

[10] Winston S. Churchill, *The Gathering Storm* (Boston, 1948), p. 627.

cisions. They should be the ministers, in his view, who headed the departments most directly concerned with the politico-military problems of the war. He did not favor a War Cabinet composed mainly of ministers without portfolio. Regarding the latter kind of a Cabinet he has written:

> A group of detached statesmen, however high their nominal authority, are at a serious disadvantage in dealing with the Ministers at the head of the great departments vitally concerned. . . The War Cabinet Ministers themselves would naturally be diffident of challenging the responsible Minister, armed with all his facts and figures. They feel a natural compunction in adding to the strain upon those actually in executive control. They tend, therefore, to become more and more theoretical supervisors and commentators, reading an immense amount of material every day, but doubtful how to use their knowledge without doing more harm than good. . . Personally, when I was placed in charge I did not like having unharnessed Ministers around me. I preferred to deal with chiefs of organizations rather than counsellors. Everyone should do a good day's work and be accountable for some definite task, and then they do not make trouble for trouble's sake or to cut a figure.[11]

Secondly, the highest professional advisors and executors were closely linked to the War Cabinet. The Chiefs of Staff Committee served directly under the Prime Minister as Minister of Defence. Thus, there was no barrier of intermediate ministers or bodies to blur a complete understanding between the top political and military officers of the government. According to Churchill,

> The key-change which occurred on my taking over was, of course, the supervision and direction of the Chiefs of Staff Committee by a Minister of Defence with undefined powers. As this Minister was also the Prime Minister, he had all the rights inherent in that office, including very wide powers of selection and removal of all professional and political personages. Thus for the first time the Chiefs of Staff Committee assumed its due and proper place in direct daily contact with the executive Head of the Government, and in accord with him had full control over the conduct of the war and the armed forces.[12]

Another feature of British war administration at the highest level was the integration of staff services responsible to the principal political and military authorities. The War Cabinet Secretariat served the War Cabinet, the Prime Minister in his capacity as Minister of Defence, the Defence Committee, and the Chiefs of Staff Committee. Its head was a civil servant,

---

[11] *The Gathering Storm,* pp. 418-19. In spite of these views, only the Foreign Secretary headed a major department in Churchill's original War Cabinet. Later changes brought in ministers charged with important departmental responsibilities.

[12] *Their Finest Hour* (Boston, 1949), p. 16.

Sir Edward Bridges, and he had associated with him a Deputy Secretary (Military), Lieutenant-General Sir Hastings (later Lord) Ismay. General Ismay was also the personal representative of the Minister of Defence on the Chiefs of Staff Committee. The combined secretariat was composed of both civilian and military officers.

It would be difficult to overemphasize the importance of the secretariat in giving order and continuity to British defense administration during half a century of peace and war. The history of this institution begins with the establishment of the Committee of Imperial Defence in 1904. In 1912 Sir Maurice (later Lord) Hankey became the secretary of the Committee, after having served four years as assistant secretary, and until 1938 this distinguished civil servant was the designer and director of one of the most important contributions to the structure and functioning of modern British government. In addition to being secretary of the Committee of Imperial Defence, Hankey was secretary of the War Cabinet and the Imperial War Cabinet from 1916 to 1919, secretary of the Cabinet from 1919 to 1938, Clerk of the Privy Council from 1923 to 1938, and secretary of several Imperial Conferences. He was succeeded by Bridges. Thus, for almost half a century and while several Prime Ministers held office, two able civil servants maintained a secretariat to serve the highest policy-making centers of the government.

5. Postwar Defense Organization

When the Labour Party attained power in July, 1945, Attlee, the Prime Minister, re-established the prewar type of Cabinet. However, the advantages of the position of Minister of Defence had been sufficiently proved to justify a continuance of the office, and it was given a statutory basis in the Ministry of Defence Act, 1946. In general, this act continued the concept of defense organization that had been developed during the war. The idea of combining the service departments into one ministry was rejected, and a ministry to co-ordinate their activities and to be responsible for certain common services was created. The Ministry of Defence, it has been said, was 'conceived, primarily, as a co-ordinating mechanism to insure consistent programs among the armed services.' [13]

The entire defense establishment is represented in the Cabinet by the Minister of Defence. Besides serving as deputy chairman of the Defence Committee, he has the following principal functions:

(a) The apportionment, in broad outline, of available resources between the three Services in accordance with the strategic policy laid down by the Defence Committee. This will include the framing of general policy to govern research and development, and the correlation of production programmes.

---

[13] C. F. Robinson, 'British Organization for Defense,' *Public Administration Review,* Summer 1948, pp. 184-5.

(b) The settlement of questions of general administration on which a common policy for the three Services is desirable.

(c) The administration of inter-Service organizations, such as Combined Operations Headquarters and the Joint Intelligence Bureau.[14]

The Minister of Defence is advised by the Chiefs of Staff Committee. In addition, he has a comparatively small civilian staff, headed by a Permanent Secretary. The Ministry of Defence operates principally through a considerable number of interdepartmental committees, which have their secretariats located in the Ministry.

The organization of each of the service ministries has been left unchanged. The Admiralty is administered by a board of 11 members. The ranking member and the minister responsible to Parliament for the administration of the Royal Navy is the First Lord of the Admiralty. The other members are two junior ministers known as the Parliamentary and Financial Secretary and the Civil Lord, five high ranking naval officers known as Sea Lords, the Deputy and Assistant Chiefs of Naval Staff, and the Permanent Secretary of the department. Each of these members of the Board supervises a part of the naval administration. The command of the naval forces is vested in the First Sea Lord and Chief of Naval Staff, an Admiral of the Fleet appointed by the Crown upon the recommendation of the First Lord.

The War Office is headed by the Secretary of State for War, who is assisted in his ministerial and parliamentary duties by a junior minister, the Parliamentary Under Secretary of State and Financial Secretary. Policies for the War Office and the army establishment are determined by the Army Council, a body composed of ministerial and service members. The Secretary's principal military advisor and the head of the Army Staff is the Chief of the Imperial General Staff. Under the Army Staff come the commands in Germany, the Far East, the Middle East, and wherever for strategical reasons British troops are stationed.

The youngest of the service departments, the Air Ministry, is headed by the Secretary of State for Air. He is assisted by a junior minister, the Parliamentary Under Secretary of State, and departmental policy is established by an Air Council composed of ministerial and high ranking service members. The Air Secretary's principal professional advisor is the Chief of the Air Staff, a Marshal of the Royal Air Force.

A department closely associated with the service departments is the Ministry of Supply. This ministry is responsible for the procurement of practically all weapons and equipment used by the army and the Royal Air Force, and it administers research and development work in the military field. The Admiralty continues to be responsible for most naval procurement. Since the Ministry of Supply has important functions with respect to civilian procurement, it is not subordinated to the Ministry of Defence

---

[14] Cmd. 6923 (1946).

in the way the service departments are, but it is represented on a number of the co-ordinating committees through which the Defence Ministry discharges its responsibilities. The Minister of Supply is assisted by two junior ministers who share some of his parliamentary work and supervise departmental activities.

Immediately after World War II the United Kingdom, like the other western powers, reduced its armed forces to a small percentage of their 1945 peak of more than five million. Conscription was continued, however, in order to provide manpower for Britain's still heavy military burdens and to insure a reservoir of trained reserves. The production of military equipment was drastically cut, and emphasis placed upon research and development. These postwar policies had to be modified in 1950. The continuing threat posed by a heavily armed Soviet state and its communist satellites forced the British Government, along with its allies, to embark on programs to place more men under arms and to raise sharply the production of military equipment. In 1951 the Government announced a plan of rearmament to cost £4.7 billion over a three-year period.

Probably at no previous time in modern history has the problem of defense presented so many difficult choices to a British Government. The precarious nature of Britain's position with respect to international trade and finance has had direct repercussions upon defense policy. It has been generally recognized that the achievement of economic viability must have first claim upon British resources; unless the United Kingdom regains some measure of its former economic strength it cannot long play a leading part in insuring its own security and that of the dependent Empire. At the same time considerable military forces must be kept in being in order to provide against dangers which arise out of the unsettled state of the postwar world. It would be helpful to Britain's economy if some of the manpower and supplies now going into national defense could be diverted to civilian purposes. To make substantial cuts in defense expenditure, however, would be to expose the country and its world-wide interests to heavy risks.

The fact remains that only a fundamental change in the climate of international relations can reduce the importance of defense when compared with the other policy concerns of a British Government.

XIX

Policy and Administration: The Social Services

A field of public policy and administration which has been absorbing an increasing share of the resources of the state is that generally termed the social services. The activities included under this heading are those designed to protect the British people from the misfortunes attending life in a modern industrialized society and to enlarge their opportunities for healthful and rewarding lives. So extensive and comprehensive are the present-day social services that the name 'Welfare State' is given to the entire British polity.

Some notion of the scope and scale of the social services may be gained by looking at a few figures on the money devoted to them. The annual expenditure of the national government, the local authorities, and the National Insurance Fund amounted in 1949 to approximately £4120 million, and of this sum about 43 per cent, or £1800 million, went to the social services. This money was raised by national and local taxation and by contributions of employers and employees. In the budget for 1951-2 the Chancellor of the Exchequer allotted £1615 million to the social services, which represented 38 per cent of the estimated expenditure of the national government. As an indication of the expansion of the social services, it is calculated that in 50 years their cost has risen from about 17s. 7d. per person to £32 1s. 4d.[1] In terms of the money values of 1900, this represents an increase of more than nine-fold. It is a larger increase than has occurred under any other major heading of the British governmental budget.

The main trends during the past few decades in the development and administration of the social services, as summarized by the Accountant-General of the Scottish Health Department, have been the following:

(1) The evolution of public social services out of voluntary social services;

(2) The movement away from a comprehensive poor law service based on destitution to a number of specialized services based on common citizenship;

(3) The widening of the administrative unit from the local authority to the State, operating sometimes on a regional basis;

---

[1] *The Times*, 15 August 1951.

(4) The corresponding transfer of the major share of the financial burden from the local authorities to the Exchequer; and

(5) The adoption by the State, borrowing from the experience of friendly societies and trade unions, of the principle of mutual insurance for the payment of cash benefits during sickness and unemployment and for the payment of pensions and allowances for old age and to widows and orphans—replacing the poor relief which was the only source of assistance to former generations in similar circumstances.[2]

1. *Education*

One of the oldest and most important of the social services is public education. England was slow, compared to many other countries, in providing for publicly supported educational services.[3] At the beginning of the nineteenth century education was provided by privately endowed and maintained institutions, many of which were church connected. The two old universities of Oxford and Cambridge had richly endowed colleges, and there were a considerable number of preparatory schools supported by the income from endowments and the fees of their students. In addition, there were local schools dependent upon charity and tuition charges.

The first public assistance to education began in the 1830's with the appropriation by Parliament of a modest subsidy to be distributed to privately controlled primary schools. Not until 1870 did Parliament undertake to provide a comprehensive educational system that would insure a rudimentary education for every child in the kingdom. The Act of 1870 required every county and borough to appoint an education board and to provide primary schools if the existing private institutions were inadequate. At the national level, supervision over education was in the hands of a Privy Council committee. This committee was transformed in 1899 into a Board of Education headed by a member of the ministry known as the President.

In 1902 an education act, chiefly the work of an able civil servant, Sir Robert Morant, abolished the school boards which had been established under the Act of 1870 and made the county councils and the larger borough councils the education authorities for their areas. These councils were required to provide primary and secondary educational facilities to supplement those provided by privately supported institutions. Since then the

---

[2] Ibid. 15 August 1951.

[3] This was not for lack of an example because, as Macaulay tells us, the Parliament of Scotland passed an act in 1696 requiring 'that every parish in the realm should provide a commodious schoolhouse and should pay a moderate stipend to a schoolmaster.' The historian continues: 'The effect could not be immediately felt. But, before one generation had passed away, it began to be evident that the common people of Scotland were superior in intelligence to the common people of any other country in Europe.' Lord Macaulay, *History of England* (Philadelphia, 1861), vol. IV, p. 542.

national government has increasingly supported and supervised the educational system and today is spending over £250 million a year for this purpose. This is almost a three-fold increase over the prewar expenditure.

The present system of public education in England and Wales is based upon a comprehensive statute passed by Parliament in 1944. The principles embodied in the act had been presented in a white paper, *Educational Reconstruction,* laid before Parliament the previous year.[4] Authority to provide and develop a national policy on public education and to supervise the educational system is vested in the Minister of Education. In addition to the civil servants of his department, the minister is advised by a Central Advisory Council for England and one for Wales.

The provision of schools and their ancillary services required by the Act of 1944 is the responsibility of 146 local education authorities, which are county councils and county borough councils. Each council has an education committee to consider policy matters and to supervise its school system, and day-to-day administration is carried on by the council's education officer and his staff. The authors of the Act of 1944 recognized that in some of the larger counties educational administration would be far removed from its local patrons, so it was provided that the more populous counties should be subdivided into areas of not less than 60,000 persons. Each of these divisions has a divisional executive which, under the terms of an agreement made with the county council and approved by the Ministry, is immediately responsible for school administration. A divisional executive is composed of representatives of the county council and other local government units within the division and of private citizens who are co-opted on the basis of interest and experience. Working under the divisional executive is a divisional education officer. Through the divisional executives and their education officers 'an attempt is being made to meet the inherent weaknesses of large-scale organization—overstandardization and neglect of individual and local needs.'[5]

Considerable autonomy remains with the county and borough councils, but they are subject to the supervision of the Ministry in respect to the standard of school buildings, the pay and qualifications of teachers, and the general curricula of their schools. The Ministry has a corps of about 500 inspectors to visit local school systems. Since all local educational authorities are heavily dependent upon grants from the central government, compliance with the Ministry's standards and directives can be obtained by the withdrawal, or the threat of withdrawal, of financial support. This method of control, however, is unwieldy and rarely practical. The purposes of control and supervision are better obtained by the device of the development plan. In accordance with the Education Act of 1944, each local education authority prepares a plan covering in detail its educational program and submits it to the Minister. After negotiations be-

[4] Cmd. 6458 (1943).

[5] Emmeline W. Cohen, 'Aspects of Local Government in England and Wales,' *Public Administration Review,* Autumn 1951, pp. 255-6.

tween local and national officials and agreement upon amendments which the Ministry wishes to see made, the Minister approves the plan and issues a local education order. The Ministry can then supervise the execution of this binding order.

The Act of 1944 considerably reorganized and extended the schooling available in publicly supported institutions. It required each local education authority to provide free full-time schooling for children between the ages of 5 and 15 and free part-time schooling for youths between 15 and 18. The schooling is given in three related stages—primary education to the age of 11, secondary education to the age of 15, and further education above 15. Beyond the primary school stage, efforts are made to provide special schools and curricula for the varying needs and aptitudes of pupils. New county colleges, which are being established, are envisaged as not only places of part-time instruction for youths between 15 and 18 but also as centers for leisure-time activities and recreation.

Lying outside the system of council schools there is a large number of 'voluntary' and independent schools. The Act of 1944 sought to relate them more closely with the national educational program. The voluntary schools, most of which are church connected, were offered financial assistance to enable them to meet and maintain Ministry standards. The independent schools receive no grants of public money, but they must be registered with the Ministry and their equipment and educational programs are subject to official inspection. Among the independent schools are such widely known 'public' schools as Eton, Harrow, Rugby, Winchester, Charterhouse, and St. Paul's.

In the field of higher education the central government has no control, but it supports and, to some extent, influences university development through financial grants. These grants, amounting to £23,400,000 in the financial year 1950-51, provide more than half the income of the universities. Besides the Treasury the universities deal with a number of government departments—the Ministry of Education, the Ministry of Agriculture, the Ministry of Supply, the Department of Scientific and Industrial Research, the Colonial Office, the Civil Service Commission—which have money to spend on research or which recruit their graduates. It has been said that this 'jumble of departments controls the flow of students, the provision of jobs for graduates, and the finance of research, and between them they settle the policy of the Universities and of other bodies responsible for higher education. Or rather there are left in the interstices of interdepartmental confusion large spaces in which the Universities can still make their own policy, even though they are now financially dependent on the State; academic freedom depends in part on inefficiency in the machinery of Government.' [6]

In the past century the facilities provided by Oxford and Cambridge

---

[6] W. J. M. Mackenzie, 'The Structure of Central Administration,' *British Government since* 1918 (London, 1950), p. 66.

338–

have been supplemented by the University of London and a dozen or more provincial universities which have been established. In addition, there are several important universities in Scotland and one in Northern Ireland. Altogether there are 17 degree-granting universities in the United Kingdom. The number of students attending universities has increased considerably during the postwar period, and it is currently about 85,000. Approximately half the students receive scholarship aid.

After more than a century of expansion Britain has developed a comprehensive educational system. Parents may send a child to elementary and secondary schools administered by the county authorities in accordance with national standards and supported partly by grants from the Exchequer. Or they may choose—and the upper-middle and aristocratic classes usually do choose—a privately managed school, which must conform, as well, to the standards of the Ministry of Education. Above the secondary schools there are technical schools and universities.

One of the principal weaknesses of the educational system has been its failure to train a sufficient number of students in the scientific and technical fields. The universities have produced outstanding figures in the pure sciences—in mathematics, physics, astronomy, chemistry, and medicine, but a gap has tended to exist between them and the competent, skilled workman. Britain has lacked a considerable group of well-educated and trained people to apply the results of scientific research in industrial technology. This deficiency has not gone unnoticed, and since the war the government and the universities have endeavored to give more attention to the scientific and technical fields.

In recent years the British government has given substantial support to activities of a cultural and artistic nature. This governmental interest in the arts is not new—it can be traced back at least as far as the founding of the British Museum in 1753—but since World War II a number of lines of artistic endeavor have been subsidized on a greatly expanded scale.

Much of this activity is sponsored and supervised by the Arts Council of Great Britain, an organization founded in 1946 to continue and expand the wartime program of C.E.M.A., the Council for the Encouragement of Music and the Arts. By its royal charter, the objectives of the Arts Council are to develop 'a greater knowledge, understanding and practice of fine arts exclusively, and in particular to increase the accessibility of the fine arts to the public . . . to improve the standard of execution of the fine arts and to advise and cooperate with . . . government departments, local authorities and other bodies on matters concerned directly or indirectly with those objects.'

The Arts Council consists of a chairman, a vice-chairman, and 14 non-salaried members, all of whom are appointed by the Chancellor of the Exchequer after consultation with the Minister of Education and the Secretary of State for Scotland. Under a secretary-general the Council has a staff to administer its activities, and many leading figures of the artistic world are co-opted for committees and advisory panels. In the financial year 1950-51, the Treasury's grant to the Council amounted to £ 675,000.

Treasury control is maintained through a Treasury assessor to the Council, but there is no governmental direction on policy. The Council carries out its purposes largely by means of grants, loans, or financial guarantees to associated organizations, which are theaters, orchestras, arts clubs, music festivals, and drama and opera companies. Receiving support have been such well-known activities as the Edinburgh International Festival of Music and Drama, the London Philharmonic Orchestra, the Covent Garden Opera Company, the Sadler's Wells Ballet, and the Old Vic Theatre.

Directed at even a larger audience are the educational and entertainment activities of the British Broadcasting Corporation. The B.B.C., established as a public monopoly in 1927, is financed by the license fees paid by the owners of radio and television sets and by a Parliamentary grant. In the financial year 1948-9, the B.B.C.'s net income from licenses amounted to £9,444,472; from its publications, £989,544, and from Parliament, £17,285,000.

The B.B.C. is controlled by a Board of Governors consisting of nine members appointed on the advice of the Prime Minister. Three members represent Scotland, Wales, and Northern Ireland. The Board appoints a director-general to manage the corporation's activities. Questions concerning B.B.C. policy are answered in Parliament by the Postmaster-General. In 1952 when Parliament renewed the Corporation's charter for a ten-year period, the Government announced its intention to authorize, at a future date, a limited number of commercial television stations. The public service character and the political independence of the B.B.C. were reaffirmed.

The principal agent for bringing the educational and cultural accomplishments of Britain to the notice of Commonwealth and foreign countries is the British Council, a semi-independent organization established in 1934 and supported by an annual Parliamentary grant. The British Council sponsors the overseas tours of musical and theatrical companies, arranges the exchange of teachers and students, and maintains libraries and information offices in foreign cities. It is the government's chief instrumentality for carrying out cultural conventions agreed to under the auspices of the United Nations.

2. *Social Security*

The relief of the poor and unemployed has been accepted as a public responsibility in England for several hundred years. By the Elizabethan Poor Laws (1597-1601) the duty of caring for the indigent and providing work for the idle was vested in parish overseers of the poor, who were supervised by the justices of the peace and the latter in turn by the Privy Council. Money for poor relief purposes was provided by local taxation. Other acts of this kind were passed in the seventeenth and eighteenth centuries, and the principle of local responsibility was maintained.[7] In 1834

---

[7] According to Professor Trevelyan, the early measures for the relief of the poor, harsh and inadequate as they often were, had salutary social effects. 'The worst hor-

a new poor law introduced a form of national supervision by creating a central body, the Poor Law Commissioners, to insure that the local authorities, the guardians, did not neglect their duties.

As Britain developed into a highly industrialized nation, the measures which were practiced before the industrial revolution changed the face of the country became quite inadequate. Large urban populations whose livelihood was affected by trade cycles and business conditions far beyond their control could not be treated in the same fashion as rural communities and towns with handicraft industries. Consequently, new programs for protecting the working classes from the principal social dangers which threatened them were advocated, and these always involved the assumption of major responsibility by the central government.

The foundations of the present system of social security were laid by the Liberal Government that took office in 1906. In 1908 it established a program of noncontributory old age pensions, and the next year a system of labor exchanges. In 1911 Parliament passed the National Insurance Act under the urging of Lloyd George, Chancellor of the Exchequer, and Churchill, President of the Board of Trade. The act provided for a scheme of health insurance financed by premiums paid by employees, employers, and the state and administered through unofficial, nonprofit approved societies. In addition, it established a system of unemployment insurance. Between the two World Wars a good many changes in the scope and administration of the social security program were made. Unemployment insurance was extended to additional classes of workers. An act of 1925 set up a contributory pensions scheme for widows and orphans. In 1931 the support of the more or less permanently unemployed was undertaken by the national government, the Unemployment Assistance Board being established in 1934 to administer this aid. All persons in need of relief who did not qualify for one of the national programs were a responsibility of the public assistance committees of local governments and their support fell on the rates.

Although by the outbreak of war in 1939 Britain had gone far in establishing important schemes of social security, there were many who believed that the existing programs were inadequate and that their administration was poorly organized. Consequently, in 1941 the coalition Gov-

----

rors of failure, of unemployment and of unprovided old age were not suffered by the poor in England to the same extent as in the continental countries of the *ancien regime*. The regiments of beggars, such as continued to swarm in the streets of Italy, and of France under Louis XIV, were no longer known over here. The scandal and danger of such congregations had alarmed the Tudor and early Stuart governments; the Poor Law was meant to prevent them, and did prevent them by the only practical method, the relief of distress and the provision of work. That is one reason why there was never anything like the French Revolution in our country, and why through all our political, religious and social feuds from the Seventeenth to the Nineteenth Centuries the quiet and orderly habits of the people, even in times of distress, continued upon the whole as a national characteristic.' G. M. Trevelyan, *English Social History* (New York, 1942), p. 230.

ernment appointed an interdepartmental Committee on Social Insurance and Allied Services to make a study and submit recommendations covering the whole field of social security. The committee's report, named for the chairman the Beveridge Report, achieved a fame quite unusual for official documents.[8] Its publication 'made a deep impression on public opinion, even at a time when the country was passing through perhaps the greatest crisis in its history.'[9] The following explanation has been given for the reception accorded the report:

> The effect of the tremendous upheaval of the war upon the established order in so many parts of the world had crystallized the vague and ill-formed demands of the British people for sweeping reforms in the system of social security, and for an imaginative program based on the National Minimum. 'A revolutionary moment in the world's history is a time for revolutions, not for patching,' declared the Beveridge Report. These words aptly matched the sentiments of the British public at this time. The effect of wartime full employment on the standard of living, and the care of the dependents of those fighting the war, made people demand that the relief of want possible in wartime and the full employment of the manpower of the nation should be achieved in peace as part of a permanent policy.[10]

While the wartime Government was not willing to adopt immediately the recommendations of the Beveridge Report, it issued two white papers setting forth the schemes to be introduced upon the conclusion of hostilities.[11] It created, moreover, a Ministry of National Insurance to administer major portions of the social security program. Beginning in 1945 a series of statutes revised and supplemented the existing social security system along the lines the Beveridge Report had recommended. These included the Family Allowances Act of 1945; the National Insurance, the National Insurance (Industrial Injuries), and the National Health Service Acts of 1946; and the National Assistance and the Childrens Acts of 1948.

The various programs of social security now in operation in Britain can be only briefly described; their details and the administration of each are complicated and would require a book in themselves. The principal programs and the assistance they provide are as follows:

(1) *Retirement Pensions.* The scheme provides weekly pensions of 32s. 6d. at the age of 65 for men and 60 for women. The scheme covers employed persons, the self-employed, and persons not gainfully employed.

(2) *Unemployment Relief.* Unemployment benefits of 26s. weekly are paid to insured persons for a maximum of 180 days. After 13

---

[8] Cmd. 6406 (1942).

[9] Barbara Lewis and R. H. B. Condie, 'The British Social Security Program,' *The Journal of Politics,* May 1950, p. 336.

[10] Ibid. p. 337.

[11] Cmd. 6550 and Cmd. 6551 (1944).

weeks of further employment a person is eligible to receive benefits for another 180-day period. Provision is also made for local tribunals to authorize grants after hearing applications from persons who have exhausted their regular benefits.

(3) *Sickness Benefits.* Sick persons are entitled to a weekly payment which varies according to their individual circumstances and the number of their dependents. The standard rate is 26s. a week. In most cases individuals who become totally disabled are entitled to benefits until they reach an age qualifying them for old age pensions.

(4) *Maternity Grants and Allowances.* Mothers receive £4 for each child at birth and an additional allowance for 13 weeks which varies, depending upon whether or not they are employed.

(5) *Widows and Orphans.* Widows and the guardians of orphans are entitled to benefits to supplement such personal income as they may have.

(6) *Death Grants.* The state pays £20 toward the cost of funeral expenses.

(7) *Workmen's Compensation.* For injuries arising out of employment, workers are entitled to benefits which vary according to the severity of the accident. The basic benefit is 55s. a week.

(8) *National Assistance Grants.* Weekly grants in money or kind to persons unable to subsist without poor relief. Recipients are subject to a means test.

Retirement pensions, unemployment compensation, sickness benefits, widows' and orphans' benefits, and workmen's compensation for injuries are insurance schemes, and benefits are paid from the National Insurance Fund to which employers, employees, and the national government contribute. Insured persons and their employers pay standard premiums. An adult male worker pays 4s. 11d. weekly, and his employer 4s. 2d. For women the corresponding payments are 3s. 10d. and 3s. 3d. The contributions of self-employed persons are about a third more. Most of the schemes pay a standard weekly benefit ranging from 26s. to 32s. for an insured person, plus 16s. for any adult dependent, and 8s. for each child. The other social security schemes are financed by direct grants from the Exchequer. The cost to the Exchequer of the insurance schemes amounted in 1950 to about £214 million while the noninsurance types of assistance required almost £84 million.

3. *Health, Housing, and Food*

One of the most recent and most publicized additions to the social services program of the British government is the National Health Service, inaugurated in 1948. This program of socialized medicine entitles every inhabitant of the United Kingdom to virtually free medical care as frequently and for as long a duration as required. Medical care includes the professional services of physicians, surgeons, and dentists, hospitalization, and the supply of medicines and surgical devices. All doctors and dentists electing to join the National Health Service are paid fees from the national treasury in accordance with the number of patients they treat. Hospitals and clinics are supported by grants from public funds. Pharmacists receive payment for the prescriptions they fill. Doctors not choosing to enter the scheme may continue to practice and to charge their customary fees, and the physicians and dentists who have enrolled may continue to treat private patients. There are also private nursing homes to which patients may go and pay the established charges.

The costs of the National Health Service have far exceeded early estimates and have risen each year of operation. When the Service was proposed in 1946 its cost was estimated at £126 million. The cost during the first year of operation proved to be £278 million and the next year £359 million. The estimate for 1950-51 was set at £393 million, for 1951-2 at £398 million, and for 1952-3 at £393 million. Whether the rising costs of the Service were caused by its novelty or by needed treatment that could not be previously afforded, or whether they represented the permanent order of demand for medical care cannot yet be determined. In an effort to discourage frivolous requests for drugs and medicines the government imposed a charge of one shilling for each prescription, and beginning in 1951 it required each patient to pay half the cost of false teeth and eye glasses. Additional small charges for dental treatment and surgical appliances were imposed in 1952.

Besides costing much more than expected, the Health Service has been criticized for the slow and inadequate treatment provided. Its defenders have either disputed this criticism or have replied that it takes time to provide new facilities and that the heavy demands on the service are a measure of the need which existed. Some branches of the medical profession have accepted the new system with a good deal less than enthusiasm. Many doctors dislike the principle of socialized medicine; others have criticized the administration of the Service. With the public generally, however, the Service has proved to be popular, and the Conservative Party has acknowledged it to be a permanent part of the British program of social services.

The Ministry of Health is the department charged with the administration of the National Health Service, although there is a delegation of some aspects of the program to regional or local bodies. Regional hospital boards are in charge of hospital and specialist services, and county and borough councils manage local health centers and clinics. Local executive councils, composed of members appointed by the Minister of Health, local government authorities, and the participating doctors, dentists, and pharmacists of the area, have supervision over the members of these professions. There are in addition numerous advisory councils on different types of health and medical problems.

As the state has assumed increasing responsibility for individual welfare, the pressure has grown for it to assist in the provision of additional and improved housing. The demand for housing and the recognition that there

344–

was a public responsibility to supply it were heightened, of course, by the bomb damage which Britain suffered during World War II. Thousands of dwellings were totally destroyed, and it is estimated that one house out of five suffered some damage from enemy action. The postwar housing situation was made doubly acute by the fact that almost all construction ceased during the war years.

At the end of the war the Government immediately embarked upon a large-scale housing program. It has been carried out principally by grants to local authorities whose construction projects are under the general supervision of a department of the national government, the Ministry of Health until 1951 and now the Ministry of Housing and Local Government. By the end of July 1951, there had been constructed 929,569 new permanent houses and 157,146 temporary ones.[12] Most of the available labor and materials were channeled into public housing schemes, and private builders accounted for only about 200,000 of the new permanent houses. Despite the construction of the past few years, the demand for housing remains high and the central government will undoubtedly continue to support the program with generous grants. In 1950 the cost to the national Exchequer was £66,400,000.

A policy which came out of the war period and which is still a feature of the general welfare program of the British government is the subsidization of food. In an effort to keep the cost of living as low as possible and thus prevent wage claims, which would have accentuated the powerful inflationary pressures of the war years, the national government subsidized the basic items of the British diet. Until the financial year 1952-3, the cost of this program amounted to about £400 million annually, and it was, therefore, the most expensive of the social services. In 1952 the Chancellor of the Exchequer, stating that one of the objects of his budget was 'to restore a sense of reality to our personal as well as our national accounts,' announced that the Government proposed to allow food prices to rise to a point where the subsidies could be held to £250 million annually.[13]

Food subsidies are not regarded in Britain as an essential part of a social security or social welfare program, and they probably would have been abolished, or curtailed more sharply than they have, except for certain conditions facing British Governments since 1945. Inflation has been almost as serious a problem as it was during the war, and one way of persuading workers to be moderate in their wage demands has been to hold the basic items of their diet at a low price level. There are political considerations involved, too. Subsidies once granted are always difficult to withdraw. People get accustomed to the subsidized prices of bread, meat, tea, cheese, and other standard items, and marked advances would evoke sharp protests. Governments, therefore, have been cautious in moving toward the elimination of the food subsidies.

---

[12] *The Times,* 7 September 1951.
[13] *The Times,* 12 March 1952.

4. *Policy and Administration*

The general principle of the central government's responsibility for social welfare is not a political issue in the United Kingdom. Political parties dispute over the cost and administration of the various social welfare programs, but no group advocates their abolition or even the substantial curtailment of their services. After the Beveridge Report appeared, it became the creed of all political parties. The report's recommendations of 'cradle to the grave' social security were accepted as the general program which any postwar Government would have to introduce. The Labour Party claims great credit for having expanded the older social services and for having introduced the National Health Service. The Conservatives point to programs initiated or extended during their periods in power and remind voters that the Beveridge Report was endorsed in principle by a coalition Government. When in opposition, they confine their criticism to alleged inefficiencies and wasteful administration.

In the administration of the social services the British have built, in general, on familiar patterns. In education and housing they have followed the grant-in-aid principle by which the central government joins with local authorities in sponsoring and administering a service. The role of the national government is to establish the outlines of a program and to supply a share of its cost. It also maintains a supervisory watch over the administration by local authorities and sees that money is spent in accordance with the regulations prescribed and that standards of administration are maintained. The role of local authorities, county councils and borough councils, is to prepare plans, obtain the approval of the national ministry concerned, and to administer the program through its agencies and employees. This type of administration permits some flexibility in accordance with varying local conditions, stimulates local responsibility, and helps to equalize the burdens as between richer and poorer sections of the country.

Other programs are directly administered by the national government. For them the usual organization of a government department is employed and the regular fiscal and personnel policies are followed. Some of them require a larger field organization than is common with other government departments, but there is no substantial deviation from typical administrative practices.

The Ministry of National Insurance has attempted to make its administrative procedures simple and to provide prompt and convenient service for citizens in need. A person losing his employment may apply immediately for his weekly benefit at one of the hundreds of local offices of the Ministry, and an insurance officer will assist him in preparing his claim. Unemployment benefits are usually paid at local labor exchanges, while for other insurance grants or benefits recipients receive vouchers cashable at post offices. Local post offices also sell the stamps representing the payment of contributions by insured persons. Large employers handle the contributions of their workers, deducting from wages the weekly premiums and

346–

adding their own contributions. Should an insured person be dissatisfied with the claim allowed by an insurance officer, he may appeal to a local tribunal consisting of an independent chairman and two members drawn from panels representing employers and employees. The hearing procedure of a local tribunal is simple and informal. In some cases an appeal may be carried to the National Insurance Commissioner, an officer independent of the minister. Applicants for national assistance, poor relief, apply to a local officer of the National Assistance Board. The local officer, guided by national regulations, may grant aid in money or kind. Dissatisfied applicants may appeal to one of the Board's local tribunals.

There has been a trend toward greater centralization in public welfare administration. In some cases this has meant the national government's assumption of responsibility for a service; in others the result has been closer control and supervision by Whitehall over local authorities. Within the national government the principle of organization on the basis of functional responsibility has generally been followed. Thus, each of the principal forms of social insurance is administered by the Ministry of National Insurance, various direct grants to needy individuals by the National Assistance Board, the National Health Service by the Ministry of Health, public education by the Ministry of Education, and public housing by the Ministry of Housing and Local Government. Since the programs of these agencies touch at many points, a good deal of interdepartmental co-ordination is called for. It must also occur in the field, because in many instances the people affected by their activities are the same.

In conclusion, two observations may be made about the postwar programs of social welfare in Great Britain. The first concerns their success in terms of social improvement. Unemployment, destitution, disease, and dependency in old age are social evils which can seriously affect social stability and the morale of the productive elements of a nation. Ignorance and lack of training are great handicaps for a country seeking to be a leading industrial power. Inadequate housing can reduce the efficiency of the working population and thus increase the costs of production. All these are generally recognized factors, and their elimination or amelioration is accepted as contributing to greater national well-being.

The direct effects of welfare measures upon health, public morale, and social stability in Great Britain can only be judged by comparing contemporary British conditions with those existing at earlier times and with those in some other countries. The physical condition of the British population has undoubtedly improved as vital statistics indicate. There has been a lengthening of the life span and a decrease in the death rate, and for these trends the social service programs are entitled to some credit. Britain has been one of the most orderly and stable of modern countries. Revolutionary political movements have made no headway, and the attachment of the great mass of the people to constitutional processes has been firm. Whereas in a number of the continental countries the Communists have enlisted mass political followings, they have had singularly poor success in Great

−347

Britain. There are many considerations involved in such comparisons, but certainly an important one is the scope and character of social welfare policies.

The second observation relates to the cost of the social services. They now account for a large share of governmental expenditure in Britain, and the tendency is for the cost to rise rather than decrease. It is estimated, for example, that the expenditure on retirement pensions will increase from £238 million in 1948 to £501 million in 1978 because of the gradual 'aging' of the population.[14] This does not take into account the possibility of increases in the scale of benefits, for which pressure is constantly being exerted. Each one of the social services is a desirable end in itself, and persuasive arguments can be advanced for its continuance at the present, or even higher, level of benefit. Over a period of years each one will probably conduce to greater national well-being. The difficulty is that Britain faces a number of short-term problems of a critical nature, and their solution appears to depend upon the country rapidly becoming a more efficient workshop. By apportioning a large part of the national product to the social services the British people have, in a sense, set themselves very high goals. Only a rapid increase in productivity will enable them to meet their many commitments, including the postwar standard of social services.

No final judgment can be passed on the total British program of social welfare. Obviously some of the services are necessary to alleviate social ills which are concomitant with an industrial society and which the working classes, armed with the vote, are not inclined to tolerate. Others have undoubtedly contributed to the high measure of social stability which Britain has enjoyed. It may be, however, that the British public has placed its social welfare goals too high and sought to reach them too quickly. The answer will be given when competition in world markets sharpens and price determines the foreigner's choice.

A good deal of criticism has been voiced in the United States, and some in Britain too, about American 'subsidization' of the British welfare state through loans, grants under the Marshall Plan, and military aid programs. It is argued that without American assistance the Labour Government after 1945 would have been unable to carry out many of its socialist objectives. This view is fallacious, however, for the British social welfare programs have been financed by redistributing the wealth within the country, that is, by levying heavy taxes in accordance with ability to pay and appropriating the proceeds to education, pensions, medical attention, housing, and other welfare programs. Financial aid from the United States has undoubtedly enabled the British government to maintain a tolerable standard of living for its people, because the lack of sufficient dollar exchange would have prevented Britain from buying food and raw materials

---

[14] According to the government actuary, the increase in old age pensions granted in 1951 will cost £39 million the first year but may reach 'considerably more than double this figure' in 25 years. *The Times*, 19 April 1951.

desperately needed during the postwar years. But such aid would have been required regardless of the domestic policies of the Government of the United Kingdom. If the United States has any complaint, it is along the line that high British taxation to sustain ambitious programs of social welfare raises the costs of production and discourages incentive, with the result that Britain is a less effective competitor in the world trade which is essential for her livelihood. On the other hand, the political and social stability which has characterized the British society has made the United Kingdom the most dependable major ally of the United States during a critical period of history.

XX

Policy and Administration: Industry

A good share of the time of Parliament, many policy statements of political parties, and a great deal of administrative activity of government departments are devoted to the regulation, control, and promotion of British industry. These matters are of great importance in all modern states. They are of cardinal importance in Britain because it is a highly industrialized country which depends for the maintenance of its standard of living upon the nation's ability to compete with other industrial powers, some of which are better endowed with natural resources than the United Kingdom.

1. *Trends in State Policy*

Historically, the British nation has gone through several phases in its approach to the general problems of the control and management of its economic life. Before the nineteenth century, it was commonly accepted that the state might control and foster industry and trade. Intervention in economic affairs was regarded as a usual power of the political sovereign. Consequently, the central government created monopolies in various industries and trades, awarded commercial rights in overseas territories and in domestic markets, restricted trade to British ships, set wage rates, and in other ways took an active interest in economic affairs.

Toward the end of the eighteenth and in the beginning of the nineteenth century, this governmental intervention began to be questioned, and it was argued that industry and trade would expand and Britain would grow more prosperous if the state would remove its controlling hand and allow the uninfluenced forces of the market to shape the character of the British economy. This philosophy is termed *laissez faire*. It found a ready acceptance in early nineteenth-century Britain. The machine age was coming into existence, and British businessmen and traders were eager to exploit, without restrictions and state regulation, all the possibilities of the new sources of power and opportunities for trade. As the manufacturing and commercial classes grew in wealth and political power, they converted most of their countrymen to the *laissez-faire* doctrine and were able to repeal many of the monopolistic and restrictive laws and practices of earlier generations. Only the agricultural interests remained unconvinced, and they were finally overridden when Parliament removed the protective duties on

350–

grain in the great free trade battle of 1846. Thereafter for several decades, the ruling principle in economic policy directed the state to withhold its regulatory power over domestic manufacture and trade and to allow goods to enter and to leave the kingdom unburdened by protective duties. Because Britain grew prosperous and powerful, this principle came to have an almost unchallengeable validity among politicians, businessmen, and the public at large. It became an article of faith in Victorian Britain.

Even in the heyday of its acceptance, however, the doctrine of *laissez faire* was never applied to the full. The early nineteenth century was also a period in which humanitarian sentiments were gaining strength, and these occasionally brought modifications in the application of basic economic doctrine. Working conditions in factories and mines aroused reformers to demand protection for employees who were in no position to bargain to protect their own health and safety. Consequently, a series of factory acts began the regulation of the employment of women and children, the hours of labor, and the conditions of work in dangerous and unhealthful industries. Parliament did not permit colonists in British territories overseas to learn for themselves the ultimate lack of economy in slave labor but passed an emancipation act in 1834.

Toward the close of the nineteenth century, although free trade and the policy of nonintervention remained dominant, a growing concern about foreign competition and a desire for more positive action in economic matters were manifested. This feeling was strong enough before World War I for the Conservative Party to espouse protectionism. The party's supporters among the landowning and agricultural classes had never been thoroughly converted to free trade, and now many business groups were having their doubts. It was not a winning issue, however, until the great business depression of the 1930's made the country willing to try new economic policies. Already the world situation and the British position had changed so markedly that most Britons were persuaded that different policies were required. Great Britain was no longer the pre-eminent industrial power in the world, and she was being challenged in nearly all her traditional markets by strong competing nations which followed protectionist policies to the detriment of British trade. Even the dominions and India were protecting their domestic producers from the threat of British as well as foreign competition. So it came about that Britain abandoned free trade and joined the ranks of the protectionist nations.

Besides a change in policy toward tariffs, there were developments with respect to other aspects of British economic affairs. While much lip service was paid to the principles of free enterprise, there was in practice a growing amount of state control and intervention in business and industry. Statutory enactments provided for the closer supervision of business corporations, for the regulation of the rates and services of public utilities, for the protection of trade unions, and for the guarding of the public against many commercial abuses and malpractices. Of great significance, too, was the appearance in British political life of a party which espoused socialism and which frankly called upon the state to use its power for the planning and control of economic forces in the interest of the worker's welfare. The Labour Party became after World War I one of the two major political organizations of the country and supplanted the Liberal Party and its basic tenets of free trade.

The two dominant political parties in present-day Britain are both advocates of state intervention to control and influence economic affairs. They differ widely on the kinds and degrees of intervention, but neither is an advocate of free trade or free enterprise as such terms were understood by earlier generations. The Conservative Party proclaims its belief in capitalism and is opposed to the extension of the sphere of public ownership. In power, it may undo some of the socialization of recent Labour Governments; it will by no means restore a relatively free economy of the nineteenth-century type. The Labour Party believes in the state planning of all aspects of the country's economic life and considers that large areas of economic activity can only be controlled and managed in the public interest when they are directly owned and administered by public authorities. It is probable that the question of how much state intervention there shall be and what form it shall take will be a major domestic issue in British politics for many years to come.

A British Government framing measures to regulate and control economic affairs faces no formal constitutional barriers. The Cabinet may propose and Parliament may enact laws providing for any kind of control and management that in their wisdom the situation appears to require. The only restraints are the conventional ones that depend upon public opinion for their enforcement. No Government at the present time could pass and enforce laws that allowed property to be seized without providing for reasonable compensation to the owners or that created authorities immune from all Parliamentary and judicial control. Differences arise over issues of compensation, official power, and methods of securing responsibility, but there remains a recognition that in its intervention into economic affairs the state must not act unfairly or arbitrarily.

The present-day British government intervenes in economic affairs in two principal ways. First, it regulates and influences industry and commerce by such devices and measures as inspection, direct orders, taxation, subsidies, and co-operative marketing schemes. These devices and measures are administered by government departments on the authority of Parliamentary statutes. Secondly, the state owns and operates very important segments of the British economy. Surveys of governmental activity under the first heading with respect to agriculture and manufacturing will illustrate the scope and nature of current policy. A following section will consider the nationalized industries.

2. *Governmental Regulation: Agriculture*

The preoccupation of nineteenth-century Britain with manufacturing, commerce, and finance left agriculture a neglected industry. With protection by tariffs withdrawn, agriculture was exposed to heavy foreign competition

352–

when the tramp steamer began to bring the produce of the new lands across the ocean to British ports. The decline of the farmer was deplored, but he was considered a sacrifice to the larger national interest. However, this industry relatively unimportant in peace became of great value in time of war. Since the period of the First World War, therefore, efforts have been made to revive British agriculture and to make it a prosperous part of the economy. There is no prospect of the United Kingdom's being able to feed its population from its own resources—there are too many mouths for that. But by intensive cultivation of the land something over half the nation's present requirements are being supplied from domestic sources. National security dictates that agriculture not be neglected again, and this reason has been reinforced since World War II by the necessity of conserving foreign exchange. The less the British must spend on overseas purchases of food the more they can spend on other requirements of their economy.

The administration of agricultural policy is vested mainly in the Ministry of Agriculture and Fisheries, which was given its present name in 1919. It developed from a Board of Agriculture established in 1889, and functions pertaining to fisheries were added in 1903. The Minister is usually a member of the Cabinet. The responsibilities of the Ministry include the use and improvement of land, agricultural education and research, animal diseases, credit and marketing schemes, the regulation of agricultural wages, the regulation of fisheries, and the management of the Royal Botanic Gardens at Kew. The Minister of Agriculture and Fisheries is assisted by two Parliamentary Secretaries, and there is a Permanent Secretary as his chief adviser and as the head of the administrative organization.

Most of the agricultural legislation between the wars was designed to aid farmers in obtaining credit, to stabilize crop prices, and to provide better marketing methods. By an act of 1923 the Minister of Agriculture was authorized to encourage the establishment of credit societies to which the state contributed 50 per cent of the capital. In 1928 an Agricultural Mortgage Corporation was created to provide medium- and long-term loans. An independent Wheat Commission was set up in 1932 to administer a subsidy scheme designed to give stable prices to wheat growers. The fund from which the subsidies were paid was created by levies on imported and domestically produced flour. The Agricultural Marketing Acts of 1931 and 1933 provided for the establishment of producers' marketing boards for a number of farm products. When a marketing scheme—for milk, bacon, tomatoes, or some other product—was adopted by a majority of producers, it was laid before Parliament by the Minister of Agriculture and, if approved, it became legally binding upon all producers. The marketing boards have been described as 'guild type' administrative agencies. The producers elect a majority of the board members, and the Minister of Agriculture appoints additional ones from outside the specialty of the producers. 'The purpose of the Boards,' Sir Arthur Street said, 'was to protect home producers from disastrous falls in prices in an era of temporary glut and to help producers to help themselves by encouraging more efficient methods of marketing and production.'[1] The Agricultural Marketing Acts further provided for development schemes which embraced the processors as well as the primary producers.

Outright subsidies from the Exchequer were provided to farmers by the Agriculture Act of 1937 and the Livestock Industry Act of 1937. The first act established a Land Fertility Commission to administer the subsidy scheme, and the second a Livestock Commission. 'Generally, the intention was that the Government should grant a subsidy but that the industry should adopt measures to make itself more efficient in the national, as well as in its own, interest.'[2]

During World War II it was necessary that every arable acre in Britain be cultivated as efficiently as possible. The Minister of Agriculture and executive committees in each county were empowered to insure that this was done. Much of the wartime control was continued in effect by the Agriculture Act of 1947. 'This Act,' Professor Zink has commented, 'does not nationalize the land, but it does provide a measure of public control which some would regard as rather closely related in spirit to the various nationalization acts.'[3] In an effort to stabilize the industry as much as possible, the Minister is empowered to survey domestic and foreign agricultural conditions and then set prices for all crops, except horticulture, a year—in some cases two years—in advance. He is further authorized, in co-operation with the Minister of Food, to guarantee markets for domestic farm products. Agricultural policies and programs designed to give producers assured prices and markets are not unusual; most modern states protect their farmers with measures of this nature. Additional provisions of the act of 1947, however, are more exceptional. The act provides that land not efficiently cultivated can be placed under governmental supervision, including directions to the farmer about what crops he is to plant and how he is to cultivate them. If after a year's supervision the yield remains unsatisfactory, the Minister of Agriculture may dispossess the farmer, purchase the land, and lease it to a more satisfactory tenant. The act also provides that good agricultural land shall not be diverted to less important uses and that the Ministry of Agriculture may reclaim and cultivate land that private owners are not able to develop.[4] A National Agri-

---

[1] 'Quasi-Government Bodies since 1918,' *British Government since 1918* (London, 1950), p. 166.

[2] Sir Arthur Street, op. cit. p. 169.

[3] Harold Zink, 'The New Role of the Government in Britain,' *The Western Political Quarterly,* December 1948, p. 418. In a debate on the Speech from the Throne in 1950 the Minister of Agriculture disavowed any intention on the part of the Labour Government to nationalize land. *The New York Times,* 9 March 1950.

[4] These actions by the minister are taken on the recommendation of county agricultural committees which have majorities drawn from panels nominated by farmers', landowners', and agricultural workers' organizations. From the committees, appeals may be taken to tribunals composed of a lawyer as chairman and representatives of

cultural Land Commission, responsible to the Minister, is the administrative agency for acquiring and developing land as provided for in the statute. As a result of the Agriculture Act of 1947 and other legislation pertaining to farming and the marketing of crops, the farmer is assisted in many ways and protected against serious loss, except from the natural hazards over which no government has control. He must, however, produce as efficiently as his land and equipment permit. Land is too precious in Britain and food so necessary that wasteful cultivation cannot be tolerated.

3. *Governmental Regulation: Manufacturing, Mining, and Commerce*

Turning now to other segments of the British economy, we find that the state has intervened on an increasing scale in manufacturing, mining, and commerce. In the beginning governmental intervention was mainly of a restrictive or protective character. A series of factory acts, dating from more than a century ago, imposed restrictions upon employers with respect to the employment of women and children, sanitary and safety conditions in factories, hours of work, and similar matters. An inspectorate of the Home Office, later transferred to the Ministry of Labour, enforced the provisions of the factory acts. Other protective legislation extended the liability of employers for accidents and injuries to workmen. The law concerning joint stock companies was tightened to provide protection to investors and shareholders against deception and fraud. These measures by and large were designed to curb the social evils of unbridled competition and to protect the public and the workers from exploitation by unethical business interests. Many pages of the statute books in the United States contain comparable kinds of legislation.

While protective and regulatory measures have been extended and amplified continuously, the British government has felt the necessity of taking more positive forms of action with respect to business and industry. Much of this intervention has been prompted by problems arising out of the changing state of the British economy. Great industries, coal mining and cotton textiles for example, which once were flourishing and contributed largely to the nation's prosperity, have fallen on hard times. Unable to reorganize efficiently, attract new capital, give their workers a respectable standard of living, or find adequate markets, they have become national problems demanding the attention of Governments and Parliament. The character of governmental action has ranged from limited types of assistance to public ownership and management. It will not be possible to review

---

farmers and landowners. The minister cannot override the tribunal. With respect to control over agricultural efficiency, the act of 1947 has been interpreted by one writer to mean that, at worst, 'a bad farmer gets tried by his peers, with right of appeal, and his peers are not likely to be too hard on him. The industry is not being disciplined from without, but is being asked to maintain a very modest level of professional competence, determined and imposed by itself.' Peter Self, 'A Policy for Agriculture,' *Political Quarterly,* April-June 1948, pp. 144-5.

in any comprehensive way what has been done during the last few decades, but we can consider several typical kinds of policies and programs.

The coal mining industry has been a chronic problem for many years. Immediately after World War I it enjoyed a brief boom, repeated during the French occupation of the Ruhr, but soon the export markets declined, prices and wages fell, and unemployment rose. Strikes paralyzed the industry for long periods and engendered much bitterness which can still be detected in British politics. In 1930 Parliament passed the Coal Act with the objects of aiding a reorganization of the industry and improving its business methods. An independent body, the Coal Mines Reorganization Commission, was established to promote the amalgamation of mining properties into efficient units. Its achievements were negligible. The act of 1930 also empowered the coal companies to organize national and local bodies to set production quotas and arrange co-operative marketing. The industry remained 'sick,' however, and there was comparatively little opposition to the trial of nationalization as a remedy when proposed by the Labour Government after World War II.

The cotton textile industry was another which fell into a slump. Foreign manufacturers, utilizing more modern machine methods or, like the Japanese, paying much lower wages, invaded many traditional British markets. New capital needed to modernize the industry was not easily raised in view of the poor prospects for profits. In the late 1930's Parliament sought to promote some reorganization within the industry. The Cotton Spinning Industry Act, 1936, created a Cotton Spindles Board empowered to scrap redundant spindles and to compensate their owners from a levy on other manufacturers. The Cotton Industry (Reorganization) Act, 1939, set up a Cotton Industry Board for the purpose of co-ordinating all branches of cotton textile manufacturing and reorganizing its structure. After World War II, which produced severe dislocations in the industry, cotton was the first industry to be treated under the Industrial Organization and Development Act of 1947. A development council, termed the Cotton Board, was established to endeavor to accomplish the reorganization and modernization of the industry that had been recommended by a number of private and official studies. The Board is composed of a chairman and two independent members appointed by the President of the Board of Trade, and four members representing manufacturers and four representing textile workers. Most of the Board's powers are advisory, although it is authorized to collect a levy on the industry to facilitate reorganization schemes. The Cotton Board was the precursor and model of development councils for several other industries which were suffering from weaknesses of various sorts. The objective in all cases was to provide a mechanism whereby the industry could eliminate inefficient units, increase the productivity of the remainder of the industry, maintain employment at a high level, and compete effectively in foreign markets. The industries for which development councils have been named include furniture, clothing, pottery, and jewelry.

Besides seeking to assist long-established industries suffering some of the infirmities of their age, the state has attempted to foster younger ones. A method employed has been tariff protection. The Conservative Government of 1924-9, while forced to eschew protection in general because a large part of the electorate was still unconvinced of its desirability, introduced a number of 'safeguarding' duties to protect such industries as rayon textiles, automobiles, and tires.[5] After the National Government was returned in 1931 with a mandate to introduce protection, the range of duties was extended. Armed with its new weapon of protection, the Government was prepared to meet representatives of the dominions at Ottawa in 1932 to negotiate agreements giving each other preferential markets within their countries. Thus, in exchange for preferences to the agricultural and raw material producers of the dominions, Great Britain obtained advantages for many of her manufacturers.

Since World War II provision has been made for financial assistance to companies that cannot obtain credit from the normal sources. Large industrial undertakings needing short- or medium-term loans may apply to the Finance Corporation for Industry, a private institution established in 1945 by the Bank of England and a group of insurance and trust companies. The Industrial and Finance Corporation, another private institution, was set up the same year to provide medium- and long-term loans for small business firms. It was established by the Bank of England and the large commercial banks of the country. Although the two corporations are privately managed institutions and do not receive directions from the Government, they work in close co-operation with the departments concerned with the control and promotion of industry.

British industry receives benefits from government-sponsored research. Grants to universities finance research which leads to results having commercial applications, and the Department of Scientific and Industrial Research keeps the interests of industry to the forefront in its programs. During the operation of the Marshall Plan, the British government sent a number of groups of industrialists and trade unionists, productivity teams, to visit factories and mills in the United States and to recommend production practices suitable for adoption at home.

In recent years the state has turned its attention to the problem of monopolistic conditions and practices in industry. Parliament has seldom exhibited much concern over monopolies, and there are no statutes comparable to the anti-trust legislation in the United States. Cartels, closely knit trade associations, and industry-wide agreements on prices and markets have been common features of British business. In 1948 Parliament passed the Restrictive Practices (Inquiry and Control) Act which created a Monopolies and Restrictive Practices Commission to investigate conditions in particular industries. The President of the Board of Trade selects the subjects of investigation, and the Commission's reports are made to

---

[5] Some protective duties were imposed during World War I, but they were repealed by the first Labour Government in 1924.

him. On the basis of the Commission's findings the minister may lay an order before Parliament prohibiting the monopolistic and restrictive practices uncovered. The first inquiry was directed at the manufacturers of dental equipment.[6]

Many forms of governmental control and regulation were introduced during World War II when virtually the whole of British industry was mobilized for the prosecution of the war. National planning, reconstruction activities, shortages of foreign exchange, and the requirements of rearmament have necessitated the continuance of a large part of the regulatory system. Thus, the bulk purchase of raw materials and their allocation to industry, the specification of standardized or 'utility' lines of manufactured goods, price-fixing, and the division of production between the domestic and the export markets remain as major features of state control of British industry.

Several departments of the government are involved in the control and supervision of industry. The Treasury maintains a watch over the whole economy, and its planning measures set the limits within which individual industries must operate. Furthermore, the Treasury's fiscal and credit policies affect all lines of business and industry. The Board of Trade is the department administering most of the machinery of control and regulation. Other departments having functions in this field include the Ministry of Supply, the Ministry of Labour, the Ministry of Transport, and the Ministry of Housing and Local Government. With so many ministries involved, problems concerning business and industry frequently must be dealt with and co-ordinated in Cabinet and interdepartmental committees.

4. The Nationalized Industries

A second major type of intervention in economic affairs is that represented by the public corporation. This is the administrative form which has been selected for the industries and some of the services which have been socialized or nationalized. It is also being employed for the development of new communities under the New Towns Act, 1946. While the number

---

[6] Writing in *The Times,* 'The Problem of Monopoly,' Sir Henry Clay, an economist and Warden of Nuffield College, Oxford, criticized the vagueness of the Restrictive Practices Act and the piecemeal approach adopted. The act 'provides a procedure by which a Minister can issue Orders to individual persons—or firms or particular trades—based on no general rules laid down by statute or court decisions, which nevertheless are to have the force of law. . . True, Parliament has to endorse the blank cheque, which it has given the Minister, for the commission to fill in in each case; but Parliament has a great deal to do, and, as the debates showed, is not very well informed or judicial on this subject. The United States, so often cited in this problem, and pre-Nazi Germany, so seldom studied, proceeded by the normal Parliamentary method of legislation and interpretation of the law in the courts. The "useful case law," which the President of the Board of Trade expects the commission to build up without any foundation in statute or common law will be a legal curiosity.' 19 January 1951.

of public corporations has grown in recent years, the form is not an innovation in British affairs. Before 1939 there were several large public corporations in existence. The Port of London Authority, which owns and
manages the docks and harbor facilities along the lower Thames, had been
established in 1908; the Central Electricity Board, owner and manager of
the national grid system, had been set up in 1926; the British Broadcasting
Corporation was chartered in 1927 and given a monopoly of radio broadcasting in the United Kingdom; and the London Passenger Transport
Board, which owned and operated the tubes, busses, and tramways of the
metropolitan area, was created in 1933. To these were added between
1945 and 1951 a considerable number of other major public corporations.
These included the Bank of England, the National Coal Board, the British
Overseas Airways Corporation, British European Airways, the British Electricity Authority, the Gas Council (a federation of 12 area boards, each a
public corporation), the Raw Cotton Commission, the British Transport
Commission, the Colonial Development Corporation, the Overseas Food
Corporation, and the Iron and Steel Corporation. In most of these instances the government bought out private owners and vested ownership
in a public corporation; in some cases properties and facilities were purchased from local authorities.

The reasons for selecting the industries affected were various. Labour
Party leaders have declared that the presence of one or a number of conditions in an industry strongly suggests that it should be transferred from
private to public hands. These conditions include: (1) the presence of a
monopolistic situation; (2) the inability of private owners to bring about
reorganization or modernization which the industry appears to require;
and (3) the importance of the industry to the total economy of the nation.
All of the industries and public services selected for nationalization since
1945 are deemed by the Labour Party to have been eligible under one or
more of the above-mentioned criteria. Thus, the Bank of England as the
central bank of the nation occupied a monopolistic position, and its functions were regarded as basic to the management of the whole economy.
The coal industry not only was Britain's greatest power resource but also
suffered from disorganization, lack of new capital for modernization and
chronic labor troubles. The railroads and highway transport qualified on
the grounds of basic services and partial if not complete monopolies. The
iron and steel industry was deemed eligible because of its fundamental
importance to a nation like Great Britain and because the former private
owners of many of the companies had, in the Labour Party's opinion, been
unprogressive and lacking in foresight in the days before 1939.

Conceivably the nationalized industries could have been organized as
government departments, or branches of existing departments, under ministers responsible to Parliament. They would then have taken their places
alongside the Post Office which also is a large service agency. The administrative form of a public corporation, however, was deemed more suitable.
Several considerations led to this choice. In the first instance, the func-

tions of the controlling authorities of the nationalized industries are primarily administrative and managerial; they are more akin to those faced by the managements of large business corporations than to those of ministers in typical government departments. Policy is laid down in a basic statute, and it is fairly permanent and straightforward—to mine the coal required by the nation's economy, to operate a system of overseas airlines, or to generate and distribute electric power. This is not to suggest that the managers of nationalized industries do not consider and decide policy questions, for the line between policy and administration is not so clear that a definite partition can be made; the point is that, in the main, their job is to carry out policy already set by the politicians.

As a second consideration, the corporate form of organization provides a flexibility of administration that is not possible with a government department. It is deemed desirable that the managing authorities of the nationalized industries have considerable freedom with respect to internal organization and concerning personnel, financial, and operating practices. The continuous accountability imposed on government departments would hamper the operations of the nationalized industries and would require a fairly rigid centralization of authority. If the Minister of Transport were responsible for questions in the House of Commons about the service given by the stationmaster at Stow-on-the-Wold in the way the Foreign Secretary would answer for the activities of a British consul in Bangkok or the Secretary of State for War about the court-martial of a sergeant, the Transport Commission would have to establish the controls and keep the records of a Whitehall department. Any big organization is naturally bureaucratic in its methods, but the relief from day-to-day accountability means that a public corporation can be more flexible in its administration.

As another consideration, the corporate form of organization is favored because it permits the financial operations of each nationalized industry to be dealt with in the fashion of a private business. Each public corporation is selling a product or a service—coal, gas, transportation—and the intent is that it shall conduct its affairs in such a way that it breaks even on its operations. Government departments, on the other hand, are not usually dispensing financially measurable commodities or services. How can one measure the cost of foreign policy, of military security, or of the administration of justice? To be sure, administration in these fields can be judged to some extent by business criteria; seemingly wasteful or uneconomical expenditure on staff, offices, and supplies can be challenged. The resulting service, however, can only be evaluated in relation to its contribution or detraction from the nation's well-being. It is deemed desirable, therefore, to separate those governmental services whose support out of the public treasury is determined on broad grounds of national policy from those selling a commercial-type product or service. The use of the public corporation for activities of the latter kind allows its finances to be segregated and its efficiency to be evaluated by commercial criteria.

360–

5. *Some Problems Raised by Nationalization*

The increase in the number of public corporations has brought to the fore several important problems which are debated in Parliament, in party conferences, and in the press. These problems may be classified for purposes of discussion under the following headings: (1) the maintenance of public control and responsibility; (2) the internal organization of the public corporations; (3) personnel policies relating to public corporations; and (4) economic policy and the public corporations.

Concerning the maintenance of public control and responsibility, it is universally accepted that the nationalized industries are ultimately accountable to Parliament as the representative of their stockholders, the people of the United Kingdom. Parliament launched the corporations, and they remain subject to its sovereign jurisdiction. Several of them are managing industries or services of such importance to the national economy that Parliament is bound to be interested in their affairs. It is recognized, however, that the reasons for employing the corporate form in the case of the nationalized industries would be largely vitiated if Parliament attempted to supervise them in the manner of an ordinary government department. The problem arises, therefore, of how Parliament shall discharge its basic responsibility without interfering too frequently and in too much detail. In practical terms the questions are: what responsibility should the minister assume concerning the affairs of a public corporation and what reports are due Parliament on the activities of a corporation.

A partial answer to the first question is provided by the statutes establishing the public corporations. They empower a minister to appoint and remove the members of the board of the corporation and to give general directions to the board. In individual cases, a minister may have other duties and responsibilities with respect to a corporation. It is agreed that a minister is responsible to Parliament in the normal manner for his statutory duties. He must answer in debate and during the question hour for his performance of these duties. It is further agreed that he should not reply to questions concerning the usual day-to-day operations of a corporation. There remains, however, an area of controversy between these two accepted principles. During the past few years an effort has been made to establish some criteria concerning the kinds of questions that ministers should answer about the affairs of the nationalized industries. On one occasion the Labour Leader of the House of Commons, when questions about the responsibility of ministers for the Overseas Food Corporation and the Colonial Development Corporation had been raised on the motion for adjournment, stated that

> . . . broadly speaking, subject to the Speaker's rulings, Parliamentary questions in connection with these corporations which the ministers concerned would feel it right to answer would fall into the following categories: (1) Questions relating to the discharge of their specific statutory duties under the Overseas Resources Development

Act, 1948. (2) Questions arising from the provisions of Sections 7 and 8 relating to consultations with colonial governments about consulting local interests on safety, health, and welfare of employees. (3) Questions to the Colonial Secretary relating to the discharge by colonial governments of their general responsibilities which might bear upon the activities of the corporations. (4) Subject to the discretion of ministers to decline to reply, questions seeking for statements on matters of public importance allowed by the Speaker under his ruling.[7]

In general, the position of Labour Governments has been that questions about the nationalized industries are in order when they deal with a matter for which a minister is statutorily responsible but that they are not in order if they deal with matters of management which fall within the province of the board of a corporation. 'My Lords, this is a question of management for which the Corporation is responsible. I regret, therefore, that I am unable to assist the noble Viscount,' was a reply which the Minister of Civil Aviation gave in the House of Lords when questioned about changes made in the uniforms for employees of British European Airways.[8] Had a similar question been put to the Postmaster-General about the uniforms of postmen or to the First Lord of the Admiralty about naval uniforms, these ministers would undoubtedly have answered. The best that can be said is that there is developing a type of question which ministers consider it their responsibility to answer and a type of question which they regard as unsuitable for answer because the matter falls within the province of a board's administrative responsibility. The two types are not to date clearly defined in the minds either of ministers or of other members of Parliament. Precedents established by ministerial decision and the rulings of the Speaker over a period of years will be required before one can say with some certainty what is a legitimate question which can be addressed to a minister who has general responsibility for a nationalized industry. Very likely there will always be a debatable area on this subject.

Various proposals have come forward designed to make the control of Parliament over the nationalized industries more useful and effective. For the ordinary governmental activities the investigations and reports of the Public Accounts Committee of the House of Commons inform Parliament and the public about the progress of efficiency and economy in departmental management. The accounts of the nationalized industries are not now reviewed by the Public Accounts Committee, but suggestions have been made that they should be.[9] It has also been proposed that there

---

[7] *The Times,* 18 December 1948.

[8] 161 *H.L. Debates,* col. 1078.

[9] A former chairman of the Public Accounts Committee, Ralph Assheton, M.P., who believes that 'the power of the committee is not nearly strong enough' with respect to the financial affairs of the public corporations, has proposed that the private firms which audit their accounts should submit reports to a select committee of the

362–

should be another Parliamentary committee to receive the annual reports of the public corporations. Such a committee could get additional information and make comments on the reports so that ensuing debates in the House would have the benefit of the committee's detailed inquiries. It seems probable that Parliament will have to develop some special procedure for discharging its ultimate responsibility with respect to the public corporations. As previously mentioned, their operations are so vital to the general economy and touch the private citizen at so many points that they cannot be left in a largely insulated area of public life.[10]

Many administrative services subject to normal Parliamentary supervision are additionally under the observance of advisory councils which receive reports, confer with ministers, and submit recommendations. Most of the statutes creating the nationalized industries have provided for consumers' councils to serve as advisory bodies to the boards. In the coal industry there are two, one representing domestic and one representing industrial users. The Iron and Steel Consumers' Council, provided for in the Iron and Steel Act, 1949, has an independent chairman and 18 members—eight representing industries using iron and steel, three representing iron and steel merchants, three representing workers in consuming industries, two representing other nationalized industries, and two representing the board of the Iron and Steel Corporation. The Council is authorized 'to consider any matter, including prices, affecting the interests of consumers.' [11]

The consumers' councils have been criticized as ineffective bodies, inclined to echo the opinions and defend the policies of the boards of the corporations. Perhaps as their experience lengthens they will make more of a contribution to the administration of the nationalized industries. Sir Arthur Street, who was a member of the National Coal Board, considered that the two councils in that industry were 'performing a useful function.' [12]

Some problems of organization arising in the nationalized industries may next be considered. All of them are managed by boards appointed by min-

House of Commons in the same way the Comptroller and Auditor-General does for the regular administrative departments. *The Times,* 18 January 1951. Supporting this proposal editorially, *The Times* observed: 'The accounts of the nationalized industries should be examined as closely by the House of Commons, representing the owners, as the accounts of any company may be by its shareholders.' 19 January 1951.

[10] Soon after taking office in 1951, the Conservative Government announced its intention to appoint a select committee of the House of Commons with the following terms of reference: 'To consider present methods by which the House of Commons is informed of the affairs of the nationalized industries; to report what changes, having regard to the provisions laid down by Parliament in the various statutes, may be desirable in these methods.' *The Times,* 23 November 1951.

[11] *The Times,* 1 August 1951.

[12] 'Quasi-Government Bodies since 1918,' *British Government since 1918,* p. 167. Of the councils' work Street said, 'They can at any time bring grievances before the Minister for action, but their main purpose is to keep the Board fully attuned to the needs and wishes of the consumers of coal and to keep the consumers' representatives in touch with the Board's policies and difficulties.'

isters. This form of top management has been favored for several reasons. It permits the management of the industries to be entrusted to a group of persons of such varied experience as private business, trade union affairs, and public administration. The board form, moreover, tends to soften political criticism of the work of the nationalized industries; various bodies of opinion can feel that they have representation at the highest level of management and that major decisions have been reached after the consideration of all points of view. Finally, a board can act more independently, it is contended, than a single executive. It will not be as amenable to ministerial pressure. In Britain these reasons have been generally accepted as persuasive, and there has been no important sentiment in favor of industrial 'czars' or other single directors at the top.

Most of the boards have been composed of members with general managerial responsibilities. However, the National Coal Board, as originally organized, was an exception. The members of the N.C.B. were not only the joint directors of the industry but they had functional responsibilities as well. This form of organization did not prove satisfactory, and in 1951 the N.C.B. was reconstituted. Under the new arrangement it was composed of a chairman, two deputy chairmen, four full-time members, and five part-time members, none of whom had departmental or functional responsibilities.

Although, in general, the determination of the organizational structures below the board level has been left to the decision of the boards of the various industries, the main lines of internal organization have been prescribed in two or three of the statutes of nationalization. The gas industry, for example, has below the supervising and co-ordinating National Gas Council 12 area authorities, each a public corporation and responsible for the manufacture and distribution of gas within its area. The British Electricity Authority controls all generating facilities, except within the area of the North of Scotland Hydro-Electric Board, but distribution is in the hands of ministerially appointed area boards. These boards, however, are not public corporations, as in the case of the gas industry, and they are subject to the supervision of the B.E.A. The Transport Commission sits above a group of executives, boards of four to eight members appointed by the minister and each in charge of one of its services—railways, road haulage, road passenger transport, London transport, inland waterways, and hotels. Below each executive there are several organizational levels designed to meet the requirements of a particular service. For example, the Road Haulage Executive, which operates the long distance trucking service, has eight regional divisions, and these are divided into districts, of which there are 31. Each district headquarters supervises a number of groups. The group, under a manager, who has about 150 vehicles assigned to him, is the operational unit of the service. The organizational structure of the Road Haulage Executive has been described as 'reasonably flexible and realistically decentralized. . . There is in practice a useful degree of

364—

local decision and a welcome absence of hard-and-fast bureaucratic regulations.'[13]

Below the National Coal Board are a number of divisional coal boards appointed by the N.C.B. The next organizational level is the coal area under a manager responsible to a divisional board. The area manager supervises a group of pit managers. The N.C.B. has been the target of considerable criticism on the grounds of maintaining an unwieldy and inefficient organizational structure and failing to delegate sufficient authority to lower administrative levels. Commenting when the Board's first annual report was submitted to Parliament, *The Times* said, 'Signs are increasing, rather than decreasing, that the Board is cumbersome and slow, over-centralized and over-burdened with committees. . .'[14] To strictures of this nature, Sir Arthur Street replied:

> It would be fallacious to assume that, because the Divisional Coal Boards have been set up by the National Coal Board and are not statutory corporations like the Area Gas Boards, there is greater centralisation in the coal industry than there would otherwise be. The central functions which fall to the National Coal Board would have to be performed whatever the statutory set-up, and if there were no National Coal Board to perform these functions for the industry as a whole, then the Minister would have to perform them. He would have to co-ordinate prices and selling, settle the apportionment of capital expenditure and hold each Divisional Board to account for the way in which they spent the coal consumers' money, contrasting and comparing the results achieved by the various Divisional Boards. This would, in fact, mean greater centralisation because the Minister, being answerable to Parliament in detail for any action taken in his name, would be unable to delegate as much managerial responsibility as the National Coal Board are able to do.[15]

It was Street's opinion that too much attention was being paid to the structural organization of the nationalized industries and not enough to the caliber of people managing them. He observed that 'no amount of coloured charts can do anything for an organization if the men who fill the posts are lacking in capacity. The men in an organization and what they do will always be more important than the precise form of organization.'[16] Some would say this is an old school civil servant speaking and that he forgets that the managing personnel of the nationalized industries are people with diverse backgrounds and lacking the homogeneity and traditions of the Administrative Class, whose members function almost as much by instinct as by rule.

---

[13] *The Economist,* 2 December 1950, p. 960.
[14] 10 November 1949.
[15] 'Quasi-Government Bodies since 1918,' op. cit. p. 183.
[16] Ibid. p. 184.

Let us proceed at this point to note some of the personnel problems connected with the nationalized industries. One concerns the appointments to the boards of the corporations. Most of the nationalization acts require the minister to observe certain criteria in the appointment of board members, but these criteria are defined in terms sufficiently general to leave him considerable discretion. The Iron and Steel Act, for example, states that the chairman and the other members of the Board 'shall be appointed by the Minister from amongst persons appearing to him to be persons who have had wide experience of, and shown capacity in the production of iron ore or iron and steel, industrial or financial matters, administration and the organization of workers.' The appointments made to the boards since 1945 have frequently been criticized. A good deal of the criticism has come from enthusiasts for nationalization who have felt that ministers have been too reluctant to choose convinced believers in the policy of public ownership and management. These critics assert that too many businessmen and re-tired civil servants and military officers have been appointed. They regard many of these persons as not only lacking in conviction on the subject of nationalization but as unenterprising and wedded to routine methods of business. From laboring circles there has been criticism that an insufficient number of trade unionists and workers' representatives have been selected. At the annual meeting of the Trades Union Congress in 1950 a delegate pointed out that of some 85 members of the boards of public corporations only seven came from the ranks of organized labor. The Conservative Party, from the other direction, criticized the Labour Government for using the boards for patronage purposes, asserting that places were found for party stalwarts who did not qualify for ministerial appointments.

The Labour Government defended itself vigorously against these criticisms. At a Party Conference in 1949 Herbert Morrison, Lord President of the Council, declared that the Government 'had to find people of general competence in business or labour organization, with an aptitude for supervision, to stimulate the socialized industries to a high degree of efficiency.' [17] The task of finding satisfactory people for the higher positions in the nationalized industries has not been easy. A large proportion of the business community has been opposed to the principle of nationalization and unwilling to serve. Some competent industrialists have been politically unacceptable, for their appointment would appear to many workers as simply a continuation of private ownership under a new name. The trade unions do not possess a surplus of talent to be drawn upon. For a Labour Government it is as important that the larger unions and the Trades Union Congress be ably led as that the nationalized industries be efficiently managed, so there is nothing to be gained in depleting the unions' leadership. Under the circumstances it is not surprising that the Labour Government appointed a good many civil servants and retired military officers of high rank to the boards. They are usually politically neutral, or at least not out-

[17] *The Times,* 11 June 1949.

spokenly partisan, and they are experienced in the problems of large-scale organization.

Another personnel type problem has been the extent to which the nationalized industries should conform to civil service standards. The employees of the corporations are not civil servants in the usual sense, but the question arises as to how closely personnel policies and practices for administrative and technical staff should be related to those in the public service. In general, the boards of corporations have established their own personnel standards, and these standards have been more comparable to the practice of large private businesses than to that of the Civil Service. Salaries for the higher administrative and technical positions have exceeded the comparable ones of the Civil Service and local government service. Defending this practice before a Labour Party Conference, Herbert Morrison told his audience that it was necessary to approach the question rationally. 'For competent brains,' he asserted, 'they had to pay something towards the market rate, whatever that might be.' [18] It remains to be seen how long different policies and standards can be applied in the two large areas of public service. The distinction between public and other kinds of employment is less clear than it was a generation ago, and young people beginning careers will probably consider a position with the British Overseas Airways Corporation as much a type of public service as one with the Ministry of Works or the Post Office. They probably will note, however, that salary scales in the nationalized industries rise to higher figures than do those of the Civil Service.[19]

There has been some discussion in Labour Party and trade union circles about direct workers' representation in the management of the nationalized industries. The Labour Government resisted arguments that the trade unions are entitled to representation on the boards of industries in which large numbers of their members are employed, and in this attitude it was supported by the Trades Union Congress. Both took the position that the introduction of syndicalist principles would bring confusion into negotiations on wages and working conditions and militate against efficient management. Nevertheless, a demand for direct workers' representation appears annually at the conference of the T.U.C. For example, the National Union of Bank Employees, which desires representation on the Board of Governors of the Bank of England, sponsored a resolution of this kind at the 1949 conference. It was defeated on a card vote, 3,566,000 to 2,761,000. Similar resolutions at other conferences have suffered the same fate, but some of the unions keep the issue alive.

Nearly all the nationalized industries must grapple with serious business and commercial problems. It has been the Government's intent, as ex-

---

[18] *The Times,* 11 June 1949.

[19] For example, the Director General of the Post Office receives a salary of £4500 a year while the Chairman of the Railway Executive of the Transport Commission receives £7000.

pressed in the acts of nationalization, that the public corporations should pay their own way. Consistent profit-making is not expected but, 'taking one year with another,' they should stand on their own financial feet. This intention has proved difficult of realization in the case of several corporations. The National Coal Board managed after three or four years to report a modest surplus, but in 1951 it had a deficit of £1.8 million because of a rise in miners' wages.[20] The deficits of the Transport Commission were halted in 1951, when its annual report revealed a credit balance of £113,558. The report of the previous year showed a deficit of £14.1 million. One of the nationalized airways, B.O.A.C., managed to produce a surplus in 1951, but B.E.A. has operated at a loss. The Gas Council got off to a better start than some of the other nationalized undertakings. Its first report announced a surplus of £2633, with eight area boards showing surpluses on their operations and four showing deficits. In its second year, the nationalized gas industry did remarkably better; the Council announced a net surplus of £1,492,748.[21] The failure of the East African groundnuts scheme of the Overseas Food Corporation forced Parliament to write off a loss of approximately £36,000,000. Preventing some of the corporations from being a constant drain on the national treasury is going to require resolution on the part of ministers and trade union leaders.

The capital development of the nationalized industries presents economic problems. As stated by Sir Arthur Street, 'The industries will have to be expanded well beyond the point at which expansion would cease if they were commercial monopolies bent only on making the maximum profit. Yet they must not expand so far that the additional goods and services are provided at a loss, even though the books of the industry as a whole can be made to balance, as this would denote misapplication of national resources.'[22] The task of making provision for the optimum amount of capital development while subject to the many and frequently contradictory pressures of politicians, business interests, workers, and consumers will tax the judgment and foresight of ministers and the boards of the corporations.

6. The Record to Date

In concluding our consideration of the nationalized industries we can attempt a brief evaluation of program and administration as they have evolved to date. It must be very provisional, for the record is too short to support firm judgments. The nationalization program as pursued since 1945 has not led to the increases in productivity and efficiency that many of its advocates prophesied. The simple faith that nationalization would put everything right with a 'sick' industry has had to be revised. Coal output remains below national requirements, and the railways' losses continue

[20] The Times, 29 May 1952.
[21] Ibid. 14 March 1951; 11 December 1951.
[22] Op. cit. p. 189.

368–

to mount in spite of higher charges. There is little evidence that the workers in the nationalized undertakings find any additional stimulus to their efforts in the fact that they as citizens 'own' the public corporations. Absenteeism among miners still plagues the coal industry, and notwithstanding the highest wages in the history of British mining, the recruitment of new workers fails to meet the targets. Although the postwar period has been comparatively free of industrial unrest, strikes and slowdowns have occurred in the nationalized industries. Labor relations have probably been complicated by the workers' disposition to look beyond the board of a public corporation to the ministry and Parliament for the satisfaction of claims. It is plain that the state's new role as the employer of several million workers will lay some complex problems before ministers and Parliament.

If nationalization has not proved to be the medicine to cure the ills of some of Britain's important industries, it has not killed the patients as some opponents of socialism claimed it would. Indeed, it is difficult to see that the industries transferred to the public domain would have established any better records in private hands and they might have done considerably worse. It should be noted that two of the principal subjects of nationalization, coal and the railways, were far from flourishing under private ownership. Both required large outlays of capital if their health was to be restored, and the state was the only likely source of such capital. Furthermore, it is doubtful if private managements, particularly in the coal industry, could have maintained even the degree of worker morale that has prevailed since 1947. Of coal nationalization an American observer has written, 'For better or for worse, the political necessities of the situation did not permit any other solution or any attempt to find an alternative.' [23]

The enthusiasm for nationalization within the ranks of the Labour Party appears to have waned as experience has indicated its limitations as a solution for industrial problems. In 1949 the party issued a pamphlet, *Labour Believes in Britain,* which listed several industries and services considered either as suitable for nationalization or as due to be investigated with this end in view. Meat slaughtering, cold storage, sugar refining, cement, chemicals, and industrial insurance were among the industries and businesses mentioned. With the party having only a small majority in the House of Commons after the general election of 1950, no legislation affecting these private businesses was introduced. The party ranks held firm as the Conservatives made last-minute attacks on iron and steel nationalization before the vesting date, 15 February 1951, but Labour sentiment seemed to favor a period of consolidation and assessment before embarking on additional projects of public ownership.

When the Conservatives took office in October 1951, they had promised to restore only two nationalized industries to private hands, long-distance road transport and iron and steel. The Government introduced a bill to

---

[23] Robert Brady, *Crisis in Britain* (Berkeley, 1950), p. 108.

authorize it to sell the Transport Commission's highway equipment, amounting to 44,000 vehicles, to private operators. The denationalization of the iron and steel industry represented a more formidable administrative task. The prospects of finding private investors were not enhanced in either case by threats from Labour circles to re-enact nationalization when the party gained power again.

Some understanding between the major parties with respect to the more controversial nationalization projects appears necessary. Great industries obviously cannot be shifted back and forth between public and private ownership as party fortunes change at Westminster. Under such shuttle-cock action in Parliament, long range development would become impossible, and the managerial efficiency so vital to the success of these industries could never be achieved.

XXI

Policy and Administration: Imperial Affairs

More than any other major power the United Kingdom is concerned in the formulation and application of policy with its relations with associated nations and dependent territories. The United Kingdom as the most powerful unit in the British Commonwealth of Nations and as the center of an extensive colonial empire must always bear these connections in mind in shaping both external and domestic policy. It is no easy task to provide leadership in the Commonwealth group and to strike a satisfactory balance between conflicting claims arising out of the United Kingdom's multilateral interests.

The dominions now are comparatively important national states, and their historical traditions, geographical locations, racial compositions, and domestic problems raise matters of considerable delicacy in the United Kingdom's dealings with them. There is a strong disposition on their part for co-operation, without which the task of providing leadership would be impossible; nevertheless, much negotiating and consideration of varying points of view must enter into the development of any common understanding, to say nothing of common policy.

With the colonial empire the problem of relationships is not so difficult. The United Kingdom deals with the units of the empire, for the most part, on a bilateral basis, and the mother country is almost always in a much stronger position than the colony. Britain is interested, however, in maintaining the loyalty of colonial peoples and is required to weigh their needs and aspirations in formulating policy. In this chapter we shall consider the governmental organization and practice in the United Kingdom for developing and administering policy with respect to the Commonwealth and Empire and some of the domestic influences bearing on imperial affairs; subsequent chapters will deal with the political organization of the Commonwealth and Empire and some problems arising from the relationships of the members.

1. Britain and the Commonwealth Nations

One could scarcely say that there is any such thing as a Commonwealth policy of the British government. There is rather an attitude toward relations with the Commonwealth that is shared by all political parties. Basic in this attitude is a recognition of the independent status of the dominions and their complete freedom to determine their own policies.[1] An equally important part of the attitude is the acceptance of an obligation to make every effort compatible with the essential interest of the United Kingdom to promote the continuance of the Commonwealth as a group of especially friendly and co-operating states. Practical manifestations of this attitude were to be seen in the dealings with India on the question of retaining Commonwealth membership as a republic instead of as a constitutional monarchy. The British Government took pains to assure the Indians that the choice was freely theirs and that no reprisals would follow a decision to break the connection with the United Kingdom and the other dominions. At the same time the Indian Government was informed that an effort would be made to accommodate its intended national position within the existing company of the Commonwealth. This approach commended itself to the Parliamentary opposition as well as to the Government, and there was general satisfaction with the formula of association which was agreed to at the Prime Ministers' Conference in April 1949.

While it is difficult to describe a policy toward the Commonwealth, there are numerous policies in the imperial and Commonwealth field which are formulated and carried into effect by the British Government. These relate to such important matters as co-operation in defense, mutual assistance in trade and commerce, dominion immigration schemes, and common objectives with respect to various international problems which arise. It is obvious that some of these matters are of the greatest moment to the United Kingdom and are consequently considered and formulated at the highest political levels. The Prime Minister takes an active interest in the shaping of policies that affect the Commonwealth. On many major questions he takes personal responsibility for the discussions leading to a British position, and he explains and defends this position in Parliament. He is assisted in the development of a United Kingdom policy by two or three of the Cabinet committees which operate in this area. One of these is the Defence Committee of which he is the chairman and which studies problems and makes proposals involving military and strategic concerns. Another is the Economic Committee which deals with Britain's position in world trade and which naturally considers commercial relations with the Commonwealth nations. The recommendations of these committees will in all important instances go before the full Cabinet, and the decision there will become the policy of the British Government.

Some policy decisions of the Cabinet on imperial affairs will require Parliamentary action. When new legislation or amendments to existing legislation are necessary, the Government will introduce a bill for this

---

[1] Even when the Commonwealth nations are joined in such an important endeavor as fighting a war, the right of each to determine the strategical deployment of its forces and like matters is recognized. Readers of Churchill's history of World War II will recall his exchange of messages with the Prime Minister of Australia over the future use of dominion troops being returned from the Middle East theater. *The Hinge of Fate* (Boston, 1950), pp. 155-66.

purpose and will promote it through its various stages. The major burden of guiding legislation through Parliament will probably be taken by the Secretary of State for Commonwealth Relations, and the Prime Minister, the Foreign Secretary, the Chancellor of the Exchequer, and other ministers will participate according to the nature of the legislation and the degree to which it bears upon their special responsibilities. The House of Lords always takes an active interest in imperial affairs and any legislation in this field is certain to get serious consideration in the upper chamber. Some members of the Lords have served as governors-general, high commissioners, or in other imperial positions which give them qualifications for discussing such policy matters. Usually such debates attain the high order and indicate the feeling of responsibility which the British Government assumes in dealings between itself and the other nations of the Commonwealth.

Besides debating and passing legislation concerning Commonwealth relations, Parliament also participates in the policy field by directing questions to ministers and by holding debates on current issues. Questions about all aspects of the relations between the United Kingdom and various members of the Commonwealth appear regularly on the order paper of the House of Commons. Usually these are answered by the Secretary of State for Commonwealth Relations, or the Parliamentary Under Secretary if the Secretary is a peer, but some of them may be taken by the Prime Minister, the Foreign Secretary, the Minister of Defence, or some other appropriate minister.[2] In the House of Lords the opposition utilizes the privilege it has of raising questions for debate to introduce a discussion of some aspect of Commonwealth relations and thus to obtain from the Government a statement of policy on a particular matter. It can be said that Commonwealth affairs are under continuous Parliamentary scrutiny, and no serious problem arising between the United Kingdom and one or all of the dominions goes for long without a discussion in Parliament.

When an issue of policy which involves all the Commonwealth countries as well as the United Kingdom arises, it may be necessary to consult and seek agreement through a meeting of Commonwealth representatives. Such a meeting may be proposed by the Prime Minister in the United Kingdom, and if his dominion colleagues are agreeable, a time and place

---

[2] The following example is typical of the kind of question on Commonwealth relations directed to ministers in the House of Commons:

'Mr. Hurd (Newbury, C.) asked the Prime Minister to what extent he discussed migration policy with the Prime Ministers of Australia and New Zealand at the recent meeting of Commonwealth Prime Ministers; and if he would state the extent to which the United Kingdom will co-operate, for instance through assisted passages, in encouraging the migration of British families to the Dominions.

'Mr. Attlee (Walthamstow, West, Lab.)—The opportunity was taken to discuss future migration policy with Mr. Menzies in London, as the Assisted Passage Agreement with Australia expires on March 30. There is no such agreement with New Zealand and there have been no discussions on migration here with Mr. Holland.' 483 *H.C. Debates* 5s., col. 298.

are decided upon. The United Kingdom Government will determine its position toward the question through the regular procedure by which it formulates policy. This position may have to be modified as a result of the negotiations with the Commonwealth representatives. Minor adjustments are usually possible within the scope of the British Cabinet's policy decision, but a major amendment will go back to the Cabinet for consideration.

Problems of insufficient gravity to justify calling a conference of representatives from all the dominions may be dealt with through visits of British ministers to one or more dominion capitals. These trips may be undertaken by the Secretary of State for Commonwealth Relations or by a minister primarily concerned about a current problem. From time to time the Minister of Defence has business to discuss with a dominion government, and the President of the Board of Trade, the Minister of Food, and the Minister of Supply are occasionally required to visit Commonwealth capitals to consider matters falling within their responsibilities. When ministers from London come to the United States they usually include Ottawa in their itinerary. Between the United Kingdom and Canada there are special diplomatic and military problems arising out of the North Atlantic Treaty, and the trade and financial relations of the sterling and dollar areas are of great importance to both countries. When making visits to Commonwealth capitals British ministers are customarily accompanied by military or civilian advisors who confer with their dominion opposite numbers.

Important issues requiring consultation with the dominions are dealt with in the ways just described, but there is a great deal of daily business which does not rise to such levels. This daily grist is the responsibility of the Office of Commonwealth Relations. The evolution of this office reflects the development of Britain's relations with the present Commonwealth countries during the past century and a half.

At the beginning of the nineteenth century the administration of the colonies was vested in the War Office, and they remained in the charge of that department until the Crimean War. Then a separate Colonial Office was established under a minister known as the Secretary of State for the Colonies. Almost contemporaneously there was established, under another Secretary of State, the India Office, which succeeded to the governmental functions performed before the mutiny by the East India Company. Gradually, a separation developed within the Colonial Office between sections dealing with those colonies settled by Europeans and having a large measure of self-government and the dependencies and protectorates. The Dominions Division which existed from 1907 to 1921 developed into the Dominions Office under a Secretary of State. From 1925 until 1930 a single minister headed both the Colonial Office and the Dominions Office, but since then it has been customary for individual secretaries to occupy these posts. In 1940 British relations with Burma, previously handled by the India Office, were transferred to a separate department, although the Secretary of State for India continued to head the Burma Office. When India achieved dominion status (1947) and the independence of Burma was recognized (1948), the India and Burma Offices were abolished. The

Dominions Office was renamed the Office of Commonwealth Relations with a Secretary of State to deal with all the Commonwealth nations.

The Secretary of State for Commonwealth Relations is in constant touch with the dominion governments, usually through their ministries of external affairs. His representatives for approaching the dominion governments are the British high commissioners stationed in each capital. In London dominion high commissioners maintain close and intimate contacts with the Office of Commonwealth Relations. Thus, there is a constant flow of information and policy consultation between London and the dominion governments.[3]

The Office of Commonwealth Relations is a relatively small department organized in a fashion similar to most other ministries of the British government. In addition to the Secretary of State, there is a Parliamentary Under Secretary who shares some of the Secretary's departmental and Parliamentary duties. All other officials of the Office are permanent civil servants. A Permanent Under Secretary is the minister's principal advisor and the head of the administrative organization of the Office. The duties of the officers of the department consist principally in conferring with representatives of the dominion high commissioners' offices, preparing instructions and information reports for the United Kingdom's high commissioners in dominion capitals, and in maintaining liaison with other ministries on problems affecting Commonwealth relations. From time to time they have the responsibility of organizing a Commonwealth conference and insuring that all the necessary memoranda and data required by the United Kingdom participants are prepared and co-ordinated with the interested departments.

While the Office of Commonwealth Relations takes the lead in dealings with the Commonwealth nations, several other departments of the British government are much concerned. The Foreign Office must consult the dominions frequently about questions before international organizations such as the United Nations and the Council of Foreign Ministers. The Treasury has business with them on such matters as the blocked sterling

---

[3] In 1940 Prime Minister Churchill decided that too large a volume of information was being sent from London to the dominion governments. He, therefore, wrote the following memorandum to the Dominions Secretary: 'No departure in principle is contemplated from the practice of keeping the Dominions informed fully of the progress of the war. Specially full information must necessarily be given in respect of theatres where Dominion troops are serving, but it is not necessary to circulate this to the other Dominions not affected. Anyhow, on the whole an effort should be made not to scatter so much deadly and secret information over this very large circle. . . There is a danger that the Dominions Office Staff get into the habit of running a kind of newspaper full of deadly secrets, which are circularised to the four principal Governments with whom they deal. The idea is that the more they circulate, the better they are serving the State. Many other departments fall into the same groove, loving to collect as much secret information as possible and feeling proud to circulate it conscientiously through all official circles. I am trying steadily to restrict and counteract these tendencies, which, if unchecked, would make the conduct of war impossible.' *Their Finest Hour*, p. 707.

balances—that is, the unfunded war debts—which several of them hold, exchange controls, and the gold and dollar reserves of the sterling area. British commercial policy as administered by the Treasury and the Board of Trade is of great importance to the dominion governments. The Minister of Defence and the three service departments deal with the dominion governments on strategical plans, jointly used facilities, and military training and equipment matters. Most of this business is channeled through the Office of Comomnwealth Relations, although on specific issues British ministries may deal directly with their opposite numbers in the dominions. In total there is a very large volume of Commonwealth business which covers the whole range of governmental activity except the purely domestic. As a measure of the volume, it has been reported that whereas in 1938 London dispatched 5656 telegrams to Commonwealth governments, the number in 1949 was 21,790.[4] This substantial increase reflects the growing stature of the dominions in world affairs and the greatly expanded activity of international organizations in which they, as well as other countries, participate; it also indicates the importance the United Kingdom attaches to consultation with the Commonwealth governments.

Britain's position as the leading member of the Commonwealth has several effects upon its policies. In the first place, to the extent that the United Kingdom can speak for all the dominions as well as for itself, the London government's weight and prestige in international affairs are thereby increased. As one of the Big Three, the Big Four, or as a permanent member of the United Nations Security Council, Great Britain endeavors to expound policies and take positions that have a Commonwealth backing. When the British government is able to do this, it can claim to represent a collection of states more populous than any one of the major powers. They are states, too, which are entitled by the parts they have played in both world wars to respectful consideration by the other major nations. A British Foreign Secretary participating in a meeting of the Council of Foreign Ministers is representing primarily the United Kingdom, but his position is bolstered by the fact that he is often speaking as well for Canada, Australia, New Zealand, India, Pakistan, South Africa, and Ceylon, most of whom made substantial contributions to the allied victory over the Axis powers.

Secondly, the position of spokesman for the Commonwealth nations frequently involves considerable delay in the formulation of British policy. In order to present a united front the British government must consult each of the dominions and obtain their views upon a pending issue. There is adequate machinery for this consultation and on the whole it works quickly and efficiently, but nevertheless some delay is inevitable. Dominion cabinets must confer and reach an agreed policy and then each must transmit its views to London. There they must be reconciled with the policy decided upon by the British Cabinet, and frequently further consultations

---

[4] *The Economist,* 16 December 1950, p. 1065.

are necessary to eliminate conflicting opinions or to establish individual reservations on the part of the dominions. There is a considerable price to be paid, therefore, for the additional strength which the United Kingdom possesses in international affairs by virtue of its Commonwealth leadership.

The United Kingdom's position has another effect upon its policy formulation. This is its inability to take a positive stand upon some international issues because of lack of agreement within the Commonwealth or because of important clashes between Commonwealth members. Thus, the United Kingdom is sometimes required to take an equivocal position lest it offend a member of the Commonwealth upon some issue which the latter regards as not open to debate. Within the Commonwealth there is a general acceptance of the possibility of disagreement even to the point of opposing one another in international bodies, but the United Kingdom cannot claim too much latitude for itself without endangering the likelihood of getting agreement upon most major issues. It must stand sometimes in the position of impartiality when two dominions clash, as for example South Africa and India over the color question, or India and Pakistan over the control of Kashmir. When such differences arise the United Kingdom usually maintains a studiously impartial public attitude but endeavors to work behind the scenes to effect an acceptable agreement.

2. *Colonial Policy*

The formulation of colonial policy is not fraught with the difficulties that arise in connection with the dominions. The United Kingdom is in the position of dominance, although it endeavors to pursue policies which are widely acceptable to colonial peoples. Responsibility still rests in London, however, and the elaborate consultation carried on with the Commonwealth nations is lacking.

Present-day British colonial policy may be said to consist of three elements. The first is the idea of trusteeship for colonial areas. For a generation or more the British have justified to themselves and to the world their possession and control of the vast colonial empire which they still hold on the grounds that these territories are unprepared for independence and that they require the support and guidance of a great power to lead them into the status of nationhood. The British reason that if they did not exercise dominion over them the dependencies would revert into barbarism or would fall prey to some less benevolent imperialism. From this attitude it follows that the long-term interests of the colonial peoples must be the first consideration of British policy. The colonies must not be exploited for immediate commercial profit nor must their basic resources be alienated and their future development thwarted. The social development of colonial peoples must be encouraged so they can gradually take over the management of their own affairs. British colonial officials must endeavor to associate native leaders with their administrations in order that local interests have representation and political experience be gained.

A second element in British colonial policy is the intention to retain

control of areas of great strategic value. Since the maintenance of communications with distant parts of the world is second in importance only
to the defense of the British Isles in Britain's security plans, the colonial
possessions that are strategically located on sea and air routes are in-
valuable. To mention places such as Gibraltar, Malta, Aden, Singapore,
and the Falkland Islands is sufficient to indicate their importance in British
security considerations. While Britain was unable to prevent the capture
of some of its strategic colonies in World War II, enough of them were successfully defended to be of immense value in the military operations of
the conflict. In modern war a closely connected chain of coaling stations
is less essential than it was in the nineteenth century, but there is still need
for securely held bases where ships can be repaired, airplanes can land
and refuel, and offensive operations can be mounted. The British government, therefore, regards the colonial empire as an essential part of its
security system. It is not inclined to abandon its control of any important
strategic territory without some assurance that it will be available when
military necessity requires. In recognizing Ceylon as a self-governing dominion, the United Kingdom negotiated for the use of naval bases in the
territory. It was prepared to forego its special position in Egypt only when
a treaty could be signed providing for the security of the Suez Canal.[5]

The third element in colonial policy is the desire to integrate the economies of the colonies with that of the United Kingdom. Britain's existence
as a strong industrial nation depends upon her ability to import large
quantities of food and raw materials and to sell manufactured goods to
the rest of the world. In this scheme the colonial empire has a large part
to play. Some of the colonies are rich sources of minerals, foodstuffs, and
raw materials like rubber. As Britain finds it difficult to sell manufactured
goods to the dollar area, it becomes increasingly important to utilize
sources from which supplies can be paid for by her own exports. Vigorous
efforts are being made, therefore, to develop the potentialities of the
colonial empire and to decrease correspondingly the United Kingdom's
dependence upon the dollar area. Some of the problems being encountered
in the pursuit of these efforts will be discussed in Chapter XXIII.

The lead in developing colonial policy and the political responsibility
for administering the Empire are duties of the Secretary of State for the
Colonies who is almost invariably in the Cabinet. As a member of the
Government he is responsible to Parliament for the discharge of these
duties. The members of Parliament maintain a watchful eye over colonial
affairs. Any special occurrence, such as civil disorder in a colony, the
alleged mistreatment of natives, or financial mismanagement, will be the

---

[5] Although the treaty permits British forces to be stationed in the Canal Zone until
1956, Egyptian nationalists have been eager to obtain their earlier withdrawal; the
British government contends, however, that the security of the Middle East requires
a satisfactory substitute arrangement before it can evacuate the area. The Canal Zone
issue is complicated by Anglo-Egyptian differences over the Sudan, nominally a condominium but actually under British administration.

subject of questions to ministers and will be raised in debate. Many members are well informed on colonial matters through study and experience, and there are always a number in Parliament who can speak with authority on the West Indies, Malaya, Central Africa, and the other areas of empire. Moreover, they are prompted and assisted in raising matters in Parliament by private individuals and groups having an interest in colonial affairs.

Parliament rarely legislates directly for the colonial empire, although some general acts, for example legislation on shipping or citizenship, may apply to the colonies. The legal instruments of colonial control are orders-in-council and the letters patent and royal instructions given to colonial governors upon appointment. It should perhaps be mentioned that Parliament levies no taxes on the colonies nor exacts any tribute. A lesson learned around 1776 has never been forgotten at Westminster.

The department through which the Secretary of State for the Colonies discharges his responsibilities is the Colonial Office. He has the assistance of a Parliamentary Under Secretary of State and a Minister of State, both sitting in Parliament and usually in different houses. A Permanent Under Secretary is the Secretary's principal policy advisor and the head of the department's staff of about 1200 civil servants. Below the permanent head of the Colonial Office there are two Deputy Under Secretaries, seven Assistant Under Secretaries, and 26 Assistant Secretaries. Each of the Assistant Secretaries is in charge of one of the departments of the Office. Six of these departments have area responsibilities—East and Central Africa, Eastern, Mediterranean, Pacific, West African, and West Indian—and the rest are functional or administrative. The Office has a considerable staff of advisors to give expert assistance on such subjects as agriculture, animal health, education, forestry, labor, social welfare, and other colonial problems. Furthermore, there are advisory committees drawn mainly from outside the government aiding in the administration of these functional subjects. The existence of the advisors and the advisory committees and the subjects with which they are concerned indicate that the Colonial Office is not alone a ministry of political control over scattered dependencies of the United Kingdom but is an agency to promote economic and social development as well. As one of its senior officials has written: 'The big change of the last quarter-century is the development of the Colonial Office as a central organization for policy-making and for giving assistance, advice, and guidance to the Colonial Governments in their task of promoting the advancement and welfare of the Colonial peoples. In short, whereas the work of the Colonial Office was, in the old days, mostly of a negative kind, now it is positive and dynamic.' [6]

3. Public Attitudes on Imperial Affairs

There is little difference today between the attitudes on imperial affairs of the two leading political parties, the Labour Party and the Conservative

---

[6] Sir Charles Jeffries, *Partners for Progress* (London, 1949), p. 71.

Party. In the middle of the nineteenth century the Liberals were generally anti-imperialistic and believed that under the principles of free trade all backward areas of the world would be opened for commercial exploitation regardless of political control. The Conservatives, for reasons of prestige and strategical advantages, were more favorably disposed toward the Empire, although it was not until Disraeli made the new imperialism a basic tenet of Conservative policy that the idea was enthusiastically accepted. It may be said that from about 1875 onward the Conservatives were ardent imperialists and the Liberals rather reluctant ones. Free trade had failed to sweep the world as its early proponents predicted, and the competition of rival imperialisms drove even Liberal Governments in Great Britain to the protection and the extension of colonial holdings.

The Labour Party inherited to some extent the lack of enthusiasm of the old-time Liberals for Britain's colonial empire. Many Labourites believed that a moral issue was involved and that imperialism resulted from the desire of capitalists to exploit backward peoples and rob them of their indigenous resources. Other Labourites considered that the colonial empire was greatly overrated in an economic sense and that the working classes of Britain were supporting a system which had advantages only for relatively few businessmen, military officers, and colonial officials. These attitudes which were strong in the early years of the Labour Party have for the most part disappeared. The moral problem has been solved for many scrupulous party leaders by the concept of trusteeship. Great Britain, so they reason, is exercising a benevolent tutelage over its wards and gradually preparing them for independent life in the modern world. This is an idea of service that removes most of the unsavory characteristics associated with imperialism. A second reason for the change in attitude upon the part of the Labour Party is found in the economic support which the colonial empire brings to the United Kingdom. After 1945 a Labour Government was faced with a formidable economic problem and its solution appeared to depend upon Britain's ability to mobilize all her remaining economic assets and to integrate them into an increasingly productive whole. More and more the British are finding that their investments in areas under foreign political control are being expropriated or liquidated under circumstances unfavorable to their former owners. The railways and other public utilities in Latin America, in which much British capital was invested, are being purchased by the governments where they are located. In Central and Eastern Europe, Communist regimes have expropriated important British investments. Nationalist and anti-foreign campaigns in the countries of the Near and Middle East have placed British holdings in jeopardy, and in the Far East revolutionary movements have made British commercial prospects exceedingly dim. Along with the loss of investments which formerly added to the invisible exports of the United Kingdom and which usually helped to channel British trade in the direction of their location, the United Kingdom is finding many barriers raised to profitable commercial relations. The British hope that after the dislocations of the

380–

last war subside, they will be able to re-establish many of these commercial relationships. In the meantime, however, they must depend increasingly upon their colonial empire for secure sources of raw materials and for markets for manufactured goods. As an example, should Malaya fall into the anarchy which ensued with the independence of Burma, the British would be deprived of a large source of rubber and tin and one of the most important dollar earning areas of the empire. The Labour Government considered it necessary, therefore, for Britain to retain the existing colonial empire in its own economic self-interest. It could assuage such qualms of conscience as arose from the party's anti-imperialistic past by pointing to the new doctrine of trusteeship and by advancing the argument that British rule is more advantageous to the native populations than that of other imperialisms or the internal chaos which might ensue upon withdrawal.

The Conservative Party has never been bothered with the problem of reconciling early professions of anti-imperialism with present necessities. The Conservatives, for the most part, have believed wholeheartedly in Britain's imperial mission, and Winston Churchill voiced their sentiments when he said that he had not become the King's first minister in order to preside over the liquidation of the British Empire. Much of this attitude has come from the basic paternalistic philosophy of the party. Just as it was believed that a governing class could serve the interest of the whole country with greater effectiveness than a more democratic regime, so it was held that British colonial administrators performed a service that no one else was capable of duplicating. Within this general philosophy many special interests found a place. Bankers preferred to invest under the Union Jack, and other commercial interests felt more secure with British political control extending over their trading areas. The military services brought forth strong arguments for the acquisition and retention of various strategic regions necessary to the security of Britain and its far-flung lines of communications. The Colonial Service itself became something of a vested interest. Most of the members of the Colonial Service were drawn from the same social stratum as the military services and the higher Civil Service at home, and they took seriously the notion of Britain's imperial mission. The Conservative Party bound a large proportion of these elements together, and they were influential in determining its attitude on imperial questions. The slogans and toasts of empire always received an enthusiastic response from a Conservative audience.

Within recent years a kind of British isolationism, best exemplified by Lord Beaverbrook and his widely read newspapers, has laid heavy stress upon the maintenance and development of the colonial empire. This movement argues that Britain should cease her political and economic dependence upon the United States and with the Commonwealth and Empire form a third bloc in international affairs. Slurred over are the unwillingness of the dominions to fall into any closed system with the United Kingdom and the inability of the colonial empire, valuable as it is, to supply all the necessities of British commerce. The appeal has considerable attractive-ness, however, for a people who are reluctant to admit the necessity of leaning on any other nation and who are eager to regain a more inde-pendent position.

The political parties are influenced by a considerable body of British opinion which interests itself in imperial affairs. Within the United King-dom there are a good many people with connections of various kinds to the Commonwealth and Empire. Among them are industrialists and busi-nessmen who have extensive investments and commercial interests in the dominions and colonies. To note the branch offices or to read the annual reports of many of the banks, commercial houses, and shipping companies having their headquarters in the City of London is to see the ramifications of British industry and trade throughout the Commonwealth and Empire. There are numerous cultural and religious societies with affiliations in British overseas territories. These groups, plus the military and colonial services, contribute to a large body of retired people who have spent their active years in the dominions and colonies and who maintain a continuing interest in imperial affairs. Many of them support or are members of or-ganizations such as the Royal Empire Society, the British Empire League, the Overseas Club, and the Empire Economic Union, which by meetings, lectures, and publications keep Britain's overseas relations constantly in the public eye. While these organizations are usually politically neutral, links with the Conservative Party are often close. The party has always presented itself as the champion of the imperial interest, and it gives a sympathetic hearing to all those devoted to strengthening the Common-wealth and Empire. The Labour Party has never been as directly influ-enced by these interest groups as have its political opponents, but in recent years some of the bodies associated with the Labour movement have de-voted considerable attention to imperial affairs. In 1940 the Fabian Society established a Colonial Bureau to study the problems of the dependent em-pire and to propose solutions in keeping with Labour's objective of abol-ishing old-fashioned imperialism and substituting a reciprocally fruitful partnership between the mother country and the colonies. The Bureau's first chairman was Arthur Creech Jones, a trade union official and Labour Party politician who in 1945 became Parliamentary Under Secretary of State for the Colonies and the next year Colonial Secretary. He was also chairman of an organization known as the Friends of Africa. The Trades Union Congress has a Colonial Labour Advisory Committee, and there are other Labour oriented groups taking notice of Britain's overseas empire. Altogether the political parties and the Government in power are kept aware of the multifarious British imperial interests by the patriotic, com-mercial, cultural, and research organizations which concern themselves with the Commonwealth and Empire.

Traveling by different paths, the two principal political parties have ar-rived at practically the same point of view on imperial issues. Both acclaim the importance of the Commonwealth to the United Kingdom and are eager

382–

to maintain it as a co-operating group of nations. Responsible leaders in both parties are aware that the continuance of the Commonwealth depends upon a recognition that each member is a fully sovereign nation and that the league can develop only by the mutual agreement of its parts. Concerning the colonial empire, both parties are desirous of promoting its development and of winning the assent of dependent peoples to a continuation of the British connection. Both believe that the welfare of colonial peoples takes precedence over purely British interests and that the old days of exploitation for quick profits have gone forever. A Conservative Government will probably be somewhat more solicitous of private business interests in the colonies, while a Labour Government is inclined to emphasize native welfare and social advancement. These differences, however, are only ones of degree, and there is no sharp break in colonial policy when Governments change in London.

XXII

The British Commonwealth of Nations

History contains many examples of countries forming leagues and associations for the promotion of their mutual interests. In the modern world the most geographically widespread and the most populous is the British Commonwealth of Nations. It is an interesting association because of the historical evolution by which it has come into existence and because of the institutions through which its contacts are maintained and its purposes promoted.

1. *The Nature of the Commonwealth*

The Commonwealth consists of eight countries which are placed on all the continents except South America. These countries are Canada, Australia, New Zealand, the Union of South Africa, India, Pakistan, Ceylon, and the United Kingdom itself.[1] They differ greatly in size, population, and wealth. Canada, Australia, South Africa, and India cover vast territories, while Britain, New Zealand, and Ceylon are comparatively small in geographical size. India with about 350 million people is the largest in population; at the other extreme is New Zealand with slightly more than two million inhabitants. The people of Canada probably enjoy the highest standard of living within the Commonwealth, while the three Asian dominions are areas of comparatively low living standards. Canada, Australia, and New Zealand are peopled almost entirely by descendants of European nationalities, mainly British, and have only small indigenous populations

---

[1] Newfoundland was counted as a dominion until 1933 when financial troubles led it to revert to colonial status. Governed by a British appointed commission, Newfoundland was offered the choice after World War II of continuing the colonial administration, attempting again an independent existence as a dominion, or of joining Canada as a province. The first referendum on the question was indecisive, but at a second one there was a small majority favoring union with Canada. In 1949 Newfoundland became, therefore, the tenth province of the Canadian federation. Southern Rhodesia falls short of dominion status because its foreign relations are controlled by the United Kingdom. Representatives of Southern Rhodesia often participate in Commonwealth conferences, and its relations with the United Kingdom are handled by the Office of Commonwealth Relations. The term 'dominion' came into use to denominate the self-governing members of the British Empire at the time of the Imperial Conference of 1907. It is officially a part of the name of only two, the Dominion of Canada and the Dominion of New Zealand.

384–

remaining within their borders.[2] The 12 million people of South Africa are divided between about 2,500,000 Europeans and more than nine million Negro and colored races. The three Asian dominions are peopled almost exclusively by native, but not homogeneous, races. In the Commonwealth as a whole the people of European stock are outnumbered about six to one by people of other races.

All the dominions were at one time colonial dependencies of Great Britain. Their evolution into independent states began at different times in each one; it culminated in 1948 when Ceylon was granted dominion status. During the nineteenth century the four oldest dominions, Canada, Australia, New Zealand, and South Africa, achieved a considerable measure of home rule, either as countries within their present borders or as geographical areas embracing several individual colonies. Under the pressure of growing colonial assertiveness, the government at London gradually relinquished its supervision and permitted the colonies to manage their domestic affairs. After gaining autonomy at home, the colonial governments sought an increasing share in such foreign policy as concerned their interests. This Britain conceded, and eventually they became recognized as independent states although still maintaining a close relationship to the United Kingdom and to each other.[3] The Asian dominions advanced toward independence at a later date, and their status of equality with the older dominions was only achieved after World War II. Important landmarks along the road to dominion independence were the peace conference of Versailles, where Canada, Australia, New Zealand, South Africa, and India signed their first important treaty as separate states, and the establishment of the League of Nations in which the dominions and India, plus the Irish Free State after 1921, participated as individual members. The new position of the dominions was announced in a report of the Imperial Conference of 1926, further elaborated at the Imperial Conference of 1930, and given constitutional form by the Statute of Westminster in 1931.[4]

---

[2] In Canada there are about 120,000 North American Indians and Eskimos. The Australian aborigines are a very primitive race and number approximately 60,000. The Maoris, the natives of New Zealand, are an advanced Polynesian race and have in many respects been assimilated into the national life of the dominion.

[3] Sketching the development of dominion autonomy until the time of World War I, A. Lawrence Lowell wrote that, 'Canada, followed by the other self-governing colonies, had from time to time been asking for a greater degree of autonomy, which was always granted when the demand appeared to be serious. In fact, while it is possible to describe with some accuracy the relation of each of these colonies to the mother country at any one time, the practical situation was that they could obtain any amount of autonomy that they earnestly desired. It was perfectly understood that neither the Cabinet nor the Parliament at Westminster would resist such a demand, and hence that the nature of the connection with the mother country would be determined by the progressive wishes of the colonies.' 'The Imperial Conference,' *Foreign Affairs,* April 1927, p. 380.

[4] The dominions were defined by the Imperial Conference Committee on Inter-Imperial Relations as 'autonomous Communities within the British Empire, equal in

Between the wars there was a good deal of discussion and speculation concerning the nature of the new Commonwealth. How 'independent' were the dominions? What did 'equal in status' mean? Was the Crown really divisible into several parts? While these questions bothered the constitutional lawyers more than the politicians, they were not without practical importance. They led to such queries as: Can a member of the Commonwealth secede? Can a dominion be neutral in a war involving other Commonwealth members? Can intra-Commonwealth disputes be taken to international tribunals? Events and the actions of governments have given answers that puzzled the legal theorists. The Irish Free State remained neutral throughout World War II and in 1948 formally seceded from the Commonwealth. The action of the Crown in the United Kingdom in declaring, on 3 September 1939, that a state of war existed with Germany did not automatically make belligerents of the other Commonwealth members. Each acted independently in declaring war. Canada's declaration followed several days after that of the United Kingdom, and in South Africa a change of Government had to occur before the dominion went to war. India's accusations against racial discrimination in South Africa have been heard in the United Nations, and her dispute with Pakistan over Kashmir has been before the same international forum. The practice since 1939, therefore, leaves no doubt about the juridical status of Commonwealth members; they are independent countries possessing all the attributes of sovereignty. Such connections as they still maintain with other Commonwealth members are by their own desire, and they are free to terminate them at any time.

The present-day Commonwealth is a fact in world affairs, but it is difficult to define in the conventional terminology which we use to describe states and their relations with one another. It is much easier to say what the Commonwealth is not, than what it is. As a union of sovereign states the Commonwealth falls far short of being a confederation, and it is not a league of countries joined to achieve a limited number of objectives. The Prime Minister of Canada, Louis St. Laurent, giving his conception of the Commonwealth in a broadcast speech in London, declared:

> The Commonwealth is not a political unit, nor is it an alliance. It has no common policies. The nations of the Commonwealth make their own separate decisions in world affairs, and none is prepared to give up that right. But they have a community of interest on matters that really count. All of them have a common attachment to certain political ideals, but there is nothing exclusive about these ideals. They are ideals which could, with advantage to the world, be extended to all other nations.[5]

---

status, in no way subordinate one to another in any aspect of their domestic or external affairs, though united by a common allegiance to the Crown, and freely associated as members of the British Commonwealth of Nations.' Cmd. 2768 (1926).

[5] *The Times*, 11 January 1951.

Other Commonwealth statesmen might describe their association in different terms. Perhaps a definition of this nature would be agreeable to a majority. The British Commonwealth of Nations is a group of independent states linked by historical association with the United Kingdom and resolved to co-operate with one another to the extent permitted by their separate national interests.

2. *The Organization of the Commonwealth*

The formal political machinery of the Commonwealth is not extensive. Its most visible manifestation is the person of the monarch who is the sovereign in all the dominions except India. Thus, besides being Queen of the United Kingdom of Great Britain and Northern Ireland, Elizabeth II is also Queen in each dominion, and India recognizes her as the head of the Commonwealth. It being impossible for the monarch to be physically present in each of her dominions, she is represented by a governor-general whose powers and duties are similar to the Queen's in the United Kingdom. A governor-general exercises the royal prerogatives upon the advice of dominion ministers; he is not the agent of a Government of the United Kingdom.

In the appointment of a governor-general the monarch is advised by the dominion prime minister. Until recent years it was the practice to appoint distinguished citizens of the United Kingdom as governors-general. They were usually peers and occasionally connected with the royal house. Nowadays the governors-general are in most instances citizens of their respective countries. By requesting in 1930 the appointment of the Commonwealth's Chief Justice as Governor-General, Australia was the first dominion to break with past practice. But it reverted to the previous custom from 1945 to 1947, when a brother of King George VI, the Duke of Gloucester, served as governor-general, and again in 1952, when Field Marshal Sir William Slim was nominated for the post. New Zealand did likewise upon the expiration of the term of Lord Freyberg, a native son. Canada obtained its first native governor-general in 1952 when Vincent Massey was nominated to succeed Lord Alexander. Ceylon remains the only Commonwealth country which has never had one of its citizens holding the post of governor-general.

The Commonwealth has no permanent council or assembly in which it formulates policy or transacts business. Around the turn of the century ideas of imperial federation and the creation of central political institutions were discussed a good deal, but dominion nationalism and the physical obstacles involved in the global dispersion and the disparate populations of the self-governing colonies blocked any advances toward a federal constitution. In recent years, proposals have been made that some kind of permanent council and secretariat be established for the Commonwealth. Except for Australia and New Zealand, however, the dominions have shown no particular interest in creating such institutions. They have preferred to follow the practice of several decades of discussing their affairs

−387

in occasional meetings, formerly called imperial conferences and now termed Commonwealth conferences, which bring together ministerial and official representatives of all members.

There is no set time for the holding of such conferences, and while the venue is usually London they have met in other Commonwealth capitals. Some of the conferences have discussed a considerable range of questions; others have been limited to one or two important matters of current interest. The initiative in calling a Commonwealth conference usually is taken by the United Kingdom, although consultation with the dominion governments always occurs and their agreement to a meeting obtained. On the date set, leading ministerial representatives of each dominion assemble at the appointed place, and they are accompanied by considerable staffs of officials and experts who can serve on committees and participate in preliminary negotiations. A full-dress Commonwealth conference will bring together the prime ministers of the United Kingdom and the dominions.

The conferences do not make decisions that are automatically binding upon the members of the Commonwealth. The United Kingdom and each dominion government must take the legislative and executive action that has been agreed upon in order to make the decisions of the conference operative. The probability of each member's carrying out the agreements of a conference is high. The representatives present are prime ministers or other important members of dominion Governments, and they are unlikely to take decisions that will not command the support of their colleagues at home and their parliamentary majorities. Furthermore, the moral commitment is one of considerable weight. A change of Government in a country might prevent the fulfillment of an undertaking assumed at a Commonwealth conference, but even in such an event the moral obligation would be strong. The agreement would probably be repudiated only if it conflicted with a basic tenet of the victorious party or with one of its election pledges.

Continuous and less formal consultation is always in progress between the Governments of Commonwealth countries. On the matters of the highest importance this consultation will be between prime ministers. On other matters consultation will be between the Secretary of State for Commonwealth Relations of the United Kingdom and the ministers of external affairs in the dominions. These ministers have representatives known as high commissioners in all the Commonwealth capitals. Thus, if the Government of the United Kingdom wishes to discuss a problem with the Commonwealth of Australia it would instruct the British High Commissioner in Canberra to take up the matter with the Australian Ministry of External Affairs. Conversely, should the Australian Government desire to raise some matter with the Government of the United Kingdom it would instruct the Commonwealth's High Commissioner in London to call upon the Secretary of State for Commonwealth Relations. This kind of consultation is proceeding constantly. The high commissioners and their staffs in all the Commonwealth capitals are in daily contact with the government to which they are accredited, and a constant exchange of views is going on. In time of war, and occasionally during less critical periods, a dominion may place a ministerial representative in London. He will have access to the ministerial level of the government of the United Kingdom, and as a member of a dominion ministry he will have the authority to conduct negotiations and to take decisions which would be beyond the normal province of the nonpolitical high commissioner.

Besides the Commonwealth's machinery for dealing with important policy matters of concern to its members, there are a good many official and semi-official bodies and committees established to handle administrative, technical, and cultural subjects of interest to all or several of the countries. Some of these are governed by councils on which all Commonwealth states are represented; others are primarily British organizations to whose support dominion governments contribute. A few of them hold periodic conferences which bring together Commonwealth and colonial representatives. These bodies and committees maintain close relations with appropriate government departments in the United Kingdom, usually the Office of Commonwealth Relations or the Colonial Office.

A few examples will serve to indicate the range and character of Commonwealth co-operation at the technical level. In the scientific field there is the Imperial Institute of Entomology, a clearing house for information about insect life of economic importance; the Bureau of Hygiene and Tropical Diseases, a research and educational agency; the Imperial Institute, an organization for the collection and dissemination of information on the commercial and industrial utilization of raw materials; and the Executive Council of the Imperial Agricultural Bureaux, a body to supervise the activities of the eight research units in different parts of the Commonwealth. In the field of trade and economic affairs, there is the Imperial Shipping Committee which conducts inquiries into and reports on sea and air communications between Commonwealth countries. The Imperial War Graves Commission is responsible for the administration of military cemeteries in foreign lands. The functions of these and other bodies indicate that there is much co-operative activity which is little publicized but which, in total, constitutes a network of bonds between the members of the Commonwealth.

3. *Remnants of Dominion Subordination*

The evolution of the dominions into separate states has been sufficiently gradual and enough elements of former colonial usage have remained so that it has sometimes been difficult for the non-British world to understand just what legal and customary connections existed at any particular time between the units of the Commonwealth. The fact that so much of the development has been achieved by practice and precedent rather than by legislation or formal statements of rules has added to the perplexity of foreigners. There are now only a few vestigial instances of subordination, and they could be removed if the dominions concerned so desired. The principal ones relate to the amendment of dominion constitutions and the appellate jurisdiction of the Judicial Committee of the Privy Council.

Any amendment of the Canadian constitution, the British North America Act of 1867, until recently required action by the Parliament at Westminster. In passing amendments Parliament had always acted on the request of the Canadian government and its function was purely formal. In 1949 Canada proposed that the power to amend all provisions of the British North America Act pertaining to the federal government be vested in the Parliament at Ottawa, and the Parliament of the United Kingdom duly passed such an amendment.[6] There are now three classes of subject matter still necessitating reference to London for amendment. They are: (1) powers delegated to the provinces by the British North America Act; (2) special provincial rights with respect to education and language; (3) provisions requiring annual meetings of Parliament and limiting its life to five years except in times of war, invasion, or insurrection. In case of doubt the Supreme Court of Canada will decide whether or not a proposed amendment falls within one of these excepted categories and thus must be submitted to Westminster for enactment. The United Kingdom Parliament remains, therefore, a guarantor of provincial legislative powers, of Quebec's cultural autonomy, and of the Canadian Parliament's observance of limitations on its own duration. The Parliament at Westminster would be placed in an extremely delicate position should it be requested by a Canadian Government to pass an amendment clearly falling in one of the excepted categories, for it has no desire to become involved in a constitutional controversy arising in one of the dominions. One must assume that as a practical matter the excepted categories comprise subjects that are not presently susceptible to amendment. Should public opinion within Canada change, the Parliament of the United Kingdom would undoubtedly transfer, upon appropriate Canadian request, the amending authority it now holds to Ottawa.[7]

The basic laws of the other dominions, with the exception of India, are likewise statutes of the Parliament at Westminster, but they contain provisions for their own amendment. In the cases of Australia and New

---

[6] The formality of the action of the United Kingdom Parliament is illustrated by the fact that the amending legislation passed all stages in the House of Commons on one day, 2 December 1949.

[7] The amendment of the Canadian constitution raises subjects complex enough to baffle skilled legal experts. As an American scholar has pointed out, 'From the beginning this process has been surrounded with a certain mysterious imprecision, deriving from the fact that Canada's basic constitutional statute—the British North America Act, 1867—contained no provision for its own amendment.' The United Kingdom Parliament has passed a number of amending statutes, and there has been the usual constitutional development by law, convention, and judicial decision. Today 'no one can say with authority exactly what constitutes the formal written constitution,' nor is there 'even general agreement concerning the number of times that the British North America Act, 1867, has been amended and what these amendments are.' William S. Livingston, 'The Amending Power of the Canadian Parliament,' *The American Political Science Review,* June 1951, pp. 437-8.

Zealand the amending procedure which existed prior to the passage of the Statute of Westminster, 1931, was confirmed, at their request, and no additional power to repeal or alter their fundamental laws was conferred. Consequently, an amendment of the Statute of Westminster would be required to change the method of dominion amendment.[8] The Parliament of the Union of South Africa is legally competent to amend the South Africa Act, 1910, since the Statute of Westminster imposed no restraint and made the Colonial Laws Validity Act, 1865, inapplicable to United Kingdom legislation which formed part of the law of a dominion. In 1952 an acute controversy developed in the Union over the Parliament's power to alter the so-called entrenched clauses, which by the Act of 1910 required two-thirds votes in the legislative houses. The constitutional issue was a domestic one; no question of any power of the Parliament in London over South African affairs was involved.

Today there is no legislative subordination of a dominion to the Parliament of the United Kingdom. No laws enacted by the Parliament at Westminster extend to a dominion unless a dominion expressly requests to be included. Moreover, no dominion legislation is invalid because it is in conflict with the law of the United Kingdom. Formerly, a governor-general, acting on instructions from the Crown, could refuse to assent to dominion legislation, and the Government of the United Kingdom could disallow statutes to which the assent had been given. Moreover, a governor-general's instructions required him to reserve bills on certain subjects for decision by the Government in London. Except for reservation, these powers had fallen into disuse before the meeting of the Imperial Conference of 1926. This conference found the whole subject of the operation of dominion legislation 'so complex that there would be grave danger in attempting any immediate pronouncement other than a statement of certain principles,' but it recommended, in effect, the discontinuance of the practice of reservation.[9] The complexities of the subject were studied by a committee of legal authorities which reported to the Imperial Conference of 1930. Out of this work came the Statute of Westminster, 1931, which recognized the full legislative competence of dominion parliaments. The governors-general now signify the royal assent to all dominion legislation just as the Queen does in the United Kingdom. Both in theory and practice, therefore, the dominions are empowered to enact any legislation authorized by their constitutions, and there is no review by the British Government nor is there any question of invalidity because of conflict with the law of the United Kingdom.

There remains an element of subordination of some of the dominions to the United Kingdom in respect to appeals to the Judicial Committee of

---

[8] The constitution of the Commonwealth of Australia has proved difficult to amend. Amendments adopted by the federal Parliament must be submitted to a referendum in which not only a national majority but majority votes in 4 of the 6 states are required. Only 4 of 23 amendments submitted have won approval.

[9] Cmd. 2768 (1926).

the Privy Council. It will be recalled that the authority of the Judicial Committee grew out of the right of the British subject to appeal to the Crown after he had exhausted the appellate procedure available to him in the colony where he resided. The right to carry such appeals to the Judicial Committee was barred by the Irish Free State before it seceded from the Commonwealth, and India took similar action in 1948. Canada abolished appeals to the Judicial Committee in 1949, and the Union of South Africa and Pakistan ended them in 1950. Jurisdiction with respect to Australia, New Zealand, and Ceylon, will probably disappear in time. This movement to restrict the appellate procedure to dominion courts has resulted primarily from nationalistic sentiment which dislikes the idea of carrying appeals beyond the highest dominion court. Moreover, the expense imposed on litigants by counsel fees and travel to London was an argument against continuing the practice. The reputation of the Judicial Committee has been high, even in the dominions where further appeals to London have been barred. There has been a general recognition that it provided a standard of judicial integrity and a helpful guide to the interpretation of law during the years when the courts and the legal profession in the dominions were advancing to maturity.

4. *Commonwealth Co-operation*

The areas within which Commonwealth co-operation is strong may be discussed under four main headings: foreign affairs, defense policy, economic relations, and immigration. In all these matters there is a great deal of consultation among members of the Commonwealth, and a considerable measure of agreement on common policies is achieved. The first three are subjects of great interest to all parts of the Commonwealth, while the last, immigration, concerns the lightly-populated dominions.

There is no such thing as a Commonwealth foreign policy. Each of the units of the Commonwealth has policies of its own which are established by the dominion's cabinet and parliament and administered by its ministry of external affairs. Each dominion Government is responsible to its parliament and ultimately to its own electorate for its conduct of the foreign relations of the country. However, a considerable amount of agreement is always present among the Commonwealth countries, and on some of the major issues of world affairs a common policy emerges.

There are several reasons for this unanimity and for agreement to act in concert. For one thing, the dominions are all democratic states, and their public opinions and their Governments tend to react alike when faced with the major problems of foreign policy. In the present state of world affairs, they all dislike communist totalitarianism and they prefer a world order in which trade and cultural activities are not limited by iron curtains. The British concept of the rule of law is generally admired and practiced, and there is considerable antipathy toward those states and political systems which deny it. Consequently, there is a cultural base for common action in the field of foreign affairs. Whether the instinctive reactions of

392–

the Asian dominions to important questions of foreign affairs will run parallel to those of the other Commonwealth countries remains to be seen. It is plain that their peoples and governments are swayed by crosswinds of nationalism and anti-imperialism to an extent not felt in such countries as Canada, Australia, and New Zealand. Nevertheless, their political leaders joined in the following words of the communiqué issued at the close of the Commonwealth Prime Ministers' conference in 1951: 'We all have deep within us a faith in the existence of a purpose of justice in the world, and we believe it to be our duty to forward it by everything we do. . . It is our firm belief that the rule of law should govern human conduct; and we are prepared to accept whatever sacrifices may be necessary to uphold, with all other nations, those principles of international law and order which are essential conditions for world peace and progress.' [10]

In the second place, no one of the dominions ranks as a great power and all desire the support of allies. This sense of dependence varies from dominion to dominion, and from time to time, but it forms a bond which expresses itself in common policy. There is a general realization that separately the dominions would be less influential in international affairs without the support of fellow-members of the Commonwealth. A country such as Australia with approximately eight million inhabitants is a relatively small member of the family of nations, but joined in close co-operative ties with the United Kingdom and the other dominions it takes on added stature. India and Pakistan are large if population alone is considered, but their industrial backwardness tends to depreciate their international status. Thirdly, the prestige of the United Kingdom and its long experience as a great power are advantages in which all members of the Commonwealth share. They know that the principal member of the Commonwealth is always conscious of their interests and that when representatives of the great powers meet and confer, they, in a sense, will be represented in these councils.

Common policies in the field of foreign affairs are arrived at principally through the machinery of consultation. The United Kingdom keeps the dominion governments informed of its views on all major issues of foreign policy, and the dominions for their part express their opinions to the government in London and to the governments of the other dominions. By this method of consultation a measure of agreement is arrived at and the differences of viewpoint are set forth. Frequently it is possible to resolve the divergencies of view and to agree upon a common policy. If there are issues upon which one or more dominions feel that they cannot compromise they are at liberty to maintain their positions. Besides the regular machinery for consultation between government and government, there is informal consultation at the seat of the United Nations and often at international conferences in which the British Commonwealth nations are repsented. Common policies do not always result from these conferences, but

---

[10] *The New York Times,* 13 January 1951.

each member of the Commonwealth knows where the others stand and is prepared to adapt its policies to the degree possible to a common position.

The power and influence of the United States are so great in world affairs that policy formulation by the Commonwealth nations is bound to be affected. For Britain, the maintenance of close ties with the United States is a cardinal principle of foreign policy. Canada, Australia, New Zealand, and South Africa likewise believe that on fundamental issues they must march alongside the United States. India and Pakistan, while individually friendly, are less certain in their attitude. The Commonwealth sometimes has the problem, therefore, of reconciling the desire of some of its members for co-operation with the United States and the reluctance of others to be too closely associated with policies originating in Washington. The product of reconciliation may be a poor compromise or an attempt at evading the issue. Occasionally no agreement is possible; India, for example, refused to accept the invitation of the governments of the United States and the United Kingdom to attend the conference at San Francisco to sign a peace treaty with Japan.

In the field of defense, Commonwealth co-operation is probably more close than it is in foreign policy. Since the United Kingdom is the only major military power in the Commonwealth, the members' sense of dependence is somewhat greater. All the dominion military forces are organized and trained along British lines, and most of them depend upon the United Kingdom for weapons and equipment.[11] Their military staffs are closely connected, and there is a considerable exchange of personnel and information. Collaboration along these lines facilitates such joint action as was exemplified in the formation of the 1st Commonwealth Division from among British, Canadian, Australian, and New Zealand troops sent to Korea.

Strategic planning embracing the United Kingdom and most of the dominions is always in progress, and this leads to commitments for future co-operation. In Australia at Woomera the Commonwealth has experimental facilities for long range weapons which would not be possible in a small and congested country like the United Kingdom. Canada undertakes to operate a training scheme for air force pilots and crews from all the Commonwealth countries. Members of the armed forces of the Commonwealth countries attend service schools in the United Kingdom where they get training on a scale which could not be afforded by the dominions individually. They all share in the results of research and experimentation which is carried on by the United Kingdom and which would be beyond

---

[11] Canada maintains equally close military ties with the United States. Since the Hyde Park Agreement and the establishment of the Canadian-American Joint Defence Board during World War II, the co-operation between the two countries has been continuous, and it has been reinforced by their common membership in the North Atlantic Treaty Organization. In strategical planning, military training, and munitions production Canada almost certainly will increasingly integrate her defense effort with that of the United States.

the financial and industrial capabilities of most of the nations. All in all, the members of the Commonwealth are convinced that the advantages of co-operation and common policies greatly enhance their individual security.

While the British government desires to foster the Commonwealth as a world-wide association of co-operating states, it is prepared to recognize that the dominions may find it expedient to promote their individual interests by regional political and defense agreements. Australia and New Zealand led the way in the creation of regional arrangements between dominions when in 1944 they joined in a defense agreement. This provided for the consultation of the two governments on matters affecting the security of the Southwest Pacific area and arranged for the sharing of military facilities in that part of the world. It is the only agreement of its kind limited to Commonwealth countries.[12] The United Kingdom and Canada are parties to the North Atlantic Treaty. The British government would probably like to promote a regional arrangement of the three South Asian dominions designed to aid their mutual security, but such an agreement is not practical until India and Pakistan settle the major issues which presently divide them and Ceylon is satisfied that its large neighbor, India, has no designs upon it.

The economic ties among most members of the Commonwealth are strong, and a considerable measure of agreement on policy is obtained. Canada excepted, all are members of the sterling area, which means that their financial stability is linked with that of the United Kingdom.[13] Within the sterling area all currencies are convertible and trade is carried on without exchange restrictions. The reserves of gold and dollars of all sterling area countries are held in London, and they form a common pool upon which the currencies of the individual members are founded. The importance of the maintenance of these common reserves leads the Commonwealth members to agree to pursue mutually helpful financial and commercial policies. For example, in early 1949 when the drop in the gold and dollar reserves became alarming all the sterling members of the Commonwealth agreed to restrict their dollar purchases by at least 25 per cent and to push exports to dollar areas as vigorously as they could. Again in 1952, the finance ministers of all the Commonwealth countries met in London to discuss measures to halt the drain on the reserves and to bring their external payments into balance.

The willingness of Commonwealth countries to co-operate in financial matters stems from their commercial interdependence. Great Britain is

---

[12] The Australian-New Zealand agreement may, for practical purposes, be superseded by the security pact negotiated by these nations and the United States in connection with the peace treaty for Japan. The two dominions felt that they could not agree to a peace treaty permitting Japanese rearmament unless their security was guaranteed by the United States.

[13] The boundaries of the sterling area are not exactly coterminous with those of the Commonwealth and Empire, for such independent countries as Burma, Iraq, and Iceland are members of the sterling area.

their major market and their principal source of imports. The Commonwealth is by no means a closed economic system, for all its members have important commercial connections with non-sterling countries of the world. It is the area, however, on which their livelihood chiefly depends and in whose prosperity they have a vital interest. Trade between the Commonwealth countries has expanded considerably since World War II, in large part because of the dollar shortage. In 1950, 43 per cent of the imports of the United Kingdom came from Commonwealth and Empire sources, and 47 per cent of its exports went to these countries. The prewar percentages were 37 and 41, respectively.[14]

Besides federation schemes, imperialists of 50 years ago talked a great deal about the development of the British Empire into a kind of *zollverein* behind whose tariff walls free trade principles would be practiced. Joseph Chamberlain, Colonial Secretary from 1900 to 1903, was a leading advovate of an imperial customs union. There were major obstacles standing in the way, however, for the dominions desired to encourage diversified economies and to use their autonomy in fiscal matters to protect young industries.[15] The British electorate, moreover, was not ready to abandon free trade. Consequently this concept of imperial unity was never realized.

A considerably restricted version was established as a result of the Ottawa Conference of 1932. The United Kingdom had just reversed its free-trade policy by imposing a basic duty of 10 per cent ad valorem on imports and was prepared to bargain with the Commonwealth countries for reciprocal tariff concessions. A series of agreements resulted which give Commonwealth members preferential duties on imports into the United Kingdom in return for lower duties on British exports. Fruits from Commonwealth nations, for example, pay a lower duty than imports from other countries, while motor cars manufactured in Great Britain enjoy a preference in dominion markets by virtue of reduced tariffs. Imperial preference has become a basic feature of the fiscal and commercial policies of the United Kingdom and other Commonwealth members, and they have not been prepared to agree to its abolition or serious impairment at the postwar conferences on international trade.

---

[14] *The Times,* 21 April 1951.

[15] Speaking about empire free trade at the Imperial Conference of 1930, N. C. Havenga, then South African Minister of Finance, summed up the dominions' attitude when he said that the Union 'cannot afford, and is not prepared to subscribe to, such a policy.' He continued: 'Manufacturing industries have been established in the Union which could not exist even against Empire competition without a protective tariff. Those industries, many of them branches of or allied to British houses, now form an indispensable part of the structure of our country, they contribute to our prosperity and afford employment to a large section of our population which cannot be absorbed in agriculture or mining. Our policy is to build up and maintain such industries as are natural to the country or which we consider essential to its development, and we cannot subscribe to any agreement which would endanger their existence.' Cmd. 3718 (1930), p. 69.

In addition to imperial preference, close commercial relations are fostered by long-term trade agreements between the United Kingdom and members of the Commonwealth. At the close of World War II Britain and Canada entered into a five-year wheat agreement designed to give the dominion's farmers an assured market and the United Kingdom a stable price for this basic import. Agreements with New Zealand have dealt with dairy products, and a 15-year meat scheme has been negotiated with Australia which, it is hoped, will encourage growers to increase their production to meet the demands of a settled market. Sugar has been the subject of another Commonwealth trade plan. An eight-year agreement, beginning in 1952, imposes export quotas on the principal producing areas—Australia, British West Indies, British Honduras, East Africa, Fiji, Mauritius, and South Africa—and obligates the United Kingdom to purchase fixed quantities of sugar at a uniform, negotiated price.

All of the older dominions have co-operated to some extent with the United Kingdom in the development of immigration schemes. Being sparsely populated countries they are eager to receive immigrants who will contribute to the development of their resources. They prefer, for the most part, people of British stock. British immigrants quickly adapt themselves in the dominion societies and do not raise the problems of cultural adjustment posed by more alien nationalities. The only one of the older dominions which has been reluctant to receive large numbers of immigrants from the United Kingdom is the Union of South Africa. In that dominion the dominant Dutch-Boer stock has been fearful of being submerged by the British element and obstructed in the fulfillment of its goal of establishing an Afrikaans republic. All of the older dominions bar non-white immigrants. Australia is particularly strict in this respect and with Asia's teeming millions at hand refuses to compromise its standing policy of a white Australia. It is prepared to receive immigrants from continental Europe and currently pursues a policy of admitting one for every two persons from the United Kingdom.

The British government, for its part, has been interested in co-operating with the dominions in the development of immigration schemes. It recognizes the value in terms of future Commonwealth development of having a steady flow of British emigrants to the dominions. In view of the reduced security situation of the British Isles, it is also conscious of the importance of the growth of industrial power in friendly countries of less vulnerability. The United Kingdom has been prepared, therefore, to give financial aid, in co-operation with the dominions, to people who desire to settle overseas. In the period 1945-51, British emigration to Canada amounted to 217,873 persons, and to South Africa 89,321 persons. From 1945-52, Australia received 313,000 and New Zealand 72,898.[16] A large proportion of the emigrants received free or assisted passage overseas. In 1951, 42,300 per-

---

[16] *The Sunday Times,* 22 June 1952.

sons sailed from the British Isles to Australia under the Commonwealth's assisted-passage agreement with the United Kingdom.[17]

While the British government has continued to support migration to the dominions, there have been questions raised concerning the advisability of the policy. The dominions are desirous of receiving young and skilled workers, and such people have been urgently needed in postwar Britain in its efforts to raise industrial production. Some Britons have misgivings about encouraging young workers to leave and thus contributing to the labor shortages which have plagued some of Britain's industries. It seems likely though that the general advantages to be derived from strengthening Commonwealth ties will be considered to outweigh the harm which comes from reducing the labor force in the United Kingdom.

5. Stresses within the Commonwealth

Predictions concerning the disruption of the Commonwealth have so often been disproved that one is entitled to believe it has a long life ahead of it. The Commonwealth has shown itself to be adaptable to new conditions, and it has survived crises which threatened its existence. Two world wars starting in Europe and immediately involving the United Kingdom imposed strains upon the Commonwealth. Britain's enemies were, however, to see all members of the Commonwealth join in the struggles and to witness the emergence of the British association of states in as vigorous a condition as when the conflicts began. The problem of Indian independence was expected to be a serious threat to the continuation of the Commonwealth, but that difficulty was surmounted. Without attempting to define relationships and obligations in precise terms, the Commonwealth has shown itself capable of absorbing many stresses and strains and still retain its basic integrity.

One strain to which the Commonwealth has been subjected is that represented by the term 'republicanism.' In those dominions in which the people are not predominantly of British stock, the monarchical form of government has represented to many of them continuing subordination. Even though the Crown has chiefly symbolic significance and the monarch is represented by a governor-general appointed on the advice of dominion ministers, nevertheless the feeling remains that full independence has not been achieved and that former elements of colonial status remain. This attitude toward the monarchical form of government has been strong in India, and it resulted in the drafting of a constitution which substituted an elected president for the royally appointed governor-general. To large numbers of Indians this change effectively removed the last trace of the British Raj and Indian subordination. There was considerable feeling throughout the Commonwealth that the action of the Indian constitutional assembly made the continuation of India within the Commonwealth an impossibility, since it had been assumed that the symbol of the Crown was

---

[17] *The Times,* 19 December 1951.

to remain the effective tie uniting the dominions and differentiating them from other independent states which have close associations with the United Kingdom. When Indian political leaders expressed a desire to retain their connection with the Commonwealth, a search for an acceptable formula was undertaken. This search culminated successfully at a conference of dominion prime ministers meeting in London in 1949, and the formula provided that all dominions would recognize the King as Head of the Commonwealth but might individually have any form of government desired by their own peoples.

Another dominion in which sentiment for republican institutions is strong is the Union of South Africa, and it seems probable that the Indian precedent will one day be followed by the Union. The eventual establishment of a republic has been an article of faith among the more nationalistic Boer elements in South Africa, and they have dominated the political scene there during the past few years. When Prime Minister Malan returned from the conference at which the formula for continued Indian membership in the Commonwealth had been agreed upon, he said that he believed South Africa's greatest chance of unity was in a republic, but that there were more urgent matters to be attended to presently. Malan interpreted the recognition of the King as Head of the Commonwealth as not implying that the Crown had any formal constitutional function, stating that this recognition 'did not in any way suggest that the Commonwealth was or resembled a super state.' [18] That many nationalistic politicians of the Union do not consider the continuance of the monarchical form as a *sine qua non* of Commonwealth membership is suggested by Malan's concluding remark on this occasion when he said that 'in any case South Africa should never leave the Commonwealth.' [19]

There is no important republican sentiment in any of the other dominions. No responsible political group sees any advantage in substituting a president for a governor-general and for amending the constitutional language of the dominion to eliminate the nomenclature of monarchy. On the other hand, they believe, for the most part, that there are certain advantages in the continuation of the present system. It in no sense limits their independence of action, and it works very satisfactorily in practice.

Perhaps the most dangerous strain upon the Commonwealth concept arises from the racial minority problem. India's relations with her sister dominions are seriously affected on this account. There are about 300,000 Indians permanently residing in the Union of South Africa where they suffer various disabilities in connection with the franchise, property ownership, and other civil rights. As the white element in South Africa adopts more repressive measures of segregation and discrimination, the position of the Indians becomes less and less favorable, and they look to New Delhi to support their claims for better treatment. The Indian government

---

[18] *The Times,* 12 May 1949.
[19] Ibid. 12 May 1949.

has been willing to champion their cause, even to the extent of bringing an accusation against South Africa before the United Nations. Efforts by the United Kingdom and other countries to have the Indian and the South African governments seek some accommodation through bilateral negotiations have not proved successful. The South African government takes the position that only the repatriation of its Indian population can solve the problem, while the Indian government counters that the return of such a large number to an already densely populated country is physically and financially impossible. Moreover, most of the Indian community has no desire to leave the land where it has been settled for several generations and where even under policies of segregation and discrimination most of its members are probably better off than they could be in India. The problem appears fated to remain a source of bitterness between the two dominions.

India also has a serious minority problem affecting its relations with Pakistan. When the Indian Empire was divided in 1947 into the two dominions of India and Pakistan, it was impossible to draw boundaries which enclosed all their respective Hindu and Moslem peoples. Millions of Moslems were left in India, and a good many Hindus found themselves within the borders of Pakistan. When the division was declared, communal rioting broke out in many places and millions of people decided that their only security lay in joining their co-religionists. Consequently, the world observed the spectacle of refugee masses fleeing from Pakistan into India, or in the opposite direction, carrying what few possessions they could rescue and running the gauntlet of hostile crowds along almost every mile of their terrible journey. How many perished in this exchange of populations will never be known. After the original period of rioting and panic subsided there still remained many Hindus within Pakistan and Moslems within India. As a result of their religious intolerance, communal strife has periodically occurred. Upon an occasion of serious outbreaks each government becomes apprehensive that its neighbor will intervene to protect the victims of these disorders and provoke warfare between their military forces. In 1950 the threat of major hostilities was only averted by an agreement between the Prime Ministers of India and Pakistan in which they promised to restrain their more ardent political and religious elements and to insure that minority groups received the protection of the civil authorities. The problem remains a source of serious friction between the two dominions.

An Indian minority in Ceylon has caused some strain between the two dominions concerned. In 1949 Ceylon adopted a nationality act which required its Indian minority, amounting to approximately one-eighth of the dominion's population, to choose between Indian or Ceylonese citizenship. Those choosing Indian citizenship were to be denied the franchise in Ceylon; those choosing Ceylonese nationality were to be deprived of the right to remit earnings to dependents in India. There are large Indian minorities in Malaya, East Africa, and the West Indies, and it appears

400–

probable that, if and when these areas advance to dominion status, the civil rights of these groups will raise serious problems. They look to India to protect them, and if the South African precedent is followed, it can be expected that the Indian government will show considerable interest in the treatment accorded these minority groups.

The colonial policy of the United Kingdom government gives rise to Commonwealth problems. The idea that Britain is to assist the native populations of her colonial areas to advance politically, economically, and culturally and gradually to assume more governmental responsibility runs counter to the policies of the Union of South Africa for dealing with the native population. The dominant white element in this dominion foresees only trouble from efforts to advance the social condition of the African natives and opposes the policies pursued in the British colonies. In this opposition the South Africans are joined by a good many white settlers of East Africa and the Rhodesias. The problem is serious in connection with the three high commission territories of Basutoland, Swaziland, and Bechuanaland which are either enclaves in South Africa or contiguous to the Union. Withheld from the territory of the Union at the time the dominion was established in 1910, their incorporation has long been sought by the Union. The United Kingdom has resisted chiefly because public opinion in England objects to the South African policies in regard to natives and believes that the British government would be unfaithful to the concept of trusteeship should it agree to the incorporation of the high commission territories. Since the areas are economically dependent upon the Union, South Africa has a means of exerting strong pressure should it desire to do so.

When in 1951 a more autonomous colonial regime was inaugurated in the Gold Coast, Prime Minister Malan raised the question of Britain's right to hold out the prospect of eventual Commonwealth membership to the colonies. He said:

Here we have a glaring anomaly in existing Commonwealth relations. The Commonwealth is a closed group, all free and all equal, and consequently one would expect that in admitting a new member all would have an equal say, because it may affect the whole complexion and character of the group. But what do we find? Acting on her own, and without consultation with or the approval of other Commonwealth members, Britain recently admitted India, Pakistan, and Ceylon to the Commonwealth, and now intends to continue the process without restriction and in the same way.

It is true that as colonies these territories belong to Britain alone, but as prospective members of the Commonwealth there are others who have just as much interest in their position, and who should have an equal say as to whether they should be admitted or not. This anomaly should be removed without delay.

The Commonwealth can and could in the past exist only as a result of a feeling of solidarity between its members. This feeling of solidarity could and does exist only on the basis of two things, namely specific common interest and sufficient homogeneity of cultural and political outlook.[20]

And the South African Prime Minister asked:

> But now, as the result of latest events and declarations of policy, the question necessarily arises—what greater solidarity or common interests or homogeneity does there exist, for example, between South Africa and India than exists between South Africa and Holland, or Belgium, or France, or Germany, or, for example, between Australia and the Negro State in West Africa than between Australia and the United States? To this question there can be only one answer.[21]

Malan has exposed a strain on the Commonwealth structure which cannot easily be relieved. The United Kingdom has been picturing to colonial peoples a goal of self-government within the Commonwealth as the natural fulfillment of their political evolution. If admission to the group is to require the consent of all current members, can the United Kingdom continue to give assurances of eventual entry to the select circle? Will colonial peoples continue to accept such assurances knowing the opposition of at least the Union of South Africa to their admission? May they not reason that independence outside the Commonwealth is the only objective promising them real equality of status? While questions of this kind will be asked in discussions of imperial affairs, Britain will probably not seek answers at this stage. Most of the colonies are far from a condition making independence, within or without the Commonwealth, a practical matter. When the issue of adding a West African or a West Indian dominion arises there may well have been developments pointing to the proper solution. Conceivably the views of South Africa concerning the proper political development of the African continent may have changed.

6. *Future Trends*

The future history of the British Commonwealth of Nations will depend upon developments within the group of countries now belonging and upon the course of world politics in general. Britain's own future political and economic strength will be a major determinant. The foundations of the Commonwealth were laid at a time when Britain's power was at its zenith. London was the most important diplomatic capital in the world, the Royal

---

[20] *The Times,* 24 February 1951. L. S. Amery, in a letter to *The Times,* disputed Malan's statement that the Asian dominions had been admitted to the Commonwealth without the consent of the other members. Recalling India's place in the councils of the Commonwealth from the period of World War I to the Prime Ministers' Conference of 1949, he said: 'The Commonwealth has, in fact, in relation to India—and, by inference, to Pakistan and Ceylon—so far followed the constitutional principle which, rightly in my opinion, Dr. Malan has laid down.' 1 March 1951.

[21] Ibid. 24 February 1951.

Navy was dominant on all the oceans, and the City of London was the nerve center of world trade. This combination of power has moved 3000 miles westward. Britain remains a strong country, but it is improbable that she will ever recover the relative position which she occupied at the beginning of the twentieth century.

As Britain has declined in strength, compared to other world powers, the dominions have grown in population, wealth, and military potential. They are obviously less dependent upon Great Britain than they were two or three generations ago. Should the next half century witness an appreciable decline in the political, economic, and military importance of the United Kingdom, it seems likely that the Commonwealth connection would be dissolved for all practical purposes. The dominions in their own self-interest would seek to attach themselves to more important sources of power. But should the United Kingdom exhibit the vigor which it has displayed at previous times, the chances are good that it will remain the center of a functioning Commonwealth. It is still the most influential member of the Commonwealth, politically and economically, and it disposes the greatest military power.

There are advantages to the dominions in maintaining a connection with a country that is strong but still not so powerful that it can afford to ignore their interests. Economically, the Commonwealth continues to offer advantages to the dominions. Although they are all interested in further industrialization, they are primarily producers of raw materials and basic commodities, and Great Britain remains the most important importer of such products. It would be difficult for most of them to establish the same level of complementary trade with other countries that now exists with Britain. Finally, while the world remains sharply divided into the free and the totalitarian nations, there are excellent reasons for the dominions to remain a close co-operating group. It is not entirely a matter of military security, although that is important, but it is a feeling of community in a group of states that share a common concept of how the world should be organized and the part that nations should play in advancing human civilization.

The Commonwealth has shown itself to be sufficiently flexible and adaptable to surmount all the strains and stresses that have confronted it to date. There remain serious problems facing all its members or groups of its members, and they may prove to be its eventual undoing. Likewise, new problems will undoubtedly appear to threaten the continuance of this association of states. If future political leaders arise possessing the largeness of mind and the ability to lead their publics that have characterized past statesmen in Britain and the dominions, there is a good chance of the British Commonwealth surviving as a vital part of the world community.

XXIII

The Colonial Empire

The story of how Britain became the center of the world's largest and most populous empire has been told many times. It includes the accounts of the daring explorers and adventurers who sailed to far corners of the world in search of profitable trade, of earnest folk seeking religious liberty or opportunities for social advancement in rude communities beyond the seas, of innumerable campaigns and wars against European rivals and native rulers, and of fabulous riches brought back from the exotic lands of the East.

1. *The Periods of Colonial Expansion*

Moving both eastward and westward, the English established in the 150 years between 1600 and 1750 a very sizeable empire. It consisted of a good part of India, 13 growing colonies on the mainland of North America, and a number of useful island outposts. This empire was considerably enlarged by the cession of French Canada in 1763, but it soon thereafter suffered a serious contraction when the other British colonies on the American continent declared their independence and sustained it militarily against the mother country. After the loss of the 13 American colonies, British overseas interests largely turned eastward where the profits of the trade with India held great attractions.

The first part of the nineteenth century saw few possessions added to the Empire; indeed, a spirit of anti-imperialism gathered considerable strength in England. According to tenets of the dominant political and economic philosophy of the time, colonies were a financial burden and trade moved between advanced and backward areas irrespective of political links. The attention of most British politicians was centered upon advocating or resisting domestic reforms, and there was little official interest in promoting imperial expansion or development. It was generally expected that the colonies to which settlers from the British Isles had migrated would soon become independent and that England's responsibility for their protection and well-being would end.

This anti-imperialist sentiment was succeeded during the latter half of the nineteenth century by a new interest in colonial expansion. The outstanding aspect of the new imperialism was the competition that developed among the European powers to stake out possessions on the continent of

404–

Africa. The British already had footholds there in the former Dutch colony at the Cape of Good Hope and in West African trading posts, and they were successful in adding a considerable part of the rest of the continent to their imperial domain. At the same time, they were expanding in the Far East, acquiring territory either on the mainland of Asia or among the Pacific islands. The latest period of colonial expansion continued until 1919 when Britain succeeded to a share of the German and Turkish empires conquered during World War I. Since 1919 the tendency has been for the Empire to contract rather than expand. Nationalist sentiment in the colonial dependencies has increased, and Britain has had neither the resources nor the desire to maintain overseas possessions by force alone. It is probably significant that World War II was the first major conflict in almost 400 years that did not result in an enlargement of Britain's colonial empire.

While the growth of the Empire appears definitely to have ceased, it remains large both in terms of area and population. It amounts to approximately 3,366,049 square miles of territory, and its inhabitants number 77,050,225 people belonging to scores of races and nationalities. The Empire includes such tiny specks on the ocean wastes as Pitcairn Island, the two square miles made famous by *Mutiny on the Bounty,* and such large territories as Nigeria whose 338,593 square miles are more than three times those of the mother country.

2. *The Control of the Empire*

The political organization of the Empire follows no standard pattern. The Empire consists of territories that are direct colonial dependencies, of native states over which the British have a protectorate, and of countries that are administered as mandates or trusteeships. It includes, as Professor Elliott once said, 'every shade of dependency which political ingenuity has been able to devise.' [1] Currently, 34 units of the Empire are classified as colonies or as colonies and protectorates, 12 as protectorates, three as trust territories, and three as condominiums (i.e. rule is shared with another power).

In addition to the variety of constitutional relationships between Britain and the units of the Empire, there is also a diversity with respect to local self-government. Some of the territories are directly ruled by a British governor, and the inhabitants have practically no voice in the colonial administration. Others are self-governing in all their domestic affairs. In between these two extremes there are colonies in various stages of political development. It is an empire that is constantly in transition, for scarcely a year passes that some new colonial constitution is not promulgated which advances a colony farther along the road to local autonomy.

---

[1] W. Y. Elliott, 'The Riddle of the British Commonwealth,' *Foreign Affairs,* April 1930, p. 460.

Whatever the constitutional position of the different dependent areas, they are all subject to a measure of control from London. The administrative department which exercises this control is, with a few exceptions, the Colonial Office.[2] The head of the Colonial Office is the Secretary of State for the Colonies. He is almost invariably a member of the Cabinet.

Colonial problems are occasionally discussed by the Cabinet and policy decisions taken, but in the competition with important domestic issues, with foreign affairs, and with the relations between members of the Commonwealth, colonial problems do not usually stand high on the Cabinet's agenda. Nevertheless, some developments within the colonial empire require Cabinet consideration and the determination of policy by the highest political authorities. It may be safely assumed that within recent years the British Cabinet has considered such matters as the suppression of terrorism in Malaya, the threat to Hong Kong, the elevation of Ceylon from colonial to dominion status, and nationalist movements in West Africa.

Some of these important problems involve other ministries of the British government. For example, the Ministry of Defence and the service departments would naturally be much concerned about the Malayan situation, since they must provide the forces to support the police action in that area. In a critical situation such as that existing in Hong Kong the Foreign Office would be vitally concerned, for the policy with respect to the future of that Crown colony is intimately connected with Britain's entire position in the Far East and her relations with China and the other Asiatic nations. The Foreign Office is also involved when colonial issues arise in the United Nations. The Treasury is an interested party in the handling of many colonial problems. For instance, the rubber and tin of Malaya are among the largest dollar-earning exports of the sterling area, and the Chancellor of the Exchequer is concerned when internal disturbances affect the producing capabilities of this colonial region. The responsibilities of the Colonial Office and the Commonwealth Relations Office touch at many points. The dominions of Australia and New Zealand are concerned about British colonies in the Pacific; India, Pakistan, and Ceylon have a considerable interest in all South East Asian affairs, and the Union of South Africa constantly keeps an eye on developments in the vast colonial area to the north. It may be said, therefore, that all the ministries dealing with foreign relations, Britain's military responsibilities, and her financial and economic affairs are interested parties in major policy matters respecting the colonial empire.

Into the Colonial Office flows a large volume of reports from royal governors and their administrative officials and from persons at home and abroad who are concerned with colonial affairs. Outward from the Office

---

[2] The colony of Basutoland and the protectorates of Bechunanaland and Swaziland—known as High Commission Territories—are administered through the Commonwealth Relations Office, while the condominium of the Anglo-Egyptian Sudan is administered through the Foreign Office.

goes a stream of instructions to colonial governors. Besides the instructions to governors, the Colonial Office exercises its control through its approval or disapproval of colonial legislation and through its review of the financial affairs of the various colonies. The degree of control exercised varies with the political development of the respective dependencies. It will be slight in the case of a colony, Malta for example, which enjoys almost complete self-government, and it will be considerable for some like the Fiji Islands and Nigeria which are much less advanced with respect to local autonomy.

3. *The Government of a Colony*

The basic law of a Crown colony is laid down in orders-in-council, royal instructions, and letters patent. Orders-in-council are used to describe the general political organization of the colony, and they indicate the principal institutions of government to be established and the powers to be exercised. Guarantees of the rights and privileges of special areas or classes of the population may be included. Royal instructions give the governor additional guidance about the organization and functioning of the colonial government. Letters patent confer authority on the governor as the chief executive and commander-in-chief to make appointments, discipline officials, grant pardons, and perform other acts.

In each of the Crown colonies the colonial government is headed by a governor. He is a senior officer, with few exceptions, in the Colonial Service, and he has probably had experience in a number of colonies before reaching the rank of governor.[3] In some of the less advanced colonies the governor has far-reaching powers over all aspects of the colonial government, while in others his powers are limited by the constitutional authority of colonial legislatures and native ministers. The governor of a self-governing colony occupies a position not too dissimilar from that of a governor-general in a dominion, although he possesses reserve powers which can be called into play in an emergency.

In a fairly common type of colonial dependency, the governor is assisted by an executive council. This advisory body usually consists of British officers of the Colonial Service, but there may be appointed representatives of the native population. A good many official actions must be taken by the governor-in-council. The governor is not required to accept the council's advice, but if he acts contrary to the views of a majority of its members he must report the matter to the Colonial Office.

The governor heads an administrative establishment of several departments, the number varying according to the size and the character of a colony's problems. Below the governor the chief official in a colony is the colonial secretary. He is in charge of an office known as the secretariat,

---

[3] In 1949 Lord Baldwin, son of the former Prime Minister, was the only 'political,' i.e. non-career, governor. Fortress colonies, such as Gibraltar and Malta, frequently have high ranking military officers as governors.

which deals with the political, general administrative, and financial affairs of the colonial government. Departments concerned with such activities as agriculture, education, mines, health, transportation, and police are under professionally qualified officers.

Colonies fairly well advanced in self-government have a colonial assembly or legislative council. This body is composed of official, nominated, and elected elements in proportions varying according to the colony's autonomy. The greater the self-government the smaller are the official and nominated groups. In a number of colonies the governor presides over the legislative council, but in the more advanced colonies the assemblies have speakers who follow the practice, and in some cases the dress, of their model at Westminster. Draft ordinances are introduced after consideration by the executive council, and they are debated and passed. While the governor is empowered to signify the royal assent to most legislation passed by the colonial assembly, he must reserve certain measures for approval by the Secretary of State. For example, legislation which confers special rights or privileges upon European residents must be reserved. The Secretary of State, moreover, may disallow colonial ordinances after they have received the governor's approval, but such action is rare. Besides passing ordinances the colonial assembly debates and approves an annual budget. The budget is prepared by the financial secretary of the colony who introduces it in the colony's legislative council. Most colonial budgets must be referred to London for approval before becoming effective.

Local government and administration in the colonies vary according to the degree of social advancement existing in particular territories. In a colony enjoying considerable political autonomy and having social institutions of a European character—Jamaica, for example—there are counties, parishes, and towns with elected councils in charge of municipal affairs. In less advanced colonies, the British have generally practiced indirect rule, leaving local affairs in the hands of the traditional native authorities but supplying guidance and supervision by district officers. The district officers, who belong to the Colonial Service, administer and enforce colonial ordinances and advise native chiefs and headmen. They only impose their authority when the native administration transgresses the policies of the colonial government.[4]

Each colony has a judicial department with a high court and such inferior courts as its size and development warrant. For the most part these

---

[4] In eastern Nigeria, where indirect rule has never been very successful because of weak tribal organizations among the natives, the colonial government is attempting to introduce a system of local government similar to that of England. The first county council was inaugurated in 1951, and the hope is that within ten years a complete system of parish, district, and county councils will be operating. That the experiment faces some problems is indicated by the temperament of the tribe concerned, the Ibibios. These people are described as 'one of the less sophisticated of African tribes' and 'prone to sudden violence.' Moreover, about thirty of the forty councilmen first chosen were illiterate. *The Times,* 19 April 1951.

courts adjudicate according to native law, although the applicable British laws and the ordinances of the colony have precedence. Appeals from colonial courts may go to the Judicial Committee of Privy Council sitting in London, and it hears a dozen or so such appeals each term. Most of the colonial judges are Britons, but the number of natives appointed to judicial office in the colonies is increasing. As a rule, the latter have had their legal training in England and been admitted to the bar there.

In protectorates, territories under trusteeship, and other areas that are not direct dependencies of the British Crown, the colonial administration varies somewhat from the typical pattern of a Crown colony. In the protectorates the native government continues to exist, and British control is exercised through a resident at the seat of the local ruler. The resident will be mostly concerned with the external relations of the protectorate, but he will also give advice upon internal policies and problems. The extent to which this advice will be given and followed depends upon the degree of advancement of the local culture and upon the personalities of the ruler and the resident. In some protectorates the resident is the real power behind the throne, while in others the native ruler continues to exercise broad authority in domestic matters. In the territories under United Nations trusteeship, the form of government is similar to that in the colonies, local autonomy varying with the degree of advancement of the native population. For these territories the British government is required to make reports to the Trusteeship Council of the United Nations and to observe certain international agreements with respect to trade and the promotion of political, economic, and social advancement.

The colonial governments do not have direct representation in London. Their dealings with the British government are through the Colonial Office. They do maintain, however, crown agents whose principal function is the purchase of supplies for the account of their respective colonies. The crown agents also do some recruiting for educational and social welfare positions not normally filled by officers of the Colonial Service.

4. *The Colonial Service*

The British complement in all the colonial governments belongs to the Colonial Service. While the term 'Colonial Service' has been in use for a long time it is only recently that a unified organization has been established. Before 1930 the administrative service of each colony was a separate entity to which an officer was appointed with no assurance that he would have an opportunity to serve elsewhere in the colonial empire. Among the higher officers there was in practice a considerable interchange, but more junior officers often found their promotional prospects limited to the colony where they were first appointed, and it might prove to be small and poor. In 1930 the Colonial Office began to unify the various functional branches of the Colonial Service in order to utilize its officers more effectively and to improve their career prospects. There are now some 19 unified services, including the Colonial Administrative Service, the Colonial

Audit Service, the Colonial Customs Service, the Colonial Agricultural Service, the Colonial Mines Service, and the Colonial Police Service. An officer is still appointed by a governor to a post in a colony's government service, but he is eligible for transfer to other territories where his functional service operates.

The central administration of the Colonial Service is vested in the Colonial Office. The Colonial Service Division of the Office deals with the selection, training, promotion, transfer, and other conditions of service of the professional and higher administrative ranks of the Service, positions generally filled by British officials. While the Colonial Office establishes the qualifications for various positions in the Service, recruitment is performed by the Civil Service Commission which employs selection methods similar to those used for the Administrative Class and the professional grades of the Home Civil Service.

Successful candidates are given a training course in their specialized fields. Officers entering the Colonial Administrative Service, for example, go to Oxford or Cambridge where they spend several months studying colonial law, history, economics, and public administration. Those recruited for the Colonial Medical Service take a course in tropical medicine at one of the British universities, while the entrants to the Colonial Agricultural Service study at the Imperial College of Tropical Agriculture in Trinidad. Also, before leaving for their posts, young officers are instructed in the language and social customs of the colonies to which they are going. Following their basic training they spend a two-year probationary period in the field and then return to England for an advanced course of instruction.

Each officer of the service is officially appointed by the governor of the colony in which he serves, and his salary is paid by the colonial government. Into his file in the Colonial Office go confidential reports about his work from the governor, and these form the basis of judgment when he is considered for promotion and transfer. An officer, particularly one in the Colonial Administrative Service, may serve in half a dozen colonies during the course of his career.

By and large, the Colonial Service has attracted a good type of recruit. When war has not interfered with the careers of young men, those entering the Service have had the normal university training, and the doctors, lawyers, engineers, and other professional officers have taken the necessary courses to qualify in their specialties. Belonging to the Colonial Service carries a good deal of prestige in the eyes of the British public, and prominent members of the service receive various honors, including knighthoods and an occasional peerage.

Besides the officers of the Colonial Service, the government of a colony has many other officials and employees. Most of them are drawn from the native population, and in a typical colony they will comprise about nine-tenths of the public service. Although the great majority of senior and professional positions are filled by Europeans, native officials are eligible

410–

for appointment to the higher posts, and they are serving in increasing numbers. In the Gold Coast about ten per cent of some 850 senior posts in the colonial government are occupied by native officials.[5] It is expected that throughout the colonial empire the proportion of natives in responsible positions will rise as educational opportunities increase and as they gain experience. The Colonial Office encourages the employment of native officials in administrative and professional positions and has an allocation of £1,000,000 under the Colonial Development and Welfare Acts to assist promising candidates to obtain the necessary education and training. In 1950 there were about 1500 colonial students in England under the scheme.[6]

5. *Major Problems of Colonial Government*

One of the major problems of the colonial empire concerns the development of the different units toward self-government. The British government has accepted as a basic colonial policy the obligation to guide the inhabitants of dependent areas toward autonomy and to foster their responsibility in political affairs. The determination of the pace of progress toward local self-government is a rather difficult matter. Within most colonies there are culturally advanced groups which are eager for greater political power, and they exert constant pressure upon the Colonial Office for more speed in devolving responsibility upon the colony. At the same time, there are frequently backward, uneducated elements of the population for the protection of whose interests the British government considers itself responsible. They often fear, usually with some reason, that they may be exploited by their more advanced fellow-citizens if British rule is relaxed. The problem of colonial policy in this matter, therefore, is to grant responsibility fast enough to satisfy the aspirations of the better-educated native elements and still retain sufficient control to protect the rights and interests of the backward groups.

The trend of political development has been fairly consistent throughout the colonial empire. A colony that starts with an appointed British governor and an executive council of officers of the Colonial Service has the council gradually changed by the inclusion of native representatives. In the beginning, the native representatives are nominated by the governor, but one or more may be elected. The next stage is the provision of a legislative council. As a first step, it probably consists of official, nominated, and elected members, but as the colony gains experience in democratic practices the popular element is increased. A further stage is reached when members of the executive council become responsible to the legislative assembly and finally are drawn from the latter body as ministers are from the Parliament at Westminster. Government by political parties which sup-

---

[5] Sir Charles Jeffries, *Partners for Progress* (London, 1949), p. 58.
[6] *The Economist,* 11 March 1950, p. 519.

port and oppose the ministers is then in order. Even at this stage the governor retains reserve powers which may be exercised should there be a breakdown in the government of the colony. He also controls external relations and defense.

The political advancement of the colonies is not only complicated by the wide range of cultural development among the native inhabitants of many areas, but it is also affected by the mixed populations found in a number of them. The Crown colony of Mauritius, for instance, has a mixed population of Indians, French, British, Chinese, and coloreds. The colony received a new constitution in 1947 which provided for a legislative council of 19 elected seats and 12 nominated seats. In the first election under this constitution the Indians, who constitute a majority of the population, won 11 seats while seven were won by colored candidates and one by a white candidate. The colony of Singapore has the kind of cosmopolitan population associated with the great crossroads of world commerce. There are nine elected seats in the colony's legislative council, and after an election in 1951 they were held by three Indians, three Chinese, one Ceylonese, one Eurasian, and one Englishman. Not all colonies have quite as complicated an ethnic structure as Mauritius and Singapore, but situations of this kind are by no means uncommon. In a few, Kenya for example, there is an important European element which is determined to seek the development of the colony as an area of white settlement and is hostile to any augmentation of the political power of the native Africans or the numerous Indian immigrants.

Another problem concerning the political development of colonial areas arises in those colonies where the British practice indirect rule. If indirect rule is strictly adhered to, the colonial administration makes little change in tribal customs and practices. Native chiefs and their headmen are permitted to rule according to their traditional customs and are restrained from only those practices which go against the basic principles of European civilization. Indirect rule results in very slow advancement toward western concepts of democracy, freedom, and justice. This policy probably satisfies the majority of the natives, but for those who acquire some education along European lines it produces a sense of frustration and a belief that the British are deliberately retarding the colony's political development.

In addition to the political tutelage of colonial peoples, the British government is pledged to their economic and social development. The British recognize that the policy of developing the colonial empire economically and socially is one of enlightened self-interest. The more the resources of the colonies can be developed, the better will be the United Kingdom's position in international trade. From them she can obtain an increasing supply of raw materials which now, in many cases, have to be purchased with scarce dollars or forfeited, and the direct sale of colonial products to the western world aids Britain in her efforts to earn hard currencies. The social improvement of the colonial populations will also benefit Britain's

412–

trading position. The productivity of native labor, usually very low, can be expected to increase with advances in the fields of education and public health. Social progress enhances the desires of native populations for manufactured goods, and most of this market will be taken by British industry and British merchants.

Recognizing the importance of developing the colonial empire economically and socially, the British Parliament has passed two Colonial Development and Welfare Acts, one in 1940 and another in 1945. Under the Act of 1940, £30 million were contributed, and under the more comprehensive Act of 1945, the United Kingdom provided £120 million to be spent over a ten-year period ending in 1956. Grants are made for a wide range of social and economic projects designed to raise living standards and to promote the development of colonial resources. A sum not to exceed £2.5 million annually may be spent on research.

Projects under the Colonial Development and Welfare Acts are prepared by individual colonies and submitted to the Colonial Secretary. He is advised in these matters by the Colonial Economic and Development Council. The purposes, administration and financing of individual projects are carefully reviewed in the light of a colony's needs, available resources, and future ability to support the scheme. A colonial government is expected to contribute to the expenses of a project with the balance provided by grants and loans.

Projects approved for aid include research into the habits of the tsetse fly and into the nature of a number of tropical diseases; the construction and equipment of schools, colleges, and technical institutes; the construction of roads, airports, harbors, reservoirs, and water and sewage systems; pilot schemes in agriculture, fisheries, and animal husbandry; and training programs for doctors, nurses, and public health specialists. An effort is made to maintain a proper distribution among research, basic economic development, and social welfare projects.

As a means of providing additional assistance to dependent territories, Parliament in 1948 passed the Overseas Resources Development Act which created the Colonial Development Corporation and the Overseas Food Corporation. The first corporation has resources amounting to £110 million to finance general development projects, and the second has resources of £55 million to promote food production schemes in overseas territories.

The most ambitious project of the Overseas Food Corporation has been the East African groundnuts scheme. This project involved the clearing of thousands of acres in Kenya and Tanganyika, constructing the necessary transportation and living facilities, and raising peanuts for vegetable oils. The scheme was launched with considerable fanfare, but the results have not risen to expectations. Various aspects of the development proved more difficult than had been anticipated, and costs mounted rapidly as the work progressed. In 1951 the Government announced that the Corporation had lost £36,500,000 on the project and that the original targets in acreage and yield were being drastically reduced.[7] Administration of the project was transferred from the Ministry of Food to the Colonial Office.

Misfortune also overtook another African development project, the raising of poultry in Gambia. This scheme, administered by the Colonial Development Corporation, was designed to provide Britain with 20 million eggs and one million pounds of poultry annually. Disease and the unsuitability of the soil for growing feedstuffs brought the project to an end with a loss of £825,000.[8] A joint scheme of the Overseas Food Corporation and the government of Queensland, in Australia, to raise sorghum, cattle, and hogs fared somewhat better, but drought and other difficulties prevented the realization of the original plans, and at the end of 1951 the project was operating at a loss.

In a report on its operations from 1948 through 1951, the Colonial Development Corporation announced a deficiency of £4,594,000, including a loss of more than £1 million on abandoned undertakings. The deficiency in 1951 was £2,905,290.[9] At that time it had fifty-three schemes in operation for which capital of almost £36 million had been sanctioned. The causes of the Corporation's troubles appear to include cases of both bad luck and inefficient management. One major difficulty facing the Corporation has been the vagueness of its charter. Designed to operate in an area between welfare grants and ordinary commercial investment, it has had trouble finding projects which give reasonable promise of the Corporation earning interest and repaying capital. The Colonial Development and Welfare Fund is available for non-commercial schemes in the colonies, and private capital is attracted to projects offering the prospect of profits.

The experiences of the postwar years have induced a more realistic appraisal of the potentialities of colonial development. Much can be done in clearing jungle and bush, in introducing new crops and improving indigenous ones, and in increasing the productivity of native labor, but the task is a long term one requiring a great deal of experimentation and patience as well as capital. Spectacular results are unlikely. Failures occur even after careful planning and the collection of much expert advice. Britain will persevere in efforts to develop colonial resources, but Parliament will probably be cautious in approving large-scale projects promising quick returns.

The much publicized failures in colonial development tend to obscure the successes. Nearly every colony can point to schemes which have improved its economy or the well-being of its people. Improvements are constantly being made in agriculture and animal husbandry; modern medical and health practices are replacing the witch doctor and his charms and magic potions. Under the Colonial Development and Welfare Acts £10

---

[7] Cmd. 8125 (1951). At the start the Overseas Food Corporation planned to clear 3,210,000 acres of bush by 1953. It revised the target to 255,000 acres by 1957.

[8] *The New York Times*, 1 March 1951.

[9] *The Times*, 3 May 1952.

million have been earmarked for research work, and the use of this sum, under the guidance of the Colonial Research Council, will undoubtedly contribute to further progress.

6. *Regionalism in the Colonial Empire*

In recent years the British government has concluded that many colonial problems could be attacked more profitably in terms of regions instead of individual colonies. Some colonies are too small for efficient development as independent units and others are contiguous to areas sharing the same political, economic, and social problems. It has appeared desirable, therefore, to approach a number of colonial problems along regional lines.

One natural regional grouping has been the East African area which includes the colonies of Uganda and Kenya and the trust territory of Tanganyika. For these three dependencies there has been established an East Africa High Commission consisting of their governors and supported by a secretariat of Colonial Service officers. The High Commission meets periodically to consider such matters as the defense of the area, the improvement of communication facilities, and racial problems.

In Central Africa there is a strong movement among the European population for closer relations between Southern Rhodesia, Northern Rhodesia, and Nyasaland. In 1944 their governments established the Central African Council to co-ordinate a few of the essential services of the region, but most of the white residents favor a federation of the three territories and their eventual development into a dominion, occasionally given the name of Capricorn. The Colonial Office has been reluctant to encourage this movement because it fears that the interests of the African natives would be insufficiently protected in a white dominated dominion. The trend of events in the Union of South Africa lends substance to these apprehensions. It seems likely, however, that the common interests of the territories in improving communications and in developing the area in other ways will lead them to closer political connections.

No definite proposal for the political unification of the British colonies in West Africa has been advanced, although there is considerable co-operation among the colonial governments on common problems that they face. Some of these co-operative endeavors have also included the colonial administrations of adjoining French territories. Among the educated natives of West Africa there appears to be developing some community of interest, although perhaps only that of opposition to their imperial rulers, and this may eventually lead to closer political ties.

The British possessions in the Caribbean form another regional group where the movement for federation has gained considerable momentum. At a meeting in 1947 of representatives of the West Indian colonies, federation was approved in principle, and the response of the Colonial Office was generally favorable. A committee appointed at the meeting prepared a draft constitution which, like the constitutions of the United States and Australia, envisages a federal government of delegated powers with other powers remaining with the individual colonies. In the case of these colonies, the impetus toward unification of some kind arises principally from their economic and social problems, for they all have achieved a considerable degree of local self-government. Possibly the evolution here will be in the direction of a West Indies dominion, although the dependence of the colonies upon financial support from the United Kingdom will rule out the achievement of such a status for some time to come. There is another line of development affecting these colonies. This has taken the form of a Caribbean Commission in which British, French, and Dutch authorities sit along with representatives of the United States. The purposes of the Caribbean Commission are to promote the economic and social advancement of the area and to share the experiences of the different colonial administrations. The Commission has no control over the colonial governments.

In Southeast Asia a still different type of regional arrangement has been established. At the close of World War II the British government appointed a Commissioner-General for Southeast Asia with headquarters at Singapore. His authority extends over the federation of Malaya, the colonies of Singapore, British North Borneo, and Sarawak, and the protected state of Brunei. While each of these dependencies has its own colonial government, the Commissioner-General serves as a co-ordinating authority and has the power to deal with the common problems which affect British interests in this part of the world. With the communist menace overhanging the area, the Commissioner-General is largely concerned with measures to bolster the military and political defenses against this enemy. He is also concerned with gaining the co-operation of such independent states as Siam and Indonesia and the French authorities in Indo-China to strengthen the rich and populous region against the threat posed by a Communist China. Since the British believe that an improvement in living standards and gradual political development are the only permanent barriers to Communist encroachment, the Commissioner-General recommends to the home government various steps in these fields which he believes can be advantageously taken. These colonies will be among the principal beneficiaries of the Colombo Plan, a six-year development scheme projected by the British Commonwealth to assist the countries of South and Southeast Asia. An expenditure of £1,868 million is proposed, principally for improved communications services and agricultural development. At a conference in London in 1950 a Council of Technical Co-operation was established to supervise the expenditure of £8 million to train native technicians who will be needed as various projects take shape.

Within the general framework of British colonial policy, developments are taking place constantly which change the political organization of individual territories and their relations with the mother country. There is a general movement toward devolving more responsibility upon colonial populations and guiding them into the management of their own affairs. There are also ambitious programs of economic and social development designed to improve living standards throughout the colonial empire and

416–

indirectly to make it of more value to the United Kingdom. Although a general pattern of colonial government is maintained, considerable experimentation, particularly with respect to regional arrangements, is going forward. It is the British hope that colonial populations will see in their tie with the United Kingdom the best means of realizing their political aspirations, their economic prosperity, and their cultural advancement.

Selected Bibliography

The literature pertaining to the history, organization, and practice of British government is very extensive. The selection of books listed here is arranged according to the chapter or chapters of this book to which they most closely relate. Included also is a list of biographical works by or about some of the leading figures in the public life of modern Britain. Additional readings of value are to be found in the files of *The Political Quarterly* and in *Public Administration,* the journal of the Institute of Public Administration. Scholarly journals published in the United States frequently contain useful articles concerning British government. The official publications of H. M. Stationery Office, including *Parliamentary Debates* (Hansard), reports of Parliamentary committees, and the command papers series, are basic sources of information.

GENERAL (Chapter I)

Barker, Sir Ernest, ed., *The Character of England,* Oxford, 1947.
Brinton, Crane, *The United States and Britain,* Cambridge, Mass., 1947.
Brogan, D. W., *The English People,* New York, 1943.
Clarke, C. F. O., *Britain Today,* Cambridge, Mass., 1951.
Gooch, R. K., *The Government of England,* New York, 1947.
Lewis, Roy and Maude, Angus, *The English Middle Classes,* New York, 1950.
Smith, Wilfred, *An Economic Geography of Great Britain,* London, 1949.
The History of The Times, 4 vols., London, 1932-52.
Trevelyan, G. M., *English Social History,* London, 1942.
Watkins, Ernest, *The Cautious Revolution: Britain Today and Tomorrow,* New York, 1950.

THE CONSTITUTION (Chapters II & III)

Adams, George Burton, *Constitutional History of England,* rev. by Robert L. Schuyler, London, 1941.
Amery, L. S., *Thoughts on the Constitution,* Oxford, 1947.
Anson, Sir William R., *The Law and Custom of the Constitution,* 2 vols., 5th ed. vol. I and 4th ed. vol. II, Oxford, 1922-35.
Chrimes, S. B., *English Constitutional History,* London, 1947.
Denning, Sir Alfred, *Freedom Under Law,* London, 1949.
Greaves, H. R. G., *British Constitution,* New York, 1938.
Dicey, A. V., *An Introduction to the Study of the Law of the Constitution,* 9th ed., London, 1939.

SELECTED BIBLIOGRAPHY

Jennings, Sir Ivor, *The Law and the Constitution,* 3rd ed., London, 1943.

——, *The British Constitution,* 3rd ed., Cambridge, 1950.

Keir, Sir D. L. and Lawson, F. H., *Cases in Constitutional Law,* 3rd ed. rev., London, 1948.

Keith, Arthur Berriedale, *The Constitution of England from Queen Victoria to George VI,* London, 1940.

Wade, E. C. S. and Phillips, G. Godfrey, *Constitutional Law,* 4th ed., London, 1950.

THE MONARCHY (Chapter IV)

A King's Story: The Memoirs of the Duke of Windsor, New York, 1951.

Hardie, F., *The Political Influence of Queen Victoria, 1861-1901,* London, 1935.

Lee, Sidney, *King Edward VII, a Biography,* 2 vols., New York, 1925-7.

MacDonagh, M., *The English King,* London, 1929.

Marriott, Sir John A. R., *Queen Victoria and Her Ministers,* London, 1933.

Nicolson, Harold, *King George V,* London, 1952.

Ponsonby, Sir Frederick, *Recollections of Three Reigns,* London, 1951

THE CABINET (Chapter V)

Fitzroy, Sir Almeric, *The History of the Privy Council,* London, 1928.

Hankey, Lord, *Diplomacy by Conference,* New York, 1946.

Jennings, Sir Ivor, *Cabinet Government,* 2nd ed., Cambridge, 1951.

Mersey, Lord [Bigham, C.], *The Prime Ministers of Britain, 1721-1921,* London, 1922.

Keith, Arthur Berriedale, *The British Cabinet System,* 2nd ed. by N. H. Gibbs, London, 1952.

Muir, Ramsay, *How Britain is Governed,* New York, 1930.

PARLIAMENT (Chapters VI, VII, VIII & IX)

Bossom, Alfred C., *Our House,* London, 1948.

Campion, Lord, ed., *Parliament: a Survey,* London, 1952.

Chubb, Basil, *The Control of Public Expenditure,* Oxford, 1952.

Herbert, Sir Alan P., *Independent Member,* New York, 1951.

Hollis, Christopher, *Can Parliament Survive?,* London, 1949.

Ilbert, Sir Courtenay, *Parliament: Its History, Constitution, and Practice,* 3rd ed. rev. by Sir Cecil Carr, London, 1950.

Jennings, Sir Ivor, *Parliament,* Cambridge, 1948.

Bailey, Sidney D., ed., *Parliamentary Government in Britain,* Hansard Society, London, 1949.

Taylor, Eric, *The House of Commons at Work,* London, 1951.

POLITICAL PARTIES AND ELECTIONS (Chapters X, XI & XII)

Attlee, C. R., *The Labour Party in Perspective,* rep., London, 1949.

Butler, D. E., *The British General Election of 1951,* London, 1952.

Cole, G. D. H., *A History of the Labour Party from 1914,* London, 1948.

McCallum, R. B. and Readman, Alison, *The British General Election of 1945,* London, 1947.

Muir, Ramsay, *How Britain is Governed,* New York, 1930.

420–

Nicholas, H. G., *The British General Election of 1950,* London, 1951.
Pollock, James K., *Money and Politics Abroad,* New York, 1932.
————, Laing, Lionel H., Eldersveld, Samuel J., Jenkin, Thomas P., and Scamman, Richard M., *British Election Studies, 1950,* Ann Arbor, 1951.
Ross, J. F. S., *Parliamentary Representation,* London, 1948.
Smellie, K. B., *A Hundred Years of English Government,* New York, 1937.
Somervell, D. C., *British Politics Since 1900,* New York, 1950.
The British Party System, Hansard Society, London, 1952.
Tracey, Herbert, *The British Labour Party: Its History, Growth, Policy, and Leaders,* 3 vols., London, 1948.
Williams, Francis, *Fifty Years' March: The Rise of the Labour Party,* London, 1949.
————, *Socialist Britain: Its Background, Its Present, and an Estimate of Its Future,* New York, 1949.

THE ADMINISTRATION OF JUSTICE (Chapter XIII)

Friedmann, W., *Law and Social Change in Contemporary Britain,* London, 1952.
Griffith, J. A. G. and Street, H., *Principles of Administrative Law,* London, 1952.
Holdsworth, Sir William, *The History of English Law,* 12 vols., London, 1903-38.
Lawson, F. H., *The Rational Strength of English Law,* London, 1951.
Patterson, C. Perry, *The Administration of Justice in Great Britain,* Austin, 1936.
Pendleton, Howard, *Criminal Justice in England,* London, 1931.
Robson, W. A., *Justice and Administrative Law,* 3rd ed., London, 1951.

THE NATIONAL ADMINISTRATION (Chapters XIV & XV)

Critchley, T. A., *The Civil Service Today,* London, 1950.
Finer, S. E., *A Primer of Public Administration,* London, 1950.
Greaves, H. R. G., *The Civil Service in the Changing State,* London, 1948.
Monck, Bosworth, *How the Civil Service Works,* London, 1951.
Robinson, Howard, *The British Post Office: A History,* Princeton, 1948.
Robson, W. A., ed., *The British Civil Servant,* London, 1937.
Smellie, K. B., *A Hundred Years of English Government,* New York, 1937.
Stout, H. M., *Public Service in Great Britain,* Chapel Hill, 1938.
The Reform of the Higher Civil Service, The Fabian Society, London, 1948.
White, Leonard D., *Whitley Councils in the British Civil Service,* Chicago, 1933.

LOCAL GOVERNMENT (Chapters XVI & XVII)

Carlson, Reynold E., *British Block Grants and Central-Local Finance,* Baltimore, 1947.
Cole, G. D. H., *Local and Regional Government,* London, 1948.
Finer, Herman, *English Local Government,* 4th ed., London, 1950.
Hasluck, E. L., *Local Government,* 2nd ed., Cambridge, 1948.
Morrison, Herbert, *How London Is Governed,* London, 1949.
Oakes, Sir Cecil and Dacey, H. W., *Local Government and Local Government Finance,* 9th ed., London, 1950.
Robson, W. A., *The Government and Misgovernment of London,* 2nd ed., London, 1948.
————, *The Development of Local Government,* 2nd ed., London, 1948.
Smellie, K. B., *A History of Local Government,* London, 1946.
Warren, J. H., *The English Local Government System,* London, 1946.

SELECTED BIBLIOGRAPHY

NATIONAL SECURITY (Chapter XVIII)

Ashton-Gwatkin, Frank J., *The British Foreign Service,* Syracuse, N. Y., 1950.
Chester, D. N., ed., *Lessons of the British War Economy,* Cambridge, 1951.
Hankey, Lord, *Government Control in War,* Cambridge, 1945.
Hart, Liddell, *When Britain Goes to War,* rev. ed., London, 1936.
London, Kurt, *How Foreign Policy is Made,* New York, 1949.
Webster, Sir Charles, Jacob, Sir Ian, and Robinson, E. A. G., *United Kingdom Policy: Foreign, Strategic, Economic,* London, 1950.
Windrich, Elaine, *British Labour's Foreign Policy,* Stanford, Calif., 1952.

THE SOCIAL SERVICES (Chapter XIX)

Education 1900-1950, H. M. S. O., Cmd. 8244, London, 1951.
Marsh, David C., *National Insurance and Assistance in Great Britain,* London, 1951.
Peacock, Alan T., *The Economics of National Insurance,* London, 1951.
Report of the Committee on Social Insurance and Allied Services [The Beveridge Report], H. M. S. O., Cmd. 6406, London, 1942.
Robson, W. A., ed., *Social Security,* 3rd ed., London, 1948.
Ross, Sir James Stirling, *The National Health Service in Great Britain,* Oxford, 1952.

INDUSTRY (Chapter XX)

Accountability to Parliament, Acton Society Trust, London, 1950.
Allen, G. C., *British Industries and their Organization,* 3rd ed., London, 1951.
Brady, Robert, *Crisis in Britain,* Berkeley, Calif., 1951.
Hutchison, Keith, *The Decline and Fall of British Capitalism,* New York, 1950.
Men on the Boards: A Study of the Composition of the Boards of Nationalized Industry, Acton Society Trust, London, 1951.
Powers of the Minister, Acton Society Trust, London, 1951.
Robson, W. A., ed., *Problems of Nationalized Industry,* London, 1952.

THE COMMONWEALTH AND EMPIRE (Chapters XXI, XXII & XXIII)

Bailey, Sidney D., ed., *Parliamentary Government in the Commonwealth,* Hansard Society, London, 1951.
Brady, Alexander, *Democracy in the Dominions,* London, 1950.
Elliott, W. Y., *The New British Empire,* New York, 1932.
Hailey, Lord, *Native Administration in British African Territories,* H. M. S. O., London, 1951.
Harvey, Heather J., *Consultation and Cooperation in the Commonwealth,* London, 1951.
Hinden, Rita, ed., *Local Government and the Colonies; a Report to the Fabian Colonial Bureau,* London, 1950.
Jeffries, Sir Charles, *Partners for Progress,* London, 1949.
Keith, Arthur Berriedale, *The Dominions as Sovereign States: Their Constitutions and Governments,* London, 1938.
Mansergh, Nicholas, *Survey of British Commonwealth Affairs: Problems of External Policy,* 1931-39, Oxford, 1952.
Sinnett, W. E., *The British Colonial Empire,* 2nd ed., London, 1949.
Soward, F. W., ed., *The Changing Commonwealth* (Proceedings of the Fourth Unofficial Commonwealth Relations Conference, September, 1949), London, 1950.

BIOGRAPHY

Estorick, Eric, *Stafford Cripps,* London, 1949.
Feiling, Keith, *The Life of Neville Chamberlain,* London, 1946.
Oxford and Asquith, Lord, *Fifty Years of British Parliament,* 2 vols., Boston, 1926.
Postgate, Raymond, *The Life of George Lansbury,* London, 1951.
Reith, Lord, *Into the Wind,* London, 1949.
Retrospect. The Memoirs of the Rt. Hon. Viscount Simon, G. C. S. I., G. C. V. O., London, 1952.
Samuel, Lord, *Memoirs,* London, 1945.
War Memoirs of David Lloyd George, 6 vols., London, 1933-6.
Williams, Francis, *Ernest Bevin: Portrait of a Great Englishman,* London, 1952.
Young, G. M., *Stanley Baldwin,* London, 1952.

Index